Max Trescott's G1000 and Perspective Glass Cockpit Handbook

Max Trescott

2008 National Certificated Flight Instructor of the Year

Master CFI, Master Ground Instructor, Cirrus CSIP

Max Trescott's G1000 and Perspective Glass Cockpit Handbook
By Max Trescott

Glass Cockpit Publishing
P.O. Box 4061
Mountain View, CA 94040
www.glasscockpitbooks.com

Fifh Edition, 2012
Published 2012 by Glass Cockpit Publishing
Acknowledgements
Interior Book Design and Typesetting by JustYourType.biz
Photographs: Max Trescott, except where noted
Cover Design by Abel Robinson
Rear cover photograph: Fairbanks Photography

Printed in the United States
Last digit is the print number: 9 8 7 6 5 4 3 2
ISBN 0-9777030-8-8

Contents

	Acknowledgements	iv
Chapter **1**:	The Glass Cockpit Revolution	1
Chapter **2**:	G1000 and Perspective Benefits	5
Chapter **3**:	System Overview	11
Chapter **4**:	PFD Overview	19
Chapter **5**:	Radios and Audio Panel	39
Chapter **6**:	Engine Indication System	51
Chapter **7**:	MFD Overview	61
	MAP Group Pages	65
	Waypoint Group Pages	86
	Auxiliary Group Pages	94
	Nearest Group Pages	109
Chapter **8**:	Onboard Data Link Weather	115
Chapter **9**:	Flight Planning with the G1000	131
Chapter **10**:	Autopilot Operation	149
Chapter **11**:	Instrument Flying with the G1000	167
Chapter **12**:	Electrical Systems, Component Failures and Emergencies	189
Chapter **13**:	Flying a Trip Behind the G1000	199
Chapter **14**:	Advanced G1000 and Perspective Features	209
Chapter **15**:	Flying the Perspective Glass Cockpit	247
Chapter **16**:	Very Light Jets and Turboprops	267
	Appendices	276
	Glosssary	293
	Index	300

Acknowledgements

Creating a book is a journey, and along the way, I was encouraged by an amazing set of people. I'd like to thank Tradewinds Aviation, the Cessna dealership in San Jose, CA. Alan Elpel and Erin Hay were instrumental in supporting me to get trained as a Cessna CFAI so that I can deliver training to their new airplane customers. Erin also supported me with the documentation I needed to start the book.

Also, I'd like to thank the wonderful staff at West Valley Flying Club, particularly Josh Smith, Ken Frank and Dominique Marais, who run the largest flying club in the country with many glass cockpit aircraft. Special thanks to fellow flight instructors Peter Long (now in Australia) and David Zittin, from whom I've learned so much about flying glass cockpit aircraft.

Ken Smoll and his pilot training staff at Cessna have been exceptional both at training me during my multiple visits to the factory, and in reviewing this book. I'd particularly like to thank Rosa Lee Harris, Alex Unruh, Brandy Hearting, Steve Smethers and Dean Beliera (now at Flight Safety).

G1000-equipped aircraft owners who've been helpful in many ways include Dan Baggett, Cory Lovell and particularly James Dao, John Ferrell and Dan Vivoli. Thank you for your support.

Support from industry has been outstanding. This book probably wouldn't have been possible without the tireless work of Ken Terada (formerly at Garmin, now at Flight Safety), who answered my endless stream of emails and phone calls for clarification on many points. Thank you Ken!

Thanks to Pat Groves for introducing me to the Diamond DA40 and to Seth Jayne and Terry Abst for answering many questions on the Diamond and Mooney products. Thanks also to John Rock of Tiger Aircraft, Jim Alpiser of Garmin, Randy Bolinger, Mike Schrader, and Terry Brewer of Columbia Aircraft, Ed Darnell of WxWorx and Lynn Thomas of Quest Aircraft.

I'd also like to thank aviation authors Rod Machado and Greg Brown for their encouragement and suggestions. Both were very generous with their time. Thanks also to fellow glass cockpit instructors Emily Watters of Cessna and Michael Gilbert and fellow Master CFI Susan Parson for their many suggestions. Boni Caldeira, Terry McGee and Scott Winter of Cirrus Design, CFI Peter King and SR22T owner Bob Anderson contributed to the Perspective chapter.

Other people who've contributed in various ways include Bill Van Zwoll of Garmin, Bob Kaplan, Candice Tuttle, Lew Hollerbach, Larry Olson, Jack Hocker, Ron Carmichael and of course my editor, Joan Garvin. Any mistakes you find are mine not hers, since I occasionally turned down her excellent advice.

Special thanks to my first flight instructor Dick Johnston, a former FAA Pennsylvania Flight Instructor of the Year, for whom the Wellsboro-Johnston airport in Pennsylvania is named. It's people like Dick who make aviation great. Dick, thanks for getting me started in aviation as a teenager. Thanks also to my mother Sue Trescott, who nurtured my interest in aviation and drove me to the airport for lessons when I was too young for a driver's license.

The book has been a family affair. I'd like to thank my brother-in-law and author Rob Stearns for his pragmatic advice throughout the process and my sister Carol for her inputs. My wife Laurie is a saint, and was helpful in many ways. Thanks also to my daughters Julie and Katie, who noticed that Dad spent way too much time in front of the computer, and to Sol and Betty Stuttman for their support.

Finally, a special thanks to my many flying clients with whom I've learned so much as we've flown together.

—Max Trescott

Chapter 1:
The Glass Cockpit Revolution

There's a quiet revolution going on in general aviation—one which will save lives and is destined to change forever the way small planes are flown. The glass cockpit is taking the industry by storm.

The Garmin International Inc. G1000 and Perspective are driving much of that change into small planes and into Very Light Jets (VLJ). Savvy pilots and flight instructors, seeking to stay on the leading edge of their profession, will embrace the change. If you're one of these pilots, this book will help you to transition smoothly into one of the thousands of glass cockpits now being shipped each year.

Historically, change has come extremely slowly to general aviation, particularly when compared to the consumer electronics or even the automobile industries. Many of today's airframes were designed 50 years ago and the biggest change that's occurred since then was moving the tailwheel from the back of the plane to the front! The only other major visible changes have been to the navigation receivers in the cockpit.

Yet, change is nonlinear. The airplanes I fly today are, in almost every respect, the same ones I learned to fly in over 30 years ago. Other than the advent of the nosewheel fifty years ago, the only other major changes were the introduction into the cockpit of Loran navigation receivers in the 1980s and GPS receivers in the 1990s. For those of us accustomed to seeing rapid change in other parts of our lives, change in general aviation seemingly moved on a geological timescale—the change was there, it was just hard to detect during our short life spans!

However, in the two-year period beginning in 2003, the general aviation industry converted from shipping no glass cockpits at all to equipping approximately 90% of all new small airplanes with glass cockpits! In 2003, Cirrus Design led the way by shipping the Avidyne Entegra glass cockpit in their SR20 and SR22 aircraft. In 2004, Diamond Aircraft Industries and Cessna Aircraft Company began shipping the Garmin G1000 in some models. By 2005, nearly every major manufacturer was shipping glass cockpits, and they were reporting that, when

Perspective

Owners and pilots flying the Perspective glass cockpit, introduced by Cirrus Design in 2008 for the SR22 and later for the SR20, may want to start this book by skimming Chapter 15, and these sidebars on the first page of each chapter, to understand the differences between the Perspective and the G1000. The Perspective's software is nearly identical to the G1000 with some additional features listed in Chapter 15 and 16. The Perspective hardware is totally new, though pilots familiar with the G1000 and the Garmin GFC 700 autopilot will quickly adapt to flying the Perspective glass cockpit, once they note the new locations for knobs and autopilot keys. After reviewing Chapter 15, Perspective pilots may want to return to Chapter 1 to read the entire book.

NTSB Glass Cockpit Study

The NTSB conducted a study in 2010 on whether glass cockpit-equipped general aviation aircraft are safer than aircraft with traditional round gauges. The total accident rate was essentially the same for both groups: 3.77 accidents per 100,000 hours for glass cockpit aircraft versus 3.71 for non-glass aircraft. For fatal accidents, the story was quite different. The study found the glass cockpit fatal accident rate was 1.03 accidents per 100,000 hours versus 0.43 for non-glass aircraft.

It would be easy to leap to the conclusion that glass cockpit aircraft are less safe except for one fact: glass cockpit aircraft are used very differently than their non-glass counterparts, exposing them to greater risk. The Board found that glass cockpit aircraft were more likely to be used for business and personal flying and to be flown IFR by older pilots. Non-glass airplanes had a significantly higher percentage of takeoff and landing accidents, were more likely to be used for instruction, and were flown on shorter flights. Glass aircraft averaged trips of 96 miles, exposing them to more weather and terrain dangers, while non-glass aircraft averaged trips of just 25 miles. For my full article, use the QR code below or enter the following search term into Google: NTSB study site:maxtrescott.com

offered as an option, over 90% of their customers were choosing the new glass cockpits!

No one could have predicted the rapidity of this change, least of all the hundreds of thousands of pilots around the world who will eventually use them. While the manufacturers were able to make a total shift to "glass" in two years, training pilots will take longer, since the more than 200,000 airplanes that exist today without glass cockpits will continue to constitute the majority of the fleet for years to come.

The advent of the glass cockpit comes at a time when there's been a rebound in the industry. In the past, small changes in the economy have been amplified into huge swings in the production of small aircraft. Hence the saying "when the economy gets a cough, general aviation gets double pneumonia." While past upswings in new airplane sales were driven by the economy, the current renaissance is driven by innovations such as the glass cockpit and safety systems such as parachutes and airbags. Hopefully the current growth cycle will continue and glass cockpit aircraft become widely available.

Glass Cockpit Benefits vs. Risks

To many pilots, the benefits of glass cockpits are not intuitively obvious until they've flown in one. Until then, it's easier to focus on the perceived increase in risk posed by using a system more heavily dependent upon an aircraft's electrical system. "You won't find me flying one of those in the clouds," was the comment of one flight school manager.

What they may not realize is that the electrical systems of glass cockpit aircraft have been beefed up, and the glass cockpits themselves have tremendous redundancy. Whereas in the past, electrical system failures were common and often went unnoticed until the battery was completely drained, the new systems notify pilots immediately of a problem. In addition, standby batteries are often included to allow even more time to land or reach fair weather.

Single points of failure have also been largely eliminated. Today, most critical components have multiple backups. Losing any one component still leaves modern glass cockpit pilots with far more instrumentation and data than they normally would have after losing a component in traditional aircraft.

The benefits of flying any glass cockpit system are substantial. The biggest benefit is that the equipment frees a properly trained glass cockpit pilot from mundane tasks, such as keeping the wings level, while providing the information needed for him or her to make decisions about more important tasks. These include monitoring the current weather versus the forecast, both en route and at the destination, monitoring aircraft performance and fuel consumption, and continually evaluating alternatives throughout the flight.

Another major benefit is the reduced workload associated with maintaining an instrument scan. While it's not initially obvious, scanning a round gauge panel requires the eye to jump across at least two boundaries—the edges of adjacent instruments—before refocusing on the center of another instrument. By contrast, glass panels have no artificial boundaries between instruments, and it's less tiring for the eye.

According to a University of Iowa study, glass cockpits lead to increased situational awareness on three levels. First, they lead to a better perception of the current environment, since data is presented in ways that pilots can more quickly absorb. Next, they increase comprehension of the current situation. Finally, they provide a better projection of the future status of the pilot and aircraft. They also decrease pilot workload, since data is presented in a more integrated format on larger displays.

System reliability is also enhanced. Traditional mechanical gyros have a lifetime of perhaps 1000-1500 hours. As they get older, Heading Indicators, for example, drift and need frequent adjustment so they remain synchronized with the compass. In contrast, the modern Attitude Heading Reference Systems (AHRS) last five to ten times longer and never need resetting, since they're automatically slaved to an electronic compass.

Traditional gyros are often driven by vacuum pumps with a lifetime of as little as 500 hours and, when these pumps fail, the gyros fail in an insidious fashion. When a pump fails, the gyros, which run at 18,000 rpm, slowly spin down over five minutes. As they slow, they start to tilt almost imperceptibly. An unsuspecting pilot, who has received virtually no warning of the vacuum pump failure, may follow the tilt of the gyro and slowly lead the plane into an unusual flight attitude. If this occurs while in the clouds, the result can be fatal. Modern glass cockpits don't use vacuum pumps for any of the primary flight instruments. Also, when a failure does occur, it's immediately obvious since a large red X replaces a portion of the instrument display.

One very real danger is that glass cockpits draw pilots' attention into the cockpit and away from scanning outside for other aircraft and terrain, particularly during transition training. The brilliant color displays demand attention, and even the most conscientious pilots will find themselves looking outside less. However, one study has shown that the traffic displays found in most glass cockpits, which graphically depict the location of other airplanes in the vicinity, actually help glass cockpit pilots visually spot traffic faster than pilots in traditional cockpits. Also, a large manufacturer's training department reports that after G1000 transition training is completed, pilots are returning to looking more outside the cockpit. If you do want to go "heads down" to focus on the system, you should advise your copilot, so that he or she will dedicate themselves to looking outside for traffic.

Another potential risk is the increased mental workload due to the inherently more complex software interface of glass cockpits.

Programming the systems can distract a pilot from the primary task of flying the aircraft. There is also some risk of dependency upon the automation. To stay proficient, pilots will need to balance the time they spend hand flying an aircraft versus using the autopilot, so that their skills remain sharp in both areas. This risk may be somewhat overstated, however. Airline pilots work with high levels of automation, and little is said of any degradation in their basic flying skills.

Enhanced Safety & More Training

The biggest legacy of glass cockpits is bound to be the enhanced safety they provide. For example, terrain awareness databases built into most glass cockpits, that show whether the rocks are above or below you, should save thousands of lives in future decades. The use of the advanced autopilots found in these aircraft will also lighten pilot workloads and enhance safety.

Already lives are being saved by a simple advancement that predated glass cockpits by only a few years—the low fuel indicator. Cessna started shipping their aircraft with these warning indicators in the late 1990s, and they're now integrated into the G1000-equipped aircraft Cessna ships. Over 5,000 aircraft have these indicators, and none has had a fuel exhaustion accident. In contrast, in 2003, 147 general aviation aircraft accidents in the United States, or nearly 10% of accidents, were caused by fuel mismanagement. Other recent safety innovations include carbon monoxide monitors, shipped first on Columbia aircraft, and airbags shipped first on Cessnas.

An Air Safety Foundation publication on Technically Advanced Aircraft (TAA)—which includes all aircraft with glass cockpits—states that these aircraft have the potential for increased safety, but to "obtain this available safety, pilots must receive additional training in the specific TAA systems in their aircraft." Also, piloting in the future will require "a more mental approach."

Pilots accustomed to flying the gauges will find a paradigm shift as they transition into TAA aircraft. In addition to getting the feel for flying and landing a new aircraft, they'll now need to spend additional time learning to "navigate" through the software menus and softkeys. Most pilots will rise to this new challenge, though some will prefer the old methods of navigating an airplane.

Summary

The glass cockpits are here and they're bringing unprecedented levels of information, automation and potential safety into the small aircraft cockpit. Now, the challenge is for the pilot community to get additional training and develop a new orientation toward "programming the cockpit" so they can derive the full benefits of these new technologies. The bottom line is that glass cockpits are here to stay, and savvy pilots are already flying these safer, easier to manage aircraft, which are even more fun to fly!

Chapter 2:
G1000 and Perspective Benefits

Some glass cockpit benefits are common to all systems and were previously discussed. Others are unique to each avionics manufacturer's design. The field is not static, however. Relatively few features are proprietary and manufacturers continue to play a game of leapfrog with each other. While some benefits discussed here are unique to the G1000 and Perspective now, by the time you read this they may have been incorporated into other manufacturers' glass cockpit products.

Gary Burrell and Min Kao, former employees of King/Bendix®, founded Garmin in 1989, and used a contraction of their respective first names to name the company. It's been said they envisioned a product like the G1000 from the time they founded the company. Since 1997, they've shipped over 100,000 GNS 430 and GNS 530 GPS units. If you're proficient in using one of these units, your transition to the G1000 will be easier, since many of the programming steps are similar, if not identical.

Aviate, Navigate & Communicate on a Single Display

The single biggest benefit of the G1000 and Perspective, compared to competitive products, is that it allows you to aviate, navigate and communicate from a single 10-inch or 12-inch display. In contrast, competitive products have pilots looking in multiple places to see data and reaching in multiple places to operate controls.

The disadvantage of this should be obvious. Pilots need to check their primary instruments constantly to monitor the attitude of their aircraft to verify that it's flying straight and level, climbing with wings level or whatever the case may be. It's easy to get distracted while flying and failing to monitor airplane instruments can be fatal. Two accidents, which occurred while operating IFR in the clouds, clearly illustrate this point.

In 2000, an aircraft climbing out of Santa Rosa, Calif., on an IFR departure, was performing well until the pilot got a call from the controller pointing out that his transponder was not operating. Shortly thereafter, the airplane spun out of the clouds and crashed into a lake, although radar did capture one report from the now operating transponder. This accident would not have occurred in a G1000-equipped aircraft. Not only would the pilot have a 10-inch wide horizon showing him whether his wings were level, but the transponder would have automatically switched to the ALT mode as soon as the plane took off and started flying faster than 30 knots.

Another crash occurred in 2003, while an aircraft was on an instrument approach to the Reid-Hillview airport in San Jose, Calif. In this case, a controller gave the pilot an incorrect tower frequency. The pilot spent more than a minute changing frequency, calling the wrong tower, entering the correct frequency and calling the correct tower. About that time, he noticed that he was in a descending right turn, that he had turned 90° from his course, and was impacting terrain. In a G1000-equipped aircraft, the pilot would have been looking in the upper right hand corner of the PFD (Primary Flight Display) to set frequencies. He would not have been able to miss the 10-inch wide horizon tilting to the right as he descended into terrain.

The lesson is simple. Pilots cannot afford to be distracted from their primary task of flying the airplane. With the increasingly complex airspace and increasingly complex aircraft systems, a pilot can get overloaded to the point where he cannot keep up with the demands of flying the airplane. Having to look away from the instruments and reach for controls that are not adjacent to the instruments contributes to these distractions and makes it more difficult to fly safely.

These accidents could also have been prevented if the pilots were using their autopilots. All glass cockpit aircraft are equipped with modern autopilots that work far better than most older ones. FITS (FAA Industry Training Standards) strongly emphasizes use of the autopilot, particularly when pilots are programming the system. Use of the autopilot also reduces the workload and frees pilots to concentrate on higher level tasks.

Integrated, Customizable Information

From a human factors standpoint, the G1000 is unique in that it tightly integrates all relevant information onto a single display panel and has all of the relevant controls adjacent to the display. With the exception of the engine instruments, which are on the MFD (Multifunction Display) during flight and don't require constant attention, a G1000 pilot can do everything from the PFD. For example, a pilot can modify a flight plan, monitor his position on a map, monitor other nearby aircraft, set all radio and navigation receivers, call up information on nearest airports and monitor flight and navigation instruments—all from a single display. This is close to finding the Holy Grail of flight instrumentation in a small plane.

You can easily add and subtract information from the G1000 PFD as desired. In a minimalist configuration, the display shows the primary flight instruments, radio frequencies and status information on the transponder and the next GPS waypoint. From that base configuration, you can add a map to the PFD and configure whether it displays various combinations of topography, traffic, lightning, terrain awareness, and obstructions. The map range can be adjusted manually or automatically.

In another part of the display, you can choose to bring up, modify and continuously display the flight plan. Alternatively, information on the nearest airports can be displayed, or system status alerts can be reviewed. If the aircraft is so equipped, DME, ADF and RMI bearing information can be added to the display.

If you're a renter, or an owner who has your aircraft on leaseback, you will need to check the settings before you take off, since the prior pilot may have customized the settings for his or her preferences. For example, it could be confusing if you didn't notice that the map is in the North Up orientation, when you're used to flying with Track Up.

TIP

Don't touch the displays with your finger! You'll leave oil on the screens and could scratch them. The scratches cannot be repaired, but you can place a protective film onto the display. The film can be ordered from many companies; be sure to specify the size precisely.

Clean the display only with a solution and soft microfiber cloth that's safe for anti-reflective coatings. Do not use eyeglass solutions that contain ammonia. Eyeglass solutions labeled for use on anti-reflective and mirror coatings are safe to use. Never wipe or clean with a cloth alone—always use the solution in conjunction with the cloth.

Multiple Paths Simplify Reaching Your Data

The G1000 and Perspective employ the same technique that good software developers have used for some time. Some software is intuitively obvious—if you happen to think exactly like the developer! If you don't, it can be very frustrating and nearly impossible to figure out.

Other software seems intuitively obvious at first, since when you try something, it often seems to work the way you want it to. The trick, which may not be obvious, is that the software developers have built in alternate ways to perform a function. Not only does the software seem like it's designed for your preferences, but it's designed for other people's preferences, too!

The G1000 is similar in that it often has multiple ways to perform a function. If you're familiar with programming a GNS 430 or GNS 530, your preferred way to load an instrument approach may be through the PROC and MENU keys. You might not even notice that softkeys, located along the bottom of the display, will also allow you to load an approach. The functions of softkeys change with context, and often they are the fastest way to reach information on the G1000.

In some cases, you're forced to use a particular user interface. For example, the Flight Management System (FMS) knobs are used heavily to program the G1000 system. Often, you can use only the larger or the smaller of these concentric knobs to perform a particular function. Use the wrong knob, and you get something different from what you intended. In other cases, however, software designers made it easier by allowing you to use either knob to make a selection.

Since this book is intended to be a comprehensive treatment of the G1000, we've tried to present all of the different ways—some of which aren't found in the current manuals—you can access a function. As a user, however, you only need to remember one way to perform an operation. In general, you'll find that using the softkeys on the MFD will save keystrokes versus using the MENU and PROC keys. However, if you want to learn one set of techniques for programming the GPS that works equally well on both the MFD and the PFD, you may want to focus on learning to use the MENU and PROC keys.

Information, Not Just Data

We live in a world where we're surrounded by *data* and somehow we're expected to process it to derive the *information* we need. The G1000 does an outstanding job of taking that raw data and turning it into useful information.

In one of the simplest cases, the airspeed display tape has "Speed bugs," which point to some of the many, important to remember airspeeds. As a flight instructor, I'm constantly jumping into different airplanes and one of the first things I ask a client is what the Vx and Vy airspeeds are for their airplane. This tells me two things—whether they know them, and whether they're what I think they are.

The G1000 takes care of this issue. As the aircraft accelerates and reaches rotation speed, a reference bug labeled "Vr" appears alongside the speed tape. Now, pilots don't need to remember Vr—they know to rotate when they reach the first speed bug. Other bugs for the best angle of climb Vx, best rate of climb Vy, and best glide speed Vg are included in the G1000. The manufacturers' specified speeds are loaded into the system, though you can change those values or turn off the bugs all together.

Human factors specialists determined years ago that humans can grasp data more quickly when it's presented graphically. The G1000's Fuel Range Ring is a great example of this. It's one of my favorite features, which is ironic, since I originally scoffed at its usefulness.

The first time I flew back from the Cessna factory in Kansas with a client in a new T206, we wanted to avoid making an extra fuel stop. The MFD showed our destination airport between the fuel range ring that indicated our time to fuel exhaustion and the ring that indicated our time to reaching reserve fuel (which we had defined as one hour of fuel).

Uncomfortable with that, yet still wanting to reach our destination, we began experimenting with different power and mixture settings. Very quickly, we found power settings that moved the reserve range ring beyond the destination airport, and indeed we arrived with nearly 20 gallons remaining in the tanks. With other glass cockpits, we could have found the same *data* manually, but with the Fuel Range Ring we got instant *information* graphically.

Display Redundancy

Much is made—sometimes too much—of what will happen under various flying scenarios. For example, some pilots worry out of proportion about infrequent scenarios—such as engine failure and midair collision—versus more frequent occurrences such as night flight (which has several times the daytime accident rate) and the almost always fatal inadvertent VFR into IMC accidents.

Likewise, when pilots think of glass cockpits, they're quick to worry about what will happen if the display fails, when it's more likely that an alternator will fail. Nonetheless, the G1000 is unique in its ability to continue displaying the primary flight instruments even after a PFD failure! Its unique reversionary mode recombines data from the PFD and MFD to create a new combination of information that appears on whichever display is still functional.

Lose a PFD and you still see the flight instruments and engine display, though you have to look at the right side display. Lose an MFD and you get the same combined information on the left side display. In the unlikely event you lose both displays (and you don't wake up from having a nightmare), you still have use of the three standby instruments.

Obviously, the loss of an alternator and subsequent draining of the battery would lead to the loss of both displays. However, all G1000 and Perspective implementations include an additional battery and sometimes a second alternator. This provides much redundancy and virtually eliminates single points of failure where losing a single component would result in disaster.

Real-time Data

Real-time data is available in most glass cockpits, so while this is not a large G1000 differentiator, it's still worth describing the benefits. Traffic Information Service (TIS) and Traffic Advisory Systems (TAS) are common functions; both make visually spotting other aircraft much easier. Stormscopes® provide real-time lightning data, and in-cockpit weather services provide near real-time displays of virtually the same graphical weather products that you're able to get sitting in front of your computer on the ground.

For example, you can call up a satellite picture to see whether clouds have moved in from the coast obscuring your home airport, or another weather product showing the cloud top heights so you can estimate the severity of a storm and whether you're likely to encounter freezing rain. Radar pictures, mapped in near real-time relative to your current position in the air, can also be called up so that you can see where cells are located and plan a route around them.

Note that you shouldn't use these radar pictures to pick your way through storm cells. Rather, use them strategically to steer well around the weather. Remember too that the radar data is a minimum of eight minutes old, and much can change in that time.

Some in-cockpit weather solutions provide SIGMETs and AIRMETs. These warnings of significant weather, are virtually indecipherable when given over the phone by Flight Service Stations, unless you happen to know the location of every VOR they reference to describe the boundaries of the affected area. Via the G1000, SIGMETs

IFR Rating in a Glass Cockpit or Round Gauge Plane?

If you're studying for the instrument rating, you may be wondering whether to do your IFR training in a round gauge (sometimes called steam gauge) airplane or in a modern glass cockpit aircraft such as the Garmin G1000, Avidyne, or Cirrus Perspective. Like many of life's questions, the answer is: "It depends."

If your goal is to get an instrument rating at the lowest possible cost—and I hope it's not—then, of course, round gauge airplanes are less expensive to fly. Frankly, getting the best IFR training has more to do with the quality of instruction than the price of the airplane, so if you need to save a few bucks, use a round gauge airplane, but pay for a great instructor.

In general, it makes sense to learn in the type of plane in which you'll ultimately do your IFR flying. If your goal is to make IFR trips in the safest airplane, than I highly recommend you train and fly in glass cockpit aircraft.

For my full article, use the QR code below or enter the following search term into Google: Instrument Rating site:maxtrescott.com

and AIRMETs are shown graphically on a map, and you can read the full text of the warnings. Real-time Temporary Flight Restriction (TFR) data is also available.

Summary

Each manufacturer's glass cockpit implementation has unique strengths and weaknesses and all will improve over time as new revisions are introduced. All of them can help general aviation reach new levels of safety. What's most important is that you as a pilot fully understand all of the nuances of the system you fly, so that you always know what the system is doing now and how to make it do what you need to do next. Ultimately, fully understanding your system is going to reduce your workload, enhance safety and make flying even more enjoyable.

Chapter 3:
System Overview

The G1000 and Perspective are a flexible system of interchangeable hardware modules and software tailored to the needs of individual aircraft manufacturers. Piston-powered aircraft have the two-display version, while high-end aircraft like the Cessna Mustang jet use a three-display version. While it's not necessary to understand the system architecture to operate the G1000—and you can skip ahead to Chapter 4 if you wish—knowing the architecture can be helpful in understanding the ramifications of the failure of one or more system components.

In addition to the displays, there are a number of hardware modules that make up the system (figure 3-1). In most aircraft, these are located in the tail cone; in others the modules are behind the instrument panel, but hidden from view. Placing the electronics in the tail adds one aerodynamic benefit. In most aircraft, the wing provides lift, while the horizontal stabilizer actually generates a downward force, balancing the aircraft around its center of gravity, but also requiring the wing to generate additional lift. Placing the electronics in the tail reduces the amount of down force required from the tail, the amount of lift required from the wing, and makes the aircraft slightly faster.

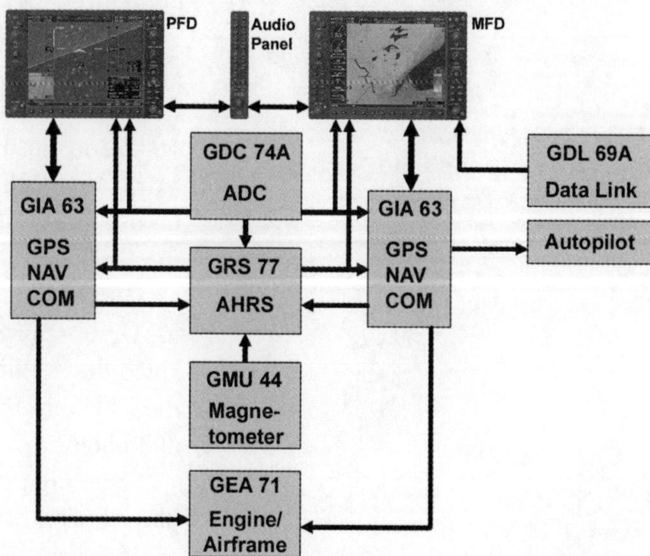

Figure 3-1 The G1000 is a modular system.

All hardware modules are line replaceable units (LRU) for quick service. A technician pulls out the faulty unit and replaces it with a known good unit from inventory. The faulty unit is repaired, goes back into inventory, and eventually into another aircraft. Your module that started life in a Mooney may end up in a Mustang jet! You may also save time by not having to take your airplane to a separate avionics shop, as some aircraft service centers will be authorized to swap G1000 LRUs. Finally, one-stop shopping when you take your plane in for maintenance!

While much of the hardware may be the same, whether you're flying jets or propeller-driven aircraft, the software is different—though similar—for each model. Thus when you jump from one G1000 aircraft into another, the instruments will appear the same, but the implementation of some features may vary, or may not exist at all if a manufacturer chose not to implement them.

When you buy a new plane, not only will you receive a copy of the Pilot Operating Handbook (POH), but you'll also receive a CD with a copy of the software loaded onto your system. In some cases, maintenance personnel may need this disk to reload the software onto your system after it's been serviced. You'll want to keep the CD in a safe place, particularly if it's a rental aircraft used by many people. In addition, when the G1000 is first turned on, you should verify that the aircraft's software version is correct—in case software for another airplane model was inadvertently loaded after your system was serviced.

G1000 Displays

Figure 3-2 Manufacturers can now choose from 10, 12, and 15-inch displays. *© Garmin Ltd. or its affiliates*

The most prominent part of the system is the full-color displays that pilots use to interact with the system. G1000 Aircraft with non-integrated autopilots use two GDU 1040s, which are 10.4-inch diagonal displays that are physically identical (figure 3-2). That keeps costs down, since service centers will only need to stock a single part which can be used to replace either display. The display on the left (pilot's side) is configured through software as a PFD, while the display on the right is configured as a MFD.

G1000 aircraft using the integrated GFC 700 autopilot use a different MFD display with additional keys that control the autopilot. The Columbia 400i (now called the Cessna Corvalis TT) uses the GDU 1042 and the Beechcraft G36 uses the GDU 1043, which includes an extra key for the yaw damper. Cessna aircraft with the GFC 700 autopilot use a pair of GDU 1044Bs with autopilot keys on both the MFD and the PFD.

Perspective aircraft use either 10- or 12-inch displays for the PFD and MFD; most owners choose the larger displays. They have fewer knobs, since they eliminate the G1000's redundant knobs along the left side of the PFD and the right side of the MFD. See Chapter 15 for more details and photos.

Some high-end aircraft, such as the Cessna Mustang, use a three-display version of the G1000. In these installations, the outer two displays are identical 10.4-inch displays, both configured as PFDs, so the pilot and copilot have identical views of the primary flight instruments. A third 15-inch display, located in the center of the instrument panel, serves as a MFD. Garmin also sells a 12-inch version of the display, giving manufacturers yet another option for tailoring the G1000 to their aircraft.

The GDU 1040/1042/1043/1044B displays use thin-film transistor (TFT) technology, which provides a wider viewing angle than older flat panel displays, and is easily readable in most sunlight conditions. Physically, each 10-inch display is 7.7 by 11.8 inches and 3.5 inches deep. Electrically, it's an XGA type display with 1024x768 pixels of resolution and capable of displaying 262,144 colors. The color capability is fully used when displaying topographical maps, which appear equal in quality to a printed map. A built-in graphics accelerator refreshes the display 30 times a second, rendering excellent, flicker-free graphics.

Cockpit lighting in many general aviation (G.A.) aircraft has been atrocious, and here the G1000 shines—literally. Backlighting has been added to the displays, and pilots can control the intensity of each display individually as well as adjust lighting of the engraved labels on the display bezel.

Each display has two slots for SD-type memory cards. The lower slot is occupied by a memory card which contains the terrain and obstruction databases. Pull that card and the data's gone. The other slots are used to update the internal GPS databases and, by some manufacturers, to provide electronic checklist capability.

GIA 63 and GIA 63W Integrated Avionics Units

If the G1000 displays are the beauty of the system, then the two GIA 63, or GIA 63W for WAAS-capable systems, integrated avionics units are close to being the dual brains of the system (figure 3-3). Each of the units, designated GIA1 and GIA2, contains a complete GPS receiver, VHF COM radio, and VHF NAV receiver. These functions are relatively independent of each other so if, for example, the COM radio fails, the GPS and NAV receivers in that LRU might continue to operate. In addition, if an entire GIA 63 fails, the second GIA 63 will still provide GPS, COM and NAV receiver functions for the aircraft, though some autopilot functionality will be lost.

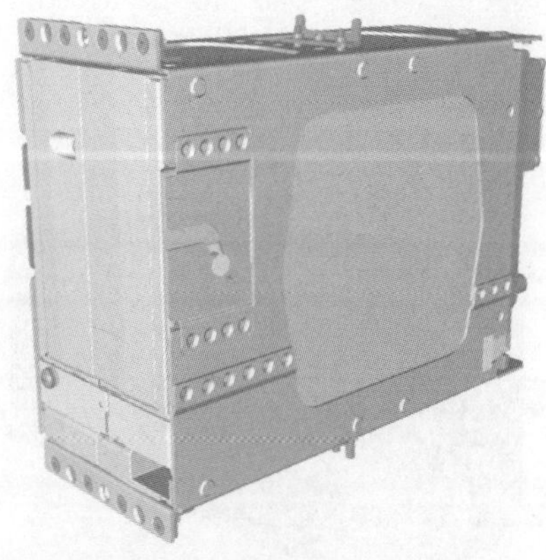

Figure 3-3 The GIA 63 is similar in functionality to the Garmin GNS 530.
© Garmin Ltd. or its affiliates

The first GPS, either GPS1 or GPS2, to acquire a signal becomes the active GPS. The other one becomes a hot spare which can take over at any time. If the active GPS subsequently fails, the hot spare becomes active and there is no loss of functionality.

The COM portion of the unit has 16 watts of transmit power and is designed for 8.33 kHz radio channel spacing, now in use in some parts of the world. You can easily reconfigure the system from 25 kHz spacing to 8.33 kHz spacing by making a change on the System Setup page in the AUX page group.

The GIA 63s communicate with both displays via a High-Speed Data Bus (HSDB) Ethernet connection. When the GPS database is updated by the user though slots in the displays, a copy of the data is stored in both GIA 63s, so it is still available if one unit fails. Updating the system is quick and easy since you only have to update the two displays, taking 20 to 30 seconds each.

To update the database, download data from the Internet via a subscription service onto a SD card. Insert the card into the PFD's slot and turn on the master switch. The system will ask if you want to update the database. Press the ENT key for yes or the CLR key for no. After the update is complete, move the SD card to the MFD's slot, turn on the Master Switch (and, for some manufacturers, an Avionics switch) and repeat the process.

Audio Panels

The system audio panels provide many modern features. The GMA 1347 (figure 5-1) is used in G1000 systems. Perspective aircraft use the GMA 347 (figure 15-8) and, beginning in 2012, the GMA 350 (figure 15-9). All let you select the radios on which you're transmitting and receiving and listen to any of the navigation radios to identify a station. They also integrate an intercom system, marker beacon receiver and a digital clearance recorder.

The GMA 1347 is mounted in G1000 aircraft between the PFD and MFD. It includes a Display Backup button, which can be pushed in an emergency if one of the displays fails. When pushed, it displays the primary instruments on whichever display remains. The GMA 347 and GMA 350 are located in the central radio stack of Perspective aircraft. The Display Backup button in these aircraft is located between the PFD and MFD, not on the audio panel.

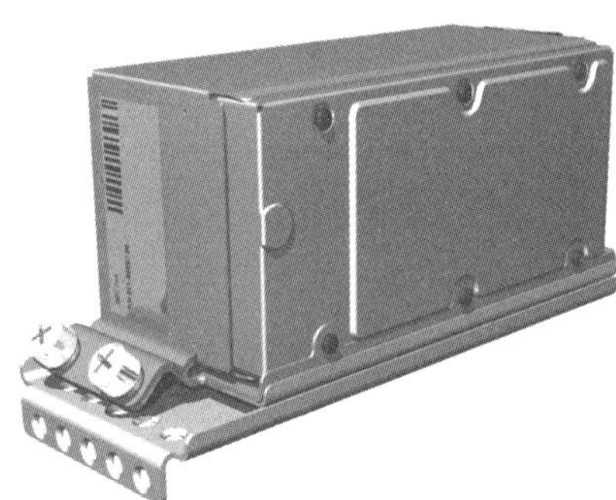

Figure 3-4 The GDC 74A processes air data from the pitot-static system. *© Garmin Ltd. or its affiliates*

GDC 74A Air Data Computer

The GDC 74A Air Data Computer (figure 3-4) processes information from the pitot-static lines, which bring in data about the air outside the plane. For example, it provides information on pressure, altitude, indicated airspeed, vertical speed, outside wind direction and strength, and total air temperature.

Vertical speed information has the same lag (approximately 6 seconds) that you find in a traditional VSI, so don't chase these indications excessively. Total air temperature, which includes the heating effects of the airplane moving through the air, is used to calculate outside air temperature (OAT). The GDC 74A also provides altitude information to the transponder.

Figure 3-5 The AHRS is a solid-state replacement for mechanical gyros. *© Garmin Ltd. or its affiliates*

GRS 77 Attitude Heading and Reference System

The GRS 77 Attitude Heading and Reference System (figure 3-5) or AHRS is one of the key components that helped bring glass cockpit technology into the price range of general aviation aircraft. This AHRS was developed initially by Sequoia Instruments, which Garmin purchased in 2001. It was the one of the first low-cost, solid-state replacements for mechanical gyros.

Historically, gyros were first replaced in military aircraft using expensive laser-ring gyros that cost $75,000 and up. The GRS 77 includes three rate sensors, three accelerometers, and two 2-axis tilt sensors for position data. It's unique in that it also uses GPS and magnetometer data to provide an accurate reference at a relatively low cost. If either of those external sources is unavailable or sending invalid data, then data from the air data computer is also used.

Figure 3-6 The Magnetometer senses an airplane's heading. *© Garmin Ltd. or its affiliates*

It's also fast to initialize. On the ground during start-up, all instruments are usually available within 45 seconds. In addition, the GRS 77 AHRS can be reinitialized in flight, should power be interrupted. Reinitialization can occur even while the airplane is in a bank of up to 20°, and some factory pilots have seen it reinitialize in up to a 45° bank. In contrast, the reference systems in some other glass cockpits, including jet aircraft, require that the system remain motionless for several minutes during initialization and the systems cannot be reinitialized in flight.

GMU 44 3 axis magnetometer

Future pilots may never have to adjust a Directional Gyro or Heading Indicator to the correct compass setting again—and again if the gyro is wearing out—because of the GMU 44 3-axis magnetometer (figure 3-6). Generally located in the wing, this device does the work of a compass, but with a digital output of the correct heading.

Traditional one-axis flux valves weren't accurate during climb out, particularly during turns. Magnetometers in older general aviation aircraft often didn't work well since they couldn't be located far enough away from the avionics in the front panel. This problem is solved by locating many of the G1000 avionics in the tail cone.

Many older magnetometer installations had a Free/Slave switch on the instrument panel, which was occasionally needed to sync up the reading from the magnetometer with a compass. There is no such switch in a G1000 or Perspective cockpit—it's all automatic.

Mechanics still need to exercise caution when working on the magnetometer. They must use a composite screwdriver or demagnetize their screwdriver. Otherwise, they may damage this sensitive instrument.

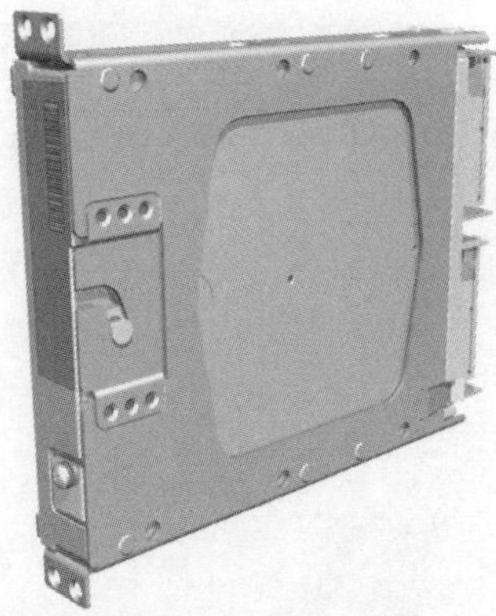

Figure 3-7 The GEA 71 monitors engine parameters and all G1000 system components. *© Garmin Ltd. or its affiliates*

GEA 71 Engine/Airframe Unit

The GEA 71 Engine/Airframe Unit (figure 3-7) monitors engine parameters, avionics, and all system components. The layout of the engine information on the G1000 display varies among aircraft models, and represents one of the biggest differences between systems. Unlike other glass cockpit systems which have a single page for all engine data, most G1000 implementations display the most important data on one page, and other engine-related data on two other pages. While some engine data is not continuously available for view, the system provides alerts if needed.

Figure 3-8 The Garmin Data Link is required to receive weather data via SiriusXM Satellite. *© Garmin Ltd. or its affiliates*

GDL 69A Garmin Data Link

The GDL 69A Garmin Data Link is optional (figure 3-8). When installed, it provides radio and aviation weather data through a subscription service from SiriusXM. For example, current textual METARs (latest weather observation) and Terminal Aerodrome Forecasts (TAFs) can be displayed for any airport. Graphical weather products, such as radar and satellite imagery, can be displayed relative to the aircraft's position. See Chapter 8 for more details on this system. A less expensive GDL 69 is available which has weather capability but no satellite radio capability.

Figure 3-9 The alphanumeric keypad in the Columbia 350i and 400i. *© Garmin Ltd. or its affiliates*

Alphanumeric Keypad

The Cirrus Perspective ships with an alphanumeric keypad (figure 15-7) as does the Corvalis TTX (figure 3-9) and the Cessna Mustang. GA pilots can

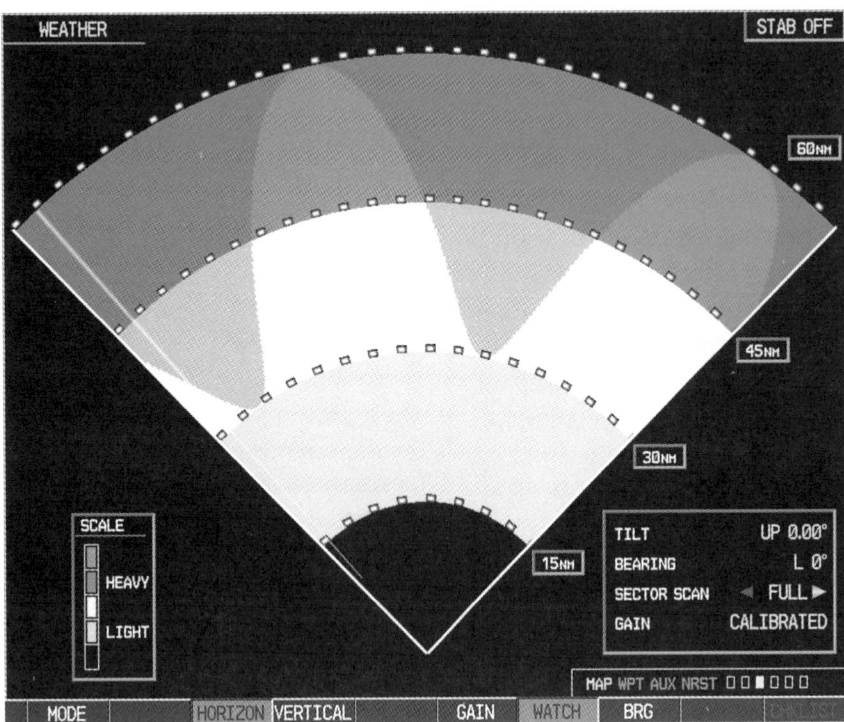

Figure 3-10 The Weather page from a radar equipped Baron. *© Garmin Ltd. or its affiliates*

only hope that keypads become available in all G1000-equipped aircraft, as this will save considerable knob twisting when entering identifiers into a flight plan.

GWX 68 Radar

The GWX 68 is an airborne radar unit, currently available only in the Beechcraft G58 Baron and Cessna Citation Mustang, though you'll probably find it available in the future in other G1000-equipped Very Light Jets (figure 3-10). It provides a real-time view of precipitation in the vicinity of the aircraft and is available with either a 10-inch or 12-inch phased array antenna. It features a weather avoidance range of as much as 305 nm.

Its features include:

- Selectable Ranges: from 2.5 to 320 nm
- Vertical Scan Angle: up to 60 degrees
- Altitude: 50,000 ft (unpressurized)
- Horizontal and vertical scan modes
- Weather and ground mapping modes

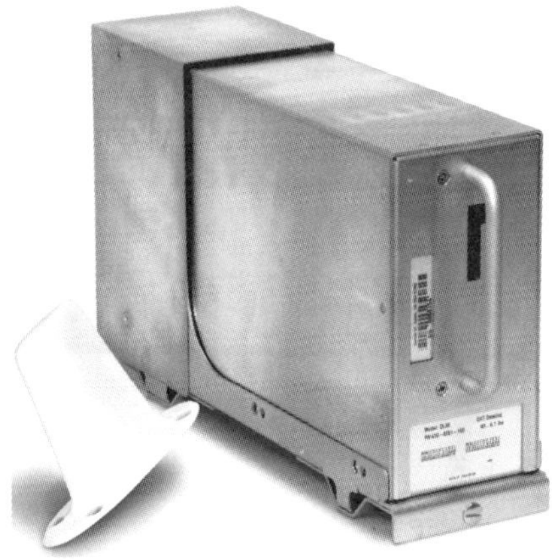

Figure 3-11 The ADS-B transceiver broadcasts your aircraft location and receives traffic and FIS-B weather data. *© Garmin Ltd. or its affiliates*

GDL 90 ADS-B Data Link Transceiver

The optional Automatic Dependent Surveillance-Broadcast (ADS-B) data link transceiver (figure 3-11) broadcasts aircraft position, airspeed, projected track, altitude and identification to other similarly equipped aircraft and to a growing network of ground stations. It includes Flight Information Service-Broadcast (FIS-B), which displays traffic, weather and other information broadcast from ground stations. The FAA's network of ADS-B ground stations in the U.S. is nearly complete and all aircraft must be equipped with ADS-B Out before January 1, 2020.

Autopilot

When the G1000 was first introduced, Garmin didn't have an autopilot product, so the G1000 was interfaced to other manufacturers' equipment. For example, both Cessna and Diamond propeller-driven aircraft incorporated the Honeywell (formerly Bendix/King) KAP 140 autopilot, while Mooney and Tiger used S-Tec autopilots.

Subsequently, Garmin developed its own autopilot, the GFC 700. To allow more precise control of speed and torque and increase reliability, Garmin chose to distribute the electronic controls among the servos that move the control surfaces, rather than consolidate them centrally. In most G1000 aircraft, the GFC 700 controls are on the MFD. A separate control panel, the GMC 705, is used in the Cirrus Perspective (figure 15-16) and some turboprop and jet aircraft use the GMC 710 control panel.

Competitive glass cockpit manufacturers point out that G1000-equipped aircraft without the GFC 700 autopilot are not fully integrated. While that's true, the most visible disadvantage of a nonintegrated autopilot—and it's minor—is that pilots must set their altitude reference twice, once on the G1000 and again on the autopilot, instead of once with an integrated autopilot. This is a minor inconvenience compared to the many advantages of the G1000.

Most G1000 nonintegrated autopilot installations include GPS roll steering, though KAP140-equipped models of the Diamond DA40 did not. GPS roll steering takes your current location and groundspeed, compares it with the flight plan, and calculates accurate intercept angles and initiation of turns. GIA2 provides this information to the autopilot, which enables it to roll the plane precisely out on course, without the under or overshoot common with systems connected directly to a CDI or HSI needle. A system without roll steering will still track a GPS signal, but will not handle intercepts and turns as well.

Nonintegrated autopilot systems ship with one mechanical gyro—an electric turn coordinator—though it's not visible to the pilot. It's needed to provide roll rate information to the autopilot. Should the AHRS fail, it allows nonintegrated autopilots to continue to operate in some modes.

GSR 56 Iridium Transceiver

The GSR 56 Iridium Transceiver (figure 3-12) provides voice communication via the pilot and copilot headsets. The unit sends and receives voice data and text messages through the Iridium satellite network. It connects to GIA1 via RS-232. Email messages are limited to 160 characters, including the email address. The transceiver is also used to receive worldwide weather text and graphics from Garmin Flight Data Services.

Figure 3-12 The Iridium transceiver is used for phone calls, text and email messages, and worldwide weather data from Garmin Flight Data Services. *© Garmin Ltd. or its affiliates*

Standby Instruments

Each manufacturer chooses what backup or standby instruments to include with their aircraft. Typically there are three—an airspeed indicator, mechanical attitude indicator and an altimeter. Some manufacturers, like Cessna and Tiger, choose to include a vacuum pump to drive the standby attitude indicator to provide another level of redundancy, while others, such as Diamond and Cirrus, use an electric standby attitude indicator.

G1000 and Perspective Limitations

As a pilot, you should carefully read the limitations for your aircraft. In particular, you should pay attention to the limitations for your autopilot and the preflight test of the autopilot that may be required by your aircraft's manufacturer.

There are also G1000 limitations that vary by manufacturer. You can find these in your FAA Aircraft Flight Manual or Flight Manual Supplement. A few examples of limitations that you might find include:

- Operation is prohibited north of 70° N or south of 70° S latitudes. In addition, operations are not authorized in the following two regions: 1) north of 65° N between 75°W and 120°W longitude (northern Canada) and 2) south of 55°S between 120°E and 165°E longitude (region south of Australia and New Zealand).
- Navigation must not be predicated upon the use of the Terrain or Obstacle data displayed by the G1000.
- Use of the Traffic Map to maneuver the airplane to avoid traffic is prohibited.
- Use of the Weather Map page for hazardous weather (thunderstorm) penetration is prohibited.

Most aircraft will have more G1000 limitations than those listed above. FITS training typically includes a review of all limitations and you're strongly encourage to read all of the limitations for your aircraft.

Summary

As you can see, the G1000 and Perspective's modular architecture gives it a flexibility not usually found in general aviation avionics. It makes it easier to add new features through software revisions and the addition of new LRUs or external devices connected to the Ethernet bus. The use of LRUs makes troubleshooting and servicing simpler. As a result, we can expect the system to evolve and add new capabilities for years to come. Now let's learn how to use the main interface of this exciting system, the Primary Flight Display.

Chapter 4:
PFD Overview

The most visible difference in any glass cockpit aircraft is the Primary Flight Display (PFD) directly in front of the pilot. Many older aircraft already have Multifunction displays (MFD), or a moving map on the GPS receiver, but these planes still use the traditional six round gauges or primary flight instruments, variations of which have been in the airplane virtually since it was invented over 100 years ago. PFDs, however, display flight information in new ways that allow you to quickly synthesize a mental picture of the plane's current situation and its trend for the near future. Initially, it can be confusing but, when fully understood, the PFD simplifies pilot workloads.

In the old paradigm, the primary instruments served two functions: they directly measured some parameter and they displayed this data. In contrast, PFDs display only data; the actual measurement occurs through sensors located elsewhere in the plane.

The most prominent feature of the PFD is the horizontal line, which separates the blue, upper half of the screen representing the sky from the brown, lower half of the screen representing the ground. In traditional aircraft, this line is less than two-inches wide and is found in the attitude indicator. Instrument pilots constantly work to match a miniature airplane with the line to keep an airplane in the clouds flying level. Since the traditional display is so small and there are so many instruments to monitor, it's easy to get distracted and not notice if the airplane transitions from straight-and-level flight into an unusual attitude.

In the G1000 and Perspective, however, you will find that is virtually impossible. The horizontal line is so prominent and the PFD so large and bright that it is nearly impossible not to notice—even through peripheral vision—when the airplane begins to inadvertently enter a turn. This is one of the many contributions that the G1000 makes to increasing safety. This chapter discusses virtually all functions accessed through the PFD, except for radio operation discussed in Chapter 5 and flight planning and instrument procedures, which are similar for both the PFD and MFD, discussed in Chapters 9 and 11.

Perspective

Most of the PFD features are the same for the G1000 and Perspective. The CRS, HDG and ALT knobs, found on the PFD in G1000 systems, are found on the Perspective's center console. The Perspective displays % Power in the upper left instead of the NAV radio frequencies. The Perspective's background colors are gradients, not solid colors. The Current Track Bug, a powerful feature added in later G1000 versions and described in Chapter 14, has dashed lines that make it more visible in the Perspective (figure 15-3). Early versions of the Perspective software had only one bearing pointer; later versions have two bearing pointers, like the G1000. The Perspective's BARO knob can be pushed to set the altimeter to standard pressure, which is 29.92. The latest Perspective software replaces the BRG (bearing) field at the top of the PFD with ETE (estimated time to next waypoint). The Perspective PFD has several new softkeys, described in Chapter 15.

Organization

The primary flight instruments occupy the center of the display (figure 4-1). While traditional aircraft have six primary instruments, airspeed, attitude indicator, altimeter, heading indicator, turn coordinator and vertical speed, the G1000 and Perspective group this information into four information displays. Airspeed is to the left, attitude and slip/skid information in the upper center, altitude and vertical speed to the right, and heading and rate of turn information in the lower center of the screen as part of a horizontal situation indicator (HSI).

In the upper left of the PFD, VHF navigation frequencies are shown on the G1000 and % Power is shown on the Perspective. The Navigation Status bar—showing distance and direction to the next waypoint—is in the center and communication frequencies in the upper right corner. Along the bottom, the outside air temperature is displayed on the lower left and the transponder status bar and system time are displayed to the lower right.

One of the system's most distinguishing features, softkeys, are along the bottom of the display. Softkey labels correspond to the keys below and change depending upon the context. Pushing a key implements a function or leads to a hierarchical set of additional softkey choices. You'll want to pay particular attention to the softkeys, which are utilized extensively throughout the PFD and MFD, as they often access functions faster than the MENU key which GNS 430 and GNS 530 users are accustomed to using.

Note the significance of color. Cyan (light blue) is used for items that are pilot adjustable, such as the altitude and heading bugs. Green is for items actively in use, such as the transponder, COM and NAV frequencies. Yellow, representing caution, marks the smooth air penetration range on the airspeed display and is used for some annunciators, such as low fuel indications, that appear on the display. Red is for warnings. It's used at both the upper and lower speeds of the airspeed display and for the most serious Warning annunciators. Magenta represents rate of turn, trend vectors, and anything derived from the GPS signal, such as the active leg of a GPS flight plan.

Radio Display and Controls

Radio frequencies are displayed in the upper corners of the PFD and MFD. Communication frequencies are shown in the upper right of both displays on the G1000, but only on the PFD for the Perspective. VHF navigation frequencies are shown in the upper left of both displays on the G1000, but only on the MFD for the Perspective. The top line is for NAV1 and COM1 and the second line is for NAV2 and COM2.

Like most modern radios, two frequencies are shown for each radio: the active frequency being used and a standby frequency where new frequencies are entered. They're not labeled, however, so you'll need to remember which is which. One way to identify each on the G1000 is to remember that standby frequencies are toward the outside of the screen

TIP

To remember which frequencies are standby versus active, on the G1000, look for the light-blue colored tuning box. It's around the standby frequency where you can dial in a new frequency. On the Perspective, a smaller font is used for standby frequencies.

Figure 4-1 The primary flight instruments occupy the center of the PFD. Radio frequencies and the Navigation Status bar are at the top. The knobs shown on the left do not exist on the Perspective. *© Garmin Ltd. or its affiliates*

closer to the tuning knobs, and active frequencies are toward the center of the screen.

The G1000's PFD control knobs are located on both sides of the display bezel. All G1000 control knobs are duplicated on the MFD display bezel and, in many cases, they perform the identical function. While not obvious at first, this has the effect of grouping one set of all controls together between the PFD and MFD display screens. Some MFD functions, however, such as the range control/pointer knob and FMS knobs, need to be performed by the controls to the right of the MFD. Train yourself to use your right hand and only use the controls in the center and to the lower right of the MFD (figure 4-2). There's never a need to use the knobs to the left of the PFD and the upper right of the MFD. The Perspective has no knobs on the left side of the PFD or the right side of the MFD.

To select a radio frequency, use two pairs of concentric knobs, one to the left of each display labeled NAV and to the right labeled COM. The larger knob selects the MegaHertz, or numbers to the left of the decimal point and the smaller knob selects the kiloHertz numbers to the right of the decimal point. Radio frequencies can also be auto-tuned from several pages, including the Nearest and Airport Waypoint pages. This is usually faster than manually dialing frequencies with the NAV and COM knobs, particularly if you're loading multiple frequencies at one time. Use of the radios and audio panel is discussed in more detail in Chapter 5.

Figure 4-2 Use just the controls between the displays and to the lower right of the MFD. *© Garmin Ltd. or its affiliates*

Status Bars

The Navigation Status bar (figure 4-3), in the upper center of the display, shows four parameters about the active GPS waypoint. It lists the waypoint name, the distance to it in nautical miles, the DTK or desired track to the waypoint and the TRK, the plane's current track across the ground.† These navigation parameters were defined as part of the certification process and are not user configurable. However, the Navigation Status bar on the MFD is user configurable, so if you have a favorite set of navigation parameters you prefer to monitor, set the MFD to display them.

Figure 4-3 The PFD's Navigation Status bar always shows distance and track to the active waypoint. *© Garmin Ltd. or its affiliates*

The system time box, in the lower right corner, derives its time from the GPS. You cannot change the actual time, but you can change the format in which it's displayed, such as 12 or 24 hour time or local versus Zulu time. The transponder status bar, to the left of the system time box, shows the current operating mode, ground, standby, ON or ALT, and the current squawk code, all of which can be set through the softkeys described later in this chapter. Outside air temperature, in the lower left, can be configured to display in either °F or °C.

Airspeed Display

The airspeed indicator is a tape style display, with the indicated airspeed always displayed in the center and an additional 30 knots displayed above and below it (figure 4-4). The benefit of this type of display is that you always look in the same spot for the airspeed. With a traditional gauge, you might have to look around the full instrument to find the current airspeed.

The airspeed starts to indicate when the plane is faster than 20 knots and traditional color markings are used to indicate different speed ranges. White is used for the flap operating range, green for the normal operating range, yellow for the caution range and red to indicate the never exceed speed. In addition, red is used for low speed awareness when within 20 knots of stall speed. Above the never exceed speed, a barber pole type display with alternating red and white diagonal stripes is shown.

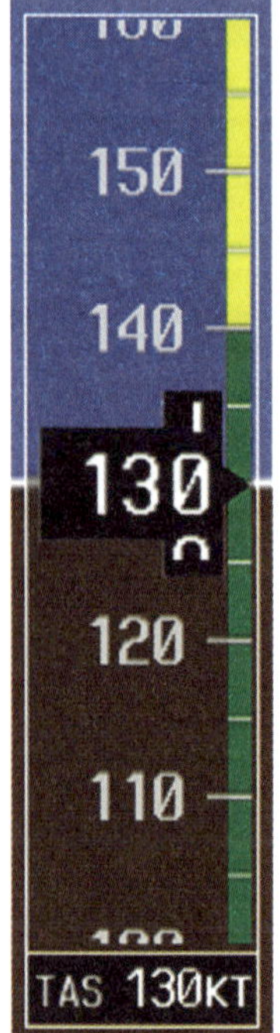

Figure 4-4 Airspeed indicator with True Airspeed (TAS) shown at the bottom. *© Garmin Ltd. or its affiliates*

† See page 210 for updates to this feature.

One benefit of glass cockpits is that the computer processing power can be used to generate additional information not found on traditional airspeed indicators. For example, true airspeed is continuously displayed in a box below the airspeed indicator. Also, the PFD displays several types of "trend vectors" that extrapolate current data and predict the aircraft's performance six seconds into the future. One of these is an airspeed trend vector, shown by a magenta line above or below the current airspeed, which extends out to the predicted future airspeed. The trend vector appears anytime the airplane is accelerating or decelerating (figure 4-5).

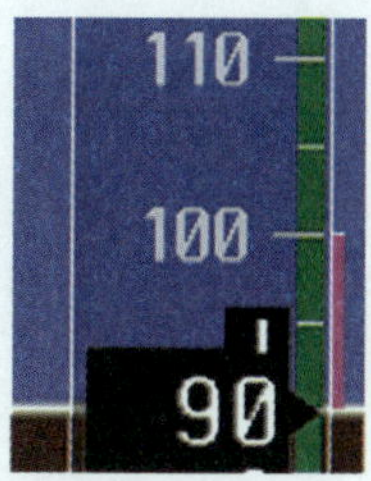

Figure 4-5 Airspeed trend vector shows aircraft will be at 100 knots in 6 seconds. *© Garmin Ltd. or its affiliates*

One disadvantage of the tape style display is that when initially transitioning to a glass cockpit, it takes a little more effort to read the numbers, compared to a traditional airspeed indicator where you get an instant sense of the airspeed by glancing at the pointer. This disadvantage is offset by the presence of Vspeed reference bugs. Also, experience in the field is showing that over time, pilots do accommodate to referencing numbers rather than needle positions.

One of the first things you need to know about an aircraft is its rotation speed, best angle and best rate of climb speeds. The G1000 and Perspective make it easy to identify each of these speeds by adding speed bugs along the right side of the airspeed tape. The aircraft manufacturer specifies the reference speeds to be displayed, though you can enable, disable or change these values. For example, if flying a short field takeoff at less than gross weight, you could reset Vr to a more appropriate speed, though it will reset to the manufacturer's default speed after power shutdown. Changing the speed bugs is discussed later in this chapter.

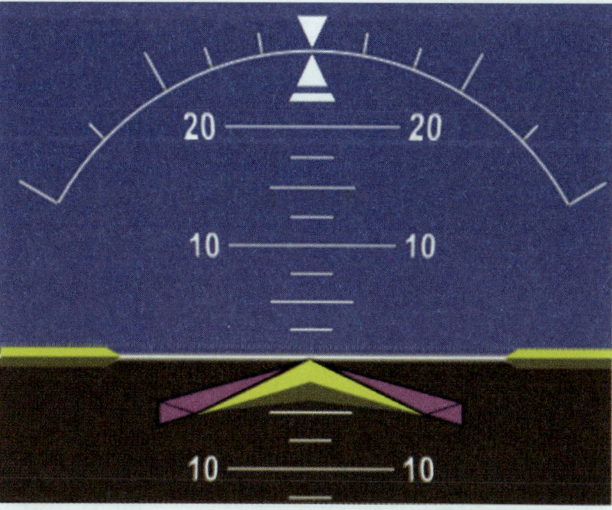

Figure 4-6 Attitude indicator shown in straight and level flight. *© Garmin Ltd. or its affiliates*

Attitude Indicator

The attitude indicator, located in the upper center of the PFD, is similar to a traditional attitude indicator, except that an inverted "V" replaces the miniature airplane in the center (figure 4-6). For aircraft with a Flight Director, discussed in more detail in Chapter 10, command bars rest above the inverted "V."

Pitch is indicated by major marks every 10° and minor marks every 5°. Should the pitch exceed 50° above or 30° below the horizon, large red pitch warning chevrons appear on the display (figure 4-6A). Unlike a traditional mechanical gyro which can "tumble" at extreme attitudes, the electronic AHRS is immune to this type of problem.

Figure 4-6A These chevrons indicate that the aircraft is pitched up beyond normal. *© Garmin Ltd. or its affiliates*

Bank angles are marked in the traditional fashion with major tick marks at 30° and 60° and minor tick marks at 10° and 20°. There is an additional mark at 45°, not found on traditional gyros, which is very useful for practicing steep turns. Most G1000-equipped aircraft are not certified beyond 60° of bank. Should an unusual attitude occur, the

PFD is de-cluttered by the automatic removal of the Inset Map, flight plan and true airspeed boxes.

The slip/skid indicator is a small trapezoid located below the two triangles at the top of the attitude indicator. It moves in the same way as the traditional ball in a turn coordinator. In other words, if the trapezoid is to the right of center, you'll need to apply additional right rudder to force it back to the center.

Altimeter and Vertical Speed Indicator

The altimeter uses a tape-style display located on the right side of the PFD (figure 4-7). The tape extends 300 feet above and below the center, where the current altitude is shown in larger numbers. Numeric values and major tick marks are shown every 100 feet and minor tick marks every 20 feet. Like the airspeed indicator, a magenta trend vector, located on the left side of the display (though earlier versions had it on the right side), extends up or down to the altitude at which you're predicted to be in six seconds, based upon the current rate of climb or descent.

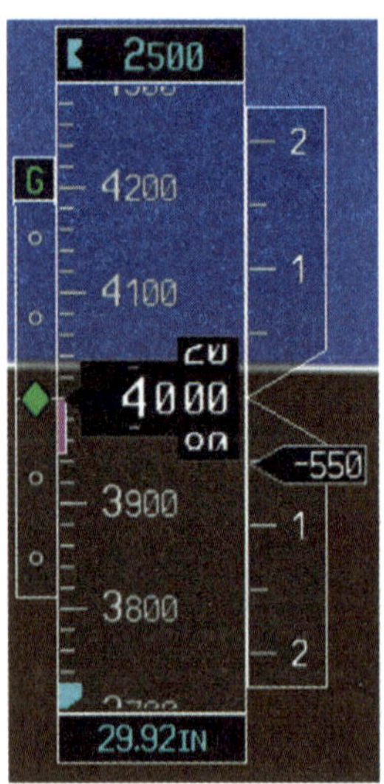

Figure 4-7 The altimeter is in the center, the glide slope indicator is on the left, and the vertical speed indicator is on the right. *© Garmin Ltd. or its affiliates*

The vertical speed indicator is displayed as a numeric value in a box to the right of the altimeter display; it begins displaying whenever the climb or descent rate exceeds 100 feet per minute. As the vertical speed changes, the display box moves up and down alongside the VSI markings, providing both an analog and digital indication. Numeric labels and major marks appear every 1000 feet, and minor tick marks are used every 500 feet.

The altitude reference, shown in a box at the top of the tape, is set by the ALT knobs, located on the bezel to the lower left of either display. The reference altitude provides two functions. In all aircraft, it sets the cyan Altitude Reference Bug, displayed along the left side of the tape when that altitude is on scale. If the reference altitude is off-scale, the reference bug stays at either the top or bottom of the display. You'll find this bug invaluable in flight, as it quickly shows whether you've deviated from your target altitude. Instead of having to read the digits to determine your exact altitude, simply fly the plane so that the cyan reference bug remains centered.

The second function of the reference altitude is to provide altitude level off information from the G1000 or Perspective to the autopilot. This works in aircraft with the Garmin integrated autopilot. For nonintegrated autopilot installations, such as in Mooney, Tiger and older piston-powered Cessna and Diamond aircraft, you'll need to set the altitude reference manually on both the G1000 and the autopilot. The glide slope indicator appears on the left side of the tape whenever an ILS frequency is tuned in the active navigation receiver. The glide slope is indicated by a green diamond which moves up and down along the side of the display, much like a conventional glide slope display needle. A magenta diamond is used for WAAS approaches. The marker beacon annunciators, blue for the outer marker (figure 4-8), amber for the middle marker and white for the inner marker, are displayed just to the left of the reference altitude.

TIP

When climbing or descending, you can use the altitude trend vector and altitude reference bug to manage your level off. First, set the altitude reference to your desired altitude using the ALT knobs. As you approach your designated altitude, start to level off when the altitude trend vector is opposite the altitude reference bug. Continue to pitch to keep them matched to each other until you're at your target altitude.

The barometric setting box is located below the altitude display. To set it, use the BARO knob, the larger of a pair of concentric knobs located in the middle of the right side of both display bezels. You can switch the barometric pressure display from inches of mercury to hectopascals by pressing the PFD softkey and then the METRIC softkey.†

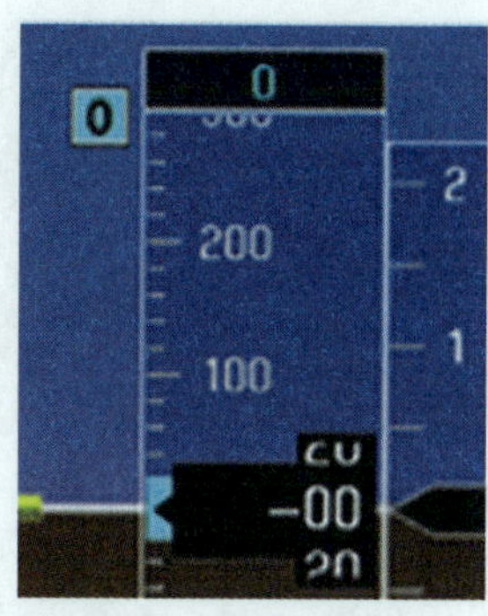

Figure 4-8 The blue "O" indicates you're passing over the outer marker. *© Garmin Ltd. or its affiliates*

Horizontal Situation Indicator

The horizontal situation indicator (HSI), located in the lower center of the PFD, is similar to a traditional HSI. If you are unfamiliar with an HSI, it combines the functions of a Directional Gyro (DG) or Heading Indicator (HI) with a course deviation indicator (CDI) or course pointer, such as you'd use with a VOR receiver to display navigation information. While initially confusing to neophytes, most experienced pilots prefer using an HSI, since the CDI needle turns with the rotating compass card, presenting a graphical indication of where the desired course is located and what intercept angle to use (figure 4-9).

Figure 4-9 HSI with GPS CDI needle selected. *© Garmin Ltd. or its affiliates*

The HSI can be presented in two forms, either a 360° display as shown in figure 4-9, or a 140° arc display which shows just the top third of the HSI presented in a 3-D projection. You can switch between the two by pressing the PFD softkey and then the 360 HSI or ARC HSI softkey.† Most pilots prefer the 360° view. The 140° arc view is useful when the optional Synthetic Vision Technology is displaying nearby terrain and obstacles.

The turn rate indicator is located along the top of the rotating compass card, and uses half tick marks at 9° and full tick marks at 18° to the left and right of center. In a turn, a magenta line extends to the left or right to display the number of degrees the plane is projected to turn in the next six seconds. In a standard rate or 2-minute turn, a plane turns 3° per second. Thus, when the magenta line extends to 18°, the airplane is established in a standard rate turn (figure 4-10). If the projected turn extends to 25° or beyond, an arrowhead appears on the magenta line (figure 4-11).

The HSI is automatically slaved to the GMU 44 3 axis magnetometer, so it continuously displays the correct heading and there is never a need to adjust it to the compass heading as required with a traditional DG. There is no free/slave switch, found in many traditional HSI installations, for you to adjust the slaving between the HSI and magnetometer; the system does that work automatically.

Figure 4-10 Major 18° tick marks indicate a standard rate turn. In six seconds, this aircraft will be on a heading of 80°. *© Garmin Ltd. or its affiliates*

The airplane's current heading is displayed numerically in the Heading Box at the top of the HSI. Just below it is the light-blue heading reference Bug (figure 4-15), set by the user with the HDG knob located in the middle on the left side of both G1000 display bezels and on the Perspective's central console. When the pilot turns the HDG knob, the

† See page 213 for updates to this feature.

Figure 4-11 A trend vector with an arrowhead indicates the aircraft will turn more than 25° in six seconds. *© Garmin Ltd. or its affiliates*

newly selected heading appears digitally in a box to the left of the current heading. In the Perspective and some G1000 versions, the heading box is removed after three seconds.

The HDG knob and heading reference bug are used in two ways. First, the heading reference bug provides you with a large visual reference for maintaining heading that is faster and easier to use than reading the numeric display. Also, turning the HDG knob sends a signal to the autopilot used for steering the aircraft when the autopilot's heading mode is engaged. This is true for both integrated and nonintegrated autopilots.

To use the heading reference bug in flight, you might initially push the HDG knob to synchronize the cyan bug with the current heading. Next, engage the autopilot in the heading mode. Then, turn the HDG knob to move the heading reference bug to a new heading and the autopilot will turn the airplane to fly the new heading.

Navigation with the HSI

The CDI or course pointer in the center of the HSI is magenta when the GPS is used for course navigation and green when either the NAV1 or NAV2 VOR receivers are used. Labels, such as a magenta "GPS", appear just above the HSI's miniature airplane to identify the navigation source. In some G1000 software versions, a green "NAV1" or "NAV2" label is displayed when a VOR receiver is selected. Others display LOC1 or LOC2 and VOR1 or VOR2 depending upon whether a localizer or VOR frequency is currently active in the NAV1 or NAV2 receiver. In all cases, you'll select the navigation source by pressing the CDI softkey one or more times until the desired CDI needle is displayed in the HSI.

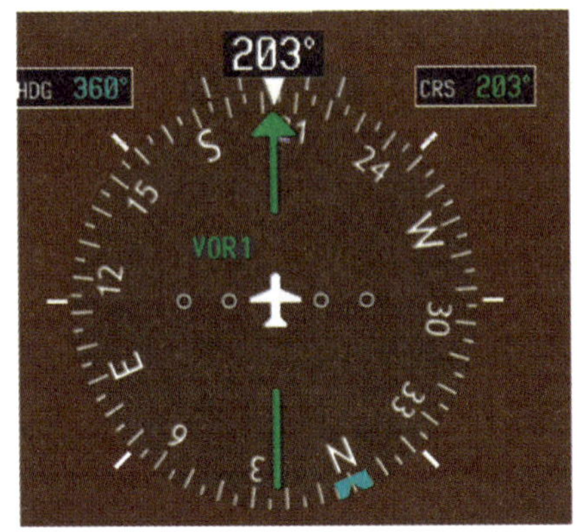

Figure 4-12 The missing D-bar, in the center of the needle, indicates an invalid signal. *© Garmin Ltd. or its affiliates*

Before using the CDI needle for navigation, you should verify the integrity of the navigation source. In all cases, a missing D-bar, the center portion of the CDI needle that moves left and right, or a large red X on the HSI, signifies the lack of a valid signal and that the CDI should not be used (figure 4-12). If both GPS1 and GPS2 were to fail, or if the GPS was not receiving enough satellites to perform a "RAIM" test, you would be warned by a magenta INTEG label in the center of the HSI.

Figure 4-13 NAV1 is tuned to SJC; NAV2, which is green since it's currently selected on the HSI, is tuned to SNS. *© Garmin Ltd. or its affiliates*

VHF navigation signals send a station identifier in Morse code if the station is operating properly. The system decodes these signals and, when it detects valid Morse identifiers, it displays them to the right of the active NAV frequencies (figure 4-13). You should validate NAV1 and NAV2 signals by looking to see if the station identifier is displayed and also turn up the NAV volume to listen to the Morse code as a double check. In some rare cases, the system is unable to decode the Morse code if it's transmitted too rapidly by the navigation signal.

You can set the CDI course with the CRS knob, the smaller of a pair of concentric knobs located in the middle of the right side of both G1000 display bezels and on the Perspective's console. The knob is easy to identify since it's the only one which is triangular in shape chosen to resemble the arrow head of the CDI needle. Each click of the knob turns the CDI pointer one degree. As you turn the CRS knob, the newly selected course appears digitally in a box to the right of the Heading Box. If you push the CRS knob, it will automatically center the CDI needle.

The CRS knob is used to set the desired course whenever you're flying to or from a VOR, or when navigating via GPS in the OBS mode, discussed in Chapter 11. The CDI needle is automatically set to the correct course whenever a localizer frequency is selected on the NAV1 or NAV2 receiver and that CDI pointer is displayed, a localizer or ILS instrument approach is loaded or whenever the GPS is operating in the leg mode, in which it sequences through the waypoints in the active flight plan. When tuned to a localizer, you can still adjust the CDI with the CRS knob, though there's no reason to since the correct bearing of the final approach course for the localizer was automatically selected. However in the GPS's auto-sequencing mode, the CRS knob is inactive and the bearing cannot be changed.

The CDI needle operates in the traditional fashion, with the center portion of the needle or "D-bar" moving left or right of center to indicate the location of the desired course. When displaying a VOR signal from a NAV receiver, traditional CDIs display 10° to the left and right of center and have five dots on both sides. Each dot is therefore equivalent to 2° of deflection from the desired course. The G1000 also displays 10° on each side of center, but has only two dots on each side of the display or 5° per dot of deflection (figure 4-14).

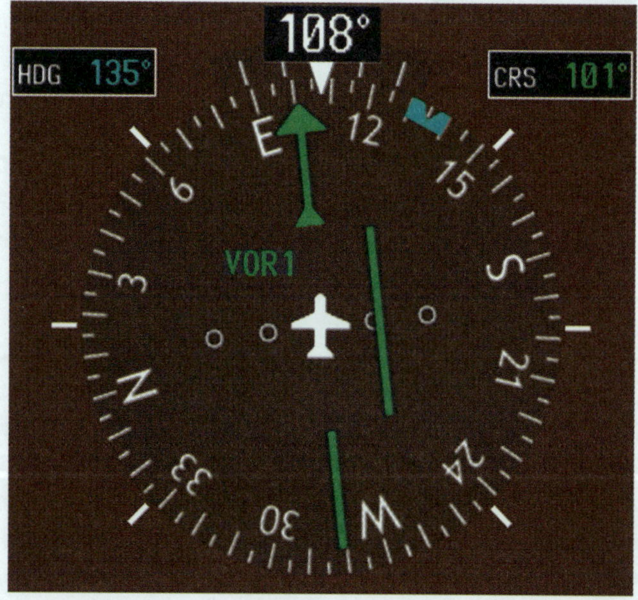

Figure 4-14 The NAV1 radio is currently selected on the HSI. *© Garmin Ltd. or its affiliates*

When the CDI is used for GPS navigation, the scale depends upon the receiver's current mode. Typically, the GPS mode is selected automatically, though you can choose to manually override the settings. For non-WAAS-equipped aircraft, when the enroute mode is active, "ENR" is displayed on the HSI, and the CDI scale displays 5 nm on each side of the center, or 10 nm total.† Thus, each dot represents a deviation of 2.5 nm from the desired course. In the terminal mode, "TERM" is displayed and the CDI scaling changes to 1 nm on each side of center, or 2 nm total. In the approach mode, "APR" is displayed and the scaling is reduced to 0.3 nm on each side of center or 0.6 nm total.

When departing an airport, the GPS is initially in terminal mode. As the airplane reaches a point 30 miles from the departure airport, the GPS switches to enroute mode, and the CDI scale gradually changes to 10 nm full scale, which has the effect of making any deviation from course appear to be less (figure 4-15).

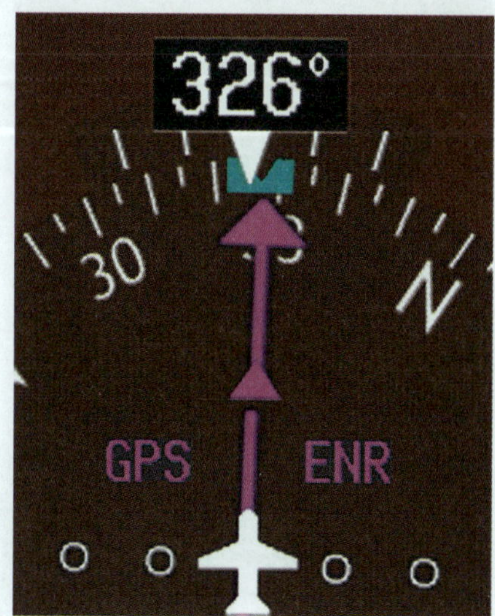

Figure 4-15 GPS is currently in the ENR or enroute mode. *© Garmin Ltd. or its affiliates*

Approaching the destination airport, the GPS cycles from enroute to

† See page 224 for updates to this feature.

Figure 4-16 Yellow low fuel Cautions are displayed in the annunciator window. *© Garmin Ltd. or its affiliates*

terminal mode 30 nm before the airport and the full scale display changes to 2 nm. This re-scaling of the CDI occurs slowly so that you don't perceive any existing deviation from course—which will appear to be a larger deviation after the mode change occurs—as a rapid turn away from the desired course.

If an instrument approach was selected for the destination airport, the GPS switches to the approach mode 2 nm before the final approach fix (FAF), which is typically four to seven miles away from the airport. Full scale is now 0.6 nm, giving the greatest possible sensitivity for flying the approach. Instrument approaches are discussed more fully in Chapter 11, and WAAS approaches are covered in Chapter 14.

Annunciators and Alerts

Annunciators are displayed to the right of the vertical speed indicator and are used to draw the pilot's attention to unusual conditions. Prior to glass cockpits, these were displayed in the form of warning lights, though most general aviation aircraft had relatively few of them and system failures often went unnoticed. For example, undetected alternator failures can drain an airplane's main battery and go unrecognized until the loss of the radio, lights and all other electrically powered devices. In contrast, the G1000 and Perspective annunciators make it far more likely that you will recognize system failures immediately before they become more serious (figure 4-16).

The annunciators are organized into groups, based on their severity. Warnings are the most severe and demand immediate attention. A new warning appears above a white line at the top of the annunciators as a flashing red label accompanied by a chime that rings every two seconds and a softkey that flashes "WARNING." Pressing the softkey silences the chime, stops the annunciator from flashing, removes the white line and re-sequences the warning within the list of all annunciators based upon a priority assigned by the manufacturer.

A Caution is less severe and is signaled by a yellow label in the annunciator list, a single chime and a softkey that flashes "CAUTION." Press the softkey to stop it from flashing.

Advisories are the lowest level and do not appear in the annunciator list. Instead, a flashing ADVISORY softkey alerts you. Press the softkey to stop it from flashing.

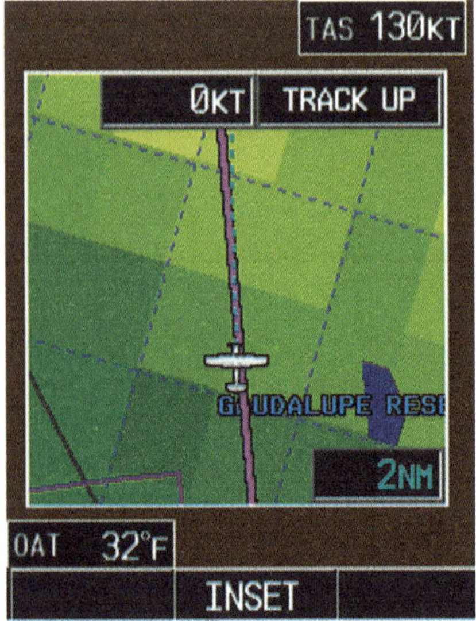

Figure 4-17 The INSET softkey enables the Inset map in the lower left corner of the PFD. *© Garmin Ltd. or its affiliates*

An Alerts window in the lower right corner of the PFD displays more details on any system WARNING, CAUTION or ADVISORY. This window is opened by pressing the ALERTS softkey and can list up to 64 alerts. Aircraft manufacturers define the alerts and their priorities, so annunciators can differ from one aircraft model to another. A complete list of Warning and Caution alerts for each manufacturer can be found in the Appendix.

Another form of alerts is Traffic Advisories, which occur whenever another aircraft displayed by TIS is within a half mile and 500 feet vertically of your aircraft, or is predicted to become a conflict within the next 34 seconds. Three things happen when a traffic advisory occurs.

First, the Inset Map is enabled and the conflicting traffic is displayed. A single "Traffic" voice message sounds and a flashing "TRAFFIC" Annunciator appears to the top left of the attitude indicator (figure 4-6). The annunciator, black text on a yellow background, flashes for five seconds and remains displayed until threat aircraft are no longer detected in the immediate vicinity. For each additional threat aircraft, a new aural alert and visual annunciator is displayed.†

Softkey Functions

Softkeys, located along the bottom of both displays, are used extensively throughout the G1000 and Perspective to give you rapid access to many additional functions. Pushing a key often leads to additional softkey choices which can lead to even more softkeys in a nested hierarchy. In all cases, press the BACK softkey, located on the second softkey from the far right, to return to the next higher level menu of softkeys. Also, a timeout system automatically returns you to the higher level of softkeys if no keys are pressed for approximately 45 seconds. The following systems are accessed through the softkeys.

Inset Map

The Inset Map (figure 4-17) appears in the lower left corner of the PFD, and is a smaller version of the MFD's navigation map.† You can enable it by pressing the INSET softkey, which leads to a sub-menu of additional softkey choices for configuring the map. While you can choose which map layers to add to the Inset Map and change the map range, many of the map features and orientation are dictated by the map settings on the MFD and cannot be set separately for the Inset Map.

After you press the INSET softkey, the following softkeys appear and are used to add or subtract information from the Inset Map:

OFF – turns the Inset Map off and returns the softkeys back to the higher level menu.

DCLTR – selects one of four levels of information to display on the map. Successive presses of the DCLTR softkey step through four levels and progressively remove information from the display. You'll find more details on the declutter function in the Appendix.

Whenever you press one of the following softkeys, it turns gray, indicating that the map layer selected was added to the Inset Map. Press the softkey a second time to deselect a particular map layer. More information on each of these layers of map information is included in Chapter 7.

TRAFFIC – Adds Mode S TIS or TAS data to the map. In recent software versions, the TRAFFIC softkey is replaced with TRFC-1 and TRFC-2, which alternate with each other.

TRFC-1 – Adds Mode S TIS or TAS data to the map.

TRFC-2 – Removes all map information except TIS or TAS traffic.

TOPO – enables the topographic map which uses color to signify land elevation.

† See pages 212-13 for updates to these features.

TERRAIN – enables terrain data.

STRMSCP – enables the display of lightning strike data out to 200 nm, when the WX-500 Stormscope option is installed in an aircraft. The STRMSCP and XM LTNG softkeys are mutually exclusive since only one source of lightning data can be displayed at a time. Pressing one of these keys deselects the other.

NEXRAD - enables the display of weather data and graphics, when the Garmin data link option is installed in an aircraft and the user has a subscription to the SiriusXM aviation package.

XM LTNG - enables the display of lightning strikes, when the Garmin data link option is installed in an aircraft and the user has a subscription to the SiriusXM aviation package. The STRMSCP and XM LTNG softkeys are mutually exclusive since only one source of lightning data can be displayed at a time.

METAR – enables the display of METAR weather information.

WX LGND – Displays icon and age for weather products.

BACK – returns the softkeys to the higher level menu while retaining whatever selections were made to the Inset Map.

You can zoom the Inset Map in and out by turning the range knob in the middle of the bezel's right side. The map range varies from 500 feet to 2000 nm.

Generally the Inset Map is centered on the airplane's current location. However, you can pan the map with the joystick to view other areas. This is useful for looking ahead along a route of flight or for getting more information about an object, such as the height of an obstruction like a broadcast tower. You can enable the panning pointer by pushing the range/joystick knob. Then, move the joystick to shift the pointer and highlight an object or to view other areas of the map.

When the pointer is placed on an object, with the exception of the magenta route lines created by a flight plan, the name of the object appears for four seconds. Pushing the joystick cancels the panning mode and returns to a map centered on the aircraft's current position. The joystick for the MFD, located on the G1000's MFD bezel and the Perspective's console, operates in the same fashion, but can also be used to get additional information, such as the vertical limits of Class B, C, D and other airspace.

TIP

One of the more consistent "gotchas" I see in the G1000 are pilots taking off squawking a prior squawk code instead of 1200. Since the G1000 saves the transponder code when it's powered down and the transponder numbers are relatively small, this is an easy mistake to make. Therefore I recommend that people verify the squawk code as part of the "transponder" item on the pre-takeoff checklist.

Transponder

The transponder is accessed through softkeys on the PFD.† Most G1000 installations use a Mode S transponder that displays TIS data, showing nearby aircraft on the PFD and MFD maps. The TIS function is described in more detail in Chapter 7.

The transponder generally operates in the automatic mode, though it can also be controlled manually. In the automatic mode, it starts in the Ground mode, and a green GND label appears in the transponder status bar in the lower right corner of the PFD display (figure 4-18). In

† See page 212 for updates to this feature.

Ground mode, no Mode A or Mode C signals are sent, however, data transmissions related to the mode S traffic capabilities are still enabled.

Figure 4-18 Transponder Status window, labeled XPDR, appears in the lower right corner of the PFD. *© Garmin Ltd. or its affiliates*

Altitude mode is automatically selected whenever the aircraft exceeds approximately 30 knots. The transponder then begins transmitting Mode C altitude data and a green ALT label appears in the transponder status bar. When the transponder is interrogated, usually by ground-based radar but also by other aircraft with traffic collision avoidance systems (TCAS) and traffic collision avoidance devices (TCAD), a green R label appears, signifying a reply was sent.

The automatic mode can be overridden. For example, if air traffic control (ATC) notices that the altitude sent by your transponder differs by more than 300 feet from the actual altitude, they may ask you to "stop squawking altitude." This requires that the transponder be switched from the ALT mode, where it transmits Mode C altitude data, to the ON mode, where it transmits Mode A data but no altitude information. In this case, you would press the XPDR (meaning transponder) softkey and then the ON softkey to stop the transmission of altitude data. Other softkeys on this sub-menu control additional transponder functions.

These softkeys and their functions are:

STBY — manually selects the standby mode where no data (including mode S) is transmitted.

ALT — manually selects Mode C and transmits altitude data.

VFR — sets the transponder code to "1200," the standard code for VFR aircraft.

CODE — selects an additional sub-menu for entering a discrete transponder code. The numbers 0 through 7 are each assigned a softkey, which allows you to enter a four digit squawk code. A BKSP or backspace softkey on this sub-menu lets you back up if you enter one or more digits incorrectly.

IDENT — enables the ident function, which makes your aircraft more visible on ATC radar. Another IDENT softkey appears on the upper level of softkeys, so that you can access it at any time without needing to push the XPDR softkey to reach the sub-menu.

Airspeed Reference Speed Bugs and Timer

The TMR/REF softkey brings up the Timer/References window in the lower right corner of the PFD (figure 4-19). Press the TMR/REF softkey again or press the CLR key to close the Timer/References window. The first line in the window displays information about the general purpose timer. You can use this to time anything, such as length of a leg while flying a holding pattern, or to time an instrument approach. The timer can be configured to count up from zero, or to count down from a user-specified amount of time. When the time expires in the count down mode, an Alert message is sent advising that the "Timer has expired."

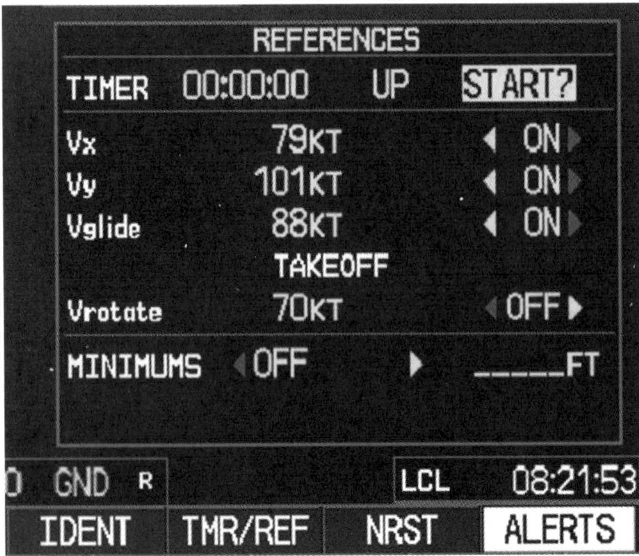

Figure 4-19 The Timer/References window includes a timer and reference bugs that show best glide, Vr, Vx and Vy airspeeds. *© Garmin Ltd. or its affiliates*

Initially, the upper right field is highlighted by a flashing cursor and the label "START?" Press the ENT key to start the timer, which changes the field to a flashing "STOP?" Press the ENT key again to stop the timer and change the field to a flashing "RESET?" Pressing the ENT key again brings up the "START?" label and resets the timer to zero or, if a time was preset in the time field, back to the preset time.

The large FMS knob is used to select other fields in the Timer/References window. Turn it one click counterclockwise to highlight the UP/DOWN field, turn the small FMS knob to select UP or DOWN timing and press the ENT key. Turning the large FMS knob an additional click counterclockwise selects the time field. Then turn the large and small FMS knobs to select the number of hours, minutes and seconds from which to count up or down. You can make changes to the time and the UP/DOWN field while the timer is still running.

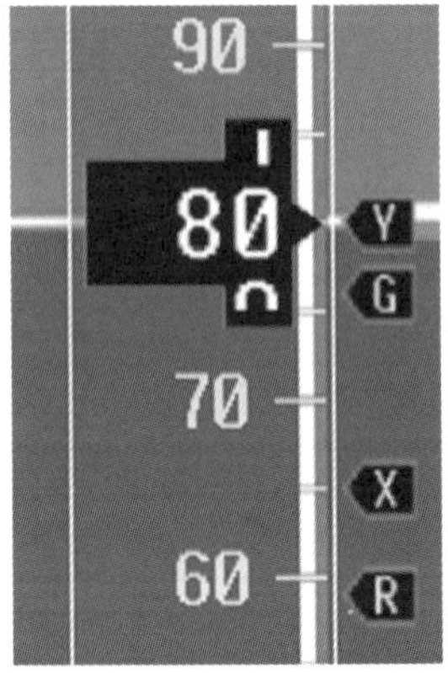

Figure 4-20 Speed bug labels appear on the right side of the airspeed indicator. 80 knots is the Vy airspeed for this aircraft. *© Garmin Ltd. or its affiliates*

The airspeed reference bugs are also accessed through the Timer/References window, where they are enabled or disabled and their values are changed. As mentioned earlier, speed bugs help you recognize important speeds for the airplane and, since they move with the airspeed display tape, they make it easier to recognize any deviation from a target speed (figure 4-20).

For example, as the aircraft accelerates on the runway, you can start to pull back on the yoke at Vr, when the bug for rotation speed reaches the center of the airspeed display tape. While climbing, additional speed bugs make it easy to identify and maintain Vx, the best angle of climb speed, and Vy, the best rate of climb speed. The G1000 also displays the airplane's best glide speed, which would be used in the event of an engine failure.

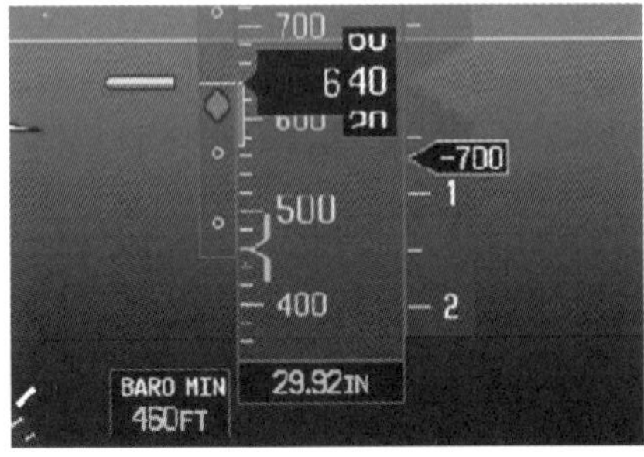

Figure 4-20A Both the BARO MIN box and the MDA/DA bug on the altimeter are indicating the 460-foot minimums set for an approach. *© Garmin Ltd. or its affiliates*

To change a speed bug, turn the large FMS knob to highlight a particular speed bug value. You can select a new speed by turning the small FMS knob and pressing the ENT key. An asterisk appears whenever the speed is different than the default speed set by the aircraft manufacturer. All speed bugs return to their default speeds after the G1000 is turned off, or after pressing the MENU key, turning either FMS knob to highlight "Restore Defaults" and pressing the ENT key.

Speed bugs can be enabled or disabled individually by turning the large FMS knob to highlight the ON/OFF field for a particular speed bug. ON or OFF is selected by turning the small FMS knob and pressing the ENT key. All speed bugs can be turned on or off simultaneously by pressing the MENU key, turning either FMS knob to highlight "All References On" or "All References Off" and pressing the ENT key.

MDA/DA Alerting

The TMR/REF window (figure 4-19) includes a function that lets you set a minimum decision height (MDA) or decision altitude (DA) for use with flying an instrument approach. To set an altitude, turn the large FMS knob to highlight the BARO MIN field (MINIMUMS field in some aircraft) and use the small FMS knob to select ON. Then scroll to the next field and set an altitude with the small FMS knob or, in some aircraft, the keypad.

As the aircraft descends to within 2,500 feet of the altitude set, a BARO MIN box (figure 4-20A) appears with the minimum altitude in cyan and, within 300 feet of the minimum altitude, a MDA/DA bug comes into view. Both the text and bug turn white at 100 feet above the minimum altitude. As the aircraft reaches the minimum altitude, the text and bug turn yellow and an aural "MINIMUMS, MINIMUMS" is heard. If the aircraft climbs more than 50 feet after reaching the minimum altitude, alerting is disabled. On the ground alerting is inhibited.

Nearest Airports Softkey

Most GPS receivers have a way to determine the direction and distance to the nearest airports rapidly. This is useful in an emergency if you need to land immediately. The function allows you to evaluate alternatives quickly, perhaps based upon the distance to the airport or, for higher performance aircraft, the runway length, and can provide direct GPS guidance to the airport.

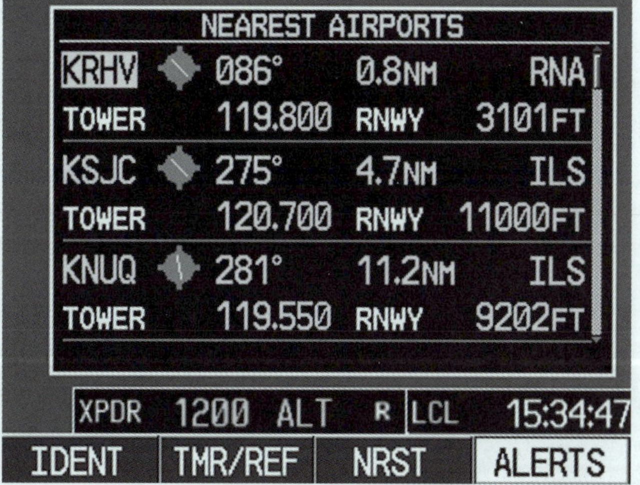

Figure 4-21 The NRST softkey is the fastest way to get information on the nearest airports. *© Garmin Ltd. or its affiliates*

Garmin 430/530 users are used to accessing this function with the FMS knobs, and you can still do this through the MFD display. However, the system goes a step further in that it also provides a NRST softkey on the PFD, which gives you instant access to a subset of information about the nearest airports. More detailed information about the airports and about other nearby facilities such as VORs, NDBs, intersections, ATC frequencies and user waypoints, is found through the MFD.

Press the NRST softkey to bring up the Nearest Airports window in the lower right corner of the PFD, which displays the first three of the 25 nearest airports. Scroll down with either FMS knob to display additional airports (figure 4-21). The display shows the most critical data for each airport and you can get additional information by selecting an airport from the list and pressing the ENT key.

The following information is shown for each airport:

- Three or four letter airport identifier
- Symbol for the type of airport
- Magnetic course to the airport
- Distance to the airport in nautical miles
- Best type of instrument approach available (VFR is listed if there are no approaches)
- Primary communication frequency such as tower or CTAF
- Length of longest hard surface runway (or longest soft surface if there are no hard runways)

TIP

The Nearest Airports window closes after using the Direct-to key to fly direct to an airport on the list. Therefore, if you also want to load a frequency from this page, do that before using the Direct-to key. You can do this in the opposite order, but you'll need to press the NRST softkey again to re-open the window after using the Direct-to key.

Additional information is available by scrolling either FMS knob, highlighting an airport identifier and pushing the ENT key. A new Airport Information window displays additional information including the airport name, the city and state, the type of airport (e.g. public, military), field elevation, longitude and latitude coordinates and the type of fuel services available. Should you wish, you can also use this window to get the same information about any airport by using the FMS knobs to scroll to the airport identifier, airport name or city, entering the characters for another airport and pressing the ENT key. To return to the Nearest Airports window, turn the FMS knobs to highlight the BACK field, and press the ENT key.

The G1000 also makes it easy to navigate to the nearest airport. From the Nearest Airports window, scroll either FMS knob to the identifier for the airport you've chosen, press the Direct-to key and then press the ENT key twice. Or, while looking at more detailed airport information on the Airport Information window, you can press the Direct-to key and then the ENT key twice.

A magenta line will appear on the PFD's Inset Map and the MFD map leading you from your present position to the selected airport. If the CDI pointer is already selected for GPS, then course guidance also appears on the HSI. If, however, the green NAV1 or NAV2 CDI needle was in use, you must push the CDI softkey until the magenta GPS needle appears to get course guidance.

Selecting the frequency for the chosen airport is also easy. From the Nearest Airports window, scroll either FMS knob to the frequency for the airport you've chosen and press the ENT key. The frequency is then loaded as the standby frequency for whichever NAV radio is currently selected for tuning.

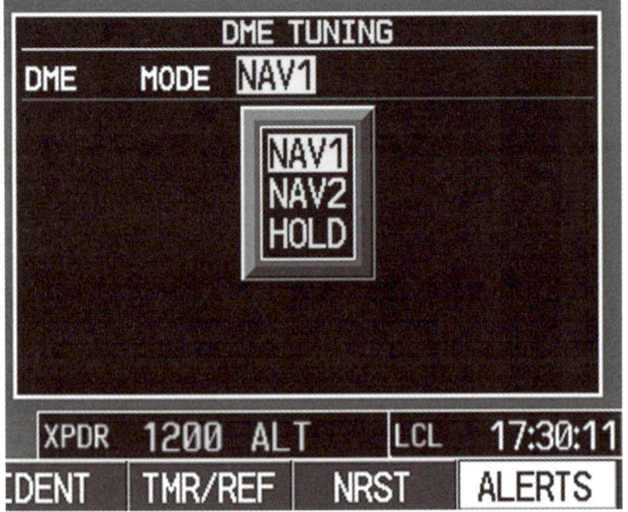

Figure 4-22 The DME Tuning box lets you select the source of DME information. *© Garmin Ltd. or its affiliates*

Additional Navigation Functions: DME

Distance Measuring Equipment (DME) is available as an option to the G1000 in some manufacturers' aircraft. When installed, this function measures and displays the distance from the aircraft to a ground-based navigation station, usually a VOR, to which the DME is tuned. The distance measured is the slant-range distance in nautical miles, which is the distance from the airplane itself (not a position on the ground under the aircraft) to the VOR station. For example, when flying directly over a VOR at 6000 feet, the DME would read 1.0 nm, not zero, since the aircraft is about 1 nautical mile above the station. Even though GPS can now make the same distance measurements, DME remains popular because it is simple to operate compared to GPS receivers.

When installed, DME is accessed through softkeys on the PFD. Two steps are required to display it. First, a source of DME data must be selected with the DME Tuning box and then the DME display box must be turned on.

Press the DME softkey to bring up the DME Tuning box in the lower right corner of the display, so you can select the source of DME information (figure 4-22). Turn the small FMS knob to select NAV1, NAV2 or HOLD. Selecting NAV1 or NAV2 means that the DME distance measured and displayed will be to the station active in the NAV1 or NAV2 receiver.

Selecting HOLD allows you to continue displaying the DME distance from whichever VOR is currently selected in the DME Tuning Box—either NAV1 or NAV2—even if that NAV receiver is subsequently tuned to another frequency. For example, if the active frequency in NAV1 is the San Jose VOR on 114.1 and the DME Tuning box says NAV1, then the distance to San Jose can be displayed. Selecting HOLD assures that the San Jose VOR will continue to be the source of DME information even after NAV1 is re-tuned to the Salinas VOR on 117.3.

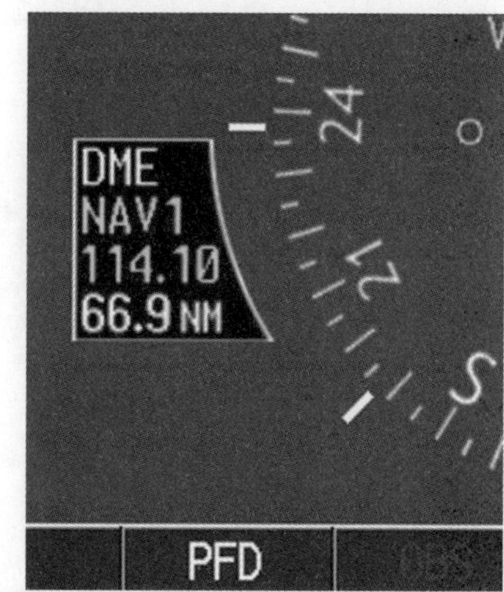

Figure 4-23 DME equipped aircraft can display distance to a VOR. *© Garmin Ltd. or its affiliates*

Once the DME source is selected, the DME display box must be enabled. This is done from the higher level menu of softkeys, which you can always reach by pushing the BACK softkey. From here, push the PFD softkey and then the DME softkey. This brings up the DME display box to the lower left of the HSI (figure 4-23). It shows which source (NAV1, NAV2 or HOLD) is selected, the frequency being used, and the distance to the station in nautical miles.

In some G1000-equipped aircraft, an Automatic Direction Finder (ADF) receiver is also available as an option. This receiver is usually accessed through the same softkey used for the DME, except that it is relabeled as a DME/ADF softkey.

Additional Navigation Functions: Bearing Pointers or RMI

Bearing pointers, not included in the original G1000 software release, are now available in most versions of the G1000 and Perspective software. These pointers are essentially the same as the Radio Magnetic Indicators (RMI) that are found in many airliner cockpits. Those indicators combine a bearing indicator with a heading indicator and one or two needles which point in the direction of whichever station (usually a VOR or ADF) is selected. The beauty of the device is that the tail of the needle gives a direct reading of the radial on which the aircraft is located, making it easier to maintain positional awareness.

Figure 4-24 Bearing pointers shown enabled for NAV1 and NAV2. *© Garmin Ltd. or its affiliates*

The bearing pointers provide an important function. Traditional cockpits usually have two VOR receivers and pilots can display information from both simultaneously. The G1000 and Perspective's HSI has a single CDI pointer that displays information for only one VOR or other navigation source at a time. Turning on the system's two bearing pointers lets you display course information for three different navigation signals simultaneously (figure 4-24). Note: early versions of the Perspective have only one bearing pointer.

This is useful when flying an instrument approach that requires two VOR signals or a localizer and a VOR signal so that you can monitor both signals simultaneously. Of course, an even easier way to maintain positional awareness is to use the MFD's moving map.

The bearing pointers are accessed through the PFD softkey. Press it to bring up a lower level menu of softkeys including the BRG1 and BRG2 softkeys. Press the BRG1 softkey to bring up a display box at the lower left corner of the HSI and a single-width, cyan-colored pointer in the center of the HSI. The BRG1 display box shows the name of either the VOR station or GPS waypoint selected and the distance to that point. Pressing the BRG1 softkey multiple times cycles between displaying NAV1 bearing data, displaying GPS bearing data and turning the BRG1 display box off.

The BRG2 softkey performs a function nearly identical to the BRG1 softkey, except that it brings up a display box at the lower right corner of the HSI and a double-width, cyan-colored pointer in the center of the HSI. Pressing the BRG2 softkey multiple times cycles between displaying NAV2 bearing data, displaying GPS bearing data and turning the BRG2 display box off.

Additional Windows

Outside air temperature is continuously displayed in a box in the lower left corner of the PFD. This information is particularly valuable to instrument pilots, as it can alert them to possible freezing conditions and the need for pitot heat. The temperature is displayed in either °C or °F, depending on a setting in the System Setup page described in Chapter 7.

The System Time box, in the lower right corner of the PFD, continuously displays the time, derived from GPS satellites, and that time cannot be changed. However, the format in which it is displayed, such as local 12-hour time, local 24-hour time, or Zulu time, can be changed. When using local time, you must also specify a time offset, specifying the number of hours between local time and Zulu time so that the correct hour is displayed. All of these time settings are made through the System Setup page described in Chapter 7.

Miscellaneous PFD Softkeys

There are several miscellaneous softkeys on the PFD. The OBS/SUSP softkey is located on the highest level of softkeys and switches the GPS from the auto-sequencing mode (which automatically sequences through each leg of the active flight plan) to the waypoint

† See page 213 for updates to this feature.

or OBS mode. In the OBS mode, a GPS waypoint is treated like a VOR, and the CDI course pointer sets a course to the waypoint. The OBS mode is discussed more in Chapter 11.

When pressed, the PFD softkey accesses a lower level menu of softkeys that include:†

- METRIC — displays the altitude and reference altitude in meters and the barometric setting in hectopascals.
- DFLTS — configures the PFD display to remove the Inset Map, display the 360° HSI, and deselect the METRIC softkey.
- STD BARO — sets the barometric pressure to 29.92. This setting is used above 18,000 feet in the United States, and above lower altitudes in many other countries. Pressing this softkey again returns the barometric pressure to the prior setting.

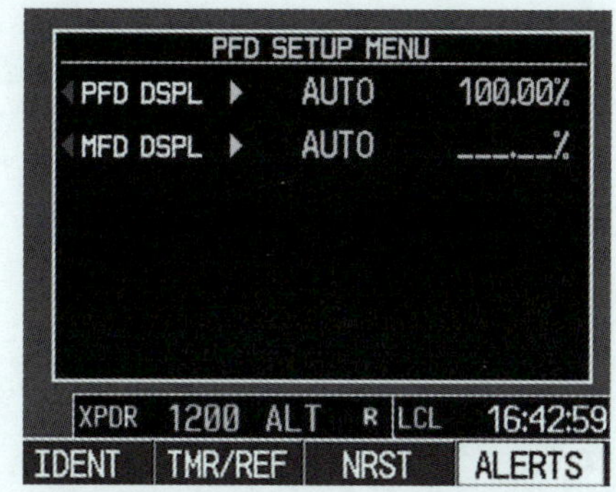

Figure 4-25 Display lighting is controlled by the MENU key on the PFD.
© Garmin Ltd. or its affiliates

Lighting

If you're used to the poor cockpit lighting in older general aviation aircraft, you'll be elated when you see the G1000 and Perspective lighting. In most implementations, manufacturers have added one or more knobs to the instrument panel which simultaneously control the backlighting of the PFD, MFD and control knob labels on the bezels. Also, an electric eye sets the brightness of the displays when AUTO is selected.

This works well, however, you may find times when you want to set the backlighting level of the MFD separately from the PFD. For example, at night the topographical map display on the MFD can still seem very bright even after the PFD is dimmed to the proper level. Or, you may want to set the backlighting for the key labels on the bezel separately.

Also, the intensity of the MFD is intentionally set higher than the PFD, since the pilot is viewing it off angle and therefore sees less light from that display. If you're in the right seat, the MFD will appear much brighter than the PFD, since you are viewing the PFD off angle and will see less light from that display. For all lighting functions of either display, use the MENU key on the PFD. Note that you cannot perform this function from the MFD unless you first push the Display Backup button, discussed in Chapter 12.

To set the PFD backlighting, press the MENU key, push the FMS knob, scroll with the large FMS knob to the first field and then use the small FMS knob to select PFD DSPL (figure 4-25). Then, scroll with the large FMS knob to the next field and use the small FMS knob to select MANUAL and press the ENT key. Finally, set the intensity percentage using the small FMS knob and press the ENT key. To return to full brightness, select AUTO. To remove the lighting window, press the MENU key.

The procedure for setting the backlighting of the key labels on the PFD is the same, except that in the first field you must scroll with the small FMS knob to select PFD KEY. Then select MANUAL and select an intensity as described above. Backlighting of the MFD and MFD key labels is identical except that you must scroll to the second line and select either MFD DSPL or MFD KEY.

Summary

While it's easy to focus attention on MFDs because of their large, colorful maps, the PFD is really the heart of the system, since every function critical to aviating, navigating and communicating is available through the PFD. This makes the G1000 and Perspective unique, because it is the only glass cockpit that allows all critical functions to be accessed through a single display. Allowing a pilot to stay focused on a single display reduces the workload and ultimately contributes to overall safety.

To become a proficient pilot in a G1000 or Perspective-equipped aircraft, start by becoming familiar with all of the functions available through the PFD. Most of those functions were discussed in this chapter, except for radio operation and flight plan programming which are discussed later. Practice operating the PFD by reviewing the diagrams in this book and by using the Garmin PC Trainer software for your aircraft. You'll find that any time you spend learning the PFD on the ground will make your first flight in a G1000 or Perspective-equipped aircraft even more enjoyable!

Chapter 5:
Radios and Audio Panel

This chapter focuses on the operation of the radios and audio panel. While many aspects of their operation are familiar to anyone who has operated modern aircraft radios, some of the functions are difficult to discern without instruction or documentation. This chapter attempts to unravel those mysteries so you won't be blindsided operating this new panel.

Radio frequencies are displayed in the upper corners of the PFD and MFD. Communication frequencies are shown in the upper right of both displays on the G1000, but only on the PFD for the Perspective. VHF navigation frequencies are shown in the upper left of both displays on the G1000, but only on the MFD for the Perspective. These radio locations are a major benefit of the system, since pilots can view and operate the radios while still keeping their eyes near the primary flight instruments.

The top line displays frequencies for the NAV1 and COM1 radios. Physically, these radios are combined with the GPS1 receiver into a single GIA 63 Integrated Avionics unit, located elsewhere in the plane. Although these three radios are housed in the same LRU, they are independent, and for example, should NAV1 fail, COM1 and GPS1 may continue to operate. The second line displays frequencies for the NAV2 and COM2 radios, physically located in a second GIA 63 that contains the GPS2 receiver.

> **Perspective**
>
> The Perspective's COM and NAV radios are operated the same as the G1000 radios, though the COM frequencies appear only on the PFD and NAV frequencies appear only on the MFD. There are subtle differences in the way the numbers are displayed: standby frequency numbers are smaller, are in cyan and are not surrounded by a white rectangle. The Perspective has a number pad (figure 15-7), which is a fast way to enter frequencies. Different audio panels, the GMA 347 and GMA 350, are used in the Perspective. Most of these audio panel keys operate the same way. The biggest differences are how the intercom volume and squelch are set.

NAV and COM Radio Tuning

Since operation of the NAV and COM radios is virtually identical, we'll treat them together. Like most modern radios, both an active and a standby frequency are shown for each NAV and COM radio. The active frequency is the one ready for use, and the standby frequency is where new frequencies are loaded. Unlike most radios, however, the frequencies aren't labeled! A user has to either remember which one is active and which is standby. One way to remember standby frequencies is that they are entered with the tuning knobs next to the frequency tuning

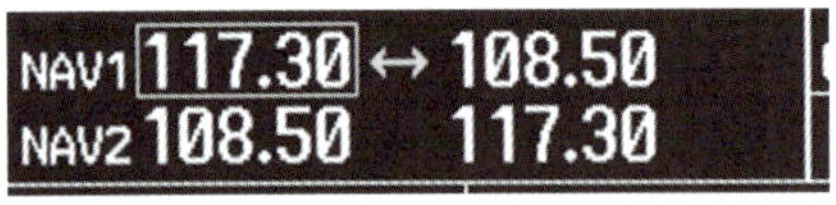

Figure 5-1 On the G1000, a light-blue tuning box surrounds the standby frequency. *© Garmin Ltd. or its affiliates*

Figure 5-2 On the Perspective, the standby frequency is displayed in light-blue in a smaller font. *© Garmin Ltd. or its affiliates*

boxes, toward the outside of the screens. Active frequencies are toward the center of the screens. The standby frequency is identified on the G1000 by a light-blue tuning box around the frequency (figure 5-1). On the Perspective, the standby frequencies are displayed using a smaller font size (figure 5-2). In addition to discerning active and standby frequencies, it is important to identify the selected frequency, which is an active frequency that's been selected on the audio panel (figure 5-3) or HSI for use.

As we've seen elsewhere on the PFD, color is significant and all frequencies are displayed with white numbers, except for the selected frequency, which is displayed in green. For the NAV radios, a frequency is selected if the green CDI needle associated with it is displayed on the HSI; if GPS is selected on the HSI, all active NAV radio frequencies are white. The selected COM frequency, displayed in green, is the active frequency selected on the audio panel for transmitting.

Color also indicates which radios are currently being tuned by the NAV and COM knobs. Understanding this is important since the frequency selection and volume control knobs are shared and can only control one radio at a time. Garmin 430/530 users are already accustomed to sharing a single set of concentric frequency control knobs that control one radio at a time and are switched between radios by pushing the center of either the NAV or COM knobs. That's also true on the G1000 and Perspective, but what's unique is that the volume controls are also shared! So, it's important to know which radio you're controlling with the knobs.

Cyan, a light-blue color, is used for objects that are user adjustable and it's used to indicate the radio being operated by the bezel controls. A cyan-colored double arrow is located between the active and standby fields. On the G1000, a cyan tuning box surrounds the tunable standby frequency; on the Perspective, the standby frequency is displayed in cyan in a smaller font. Pushing the button in the center of either the NAV or COM knobs selects the other radio for adjustment and moves the cyan indicators up or down. To tune a radio, look for the cyan arrow. If it's on the correct radio, turn the concentric NAV or COM knobs to set the new frequency.

The large knob sets the MegaHertz numbers to the left of the decimal point and the small knob sets the kiloHertz numbers. To tune the other radio, push the button in the center of the NAV or COM knobs to move the tuning box and cyan arrow.

To use a frequency you've entered, you'll need to swap the frequencies in the active and standby fields. To do this, push the Frequency Toggle key, marked with a double headed arrow. This transfers the frequency you've entered in the standby field to the active field toward the center of the screen, where it can now be used. The final step is to use the audio panel to select the active COM frequency or the CDI softkey on the PFD to select the active NAV radio frequency.

COM Radio Operation

The COM radios transmit with 16 watts of power on the VHF aviation band from 118.000 to 136.992 MHz. In the United States, 25 kHz channel spacing is used. The COM radios can easily be reconfigured through the System Setup page for 8.33 kHz spacing, which is used in some other parts of the world.

The COM radio volume can be adjusted from 0 to 100% of volume using the VOL/PUSH SQ knob. In most manufacturers' implementations of the G1000, turning the volume knob one or more clicks allows you to see at what level the volume control is set. In some early implementations, however, it's not possible to display the volume level. Where it's available, the volume percentage is displayed for approximately two seconds in place of the corresponding standby COM frequency and the word "VOLUME" replaces the COM1 or COM2 label.

One possible area of confusion on the G1000, but not the Perspective can arise when using the volume controls on both the PFD and MFD. For example, the pilot may be adjusting the volume of the selected COM radio using the VOL/PUSH SQ knob on the PFD. However, the non-flying pilot in the right seat may find that the VOL/PUSH SQ knob on the MFD is having no effect upon the volume of that radio. Usually, the problem is that the MFD's COM controls are set for the other radio. Pushing the COM knob on the MFD will set the radio controls to the selected radio and should solve the problem.

The COM radio squelch is set automatically so that the receiver is quiet when no signals are present. Sometimes, however, a weak signal may not be strong enough to open the squelch to enable the signal to be heard. Either the signal will break in and out or, if it's a weak signal, it's not heard at all. In this situation, pushing the VOL/PUSH SQ knob disables the automatic squelch so that the weak signal—and its accompanying background noise—can be heard. After you're finished listening to the signal, push the VOL/PUSH SQ knob again to re-enable the automatic squelch and remove the background noise.

Whenever a pilot is transmitting, a white "TX" indicator appears to the right of the active COM frequency. Anytime you suspect that your push-to-talk button is not working, look to see if "TX" appears when you push the button. Also, a white "RX" indicator appears whenever a signal is being received, except in some early G1000 implementations.

Stuck microphones are common, particularly in training environments where a student or instructor continue to grip the push-to-talk button. The system limits these transmissions by automatically timing out after 35 seconds and shutting off the transmitter. In addition, an alert appears in the Alerts window to notify the pilot of the possible stuck microphone.

The G1000 and Perspective makes it easy to get to the emergency frequency of 121.5 MHz. Pushing and holding the Frequency Toggle key for two seconds loads the emergency frequency into the active frequency for which toggling is enabled. Should a COM radio fail, that radio defaults to 121.5 MHz. If both displays were to fail, the pilot's headset is automatically connected to 121.5 MHz.

NAV Radio Operation

The NAV radios operate in the 108.0 to 117.95 MHz aviation band, just above the FM broadcast band used for music stations on your car radio. The receiver can tune ground-based VOR navigation stations or the Instrument Landing Systems (ILS) used for instrument approaches at many airports. Manually tuning a NAV frequency is accomplished in the same way that COM tuning is done.

VOR and ILS stations broadcast a Morse code identifier, which you can use to confirm that the correct station has been tuned. It confirms that the signal is valid and is not, for example, undergoing maintenance testing by an FAA technician. The system helps you identify and validate a signal in two ways.

First, the system incorporates a Morse code detector. When a VOR or ILS frequency is tuned on the active side of the NAV radio display, the Morse code identifier is displayed after the system verifies that the code is present. This three or four letter identifier appears to the right of the active NAV frequency. Note that this occurs even if the GPS CDI is displayed on the HSI, meaning that neither NAV radio is selected for use.

You should always listen for the Morse code identifier before trusting your life to navigating via a radio signal. NAV radios allow a user to do this by incorporating an audio filter which notches out the 1020 Hz audio frequency of the Morse code. Normally the filter is on, so that users don't have to listen to Morse code on top of other things they're trying to hear, such as a Hazardous Inflight Weather Advisory Service (HIWAS) broadcast or Flight Service Station (FSS) personnel replying to a request to open or close a flight plan.

In order to hear the Morse code, the audio filter needs to be turned off, so that you can hear the 1020 Hz audio frequency used for the code. This is done by pushing the VOL/PUSH ID knob. When the label "ID" appears between a NAV radio's active and standby frequencies, it indicates that the audio filter is off to enable you to hear the Morse code identifier for that radio. To hear the code, turn up the volume for that radio and select NAV1 or NAV2 on the audio panel. Remember, in order to use the volume control for a particular radio, the cyan frequency toggle arrow must be on the radio you're listening to; if not, press the button in the center of the NAV knobs.

To select a NAV radio, the correct frequency must be placed in the active field and that radio's CDI must be selected by the CDI softkey so that it appears in the center of the HSI. When these conditions are met, the frequency is displayed in green, indicating that it's the selected frequency.

Frequency Auto-Tuning

Auto-tuning saves time by allowing you to push a few keys to load a frequency, rather than looking it up on a map and dialing in each digit. It particularly saves time before departing from or arriving at an airport, since multiple frequencies can be loaded from a single page. New users, used to looking up and loading frequencies manually, may at first need to force themselves to use auto-tuning, until they've formed a new habit pattern and remember to use this valuable resource.

The PFD can be used to load COM frequencies from the NRST page, while the MFD can be used to load COM or NAV frequencies from many of its pages. The method of doing so is always the same. The FMS knobs are used to scroll the cursor and highlight a frequency and then the ENT key is pushed to load the frequency. NAV frequencies are loaded automatically whenever a VOR, localizer or ILS instrument approach is loaded or activated.

You should become well acquainted with the NRST softkey on the PFD—it could save your life in an emergency. Push the softkey to bring up a list of the 25 nearest airports, the bearing and distance to these airports and their COM frequencies. Then scroll with either FMS knob to highlight an airport, so that you can enter it into the GPS, or to highlight a frequency, so that you can load it into the COM radio. Highlighting a frequency and pushing the ENT key loads it into the cyan tuning box on the standby side of the COM radio. Then press the Frequency Toggle key to transfer it to the active side, and press the appropriate key on the audio panel to select the frequency for use.

Auto-Tuning with the MFD

NAV and/or COM Frequencies can be loaded from several pages in the WPT and NRST group of pages:

- WPT: Airport Information page; VOR Information page
- NRST: Nearest Airport page; Nearest VOR page, Nearest Frequencies page

Frequencies are also loaded automatically when an instrument approach is loaded.

After engine start-up, get in the habit of selecting the Airport Information page to load frequencies; just turn the MFD's large FMS knob one click to the right. Since it's the most used page in the WPT group, it's the first page in the group. If the frequencies are not already displayed, push the INFO softkey. From here, load the Automated Weather Observing System (AWOS), Automated Surface Observing System (ASOS), Automatic Terminal Information Service (ATIS), ground, tower and other frequencies by scrolling to highlight frequencies and pressing the ENT key.

Generally at engine start-up, even before you load a flight plan, the departure airport will already be displayed, since the system knows where the airplane is located. After you've loaded a flight plan that terminates at an airport, the destination airport will be displayed whenever you select the Airport Information page. Also, anytime a flight plan is loaded, you can easily get information for the departure or destination airport by pressing the MENU key, selecting "View Departure Airport" or "View Destination Airport" and pressing the ENT key.

To select a different airport from the one displayed, push the FMS knob, enter the identifier for the airport you want and press the ENT key. Alternatively—and this feature will save you time if you remember to use it—push the MENU key, select "View Recent Airport List," and press the ENT key. Then scroll with either FMS knob through the list of airports you've recently used, highlight one and press the ENT key. This is often the fastest way to select an airport on the Airport Information page.

Loading frequencies from the VOR Information page is virtually identical. To reach this page, turn the large FMS knob to WPT and the small knob until the VOR page is shown. Use the FMS knobs to enter an identifier and then scroll to highlight a frequency and push the ENT key. To save time entering a VOR, push the MENU key, select "View Recent VOR List," and press the ENT key.

The NRST group of pages on the MFD is easy to reach in an emergency. On the G1000, twist the large FMS knob to the right as much as you want—at least three clicks—and you're there. On the Perspective, turn the large FMS knob on the console to select NRST, usually the next to the last group. The first page in the group is the Nearest Airports page. COM frequencies can be loaded by highlighting a frequency and pressing the ENT key and NAV frequencies can be loaded by using the softkeys or PROC key to load an instrument approach.

The Nearest VOR Page works similarly to the other pages for loading frequencies with one exception. Once you've scrolled with the FMS knob to the desired VOR, you must then push the FREQ softkey to highlight the frequency. Then press the ENT key to load it into the NAV radio.

Use the Nearest Frequencies page to quickly load nearby Center, FSS, ASOS and ATIS frequencies. This page is easy to use if you remember to use the softkeys or the MENU key to select the type of frequency you wish to load. After selecting the page, push the FMS knob to bring up a cursor in the NEAREST ARTCC box, where you can use the FMS knobs to scroll to highlight a nearby Center frequency and push the ENT key to load it. To select an FSS or weather frequency, you must push the FSS or WX softkey or press MENU and select either "Select FSS Window" or "Select WX Window." This moves the cursor to the appropriate box, where you can then scroll to a frequency and press the ENT key to load it.

Auto-Tuning by Loading an Instrument Approach

NAV frequencies are loaded automatically when an instrument approach is loaded or activated. You can also load them manually from the Airport Information page and other pages by highlighting the frequency and pressing the ENT key.

When NAV frequencies are auto-tuned by loading an instrument approach, the frequency is loaded into the active side of the NAV1 radio *if GPS is selected* for use on the HSI. That way, the frequency is ready for use when the user selects NAV1 on the HSI to begin the approach. However, *if either NAV radio is selected* for use on the CDI—and is presumably being used for course navigation—the frequency is entered into the standby side of whichever NAV radio is selected on the HSI. This prevents you from accidentally changing your navigation source while loading an instrument approach.

Audio Panels

Mastering the audio panel of an aircraft is often given short shrift by both pilots and instructors—which may explain why so many pilots fumble around when using one! While most panels are similar, each has its own nuances, and the G1000 and Perspective audio panels are no different. Many of the functions of these audio panels are intuitively obvious to the average pilot; however, some, like the intercom's manual squelch, are more difficult to figure out without instruction or documentation.

Most G1000 systems use the GMA 1347 audio panel. Perspective aircraft use the GMA 347 (figure 15-8) and, beginning in 2012, the GMA 350 (figure 15-9).

Upon power up, the audio panels go through a self-test, which includes lighting all of the triangular annunciator lights for about two seconds. Then the audio panel restores all settings the way they were when the system was powered down. If the audio panel ever fails in flight, the system will bypass the audio panel and connect the pilot's microphone and headset directly to the COM1 audio. Dual GMA 1347 audio panels are supported in primarily jet aircraft for full redundancy.

Pressing most keys activates a function and lights the triangular annunciator above the key. Pushing it again deactivates the function and annunciator, except for the MKR/MUTE and PLAY keys, discussed later in the chapter.

The GMA 1347 and GMA 347 audio panels support three COM transceivers; the GMA 350 supports only two COM radios. Pressing one of the three microphone keys, COM1 MIC, COM2 MIC or COM3 MIC selects a radio for transmitting. At the same time, it turns the corresponding COM frequency green in the active fields on the PFD, and on the MFD in the G1000, to indicate the frequency is selected.

Receive audio is selected by pushing the COM1, COM2 or COM3 keys. Normally you won't have to push any of these, since pressing the MIC key for transmitting will simultaneously select the corresponding COM key for receiving. However, you could use the COM keys so that you can listen to two COM radios simultaneously. For example, when approaching your destination airport, you might have COM1 MIC selected to talk to approach control and then push COM2 so that you can monitor the ATIS for the destination airport at the same time. The

Figure 5-3 The G1000 audio panel is generally located between the PFD and MFD. The Perspective audio panel is shown in figure 15-8. *© Garmin Ltd. or its affiliates*

TIP

Pressing the COM knob switches the frequency tuning box between COM1 and COM2, however pressing the audio panel's COM/MIC keys also moves the tuning box. Therefore, if you need to move the tuning box and press a COM/MIC key to make an active frequency the selected frequency, you can do both with a single key push: just press the COM/MIC1 or COM/MIC2 key.

GMA 1347 can be configured to automatically mute the secondary audio (in this example, COM2), whenever a signal is received on the primary receiver. To configure this, you must contact your authorized avionics service center.

The COM 1/2 key allows, in some installations, the pilot and copilot to talk simultaneously on separate radios. When activated, the pilot can transmit on COM1 and the copilot can transmit on COM2. Note, that while the pilot can still continue to monitor any other audio sources selected, such as NAV1, DME, MKR audio, etc, the copilot can only hear COM2 audio.

The ability to transmit simultaneously on two frequencies is directly affected by the distance between the COM antennas and how close the transmit frequencies are to each other. In some cases, transmitting on one frequency will interfere with the other COM radio receiver. This is identified by a decrease in sensitivity of the other COM receiver, by the squelch circuit opening and closing during the transmissions or by hearing a large amount of background noise. Some manufacturers disable the COM 1/2 key function in their aircraft to avoid these problems.

The TEL key can be configured to support wiring a telephone in through the audio panel. You can work with an authorized avionics dealer to enable this function.

The Passenger Address mode is used to make in-cabin announcements over the aircraft's speaker. To enable it on the G1000, press the PA key; in Perspective systems, hold the SPKR kcy for two seconds. Then start talking to make seat belt and emergency exit announcements to your passengers. Don't worry about accidentally transmitting over the radio at the same time; transmitting and receiving is inhibited whenever PA is selected.

The SPKR key is used to direct audio from any of the radios over the speaker. This can be used on the ground to listen to the ATIS prior to starting the plane or in flight, particularly if a headset fails, and you need to listen to the radios through the overhead speaker.

Navigation Keys

The audio panel has a built-in marker beacon receiver used to determine when certain points are passed while flying an ILS approach. All of the beacons transmit on 75 MHz and send up a narrow radio beam, so that only one beacon is heard when passing directly overhead. Some ILSs have no beacons and the FAA is decommissioning others, particularly middle markers, so their importance is slowly diminishing over time.

Outer markers are typically located four to seven miles from an airport with an ILS, and they transmit a series of Morse code dashes with a relatively low frequency (400 Hz) audio tone. When received, a blue "O" annunciator appears on the PFD. Middle markers are typically 3,500 feet from the runway threshold, transmit a series of alternating Morse code dots and dashes at 1,300 Hz, display an amber "M" annunciator on the PFD, and signal that you are approximately 200 feet above the ground and should either land, if you can see the runway, or perform a go-around. Middle markers are not essential to an instrument approach, since this position can also be determined by staying on the glide slope and noting by the altimeter when you're 200 feet above the ground. The inner marker, used in relatively few installations at major airports where a lower descent on the ILS is permitted, is indicated by a series of Morse code dots at the relatively high frequency of 3,000 Hz and by the display of a white "I" annunciator on the PFD.

In order to hear the Morse code audio associated with a marker beacon, you must push the MKR/MUTE key once so that the annunciator light is illuminated. While the marker beacon is audible, the audio can be muted by pushing the MKR/MUTE key one additional time. The audio then returns when you pass over another marker beacon and can be muted by pushing the MKR/MUTE key again. Note, however, that pushing the MKR/MUTE key when the audio is already muted will turn the markers off! If in doubt, check the annunciator light to confirm that the marker beacon audio is still on. Also, the marker beacon annunciators that appear on the PFD will always appear regardless of the position of the MKR/MUTE key.

The HI SENS key on the GMA 1347 and the SENS key on the GMA 347 increase the sensitivity of the marker beacon receiver. The GMA 350 uses an external switch to set marker sensitivity. When the MKR/MUTE key is on and high sensitivity is selected, audio from marker beacons will be heard sooner, effectively enlarging the area in which you can hear a beacon.

The audio panel is also used to listen to navigation receivers to verify the presence of the Morse code identifier and hence the validity of the signal. Pilots are accustomed to pushing the NAV1 and NAV2 keys so that they can hear the audio from these respective VHF receivers. Pushing the ADF key allows you to monitor an NDB signal, usually while on an instrument approach or to listen to an AM broadcast station. Relatively few new glass cockpit aircraft are shipping with ADF receivers however, since GPS technology has largely supplanted the need for this form of navigation.

According to some designated pilot examiners (DPEs), the DME is the radio pilots most often forget to identify on their instrument checkride. Pushing the DME key allows you to monitor the Morse code identifier—if your aircraft is DME equipped—though it transmits only once every 30 seconds. The AUX key is available to monitor any other optional radios installed by an authorized avionics shop.

Music

You can plug in a source of music, called MUSIC 1, through an auxiliary jack and listen to it through the intercom. Note, however, that in some aircraft there is no volume level for MUSIC 1; you must control it using the volume control on your external music device. The music can be configured to mute anytime there is activity from a radio or marker beacon. After the activity ceases, the music returns to its original level over a period of several seconds.

This muting function can be toggled on and off by pressing and holding the MKR/MUTE key for 3 seconds. A single beep indicates that music muting is enabled and two beeps indicate that it is disabled. You can also configure the music to mute whenever anyone talks on the intercom, but you'll need to contact your authorized avionics service center to set that up.

MUSIC 2 is the SiriusXM Radio audio for aircraft with a GDL 69A and a satellite radio subscription. Its volume is adjusted through the XM Information page, described in Chapter 7. Note that in many aircraft with a GDL 69A, MUSIC 1 and MUSIC 2 are combined.

Intercom Manual Squelch and Volume

The intercom's squelch and volume are controlled by a shared set of knobs and their operation is not intuitive. In some G1000 installations, the intercom's automatic squelch setting may be a little tight for some headset microphones, resulting in clipped speech. To resolve this, use the MAN SQ key and adjust the squelch manually.

Pressing the MAN SQ key lights the annunciator above it and lights either the VOL or SQ label located near the bottom of the audio panel. The actual label that's lit depends upon whether the volume or squelch was last set by the user. If SQ is not lit, push the center of the concentric volume/squelch knobs once to light the SQ label.

When *both* the MAN SQ annunciator and SQ label are lit, the small knob controls the squelch setting of the pilot's microphone and the large knob controls the squelch setting of the copilot's microphone. Adjustment of either knob should be made to just the point where the background noise first goes away when the pilot or copilot is not speaking. After the squelches are set manually, do NOT push the MAN SQ key again. Doing so will revert the squelch back to the automatic setting. To retain the manual squelch settings, the annunciator above the MAN SQ key must stay lit.

The same concentric volume/squelch knobs used to manually adjust the squelch are also used to set the intercom volume. If the MAN SQ annunciator is off, the knobs are automatically set to control the volume. Turning the small knob adjusts the intercom volume for the pilot and turning the large knob adjusts the volume for the copilot. Note that this does not affect the volume at which the radios are heard; it affects only the volume of the crew and passenger voices and music heard over the intercom.

If the MAN SQ annunciator is on, the knobs can control either the volume or the squelch function. Pushing the center of the concentric volume/squelch knobs will toggle their function between controlling the volume or squelch. If the VOL label is lit, use the knobs to adjust the pilot and copilot volumes. If the manual squelch was previously set and the SQ label is illuminated, push the center of the concentric volume/squelch knobs once to light the VOL label. The manual squelch

Perspective Manual Squelch

To turn on the manual squelch on the Perspective's GMA 347 audio panel, press the center knob on the left side of the panel. Then turn the outer left knob to set the intercom squelch setting on the pilot's microphone. Turn the right outer knob to set the squelch setting of the copilot and passenger microphones.

To set the manual squelch on the Perspective's GMA 350 audio panel, turn the large knob to put the cursor on MAN SQ. Then turn the smaller knob to adjust the intercom squelch setting to the point where the background noise first goes away.

setting will be saved and the knobs can now be used to adjust the pilot and copilot intercom volumes.

Intercom Isolation Modes

The intercom has four isolation modes, which provide a variety of ways to isolate the pilot, copilot, crew (both the pilot and copilot), and passengers from each other. This essentially splits the intercom into two separate audio channels. One channel connects the designated pilot or crew to the selected radios, while everyone else in the plane is grouped together on the other channel. This allows the isolated pilot or crew to communicate effectively on the radio without distractions.

All four isolation modes are controlled by the PILOT and COPLT keys. When neither annunciator is illuminated above these keys, the intercom operates in the ALL mode and all pilots and passengers can hear each other and music. The pilot and copilot hear the MUSIC 1 channel, which can be set up to mute whenever anyone talks or there's activity on a selected radio, and the passengers hear the MUSIC 2 channel, which is never muted.

Pressing the PILOT key illuminates the annunciator above that key and connects the pilot to the selected radios, but isolates him or her from everyone else. The copilot and passengers can talk to each other and each hears their respective music: MUSIC 1 for the copilot and MUSIC 2 for the passengers.

Pressing the COPLT key illuminates the annunciator above that key and connects the copilot to the selected radios while isolating him or her from everyone else. The pilot and passengers can talk to each other and each hears their respective music: MUSIC 1 for the pilot and MUSIC 2 for the passengers.

Pressing both the PILOT and COPLT keys illuminates both annunciators and selects the CREW mode, which connects the pilot and copilot to each other and to the selected radios. The passengers can hear each other and MUSIC 2.

Digital Clearance Recorder

The concept of a digital clearance recorder—which records instructions from ATC and allows a pilot to play them back to verify what was heard—has been around for awhile. It finally functions well in the G1000 and Perspective. Early recorders would record for perhaps 30 seconds, but required playing back the entire 30 seconds to get the last few bits of information. This is an eternity for controllers who expect an immediate read back of instructions, rendering the recorders impractical in most situations.

The audio panel will record up to 2½ minutes of incoming signals from the COM radios, but it records each incoming transmission separately. When the memory is full, the digital clearance recorder begins recording over the oldest memory block.

Pressing the PLAY key once plays back just the most recent transmission. Pressing the key twice plays the next oldest transmission and additional key presses bring up earlier transmissions in sequence. This makes it easy to retrieve the most recently received information without having to listen to all information that was recorded.

The quality of the playback is exceptional. It is so good in fact that crew members should alert each other whenever they are about to use the playback function. If one pilot doesn't notice that the other pilot has pressed the PLAY key, he or she could easily think that ATC is repeating a transmission and call ATC to respond to what they heard being played back.

During playback, the PLAY annunciator blinks approximately once a second. Playback can be halted at anytime by pressing the MKR/MUTE key. If a new radio transmission comes in during playback, playback is halted and the new transmission is recorded.

Display Backup

The large, red Display Backup button at the bottom of the GMA 1347 audio panel is for emergency use and switches the G1000 displays into reversionary mode, discussed further in Chapter 12 on emergencies. In the Perspective, the Display Backup button is between the PFD and MFD. Briefly, pushing the button combines the primary flight instruments with the engine indication system and displays them on both the PFD and MFD or, if one display has failed, on whichever display is still working.

Summary

Understanding the radios and the audio panel is crucial for the successful operation of an aircraft. Therefore, you'll want to review this chapter to understand the audio panel thoroughly, so that you don't pay to learn it while the engine is running!

Engine instrumentation is also often poorly understood, perhaps because so many GA aircraft have so little of it. Ironically, understanding and using it properly will cut your flying costs—both in terms of fuel usage and in engine overhaul costs—more than any other factor. Any time you invest in understanding engine instrumentation, discussed in the next chapter, will pay huge dividends over the lifetime of your aircraft.

Chapter 6: Engine Indication System

Savvy aircraft owners know that there's no better investment than having sophisticated engine monitoring equipment aboard to help maximize the life of the engine and to detect problems early. This is particularly true of the larger six-cylinder engines, which are far more susceptible to overheating and may not reach the manufacturer's time between overhaul (TBO) specification if they're not operated properly. As a G1000 or Perspective owner or renter pilot, you will find that your aircraft includes engine monitoring equipment that rivals the best of the aftermarket solutions available. Knowing how to use the engine indication system (EIS) properly can save you or the owner thousands of dollars by extending the life of the engine and postponing the need for overhaul or replacement.

The engine indication system is the part of the G1000 system that varies the most from manufacturer to manufacturer and even across airplane models within a manufacturer's line of aircraft. Therefore, it's important that you become familiar with the documentation for the engine indication system in the aircraft you fly and follow that documentation wherever it may conflict with this book.

Traditional engine monitoring systems

Most older aircraft have a cylinder head temperature (CHT) gauge, which monitors the temperature of just one of the four or six cylinders in the engine. This is a major limitation, as some cylinders will be hotter than others and the gauge might not be installed in the hottest cylinder. The gauge uses a thermocouple probe to measure the temperature of the block of metal forming the top of the cylinder.

Thermocouples are still used in modern engine monitoring systems and they're made by bonding two dissimilar metals together. When heated, the thermocouple generates a small voltage proportional to the temperature. These devices are relatively slow to react to changes in temperature, so you should turn the mixture control slowly when leaning an engine.

Perspective

The Perspective EIS displays critical data in the same way as the G1000: along the left side of the MFD (figure 15-10). But unlike most G1000 implementations, the Perspective has a full screen engine page on the MFD that displays all engine, fuel, fuel calculations, electrical, and air density data (see figure in Appendix D). Pressing the MFD's ENGINE softkey displays this EIS – Engine page. The Perspective differs from the G1000 in that it forces you to view an Initial Usable Fuel screen (figure 15-11) after engine startup. This makes it almost impossible to forget to set the fuel totalizer, a common issue among G1000 users. Most G1000 implementations display a "tach time" on one of the engine pages, but the Perspective uses mechanical Hobbs meters instead.

Figure 6-1 Older EGT gauges monitor only one cylinder. © *Max Trescott*

Monitoring cylinder head temperature is important, since cylinders can overheat and require early replacement which can cost thousands of dollars. Overheating occurs when the air flow cooling the cylinder is low relative to the power being developed. This is most likely to occur at full power settings, particularly when climbing rapidly at low airspeeds, which results in less air flowing over the engine.

Turbocharged engines may also overheat in cruise at higher altitudes, since they can still develop high power—unlike normally aspirated engines which lose power with altitude because of the thinner air—yet are cooled by the less dense air found at higher altitudes. Whenever you encounter high cylinder head temperatures, take one or more of the following actions: reduce the rate of climb, reduce engine power, enrich the mixture or, when installed, open the cowl flaps further.

Slightly more sophisticated systems include an exhaust gas temperature (EGT) gauge (figure 6-1), as an aid to leaning the fuel mixture. A single thermocouple is used to measure the temperature of the exhaust gases after they exit the cylinder. Typically, the leaning procedure includes leaning the mixture slowly and stopping when the EGT reaches a maximum or "peak" temperature. From there, the mixture is enriched until the temperature drops some number of degrees below the peak temperature. The exact number of degrees varies upon whether the pilot is seeking best power (fastest speed but at a higher fuel flow) or a best economy power setting which results in a lower speed but a more efficient use of fuel.

Again, these systems are of limited value, since the older EGT gauges monitor the exhaust temperature from a single cylinder, yet not all cylinders will reach their "peak" at the same time. Ideally, the cylinder that peaks first should be monitored, so that all other cylinders will be running a richer mixture and will run slightly cooler. However, there's no guarantee that the first cylinder to peak is the one being monitored in these older installations.

In contrast, modern engine monitoring systems measure all of the cylinders in an engine. Thus, a six-cylinder engine will have six thermocouples measuring each of the CHT temperatures and another six measuring all of the EGT temperatures. Turbocharged engines often have a thirteenth probe to monitor the turbine inlet temperature (TIT), which is the temperature of the exhaust gases entering the turbocharger. Other typical options are oil temperature, outside air temperature, fuel flow rate and tools for assisting in the leaning process. The G1000 and Perspective engine indication system includes all of these modern capabilities. Perspective users may want to skip ahead now to pages 252-3.

G1000 Engine Page

Every G1000 system has multiple pages of engine information. The Engine page (figure 6-2) is displayed by default and shows all critical engine, fuel and electrical indicators. Softkeys are used to access the System page and a third engine page called, depending upon the manufacturer, the Fuel or Lean page. Engine pages for many G1000 and Perspective aircraft are shown in Appendix D.

Before you start a G1000-equipped aircraft, turn on the PFD using the standby battery switch, master switch or as specified by your checklist. In some installations, such as the Diamond DA40, the MFD is also on at engine start. If only the PFD is on, such as in Cessna installations, the default Engine page will initially be displayed on the PFD (figure 12-2). After engine start, the Engine page shifts to the MFD when that display is turned on, usually through the avionics master switch. For aircraft such as the DA40, where both the PFD and MFD are on at engine start, the Engine page is initially displayed on the PFD, but shifts to the MFD after that display completes its self-test and the ENT key is pushed.

The Engine page in all G1000-equipped, piston-powered aircraft includes a tachometer, located near the top of the page. It displays revolutions per minute (rpm) in both an analog and a digital format. With just a quick glance, the analog needle tells you the approximate power setting. To set the power more precisely, use the digital readout below it.

The tachometer uses color bands. Green indicates the normal operating range, white is used for below normal operating ranges and red indicates the maximum speed. In some aircraft, such as the Cessna 206, white also indicates the above normal operating range.

Most aircraft with constant-speed props, which includes all G1000-equipped aircraft except the Cessna 172SP, Diamond DA40F and Tiger AG-5B, also have a manifold pressure gauge displayed at the top of the Engine page. Manifold pressure, set by the throttle, uses the same analog needle plus digital display used by the tachometer. Green indicates the normal operating range, while white indicates the above and below normal operating ranges. Turbocharged aircraft, such as the Cessna T206, use red to indicate maximum manifold pressure.

An exception is the Diamond DA42 TwinStar, which has two constant-speed props, but uses an engine load indicator, rather than a manifold pressure gauge, since the engines are controlled by a Full Authority Digital Engine Control (FADEC). While it has both an analog and digital readout, the format differs from other aircraft. Instead of a round needle, the analog display uses a triangular pointer that moves up and down. The same style is used for the tachometer in this aircraft.

Most G1000 aircraft display a fuel flow indicator—something not generally found in older aircraft—beneath the engine manifold pressure and tachometer gauges. You'll find this gauge useful when priming the engine prior to start and to monitor fuel consumption. Generally this display is a horizontal bar with a moving triangular pointer that indicates gallons per hour. Green is used to indicate normal fuel flow, and some displays also include additional tick marks to indicate maximum cruise fuel flow and maximum takeoff fuel flow.

An exception is the Diamond DA42 TwinStar, which shows only a

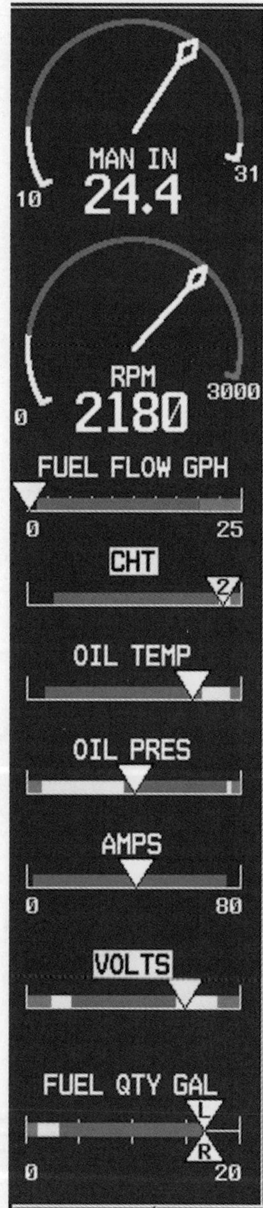

Figure 6-2 Typical Engine Page from Diamond DA40. *© Garmin Ltd. or its affiliates*

digital display—probably because of the limited space—for the fuel flows to each of its two engines. Fuel flow data is also used for computations in the Trip Planning page in the AUX group and to display the fuel range ring on the Navigation Map page.

Other engine gauges commonly found on the default Engine page are the oil temperature and oil pressure gauges. All of these gauges use the same horizontal bar format, with a moving triangular pointer that gives a relative indication. In many cases, the exact digital readout for oil pressure and oil temperature can be found by using softkeys to reach the Engine System page. Green indicates the normal range, yellow indicates caution and red is for warning.

Fuel Gauges

All default Engine pages, except Perspective, include fuel gauges. Hopefully, you've already been trained to distrust fuel gauges and always use an alternate way to verify your fuel load. The best method is to fully fuel the aircraft and personally inspect each tank to verify that it's full and that the cap is properly in place. That guarantees you a known quantity of fuel.

Next, determine your hourly fuel consumption rate by referring to your aircraft's POH and use a watch to time the number of hours you're in the air. Historically, this has been the only reliable way to assure that you don't run out of fuel.

Fuel gauges are notoriously inaccurate. Surprisingly, FAA regulations in the United States require that fuel gauges be accurate at only one point—when they register empty! Unfortunately, by the time they are guaranteed to be accurate, it's a little late to do anything except land immediately. Approximately 12% of all accidents result from fuel mismanagement issues and these accidents are entirely avoidable if you always visually verify your fuel load and use a watch to measure your flight time.

The G1000 fuel gauges use a horizontal bar presentation and triangular pointers for each tank. Green indicates normal, red indicates warning and, in some manufacturer's aircraft, yellow is used to indicate caution. White tick marks appear every 5 or 10 gallons, depending upon the capacity of the aircraft's fuel tanks.

You'll probably be surprised to learn that the fuel gauges cannot indicate full fuel in most G1000-equipped aircraft. That's because the location, shape, and position of the fuel tanks and indicators make it difficult to measure the first few gallons burned. For example in the Diamond DA40, which uses 20 gallon fuel tanks, the maximum indication is 17 gallons and any fuel above that cannot be detected. The Cessna 182 and 206 are similar: although the tanks each hold 44.5 gallons, the gauges register a maximum of 35 gallons per tank. A summary of fuel gauge differences for many G1000 equipped aircraft can be found in Appendix B.

Electrical System Status

Let's be candid. The electrical systems of older general aviation aircraft are notoriously susceptible to failure. One senior flight instructor recently told me that he has had 19 electrical failures in his flying career! This has been tolerable in older aircraft, where some gyros were run by electricity and others were powered by a vacuum pump, since an electrical failure didn't result in the loss of all the gyros. However, it's intolerable in modern glass cockpit aircraft where most, if not all, instruments are electric.

That's why some aircraft manufacturers have a second alternator and all manufacturers have a second battery in their G1000-equipped aircraft to continue providing power to some devices for at least 30 minutes after the main battery is exhausted. Furthermore, you'll know immediately when you have an alternator failure, due to the excellent annunciators and alerts in the G1000. This will give you time to start conserving power by turning off unnecessary devices. By contrast, in many older aircraft, pilots often first learn of a system failure when the battery is drained and equipment starts to fail! You'll find more about electrical systems in Chapter 12, where we'll discuss emergencies.

Most G1000-equipped aircraft display information about voltage and current on the main Engine page, though the formats differ. Exceptions are the Diamond DA42 and Columbia 350i and 400i, which displays their voltmeters and ammeters on the System page. Cessnas, for example, have a voltmeter with a digital readout at the bottom of the Engine page. Two separate numbers appear: the voltage on the main electrical bus (powered by the main battery) and the voltage on the Essentials bus (powered by both the main and standby batteries).

During normal operation, both buses should display about 28 volts with the alternator on or about 24 volts with the alternator off. Anything less suggests a dying battery or other problem with the electrical system. When outside the normal limits, the digital readouts change to yellow or red. Some other aircraft, such as the Tiger AG-5B, use a horizontal bar and triangular pointer for their voltmeter on the Engine page, but then provide a digital voltmeter on the System page.

Most Engine pages also include an ammeter, which measures the amount of current in amps flowing to or from the battery. A negative number indicates that more power is being drawn from the battery than is resupplied by the alternator. This will occur when you turn the PFD on just before engine start, since it is drawing a few amps of power, but the alternator, driven by the engine, isn't yet replenishing the battery. In flight, however, a negative current suggests that the alternator has failed and that you should try to bring the alternator back on line or start conserving power by turning off unnecessary items.

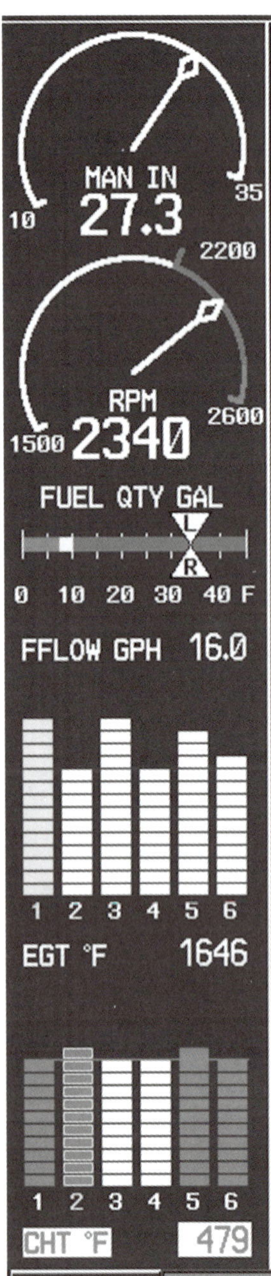

Figure 6-3 Typical Lean page from Mooney Ovation 20R. *© Garmin Ltd. or its affiliates*

Cessnas use separate digital ammeters to show the current flow to both the main battery and the standby battery. Some other manufacturers use a horizontal bar and triangular pointer for their ammeter, but provide a separate digital display on the System page.

G1000 Lean Page

Leaning an engine is critical for getting the speed and fuel flow you want, as well as for managing engine temperatures. In the introduction of this chapter, we described the generic procedure for leaning an aircraft engine. However, you should always follow the recommended leaning procedure in the POH for your aircraft. The information included in this section is advisory in nature and, where any conflict exists, you must follow your POH.

To reach the Lean page (figure 6-3), press the ENGINE softkey and then the LEAN softkey. The top of this page replicates the tachometer and, when included, the manifold pressure gauges found on the default Engine page. Below it are bar graphs for the CHT and EGT temperatures for each cylinder. Again, color is important. White indicates normal EGT and CHT temperatures, while cyan indicates the cylinder selected for digital display of its temperature. For the CHT temperatures, yellow indicates caution and red is for warning.

Below the bar graphs, a digital temperature display gives you a more precise way to measure CHT and EGT temperature for one user selectable cylinder. By default, temperatures of the hottest cylinder and the number of that cylinder are displayed; however, you can select which cylinder is displayed by pressing the CYL SLCT softkey one or more times. When a cylinder turns yellow or red, that cylinder is displayed and the CYL SLCT softkey becomes disabled until temperatures return to normal or the ASSIST softkey is pressed. Columbia aircraft continually display all temperatures and don't have a CYL SLCT softkey.

Many G1000 implementations also include on this page a fuel flow indicator and, for turbocharged aircraft, a TIT indicator, both of which are useful for engine leaning. The DA42 TwinStar and Columbia aircraft do not have a Lean page. Instead, the DA42 has a Fuel page, discussed separately below, and the Columbia 350i and 400i have a full screen System page that incorporates leaning data.

Leaning the Engine

You can lean the engine manually by watching the temperatures as you adjust the mixture, or you can press the ASSIST softkey to aid in the process. Generally, you would lean after you've reached your cruise altitude and have set the throttle and propeller controls for one of the power settings recommended by the aircraft manufacturer, though some manufacturers recommend some leaning during climb. Again, it's important to note that you should follow the leaning instructions in your POH rather than the general instructions provided here.

For normally aspirated engines, press the ASSIST softkey and slowly lean with the mixture control while watching the EGT temperatures.

When the first cylinder reaches its peak or maximum temperature, a hollow bar replaces the top bar for that cylinder on the bar chart. Then, enrich the mixture slowly while watching the "ΔPeak" display.

The Δ is the symbol for the Greek letter "Delta," used by engineers to indicate change. Thus ΔPeak means the change in temperature from the peak or maximum EGT temperature attained while leaning the mixture. Once that peak is reached and the mixture is enriched, EGT temperatures drop, and the ΔPeak display shows how much that temperature has dropped by displaying a negative temperature. Also, the bar graphs recede as temperatures lower, though the hollow bar remains at the peak temperature.

Aircraft manufacturers typically specify leaning by referencing the change in temperature from the peak temperature. For example, they might specify best power as "100° rich of peak," in which case you would enrich the mixture until the ΔPeak display shows "-100°F." Some manufacturers, such as Columbia, support lean of peak operation, and instead of "ΔPeak," they display the number of degrees "ΔRich" or "ΔLean."

Turbocharged aircraft are often leaned with a similar procedure, though instead of peak EGT, they use peak TIT as the temperature reference. The mixture is leaned until a peak TIT is detected and enriched until the ΔPeak display shows a specific temperature difference between the current and peak temperatures. One difference from normally aspirated G1000-equipped planes is that a graphical peak and hollow bar is not displayed for turbine inlet temperatures.

If your turbocharged aircraft regularly reaches the same peak temperature during leaning, you can save some wear and tear on your turbocharger by simply leaning to the final temperature, instead of leaning first to peak and then enriching back to the final temperature. That way, your turbocharger doesn't experience the higher peak temperatures. Of course, you should check with your aircraft manufacturer or mechanic before using this procedure for your airplane.

G1000 System Page

To reach the System page (figure 6-4), press the ENGINE softkey and then the SYSTEM softkey, except for the Columbia 350i and 400i, Cirrus Perspective, and later DA40 models where you just push the ENGINE softkey. The top of this page replicates the tachometer and, when included, the manifold pressure gauges found on the default Engine page. Below these, it displays numeric readouts for critical engine, fuel and electrical gauges, many of which are displayed in analog format on other pages. Numbers are displayed in white when indications are in the normal range. Their colors change to yellow for caution and red for warning when you're operating outside normal limits. Typically voltmeter, ammeter, oil temperature and oil pressure readings are displayed.

The System page probably varies more across aircraft manufacturers than any other page. For example, in Columbia, Cirrus Perspective, and later DA40 models, it's a full screen page. One of its most important

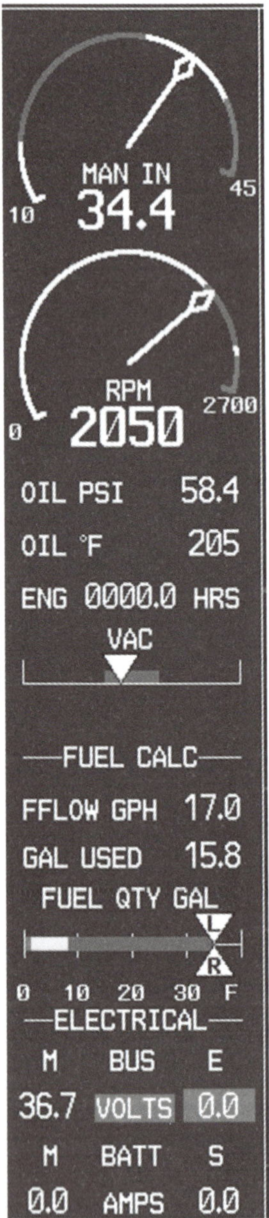

Figure 6-4 Typical System page from Cessna T206. *© Garmin Ltd. or its affiliates*

functions is the fuel totalizer, which displays the fuel flow rate, the number of gallons used and the number of gallons remaining in the tanks in all aircraft (except for Tiger AG-5B aircraft). However, in order to work correctly, *it is critical that you reset the fuel totalizer whenever you add fuel to the tanks.* Also, the fuel range ring and trip planning functions, described in Chapter 7, will not indicate properly if the fuel quantity is not reset. Since this item does not appear on some manufacturers' checklists, it is easy to forget to do this at engine start.

The fuel totalizer is reset using softkeys from the System page (except for the DA42 TwinStar, where this information is on the Fuel page). The exact implementation varies by manufacturer and revision of the G1000 software. Note that pressing the RST USED softkey does not affect the fuel quantity displayed by the fuel tank indicators; it only changes the fuel totalizer functions, such as the fuel used and fuel remaining displays, the trip planning calculations and the fuel range rings.

In some early G1000-equipped aircraft, there is only one softkey, the RST USED softkey. You should only use it when the tanks are full. Otherwise, the totalizer will indicate that you have more fuel than is actually onboard. The latest Cessna and Columbia revisions have a RST FUEL softkey instead, however the key has the opposite effect in each plane. In Cessnas, pressing the softkey sets fuel to zero; in Columbia aircraft, it sets fuel to full tanks! Pilots who fly both aircraft need to remember this difference.

Some current software versions also have INC FUEL and DEC FUEL softkeys. Pushing these keys increments or decrements the fuel totalizer by one gallon at a time, to account for adding less than full fuel to the tanks. Cessnas, however, have a GAL REM softkey which leads to additional softkeys. These keys allow you to set fuel to the tabs, to full tanks, or to add or subtract fuel in one and ten gallon increments. Additionally, some aircraft, like the Diamond DA40, display additional totalizer information on this page such as "Endurance," the time to fuel exhaustion and "Range," the distance the plane can fly in nautical miles until fuel exhaustion.

Other Functions

Most manufacturers implement on the System page some indication of the aircraft's total running time. For example, Cessna and Mooney display "ENG HRS," which is essentially the "tach time" that older aircraft display on their tachometer. This meter runs in real time when the engine is at full power and runs slower at low power settings. It indicates total engine use and is typically used by maintenance personnel to measure time between oil changes and other inspections. If you're a renter pilot, this is one of the numbers that you may be asked to log in addition to the Hobbs time.

Other aircraft, such as the Diamond DA40 and Tiger AG-5B, display "Total Time in Service," instead of engine hours. For Diamonds, this display begins incrementing when the aircraft becomes airborne, for the Tiger it increments above 800 rpm. The DA42 TwinStar also displays Total Time in Service, though it is found on the Fuel page instead.

Some aircraft, such as Cessna and Tiger, use a vacuum pump to power the standby attitude indicator, while others, like Diamond, power it electrically. The vacuum gauge for the Cessna 182 and 206 is found on the System page; in the Cessna 172, the vacuum gauge is on the main Engine page. Tiger uses a suction gauge on the instrument panel which is separate from the G1000. Columbia aircraft display oxygen pressure on this page and have a softkey for turning the oxygen on and off.

DA42 TwinStar

The DA42 TwinStar has a Fuel page instead of a Lean page (see Appendix). It contains all of the fuel totalizer functions just discussed for the System page, such as fuel quantity and fuel flow for each tank. The diesel version of this aircraft also has digital fuel temperature gauges for each tank, due to the variable density of Jet-A fuel at different temperatures. The Fuel page also displays gallons remaining, gallons used, endurance until fuel exhaustion in hours, and range in nautical miles. Total Time in Service is also shown.

The TwinStar default Engine page also differs from other manufacturers' pages in that it includes a coolant temperature gauge, since its 135-hp Thielert kerosene-powered diesel engines are liquid-cooled. Analog fuel temperature indicators for each tank also appear on this page.

The TwinStar System page is unique in that it includes a gearbox temperature indicator. The gearboxes connect each engine to its propeller and they allow the propeller to run at a lower speed than the engine. The temperatures are displayed in degrees Celsius and green, yellow, and red are used to indicate normal, caution and warning temperatures.

Summary

One strength of the G1000 and Perspective system is that manufacturers can customize it to their aircraft. Nowhere does this show up more than on the engine pages. Therefore, you'll want to get familiar with the engine pages for the particular plane you fly. If you fly different G1000- or Perspective-equipped aircraft, perhaps as a flight instructor, you'll find many similarities between the aircraft, though in some cases you may have to hunt to find a particular function, since different planes implement the same function on different pages.

If you're lucky enough to be the owner of one of these aircraft, you'll want to spend time becoming familiar with the engine pages and the manufacturer's recommendations in your POH. There's no better way to preserve your investment than to know how to operate your engine in a way that maximizes its lifetime. The system provides all of the tools to do this; it's up to you, however, to learn how to use the engine indication system and to be consistent in your use of it every time you fly the aircraft. After all, significantly overheating the cylinders a single time could lead to an early overhaul.

In the next chapter, we'll explore all of the MFD except for the EIS portion that we've just discussed. While the engine pages help you preserve the investment you've made in your engine, the rest of the MFD makes flying a joy since it helps make your flying easier and safer.

Chapter 7:
MFD Overview

If you like the PFD, you're going to love the Multifunction Display or MFD. The only downside is that it's located on the right side of the instrument panel, so you may have to arm wrestle the copilot to get to use it. In flight, this display becomes the primary way to monitor engine data and the airplane's progress along the route of flight. It also displays traffic, weather and terrain and provides access to airport and navigational aid data, trip and flight planning, and all auxiliary functions.

Some of these functions are available from the PFD, but when displayed on the MFD they are usually larger and more detailed. While the PFD serves the yeoman function of flying the airplane, the MFD is the true added value in the glass cockpit for its databases, real-time information and trip and flight planning functions. Understanding it fully will reduce your workload and make your flying safer.

Organization

Physically, the MFD hardware is identical to the PFD, except in the Perspective and aircraft with the GFC 700 autopilot. Both displays share the same part number and could be swapped by an avionics technician and still work. Thus, all of the control knobs on the bezel are identical on both units and in many cases perform the same function. For example, the ALT and HDG knobs on both displays perform identically. The radio controls also perform the same function, however, are totally independent, so you can adjust COM1 from the PFD while your copilot uses the identical knobs on the MFD to adjust COM2.

In a few cases, the controls provide similar but different functions. For example, the FMS knobs on both displays are used for data entry. However, on the MFD, you'll also use them to select the map and information pages available only on the MFD. The particular page selected by the FMS knobs is shown pictorially in the lower right corner of the display. As you probably guessed, the softkeys on the MFD are also totally different from those on the PFD.

Perspective

The CRS, HDG and ALT knobs, found on the G1000's MFD, are on the Perspective's center console. Perspective displays a Destination Airport Information window in the upper right instead of COM frequencies. Perspective's track vector is a solid blue line segment (figure 15-13). MFD page navigation varies with software version. In early Perspective aircraft, it's identical to the G1000. In later software versions, page names for every page in the currently selected group are displayed (figure 15-14). This page guide disappears after a user-settable timeout. SD data cards enable a Flight Data Logging feature to automatically store critical flight and engine data, and pilots to import and export Pilot Profiles. The Profile View (figure 14-53), now available in later G1000 versions, displays a side view of upcoming terrain, obstacles, and headwind and tailwind components for winds aloft data at the bottom of the MFD. Perspective's AUX – System Setup page is split in two; SETUP 1 and SETUP 2 softkeys are used to switch between the pages.

Figure 7-1 Navigation Status bar has four configurable data fields. *© Garmin Ltd. or its affiliates*

The engine indication system, described in the last chapter, occupies the left portion of the display. It's placed there so that you can monitor it easily during flight without having to look far from the PFD. Softkeys below it allow you to select other engine information.

You'll find the top of the MFD is similar to the PFD. The same VHF navigation frequencies shown on the PFD are displayed in the upper left corner and communication frequencies are shown in the upper right corner. Between them, a Navigation Status bar shows distance and direction to the next waypoint. Unlike the PFD, however, you can customize the four data fields in the MFD's status bar to show other navigation information (figure 7-1).

Below the communication frequencies is the wind vector window which, if enabled, shows the direction and strength of the wind while you're in flight. Next to it, the orientation of the current map (e.g. North

Figure 7-2 The MFD includes the engine instrumentation, maps and other data. *© Garmin Ltd. or its affiliates*

Up, Track Up) is displayed. You should note that while this orientation can be changed for some map pages, others are only displayed North Up, which might be confusing as you change pages. Below these boxes, map legends for the topographical and weather maps can be displayed (figure 7-2).

In the lower right corner, the current map range, set by twisting the range knob, is displayed. Alternatively, the range can be set automatically with an auto-zoom function. Ranges vary depending upon the map displayed, but the Navigation Map page, for example, can be zoomed from a 500-foot scale out to a 2000-nm scale. To the left of the map range window, the weather status bar uses icons to indicate which datalink weather products are currently selected for display.

You can open additional windows along the right side of the display. For example, pushing the FPL key brings up the Active Flight Plan window. Instrument procedures selections are also displayed in this area while using the PROC key. Also, tables of waypoint information are displayed in this area when pages from the WPT and NRST groups, described later in this chapter, are selected.

Navigating through the MFD pages

As mentioned above, the FMS knobs serve two functions. One is to select the current page viewed on the MFD and the other is to enter data and make selections. Garmin GNS 430 and GNS 530 users will quickly recognize both uses of these knobs.

Figure 7-3 This MFD page guide, used in early G1000 and Perspective aircraft, shows that the first page within the map group is selected.

Think of the pages in the MFD as organized into related groups or chapters in a book (figure 7-3). You can select four groups or chapters of pages by turning the large FMS knob. The groups are MAP, WPT (waypoint), AUX (auxiliary) and NRST (nearest). As you turn the large knob, the label for the group selected will be highlighted in cyan. Note: there's also a fifth page group that's activated by pushing the FPL key, which we discuss in Chapter 9.

Next to the group labels are a series of open squares, which represent the number of pages in the currently selected group. One of the squares will always be filled in, indicating the page within the group that's currently displayed. You can select other pages in the group by turning the small FMS knob. Each page has a name and you'll find it at the top of the MFD display just below the Navigation Status bar.

Organizationally, the most commonly used groups and pages are located at each end, so that you can reach them quickly. For example, twisting both knobs to the far left selects the Navigation Map page which is probably the one most used in flight. Twisting the large knob to the far right brings up the Nearest Airports page, which may be important in an emergency. Perspective and later G1000 versions use a different page guide (figure 7-3A).

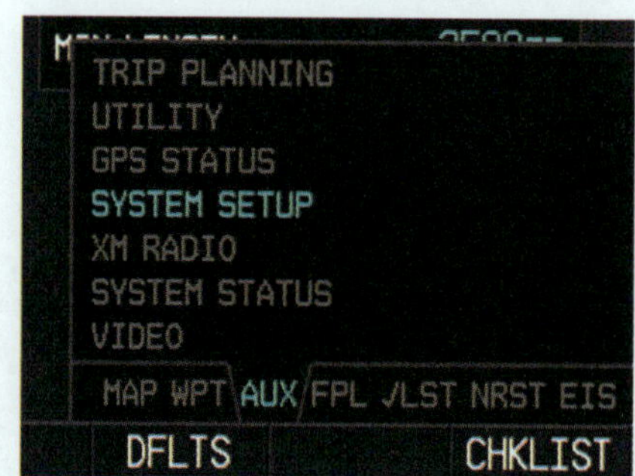

Figure 7-3A A new MFD page guide, introduced first on Perspective and now available on later G1000 versions, adds 3 additional page groups (FPL, √LST, EIS). Page names are displayed for up to 10 seconds, based on a System Setup page setting (figure 7-45).

If you ever get lost while navigating the pages and want to get back to a known state, push the CLR key and hold it for two seconds. This will take you to the Navigation Map page, which is the first page in the

MAP group. You can then get to any other page easily from this known position.

Entering Data

The FMS knobs are also used to enter data and make selections. Knowing which one to twist can occasionally confuse even experienced users, but there are some generalizations that will help you in using these knobs.

First, to make a selection or enter data, you need a cursor highlighting the field—which is a computer term for an element or category within a group—that you want to select. If you don't see a flashing white cursor, then push the FMS knob once to display one. When you've finished entering data or when you want to use the FMS knobs to select another page, push the FMS knob a second time and the cursor will disappear.

TIP

Think of the ENT key as the "yes" or "forward" key. Push it to enter data or make a selection. The CLR key, in the words of a fellow Master CFI, can be a lifesaver. Think of it as the "no" or "back" key. If you make a mistake and need to go back, press the CLR key. Or, if you've pressed a key which brings up a new window that you didn't want, press the same key a second time to remove the window. This works with the MENU, FPL, PROC and Direct-to keys. Finally, the MENU key accesses the options available for a particular page.

Often when you go to make a selection or to enter data, there will be many different fields from which to choose. For example, while entering a flight plan, you might choose to select your airport by entering either an airport identifier, airport name, city name or select from a list of recently used waypoints. The large knob will generally be used to select a particular field. In this case, you'd use it to scroll to the city name field if you know the city in which an airport is located, but don't know the airport identifier or name.

Once you've reached a particular field, you somctimcs havc to choose between two or more fixed choices. For example, when selecting an instrument approach, you need to select from among the approaches available at that airport. The small FMS is generally used to select from among choices within a particular field.

Often, once you've selected a field with the large FMS knob, you need to enter a number of characters, such as an airport identifier. Start an entry by turning the small knob until the first character is displayed. Then use the large FMS knob to select the next position (e.g. the second position in a string of four characters) and use the small FMS knob to select the next character. Remembering these general rules will help you become a pro at using the FMS knobs and accessing the many pages of information in the MFD.

This is fine when everything is going well, but what if you have to recover from a mistake during data entry? If you've pushed the FMS knob and are entering data, either intentionally or unintentionally, you can push the FMS knob again to get back where you were. Also, this removes any characters you were entering—provided you haven't pushed the ENT key.

Working with Checklists

Most manufacturers now include electronic checklists with their G1000 and Perspective aircraft, though many early aircraft shipped without this feature. Manufacturers are responsible for the content of the checklists and for any updates. As a user, you won't be able to make any changes to the checklist and you should be aware that it's intended to supplement, not replace the checklists in your POH. Also, you won't be able to use the electronic checklists for engine start in many aircraft, since in most of them the MFD doesn't come on until after engine start.

When the MFD is first powered up, it will list the current checklist file installed in the aircraft. If none exists, "CHECKLIST FILE NOT PRESENT" will be displayed and the CHKLIST softkey is grayed out.

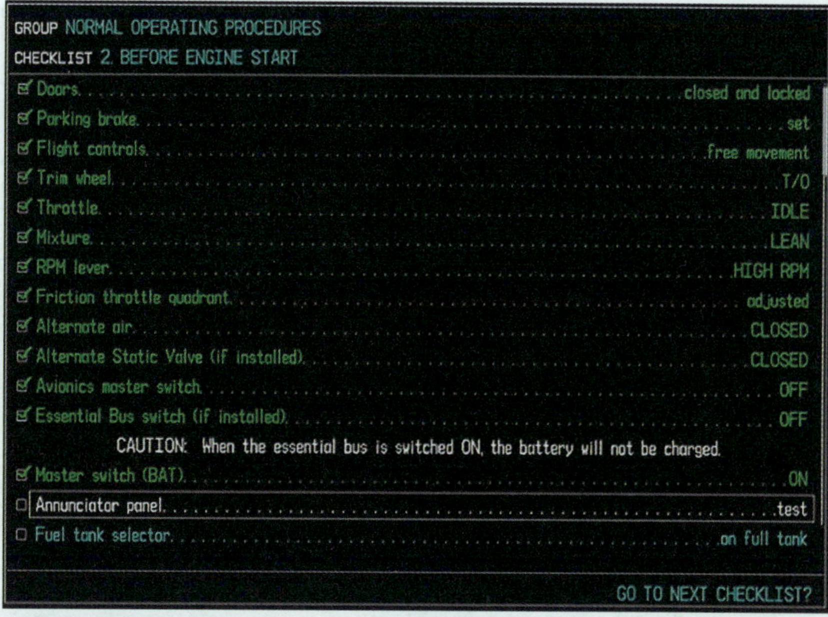

Figure 7-4 Press the ENT key to check off an item on the checklist. *© Garmin Ltd. or its affiliates*

To use the checklist, press the CHKLIST softkey from any page. Perspective and later G1000 versions use the large FMS knob to select checklists (figure 7-3A). Then, you'll want to select a particular set of procedures. Turn the large FMS knob to select the GROUP field, turn the small FMS knob to select a procedure and press the ENT key. Then select a checklist from within a group by turning the large FMS knob to the CHECKLIST field, scrolling to the desired checklist and pressing the ENT key (figure 7-4).

You can scroll to select any item, which will turn it from cyan to white. Checklist items are preceded by an open square. As you complete each item, press the ENT key or the DONE softkey to place a checkmark in the square. This turns the item cyan, moves the cursor to the next item on the list and highlights it in white. To remove a checkmark, scroll to highlight an item and press the CLR key. When you complete a checklist, "GO TO THE NEXT CHECKLIST?" is highlighted. Press the ENT key to move to the next checklist.

In an emergency, press the CHKLIST softkey and then the EMERGCY softkey, which will take you to the emergency procedures. To exit the Checklist page and return to the previous page, press the EXIT softkey or press the CLR key.

MAP Group Pages

Working with the Navigation Map Page

The Navigation Map page (figure 7-5) is the first page in the MAP group and, as mentioned above, you can reach it by pressing the CLR key for two seconds. The page is excellent for helping you maintain

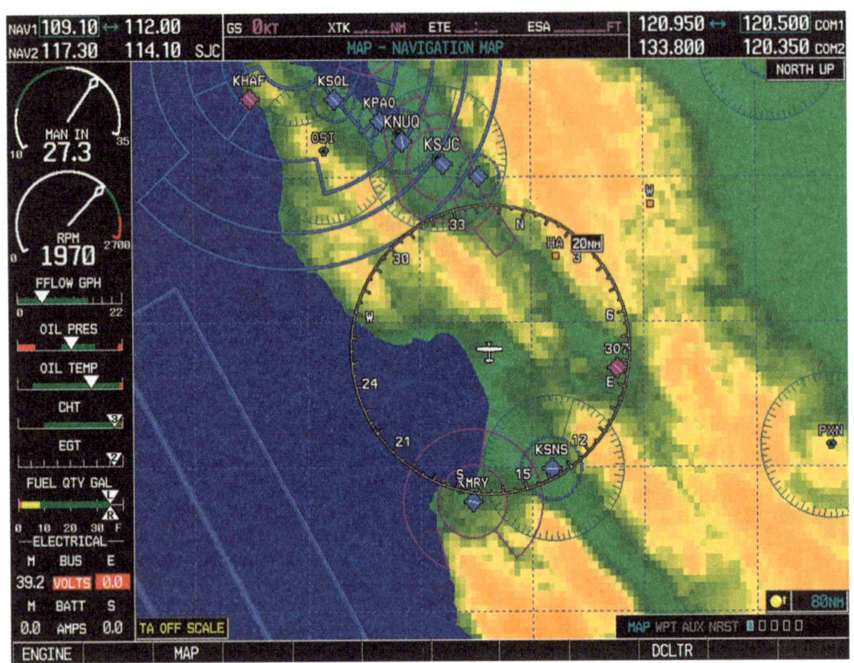

Figure 7-5 Hold the CLR key for two seconds to easily access the Navigation Map page. *© Garmin Ltd. or its affiliates*

position awareness and can be configured in dozens of ways to convey the information that's most important to you at a particular time. You'll undoubtedly use this page more than any other in flight.

The easiest way to work with this page in flight is to add or subtract layers of different information from the map. Much of this can be done with the MAP and DCLTR softkeys. The MAP softkey accesses a second level of softkeys that allow you to select, depending upon the equipment in your aircraft, a combination of topographical, traffic, Stormscope, data-link weather and terrain information to be layered onto the display (figure 7-6).

The DCLTR softkey steps you through four levels which progressively de-clutter the screen by removing more information each time you press the key. For example, one level will remove city and highway information, while another will remove VORs, intersections and special use airspace. The easiest way to use the key is to press it successively until you can view the map data you want. For a complete table of softkey de-clutter levels and the map features removed, refer to Appendix E.

TRAFFIC | TOPO | TERRAIN | STRMSCP | NEXRAD | XM LTNG

Figure 7-6 Softkeys allow you to layer a combination of information onto the map. *© Garmin Ltd. or its affiliates*

Some map features are automatically removed as you zoom out the map range. This keeps the map from getting too cluttered as you view larger areas. To some extent, you can specify at what map range the features disappear by using the MENU key.

The MENU key is used to access most map features. Many of these are preferences that you'll set once and may never change again. Others are map features that you may occasionally want to turn on and off during flight. Most of these are accessed by pressing the MENU key, choosing "MAP SETUP" and pressing the ENT key. What may not be obvious is that the first field, "GROUP," actually has several choices—only one of which is initially visible—from which to choose. You'll need to use the small FMS knob to select from the various groups of map information that you can configure.

Navigation Map Page—Topographical Information

The topographical map is certainly the most beautiful of all the map displays. It uses color to display the elevation of the land and blue to represent water. It gives you an instant sense of where you're located, unless you're over a totally flat area, since you can match the land below to the features seen on the MFD and your sectional chart.

To turn on topographical information, press the MAP softkey and then the TOPO softkey. Notice that the TOPO softkey is now grayed out, indicating that topographical data is selected. Pressing the TOPO key again turns off the topographical map. When it's off, navigation data is presented on a black background (figure 7-7).

You can also enable a legend (figure 7-8), displayed in the lower right corner of the MFD, that shows which colors correspond to each elevation. To enable it, press the MENU key, select "Map Setup," and press the ENT key. In the "GROUP" field at the top of the window, use the small FMS knob to select "Map" if it's not already displayed. Then scroll the cursor with the large FMS knob to highlight the field across from "TOPO SCALE." Use the small FMS knob to select "ON," and press the FMS knob to remove the window.

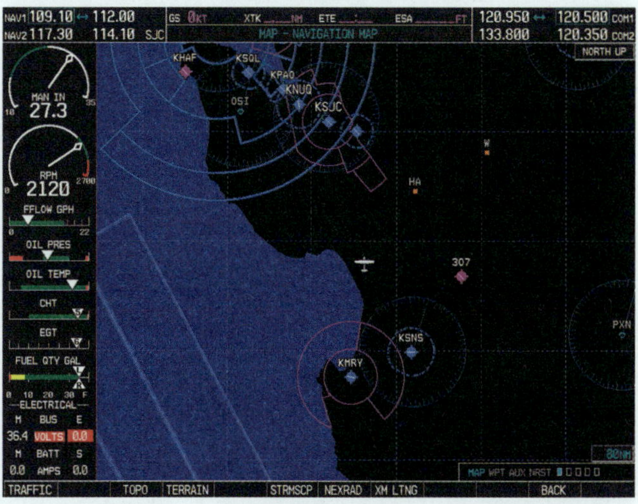

Figure 7-7 Turning off topographical data reduces brightness at night. © Garmin Ltd. or its affiliates

Note that the topographical legend or scale also displays information relevant to your flight. For example, the minimum and maximum elevations currently displayed on the Navigation Map page are listed numerically at the top of the box and graphically, by a black range indicator, to the left of the column of elevation numbers. You'll notice that as you zoom in and out, these figures change. Also, your current altitude is shown by a white line on the right side of the display. If you keep the white line above the range shown by the black line on the left, you'll be flying above all terrain currently displayed on the MFD. Finally, if you enable the map pointer by pushing the joystick, the elevation under the map pointer is indicated by a white arrow in the legend box. Map pointer position and elevation information are also displayed at the top of the MFD.

Navigation Map Page—Terrain Information

Terrain awareness information can help keep you out of the rocks, particularly at night when you may not be able to see the terrain. You can display it on the Navigation Map page by pressing the MAP softkey. Then press the TERRAIN softkey and note that it becomes gray, indicating that terrain data and a legend, in the lower right corner, are displayed. Press TERRAIN a second time to deselect terrain information. Alternatively, if you want to view only terrain data, you can select the Terrain Proximity page, which is the last page in the MAP group and is discussed later in this chapter.

The system has a database that divides the map into grids, each approximately ½ x ½ mile in size, and lists the highest land elevation within each grid. It compares your present altitude with this data and assigns a color to every grid—even those far away from your present position. If you're more than 1000 feet above a point, no change in color is made, so the topographical map color, or black if the TOPO softkey

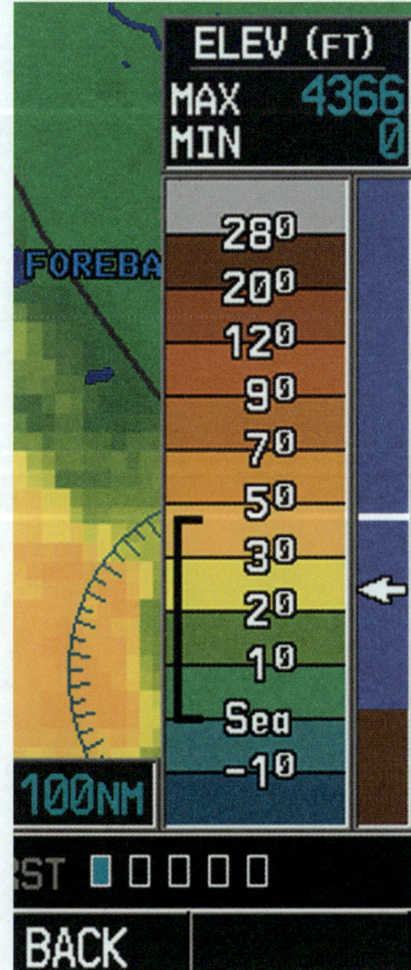

Figure 7-8 Topographical legend also indicates range of elevations displayed on map. © Garmin Ltd. or its affiliates

TIP

You may want to deselect the topographical map display at night or when in the clouds; the bright colors can be distracting in a dark cockpit. If you do this, make sure you are displaying terrain, by pushing the MAP softkey and the TERRAIN softkey. This way you'll be alerted to any high terrain in your path. Anytime—day or night—you're using TERRAIN, you'll want to deselect it after you're safely in the traffic pattern at your destination, so that you're not distracted by the entire display turning red as you approach to land!

is deselected, is displayed. If the land elevation is between 100 and 1000 feet below your current altitude, yellow is displayed. If the land elevation is above your present altitude or as much as 100 feet below you, red is displayed.

It's important to note that in almost all G1000-equipped aircraft this is a terrain awareness capability and not a terrain warning system, since it *does not provide any aural or visual warning of higher terrain.* Thus, you are totally responsible for enabling terrain information and monitoring it to assure that you maintain a safe altitude. Therefore, you may want to push the joystick and pan the map pointer along your entire route of flight to verify that your current altitude will take you above all terrain. A Terrain Awareness & Warning System (TAWS), originally found only in Beechcraft and Columbia aircraft, is now available for most G1000- and Perspective-equipped aircraft.

Navigation Map Page—Traffic Information

Traffic information from your Mode S transponder, or other traffic system, can also be layered on top of the Navigation Map page. First, press the MAP softkey and then press the TRAFFIC softkey, noting that it becomes gray, indicating that traffic data is displayed. Press TRAFFIC a second time to deselect traffic information. Alternatively, if you only want to view traffic data, you can turn to the Traffic Map page, the second page in the MAP group, which is discussed later in this chapter along with more details about using traffic information.

Traffic information from a Mode S transponder only extends out 7 miles from your present position. However, you may find that you like having the Navigation Map page zoomed out considerably farther, so that you can see your next waypoint and surrounding terrain. At high map ranges, however, traffic information is tightly clustered in the center of the map, making it difficult to see.

A solution is to set one map, such as the Inset Map on the PFD, to a relatively small range like two or three miles, so that you can see surrounding traffic and leave the MFD at a longer range. Alternatively, you can leave the MFD at a longer range and, whenever you get a traffic alert, turn the MFD's small FMS knob one click to select the TRAFFIC MAP page, which you can leave set at a smaller range.

Navigation Map Page—Weather Softkeys

There are three other softkeys, STRMSCP, NEXRAD and XM LTNG, which you can use to layer weather information onto the Navigation Map page (figure 7-5). If you have the Stormscope option in your aircraft, press the MAP softkey followed by the STRMSCP softkey to add lightning information to the page. This also brings up a box in the upper right corner of the display which tells you the rate at which strikes are being detected and the mode in which the Stormscope is operating. To select Cell or Strike mode, you'll need to go the Stormscope Map page, which is usually the third page in the MAP group. We'll discuss that page later in this chapter when we go into greater detail on the use of the Stormscope.

While using the Stormscope, you'll want to periodically clear the display of accumulated lightning strikes to get a better picture of where the current storm activity is located. To do this from the Navigation Map page, press the MENU key, scroll to select "Clear Stormscope Lightning" and press the ENT key.

If you have the Garmin Data Link module and a subscription to an aviation weather package, you can enable NEXRAD Radar images and data-link lightning images for display on the Navigation Map page. To enable radar images, press the MAP softkey followed by the NEXRAD softkey. This will bring up a legend in the upper right corner of the display, gray out the NEXRAD softkey and add radar images to the current display. NEXRAD radar is discussed in great detail in the next chapter.

To add data-link lightning to the page, press the MAP softkey followed by the XM LTNG softkey. Note that you can only display one source of lightning at a time, so Stormscope data will be deselected anytime you press the XM LTNG key. There are many differences between the two types of lightning data. You'll learn more about Stormscope data later in this chapter and about data-link lightning in the next chapter.

Navigation Map Features—Fuel Range Ring

There are several map features that you may find useful in different situations. One of my favorites is the Fuel Range Ring (figure 7-9). When enabled, this displays two yellow rings around your current position. Taking into account your current airspeed, winds aloft, fuel flow and remaining fuel, a dashed yellow ring indicates the distance you can fly until reaching your fuel reserve. An outer yellow ring indicates the distance you can fly until fuel exhaustion. All of this can be calculated manually, but the graphical Fuel Range Ring is more intuitive and easier to use.

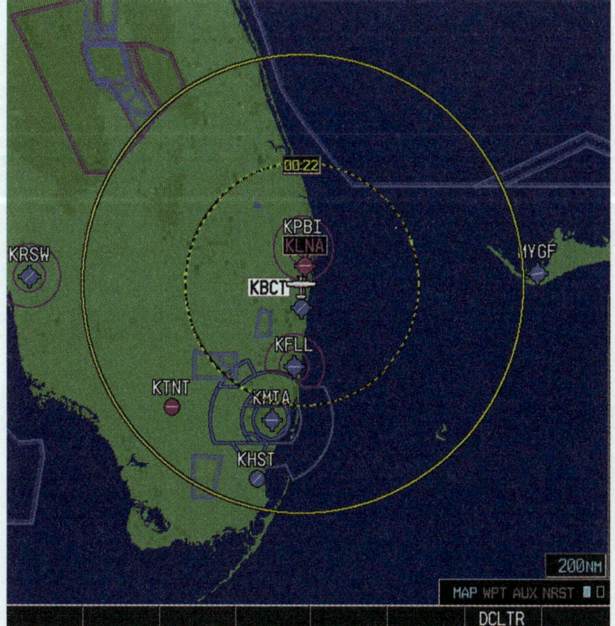

Figure 7-9 Fuel Range Rings show time and distance to reserve fuel and distance to fuel exhaustion.

© Garmin Ltd. or its affiliates

To enable the Fuel Range Ring, press the MENU key, select "Map Setup" and press the ENT key, scroll to select the "Map" group and press the ENT key. Then scroll down using the large FMS knob opposite FUEL RNG (RSV) and use the small FMS knob to select "ON." Scroll to the next field and, using both the large and small FMS knobs, enter the number of minutes of reserve fuel to be used in the calculations and press the ENT key. Push the FMS knob to remove the Map Setup window.

The Fuel Range Ring is particularly useful when flying long legs as it

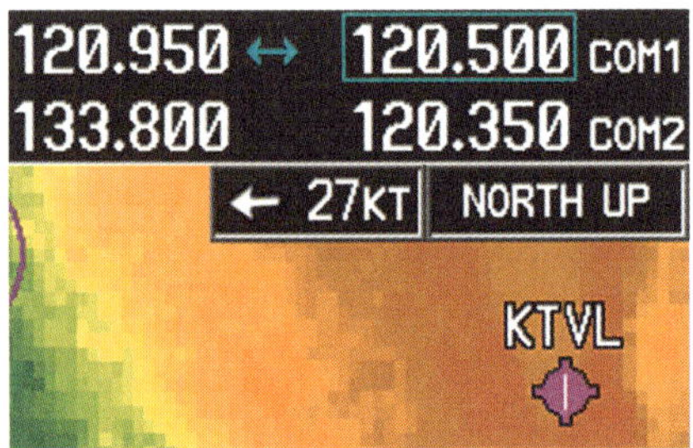

Figure 7-10 The wind vector continually displays winds aloft, in this case 27 knots from the east. *© Garmin Ltd. or its affiliates*

helps calculate whether you'll have sufficient fuel to reach your destination. Since the calculation is based upon current groundspeed, you'll want to monitor the ring throughout the flight in case winds become less favorable and you can no longer reach your destination. It's an excellent tool for watching the effects of power adjustments and fuel leaning upon your range. If, for example, you find that your destination is between the rings but you want to land with your full fuel reserves—always an excellent practice—you may be able to avoid a fuel stop by adjusting the power or leaning to a more efficient setting which moves the rings out farther and allows you to land with full reserves.

Navigation Map Features—Wind Vector

You'll never have to guess again which way the wind is blowing if you enable the Wind Vector (figure 7-10). It displays the direction and strength of the wind in a box in the upper right corner of the MFD. You'll find this useful en route while seeking an altitude with the most favorable winds or while on final approach, whether flying visually or under an instrument approach, to determine how the crosswind changes as you descend. This is a feature you'll probably set once and always leave enabled.

To enable the Wind Vector, press the MENU key, select "Map Setup" and press the ENT key, scroll to select the "Map" group and press the ENT key. Then scroll down using the large FMS knob opposite WIND VECTOR and use the small FMS knob to select "ON." Push the FMS knob to remove the Map Setup window.

Navigation Map Features—Track Vector

The track vector adds a dashed cyan arrow to the front of the aircraft symbol, which indicates the distance you will travel in the next minute (figure 7-11). The arrow helps you maintain the correct heading as you follow a course and may help you gauge when to start turning to intercept a course. The track vector is enabled in the same way as the Wind Vector, described above, except that you'll scroll to the field opposite TRACK VECTOR.†

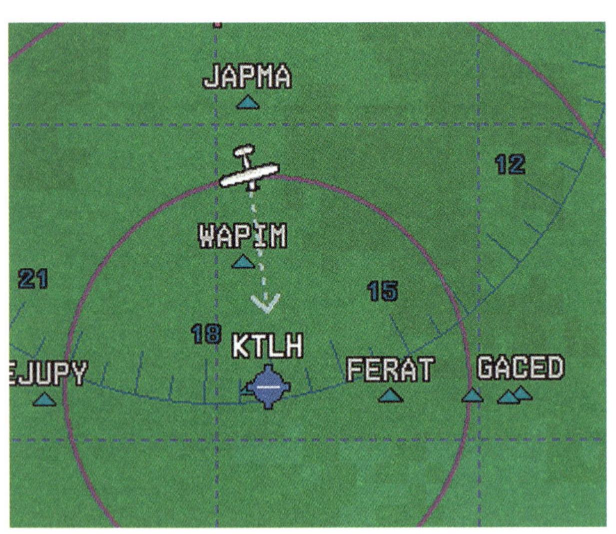

Figure 7-11 The track vector shows the distance you'll travel in the next minute. *© Garmin Ltd. or its affiliates*

Navigation Map Features—Nav Range Ring

The Nav Range Ring puts a compass card around the aircraft position indicator. This makes it easy to identify your current ground track and the heading toward any other feature on the map (figure 7-12). The distance from the aircraft position indicator to the compass card ring is labeled, and this distance changes as you zoom the map range in and out, leaving the Nav Range Ring a constant size. The distance is always one quarter of the map range.

† See page 223 for updates to this feature. For the Perspective, see figure 15-13.

Some instructors like using the Nav Range Ring to determine the heading they'll need to enter a holding pattern. Others find that it is a quick way to estimate the distance to any feature on the map. To do that, zoom the map range in or out until the Nav Range Ring is close to a feature. The distance shown on the Nav Range Ring is the approximate distance to the feature. For more precise distance measurement, push the joystick and move the map pointer over a feature. The exact distance will appear in a window at the top of the display. The Nav Range Ring is enabled in the same way as the Wind Vector, described above, except that you'll scroll to the field opposite NAV RANGE RING.

Figure 7-12 The Nav Range Ring shows compass headings and distance to compass ring. *© Garmin Ltd. or its affiliates*

Navigation Map Features—Map Orientation

The Navigation Map is the one map within the MAP group of pages for which you can change the orientation. For the other pages, you'll have to use whatever orientation that page is designed to use. There are four different orientations:

North Up — Top of the map is North
Track Up — Map aligned with ground track
DTK Up — Map aligned with Desired Track set by flight plan
Heading Up — Map aligned with aircraft's current heading

North Up can be useful for reviewing the points of a long cross country flight. Track Up, DTK Up, and Heading Up all orient the map in the direction you're going, or should be going, plus or minus wind correction. Whenever North Up is not selected, an "N" in the upper left corner of the display indicates the direction for North.

Everyone has their own particular preferences. While some people prefer North Up all the time, it can be confusing to use when you're displaying traffic. For example, if you're flying south and see an intruder aircraft displayed to the left of the airplane symbol, you'll need to look to the right to spot the aircraft! For this reason, the Track Up orientation is generally recommended.

To select a map orientation, press the MENU key, select "Map Setup" and press the ENT key, scroll to select the "Map" group and press the ENT key. Scroll down using the large FMS knob opposite ORIENTATION and use the small FMS knob to select one of the four orientations (figure 7-13). Press the ENT key, and then push the FMS knob to remove the Map Setup window.

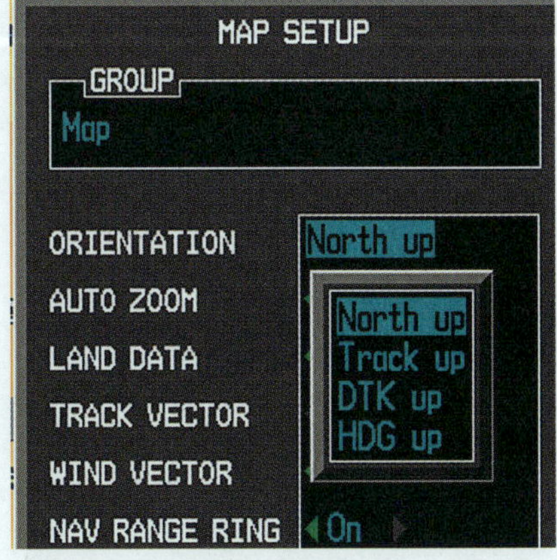

Figure 7-13 Map orientation is set with the MENU key and Map Setup command. *© Garmin Ltd. or its affiliates*

Navigation Map Features—Auto-Zoom

The auto-zoom feature keeps the active waypoint displayed and progressively zooms to lower and lower ranges as you approach a waypoint,

† See pages 222-23 for updates to this feature.

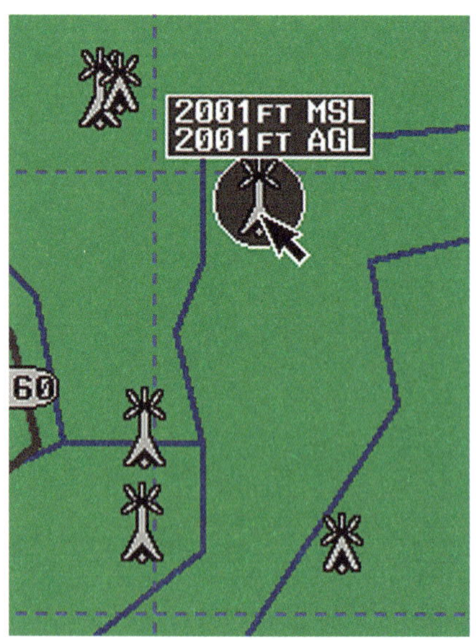

Figure 7-14 To see the height of an obstacle, pan the map pointer onto the obstacle. *© Garmin Ltd. or its affiliates*

stopping at the 1.5 nm range.† This is an alternative to manually zooming the range using the range knob. Whenever you use the range knob, auto-zoom is temporarily disabled until you reach the next waypoint.

To select auto-zoom, press the MENU key, select "Map Setup" and press the ENT key, scroll to select the "Map" group and press the ENT key. Then scroll down using the large FMS knob opposite AUTO ZOOM and use the small FMS knob to select "ON." Push the FMS knob to remove the Map Setup window.

Navigation Map Features—Obstacle Data

Most G1000 and all Perspectives have an obstacle database of broadcast towers and other obstacles. These are displayed using the same tower symbols used on sectional charts (figure 7-14). You can also set a map range setting—up to 50 nm—above which obstacles won't be displayed. So if you're flying low and need to avoid obstacles, you'll want to keep your map range set below this particular setting. Note that the G1000 does not provide any aural or visual warning of obstacles, so you must monitor the display to become aware of them.

To display obstacle data, press the MENU key, select "Map Setup" and press the ENT key, scroll to select the "Map" group and press the ENT key. Then scroll down using the large FMS knob opposite OBSTACLE DATA and use the small FMS knob to select "ON." Then scroll to the next field with the large FMS knob and use the small FMS knob to select a maximum range setting. Press the ENT key and then push the FMS knob to remove the Map Setup window. To see the height of an obstacle, push the joystick and pan the map pointer on top of the obstacle.

Navigation Map Features—Measuring Bearing and Distance

The system provides an easy way to measure the distance between any two points on the Navigation Map page. To access it, push the MENU key, scroll to "Measure Bearing/Distance" and press the ENT key. Using the Range knob, pan the map pointer to the first point and press the ENT key. Then pan the map pointer to the second point (don't push the ENT key!) and read the bearing and distance information in the upper left corner of the display. To cancel this function, press the Range knob or press MENU, scroll to "Stop Measuring" and press the ENT key.

Navigation Map Features—Land Data

You can also display land data, such as rivers, lakes, roads, borders, etc. To display land data, press the MENU key, select "Map Setup" and press the ENT key, scroll to select the "Map" group and press the ENT key. Then scroll down using the large FMS knob opposite LAND DATA and use the small FMS knob to select "ON." Press the ENT key and then push the FMS knob to remove the Map Setup window.

Navigation Map—Managing the Data

The Navigation Map page can display an abundance of information—so much so that if it were all displayed when you zoom out to the longer ranges, the screen would be totally obliterated with data and be unusable. Therefore, the G1000 has the capability for you to specify at what range settings different types of data disappear as you progressively zoom out the map. These parameters are set using the MENU key and are distributed among several map groups.

Map Group—Setting Topographical and Terrain Ranges

You can set the topographical and terrain data to turn off when you've zoomed beyond a particular map range by using the MENU key and the Map Group. Also, these data types can be totally turned on or off through the MENU key or the MAP softkeys.

To access these functions, press the MENU key, select "Map Setup" and press the ENT key, scroll to select the "Map" group and press the ENT key. Then scroll down using the large FMS knob opposite either TOPO DATA or TERRAIN DATA (figure 7-15). Use the small FMS knob to select "ON" to turn the data on or select "OFF." Scroll with the large FMS knob to the next field and use the small FMS knob to select the map range at which this data type will no longer be displayed. Press the ENT key and then push the FMS knob to remove the Map Setup window. You can verify that the data disappears at a particular map range by turning the Range knob.

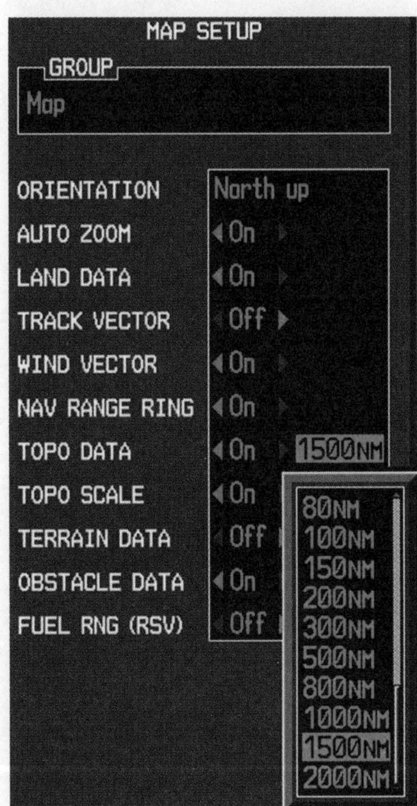

Figure 7-15 In this case, topographical data will display up to the 1500 nm range. *© Garmin Ltd. or its affiliates*

Weather Group—Setting Weather Ranges

You can turn the Stormscope data on and select its mode via the softkeys and through the MENU key using the Weather Group. From this group, you can also set the maximum map ranges at which the lightning symbol appears when lightning is detected and at which NEXRAD radar and data link lightning are displayed.

To access these functions, press the MENU key, select "Map Setup" and press the ENT key, scroll to select the "Weather" group and press the ENT key. Then scroll down using the large FMS knob to select a particular field (figure 7-16). Use the small FMS knob to turn functions on, select modes or to select the maximum map range at which a particular data type will be displayed. Press the ENT key to make a data selection and, when done, push the FMS knob to remove the Map Setup window.

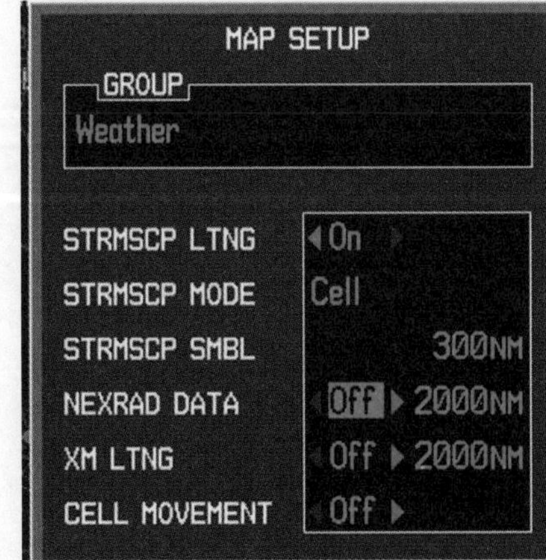

Figure 7-16 The Weather group lets you set the maximum map ranges at which the lightning symbols and NEXRAD radar appear. *© Garmin Ltd. or its affiliates*

Traffic Group—Setting Traffic Types and Ranges

Traffic information can be configured through the MENU key using the Traffic group. It allows you to turn traffic information on the Navigation Map page on and off and select the mode of operation.

To access these functions, press the MENU key, select "Map Setup," press the ENT key, scroll to select the "Traffic" group and press the ENT key. Use the small FMS knob to turn the traffic information "On" or "Off" and press the ENT key. In the next field, you can select the

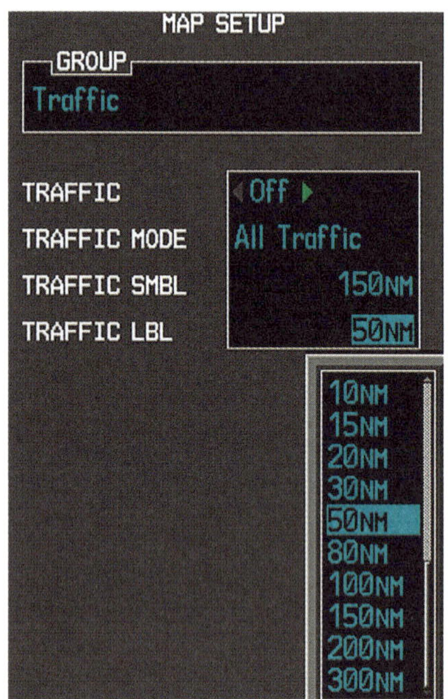

Figure 7-17 With this setting, traffic labels display up to the 50 nm range.
© Garmin Ltd. or its affiliates

Traffic Mode by scrolling with the small FMS knob and pressing the ENT key to select one of the following:

- All Traffic – display all traffic types
- TA/PA – display Traffic Advisories and Proximity Advisories
- TA Only – display only Traffic Advisories

Traffic Advisories are issued for aircraft within 1/2 mile horizontally and 500 feet vertically and are displayed in yellow. Proximity Advisories are issued for traffic that's further away, but still within 4 nm horizontally and 1200 feet vertically of your aircraft and are displayed in white.

You can also specify that traffic data be turned off when you're zoomed out beyond a particular map range. To access this, press the MENU key and select "Map Setup" and the "Traffic" group as described above. Scroll to the TRAFFIC SMBL field and use the small FMS knob to select a range up to 300 nm and press the ENT key.

Each traffic target displays the hundreds of feet separating you vertically from the traffic and shows an up or down arrow if the traffic is climbing or descending more than 500 feet per minute. You can set the map range beyond which these labels are no longer displayed with a target. Press the MENU key, go to the "Traffic" group as described above and scroll to the TRAFFIC LBL field. Use the small FMS knob to select a map range up to 300 nm and press the ENT key (figure 7-17).

Aviation Group—Configuring Aviation Data Labels and Ranges

In the Aviation Group settings, you can select the text size of labels used for airports, intersections, navaids and airspace. It also allows you to select the maximum map range at which each of these will be displayed. Finally, you can choose the maximum map range settings at which the waypoints and magenta line generated by an active flight plan are displayed.

The different types of data that can be configured include:

ACTIVE FPL (magenta line)
ACTIVE FPL WPT (flight plan waypoints)
APT: Large, medium and small airports
INT (intersections)
Runway Extensions
NDBs
VORs
CLASS B
CLASS C
CLASS D
RESTRICTED
MOA (MILITARY)
OTHER AIRSPACE (training, caution, danger, warning and alert areas)

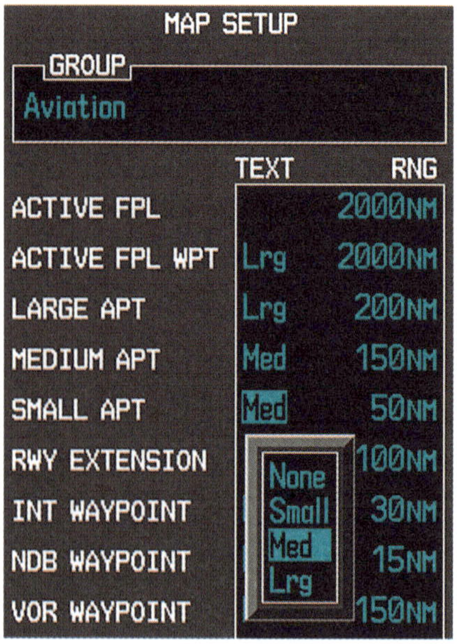

To change the text size or maximum map range for any of these parameters, press the MENU key, select "Map Setup" and press the

Figure 7-18 Here, small airport labels are set to display in medium size type.
© Garmin Ltd. or its affiliates

ENT key, scroll to select the "Aviation" group and press the ENT key. Then scroll down using the large FMS knob to select a particular field. To choose a text size, use the small FMS knob to select "None," "Small," "Med" or "Lrg" size text and press the ENT key (figure 7-18). To select the maximum map range at which a particular data type will be displayed, highlight that field, turn the small FMS knob to select a range and press the ENT key. When done, push the FMS knob to remove the Map Setup window.

TIP

To make it easy to line up with a runway, enable Runway Extensions in the Aviation Group. This turns on dashed white lines, showing the extended centerlines for all runways, of an airport that's the active waypoint.

Land Group—Configuring Labels and Ranges for Land Features

The Land Group lets you select the text size of labels for highways, railroads, cities, rivers, and lakes and to determine the maximum map range at which each of these will be displayed. You can also use it to display a grid of labeled longitude and latitude lines and to configure user-defined waypoints.

The different types of data that can be configured include:

LAT/LON (latitude/longitude)
FREEWAY
NATIONAL HWY
LOCAL HWY
LOCAL ROAD
CITY: Large, medium and small cities
STATE/PROV
RIVER/LAKE
USER WAYPOINT

To change the text size or maximum map range for any of these parameters, press the MENU key, select "Map Setup" and press the ENT key, scroll to select the "Land" group and press the ENT key (figure 7-19). Then scroll down using the large FMS knob to select a particular field. To choose a text size, use the small FMS knob to select None, Small, Med or Lrg size text and press the ENT key. To select the maximum map range at which a particular data type will be displayed, highlight that field, turn the small FMS knob to select a range and press the ENT key. When done, push the FMS knob to remove the Map Setup window.

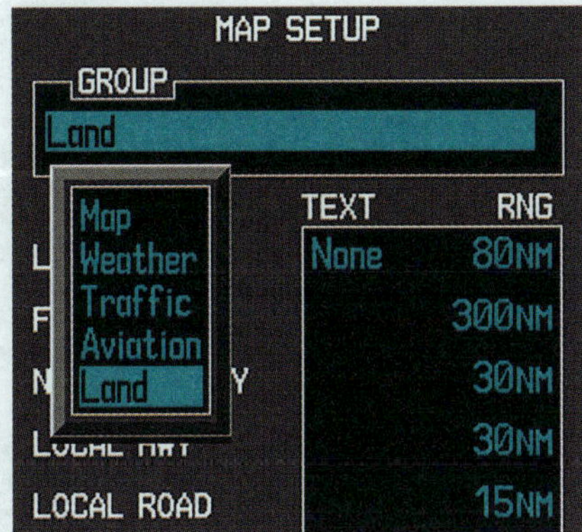

Figure 7-19 It's easy to overlook that the Group field has more than one category. You'll need to scroll to display the other categories. *© Garmin Ltd. or its affiliates*

Traffic Map Page

The Traffic Map page is an important element in attaining the increases in safety possible with glass cockpit systems. It can display Traffic Information Service (TIS), ADS-B, or Traffic Advisory Systems (TAS) data. The FAA broadcasts TIS traffic through a Mode S transponder. ADS-B traffic is received via the optional GDL 90 ADS-B Transceiver. TAS systems acquire traffic data by listening for transponder returns from nearby aircraft. They are available for the G1000 and Perspective from Garmin, L-3, Honeywell and Avidyne.

TIS is the least expensive option. We'll discuss it in detail since it's the most common traffic system in G1000 aircraft. In Perspective air-

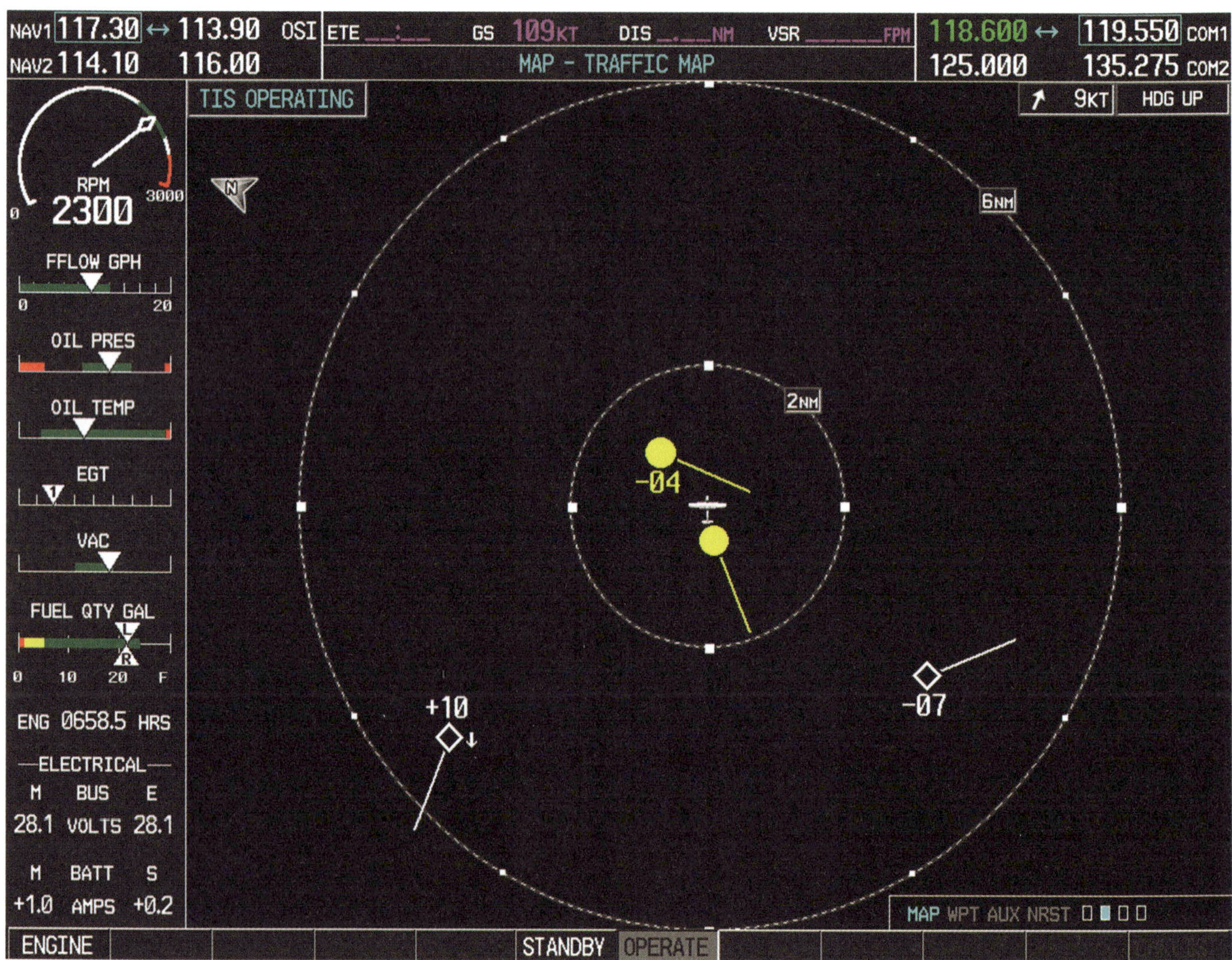

Figure 7-20 One of the yellow TA aircraft in close proximity is transmitting mode C altitude data but the other is not. *© Garmin Ltd. or its affiliates*

craft, more TAS systems have shipped. Since there are a variety of these systems, you should refer to the operating manuals for your system.

The Traffic Map page (figure 7-20) is the second page in the MAP group and you can reach it from the Navigation Map page by turning the small FMS knob one click. Two softkeys, STANDBY and OPERATE, alternate with each other. Both functions can also be accessed through the MENU key. To display traffic, press the OPERATE softkey. Press the STANDBY softkey to disable aural alerts, such as when other aircraft in the pattern are generating many traffic alerts. Later software versions have a FLT ID softkey that lets you view flight identification information for some aircraft.

The map has three ranges: 2 nm, 6 nm and 12 nm. The ranges are selected by rotating the Range knob, which is combined with the joystick. To see all traffic transmitted through TIS, you'll need to be on the 12 nm range.

Traffic Information Service

TIS transmits data on up to 8 aircraft within 7 nm horizontally, 3500 feet above and 3000 feet below your current position. (figure 7-21). It sends data on these intruder aircrafts' position, altitude, altitude trend and ground track. To be visible, however, these intruder aircraft must have an operating transponder and be within radar range.

Unlike the TCAS systems used by the airlines, TIS only provides alerts—it does not recommend maneuvers for avoiding intruder aircraft. An alert is generated anytime an aircraft is within ½ nm horizontally or within 500 feet vertically. Alerts are also generated anytime an aircraft is projected to enter this area within the next 34 seconds.

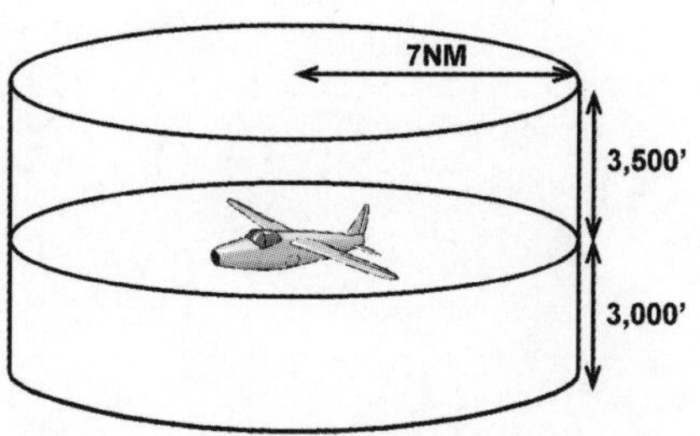

Figure 7-21 TIS only displays traffic within 7 miles and less than 3,500 feet above or 3,000 feet below your aircraft.

These alerts, called Traffic Advisories (TA), are displayed on the Traffic Map page with a solid yellow circle. A half yellow circle on the outer range ring is used if the TA aircraft is beyond the current map range. Whenever a TA is generated, an audio alert "Traffic" is heard through the audio panel, a yellow "TRAFFIC" annunciator appears on the PFD (figure 4-6) and the Inset Map on the PFD is automatically enabled.

Other traffic, which doesn't meet the criteria for a TA, is displayed as an open white diamond with a trend vector showing the aircraft's direction of travel. The intruder's altitude deviation from your altitude is displayed in hundreds of feet. Also an altitude trend arrow is displayed if the aircraft is climbing or descending at greater than 500 feet per minute.

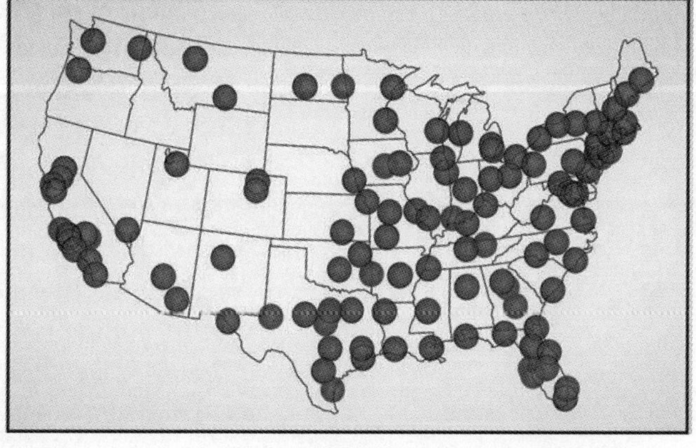

Figure 7-22 TIS data is available from some approach radar sites. *© Garmin Ltd. or its affiliates*

Traffic Information Service Limitations

TIS is only available within about 55 nm of certain FAA approach radar systems (figure 7-22). Depending upon your altitude and obstructions between your aircraft and the radar site, the actual distance at which you receive service may be less. Aircraft below you that are below the radar floor in your area will not show up. Also, if you fly directly over the radar site, you may lose TIS service since the maximum elevation of the radar is 34° and there is a "cone of silence" directly above the radar site. Finally, the altitude encoder in your aircraft must be working so that altitude deviations between you and other aircraft can be calculated. If your altitude encoder is not working, TIS data will be suppressed and no traffic is displayed.

The approach radar sweeps every 5 seconds and then transmits the TIS data on the next sweep, thus the data you receive in the cockpit is a minimum of 5 seconds old. In order to present traffic in a "real-time" position, the TIS ground station uses an algorithm to predict intruder aircraft positions at the time you will receive the data to compensate for this delay. However, if the intruder aircraft is maneuvering, their bearing information, indicated by a white line showing their direction of travel, may be inaccurate, though the position and altitude data are still generally accurate. If you make a steep turn, TIS may generate a false target at your location and altitude. Seeing a TIS target materialize right next to you can cause a scare, but the false target will usually disappear within a few radar sweeps.

Other errors can occur when a converging aircraft is on a course that crosses your course at a shallow angle. If either you or the intruder suddenly change course when you're within 1/4 nm of each other, TIS will display the intruder on the opposite side of where it actually is.

As your distance from the radar site increases, the accuracy of the system decreases. At these longer distances, TIS cannot accurately determine bearing and distance information for intruder aircraft that are close to you. Therefore, whenever you're more than 30 nm away from the radar site, TIS will display an intruder aircraft within 3/8 nm of your location either directly in front of or behind you. This is to avoid the confusion that would arise if, for example, an intruder to your right were presented to your left on the display. Thus, at longer distances from the radar site, you should assume that any aircraft displayed next to your position could be up to 3/8 nm away in any direction.

TIS Status Messages

If more than six seconds have elapsed since traffic information was updated, your Mode S transponder has missed a radar sweep. The message "AGE 00:06" appears in the lower left corner of the display to indicate the age of the data and the timer begins to increment. "TRFC COAST" also appears, indicating that the data is of reduced quality.

After 12 seconds without an update, the traffic data is removed from the display and the message "TRFC RMVD" replaces the "TRFC COAST" message. Be aware that there may still be traffic in your vicinity, but it's no longer displayed. After more than 60 seconds have elapsed, the message UNAVAILABLE or UNAVAIL is displayed and the audio alert "Traffic Unavailable" is heard through the audio panel.

A "TA OFF Range" message indicates that an intruder aircraft has been detected but is not displayed since it is beyond the currently selected range on the Traffic Map page. This message is removed when the intruder is displayed within the selected range. "NO DATA," "DATA FAILED" and "FAILED" indicate potential problems with the system and that you should consult your authorized dealer for assistance.

TAS Systems

If your aircraft includes a TAS, such as the Avidyne (formerly Ryan), Garmin GTS 800 series or the L3 SKYWATCH systems, the G1000 only displays TAS data on the Traffic page. If TAS is not configured, the system displays TIS data. The SKYWATCH HP system, for example, tracks up to 35 intruder aircraft out to 35 nm and displays the 8 most threatening aircraft. The display range is selected by rotating the MFD's Range knob.

When using TAS, the Traffic page is reached in the same way as for TIS; it's the second page in the MAP group. Also, TAS data is configured in the same way as shown in Figure 7-17. In addition to the TA and PA traffic types displayed on TIS, TAS has a third category for "Other" advisories. These are assigned to intruder aircraft within the selected vertical and horizontal range that have not yet generated a TA. A hollow white diamond is used to depict them.

The same OPERATE and STANDBY softkeys used for TIS are used for TAS. When configured for TAS, however, the Traffic page has some additional softkeys. An ALT MODE softkey brings up additional keys, which allow you to select the vertical operating limits for the system. The softkeys, modes, and vertical display limits are:

- BELOW — Look Down mode: +2,700 feet to -9,000 feet of the aircraft
- NORMAL — Normal mode: +2,700 feet to -2,700 feet of the aircraft
- ABOVE — Look Up mode: +9,000 feet to -2,700 feet of the aircraft
- UNREST — Unrestricted mode: +9,900 feet to -9,900 feet of the aircraft (mode only available with the SKYWATCH HP)

If you're using a TAS systems, you should refer to your operating manuals for instructions.

ADS-B Traffic

ADS-B stands for Automatic Dependent Surveillance-Broadcast. By January 1, 2020, all aircraft must be equipped with ADS-B Out, which broadcasts an aircraft's position. Owners can elect to also equip with ADS-B In, which allows an aircraft to receive traffic information from other ADS-B equipped aircraft, surface vehicles, and FAA ground stations. The optional GDL 90 ADS-B Transceiver provides the system with ADS-B Out and In. ADS-B traffic symbols (figure 7-22A) are displayed on the Traffic Map page.

Figure 7-22A This ADS-B traffic symbol depicts an aircraft 1300 feet below and moving to the right. The arrow shows it's descending at 500 fpm or greater. The Flight ID function is enabled, identifying the aircraft as N4450C. *© Garmin Ltd. or its affiliates*

Stormscope Map Page

Lightning data is extremely important to you as a pilot, since it's usually accompanied by moderate or severe turbulence. To help you detect and avoid lightning, many G1000 aircraft come equipped with a L-3 Stormscope® WX-500 Weather Mapping Sensor or have it available as an option. If installed, it displays on the Stormscope Map page (figure 7-23), usually the third page in the MAP group. From the Navigation Map page, turn the small FMS knob two clicks to reach this page.

The WX-500 is a passive device that detects electrical discharges—usually associated with thunderstorms—within a 200 nm radius of the aircraft. The system measures the bearing and distances to the discharges, and displays them on the Stormscope Map page. For detailed instructions on using the WX-500, refer to the system user guide.

Lightning data, collected by ground-based sensors, is also available if you have a data-link weather subscription. This data differs considerably from Stormscope lightning data and the differences between the two are discussed in detail in the next chapter.

The Stormscope Map page displays lightning strikes among range

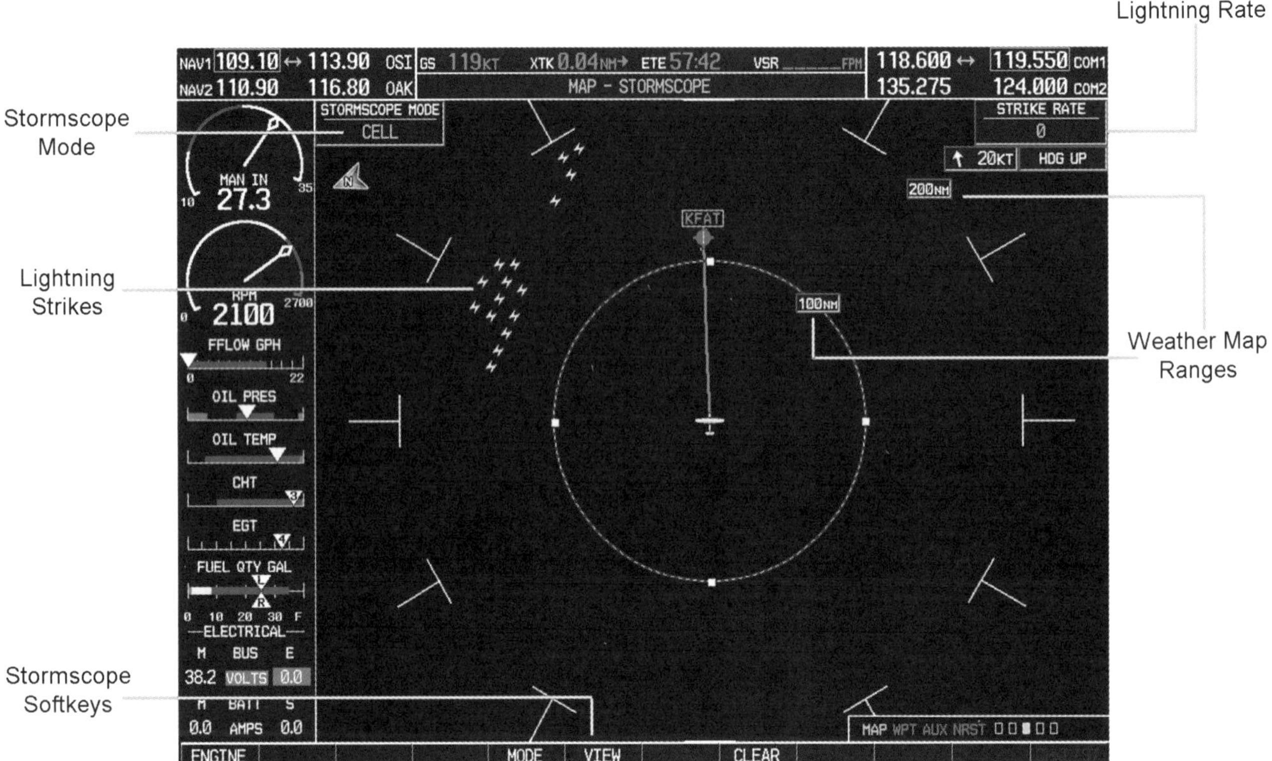

Figure 7-23 The Stormscope Map page is dedicated to displaying lightning strikes. *© Garmin Ltd. or its affiliates*

rings, indicating the distance to the strikes. The range can be adjusted by turning the range knob, which is combined with the G1000's joystick. Two views are available: a 360° view showing strikes in all directions and a 120° arc view, showing strikes ahead of the aircraft. The views can be changed by pushing the VIEW softkey and then either the 360° or the ARC softkey. You can also change views by pushing the MENU key and scrolling to select "View 360°" or "View Arc" and then the ENT key.

The upper left corner of the page displays the mode—either CELL or STRIKE—in which the system is currently operating. The upper right corner shows the Strike Rate, the relative number of strikes detected by the system. A "HDG UP" label indicates the map's heading up orientation, which cannot be changed. As the aircraft turns, the strike data rotates to maintain the proper orientation.

Stormscope data can also be displayed on the Navigation Map page. From that page, push the MAP and then the STRMSCP softkeys to enable the display. The maximum range of the Stormscope is 200 nm, so to view all strikes available in the 360° view, you'll need to select the 500 nm range.

Using Stormscope Data

The Stormscope is an excellent tool for detecting thunderstorms developing anywhere within a 200 nm radius. It's a complementary tool to NEXRAD radar imagery, discussed in the next chapter, which detects precipitation. While lightning is associated with strong updrafts and downdrafts, particularly in the developing or cumulus stage of a thunderstorm, precipitation occurs later in the dissipating stage of a storm. Thus a Stormscope issues the first warning of a developing storm and NEXRAD radar helps you track it as the storm evolves.

Lightning Age	Symbol
Strike is less than 6 seconds old	
Strike is between 6 and 60 seconds old	
Strike is between 1 and 2 minutes old	
Strike is between 2 and 3 minutes old	

Table 7-1 Lightning Age and Symbols.

Strike data is presented with symbols that indicate the age of the strike (table 7-1). A new strike is presented as a lightning symbol with a black guard band around it for the first six seconds, and then as a smaller lightning symbol for the rest of the first minute. Strikes more than a minute old are represented with a large "+" sign and strikes more than 2 minutes old are denoted with a small "+" sign. After three minutes, strikes are no longer displayed.

Older strikes may be associated with precipitation and strong downdrafts; recent strikes often contain the most severe updrafts and may not yet have a significant radar return. During times of heavy activity, you may want to clear the Stormscope Map page of data, so that you can easily identify where the new, most recent strikes appear. To clear the screen, press the CLEAR softkey or press the MENU key, scroll to "Clear Lightning Data" and press the ENT key.

The Stormscope operates in either Strike or Cell mode. Strike mode shows every discharge and is most useful during light activity, since strike data may show the beginning of a building thunderstorm sooner than cell mode. Cell mode uses a clustering algorithm to associate new strikes with nearby strikes to locate storm cells. It is most useful during periods of intense electrical activity as it will save you the time of analyzing a screen full of points to identify active cells.

The Stormscope is an excellent tool when isolated thunderstorms are forecast over a wide area. Even on hazy days with limited visibility, it will help you identify developing thunderstorms at long distances. Use it to fly well around thunderstorms, not to fly between cells. Or, if you're contemplating flying through areas of rain, use it to make sure that no lightning exists in the area. The Stormscope is most effective when used in combination with other tools such as NEXRAD radar, discussed in the next chapter. Remember to use all weather tools available at your disposal including in-flight weather advisories from Flight Watch on 122.0.

Weather Data Link Map Page

The MAP group of pages also includes a Weather Data Link Map page, if you have a Garmin Data Link module and a subscription to the data-link weather service. The next chapter is devoted to describing this page and the weather data available. You can skip ahead to this chapter now, or wait until we've finished discussing the remaining MFD pages.

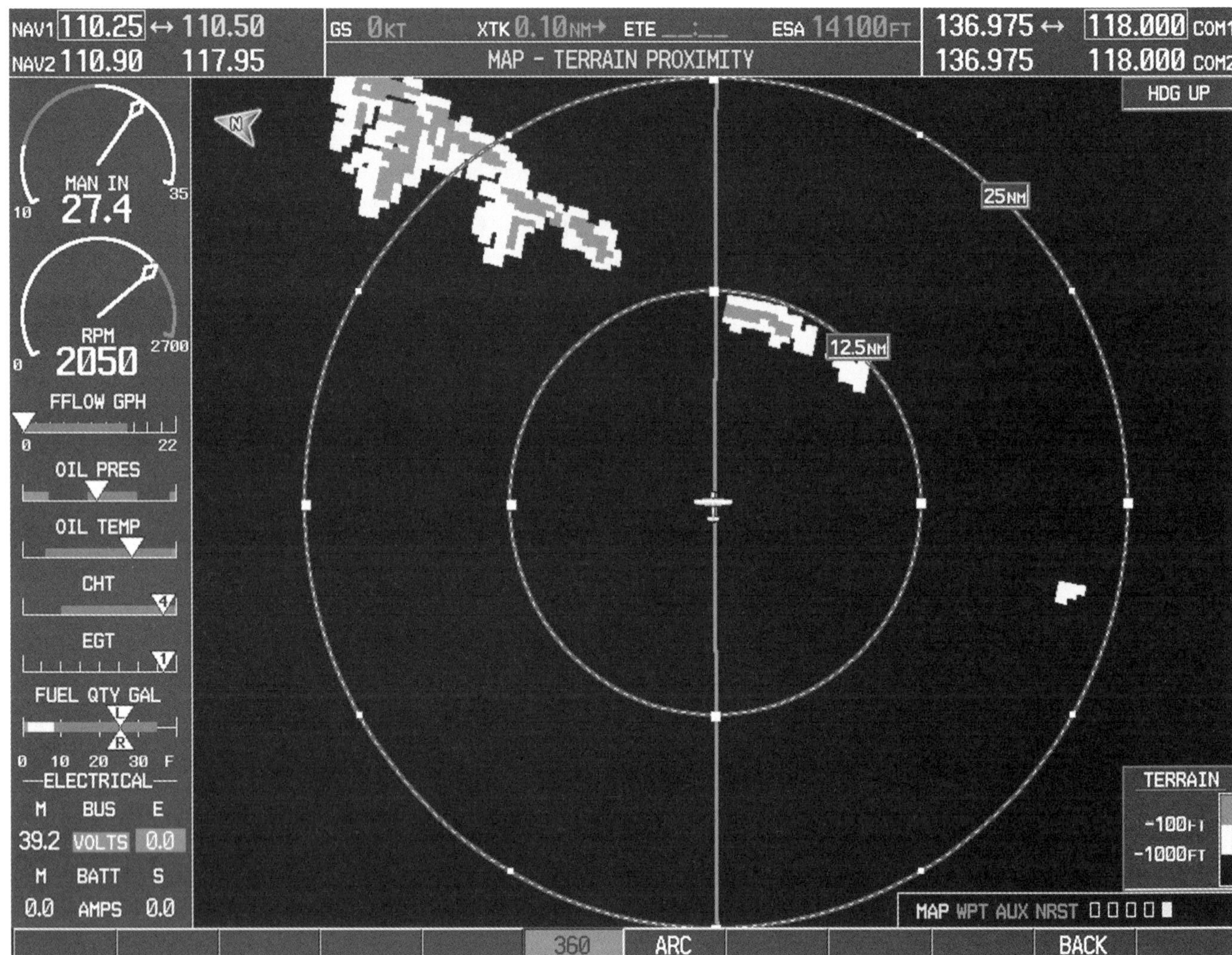

Figure 7-24 Use the Terrain Proximity page to steer around red and yellow areas of high terrain. *© Garmin Ltd. or its affiliates*

Terrain Proximity Map Page

The Terrain Proximity Map page (figure 7-24) is a dedicated page that shows only terrain information. It's a useful way to watch for terrain without any other distracting information. While you can add terrain data as a layer of information to the Navigation Map page, you may find it useful, particularly at night or in Instrument Meteorological Conditions (IMC), to use the Terrain Proximity Map page instead. It's generally the last page in the MAP group and you can reach it from the Navigation Map page by turning the small FMS knob four or more clicks.

If the land elevation is between 100 and 1000 feet below your current altitude, yellow is displayed. If the land elevation is above your present altitude or as much as 100 feet below you, red is displayed. Otherwise, the display is black.

Softkeys allow you to select a 360° or 120° arc view. To do this, press the VIEW softkey and then either the 360 or the ARC softkey. You can also use the MENU key to access these functions.

The range knob and the joystick pointer allow you to examine your entire route—or any location in the database—to see how its elevation compares with your present altitude. Later versions of the G1000 software also allow you to display aviation data, such as airports and intersections, on this page. In Perspective aircraft, aviation data is shown by default. If available, this feature is accessed by pressing the MENU key, scrolling to "Show Aviation Data" and pressing the ENT key. Aviation data is turned off by pressing the MENU key, scrolling to "Hide Aviation Data" and pressing the ENT key.

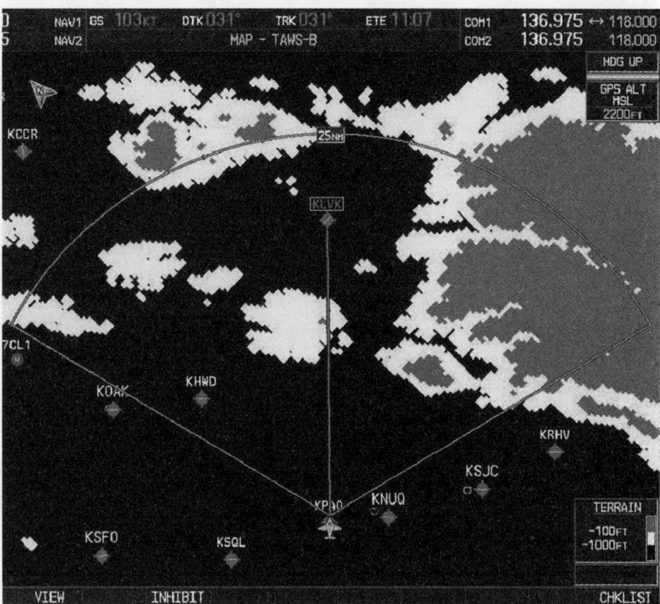

Figure 7-24A Pushing the ARC softkey removes irrelevant terrain behind you.

Note that most G1000 and some Perspective systems don't have TAWS and give no aural alerts, hence you must watch the terrain display to become aware of hazardous terrain. Also, you'll want to fly at a higher altitude than indicated by the Terrain Awareness Map page to guarantee that you clear any obstructions or tall trees that are not part of the database. The database is stored on an SD type memory card, which is inserted in one of the slots visible on the bezel of the PFD and MFD. To view terrain data, the card must remain in the slot and should be updated periodically.

TAWS—Terrain Awareness and Warning System Page

TAWS provides aural and visual alerts for hazardous terrain. It's an option in most G1000 and all Perspective aircraft. TAWS uses GPS information to determine position and altitude. GPS altitude is converted to height above geodetic sea level (GSL), which is used to determine TAWS alerts. GSL altitude accuracy is not subject to variations in pressure and temperature, making it a reliable source to calculate terrain and obstacle alerts.

In TAWS-equipped aircraft, a TAWS page replaces the Terrain Proximity page. This page is reached in the same way and has the same softkeys. Several additional MENU key options are available on the TAWS page. When flying in an area with unique terrain, the system may generate nuisance alerts. In this case, you can disable FLTA and PDA alerts (other alerts remain active). To inhibit these alerts from the TAWS page, press the MENU key, scroll to select "Inhibit TAWS," and press the ENT key. To enable alerts, press the MENU key, scroll to select "Enable TAWS," and press the ENT key.

The TAWS system performs a system self-test at power-up. You can also initiate the test manually if the aircraft is on the ground by pressing the MENU key, scrolling to "Test TAWS," and pressing the ENT key. Whenever the TAWS completes a self-test, it generates an aural "TAWS System Test, OK" message.

TAWS Functions

The FAA's technical standard order TSO-C151b prescribes the minimum operational performance standards for TAWS equipment. Per this document, the system shall provide the flight crew with sufficient information and alerting to detect a potentially hazardous terrain situation that would permit the flight crew to take effective action to prevent a controlled flight into terrain (CFIT) event. The basic TAWS functions for all TSO approved systems include the following:

1) A Forward Looking Terrain Avoidance (FLTA) function. The FLTA function looks ahead of the airplane along and below the airplane's lateral and vertical flight path and provides suitable alerts if a potential CFIT threat exists.

2) A Premature Descent Alert (PDA) function. The PDA function of the TAWS uses the airplane's current position and flight path information as determined from a suitable navigation source and airport database to determine if the airplane is hazardously below the normal (typically 3 degree) approach path for the nearest runway as defined by the alerting algorithm.

3) An appropriate visual and aural discrete signal for both caution and warning alerts.

The G1000 uses a Class B implementation of TAWS, which requires indications of imminent contact with the ground during the following airplane operations:

- Excessive Rates of Descent
- Negative Climb Rate or Altitude Loss After Takeoff
- A voice callout "Five Hundred" when the airplane descends to 500 feet above the nearest runway elevation.

Forward Looking Terrain Avoidance

Phase of Flight	Level Flight	Descending
Enroute	700 Feet	500 Feet
Terminal (Intermediate Segment)	350 Feet	300 Feet
Approach	150 Feet	100 Feet
Departure	100 Feet	100 Feet

Table 7-2 TAWS Required Terrain Clearance (RTC) by phase of Flight.

The majority of CFIT accidents have occurred because the flight crews did not have adequate situational information regarding the terrain in the vicinity of the airplane and its projected flight path. The FLTA function looks ahead of the airplane within a design search volume to provide timely alerts in the event terrain is predicted to penetrate the search volume. The search volume consists of a computed look-ahead distance, a lateral distance on both sides of the airplane's flight path, and a specified look-down distance based upon the airplane's vertical flight path. This search volume may vary as a function of phase of flight, distance from runway, and the required obstacle clearance in order to perform its intended function while minimizing nuisance alerts.

The FLTA alert is composed of two subfunctions: Required Terrain Clearance (RTC) and Required Obstacle Clearance (ROC). These provide alerts when an aircraft's flight path is above terrain or obstacles, yet is projected to fly into an area which no longer meets the minimum clearance values in Table 7-2. If an RTC or ROC alert is issued, a red or yellow "X" is displayed on the G1000's TAWS page to indicate a potential impact point. Note that during the departure phase of flight, the FLTA function must alert if the airplane is projected to be within 100 feet vertically of terrain, but shouldn't alert if the airplane is projected to be more than 400 feet above the terrain.

Imminent Terrain Impact (ITI) and Imminent Obstacle Impact (IOI) alerts are issued when an aircraft is below the elevation of terrain in its projected path. These alerts are issued when the flight path is projected to come within minimum clearance altitudes (table 7-2). At the time an ITI or IOI alert is issued, a red or yellow "X" is displayed on the G1000's TAWS page to indicate a potential impact point. RTC, ROC, ITI, and IOI alerts are inhibited during the final approach when the aircraft is below 200 feet AGL within 0.5 nm of the approach runway, or is below 125 feet within 1 nm of the runway.

Premature Descent Alert

Per TSO-C151b, approximately one third of all CFIT accidents occur during the final approach phase of flight, when the airplane is properly configured for landing and descending at a normal rate. For a variety of reasons, which include poor visibility, night time operations, loss of situational awareness, operating below minimums without adequate visual references and deviations from the published approach procedures, many airplanes have crashed into the ground short of the runway. This is particularly likely at night on "black hole" approaches, where there are few surface lights illuminating the ground leading up to the approach end of the runway.

PDA alerts are only generated during descent to land using an alerting algorithm based upon speed, distance and other parameters. Alerting ends when the aircraft is within 0.5 nm of the approach end of the runway, or when the aircraft reaches 125 feet AGL within 1 nm of the runway threshold. The TAWS unit used with the G1000 generates PDA alerts under the following scenarios:

- No Approach Loaded — Alerting becomes active when the aircraft is within 15 nm of the destination airport.
- Non-Precision Approach Loaded — Alerting becomes active when the aircraft is within 15 nm of the destination airport and the FAF is the active waypoint.

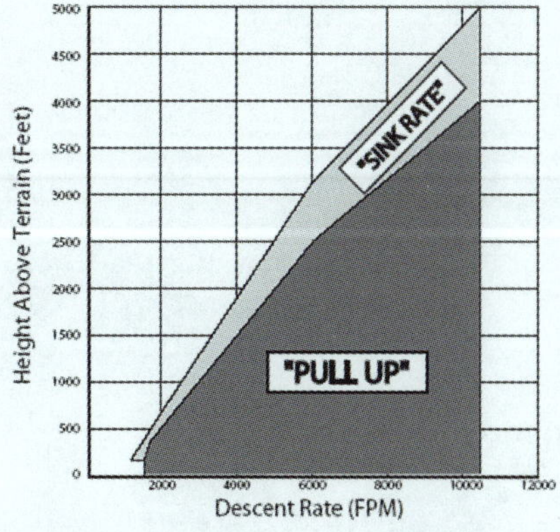

Figure 7-25 Criteria for Excessive Descent Rate Alerts. *© Garmin Ltd. or its affiliates*

- ILS Approach Loaded — Alerting becomes active when the aircraft is within 15 nm of the destination airport and the FAF is the active waypoint. Alerts are generated if the aircraft descends 0.7 degrees below the glide slope.

Excessive Descent Rate (EDR) Alert

TSO-C151b requires EDR alerts whenever an aircraft is descending into terrain at an excessive speed. Figure 7-25 shows the criteria used by the G1000 TAWS to generate two types of alerts. Alerts are based upon height above terrain and descent rate, and either a "Sink Rate" Caution or a "Pull Up" Warning is generated.

Negative Climb Rate (NCR) After Takeoff Alert

TSO-C151b requires a TAWS system to generate an alert when it determines an aircraft is losing altitude after takeoff or a missed approach. There are many accidents on record where a departing pilot crashed on takeoff by descending into the ground, usually within the first mile of departing the airport. Accidents of this type almost always happen at night, particularly when takeoff is over unlit ground or water with few visual ground references.

These accidents are usually the result of *somatogravic illusion*. According to the FAA's Instrument Flying Handbook, "...a rapid acceleration, such as experienced during takeoff, stimulates the otolith organs in the same way as tilting the head backwards. This action creates the somatogravic illusion of being in a nose-up attitude, especially in situations without good visual references. The disoriented pilot may push the aircraft into a nose-low or dive attitude. A rapid deceleration by quick reduction of the throttle(s) can have the opposite effect, with the disoriented pilot pulling the aircraft into a nose-up or stall attitude."

NCR Alerts consist of an aural "Don't Sink" or "Too Low, Terrain" message. They're accompanied by a "Terrain" annunciation on the PFD and MFD TAWS page and a pop-up alert on the MFD Navigation Map page. NCR alerting occurs during departure when the following conditions are met:

- Height above terrain is less than 700 feet
- Aircraft is within 2 nm of the airport
- Aircraft heading is still within 110° of departure heading

"Five Hundred" Aural Alert

TSO-C151b requires the voice callout "Five Hundred" during descents for landing, which is intended to provide situational awareness to a pilot when an airplane is operated normally. The feature also has an important CFIT protection function. In the event the airplane is operated unintentionally close to terrain when not in the airport area or the area for which PDA protection is provided, the 500-foot voice callout, referenced to Height above Terrain, will alert the pilot to a hazardous condition.

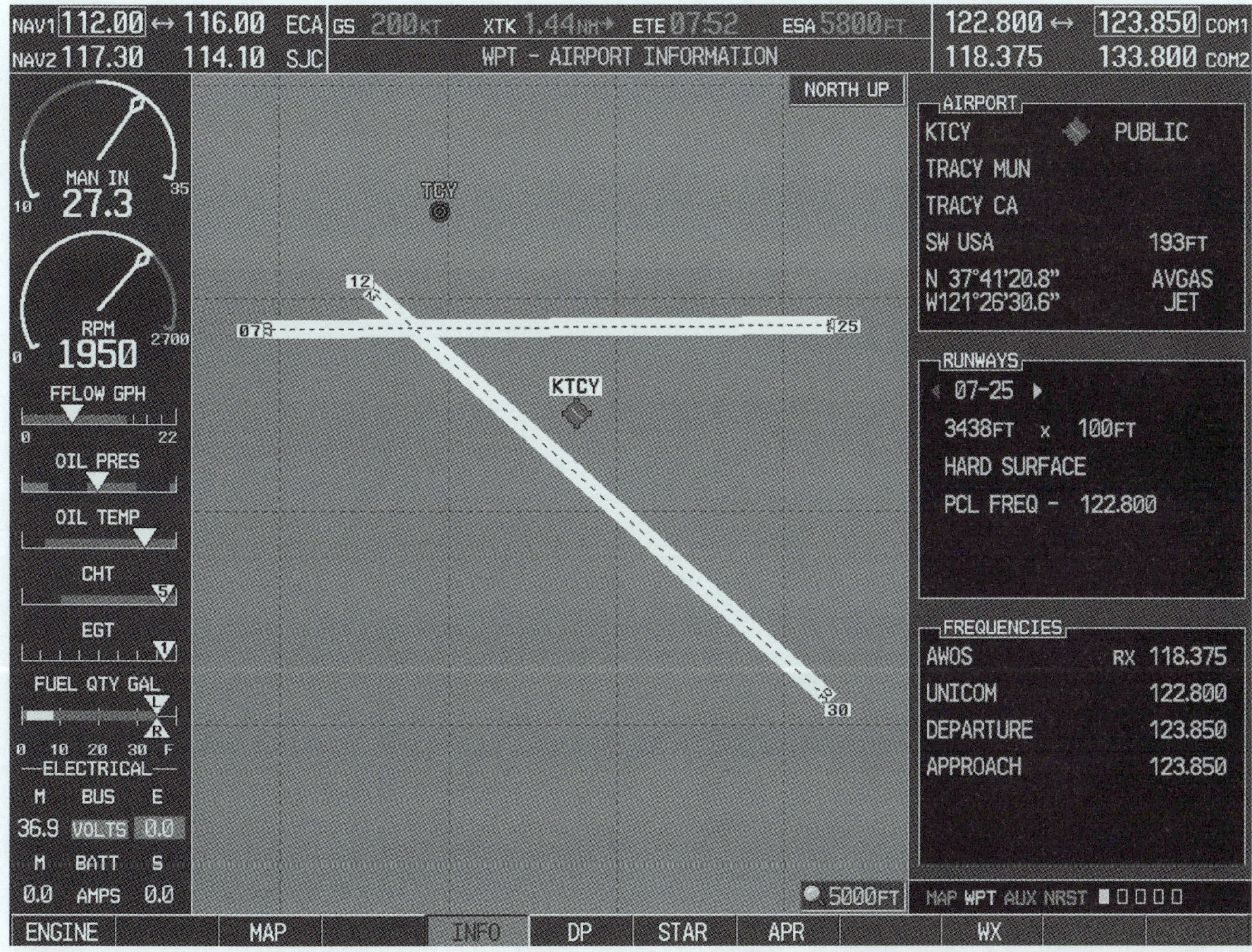

Figure 7-26 Use the Airport Information page to load frequencies and get runway information. *© Garmin Ltd. or its affiliates*

Alerting is enabled when an aircraft is more than 675 feet above terrain and is disabled when the aircraft's height above terrain is less than 500 feet. At 500 feet, the aural "five-hundred" message is heard. No PFD annunciations or pop-up alerts accompany this message.

A complete list of TAWS alert types and their corresponding aural messages and annunciators can be found in the Appendix.

WPT (Waypoint) Group Pages

The WPT page group is a treasure trove of information. Rather than scramble for charts to find a frequency or books to find a runway layout, using the WPT group of pages is a much easier way to get the information—if you remember to use it! To reach the WPT group, turn the large FMS knob until the "WPT" label is highlighted in cyan. Then turn the small FMS knob to reach a particular page within the group.

Airport Information Page

The Airport Information page (figure 7-26) is the first page in the WPT group—probably because it's the page you'll use most in this

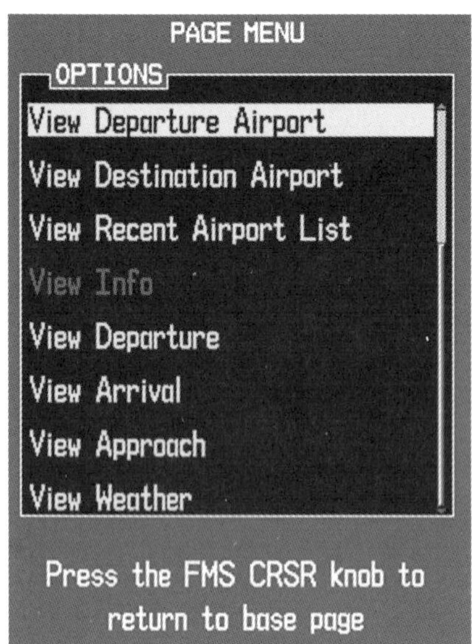

Figure 7-27 Using the MENU key saves time versus entering an airport identifier. *© Garmin Ltd. or its affiliates*

group. Train yourself to go to this page after engine start and load all of the frequencies you need—Clearance Delivery, ATIS, Ground, Tower and Departure. Later, in flight, you'll also want to use it as you near your destination to study the runway diagram, load frequencies and even review the latest METAR if you have a data-link weather subscription. As an instrument pilot, you may find it useful for examining the Standard Arrival Procedures (STAR) to see which one you're most likely to be assigned and to review the instrument approaches available.

After engine startup, the Airport Information page initially defaults to the airport where the plane is located. Later, after you've loaded a flight plan, it defaults to your destination airport. On a round-robin flight plan with multiple airports, it defaults to whichever airport is the current active waypoint.

If you need to view information on a different airport, you can use the old tried-and-true method of entering the airport identifier with the FMS knobs. Or, if you're really savvy, you can often save time by using the MENU key. Simply press the MENU key, scroll to select "View Recent Airport List," "View Departure Airport" or "View Destination Airport" (figure 7-27) and press the ENT key.

Figure 7-28 Enter the city name if you don't know the airport name or identifier. *© Garmin Ltd. or its affiliates*

If all else fails, use the FMS knobs to enter the airport identifier letter by letter. Start by pushing the FMS knob to get a cursor and then enter the identifier using the small FMS knob to select a character and the large FMS knob to select the next character position. When done, press the ENT key.

Alternatively, if you don't know the airport identifier, you can enter the full name of the airport or the city in which it is located. To enter an airport name or city name, push the FMS knob and turn the large knob one click to highlight the airport name field or two clicks to highlight the city name field. Then turn the small and large FMS knobs to enter the name (figure 7-28). If more than one airport shares the same name or city, you can scroll through them all by continuing to turn the small FMS knob. Then press the ENT key.

Airport Information Page—Using the Map

The runway map occupies the largest portion of the Airport Information page. You can zoom the map in and out using the range knob. If you want the background color to correspond to the elevation of the airport, press the MAP softkey and then the TOPO softkey. Now if the airport you're viewing is near sea level you'll see a green background; a brown background would indicate an airport located in the mountains.

Figure 7-29 The Airport Information page always has a North Up orientation. *© Garmin Ltd. or its affiliates*

In the upper right corner of the map, you'll see that it has a "North Up" orientation (figure 7-29), which cannot be changed. This may cause some initial disorientation when viewing the destination airport, particularly if you are flying with the Navigation Map page in a different orientation. An easy way to orient yourself is to look at the bottom of the HSI to see from what direction you're coming.

If, for example, you were on a heading of 240°, you'd note that the number at the bottom of the HSI is 60°, which means that you're approaching your destination airport from the northeast. Now, looking at the map on the Airport Information page, imagine yourself approaching the airport from the upper right corner of the display, which is the northeast quadrant. You should now be able to visualize which portion of the field you'll reach first, which runway you'll likely be assigned and whether the traffic pattern is close to you or on the far side of the field.

Figure 7-30 The Airport window shows the field elevation and other information. *© Garmin Ltd. or its affiliates*

Airport Information Page—Information Fields

All of the airport information can be accessed from this page, though it cannot all be displayed simultaneously. Use the softkeys, or if you prefer the MENU key, to select the different types of information available. As always, you can use the large FMS knob to scroll to any visible field.

Press the INFO softkey, or use the MENU key and select "View Info," to bring up three windows: Airport, Runways and Frequencies. The Airport window lists the airport identifier, airport name and city. It also shows the field elevation, the longitude and latitude coordinates for the airport and the type of fuel services available (figure 7-30).

Airport type, such as public, military or private is also listed. Finally, there is a colored airport symbol, similar to the ones shown on sectional charts. For example, towered airports are blue and non-towered airports are magenta. Tick marks around the airport symbol indicate that services (e.g. fuel) are available during normal working hours. Military airfields are depicted with two concentric circles and airports with other than hard-surface runways are indicated by a single circle.

TIP

When entering a three-letter identifier for a U.S. airport, you must precede the identifier with the letter K. For example, the Palo Alto, Calif., airport would be entered as KPAO, not PAO. However, airport identifiers that are a combination of letters and numbers must not be preceded by a K. For example, the Wellsboro-Johnston airport in Pennsylvania would be entered as N38, not as KN38. If, while entering characters, you want to start over at any point, press the FMS knob and the characters you've entered will be replaced with a blank field and the original flashing cursor.

The Runways window (figure 7-31) displays information on runway designations, dimensions, surface type and lighting. If there's data for additional runways, you'll see a green triangle next to the runway designation. To display the additional runway information, scroll with the large FMS knob to highlight the runway numbers, and then scroll with the small FMS knob to display information on other runways. Runway data includes the following types:

- Surface — Hard, Turf, Water, Sealed, Gravel, Dirt, Soft or Unknown
- Lighting — PCL FREQ (frequency of pilot controlled lighting), Part Time, Full Time or No Lights

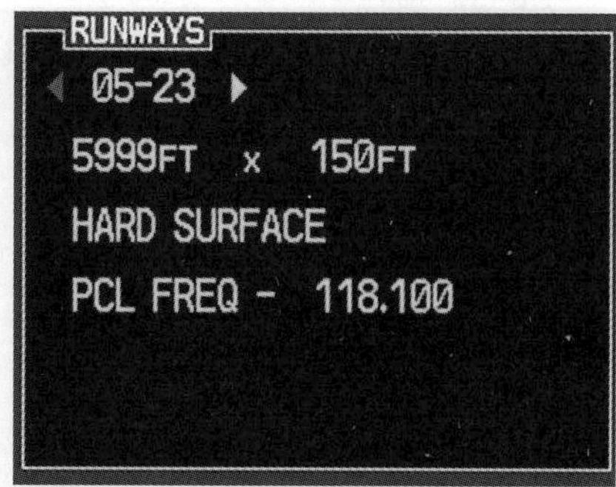

Figure 7-31 Runway information. The green triangle indicates there are more runways and you can access this data with the FMS knobs. *© Garmin Ltd. or its affiliates*

The Frequencies window lists virtually all of the frequencies that you need to know for an airport. These include, but are not limited to, ATIS or AWOS, Ground, Clearance Delivery, Tower, Class B, Class C, Approach and Arrival frequencies. In cases where multiple frequencies are used for the same function, such as Approach or Class B frequencies, a blue "i" in a circle indicates that additional information is provided on the sectors and altitude information to which these frequencies apply. In these cases, scroll the large FMS knob to highlight the type of frequency, such as "Departure" and press the ENT key to

FREQUENCIES		
ATIS	RX	124.250
CLEARANCE		121.200
GROUND		121.700
TOWER		118.100
DEPARTURE		119.200
APPROACH		127.600

Figure 7-32 You can save time by auto-tuning radio frequencies. The vertical scroll bar on the right indicates you need to scroll to see all frequencies. *© Garmin Ltd. or its affiliates*

see the additional information. Pressing the ENT key again or the CLR key will close the additional information window.

You can also load any of these frequencies directly into the NAV or COM radio, which can save you time. Note that if a scroll bar (figure 7-32) appears along the right side of the window, then there are more frequencies than can be displayed and you'll need to continue scrolling with the FMS knobs to see them all. To enter a frequency, scroll the cursor using the large FMS knob to highlight the frequency. Then press the ENT key to transfer it to the standby field of the NAV or COM radio with the tuning box. Note that if the airport has a localizer or ILS instrument approach, those frequencies will be listed and can be loaded into the NAV radio.

Other designations that appear in the frequency window are:
RX — receive only frequency (such as ATIS)
TX — transmit only
PT — part-time frequency
"i" — additional information available

Airport Information Page—IFR Information

The Airport Information page also includes detailed information pertinent to IFR operations. Chapter 11 goes into detail on using each of these functions. In brief, you can view any of the following types of procedures using the softkey labels listed below:

- DP (Departure Procedures)
- STAR (Standard Arrival Procedures)
- APR (Instrument Approach Procedures)

Once you've viewed a procedure, you can load or activate it using the MENU key. You can also select and load procedures with just the MENU key without using the softkeys.

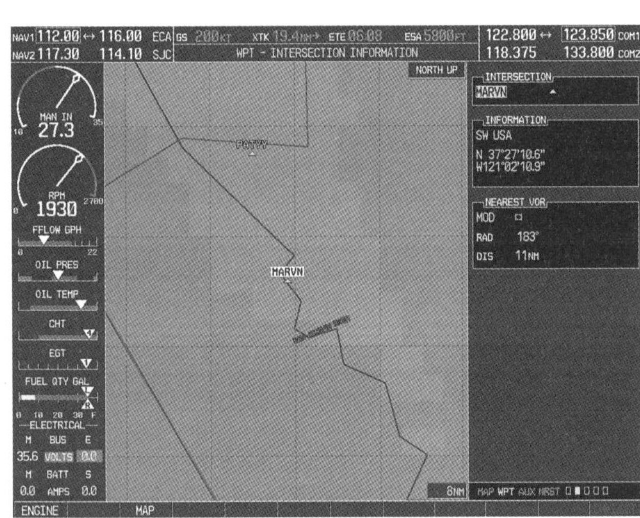

Figure 7-33 The Intersection Information page gives details on every intersection. *© Garmin Ltd. or its affiliates*

Airport Information Page—Weather

While you're reviewing information about an airport, you can easily get weather information for that airport—assuming you subscribe to an aviation weather package. To get the METAR and TAF for an airport, press the WX softkey. Full details on using data-link weather are covered in the next chapter.

Intersection Information Page

As an IFR pilot, you'll become very familiar with intersections, which are points in space usually defined by crossing VOR radials and labeled with five-letter names that are sometimes barely pronounceable. It's not unusual in flight to be instructed to fly to an intersection. If it's unfamiliar, you may want to ask how it's spelled if it's not obvious. If you want to know more about the intersection, go to the Intersection Information page (figure 7-33), the second page in the WPT group. To reach it, hold the CLR key for two seconds, turn the large FMS knob one click to the WPT group and turn the small FMS knob one click to reach the second page in the group.

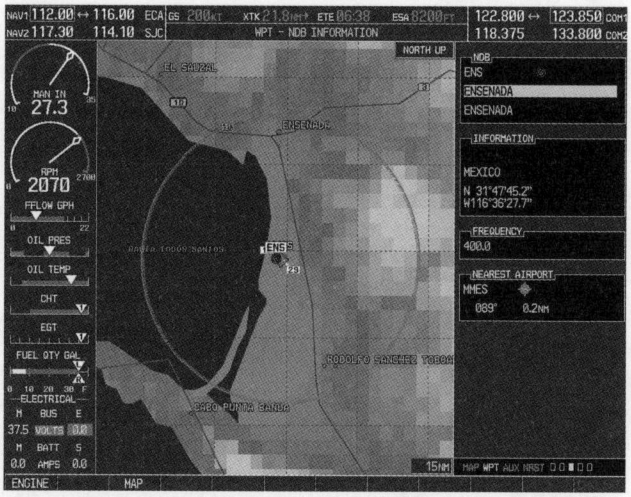

To enter a five-letter intersection identifier such as MARVN, push the FMS knob to get a cursor and then use the large and small FMS knobs to enter the characters, press the ENT key, and then push the FMS knob to remove the flashing cursor. Or, push the MENU key, select "View Recent Intersection List," scroll to an intersection, and press the ENT key.

On the left side of the page, you'll find a map centered on the intersection you've chosen. You can use the range knob to zoom in and out and press the MAP and TOPO softkeys to bring up the topographical map background. Along the right side, you'll find the Intersection identifier and symbol (a cyan triangle), the region and exact longitude and latitude coordinates where it's located and the bearing and distance to the nearest VOR. Note that the VOR might not be one used to define the intersection.

Figure 7-34 NDB Information page.
© Garmin Ltd. or its affiliates

NDB Information Page

Non-Directional Beacons (NDB) are low frequency navigational aids that are slowly being decommissioned. They are frequently associated with ILS instrument approaches and are common in remote regions that don't have other more modern navigational aids. Many modern glass cockpit aircraft no longer include an Automatic Direction Finder (ADF) receiver capable of receiving these stations directly. Instead, they use GPS to identify the location of the NDB.

To reach the NDB Information page (figure 7-34), hold the CLR key for two seconds, turn the large FMS knob one click to the WPT group and turn the small FMS knob two clicks to reach the third page in the group. You can select a NDB by entering either its identifier, the full name of the station, or the city in which it's located. To do this, push the FMS knob and then, using the large FMS knob, scroll to either the identifier, station name or city field. Turn the small and large FMS knobs to enter data, press the ENT key and push the FMS knob to remove the cursor. Or, you can press the MENU key at anytime, select "View Recent NDB List," scroll to a NDB and press the ENT key.

You can use the range knob to zoom in and out of the map that's displayed and press the MAP and TOPO softkeys to bring up the topographical map background. On the right, you'll see the NDB name, identifier, location, frequency and bearing and distance to the nearest airport.

VOR Information Page

VHF Omni-directional Radio-range (VOR) stations are ground-based navigational aids used extensively throughout the United States

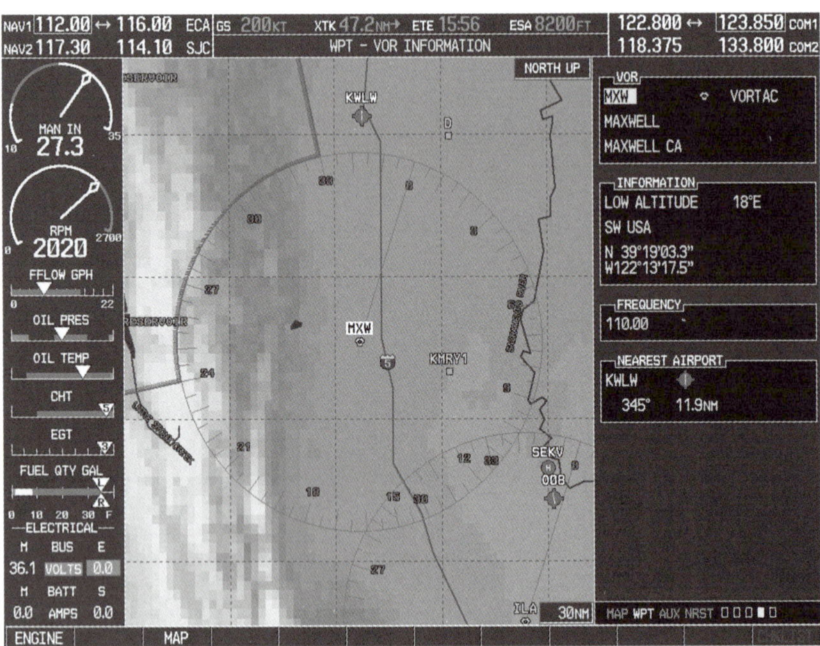

Figure 7-35 The VOR Information page also includes information on ILS installations. *© Garmin Ltd. or its affiliates*

and other countries. With the advent of GPS, it's likely that they will eventually be decommissioned, but they continue to serve as the major means of radio navigation for the thousands of non-GPS equipped aircraft.

VOR stations come in several types. If combined with a military TACAN station, it will be listed as a VORTAC and will include distance measuring equipment (DME) which will display your slant range distance to the station on a DME receiver. If it includes only DME, it's listed as a VOR-DME. There are also several classes of VOR stations. Each broadcasts with different amounts of power and can be received at different distances. They are, from high to low power: High Altitude, Low Altitude or Terminal type stations.

Instrument Landing System (ILS) signals can be received on a VOR receiver, and information about these can also be found on the VOR Information page. However, information about localizer stations, which are very similar to an ILS, is not included on this page.

To reach the VOR Information page (figure 7-35), hold the CLR key for two seconds, turn the large FMS knob one click to the WPT group and then turn the small FMS knob until you reach this page. You can select a VOR by entering either its identifier, the full name of the station or the city in which it's located. To do this, push the FMS knob and then, using the large FMS knob, scroll to either the identifier, station name or city field. Then, turn the small and large FMS knobs to enter data, press the ENT key and push the FMS knob to remove the cursor. Or, you can press the MENU key at anytime, select "View Recent VOR List," scroll to a VOR and press the ENT key.

You can use the range knob to zoom in and out of the map that's displayed and press the MAP and TOPO softkeys to bring up the topographical map background. On the right, you'll see the VOR or ILS identifier, name, city and type of station. In the Information window, you'll find the class of station and its location. Below are the frequency and bearing and distance to the nearest airport.

USER WAYPOINT
HAUS__
COMMENT
KRHV120 / 15
INFORMATION
SW USA
N 37°09'02.6"
W121°35'35.3"
REFERENCE WAYPOINTS
RAD DIS
1 KRHV 120.3° 15NM
2 ______ ___._°

Figure 7-36 You can create waypoints anywhere you'd like for any reason. *© Garmin Ltd. or its affiliates*

User Waypoint Information Page

The G1000 and Perspective let you create and store up to 1000 user-definable waypoints. These can be created for any location for any reason, such as marking where your house is located or defining a custom route to fly. Waypoints can be created from either the Navigation Map page by selecting a position on the map with the pointer or from the User Waypoint Information page by referencing a direction and distance from an existing waypoint or the directions from two existing waypoints. Once created, you can rename, delete or move a waypoint using the MENU key.

To create a new waypoint from the Navigation Map page, push the joystick and pan the map pointer to the desired location. Then press the ENT key, use the small and large FMS knobs to enter a name of up to six characters (figure 7-36) and press the ENT key. Push the FMS knob and you're done. Or, if you wish, you can enter additional information about your waypoint.

Note that the system automatically entered data in the Comment field and, in the Reference Waypoints field, selected a reference point such as an airport or VOR to define your point. You can accept these automatically generated comments and reference points or customize them using the small and large FMS knobs. Comments can be up to 25 characters long and reference points can be an airport, VOR, NDB, intersection or other user waypoint.

You can also create waypoints from the User Waypoint Information page. To reach this page, press the CLR key for two seconds, turn the large FMS knob one click to the WPT group and then turn the small FMS knob until you reach this page. To create a new waypoint, press the NEW softkey, or press the MENU key, scroll to "Create New User Waypoint" and press the ENT key. Then, use the small and large FMS knobs to enter a name of up to six characters and press the ENT key. Next, scroll with the FMS knobs to either the Information window to enter the longitude and latitude coordinates for your waypoint or to the Reference Waypoints window to enter the bearing and distance from an airport, VOR, NDB, intersection or other user waypoint to define your waypoint. Alternatively, you can define your waypoint using the bearing from two reference points. Note that as you modify the longitude/latitude information or the Reference Waypoint information, the map pans to show where your user waypoint will be located.

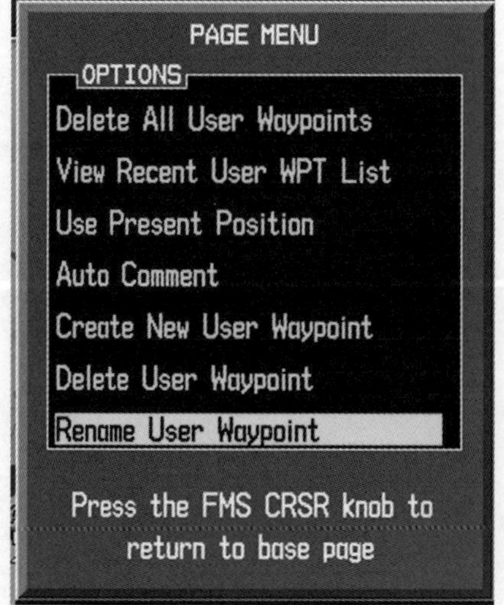

Figure 7-37 Use the MENU key to see what options are available. *© Garmin Ltd. or its affiliates*

User Waypoint Information Page—Working with Waypoints

The most common changes you'll make to a waypoint are to rename it or delete it. You can access these functions either via softkey or the MENU key. To make changes to a waypoint, press the FMS knob to get a flashing cursor and then scroll to highlight one of the waypoints in the User Waypoint List window in the lower right corner of the screen. To rename a waypoint, press the RENAME softkey, or press the MENU key and scroll to select "Rename User Waypoint" (figure 7-37) and press the ENT key. Use the FMS knobs to enter a new name and press the ENT key. To delete a waypoint, press the DELETE softkey, or press the MENU key and select "Delete User Waypoint." Press the ENT key twice.

The following additional functions are available through the MENU key:

- Delete All User Waypoints
- View Recent User WPT List
- Use Present Position
- Auto Comment

To access these functions, press the MENU key, scroll to the item and press the ENT key. To delete all user waypoints, you'll need to press the ENT key a second time to confirm your selection. "View Recent User WPT List" brings up a list of recent waypoints. Scroll to select one, press the ENT key and you'll bring up data on that waypoint.

Any time you update the location of a user waypoint, you can choose "Use Present Position," which will enter the longitude/latitude data for the aircraft's present position. To use this, enter the desired waypoint in the User Waypoint window, press the MENU key, scroll to select "Use Present Position" and press the ENT key. Note the cursor moves to highlight the longitude/latitude field. Now press the ENT key to save this information as the waypoint's new location.

The automatically generated comment for a user waypoint usually incorporates a reference waypoint, bearing and distance information. If you replaced the system-generated comment with one of your own, you can use "Auto Comment" to generate a new comment. To use this, enter the desired waypoint in the User Waypoint window, press the MENU key, scroll to select "Auto Comment" and press the ENT key. The comment generated is based upon the reference point currently used to define the waypoint.

AUX Group Pages

Trip Planning Page

Traditionally, trip planning was tedious work which required many manual calculations and therefore wasn't always done in detail. Now, the Trip Planning page makes it so easy there's never an excuse not to review your projected arrival time and fuel reserves often while flying a trip.

The Trip Planning page (figure 7-38) is the first page in the AUX group. To get there, turn the large FMS knob until AUX is highlighted in cyan and if necessary, turn the small FMS knob to find the page. The page operates in either automatic or manual mode, selected with the AUTO and MANUAL softkeys or by using the MENU key.

Trip Planning Page—Automatic Mode

Automatic mode is the easiest to use in flight, since it enters current groundspeed, fuel flow and remaining fuel on board to calculate when you'll arrive at your destination. It also generates fuel statistics, such as how much gas you'll have left when you arrive. All you have to do to analyze a trip is select a flight plan or flight plan leg or manually enter a destination. Push either the FPL softkey (not the FPL key on the bezel!)

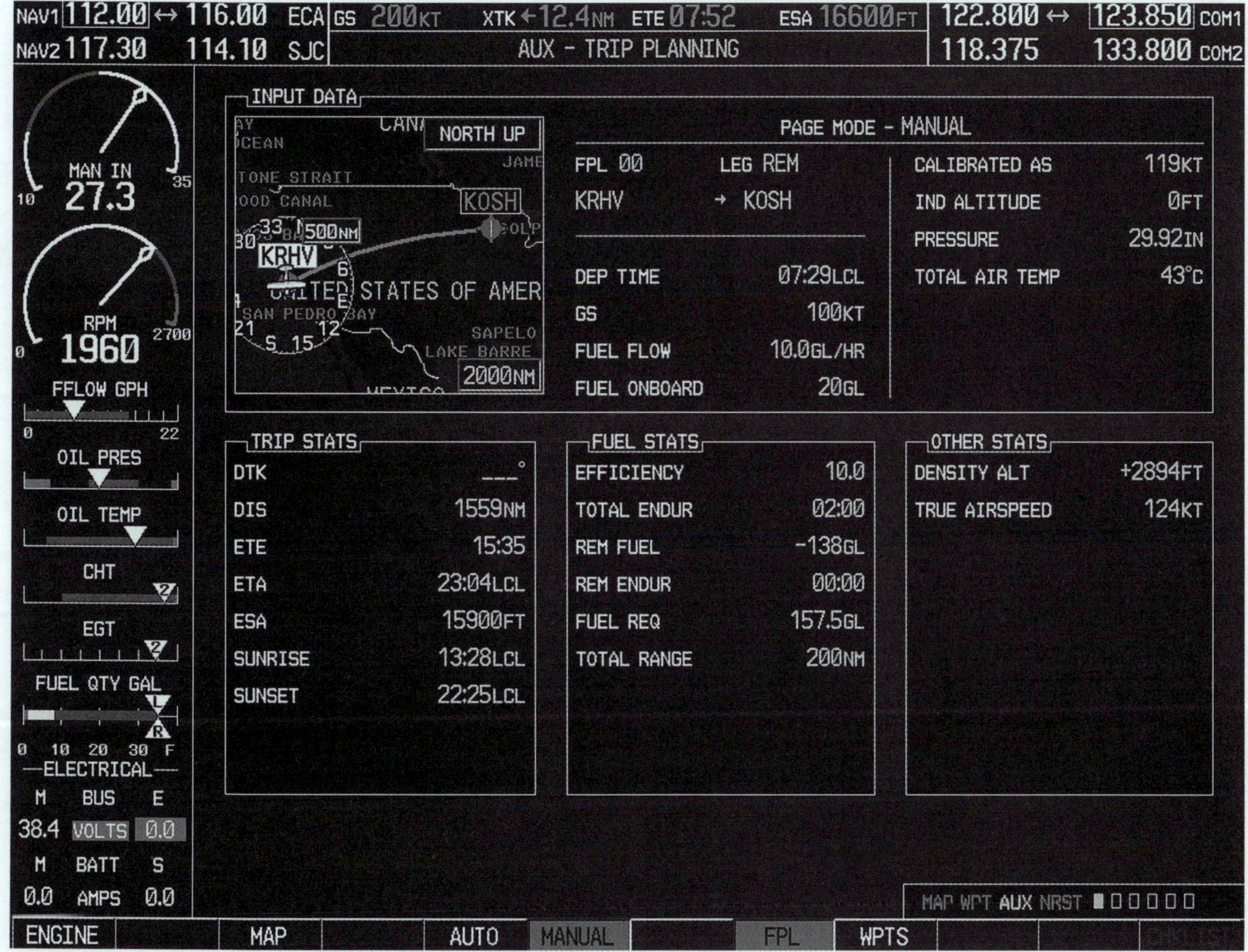

Figure 7-38 The Trip Planning page continuously calculates information for your current trip or allows you to manually analyze a future trip. *© Garmin Ltd. or its affiliates*

to select a flight plan, or the WPTS softkey to enter a destination waypoint. The MENU key can also be used to make these selections.

To use automatic mode, press the AUTO softkey or, alternatively, press the MENU key, scroll to select "Automatic Mode," and press the ENT key. To analyze, for example, the active flight plan, push the FMS knob, scroll with the large FMS knob to the FPL field and use the small FMS knob to select FPL #0, the active flight plan. Then scroll to the LEG field. Using the small FMS knob, select CUM (cumulative) for the entire flight, or a number for one of the individual legs of the flight. Then, look below in the TRIP STATS box and you'll see the following statistics updated for the flight plan leg or destination selected. The type of units used for each parameter (e.g. nautical or statute miles) is selected on the System Setup page, described later in this chapter.

- DTK (desired ground track) in degrees
- DIS (distance) in miles
- ETE (estimated time en route) in hours and minutes
- ETA (estimated time of arrival) in hours and minutes
- ESA (en route safe altitude) in feet or meters for the leg or trip based on 1000 foot clearance within 5 miles of the route or 2000

feet in mountainous areas as defined by the Airman's Information Manual.

- Sunrise and Sunset times in hours and minutes

In addition to analyzing flight plans, you can enter waypoints to define a segment for analysis. Press the WPTS softkey or press the MENU key, scroll to highlight "Waypoints Mode" and press the ENT key. Turn the small FMS knob and then use both FMS knobs to enter the first waypoint. Or, if you'd like to specify your present position as the first waypoint, press the MENU key, scroll to highlight "Set WPT to Present Position" and press the ENT key. Use the large FMS knob to scroll to the next field and enter the second waypoint using the FMS knobs or the MENU key to use your present position.

Trip Planning Page—Manual Mode

The manual mode is useful for "what if" scenarios, where you plug in a variety of parameters to see the results. It can also calculate density altitude and true airspeed. You may want to use it on the ground prior to departure to project arrival times and calculate fuel usage for your current trip or a future trip. In the air, you might use it to plan future trips, possible diversions or to see the effect of changing airspeed, fuel consumption or other parameters for your present trip. Generally in the air, however, it's easier to use the automatic mode and then make power and leaning changes to see their impact upon your current trip.

TIP

If your aircraft uses a fuel totalizer, the fuel statistics generated are NOT based upon the actual fuel in the tanks, but are calculated by the totalizer. Therefore, your start-up checklist should include pressing the ENGINE and then the SYSTEM softkey on the MFD so you can enter into the totalizer the amount of any fuel added or removed from the tanks. Otherwise, the fuel statistics generated will be inaccurate. Note: some early versions of the G1000 have only a RST USED softkey, which should only be pressed when you fill the tanks to the top.

To use the Manual mode, press the MANUAL softkey or, alternatively, press the MENU key, scroll to select "Manual Mode," and press the ENT key. Finally, select a flight plan or enter waypoints as described in the Automatic Mode section above. Then, scroll using the large FMS knob to the following fields and use the small and large FMS knobs to enter these parameters:

- DEP TIME (departure time) in hours and minutes
- GS (groundspeed) in nautical miles (or km per hour)
- FUEL FLOW in gallons per hour (or liters per hour)
- FUEL ON BOARD in gallons (or liters)

Trip Planning Page—Fuel Planning

Regardless of whether you use the automatic or the manual modes, the FUEL STATS box generates a lot of useful information. However, the way that information is generated varies depending upon what equipment your aircraft manufacturer includes in your plane (see Appendix for your aircraft's equipment). The G1000 works with the following combinations of equipment:

- No fuel sensors. You'll need to enter the fuel flow rate and fuel on board. The G1000 will use this data to continuously calculate the remaining fuel on board. Once you enter this data, it is retained until you change it.
- Fuel flow sensor and totalizer. The fuel flow rate is provided automatically, but fuel quantities are provided by a fuel totalizer

that relies upon you properly entering into the G1000 the amount of fuel you add to the tanks. See the related tip.

- Fuel Flow sensor and Fuel on Board sensors. Fuel on board is measured automatically and cannot be changed on this page. Fuel Flow is also measured, or can be entered manually, though manual entries are not retained on future views of this page.

In automatic mode, information in the FUEL STATS box is based upon your actual groundspeed and, if equipped with a fuel sensor, your actual fuel flow. These figures will change if, for example, you were to encounter strong headwinds later in the trip. In the manual mode, you'll need to specify the groundspeed, fuel flow and fuel on board. In either mode, the following data is displayed. The actual units depend upon what you select in the System Setup page.

- EFFICIENCY in nautical miles per gallon
- TOTAL ENDUR (endurance) in hours:minutes to fuel exhaustion
- REM FUEL (remaining fuel) in tanks in gallons
- REM ENDUR (remaining endurance) in hours:minutes of fuel remaining at destination
- FUEL REQ (fuel required) in gallons to reach destination
- TOTAL RANGE in nautical miles

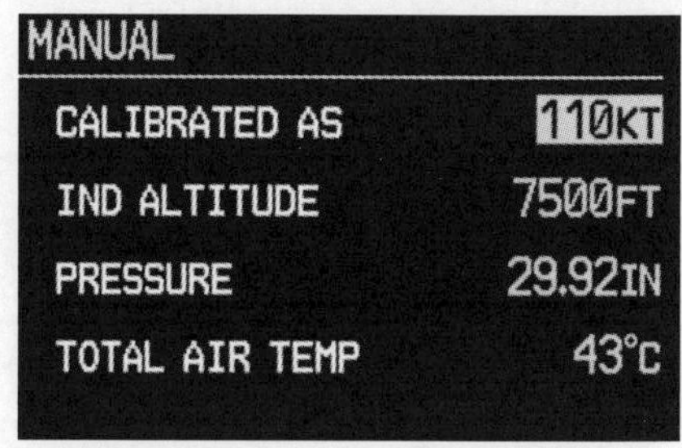

Figure 7-39 Use the Trip Planning Page to calculate density altitude and true airspeed. *© Garmin Ltd. or its affiliates*

Trip Planning Page—Density Altitude and True Airspeed

You can easily calculate density altitude and true airspeed for any set of conditions. For current conditions, it's generally easier to read the true airspeed directly from the bottom of the airspeed indicator on the PFD. The Trip Planning page, however, will allow you to calculate it for any set of conditions.

To do so, press the MANUAL softkey, push the FMS knob to get a cursor, and scroll using the large FMS knob to highlight the CALIBRATED AS (airspeed) field (figure 7-39) and enter the airspeed using the small and large FMS knobs. Scroll with the large knob and enter data in each of the following fields:

- IND ALTITUDE (indicated altitude)
- PRESSURE (barometric pressure)
- TOTAL AIR TEMP (degrees)

Using this data, the G1000 calculates and displays density altitude and true airspeed.

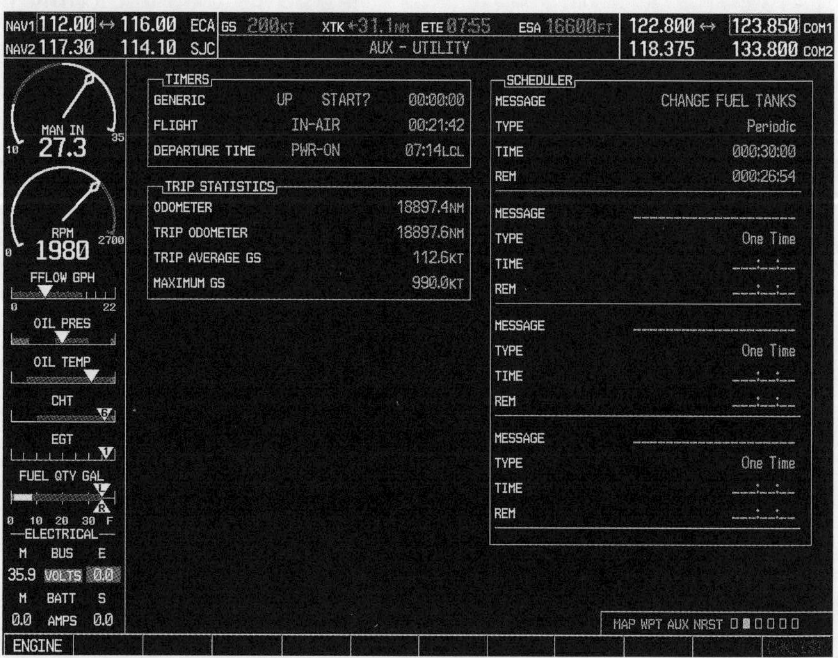

Figure 7-40 The Utility page displays timers and trip statistics and lets you schedule reminders. *© Garmin Ltd. or its affiliates*

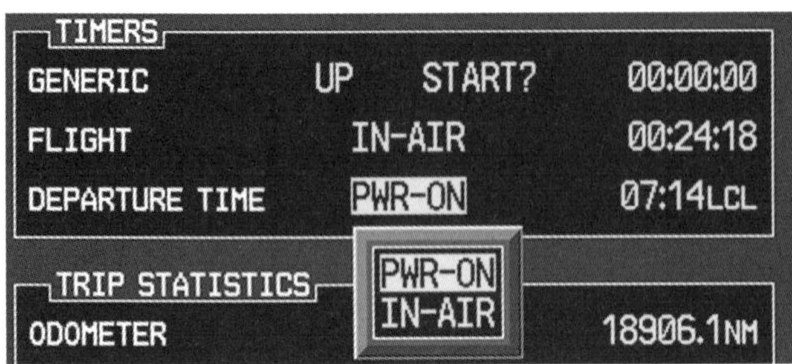

Figure 7-41 The Timer window has a generic timer and lets you set criteria for the flight timer and departure time.
© Garmin Ltd. or its affiliates

Utility Page

The utility page (figure 7-40) is usually the second page in the AUX group. To reach it, turn the large FMS knob until AUX is highlighted in cyan and turn the small FMS knob to find the page. It displays timers, trip statistics and allows you to schedule future reminders.

Utility Page—Timers and Departure Time

The Utility page includes two timers, one for general purpose up or down timing and one that records the actual flight time. It also notes the time of departure. To use any of the timers, press the FMS knob and scroll the cursor to the timer (figure 7-41). For the generic timer, the first field allows you to select UP or DOWN timing by using the small FMS knob. Scroll to the second field and successive presses of the ENT key will START, STOP and RESET the timer. Scroll to the third field and you can use the small and large FMS knobs to preset the counter with the time from which you'd like to start counting.

To use the flight timer, scroll with the large FMS knob to the first field and, using the small FMS knob, scroll to select the criteria upon which you'd like the timer to start (e.g. PWR-ON, IN-AIR or GS>30KT depending upon the version of your G1000). You can reset this timer by pressing the MENU key, scrolling to "Reset Flight Timer" and pressing the ENT key.

To set the criteria for recording the departure time, scroll with the large FMS knob to the first field and, using the small knob, scroll to select the criteria upon which you'd like the departure time to be recorded (e.g. PWR-ON, IN-AIR or GS>30KT). You can reset the departure time to the current time by pressing the MENU key, scrolling to "Reset Departure Time" and pressing the ENT key.

Utility Page—Trip Statistics

The following are displayed in the Trip Statistics box and all can be reset at any time:

- ODOMETER
- TRIP ODOMETER
- TRIP AVERAGE GS (groundspeed)
- MAXIMUM GS (groundspeed)

To reset any or all of the parameters, press the MENU key, scroll to select one of the following and press the ENT key: "Reset Trip ODOM/AVG GS," "Reset Odometer," "Reset Maximum Speed" or "Reset All."

Figure 7-42 Start a reminder by entering the message you want displayed.
© Garmin Ltd. or its affiliates

Utility Page—Scheduler

The Scheduler lets you program reminder messages based upon elapsed time or a particular date and time. Time-based messages can be periodic, such as "CHANGE FUEL TANKS" every 30 minutes, or one time after you enter the message. Event messages are based upon a particular date and time, such as "ANNUAL DUE NEXT MONTH." Since the scheduler uses the GPS receiver time, you shouldn't use it for events based upon "tach time" such as oil changes. When an event is due, the ALERTS softkey on the PFD will flash. Push the softkey and you'll see the message you programmed into the scheduler.

To use the Scheduler, push the FMS knob to get a cursor, scroll with the large FMS knob to the first blank MESSAGE line and, using the small and large FMS knobs, enter a reminder message in the 20 character field (figure 7-42). Press the ENT key and scroll with the large FMS knob to the TYPE field. Turn the small FMS knob to select one of the following and press the ENT key:

- Event — single message based upon a date and time
- One Time — occurs after time expires each time G1000 is powered up
- Periodic — recurs based on the amount of time specified

Scroll to the next field and enter a date and time (for events) or a time for one time and periodic events. Use the small and large FMS knobs to enter dates and times and then press the ENT key. For One Time and Periodic events, the REM field displays the time remaining before the message will be displayed.

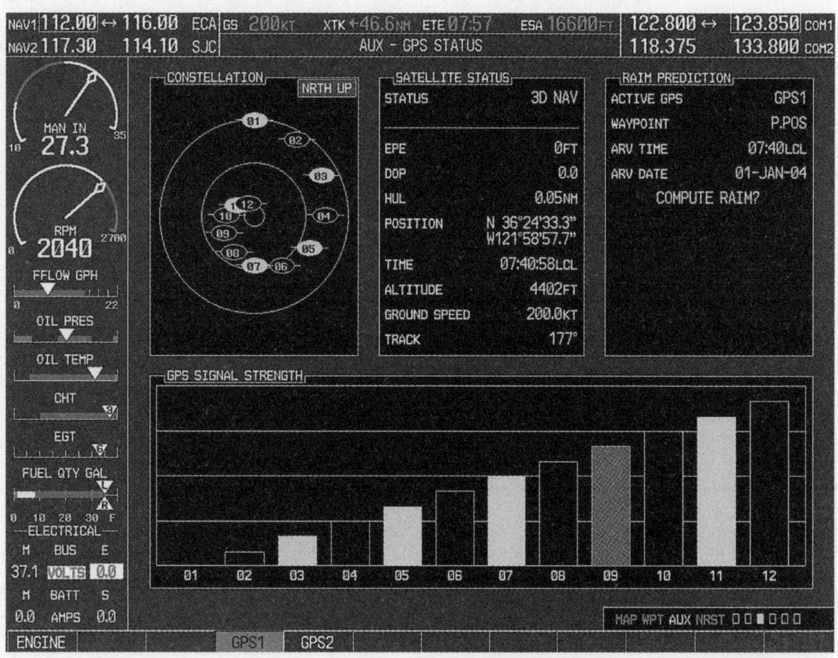

Figure 7-43 Go to the GPS Status page to verify that you have good signal strength for both GPS receivers and to calculate RAIM. *© Garmin Ltd. or its affiliates*

GPS Status Page

The GPS Status page (figure 7-43) is the third page in the AUX group. To access it, turn the large FMS knob until AUX is highlighted in cyan and turn the small FMS knob to find the page. It provides a visual reference of the status of the GPS receiver and allows you to determine in advance if the satellite configuration will allow you to use GPS when you reach your destination.

The ACTIVE GPS, which performs all GPS functions, is displayed in the upper right corner. In most aircraft, GPS1 is the first GPS receiver to receive power and become the active GPS, though occasionally GPS2 will come online first. The active GPS performs all GPS functions, while the other one is a hot spare that's ready to takeover in case of a failure.

The Constellation window, in the upper left of the display, gives a graphical representation of satellite positions. The outer ring represents the horizon, the inner ring represents 45° above the horizon and the center represents a point directly overhead. Circles represent the satellites and numbers correspond to the bar graph in the lower half of the screen that shows received signal strength. Circles and bars which are filled in indicate that a complete 30-second data transmission was received for that satellite; hollow circles and bars indicate that a complete transmission has yet to be received. If no bar is present, the receiver is still looking for a particular satellite and if a bar is checkered, the receiver has excluded that satellite's data from all calculations.

You can push softkeys GPS1 and GPS2 (or use the MENU key and select GPS1 or GPS2) to switch the bar graph display to show the signal strength for each receiver. Note that this is the best way to verify that both GPS receivers are operating, and it's highly recommended that you perform this check before takeoff.

The Satellite Status window, at the upper center of the display, shows one of the following status messages:

- ACQUIRING — The G1000 is acquiring satellite data and doesn't yet have enough data to establish its location and provide navigation guidance.
- 2D NAV — The G1000 is receiving at least three satellites and providing 2-dimensional data which is sufficient for course guidance, but which doesn't provide altitude data or the RAIM calculations required to allow using the GPS for an instrument approach.
- 3D NAV — The G1000 is receiving at least four satellites and providing 3-dimensional data including altitude.

The Satellite Status window also includes the following data:

- EPE — Estimated Position Error
- DOP — Dilution of Precision
- HUL — Horizontal Uncertainty Level
- POSITION — Longitude/Latitude coordinates of current position
- TIME — time derived from the GPS satellites
- ALTITUDE — GPS derived altitude
- GROUND SPEED
- TRACK — current ground track in degrees

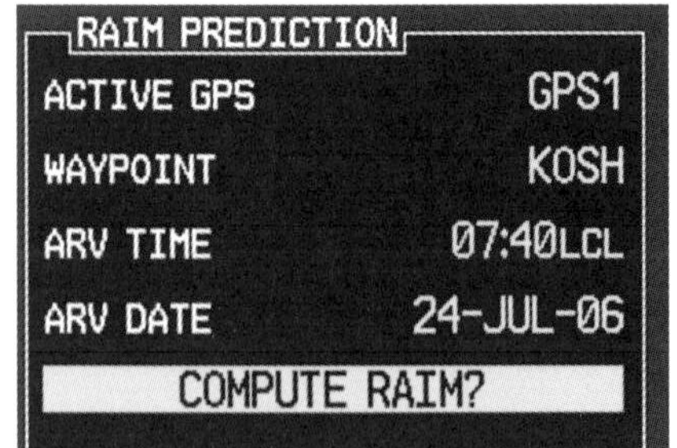

Figure 7-44 To predict RAIM, enter a waypoint, date and time, scroll to "Compute RAIM?" and press the ENT key. *© Garmin Ltd. or its affiliates*

GPS Status Page—RAIM Prediction

Receiver Autonomous Integrity Monitoring (RAIM) is a GPS receiver function that predicts, for a given location and time, the geometry of the GPS satellites and whether they will be in a position to provide the accuracy required for an instrument approach. GPS coverage is not universal, since the 24 satellites operate in low earth orbit and their positions are constantly changing. The orbits are designed so that at least five satellites will be visible most of the time; however, at higher latitudes (as you get closer to the North and South poles), RAIM warning messages are more likely to occur.

It's a good practice to check ahead of time whether you'll "have RAIM" when you arrive at your destination, particularly if you are flying in IMC. If you don't check, you may be surprised—and need to change your plans—if you receive a RAIM message while flying an instrument approach to your destination. If you receive the message outside the final approach fix (FAF), you must discontinue the approach. However, if you're inside the FAF, the receiver will continue to operate in approach mode for up to 5 minutes. You can also get a RAIM message if one or more of the satellites is providing erroneous data or if there are not enough satellites visible to calculate RAIM. For non-precision GPS approaches, a RAIM warning must be generated within 10 seconds of a fault occurring.

To predict RAIM, press the FMS knob from the GPS Status page and scroll with the large FMS knob to highlight the WAYPOINT field (figure 7-44). Using the small and large FMS knobs, enter the waypoint for which you'd like to calculate RAIM. If you're flying to a waypoint using the Direct-to key, your waypoint may already be properly loaded in this field. To check RAIM for your current position, you can press the MENU key, scroll to highlight "Set WPT to Present Position" and press the ENT key.

Next, using the large FMS knob, scroll to the ARV TIME and ARV DATE fields and use the small and large FMS knobs to enter the estimated arrival time and date at your destination. Finally, scroll to highlight "COMPUTE RAIM?" and press the ENT key. If you're predicted to have RAIM upon arrival, the field will display "RAIM AVAILABLE." Otherwise, it will display "RAIM NOT AVAILABLE" or "COMPUTING AVAILABILITY" if the computation is still in progress. If RAIM will not be available, you should plan to use a non-GPS instrument approach.

System Setup Page

The System Setup page (figure 7-45) is where you'll go to configure the many user preferences available within the G1000 and Perspective. It's the fourth page in the AUX group, and you can reach it by turning the large FMS knob until AUX is highlighted in cyan and turning the small FMS knob to find the page. Later software versions of this page include a Pilot Profile section, which allows multiple pilots to enter and save their own preferences for easy recall each time they fly the plane. Pilot Profiles are discussed at the end of this section.

The DATE/TIME box allows you to specify the format in which the time is displayed and to enter the number of hours from which your local time is offset from Universal Coordinated Time (UTC) also called GMT or Zulu time. You're not able to make any changes to the date and the actual time as both of these are derived directly from the GPS satellites which are highly accurate.

To change the time format, press the FMS knob and scroll with the large FMS knob to the TIME FORMAT field. Use the small FMS knob to select LOCAL 12hr, LOCAL 24hr or UTC and press the ENT key. To set your local time zone, push the FMS knob and scroll to the TIME OFFSET field. Use the small and large FMS knobs to enter the number

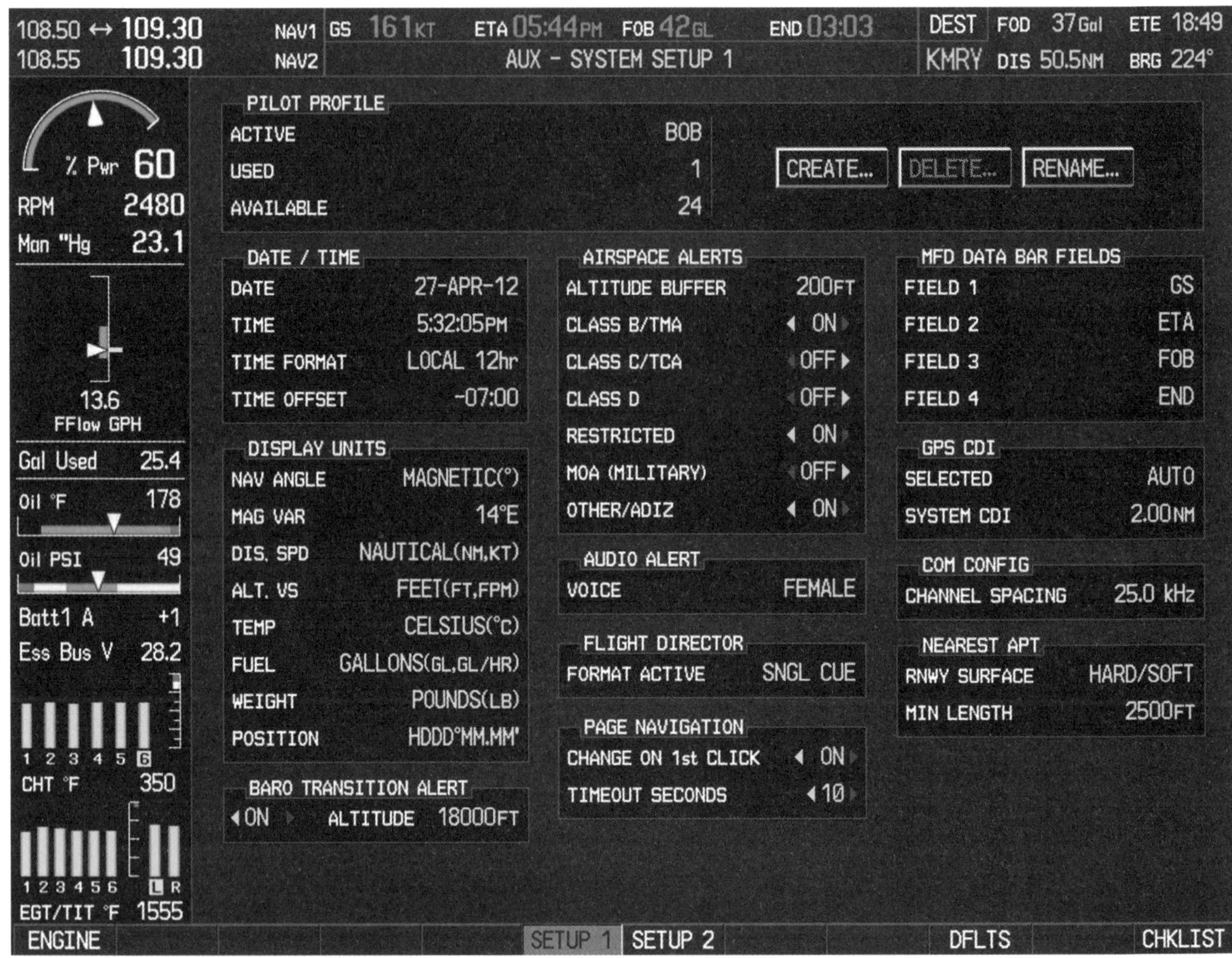

Figure 7-45 The System Setup page lets you set your preferences and store them in pilot profiles. *© Garmin Ltd. or its affiliates*

of hours and, in rare cases, the number of minutes your local time zone is offset from UTC. Press the ENT key and check the TIME field to ensure that it displays the correct local time. You'll need to adjust this field if clocks in your time zone are changed for Daylight Saving Time.

System Setup Page—Display Units and Map Datum

You can use the DISPLAY UNITS box to configure the G1000 to display data in different units. Alternatively, you can restore the units to their default values by pressing the MENU key, where "Restore Defaults" is highlighted, and then the ENT key. Default values are listed first below.

To change a data type, press the FMS knob, scroll with the large FMS knob to the desired field, turn the small FMS knob to select a data type and press the ENT key. The NAV ANGLE field lets you select whether track, course and heading information is displayed relative to true north or whether the data is corrected with the computed local magnetic variation to display data relative to magnetic north. If "True" is selected, the letter "T" follows all data to indicate this. "Auto," or "Magnetic" in later Perspective aircraft, is used to select magnetic north. The fields, their default values and alternate display units are listed below:

- NAV ANGLE: AUTO (°), TRUE (°T)
- MAG VAR: Magnetic Variation is displayed. It's not user settable
- DIS, SPD: NAUTICAL (NM, KT), METRIC (KM, KPH)
- ALT, VS: FEET (FT, FPM), METERS (MT, MPM)
- PRESS: INCHES (IN), HECTOPASCALS (HPA)†
- TEMP: CELSIUS (°C), FARENHEIT (°F)
- FUEL: GALLONS (GL, GL/HR), LITERS (LT,LT/HR)
- POSITION: HDDD°MM'SS.S", HDDD°MM.MM'

Map datums are sets of map reference points based upon a survey conducted in a region at a particular time. While many map datums cover the same region, they may show a particular point as far as a few thousand feet away from the same point using a different datum. WGS-84 is the primary datum used worldwide for GPS, though you may want to check whether another map datum is recommended for your country.

To set the map datum, press the FMS knob and scroll with the large FMS knob to highlight the MAP DATUM field. Turn the small FMS knob to select a particular datum and press the ENT key.

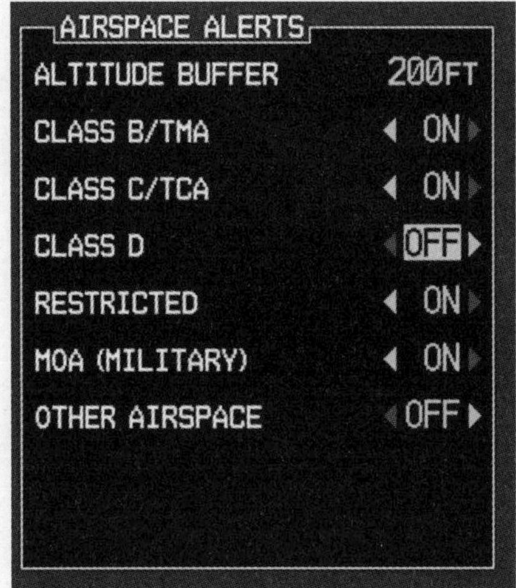

Figure 7-46 Use the Airspace Alerts to alert you to the presence of nearby airspace. *© Garmin Ltd. or its affiliates*

System Setup Page—Airspace Alerts

The AIRSPACE ALERTS box (figure 7-46) allows you to select for which types of airspace you'll receive Alerts messages on the PFD and how close in altitude to the airspace you must be to receive an alert. For example, if ALTITUDE BUFFER is set to 200 feet, the default value, and you're more than 200 feet above or below the airspace, you won't receive an alert. If you're within 200 feet vertically of the airspace and are projected to enter it, an alert message is generated. Note that turning off any alerts in this box does not change the airspace boundaries depicted on the Navigation Map page, nor does it affect any of the alerts on the Nearest Airspaces page.

Alerting can be turned on or off for the following types of airspace:

- CLASS B/TMA (Terminal Maneuvering Area)
- CLASS C/TCA (Terminal Control Area)
- CLASS D
- RESTRICTED
- MOA (MILITARY)
- OTHER AIRSPACE

To make changes to Airspace Alerts, press the FMS knob and, with the large FMS knob, scroll the cursor to highlight a field. For the ALTITUDE BUFFER field, use the small and large FMS knobs to enter an altitude and press the ENT key. For other fields, use the small FMS knob to select ON or OFF to turn altitude alerts on or off for that particular type of airspace.

† In Perspective and later G1000 versions, WEIGHT (pounds, kilograms) replaced PRESS, which can now be set with PFD softkeys.

System Setup Page—Arrival and Audio Alerts

Arrival alerts, available in more recent versions of the G1000 software, allow you to select the distance from your destination at which you'll receive an alert message. The destination is either the waypoint you've specified for Direct-to navigation or the final waypoint if you're using an active flight plan. Once you've reached that distance, the PFD Navigation Bar will display an "Arrival at (destination)" message.

To enable arrival alerts, press the FMS knob and scroll with the large knob to highlight the ON/OFF field in the ARRIVAL ALERT box. Turn the small FMS knob to select an option and press the ENT key. To set the distance, scroll the cursor with the large FMS knob to the distance field and use the small and large FMS knobs to enter a distance in nautical miles and press the ENT key.

The G1000 includes audio alerts, heard through the audio panel, to make you aware of situations like nearby traffic. You can choose to hear these alerts with either a male or female voice. To change the voice, press the FMS knob and scroll the cursor to the VOICE field in the AUDIO ALERTS box. Use the small FMS knob to select FEMALE or MALE and press the ENT key. Note that the volume of Traffic alerts can be adjusted, but you'll need an avionics technician to do it.

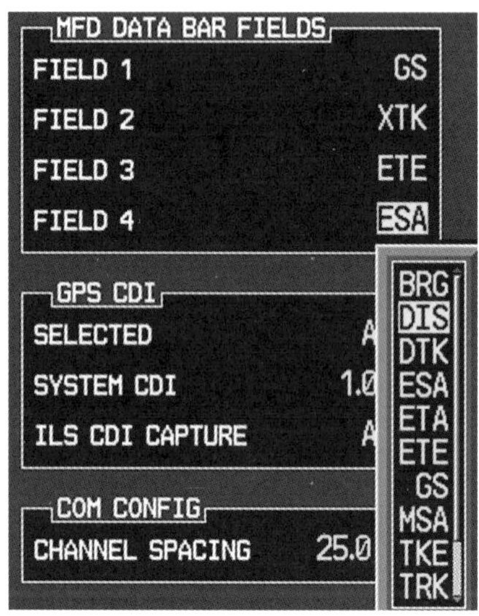

Figure 7-47 You can choose the parameters displayed in the MFD's Navigation Status bar. *© Garmin Ltd. or its affiliates*

System Setup Page—Changing the Navigation Status Bar

Both the PFD and MFD display four fields of information in a Navigation Status bar at the top of their respective displays. You cannot change the fields on the PFD, since they are specified as part of the aircraft certification; however, you can specify the ones displayed on the MFD. The default fields are, in order from left to right, groundspeed, XTK (crosstrack error in nm), ETE (estimated time en route) and ESA (en route safe altitude). You can change each of these four fields to display any of the following:†

- BRG (bearing in degrees)
- DIS (distance)
- DTK (desired track)
- ESA (en route safe altitude)
- ETA (estimated time of arrival)
- ETE (estimated time en route)
- GS (groundspeed)
- MSA (minimum safe altitude)
- TKE (track angle error)
- TRK (track)
- VSR (vertical speed required)
- XTK (crosstrack error—distance from the course)

To change the data displayed in any of the four fields, press the FMS knob and scroll the cursor to highlight one of the four fields in the MFD

TIP

XTK shows how far left or right you are from course and is particularly useful when flying instrument approaches. VSR is very useful when used in conjunction with the Vertical Navigation page, discussed in Chapter 9. It can be used to estimate the descent rate required for the final segment of a non-precision approach. To be most useful, you must look at VSR just before the final approach fix, where the system automatically turns it off.

† In Perspective and later G1000 versions, END (endurance), FOB (fuel on board), and TAS (true airspeed) can also be selected.

DATA BAR FIELDS box (figure 7-47). Then turn the small FMS knob to select an option and press the ENT key.

System Setup Page—CDI, COM Configuration

The GPS CDI box gives information about the scaling of the course deviation indicator (CDI), which is represented by four dots across the face of the HSI. A detailed discussion of the CDI can be found in the Navigation with the HSI section of Chapter 4.

When using GPS, the distance represented by the CDI scale can be either 5.0, 1.0 or 0.3 nautical miles from the center of the display to either full left or full right deflection, depending upon whether the GPS receiver is operating in en route, terminal or approach mode. The GPS will automatically cycle through these modes as it gets closer to the destination if it's operating in AUTO mode. More than 30 miles from the destination, it operates in enroute mode. Inside of 30 miles, it operates in terminal mode and, if an instrument approach is activated, it changes to approach mode two miles outside of the FAF.

If you wish to navigate more accurately all the time, you can set the CDI to 1.0 or 0.3 nm, and the higher settings won't be used. If you select 1.0 nm, the CDI will still change to 0.3 nm on an instrument approach. You can select the AUTO mode, 5.0, 1.0, or 0.3 scales by pushing the FMS knob and scrolling to the SELECTED field in the GPS CDI box. Use the small FMS knob to select a mode and press the ENT key. The current scaling is always displayed in the next field, which is labeled SYSTEM CDI. Note that WAAS-capable aircraft have a 2.0 mile scale instead of 5.0.

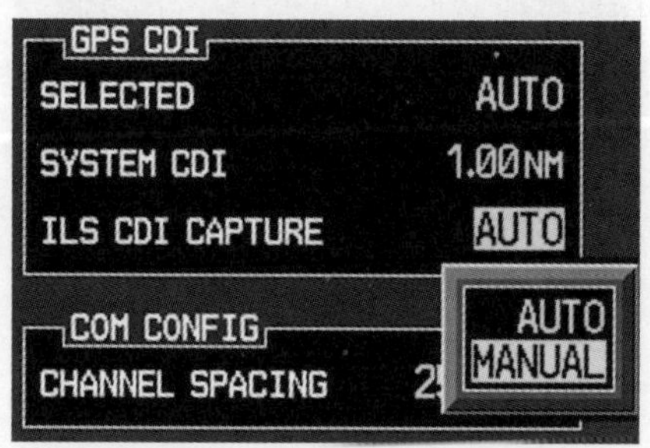

Figure 7-48 The ILS CDI Capture can automatically switch the CDI from GPS to an ILS signal. The autopilot will revert to ROL mode when the CDI switches. *© Garmin Ltd. or its affiliates*

As an instrument pilot, you always want to make sure that the HSI displays course guidance from the correct VOR or GPS receiver. For ILS approaches, it's not uncommon to navigate into the vicinity of an airport using GPS and then switch the HSI to display the ILS signal being received on NAV1 or NAV2. To protect you if you forget to switch the CDI, the G1000 has the capability to make this switch for you automatically. However, anytime the HSI switches, whether manually or automatically, the autopilot will switch to ROL mode.† This is discussed in more detail in Chapter 11. Note: Some aircraft, such as the Diamond DA40, state in the Limitations in the Airplane Flight Manual Supplement that the ILS CDI CAPTURE function must be set to Manual for autopilot coupled ILS approaches.

To set this mode, push the FMS knob and scroll the cursor to the ILS CDI CAPTURE field. Scroll with the small FMS knob to select AUTO or MANUAL and press the ENT key (figure 7-48).

The G1000 COM radios can operate with either 25 kHz spacing between channels or 8.33 kHz spacing. Currently, 25 kHz spacing is used in the United States while 8.33 kHz is used in some other countries. To set the channel spacing, push the FMS knob and scroll the cursor to the CHANNEL SPACING field. Then scroll with the small FMS knob to select 25.0 kHz or 8.33 kHz and press the ENT key.

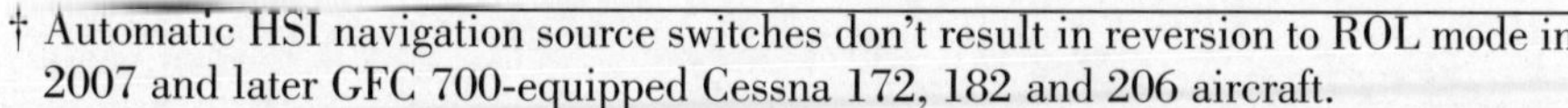

† Automatic HSI navigation source switches don't result in reversion to ROL mode in 2007 and later GFC 700-equipped Cessna 172, 182 and 206 aircraft.

System Setup Page—Nearest Airport

The NRST softkey on the PFD and the Nearest Airports page (figure 7-53) are easy ways to get information about the airports closest to your present position. However, if you have a high performance aircraft that requires a significant amount of runway to land, you may not be interested in knowing about shorter runways. In that case, use the NEAREST APT box to select your minimum criteria for an airport to appear when you push the NRST softkey or turn to the Nearest Airports page.

To set the criteria, push the FMS knob and scroll the cursor to the RNWY SURFACE field. Then scroll with the small FMS knob to select a runway surface type. Choose ANY, HARD ONLY, HARD/SOFT or WATER and press the ENT key. Then scroll to the MIN LENGTH field and, using the small and large FMS knobs, enter a minimum runway length and press the ENT key. Then press the NRST softkey on the PFD or go to the Nearest Airports page and confirm that only airports meeting your criteria are listed.

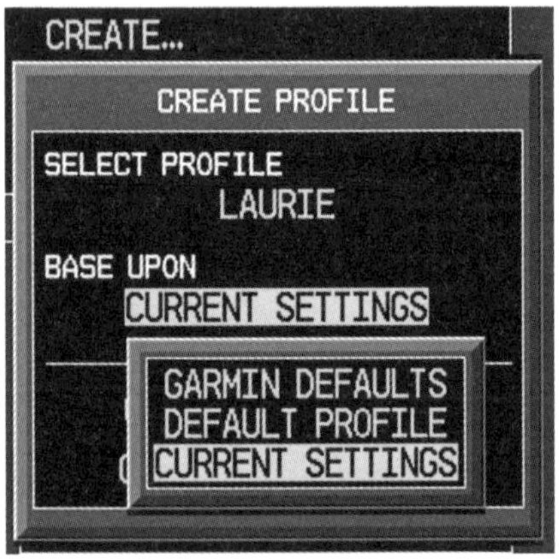

Figure 7-49 Pilot profiles make it easy for each pilot to save his or her system preferences. *© Garmin Ltd. or its affiliates*

System Setup Page—Pilot Profiles

If someone else drives your car, you know how annoying it can be to have to readjust the seat and mirrors each time. Likewise, if more than one person is flying a G1000 aircraft, each of them may have his or her own preferences for configuring the system. Pilot profiles let you create up to 25 profiles, each with its own configuration. You might use one profile for each person who flies the plane. Or, if you have different configuration preferences for different types of flight, you might create a separate profile for each. Early G1000 versions did not include pilot profiles, but most aircraft now ship with this feature.

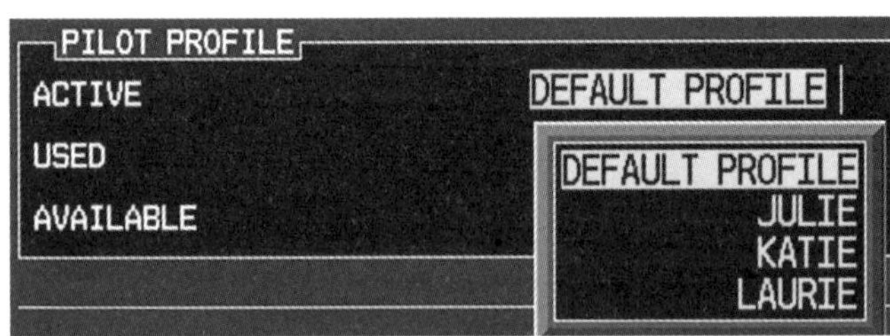

Figure 7-50 To use a profile, you must select it as the active profile. *© Garmin Ltd. or its affiliates*

To create a profile from the System Setup page, push the FMS knob and scroll with the large knob to highlight the CREATE field and press the ENT key. Then use the small and large FMS knobs to enter the name for your profile and press the ENT key. The cursor will move to the CURRENT SETTINGS field; press the ENT key to use the current settings for the profile. Alternatively, you can turn the small FMS knob to select GARMIN DEFAULTS, DEFAULT PROFILE, or the name of an existing profile, and press the ENT key (figure 7-49). Then, turn the large FMS knob to select CREATE and press the ENT key or select CANCEL and press the ENT key. Alternatively, select CREATE & ACTIVATE and press the ENT key, which will make your newly created profile active.

To use a profile, you must select it as the active profile. To do this, push the FMS knob, scroll with the large knob to the ACTIVE field and turn the small FMS knob to display the list of profiles. Scroll to highlight the desired profile (figure 7-50) and press the ENT key to make it active.

You cannot delete an active profile, so to delete a profile, first load a different one using the steps above. Then press the FMS knob, turn the large FMS knob to highlight the DELETE field and press the ENT key. Next, scroll to highlight the profile you want to delete and press the ENT key. Press the ENT key a second time to delete the profile or turn the large FMS knob to select CANCEL and press the ENT key to cancel the delete operation.

To rename a profile, press the FMS knob, turn the large FMS knob to highlight the RENAME field and press the ENT key. Next, scroll to highlight the profile you want to rename and press the ENT key. Use the small and large FMS knobs to enter a new name and press the ENT key. Press the ENT key a second time to rename the profile or turn the large FMS knob to select CANCEL and press the ENT key to cancel the rename operation.

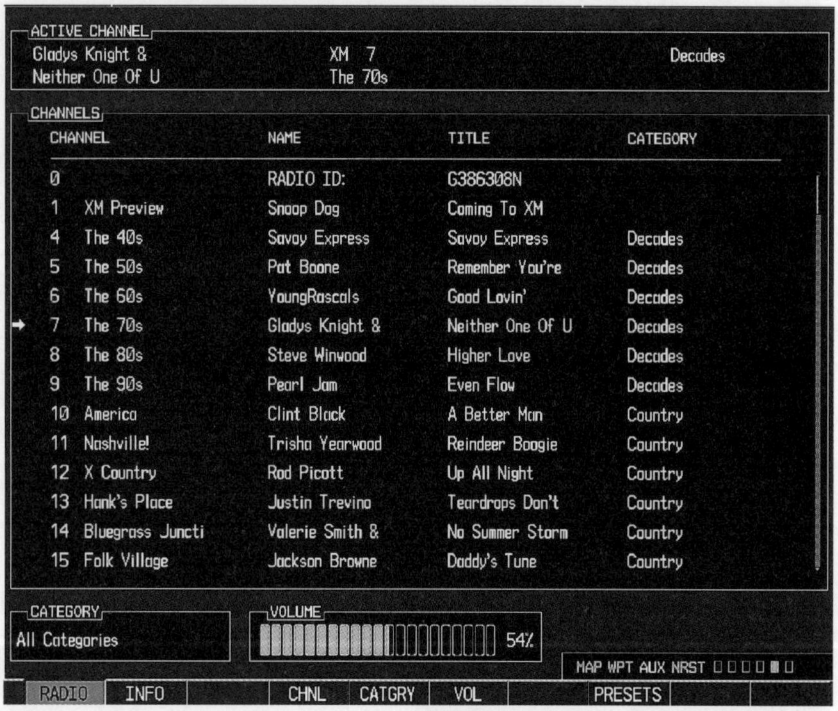

Figure 7-51 With a satellite radio subscription, you can listen to your favorite channels. *© Garmin Ltd. or its affiliates*

XM Information Page

If you have the optional GDL 69A data-link module and an aviation type subscription from SiriusXM, you're going to love this page and so will the kids! To reach this page, turn the large FMS knob until AUX is highlighted in cyan and turn the small FMS knob until you reach the page (figure 7-51). Pressing the INFO softkey or pressing the MENU key, selecting "View XM Information" and pressing the ENT key shows the list of weather products available through your subscription. The next chapter is devoted to describing these products.

To use the satellite radio system, press the RADIO softkey or press the MENU key, select "Operate Radio" and press the ENT key. There are three ways to select a channel: select from a category, press a preset softkey (much like your car radio buttons) or enter the channel number directly. If you're unfamiliar with the channel numbers, you'll want to press the CATGRY softkey and turn the small FMS knob to list the current categories of audio such as Hits, Rock, Country, etc. Highlight the desired category and press the ENT key. If you select "All Categories," you can use the CAT- and CAT+ softkeys to cycle through the categories.

Selecting a category loads all related channels into the CHANNELS window. To step through the channels, press the CHNL softkey and then the CAT- and CAT+ softkeys. Alternatively, you can push the FMS knob and scroll with the large FMS knob to highlight a channel.

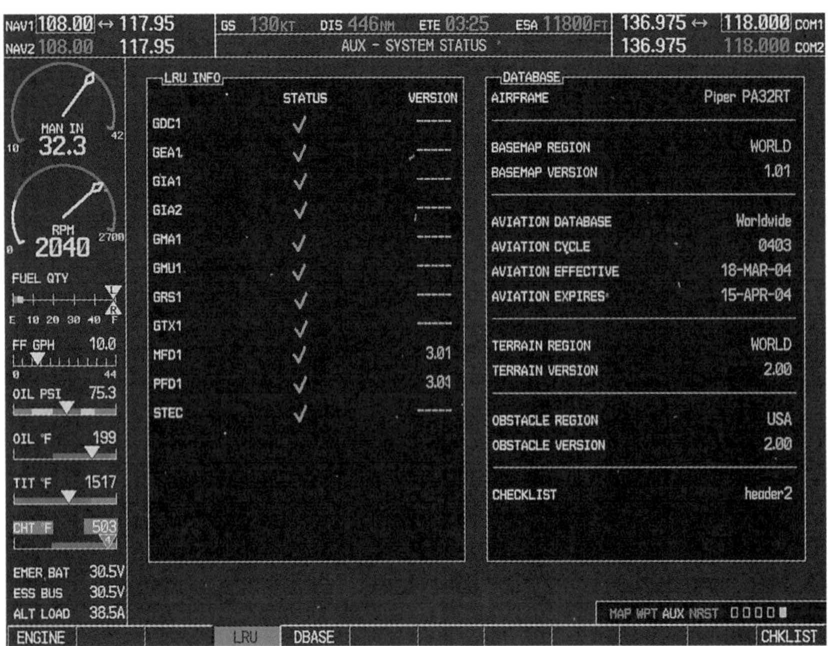

Figure 7-52 The System Status page shows the status of all system components. *© Garmin Ltd. or its affiliates*

Once you become familiar with the channels, you can enter a channel number directly. First, press the CHNL softkey and then the DIR CH softkey. Use the numbered softkeys to enter the channel number and press the ENT key.

You can also assign an individual preset key to up to 15 channels from any category. To preset a channel, select it as the active channel and then press the PRESETS softkey. Next, press the SET softkey and then one of the preset softkeys PS1 through PS15 (press the MORE softkey to reach all of these keys). To retrieve a previously set channel, press the PRESETS softkey followed by one of the PS1 through PS15 softkeys.

There are two ways to set the radio volume: using the softkeys or the FMS knobs. To select the volume control, press the VOL softkey or press the FMS knob and scroll with the large knob to highlight the "%" sign in the right corner of the VOLUME window. Then use the VOL+ and VOL- softkeys or turn the small FMS knob to change the volume. You can also use the MUTE softkey to mute the audio.

System Status Page

The System Status page (figure 7-52) is the only page where you can verify that all system components are working. For example, if your first GPS receiver (part of GIA1) has failed and the second GPS receiver has taken over for it, you might not be aware of the failure. Consider adding an item to your start-up checklist that tells you to view this page soon after engine start.

The System Status page is usually the last page in the AUX group and you can reach it by turning the large FMS knob until AUX is highlighted in cyan and turning the small FMS knob to find the page. A green checkmark indicates a component is working and a red X indicates that it has failed and that service is required. The page also indicates software versions for each component.

NRST Group Pages

Most modern GPS receivers include some type of nearest function, which gives you information about the nearest airports and is invaluable if the engine quits and you need to find a place to land quickly. In addition to airports, the G1000 and Perspective include separate pages with information on the nearest intersections, NDBs, VORs, user-defined waypoints, frequencies and airspaces.

The NRST page group is the last group and can be reached by turning the large FMS knob three or more clicks clockwise.† This makes it easy to find this group in an emergency—just give the large FMS knob a big twist and you'll reach the NRST group. Then use the small FMS knob to select a particular page within the group.

In most cases, there will be more facilities than can be displayed at one time. Whenever you see the scroll bar along the right side of a window, press the FMS knob and scroll with either knob to see the entire list and highlight a facility. This causes a white dashed line to appear on the map, connecting the airplane with the highlighted facility, which makes it easy to orient yourself.

You can also navigate directly to any airport, intersection, NDB, VOR or user defined waypoint on a NRST page. Just push the FMS knob, scroll to highlight the facility with the cursor, press the Direct-to key and press the ENT key twice.

TIP

If you own a G1000 or Perspective aircraft, you'll want to write down the software version loaded for every component in your system. Then, after each time a technician works on the system, check the System Status page to see that the correct software version—or a later version—was reloaded onto your system.

Like the WPT group pages, the NRST group pages have a large map on the left side of the page that you can zoom in and out using the range knob. The MAP softkey allows you to add layers of information to the map by pressing the appropriate softkey. These include TOPO, TRAFFIC, STRMSCP, NEXRAD, and XM LTNG softkeys. Like the WPT group maps, the NRST group maps use a "North Up" orientation, which cannot be changed.

Figure 7-53 The Nearest Airports page is one of the few pages where you need to use softkeys to access all of the information. *© Garmin Ltd. or its affiliates*

Nearest Airports Page

The Nearest Airports page (figure 7-53), the one you'll most likely need in an emergency, was purposely designed as the first page in the NRST group. Turn the large FMS knob clockwise until NRST is highlighted in cyan and turn the small FMS knob counterclockwise if you're not on the first page. The page displays up to 25 airports within 200 nm and contains information on:

- Airport identifier, symbol, bearing and distance to airport
- Airport name, nearest city, state and field elevation
- Runway designations, length, width and surface type
- Frequencies
- Instrument approaches

Most pages in the system allow you to use the large FMS knob to scroll across all of the fields. The Nearest Airports page is an exception. To move the cursor from one window to another, you must use the softkeys or the MENU key. For example, to scroll through the list of

† NRST is no longer the last group in later versions of the G1000 or the Perspective.

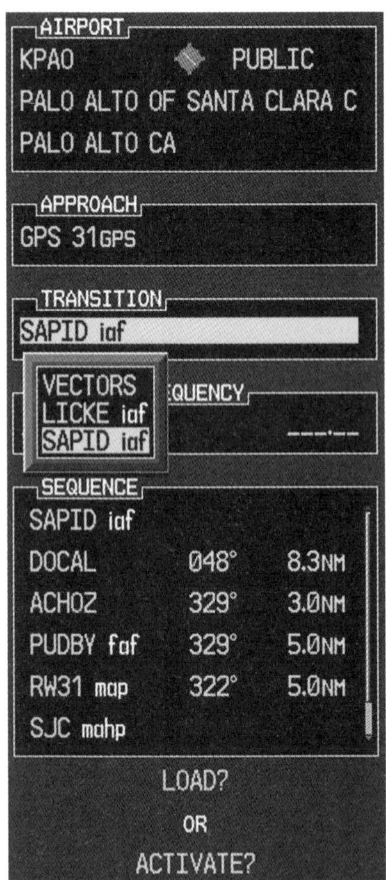

Figure 7-54 You can load an instrument approach from the Nearest Airports page by pushing the APR and LD APR softkeys. *© Garmin Ltd. or its affiliates*

nearest airports, press the APT softkey or press the MENU key, scroll to "Select Airport Window" and press the ENT key. Then press the FMS knob and scroll to select an airport. Information for that airport will now appear in the other boxes.

If there is more than one runway, a green triangle appears in the RUNWAY window. To view information on other runways, press the RNWY softkey and then scroll with the small FMS knob to view other runways. You can also use the MENU key to select the RUNWAY window.

You can load a frequency from this page directly into a COM receiver, or in the case of an ILS frequency, directly into a NAV receiver. Just press the FREQ softkey, scroll to select a frequency and press the ENT key. The frequency will be loaded into the standby side of the radio with the tuning box. Finally, press the Frequency Toggle key to transfer the frequency to the active field. You can also use the MENU key to select the FREQUENCIES window.

You can also load any instrument approach in the database for an airport. To select an approach, press the APR softkey, scroll to select an approach and press the LD APR softkey. This brings up the Approach Loading page (figure 7-54), from which you can select a transition with the small FMS knob and press the ENT key. You can then scroll to load or activate the approach and press the ENT key. Approaches can also be loaded from this page using the MENU key. Full details on loading instrument approaches can be found in Chapter 11.

Nearest Intersections Page

If you're an instrument rated pilot, you've probably had ATC direct you to fly to an intersection. If it's nearby, you may be able to find it on the Nearest Intersections page. To reach this page, turn the large FMS knob until NRST is highlighted and turn the small FMS knob to select the page.

To learn more about an intersection, press the FMS knob, scroll to highlight the intersection and press the ENT key. You'll now find information for this intersection in the INFORMATION and REFERENCE VOR windows (figure 7-55). Information displayed includes:

- Identifier, symbol, bearing and distance to the intersection
- Longitude and Latitude coordinates
- Information on the nearest VOR including identifier, symbol, frequency, bearing and distance

Nearest NDB Page

To reach the Nearest NDB page, turn the large FMS knob until NRST is highlighted and turn the small FMS knob to select the page. To learn more about a NDB, press the FMS knob, scroll to highlight the NDB and press the ENT key. You'll now find information for the NDB in the INFORMATION and FREQUENCY windows.

Information displayed includes:

- Identifier, symbol, bearing and distance to the NDB
- Longitude and Latitude coordinates
- NDB frequency in kHz

Nearest VOR Page

To reach the Nearest VOR page, turn the large FMS knob until NRST is highlighted and turn the small FMS knob to select the page. To select a VOR, press the FMS knob, scroll to highlight it and press the ENT key. You'll now find information for the VOR in the INFORMATION and FREQUENCY windows.

Information displayed includes:

- Identifier, symbol, bearing and distance to the VOR
- Longitude and Latitude coordinates
- VOR name and closest city and state
- VOR type and magnetic variation
- VOR frequency in MHz

To load a VOR frequency into a NAV receiver, press the FREQ softkey and press the ENT key. The frequency will be loaded into the standby side of the radio with the tuning box. Now, press the Frequency Toggle key to transfer the frequency to the active field. You can also use the MENU key to select the FREQUENCY window.

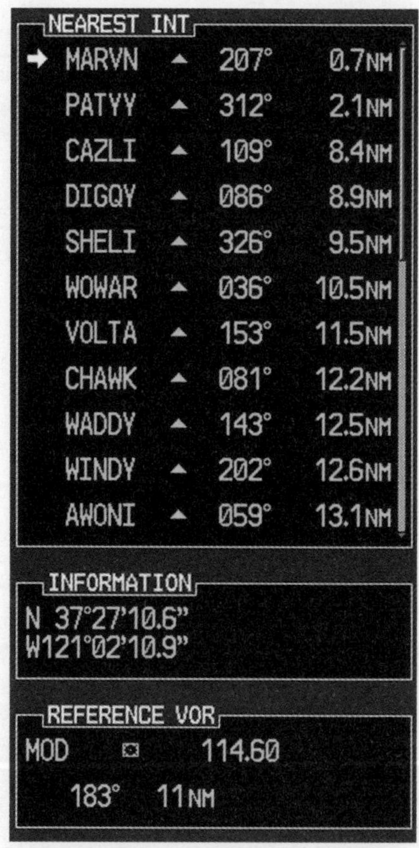

Figure 7-55 You can use the Direct-to key to navigate to a waypoint listed in the Nearest Intersections page.

Nearest User Wpts Page

This page will help you access any user-defined waypoints that you have created. To reach it, turn the large FMS knob until NRST is highlighted and turn the small FMS knob to select the page. To select a user waypoint, press the FMS knob, scroll to highlight it and press the ENT key. You'll now find information for your waypoint in the INFORMATION and REFERENCE WAYPOINTS windows (figure 7-56).

Information displayed includes:

- Identifier, symbol, bearing and distance to the user waypoint
- Waypoint comment
- Longitude and Latitude coordinates
- Identifier, bearing and distance to reference waypoint

Nearest Frequencies Page

One challenge all pilots face is finding the right frequency to use for flight following when outside major metropolitan areas, since they are not listed on sectional charts. The system makes a major contribution in that it makes it easy to find most of these frequencies. Its database includes Air Route Traffic Control Center (ARTCC), better know as "Center," and Flight Service Station (FSS) frequencies. This page doesn't, however, include Approach and Departure frequencies used in Class B and C airspace; these can be found in the Airport Information and Nearest Airspaces pages.

Like other pages in the NRST page group, a white dashed line is

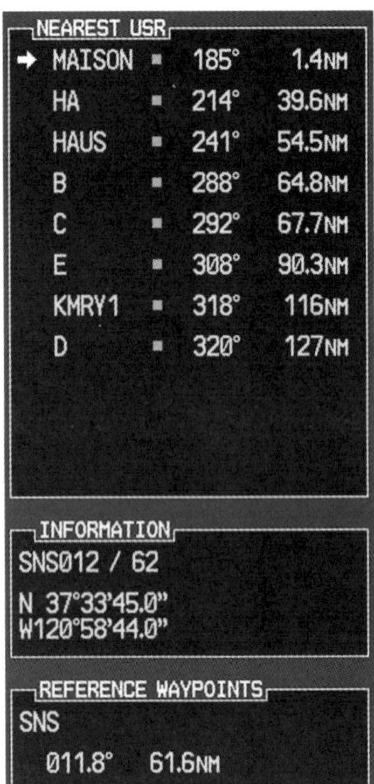

Figure 7-56 The Nearest User Wpts page lists user defined waypoints that you have created.
© Garmin Ltd. or its affiliates

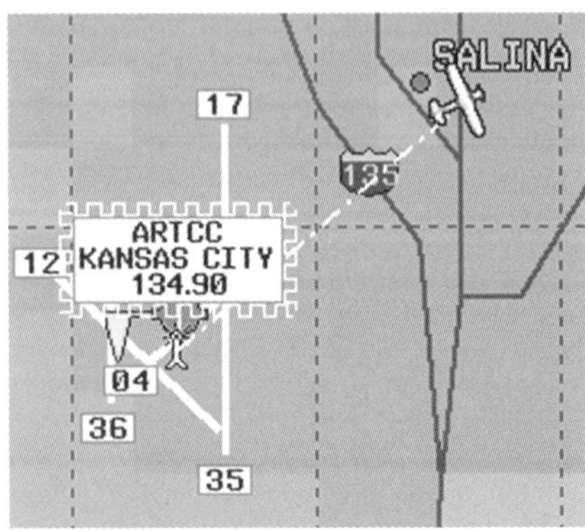

Figure 7-57 You find nearby Center and FSS frequencies on the Nearest Frequencies page. *© Garmin Ltd. or its affiliates*

drawn on the map from the airplane to the facility highlighted (figure 7-57). This is particularly useful when flying trips at lower altitudes, where you might lose radio contact with Center. If you do, go to this page and scroll through the nearby ARTCC frequencies until you find one in front of you, as shown by the dashed line. This is probably the next frequency to which you would have been handed off.

You will need to use softkeys or the MENU key to select different windows, as you cannot scroll between windows. To load a Center or FSS frequency, press the ARTCC or FSS softkey, scroll with the small FMS knob to select a facility and then scroll with the large FMS knob to select a frequency. Push the ENT key to transfer the frequency to the standby field of a radio and then press the Frequency Toggle key to transfer it to the active frequency. Bearing and distance information is also shown for these frequencies. To select a weather frequency, push the WX softkey, scroll to select a frequency and press the ENT key.

Nearest Airspaces Page

The Nearest Airspaces page is an excellent tool for tracking nearby airspace, particularly when you are flying in an unfamiliar area or in a crowded metropolitan area. Just remember to set the MFD for this page in these areas. You can still monitor your progress with the map on this page, although it is only oriented North up. Alternatively, enable airspace alerts in the System Setup page in the AUX group and each time the ALERTS softkey on the PFD flashes, press the softkey to read the message and go to the Nearest Airspaces page for more information.

This page displays and sends alert messages for the following types of airspace:

- Class B, C, D
- TCA, TMA, TRSA
- Prohibited, Restricted, MOA
- Alert, Caution, Danger, Training, Unspecified, Warning

It's easy to reach, since it's the last page in the last group. Turn the large FMS knob several clicks clockwise and then do the same with the small FMS knob.

The AIRSPACE ALERTS window (figure 7-58) shows a list of alerts prioritized according to their status label, with "Inside" alerts listed first and alerts that are still "Ahead" listed last. The different alert statuses are from highest to lowest priority:

- "Inside" — Aircraft has already entered airspace
- "Ahead < 2 nm" — Aircraft will enter airspace in less than 2 miles
- "Within 2 nm" — Airspace is within 2 miles, but aircraft won't enter on current course
- "Ahead" — Current course will take aircraft into airspace within 10 minutes

The alerts are based upon the boundaries of the airspace and the buffer altitude selected on the System Setup page in the AUX group.

For more information about a particular alert, push the ALERTS softkey, or use the MENU key. Then press the FMS knob and scroll to highlight an alert. Information about that alert is now shown in the AIRSPACE AGENCY, VERTICAL LIMITS and FREQUENCIES windows. The following information is shown:

- Type of airspace and controlling agency
- Vertical limits of the airspace
- Frequencies

To load a frequency or get more information about it, press the FREQ softkey or press the MENU key, scroll to "Select Frequency Window" and press the ENT key. To load a frequency, scroll to highlight it, press the ENT key to transfer it to a radio's standby field and then press the Frequency Toggle key to transfer it to the active field.

In cases where multiple frequencies are used for the same function, such as Approach or Class B frequencies, a blue "i" in a circle indicates that additional information is provided on the sectors and altitude information to which these frequencies apply. In these cases, scroll the large FMS knob to highlight the type of frequency, such as "Departure" and press the ENT key to see the additional information. Pressing the ENT key again or the CLR key will close the additional information window.

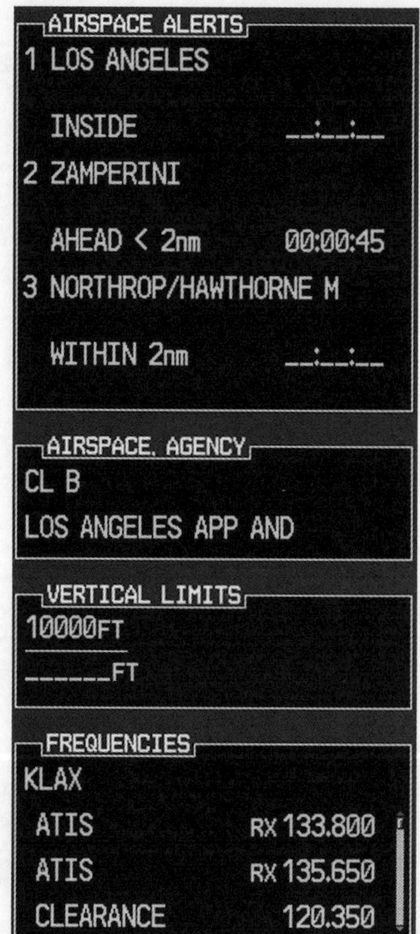

Figure 7-58 The Airspace Alerts window prioritizes alerts and gives frequencies for nearby airspace. *© Garmin Ltd. or its affiliates*

Summary

If you've gotten this far, congratulations! The MFD is a marvelous piece of technology which offers the potential to make your flying easier and safer. However, it contains a vast amount of information and managing it can at first seem daunting. Rather than try to learn it all at once, pick one or two page groups and gain familiarity with them first.

For example, the MAP page group is an excellent place to start, since it provides so much information and its most basic functions are relatively easy to use. Next, start using the WPT group, particularly the Airport Information page. Soon, you'll find yourself easily navigating the MFD and wondering what new features the next software revision will bring! When you're ready, read Chapter 14 for new features that have been added.

It's an exciting time of rapid change in aviation. Nowhere is that truer than in the rapidly emerging field of data-linked weather information, the topic of the next chapter. Hang on for the ride and have fun!

Chapter 8: Onboard Data Link Weather

Near real-time weather data, in the cockpit, is the ultimate in graphical information for general aviation pilots—at least until synthetic vision becomes available. Now, for a fee, it's available for any G1000 glass cockpit aircraft. If you're a clear skies, weekend flyer, you may not have much real world use for this data. If, however, you fly cross countries regularly, whether you're instrument rated or not, you'll find that data-link weather is an invaluable service that makes flying safer and more enjoyable. If you fly a G1000 or Perspective aircraft without a subscription to an aviation weather package, you can skip this chapter, or continue reading to see what you're missing!

Originally, the only way to receive onboard data-link weather in the G1000 or Perspective was to have a GDL 69 Data Link module, or a GDL 69A that receives weather and satellite radio for your onboard entertainment. New weather options include FIS-B weather via ADS-B and Garmin Flight Data Services (GFDS) via the GSR 56 Iridium Transceiver, described on page 130.

In addition, you need a subscription to an aviation weather package created by weather forecasters at WxWorx® and distributed via satellite through SiriusXM®. This is different from—and more expensive than—the subscription that you may already have for a satellite radio in your car. Currently, three packages are available: Aviator LT, Aviator and Aviator Pro.

If you're like the majority of pilots who fly normally aspirated aircraft at lower altitudes, the basic service meets your needs, particularly if your aircraft is also equipped with a Stormscope. Together with the NEXRAD radar, you'll be able to steer clear of problem areas. Yes, it would be nice to have the AIRMET data, but you'll get this information when you phone for a briefing before you leave, and you can always call Flight Watch on 122.0 for updates while en route.

The Aviator package is a good match for pilots flying at higher altitudes, whether they're in turbocharged aircraft or flying one of the new VLJ jets. If you're flying high in one of these planes, you're more likely to want to know how high the clouds are, where the freezing level is located and which flight level will provide the most favorable winds. If you fly at lower altitudes, particularly in cold winter locations, you may also be interested in the Aviator package. The new Aviator Pro package will be of most interest to business and commercial aviation operators.

This chapter is organized by weather product, first covering the services available with the Aviator LT subscription. Note that by the time you read this, the exact content of the aviation subscription packages may have changed, though the descriptions of the weather services themselves are less likely to change.

All of the weather services are accessed through softkeys on the MFD. Use the large FMS knob to select the MAP group of pages and then turn the small FMS knob to reach the Weather Data Link page (figure 8-1). You can simultaneously display most but not all combinations of weather information by pushing softkeys to add or subtract weather products from the display. In addition, a few of the weather products can be selected on the main Navigation Map page. For information on how to listen to SiriusXM® radio in the cockpit, turn to the XM Information page in the AUX group in Chapter 7.

Aviator LT aviation subscription package

The basic weather products package meets important needs by providing NEXRAD radar, TFR, METAR and TAF data. Table 8-1 lists the products in this package.

NEXRAD versus Airborne Radar

If you've ever watched a weather forecast on the local news, you'll recognize NEXRAD radar data. At the most basic level, it's easy to understand. Avoid flying where there's color, but if you must fly through it, try to stay in the green areas that indicate a lower intensity of radar return. Like most things that seem simple on the surface, however, there's considerably more to NEXRAD radar and we'll discuss it in detail in this section.

NEXRAD Radar is selected by pushing the NEXRAD softkey (figure 8-2) on the Weather Data Link page in the MAP group of pages. It brings up a box along the right side of the display that shows the "AGE" of the weather data and a scale for interpreting the colors on the screen. Note that the age displayed is the length of time since the weather data was received. However, at best NEXRAD radar data is approximately eight minutes old at the time that it's first received on board the aircraft and may be even older by the time you look at it.

Hence, you should use NEXRAD radar to develop strategies for avoiding wide areas of weather, not for determining where to penetrate a storm. It's highly complementary to airborne radar, such as the

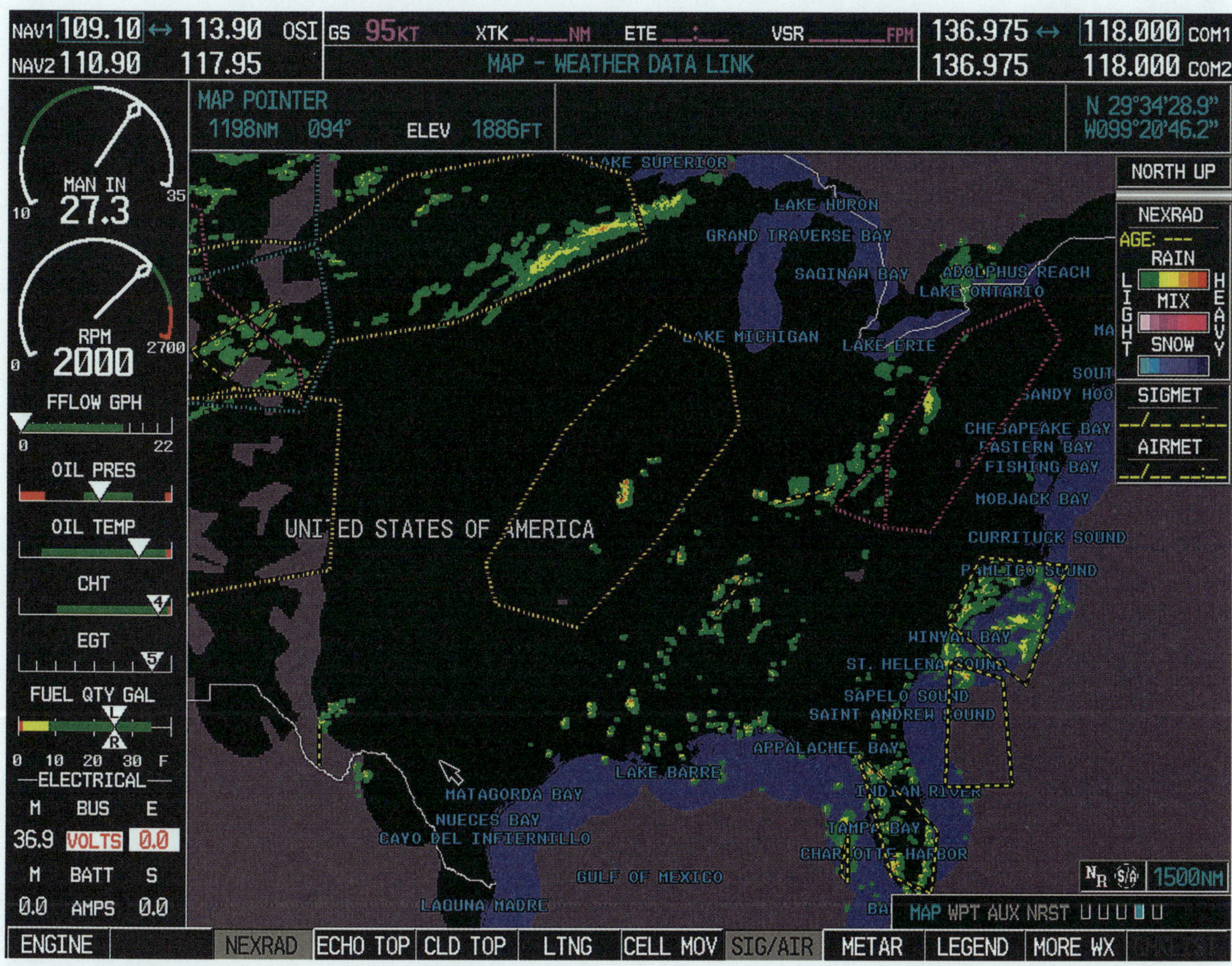

Figure 8-1 The Weather Data Link page displays weather data received through a data link module. *© Garmin Ltd. or its affiliates*

Garmin GWX 68, used in some G1000-equipped aircraft like the Beechcraft Baron.

In contrast, airborne radar data is real-time, so it can be used tactically to help determine where to penetrate an area of storms, though it does have limitations. For example, airborne radar suffers from attenuation, since heavy precipitation can block the view of weather beyond the first band of radar returns. NEXRAD data is generated from many powerful and overlapping ground radar sites and thus it can show weather that airborne radar is unable to detect. Using both types of radar data together can present a better overall picture of the weather. A full discussion of airborne radar is beyond the scope of this book, and Garmin GWX 68 radar users should refer to the approved Airplane Flight Manual Supplement for their system.

NEXRAD Radar

NEXRAD, which stands for **Nex**t Generation **Rad**ar, is a network of 159 independent WSR-88D Weather Surveillance Radar Doppler systems first deployed in 1988 and operated by the National Weather Service (NWS). It covers most of the contiguous United States, Alaska

NEXRAD | ECHO TOP | CLD TOP | LTNG | CELL MOV | SIG/AIR | METAR | LEGEND | MORE WX

Figure 8-2 Use softkeys to select which weather products to display on the Weather Data Link page. *© Garmin Ltd. or its affiliates*

Figure 8-3 WSR-88D radar located in the hills above San Jose, Calif.

and Hawaii. Doppler radar is unique in that it can determine the speed of objects as they move toward or away from the radar. This allows the NWS to detect the speed and direction of weather cells and the formation of tornados.

NEXRAD has limitations. It can detect most forms of precipitation within about 80 nm of a radar site and intense snow and rain out to about 140 nm. However, light rain or snow and drizzle from low level cloud systems may go entirely undetected.

This gap is caused because all weather radar systems have a certain amount of tilt angle, which means that farther away from the radar site, the beam is higher above the ground. The minimum tilt angle is 0.5° above the horizon. Also, many weather radar sites are located on mountain tops (figure 8-3), which puts their beams even higher above the ground.

The maximum range of the "short-range" radar product is 124 nm, and at that distance the radar beam will typically be at least 8000 feet above the ground. The maximum range of the "long-range" radar product is 248 nm and at that distance the beam will typically be at least 15,000 feet above the ground. Radar stations are located so that there is often some overlapping of beams, and storms below the outer reaches of one station may be picked up by the adjacent station.

The image displayed on your G1000 is a mosaic formed by adding together the 124 nm short-range radar returns from all of the stations, which enables you to see all weather detected by any station. Nonetheless, there are some areas, particularly in the west below 10,000 feet, which have no radar coverage, and these are marked in

Weather Product	Softkey	Description	Symbol
NEXRAD radar	NEXRAD	Color indicates intensity of precipitation. Data at least 8 minutes old.	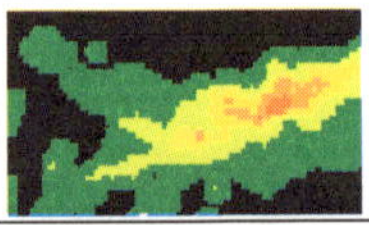
TFRs	TFRs are always on	Temporary Flight Restrictions due to national security, presidential movement, sporting events, etc.	 147
METARs	METAR	Hourly weather observations made at many airports.	 METAR WIND DIR: 10
TAFs	METAR	24 hour forecasts at selected airports.	
City Forecasts	MORE WX, SFC OFF, CURRENT	Forecast high and low temperatures and graphic for sun, clouds or showers.	 CHARLOTTE 87/66F
County Warnings	MORE WX, COUNTY	National Weather Service warnings about tornados, thunderstorms, floods and flash floods.	

Table 8-1 Aviator LT package meets basic weather needs.

grey on the G1000 when displaying NEXRAD data. Low level storms, beneath the beam tilts of adjacent stations, will also go undetected.

There are two different types of radar images: base reflectivity and composite reflectivity. Both display the echo intensity of energy reflected back to the radar site in dBZ, decibels of Z, where Z is reflectivity. Base reflectivity is a common image that's taken at the lowest tilt of 0.5° above the horizon. It's useful for detecting precipitation and hail potential.

Composite reflectivity, the type displayed on your G1000, is a composite image of data gathered from multiple tilt angles. Data gathered from each sweep at different angles is compared, and each grid square of data is painted with the highest level of reflectivity found at any height over that location. Composite reflectivity can help reveal information about the structure of a storm and the trend of its intensity.

Each radar site operates in either "clear air mode" or "precipitation mode," as selected by the radar operator. Clear air mode is the most sensitive, but also the slowest to update, since it takes longer to sample the volume of air around the radar site. In this mode, the maximum beam tilt is 4.5° above the horizon, and it takes ten minutes to collect the data to form an image.

When there's precipitation in the area, forecasters want to see higher in the atmosphere to analyze the vertical structure of a storm. Precipitation mode scans up to a beam tilt angle of 19.5° and operates at a lower sensitivity, since rain has a high reflectivity and sends back a strong signal. There are two scan speeds in this mode, and a complete radar image is updated every five or six minutes, depending upon the scan speed.

Note that since the maximum beam tilt in any mode is 19.5°, the air directly above the radar station is not sampled! Thus it's possible for a small storm directly overhead to go undetected. This area above the station is referred to as the "cone of silence."

The NEXRAD data displayed on your Garmin G1000 is shown in 2x2 km square grids. Any radar return from within a grid causes the entire grid square to be painted. The display color is determined by the strongest reflectivity or echo strength noted in the grid. The color scale begins at 10 dBZ and goes up to 75 dBZ (figure 8-4).

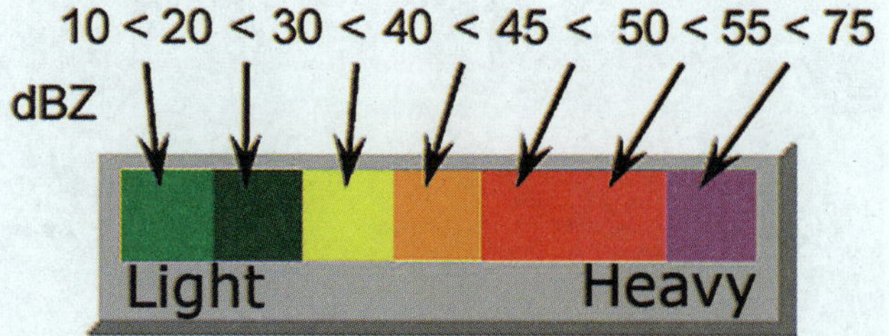

Figure 8-4 Light green shows the lightest reflectivity, while red and purple show the highest.

In clear air mode, reflectivity is measured between -28dBZ and +28dBZ. In precipitation mode, each radar site measures reflectivity from 5 to 75dBZ. While you'll never know for sure in which mode a radar site is operating, it really doesn't matter. Regardless of the mode, the reflectivity data received from the NWS is converted to the scale shown above and transmitted to your aircraft (figure 8-5).

Typically, light rain is occurring by the time 20 dBZ, the dark green color, is reached. Anything greater than 40 dBZ, the

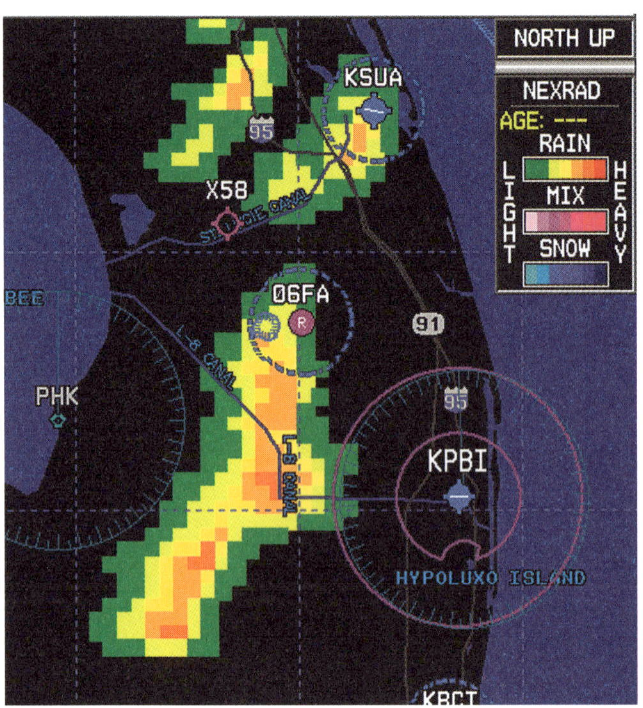

Figure 8-5 NEXRAD radar shows the location of precipitation. *© Garmin Ltd. or its affiliates*

orange color, should be considered convective activity associated with a thunderstorm. Greater amounts of turbulence are also associated with high dBZ levels. Stronger updrafts are required to hold larger, heavier raindrops aloft. Thus larger raindrops and stronger reflectivity are associated with stronger updrafts and downdrafts and hence greater turbulence.

The NEXRAD display also incorporates the Precipitation Type at Surface weather product. During the winter season, additional colors are used to display where rain, snow or mixed precipitation is most likely to occur on the ground. Greens represent rain, pinks represent mixed snow and rain, and blues represent snow (figure 8-5). Unknown precipitation below 52°N is displayed as rain regardless of actual precipitation type. Updates to this product are broadcast every 5 minutes.

Age of NEXRAD Radar Data

In the best case, some of the data you view in a NEXRAD image is at least eight minutes old. In precipitation mode, it takes five minutes to complete a scan of the atmosphere at the radar site. The data is sent to a central NWS computer where it's processed for a couple of minutes and then sent to SiriusXM®, which distributes the data your G1000 system receives. Updates are broadcast to your G1000 system every five minutes.

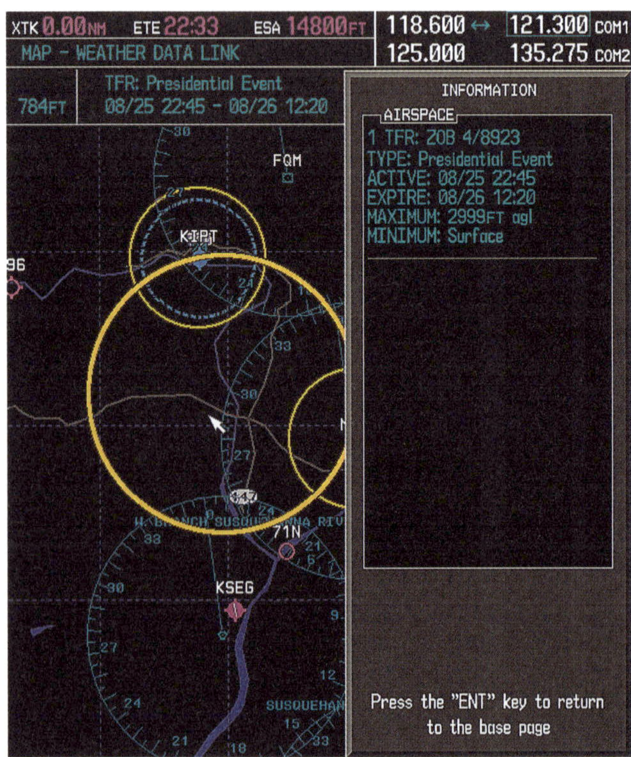

Figure 8-6 TFRs appear as yellow circles. *© Garmin Ltd. or its affiliates*

While eight minutes may not seem like a long time, consider that cumulus clouds can grow at up to 3,000 feet per minute. Thus, in eight minutes, cloud heights could have increased by 24,000 feet and evolved into a serious thunderstorm sending hail and turbulence a long distance from the clouds. Hence, your best strategy is to use NEXRAD weather data to steer well clear of any radar returns displayed. Despite its limitations, NEXRAD is one of the most useful data-link weather products, and you may want to leave it on whenever you fly.

Temporary Flight Restrictions – TFRs

Temporary Flight Restrictions exclude aircraft from portions of airspace. Traditionally, these were used for areas struck by forest fires or natural disasters to protect public-use aircraft fighting the fires or flying relief aid into the area. Since the events of 9/11, TFRs have become more frequent, and are also associated with national security, movement of the president and large sporting events (figure 8-6).

TIP
Add eight minutes to the "Age" of NEXRAD data, since the data is at least that old when it arrives on your display.

Pilots are responsible for knowing about and avoiding all TFRs along their route of flight. Inadvertently penetrating a TFR can lead to enforcement action and possibly the loss of your pilot certificates. However, identifying TFRs has been difficult at times, since they can appear with short notice and, in the case of "rolling TFRs," because they move to follow presidential motorcades.

With data-link weather in the cockpit, it's easy to identify and avoid TFRs, which appear continuously as yellow circles on the Navigation Map and Weather Data Link pages. For more details on a particular TFR, simply push the joystick knob and pan the map pointer to highlight its yellow circle. Press the ENT key for full details, such as the effective times, dates, altitudes and TFR type, displayed at the top of the MFD.

Unlike most weather products, which must be selected with a softkey to view them, TFRs are always shown on the display. They are updated every 12 minutes, so you'll always have the latest information on a TFR—even those created after you left the ground! Note that it's still highly advisable that you call a Flight Service Station before every flight to check for TFRs and NOTAMs.

METARs

METAR is the international standard for routine weather observations at airports. It's an acronym for "message d'observation météorologique pour l'aviation," French for Aviation Routine Weather Report. The METAR code uses abbreviations to communicate weather conditions in a concise, standard format. Updates to the METAR reports are broadcast every 12 minutes (figure 8-7).

The FAA's "Aviation Weather Services AC00-45E" book gives a full description of all METAR codes. A METAR report contains the following elements presented in this order:

1. Type of report
2. ICAO station identifier
3. Date and time of report
4. Modifier (as required)
5. Wind
6. Visibility
7. Runway visual range (RVR) (as required)
8. Weather phenomena
9. Sky condition
10. Temperature/dew point group
11. Altimeter
12. Remarks (RMK) (as required)

There are two types of reports: METARs, hourly observations taken between 45 minutes after the hour until the hour, and SPECI, nonroutine, special weather reports made whenever significant changes have occurred in the weather. Both reports use the same codes and format.

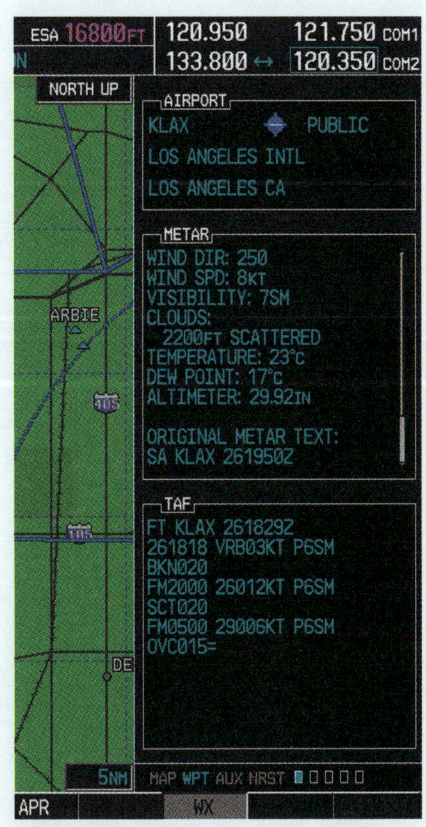

Figure 8-7 METAR data is presented in plain English and in coded format.
© Garmin Ltd. or its affiliates

To view METAR information on the G1000, press the METAR softkey on the Weather Data Link page. Colored pennant flags appear to indicate airports that have METAR information. The colors signify the category of weather present during the most recent observation. The code is:

Cyan – Visual Flight Rules (VFR) – ceilings >3,000 feet or visibility > 5 miles

Green – Marginal Visual Flight Rules (MVFR) – 1000 to 3,000 foot ceilings and/or visibility 3 to 5 miles

Yellow – Instrument Flight Rules (IFR) – 500 to 1000 foot ceilings and/or visibility 1 to 3 miles

Magenta – Low IFR – ceilings <500 feet and/or visibility < 1 mile

The flags are useful for getting a quick idea about the general weather conditions in a particular area. For example, they can indicate if weather conditions are deteriorating more rapidly than forecast and also identify frontal passages. Monitor the flags during flight and, if they change, consider changing your plans. Note that since METAR data is generally updated hourly, the change in pennant flag color may lag the passage of a storm front as depicted on NEXRAD radar.

There are a couple of ways to get METARs. From the Weather Data Link page, press the METAR softkey and then the joystick, pan the map pointer onto an airport showing a pennant and push the ENT key. In the METAR box, you'll see the plain English text for the latest report. Notice the scroll bar on the side of this box. This indicates that you can scroll down further, where you'll see the report in its original METAR coded format. To scroll, turn the large FMS knob until the cursor is in the METAR box and then scroll within the box using the small FMS knob.

You can get METAR data in nearly the same way from the Navigation Map page. Push the joystick, pan to an airport and press the ENT key. Then, press the WX softkey and you'll see METAR data if it's available for that airport. METAR data is also available from the Airport Information page in the WPT group. From this page, enter an airport identifier using the FMS knobs and ENT key and then press the WX softkey.

TAFs

The Terminal Aerodrome Forecast or TAF is a concise forecast of conditions expected during a 24-hour period within a 5-mile range of an airport's runways. The forecasts use the same codes as METARs and updates are broadcast to your G1000 every 12 minutes.

According to the FAA's "Aviation Weather Services AC00-45E," a TAF contains the following elements in the order listed:

1. Type of report
2. ICAO station identifier
3. Date and time of origin

4. Valid period date and time
5. Wind forecast
6. Visibility forecast
7. Significant weather forecast
8. Sky condition forecast
9. Nonconvective low-level wind shear forecast (optional data)
10. Forecast change indicators
11. Probability forecast

TAFs are accessed in the same ways that METARs are accessed as described above. Note that there is no separate TAF softkey; use the METAR softkey for both types of reports. A separate window, below the METAR window, gives TAF data for airports where it's available.

Note that relatively few airports issue TAFs, compared to the many airports that issue METARs. There's no easy way for you to identify which airports have TAFs, though, in general large, busier airports do. If an airport only issues METARs, then the TAF window is empty.

NWS City Forecasts

You can get a quick, graphical view of the weather forecast for major cities across the United States with the City Forecasts product (figure 8-8). Forecasts include the predicted high and low temperatures and a graphic indicating whether sunshine, partly cloudy skies or showers are forecast. Updates to the city forecasts are broadcast every 12 minutes.

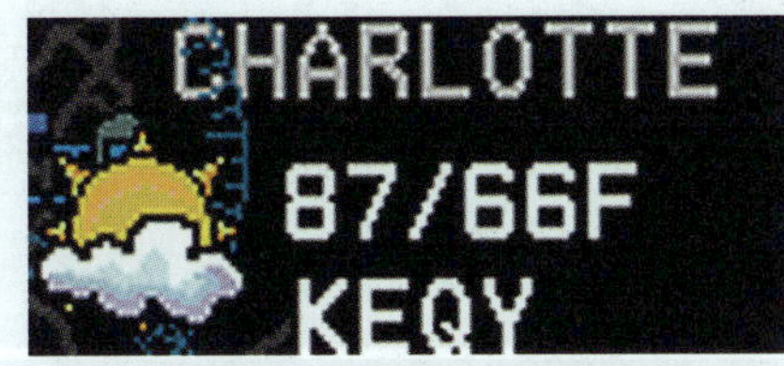

Figure 8-8 This City Forecast is for partly cloudy skies. *© Garmin Ltd. or its affiliates*

The City Forecasts are displayed whenever the Surface Weather Analysis Maps are selected. To display them on the Data Link Weather page, press the MORE WX softkey and then the SFC OFF softkey (figure 8-9). Then select the CURRENT, 12 HR, 24 HR, 36 HR or 48 HR softkey (figure 8-10) for the time period in which you're interested.

SFC OFF | FRZ LVL | WIND OFF | COUNTY | CYCLONE | LEGEND | BACK

Figure 8-9 Pressing the MORE WX softkey brings up these softkeys. *© Garmin Ltd. or its affiliates*

CURRENT | 12 HR | 24 HR | 36 HR | 48 HR | LEGEND | BACK

Figure 8-10 Pressing the SFC OFF softkey brings up these softkeys. *© Garmin Ltd. or its affiliates*

County Warnings

County warnings are generated by the NWS to notify the public about specific threats of tornados, thunderstorm, floods and flash floods. These are the same warnings you may have heard on your local radio or television station, often preceded by an emergency warning tone. You can access them by pressing the COUNTY softkey on the Weather Data Link page. Updates are broadcast every 5 minutes.

The warnings appear on the map as small colored circles (figure 8-11). Flash flood warnings are blue, flood warnings are light gray, thunderstorms are yellow and tornado warnings are red. To get details on a particular county warning, push the joystick knob and pan the map pointer to highlight its circle. This will bring up a text description of the warning at the top of the MFD.

This completes the list of products currently included in the Aviator LT aviation weather package. This package will meet your basic needs. You

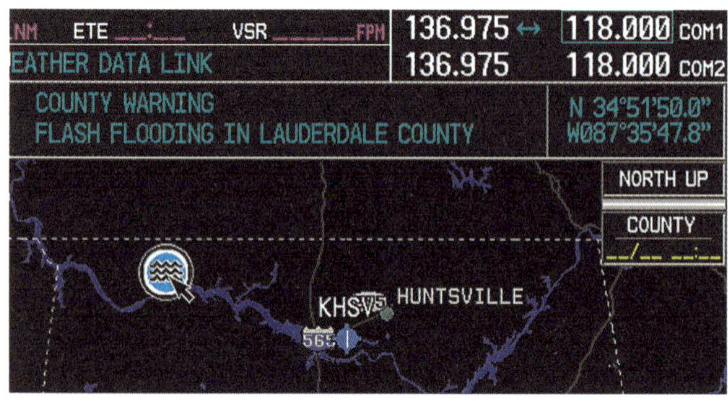

Figure 8-11 The blue circle indicates a county warning for flash flooding.
© Garmin Ltd. or its affiliates

can supplement it in flight by contacting Flight Watch on 122.0 for additional information, such as AIRMETs and SIGMETs, currently available only in the Aviator and Aviator Pro package.

Aviator aviation subscription package

The Aviator package includes the basic weather products described in the prior section and the products listed in Table 8-2.†

Weather Product	Softkey	Description	Symbol
AIRMETs	SIG/AIR	Weather hazardous to light aircraft.	
SIGMETS	SIG/AIR	Forecasts of significant weather hazardous to all aircraft.	
Echo Tops	ECHO TOP	Radar measure of maximum height of precipitation in clouds. Actual cloud tops may be higher.	
Severe Weather Storm Tracks	CELL MOV	Arrows identify strong storms, and provide information on forecasted direction/speed, hail size probability and wind shear	
Surface Analysis Weather Maps	MORE WX, SFC OFF, CURRENT OR 12 HR, etc	Shows high and low pressure systems at the earth's surface. Also shows location and direction of warm and cold fronts.	
Lightning	LTNG	Near real-time display of cloud-to-ground lightning, which occurs in later stages of storm development	
Winds Aloft	MORE WX, WIND OFF, SFC or 3000, etc.	Wind speed and direction in 3000 foot increments. Wind data updated hourly by forecasters.	
Satellite	CLD TOP	Cloud heights, based on satellite temperature measurements, in 5000 foot increments.	
Freezing Level	MORE WX, FRZ LVL	Contour lines indicate location and altitude of the freezing layer	8000FT

Table 8-2 The Aviator weather package includes all products listed in Tables 8-1 and 8-2.

† In 2008, Air reports (AIREPS), pilot reports (PIREPS) and Storm Prediction Center (SPC) Aviation Weather Watches products were added to the Aviator package.

SIGMETs

SIGMETs are forecasts of weather that extends over a widespread area and is potentially hazardous to all types of aircraft. They are unscheduled products that are valid for up to 4 hours and, over time, affect an area of at least 3,000 square miles. The G1000 can display both SIGMETs and Convective SIGMETs, which contain warnings of thunderstorm activity.

According to the Aeronautical Information Manual, SIGMETs are issued when the following weather conditions are expected to occur:

1. Severe icing not associated with thunderstorms.
2. Severe or extreme turbulence or clear air turbulence (CAT) not associated with thunderstorms.
3. Dust storms or sandstorms lowering surface or in-flight visibilities to below 3 miles.
4. Volcanic ash.

Convective SIGMETs are issued when any of the following are forecast to occur:

1. Severe thunderstorm due to:
   a. Surface winds greater than or equal to 50 knots.
   b. Hail at the surface greater than or equal to 3/4 inches in diameter.
   c. Tornadoes.
2. Embedded thunderstorms.
3. A line of thunderstorms.
4. Thunderstorms producing precipitation greater than or equal to heavy precipitation affecting 40 percent or more of an area at least 3,000 square miles.

To view SIGMETs on the G1000, go to the Weather Data Link page in the MAP group and press the SIG/AIR softkey. Then, push the joystick and pan the map pointer into one of the areas surrounded by a broken yellow line. The type of SIGMET will be listed at the top of the screen. For a full textual description of the SIGMET, press the ENT key.

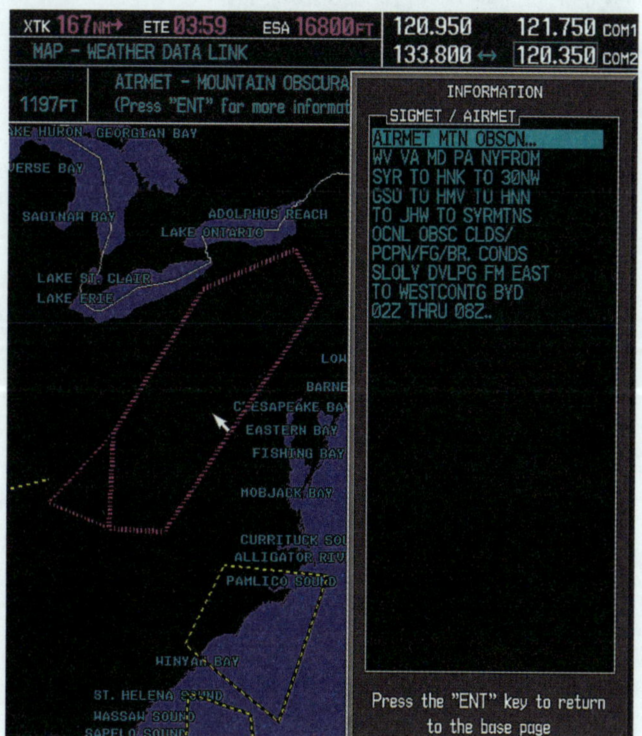

Figure 8-12 SIGMETs and AIRMETs are depicted graphically and described in text. *© Garmin Ltd. or its affiliates*

AIRMETs

AIRMETs are advisories of weather that is significant, but of lower intensity than SIGMETs. This weather should be considered hazardous to single engine and other light aircraft. They affect an area of at least 3,000 square miles and are valid for up to 6 hours (figure 8-12).

According to the Airman's Information Manual, there are three types of AIRMETs:

1. AIRMET Sierra describes IFR conditions and/or extensive mountain obscuration.
2. AIRMET Tango describes moderate turbulence, sustained surface winds of 30 knots or greater, and/or nonconvective low-level wind shear.

3. AIRMET Zulu describes moderate icing and provides freezing level heights.

AIRMETs are viewed on the G1000 in the same way as SIGMETs, though different colored boundary lines are used. The colors are:

Red – IFR or mountain obscuration

Orange – Turbulence

Cyan – Icing

To get the full textual description of an AIRMET, place the map pointer within the boundary of the AIRMET and press the ENT key.

Echo Tops

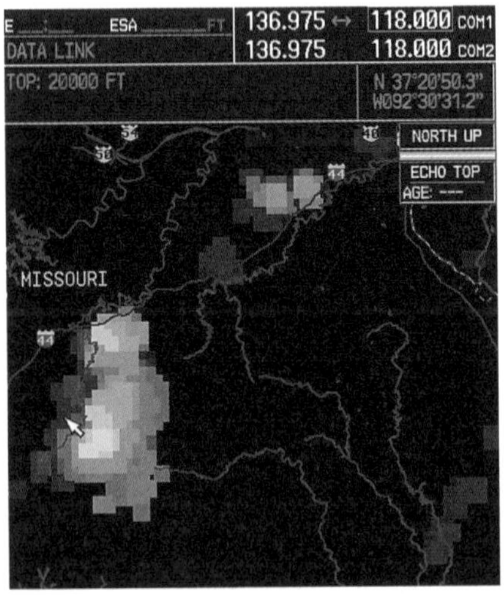

Echo tops (figure 8-13), obtained from WSR-88D radar, display the maximum height of precipitation in the clouds. The tops of the clouds, however, may actually be higher. Echo tops help indicate the relative strength of a storm, since higher tops generally mean more severe storms with stronger updrafts and more turbulence.

The maximum height of storms is generally capped by the height of the Tropopause. Over the poles, clouds may only extend up to 25,000 feet, while over the equator cloud heights can tower to over 50,000 feet. Thus, maximum echo tops will vary by region. Updates are broadcast to your G1000 every 7.5 minutes.

Echo tops should not be considered a reliable way to indicate how high you may need to fly to get above icing, even if you're flying a jet. That's because ice crystals or super-cooled water droplets may not have enough reflectivity to be detected. Thus, clouds and icing may still exist above the echo tops.

To view echo tops, go to the Weather Data Link page and press the ECHO TOP softkey. Then push the joystick and pan the map pointer over the clouds of interest. The height of the echo tops will be displayed at the top of the MFD. You can push the LEGEND softkey to see how the color corresponds to echo top heights.

Figure 8-13 Echo tops show the height of precipitation in clouds, though the cloud tops can be higher. *© Garmin Ltd. or its affiliates*

Severe Weather Storm Tracks

The Severe Weather Storm Tracks product uses arrow-like indicators to identify the location of stronger storms. In addition, it provides information on forecasted direction and speed, hail size probability and wind shear. The Severe Weather Storm Tracks are updated and broadcast to your G1000 every 1.25 minutes.

This is a new product that became available in 2006 with a software upgrade to the G1000. To view Severe Weather Storm Tracks, go to the Weather Data Link page and press the CELL MOV softkey.

Surface Analysis Weather maps

Surface Analysis Weather maps (figure 8-14) show the locations of high and low pressure systems at the earth's surface. A large "H" is used for high pressure regions, which usually denote areas of good weather, and a large "L" is for low pressure areas, which generally have poorer weather with clouds and precipitation.

The maps also depict the location of warm and cold fronts and symbols show the direction of the frontal movements. Maps are available in 12-hour increments for up to 48 hours, so they are an excellent way for you to see both the location of current weather fronts and how they are projected to move over time. Updates to the Surface Analysis Weather maps are broadcast every 12 minutes.

To display them on the Data Link Weather page, press the MORE WX softkey, then the SFC OFF softkey. Select the CURRENT, 12 HR, 24 HR, 36 HR or 48 HR softkey for the time period in which you're interested.

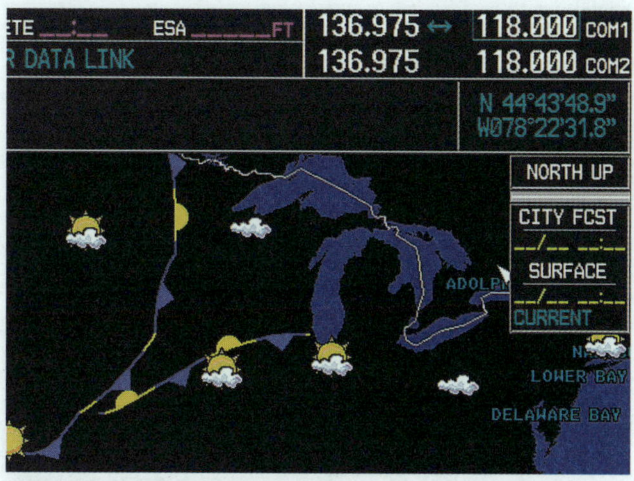

Figure 8-14 This Surface Analysis Weather map shows two stationary fronts. *© Garmin Ltd. or its affiliates*

Data-link Lightning

Lightning is a good indication that a storm is growing rapidly. Data-link lightning (figure 8-15) information differs, however, from Stormscope data, which is gathered live in the aircraft and was discussed in Chapter 7. Stormscopes detect all types of lightning, including intra-cloud (which often dominates in the early stages of thunderstorm development), cloud-to-cloud and cloud-to-ground lightning. Data-link lightning, however, only detects cloud-to-ground lightning, which accounts for about 10-20% of all lightning. According to NASA, cloud-to-ground lightning often occurs during the dissipating stages of a thunderstorm, so data-link lightning might miss a storm in the early stages of development.

The data is collected by the National Lightning Detection Network (NLDN), a private group, which sells data from their network of one hundred ground-based sensors that triangulate the location of lightning strikes. A lightning bolt is displayed in any 4 x 4 km grid that has had a cloud-to-ground lightning strike within the prior 20 minutes. The time, polarity and amplitude of the strikes are shown. However, only a single lightning bolt is shown regardless of the number of strikes that occur within a particular grid. Updates are broadcast to your G1000 every 5 minutes.

In contrast, the Stormscope will show every strike, which should assist you in determining the overall strength and location of the storm. Use both Stormscope and Data-link lightning strategically to steer well away from areas of lightning.

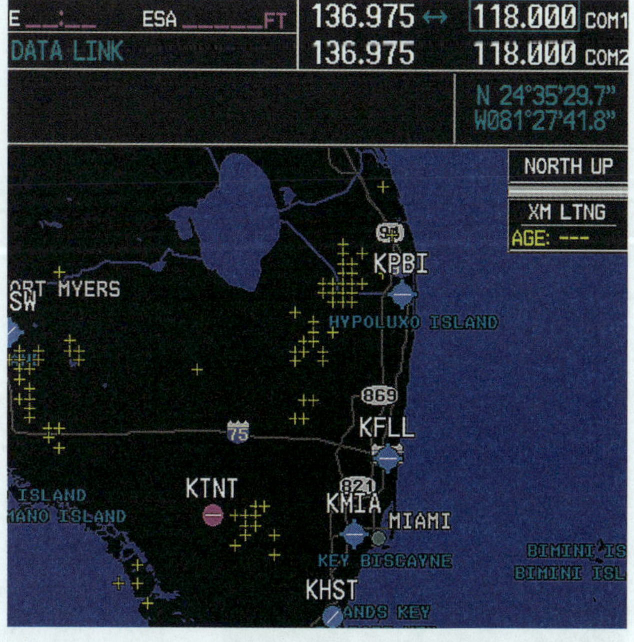

Figure 8-15 Data-link lightning only detects cloud-to-ground lightning. *© Garmin Ltd. or its affiliates*

To view data-link lightning from the Navigation Map page, press the MAP softkey and then the XM LTNG softkey. You can also view it from the Weather Data Link page by pressing the LTNG softkey. Note that you can display either data-link lightning or Stormscope lightning data, but not both at the same time

Figure 8-16 Winds aloft data is updated hourly. *© Garmin Ltd. or its affiliates*

Winds Aloft

Winds Aloft data (figure 8-16) is invaluable for selecting an altitude that gives you the best tailwind or perhaps the least headwind. Rather than climb thousands of feet to determine what the winds are doing, use the Winds Aloft data, updated hourly by the WxWorx weather forecasters, to get a graphical presentation of wind direction and velocity. These winds will generally be more accurate than the winds aloft forecast from the NWS, which are based upon data collected by balloons that are released only twice a day. Updates to the Winds Aloft product are broadcast to your G1000 every 12 minutes.

Wind speed and direction are provided from the surface up to 42,000 feet in 3,000 foot increments. To display this product from the Weather Data Link page, press the MORE WX softkey and then the WIND OFF softkey, which will bring up a new set of softkeys (figure 8-17) for different altitudes. Press, for example, the 6000 softkey to see winds at that altitude. Press the NEXT softkey to choose altitudes above 15,000 feet.

Weather speeds are displayed with standard wind symbols, which use a line to indicate wind direction and feathers along the line to indicate wind speed. Long feathers are 10 knots each while short feathers are 5 knots. For winds in excess of 50 knots, a pennant is shown. If you forget the wind symbols, just press the LEGEND softkey to see them.

PREV | OFF | SFC | 3000 | 6000 | 9000 | 12000 | 15000 | NEXT | LEGEND | BACK

Figure 8-17 Pressing the WIND OFF softkey brings up these new softkeys. *© Garmin Ltd. or its affiliates*

Satellite

Satellite imagery (figure 8-18) shows you where clouds are located and how high they are. You'll find this useful if, for example, you're flying to a coastal city and want to see if clouds have moved onshore covering your destination. Or it can give you a general idea of cloud top heights, which are determined by measuring the temperature of the cloud tops. You'll only get a relative indication of height though, since the data is presented in 5,000 foot increments.

The Satellite product uses infrared composite cloud images taken by NOAA geostationary weather satellites, the same ones which provide the satellite pictures you see on you local television news. Eight levels of cloud height are displayed and updates are broadcast to your G1000 every 15 minutes. To access this product from the Weather Data Link page, push the CLD TOP softkey.

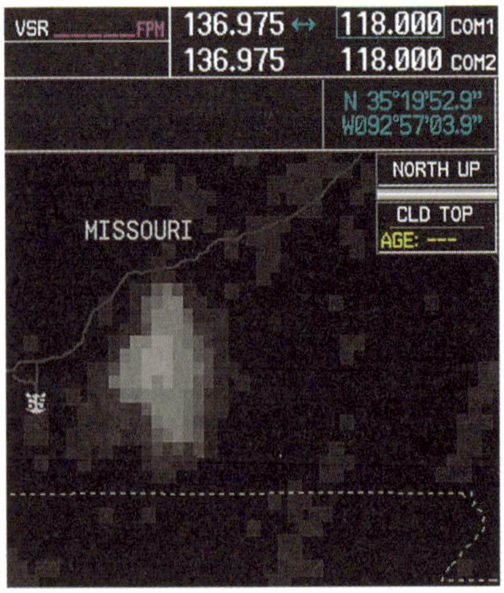

Figure 8-18 Push the CLD TOP softkey for satellite imagery. *© Garmin Ltd. or its affiliates*

Freezing Level

The Freezing Level product (figure 8-19) uses contour lines to indicate locations and altitudes where the air temperature is approximately 32°F, the temperature at which water freezes. If you fly IFR, you'll want to know the height of the freezing level, since above that level, you're likely to encounter icing in clouds. About 80% of the time, the layer of icing is no more than 4000 feet thick, so if you can rapidly climb through this layer, you may be okay. While jets and, under some circumstances, turbocharged aircraft may be able to climb through the icing layer, normally aspirated aircraft might not be able to escape the ice by climbing. Encountering icing in any aircraft is a serious matter and you should take immediate action to escape the ice.

This is a new product that becomes available in 2006 with a software upgrade to the G1000. To access it from the Weather Data Link page, push the MORE WX softkey and then the FRZ LVL softkey. Updates to your G1000 are broadcast every 15 minutes.

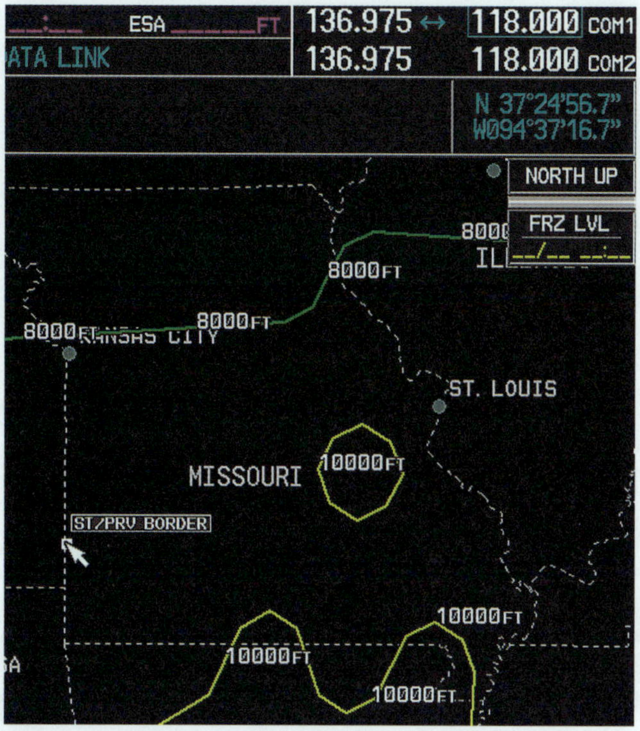

Figure 8-19 Contour lines show the location and altitude of the freezing level. *© Garmin Ltd. or its affiliates*

PIREPS and AIREPS

A Pilot Report or PIREP summarizes actual weather conditions encountered by an aircraft. An Air Report or AIREP is similar, but used primarily by commercial airlines. To display these products, press the MORE WX softkey and then the PIREPS or AIREPS softkey. Then press the joystick, pan to select a report, and press the ENT key.

Aviator Pro subscription

In July 2008, SiriusXM announced the new Aviator Pro package. It includes all of the products in the Aviator package plus the following new weather products:

Turbulence

The turbulence product (figure 8-20) is a 2-hour forecast, updated hourly, that identifies the potential for clear air turbulence. Turbulence is classified as light, moderate or severe at altitudes between 21,000 and 45,000 feet in 3,000 ft. increments.

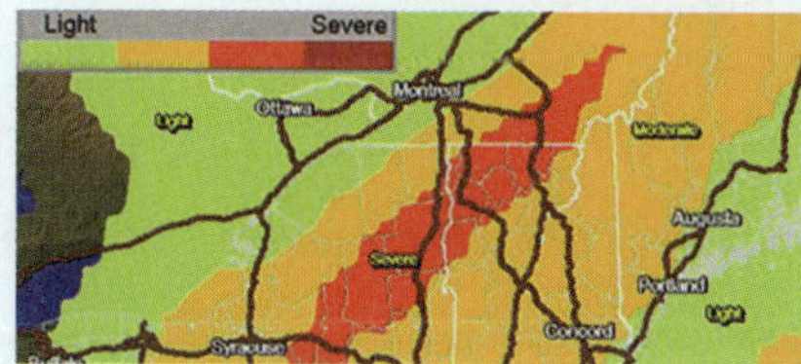

Figure 8-20 Color indicates the severity of turbulence, but only between 21,000 and 45,000 feet.

Storm Prediction Center (SPC)

The Day 1 Convective Outlook provides a text synopsis of severe thunderstorm threats across the continental United States. Threat levels are classified as slight, moderate or high. The SPC Mesoscale Discussion provides text identifying current severe weather threats before they reach the threshold for a watch to be issued. SPC Mesoscale Discussions are occasionally issued for heavy rain or convective trends.

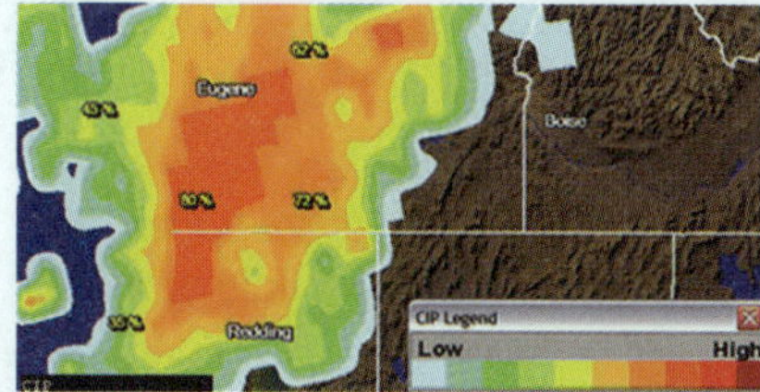

Figure 8-21 Color indicates the severity of icing between 1,000 and 30,000 feet.

Icing Current Icing Product (CIP)

The Current Icing Product (CIP) (figure 8-21), updated hourly, identifies the current icing environment by altitude from 1,000 – 30,000 feet in 3,000 ft. increments. Icing is classified by the percentage probability or by one of five levels of severity: none, trace, light, moderate or heavy.

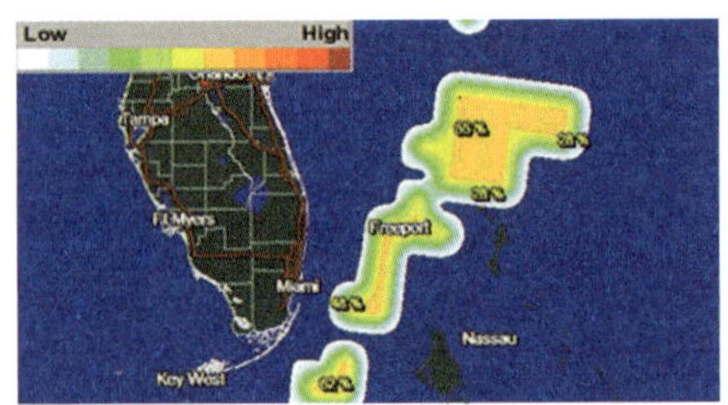

Table 8-22 Color indicates the level of probability of large, supercooled water droplets

Icing Supercooled Large Droplets (SLD)

The SLD icing product (figure 8-22) identifies the presence of large, supercooled water droplets, indicative of freezing drizzle and freezing rain aloft, at altitudes from 1,000 – 30,000 feet in 3,000 ft. increments. The product is classified by percentage of probability or one of five levels of severity: none, trace, light, moderate or heavy.

Visibility

For areas with estimated visibilities of less than ten nautical miles, the product identifies visibility in one nautical mile increments.

Hurricane Tracks

This product gives a five-day incremental forecast of hurricane location, strength, and associated wind speed and direction.

Other Weather Sources

Worldwide weather reception is available from Garmin Flight Data Services through the optional GSR 56 Iridium satellite data link. In the U.S., free FIS-B weather data, broadcast by FAA ADS-B ground stations, can be received through the optional GDL 90 ADS-B Transceiver. If you have weather from multiple services, you must select which one you'd like to view. From the Weather Data Link page press the MENU key, scroll to select a weather service (e.g. "Display FIS-B Weather"), and press the ENT key. Weather products from the three services sometimes use different names for similar products. Table 8-3 summarizes the differences.

SiriusXM Product (Softkey)	Garmin GFDS Product (Softkey)	FAA FIS-B Product (Softkey)
High-Res Radar (NEXRAD)	Precipitation (PRECIP)	Precipitation (PRECIP)
Satellite (CLD TOP)	Infrared Satellite (IR SAT)	N/A
Lightning (XM LTNG)	GFDS Lightning (DL LTNG)	N/A
SIGMETs/AIRMETs (SIG/AIR)	SIGMETs/AIRMETs (SIG/AIR)	N/A
METARs/TAFs (METAR)	METARs/TAFs (METAR)	METARs/TAFs (METAR)
Winds Aloft (WIND OFF)	Winds Aloft (WIND OFF)	N/A
Pilot Reports (PIREPS)	Pilot Reports (PIREPS)	N/A

Table 8-3 Weather services, their products, and corresponding softkey names.

Summary

Weather continues to be the cause of a significant number of aircraft accidents. However, onboard datalink weather offers the potential to eliminate these accidents—if you understand how to use it and exercise good judgment. If you can afford to fly, you probably can't afford to be without this valuable service.

If you're going to fly a glass cockpit aircraft, you'll want to use the GPS receiver in more ways than just pressing the Direct-to key. To learn the basics of GPS flight planning for any flight, read the next chapter. If you're an instrument rated pilot, read Chapter 11 to learn about flight plans and how to fly instrument approaches with the G1000.

Chapter 9:
Flight Planning with the G1000

Anyone with Garmin GNS 430 or GNS 530 experience will feel instantly at home when flight planning with the G1000 or Perspective. In fact, practicing flight planning on these panel mount systems, whether with the actual GPS or the software simulators, is excellent preparation. What experienced users may not notice at first, however, is that while they can program the G1000 or Perspective in the same way to which they are accustomed, it also offers new ways to program with fewer keystrokes! So even experienced Garmin users can benefit from this chapter by learning how to operate the system most efficiently.

For VFR flight, knowledge about the flight planning functions is nice to have, but not essential, since you can always fall back upon traditional navigation using maps, pilotage and VOR navigation. Of course, for IFR flight you'll want to know how to use the flight planning functions well.

Regardless of whether you're an instrument rated pilot, you might start by using the "Direct-to" function of the GPS, since this will address many of your needs in a VFR environment. Soon, you'll want to progress to entering and using a flight plan, which is separate from but related to the Direct-to function. Finally, as an instrument pilot, you'll want to start using procedures specific to instrument flight.

The G1000 was the first glass cockpit that let pilots flight plan from either the MFD or PFD, though there are some minor limitations to the use of the latter display. To simplify the discussion, we'll focus first on programming common to both the PFD and MFD and later discuss differences unique to flight planning with the MFD. We'll start by discussing the simpler "Direct-to navigation" and later cover navigation with flight plans. These functions, important for any flight, are discussed in this chapter, while IFR specific procedures are discussed in Chapter 11.

Direct-to Navigation vs. Active Flight Plan

The Direct-to function, accessed by pressing the Direct-to key (figure 9-9) on either the PFD or MFD, is a less powerful though easier to use alternative to the Active Flight Plan page. You'll find it useful if you want to fly a direct course from your current position to a single point, such as a nearby airport where you plan to land.

When flying to a more distant airport, you often won't fly direct, particularly if you need to avoid terrain and special use airspace such as restricted areas. In that case, you'd probably find it easier to use the FPL key and enter all of the intermediate points for your trip into the Active Flight Plan page. If, however, you didn't know how to use that page, you could alternatively use the Direct-to function and, as you reached each waypoint, enter the next waypoint. This is less convenient and may lead to brief periods of time when you don't know what heading to fly, since you haven't yet entered the next waypoint with the Direct-to function. Nonetheless, some people use this approach to fly with a GPS receiver if they don't know how to use the flight planning pages. Hopefully these people are not flying IFR!

You should treat the Flight Plan page and Direct-to navigation as separate functions and be very careful about mixing their use. For example, many people will load a series of waypoints into the Active Flight Plan page and later use the Direct-to key to enter a new waypoint and fly directly to that waypoint. What they may not realize is that the waypoint was NOT added to their flight plan, which, while still active, is no longer being used. After they reach the waypoint entered with the Direct-to key, they will no longer have course guidance as the Direct-to function is operating independently of the Active Flight Plan and can only handle one waypoint at a time. In this circumstance, you might reasonably wonder where the Active Flight Plan went (though it is still there) and resort to continuing to use the Direct-to function one waypoint at a time.

In other circumstances, however, the Direct-to key will cooperate with the Active Flight Plan page. If, for example, you have loaded a series of waypoints into a flight plan and you later use the Direct-to key to *enter a waypoint which is already loaded in the flight plan*, the Direct-to function will lead you to that point and, upon reaching it, the flight plan will sequence to the next waypoint in the plan. If you don't understand when the Direct-to key interfaces with the Active Flight Plan page and when it doesn't, you're far better off to use either one or the other, but don't mix them.

You can verify whether the active flight plan is being used by pushing the FPL key and bringing up the Active Flight Plan page. If, at the top of the page, you see the magenta Direct-to symbol followed by a waypoint (figure 9-1), you are NOT using the active flight plan, but are instead using Direct-to navigation to that waypoint. If, however, there is a magenta arrow (figure 9-5) or a "U-turn" arrow (figure 9-12) next to a waypoint in the flight plan, you are using the active flight plan.

Figure 9-1 The magenta Direct-to symbol indicates you're using Direct-to navigation to KVCV and are not navigating via the flight plan. *© Garmin Ltd. or its affiliates*

Direct-to Navigation

As mentioned above, the Direct-to key is relatively simple to use. We'll first discuss procedures that work from either the PFD or MFD and later a few extra functions available from just the MFD. First, from either display, press the Direct-to key. This brings up the Direct-to page (figure 9-2) with the destination field highlighted. You don't need to press the FMS knob first, since you already have a flashing cursor. Simply turn the small FMS knob until you reach the first letter for the desired airport, VOR, NDB, intersection or user waypoint. Then turn the large FMS knob one click to move the cursor to the next character position and use the small FMS knob to select the second letter. Continue using the large and small FMS knobs until the entire identifier is entered. Then press the ENT key twice to activate the Direct-to course function, which draws a magenta line on the maps from your current position to the destination. From there, follow the line to your destination. Note that if the destination is not in front of you, the start of the magenta line will be at a point where you'll be if you start a standard rate turn toward the destination when you press the Direct-to key.

If at any time you want to exit the Direct-to page, press the Direct-to key. Remember if the airport identifier uses all letters, precede the identifier with a K if it's a U.S. airport. For airport identifiers with a combination of letters and numbers, enter the three-letter identifier without preceding it with the letter K.

If you wander off course while flying to your destination, you may want to use the Direct-to function again so that you can fly directly to the destination from your current position, rather than reintercept the original magenta line. To do this, press the Direct-to key and then the ENT key twice. This recenters the CDI needle and redraws the magenta line from your current position. NOTE: Doing this while flying an instrument approach and navigating to the missed approach point (MAP) will cancel the approach. Instrument approaches are discussed in detail in Chapter 11.

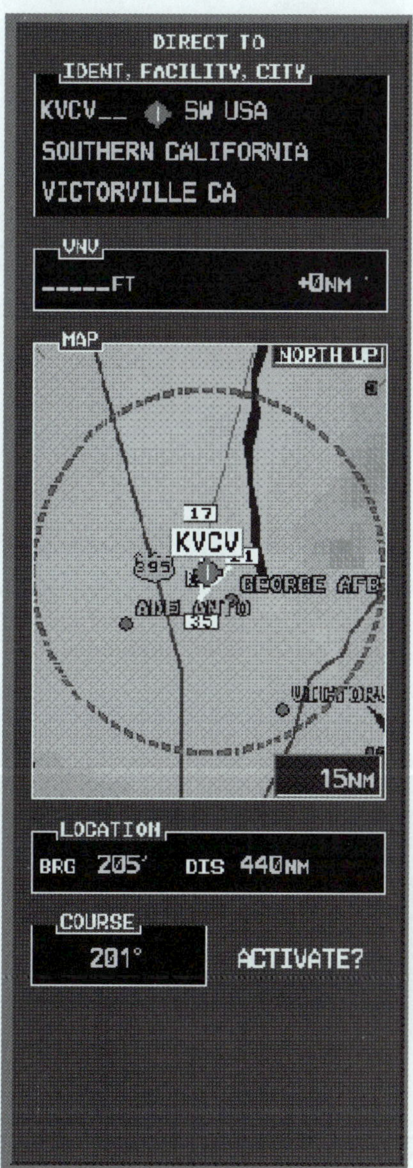

Figure 9-2 The Direct-to page allows entry of a waypoint for Direct-to navigation. MFD version of page shown. *© Garmin Ltd. or its affiliates*

Canceling Direct-to Navigation

If you later want to cancel Direct-to navigation, press the Direct-to key to bring up the Direct-to page and then press the MENU key. "Cancel Direct-to NAV" is the only menu choice for this page and pressing the ENT key completes the operation (figure 9-3). If you had an active flight plan, the system would then resume following the flight plan from the nearest leg.

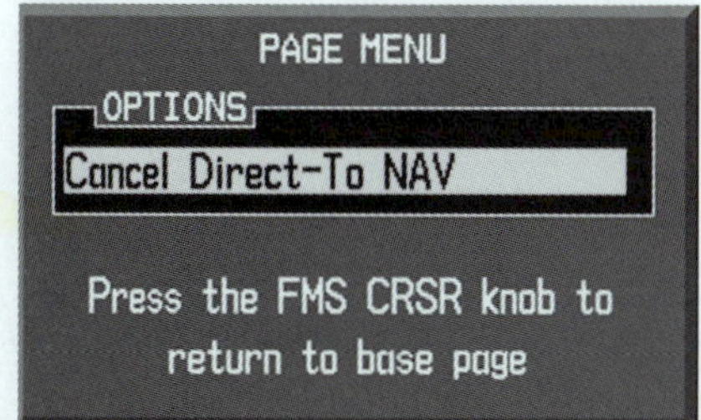

Figure 9-3 Use the MENU key to cancel Direct-to navigation. *© Garmin Ltd. or its affiliates*

Direct-to Navigation to Nearest Airport

This is an important function that could save your life if you have an emergency and need to get to the closest airport and land immediately. The fastest way to perform this function is with softkeys on the PFD. Press the NRST softkey to bring up the Nearest Airports window. Turn

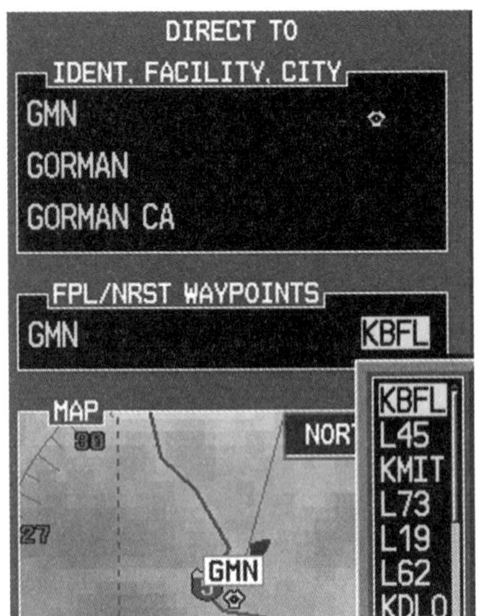

Figure 9-4 Using the NRST field can save time when entering a Direct-to waypoint. *© Garmin Ltd. or its affiliates*

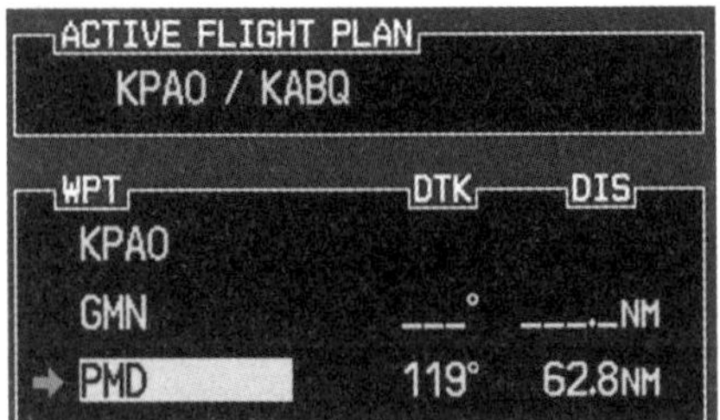

Figure 9-5 The magenta arrow indicates you're going directly to a waypoint in your flight plan. *© Garmin Ltd. or its affiliates*

TIP

To cancel Direct-to navigation, remember DME. Push the **D**irect-to, **M**ENU, and **E**NT keys to cancel direct-to navigation.

either FMS knob to highlight a nearby airport. Then press the Direct-to key and the ENT key twice to activate this function. Follow the magenta line to the airport.

On older G1000s, an alternate method was available. From either the PFD or MFD, press the Direct-to key to bring up the Direct-to page. Next, turn the large FMS knob three clicks (or four clicks if you have an active flight plan at the time) to highlight the NRST field. Then, turn the small FMS knob to select a nearby airport of your choice and press the ENT key twice (figure 9-4).

Direct-to Navigation to a Flight Plan Waypoint

The Direct-to key can be used in combination with an active flight plan. For example, suppose you used the FPL key (discussed below) to enter a series of waypoints and are now navigating using that active flight plan in the G1000 or Perspective. Sometimes, you'll want to bypass one or more waypoints and fly directly to a later waypoint in the flight plan. This could happen if you're VFR, the weather's good, and you decide to fly over a mountain rather than around it. Or, if IFR, perhaps you've negotiated with ATC to skip some intermediate waypoints and now fly directly to a waypoint closer to your destination.

There are multiple ways to skip ahead on a flight plan using the Direct-to key; all can be accessed from either the PFD or MFD. The easiest method is to press the FPL key to display the active flight plan. Press the FMS knob to turn on the cursor and then use the large FMS knob to scroll to the desired waypoint. Press the Direct-to key once and the ENT key twice. A magenta arrow appears opposite the waypoint, and you now have course navigation directly to that waypoint from the position where you used the Direct-to key (figure 9-5). Note that if your desired waypoint is the next waypoint in your flight plan (the one to which the U-turn arrow points), there's a shortcut available. Instead of pushing the FMS knob, just press the Direct-to key and the ENT key.

On older G1000s, you can also skip ahead using the Direct-to page. Press the Direct-to key and turn the large FMS knob three clicks to highlight the "FPL" field. Turning the small FMS knob will display and scroll through the list of waypoints in your active flight plan. Highlight the desired waypoint (figure 9-6) and press the ENT key twice to navigate directly from your present position to the selected waypoint. You can verify the operation by pushing the FPL key and looking for the magenta arrow opposite the desired waypoint (figure 9-5).

A third method is available, but there's never a reason to use it unless you forget the prior two methods. It takes longer and is slightly more error prone, but, if done correctly, works equally well. Press the Direct-to key to bring up the Direct-to Page. Use the large and small FMS knobs to enter a waypoint that's already in your flight plan and press the ENT key twice. You can verify that this was done correctly by pressing the FPL key and noting that the magenta arrow is opposite the selected waypoint. NOTE: This method will not work if the waypoint you entered using the Direct-to key was not already in the active flight plan, or if you enter the identifier incorrectly. Hence this method is less reliable.

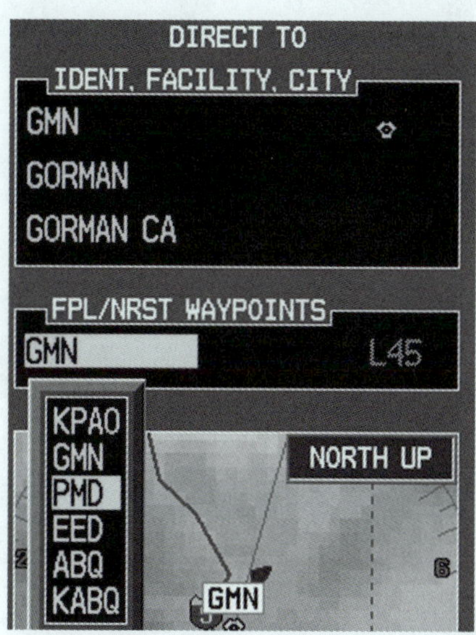

Figure 9-6 Use the Direct-to page and the FPL field to go directly to a point in your flight plan. *© Garmin Ltd. or its affiliates*

Direct-to Navigation by Facility or City name

You can also select a Direct-to destination by entering the name of the facility (e.g. airport, VOR or NDB) or city name. This is useful if you don't know the exact identifier of your destination airport. It takes longer to enter a destination this way, since you must enter more characters and because you'll have to scroll through all facilities having the same characters in common.

To enter a Direct-to destination by facility name or city name, press the Direct-to key and turn the large FMS knob one click to highlight the facility name field or two clicks to highlight the city name field. Turn the small and large FMS knobs to enter the name. If more than one facility shares the same name or city, you can scroll through them by continuing to turn the small FMS knob. Then press the ENT key twice to activate the Direct-function. This feature is available from both the PFD and MFD.

Direct-to Navigation via a Specified Course

Whenever you use Direct-to navigation, the system calculates a great circle route from your present position to your destination and guides you along that direct path. However, you may occasionally want to arrive at your destination from a particular direction. For example, you might want to line yourself up with the runway centerline miles from the airport and fly that course to the airport. The Course to Waypoint function allows you to do this from either the PFD or MFD.

First, press the Direct-to key to bring up the Direct-to page and select a destination using the FMS knobs. Then, using the large FMS knob, scroll to the bottom of the page and highlight the "Course" field (figure 9-7). Use the FMS knobs to enter the course you want to fly to the destination and press the ENT key twice. Go to the Navigation Map page and you'll find a magenta line, 500 nautical miles long, extending from your destination. You can now fly any intercept angle to that line and then follow the line to arrive at your destination on the desired course.

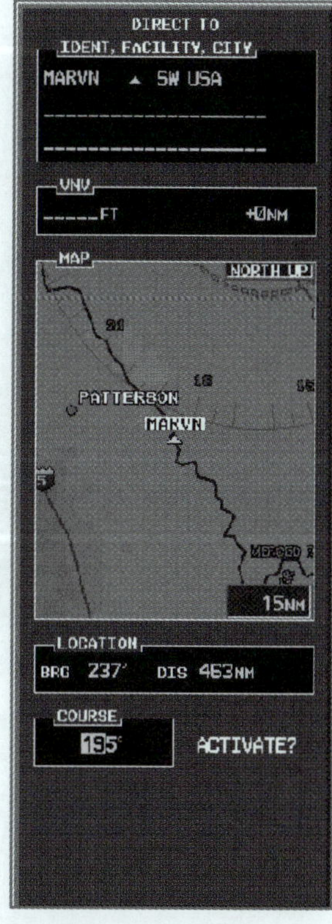

Figure 9-7 The course field, at the bottom of the Direct-to window, lets you select the direction you'll fly to a waypoint. *© Garmin Ltd. or its affiliates*

Unique MFD Direct-to Functions

There are two Direct-to functions that can only be performed from the MFD. Both can save you time, since you might not have to enter a facility identifier using the FMS knobs.

Almost any time you see a facility listed on a page, you can navigate directly to it by scrolling with the FMS knobs to highlight the identifier. Then press the Direct-to key and the ENT key twice. You can do this from all of the pages in the WPT group, such as the Airport Information

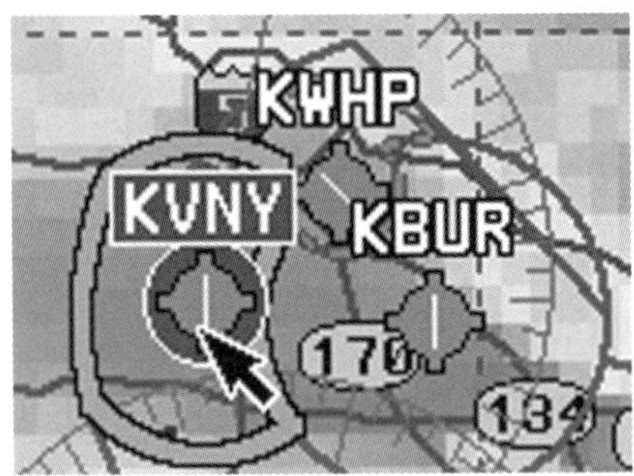

Figure 9-8 The joystick can select a Direct-to destination. *© Garmin Ltd. or its affiliates*

page or VOR Information page, for example. You can also do it from many of the NRST group pages, including the Nearest Intersections and Nearest NDB pages.

You can also enter Direct-to destinations from a map using the MFD's joystick. From the Navigation Map page, push the joystick to bring up the panning pointer. Move the joystick to place the panning pointer on your desired location (figure 9-8). Then press the Direct-to key and the ENT key twice. If there was no airport, navaid or user waypoint under the panning pointer, a new waypoint called MAPWPT is created and direct navigation will be to that waypoint.

Direct-to Navigation Summary

As you can see, using the Direct-to key is a powerful and simple way to navigate. Almost all of its functions can be used from either the PFD or MFD, which makes its use highly consistent on both displays. A more powerful and generally preferred way to navigate is with the use of flight plans, discussed in the next section.

Flight Plan Navigation

Instruction in modern TAA includes a greater focus on using the automation tools and the autopilot. This emphasis starts on the ground, where instructors encourage their clients to load a flight plan before takeoff. You can, of course, enter flight plans after you're in the air, but that further distracts you from one of your primary responsibilities, which is seeing and avoiding other aircraft. All glass panels tend to draw your eyes inside the cockpit anyway, so loading your flight plan ahead of time will help you avoid this tendency.

Figure 9-9 The Direct-to key and FPL key are used for Direct-to navigation and flight planning. *© Garmin Ltd. or its affiliates*

In Chapter 7, we discussed the four page groups—MAP, WPT, AUX and NRST—that are accessed through the large FMS knob. The flight planning functions are really a fifth chapter of pages. Instead of using the large FMS knob on the MFD, this group of three pages is selected by pushing the FPL key on the MFD (figure 9-9).† The FPL key on the PFD can also be used, but it only accesses a portion of the first of these three pages.

The first page in the group is the Active Flight Plan page, the one you'll use most of the time. Turning the small FMS knob on the MFD allows you to access the other two pages—the Flight Plan Catalog and Vertical Navigation pages—both of which are discussed later in this chapter. We'll talk first about features common to the Active Flight Plan page on both the PFD and MFD before talking about differences.

Active Flight Plan Page

The system can store up to 99 flight plans, numbered 1 through 99. Think of the Active Flight Plan page as flight plan 0 or the flight plan currently in use. It is used to create, edit and use flight plans, each of which can contain up to 31 waypoints. You can bring up the Active Flight Plan page at any time by pushing the FPL key on either the PFD or MFD.

† Latest software versions have only two pages. See pages 214-15

Along the left side of the page, you will find a list of waypoints, or empty fields if you have yet to enter waypoints. Adjacent to this are two user-definable columns. The default is for the columns to display desired track (DTK) and distance (DIS) for each waypoint. The columns are user selectable by pressing the MENU key, scrolling the FMS knob to "Change Fields" and pressing the ENT key.† Then turn the large FMS knob to select a column, the small FMS knob to select the desired field and press the ENT key (figure 9-10). Note you can choose to have different fields selected for the Flight Plan windows on the PFD and MFD. The following fields are available:

- Cumulative Distance (CUM) – total flight distance to reach a waypoint
- Distance (DIS) – length of a leg in nautical miles
- Desired Track (DTK) – ground track course (in degrees) to be flown to stay on course
- En route Safe Altitude (ESA) – safe altitude for the leg in feet
- Estimated Time of Arrival (ETA) – time at which you're predicted to arrive at waypoint
- Estimated Time En route (ETE) – number of hours and minutes required to reach the waypoint

Returning the flight plan fields back to the defaults is easy and may be necessary if multiple people fly the same plane. Press the FPL key to display the Active Flight Plan page, then press the MENU key, scroll the FMS knob to "Restore Defaults" and press the ENT key. The defaults are restored separately on both the PFD and MFD flight plan windows, so restoring one does not affect the other.

The Active Flight Plan page on the MFD has several additional fields not shown in the PFD's smaller flight plan box. These are:

- Active Leg Information – displays desired ground track and ESA for the leg
- Remaining Distance – displays remaining distance to destination
- Total Distance – displays length of entire flight plan
- FPL Estimated Safe Altitude – displays a safe altitude for the entire route

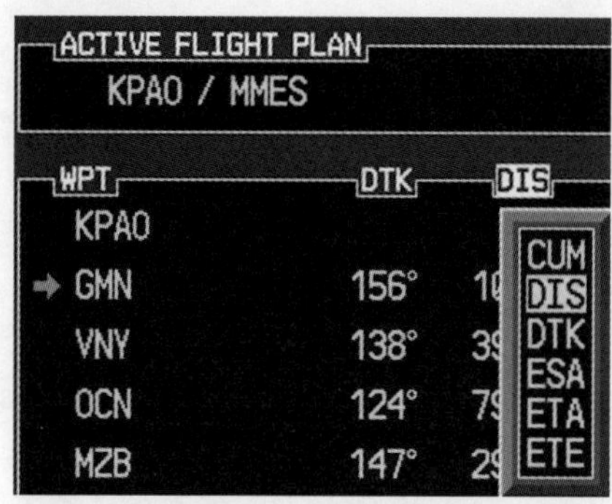

Figure 9-10 The columns in the Active Flight Plan can be changed to display two of six choices. *© Garmin Ltd. or its affiliates*

SAFETY TIP

Entering a flight plan while taxiing is the equivalent of texting while driving. Don't do it! The airlines require their crews to completely enter a flight plan before they leave the gate. That way they can give 100% of their attention to safely taxiing the aircraft. Fly like the professionals and don't do anything else while you taxi an aircraft.

Creating a Flight Plan

Creating a new flight plan is relatively easy. First, push the FPL key to bring up the Active Flight Plan page. If you enter the flight plan while on the ground, your departure airport is often already listed as the first waypoint, since the GPS receiver knows where you are located. Turn the small FMS knob one click to bring up the Waypoint Information window. Turn the small FMS knob a second click and it enters the letter K as the first character. Using the large and small FMS knobs, enter the identifier for your first waypoint and press the ENT key. Continue using the FMS knobs in the same way to enter all of your waypoints.

† Not available in most recent software versions. See page 222.

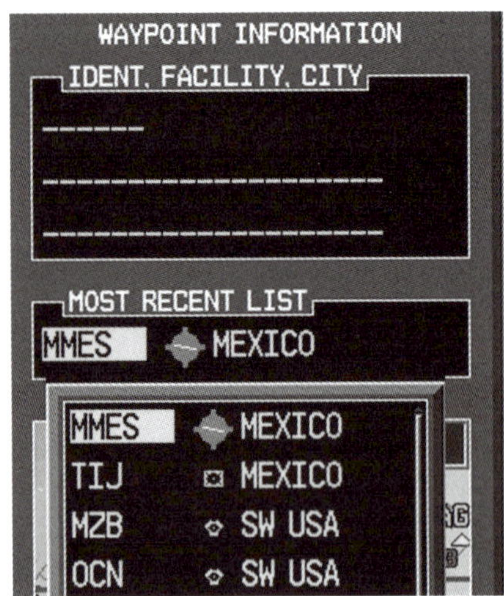

Figure 9-11 When entering waypoints, check for faster ways, like the Most Recent List, to enter a waypoint. *© Garmin Ltd. or its affiliates*

TIP

Round-robin flight plans, where you enter multiple airports into a flight plan, make it a little more difficult to use the Airport Information page and to load instrument approaches, since they will initially default to whichever airport is the active waypoint. The easiest solution is to not enter round-robin flight plans. If you do, however, just use the Direct-to key to select an airport in the flight plan. Or, if a page doesn't come up with the airport you want, enter the airport identifier manually with the FMS knobs.

It's even faster to enter a waypoint if you've recently used it in other flight plans or with the Direct-to key. After the Waypoint Information box is displayed, don't enter the identifier manually with the FMS knobs. Instead, use the large FMS knob to scroll down to the "Most Recent List" (figure 9-11) and then use the small FMS knob to scroll to highlight the desired waypoint and press the ENT key.†

Once you've entered more than two waypoints, the system will activate the first pair of waypoints as the first leg—provided you're not currently using Direct-to navigation. Activation of a leg is depicted with a magenta "U-turn" arrow (figure 9-12) leading from one waypoint to the next one in the flight plan, and by a magenta line drawn on the Navigation Map page depicting the course to be flown. You now have an active flight plan which will provide you course guidance for flying the route.

You can also create a new flight plan from the Flight Plan Catalog, the second page in the FPL group, accessible only from the MFD. Once you're on this page, the easiest way to create a flight plan is to press the NEW softkey. Or, press MENU, scroll with either FMS knob to "Create New Flight Plan" and press the ENT key. If you create a flight plan here, however, you must first store and then activate it before using it for active navigation. You'll find more details on this in the Working with Stored Flight Plans section later in this chapter.

Editing and Working with an Active Flight Plan

While creating a flight plan on the ground is relatively easy, making changes to one in flight, particularly in a high workload environment such as flying single pilot IFR, can be challenging. If you're not familiar with your system, it may be impossible. This is where less practiced users may find themselves reverting to the Direct-to key to get out of a jam. Unfortunately, changes are often necessary, particularly if you're an IFR pilot and you hear a controller call you with the dreaded words "I have a change in your routing, advise when ready to copy."

Here are the most common things that you may need to do with an active flight plan:

- Insert additional waypoints
- Delete waypoints in the active flight plan
- Fly directly to a waypoint in the flight plan
- Activate a different leg in the flight plan
- Invert the active flight plan
- Delete the active flight plan

These actions, which we cover in the next section, are made in the same way from both the PFD and MFD

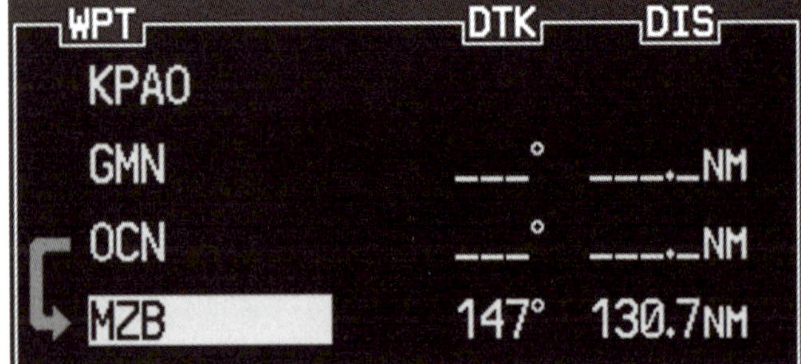

Figure 9-12 The "U-turn" arrow indicates the active leg along which you're navigating. Since MZB is highlighted, you can enter a new waypoint between OCN and MZB. *© Garmin Ltd. or its affiliates*

Insert additional waypoints in the Active Flight Plan

Inserting a new waypoint is similar to entering a waypoint when creating a new flight plan. The difference is that you must first highlight with the cursor the waypoint that will follow your new waypoint (figure

† See page 213 for updates to this feature.

9-12). If your waypoint is to be the last one in the flight plan, just highlight the blank field after the last waypoint in the plan.

G1000 users should remember that new waypoints are added *before*, not *after* the flight plan cursor. Later software updates to the Perspective continuously display a small triangle indicating that new waypoints are inserted above the cursor (figure 15-19). Also, Perspective users no longer have to first push the FMS knob to get a cursor; they can just start typing in a new identifier. That's because a new Quick Select Box of dashed white lines shows the cursor position even when the cursor is off. The box's position can be moved with the joystick.

To insert a new waypoint on the G1000, press the FPL key, push the FMS knob if needed to get a cursor and turn the large FMS knob until the cursor highlights the waypoint to follow your new waypoint. Then turn the small FMS knob to bring up the Waypoint Information window. Turn the small FMS knob one more click, enter the new identifier with the FMS knobs and press the ENT key.

If, in the course of entering a waypoint, you want to start over, just push the FMS knob once, and the characters you entered will be cleared. If you decide that you really don't want to insert a waypoint, press the FMS knob a second time to remove the Waypoint Information window.

Delete a waypoint in the Active Flight Plan

Deleting a waypoint is similar to inserting a waypoint in that you must first highlight a waypoint with the cursor. In some cases, you don't actually need to delete one or more waypoints. For example, if you want to skip some waypoints and fly directly to a point further down in your flight plan, you can do this by flying directly to a waypoint, which is described below.

If you do want to delete a waypoint, press the FPL key, push the FMS knob and turn the large FMS knob until the cursor highlights the waypoint to be deleted. Then push the CLR key. This brings up a window asking if you really want to delete the waypoint (figure 9-13). Push the ENT key to delete it or, to cancel the delete operation, turn the large FMS knob to highlight CANCEL and press the ENT key.

Figure 9-13 Use the CLR key to remove a waypoint from a flight plan.
© Garmin Ltd. or its affiliates

Fly directly to a waypoint in the Active Flight Plan

There may be times when you want to skip waypoints and fly directly to a later point in your flight plan. This could occur if you're IFR and you've negotiated with the controller to get a more direct route toward your destination. In this case, you want to fly directly from your present position to a subsequent waypoint.

To fly directly to a waypoint in the flight plan, press the FPL key, push the FMS knob and turn the large FMS knob to highlight the waypoint. Then, press the Direct-to key, and press the ENT key twice. A small magenta arrow (figure 9-5) will appear next to the waypoint and a magenta line will be drawn on the map from your present position to the waypoint. Once you reach the waypoint, the system will activate the

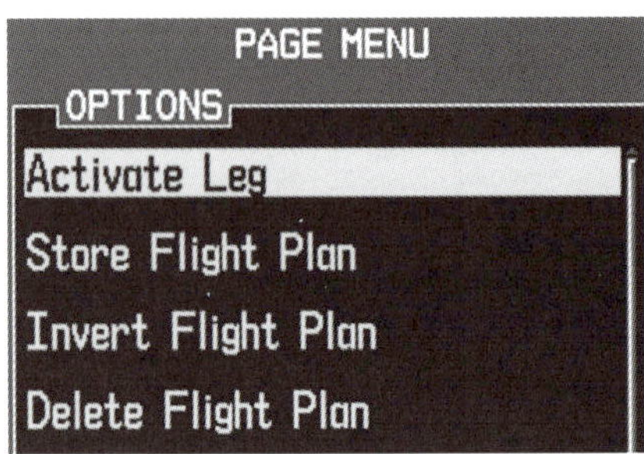

Figure 9-14 To activate a segment of a flight plan, highlight the second waypoint of the pair that define the segment, press the MENU key and select "Activate Leg." *© Garmin Ltd. or its affiliates*

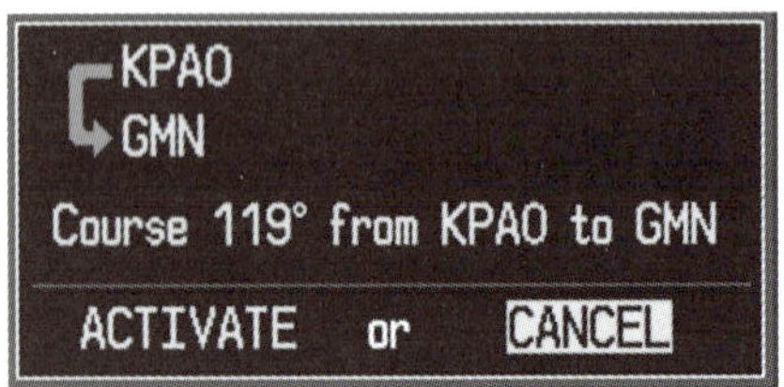

Figure 9-15 Many menus give you the choice to cancel an action you've started. *© Garmin Ltd. or its affiliates*

next leg and the magenta "U-turn" arrow will appear in the flight plan opposite the two waypoints that form the leg.

Activate a leg in the Active Flight Plan

Activating a leg in a flight plan draws a magenta line between two waypoints and provides course guidance to the segment, if the aircraft is not on it, and then along the segment. For example, an instrument pilot might be navigating along an airway between two VORs, each set up as a waypoint in the flight plan. At some point, the pilot may have turned off the airway, perhaps to avoid weather or because ATC issued a vector to avoid conflicting traffic.

Now the pilot needs to return to the airway. If he hasn't reached the next VOR, the current segment is still active and no change is required. Perhaps, however, the controller wants him to intercept the next airway, represented by the next leg of the flight plan which isn't yet active. Activating the next leg will highlight that segment on the Navigation Map page, and provide course guidance to and along that portion of the flight plan.

To activate a different leg in the flight plan, push the FMS knob and turn the large FMS knob to highlight the second waypoint that defines the leg. Then press the MENU key. "Activate Leg" should already be highlighted, since it is the first choice on the menu (figure 9-14). Press the ENT key twice to activate the leg. The magenta "U-turn" arrow will appear in the flight plan opposite the two waypoints that form the leg, and the corresponding segment on the Navigation Map page turns magenta.

LD DP	LD STAR	LD APR		ACT LEG

Figure 9-16 The ACT LEG softkey appears on the MFD after you highlight a waypoint in your flight plan. *© Garmin Ltd. or its affiliates*

Should you make an error and need to cancel selection of an active leg, you can do so after you select "Activate Leg," and press the ENT key. Before pressing the ENT key a second time, press the CLR key or scroll with the large FMS knob to "CANCEL" and then press the ENT key (figure 9-15).

You can also activate a leg from the MFD using the ACT LEG softkey (figure 9-16). Press the FPL key to open the Active Flight Plan window, press the FMS knob and scroll to highlight the second waypoint that defines the leg you want to activate. Then press the ACT LEG softkey followed by the ENT key.

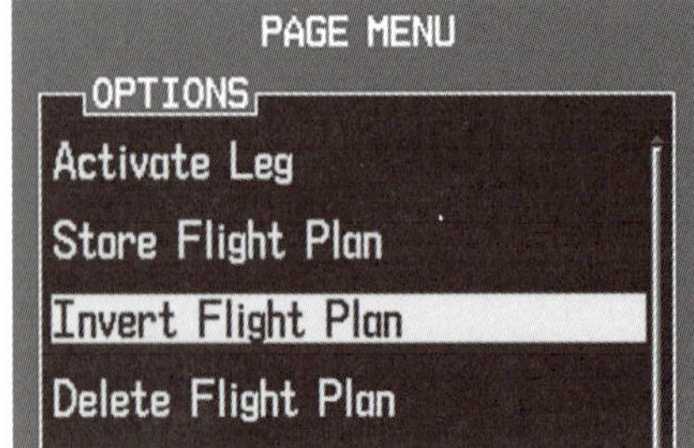

Figure 9-17 A quick way to create a return flight plan is to invert the flight plan you used going to your destination. *© Garmin Ltd. or its affiliates*

Invert the Active Flight Plan

It's common for pilots to fly to a destination and then fly back using the exact same route. If you do that, there's no need for you to re-enter a new flight plan; just invert the original flight plan.

To invert a flight plan, press the FPL key and then press the MENU key. Using either FMS knob, scroll to highlight "Invert Flight Plan" (figure 9-17) and press the ENT key twice. Should you make a mistake and need to cancel this operation before pressing the ENT key a second time, press the CLR key or scroll with the large FMS knob to "CANCEL" and then press the ENT key.

Delete the Active Flight Plan

You may want to delete an active flight plan if you no longer have any use for it. For example, if you are flying a round-robin training flight with landings at several airports, you may want to delete the flight plan after you reach your first destination so that you can enter a new flight plan for the next leg of your trip. Or, you might want to delete a plan if the changes you need to make to it are so major that you'd prefer to start over.

Before you delete the active flight plan, you may want to store it first if you have any possible future use for it. Otherwise, if the active flight plan has never been stored before, it will be irretrievably gone after you delete it. Use this function with care, particularly when dealing with long flight plans.

Note: You don't need to delete an active flight plan if you're planning to replace it with a previously stored flight plan, which is discussed in the next section. Recalling a previously stored flight plan will delete the active flight plan and replace it with the stored one.

To delete the active flight plan, first push the FPL key to display the Active Flight Plan page if it isn't already on the screen. Then press the MENU key and scroll with either FMS knob to highlight "Delete Flight Plan" (figure 9-18). Finally, press the ENT key twice to delete the flight plan. If, during the operation, you change your mind, you can press the CLR key at any time or after pressing the ENT key once, turn the large FMS knob to highlight "CANCEL" and press the ENT key to cancel the operation.

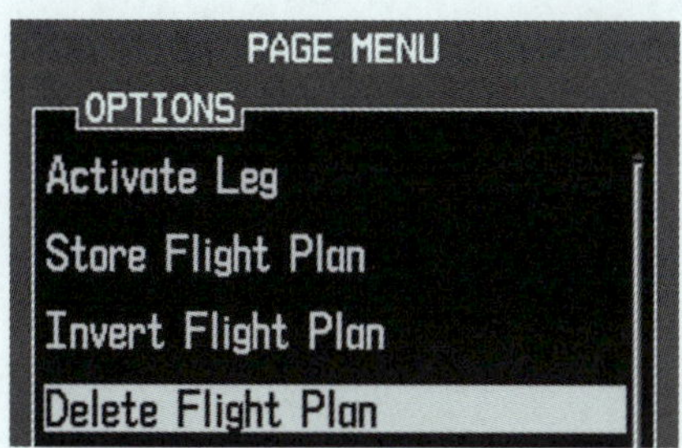

Figure 9-18 Press the MENU key to delete a flight plan. *© Garmin Ltd. or its affiliates*

TIP

On a return trip, you can save time by inverting the flight plan you used on your outbound trip. However, the active flight plan is lost when the system is shut down. So you must remember to store the flight plan before you shut down, if you want to invert it and use it on the return trip.

Storing Flight Plans and Activating Stored Flight Plans

If each time you flew, you went to a different destination, you wouldn't need to store and recall flight plans, since you'd need to create a new one each time you flew, just as we've done above. However, pilots often fly to some destinations repeatedly. Therefore the G1000 and Perspective, and all modern GPS receivers, allows you to save a flight plan that you've entered and recall it at a later date. This can save a considerable amount of time, even if some of the intermediate points change and need minor editing before use.

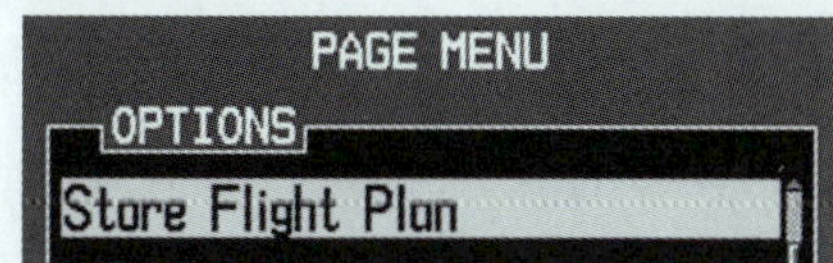

Figure 9-19 To store a flight plan at any time, push the MENU key. *© Garmin Ltd. or its affiliates*

Storing a Flight Plan

Anytime after you've created a flight plan—or even after you've started using it—you can store a flight plan for future use. First, push the FPL key to display the Active Flight Plan page if it isn't already on the screen. Then press the MENU key. "Store Flight Plan" should already be highlighted; if it's not, scroll with either FMS knob to "Store Flight Plan" (figure 9-19). Finally, press the ENT key twice to store the flight plan. If you change your mind during the operation, you can press the CLR key at any time or, after pressing the ENT key once, turn the large FMS knob to highlight "CANCEL" and press the ENT key to cancel the operation.

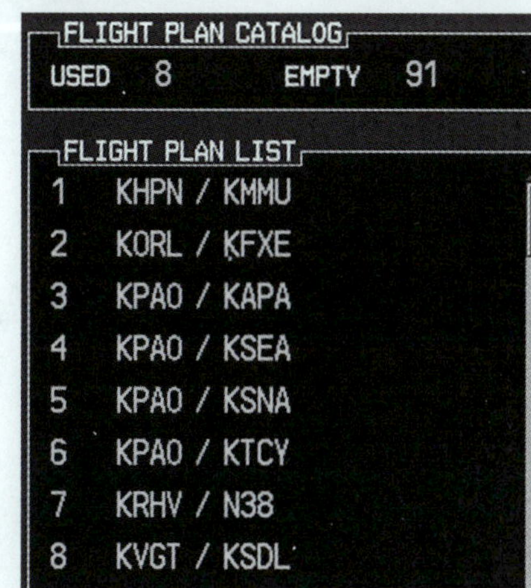

Figure 9-20 The Flight Plan Catalog page lets you store flight plans and is the second page in the FPL key group. *© Garmin Ltd. or its affiliates*

Activating a Previously Stored Flight Plan – MFD only

The system stores up to 99 flight plans, which are listed on the Flight Plan Catalog page, accessible only through the MFD. To reach this page, press the MFD's FPL key and turn the small FMS knob one click to the right. You should now see up to 12 flight plans displayed (figure 9-20). The scroll bar along the right side of the window indicates that you can scroll down to see more flight plans.

To activate a flight plan, push the FMS knob, and turn either FMS knob to highlight one of the flight plans. Once you've highlighted a flight plan, you can activate it by pressing the ACTIVE softkey and the ENT key or by pressing the MENU key, scrolling with either FMS knob to highlight "Activate Flight Plan" (figure 9-22), and pressing the ENT key twice. This flight plan now becomes the active Flight Plan 0, and the leg closest to your present position becomes the active leg, as indicated by the magenta U-turn arrow. If, during the operation, you change your mind, you can press the CLR key at any time or after pressing the ENT key once, turn the large FMS knob to highlight "CANCEL" and press the ENT key to cancel the operation.

Working with Stored Flight Plans – MFD Only

We mentioned at the beginning of this section that the flight planning functions are really a fifth chapter of pages reached by pushing the FPL key on the MFD. The first page in the group is the Active Flight Plan page. Turning the small FMS knob on the MFD allows access to the second page, the Flight Plan Catalog page. This is where you work with the up to 99 stored flight plans.

NEW	ACTIVE	INVERT	EDIT	COPY	DELETE

Figure 9-21 Use the MFD softkeys to save time when working with the Flight Plan Catalog page. *© Garmin Ltd. or its affiliates*

Experienced Garmin GNS 430 and GNS 530 users take note. There are two ways to do most of the functions in this section: the way you're familiar with using the MENU key and the easy way using softkeys! So, whenever you use the Flight Plan Catalog page, make sure you look at the softkeys (figure 9-21), as you can implement most functions faster with one.

Here are the most common things that you may need to do with a stored flight plan:

- Create a new flight plan
- Activate a previously stored flight plan (discussed in the previous section)
- Invert and activate a stored flight plan
- Edit a stored flight plan
- Copy a flight plan
- Delete a flight plan from the Flight Plan Catalog page
- Delete all flight plans from the Flight Plan Catalog page
- Sort flight plans by comment

These functions, which we cover in the next section, can only be performed through the MFD.

Create a New Flight Plan

Previously, we discussed creating a new flight plan within the Active Flight Plan page. You can also create flight plans from the Flight Plan Catalog page. The advantage of creating one here is that you can do so without disturbing Flight Plan 0, which is in use if you're currently navigating with an active flight plan.

To create a flight plan, press the MFD's FPL key and turn the small FMS knob one click to access the second page, the Flight Plan Catalog page. Then, press the NEW softkey. Alternatively, press the MENU key, scroll with either FMS knob to "Create New Flight Plan" and press the ENT key.

If you create a flight plan here, you must first store and then activate it before using it for active navigation. Storing and activating a flight plan were discussed in detail in a previous section. To review briefly, to store a flight plan, press the MENU key, select "Store Flight Plan" and press the ENT key twice. To activate a flight plan, highlight it on the Flight Plan Catalog Page, press the ACTIVE softkey and press the ENT key. Or, highlight it, press the MENU key, highlight "Activate Flight Plan" (figure 9-22) and press the ENT key twice.

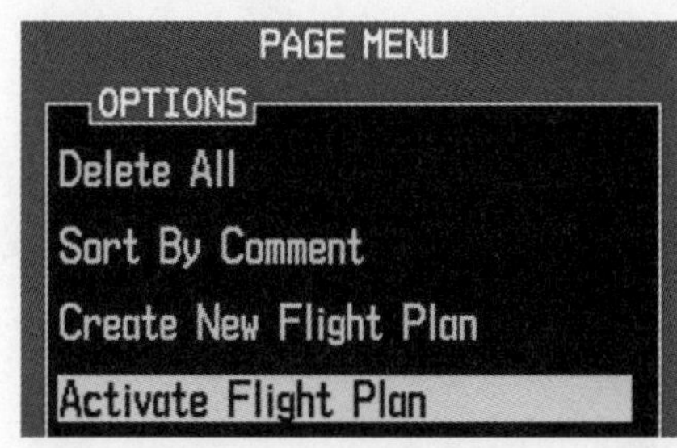

Figure 9-22 To use a stored flight plan, you must press the ACTIVE softkey or the MENU key. *© Garmin Ltd. or its affiliates*

Activate a Previously Stored Flight Plan

This was covered in the previous section.

Invert and Activate a Stored Flight Plan

It's common for pilots to fly to a destination and then fly back using the exact same route. Previously, we discussed how to invert an Active Flight Plan. You can also invert and activate a stored flight plan, which will save you the time needed to re-enter all of the waypoints in reverse.

To invert and activate a stored flight plan, press the MFD's FPL key and turn the small FMS knob one click to access the second page, the Flight Plan Catalog page. Then push the FMS knob and turn either FMS knob to highlight one of the flight plans. Once you've highlighted a flight plan, either press the INVERT softkey (figure 9-21) and the ENT key or press the MENU key and, using either FMS knob, scroll to highlight "Invert & Activate FPL" (figure 9-23) and press the ENT key twice. The Active Flight Plan page will then open and the nearest leg of the flight plan is activated. Should you make a mistake and need to cancel this operation, press the CLR key at any time or, before pressing the ENT key a second time, scroll with the large FMS knob to "CANCEL" and then press the ENT key.

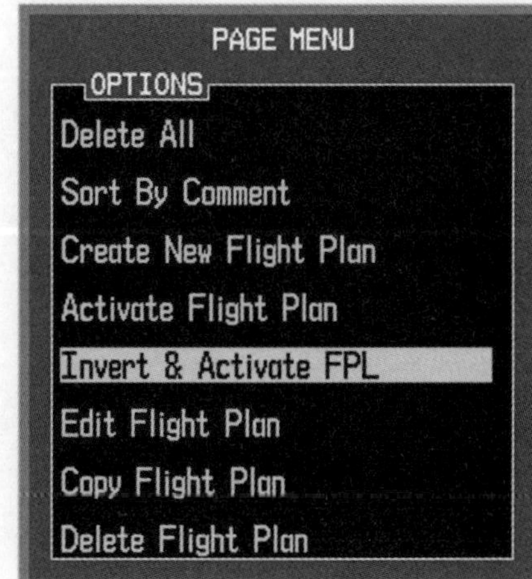

Figure 9-23 You can invert and activate a stored flight plan with the INVERT softkey or the MENU key. *© Garmin Ltd. or its affiliates*

Edit a Stored Flight Plan

If you need a flight plan similar to one you've previously stored, it may be faster and easier to edit a stored flight plan than to create a new one. Note, however, that any changes you make with the edit function will be applied to the original stored flight plan. So if you want to keep the original flight plan intact, first "Copy a Stored Flight Plan," as described in the next section, before making any changes.

To edit a stored flight plan, press the MFD's FPL key and turn the

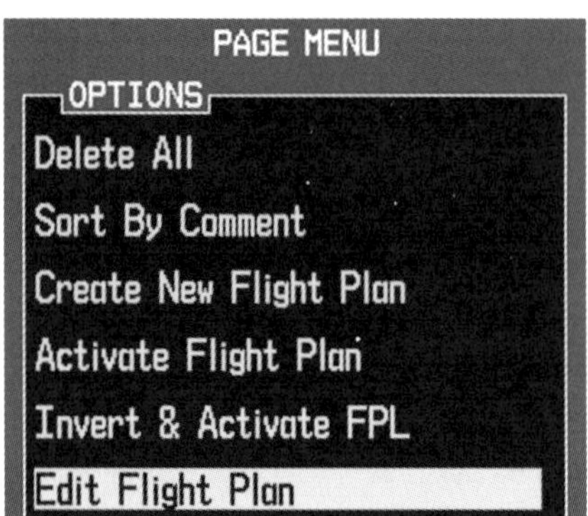

Figure 9-24 You can edit a stored flight plan with the EDIT softkey or the MENU key. *© Garmin Ltd. or its affiliates*

small FMS knob one click to access the second page, the Flight Plan Catalog page. Then push the FMS knob and turn either FMS knob to highlight one of the flight plans. Once you've highlighted a flight plan, either press the EDIT softkey (figure 9-21) or press the MENU key and, using either FMS knob, scroll to highlight "Edit Flight Plan" (figure 9-24) and press the ENT key twice. You can then add and delete waypoints and any changes you make are automatically saved in the stored flight plan; it's not necessary to store a flight plan after editing it.

Copy a Flight Plan

The copy function is useful if you need a new flight plan which is similar to one you've previously stored, but you want the original flight plan to remain unchanged. Simply copy the previous flight plan and a second copy of it will be stored in the flight plan catalog. Then you can edit the second copy with any changes you'd like, leaving the original flight plan unchanged.

To copy a stored flight plan, press the MFD's FPL key and turn the small FMS knob one click to access the second page, the Flight Plan Catalog page. Then push the FMS knob and turn either FMS knob to highlight one of the flight plans. Once you've highlighted a flight plan, press the COPY softkey (figure 9-21) and the ENT key or press the MENU key and, using either FMS knob, scroll to highlight "Copy Flight Plan" (figure 9-25) and press the ENT key twice. You can then use the Edit a Stored Flight Plan function, described above, to make changes to the flight plan copy.

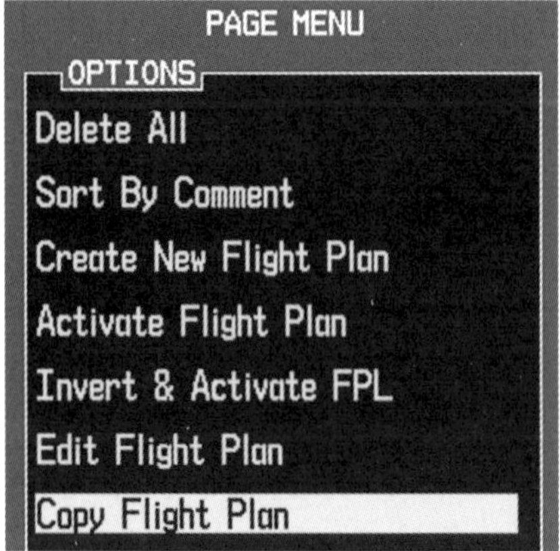

Figure 9-25 You should copy a stored flight plan first if you want to make changes to it without affecting the original flight plan. *© Garmin Ltd. or its affiliates*

Delete a Flight Plan from the Flight Plan Catalog

Once you start to get a number of flight plans stored in the flight plan catalog, you may want to do some housekeeping. For example, although the system will store up to 99 flight plans, you might not enjoy scrolling through dozens of flight plans you never use to get to a frequently used one. Occasionally deleting flight plans that you no longer use makes it easier to access the ones you do.

To delete a stored flight plan, press the MFD's FPL key and turn the small FMS knob one click to access the second page, the Flight Plan Catalog page. Then push the FMS knob and turn either FMS knob to highlight the flight plan you want to delete. Then press the CLR key or the DELETE softkey (figure 9-21) and then press the ENT key twice. Alternatively, though this is more work, after you've highlighted a flight plan, press the MENU key, scroll using either FMS knob to highlight "Delete Flight Plan" and press the ENT key twice. If you change your mind during the operation, you can use the CLR key at any time or, before pressing the ENT key a second time, scroll with the large FMS knob to "CANCEL" (figure 9-26) and then press the ENT key.

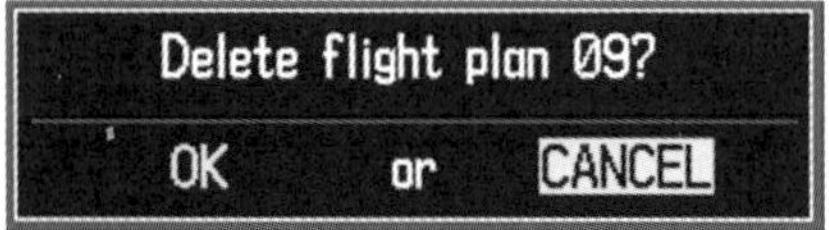

Figure 9-26 Anytime you delete something, you're given a second chance to keep it. *© Garmin Ltd. or its affiliates*

Delete All Flight Plans from the Flight Plan Catalog

It's rare that you will want to delete all flight plans, particularly if you own the plane. However, an FBO that rents an airplane may occasionally want to delete the many plans that renter pilots have stored on the system or an owner, when selling their airplane, might also want to clear out all flight plans.

To delete all stored flight plans, press the MFD's FPL key and turn the small FMS knob one click to access the second page, the Flight Plan Catalog page. Then press the MENU key, scroll using either FMS knob to highlight "Delete All" (figure 9-27) and press the ENT key twice. If you change your mind during the operation, you can use the CLR key at any time or, before pressing the ENT key a second time, scroll with the large FMS knob to "CANCEL" and then press the ENT key.

Figure 9-27 Deleting all stored flight plans can only be done with the MENU key. *© Garmin Ltd. or its affiliates*

Sort Flight Plans by Comment

After you've accumulated a large number of flight plans, you may want to sort them so that you can easily find the particular flight plan you're looking for. The system provides a sorting function which sorts flight plans by their names, as they appear on the Flight Plan Catalog page.

Figure 9-28 Sort By Comment sorts by the flight plan name. To change the name of a flight plan, edit it from the Flight Plan Catalog page. *© Garmin Ltd. or its affiliates*

To sort all stored flight plans, press the MFD's FPL key and turn the small FMS knob one click to access the second page, the Flight Plan Catalog page. Then press the MENU key, scroll using either FMS knob to highlight "Sort By Comment" (figure 9-28) and press the ENT key twice. If you change your mind during the operation, you can use the CLR key at any time or, before pressing the ENT key a second time, scroll with the large FMS knob to "CANCEL" and then press the ENT key.

The flight plans will be sorted by the departure airports and then, for flight plans leaving from the same airport, by destination airport. In the process, new flight plan numbers are assigned. The active flight plan, Flight Plan 0, remains unchanged during this operation. You can change the name of a flight plan, and hence how it is sorted, by going to the Flight Plan Catalog page, pressing the MENU key and choosing "Edit Flight Plan." Scroll to highlight the name and then use the small and large FMS knobs to enter a new name.

Closest Point of FPL

In the interest of completeness, we've included a description of the Closest Point of FPL function, though it has little practical application. The function creates a new user waypoint along a flight plan at the location closest to a chosen reference waypoint.

From an active flight plan page, press the MENU key, scroll to select "Closest Point Of FPL," press the ENT key and enter a reference waypoint. This will add a new user waypoint to your flight plan at the closest point to the reference waypoint you entered.

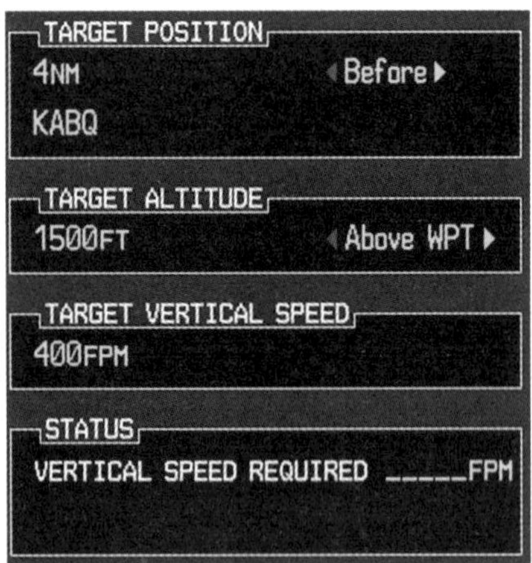

Figure 9-29 Creating a VNAV profile helps you manage the descent to your destination. *© Garmin Ltd. or its affiliates*

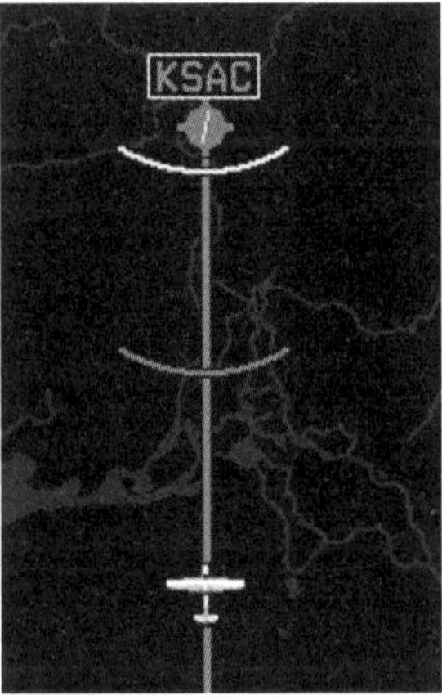

Figure 9-30 Curved lines on the Vertical Navigation page map mark the beginning and end of a descent. *© Garmin Ltd. or its affiliates*

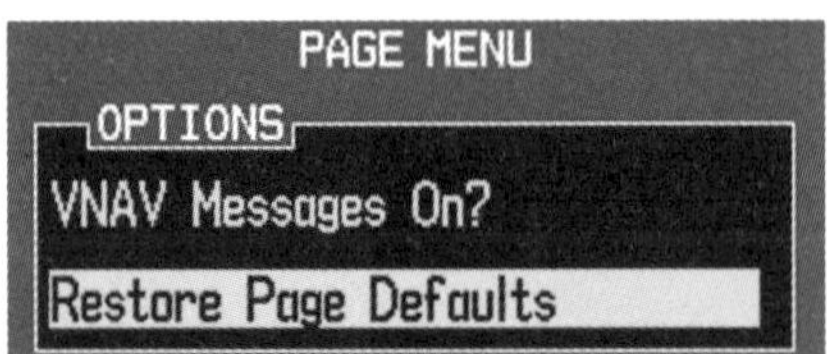

Figure 9-31 The VNAV default values are restored at power on, but you can restore them at any time with the MENU key. *© Garmin Ltd. or its affiliates*

Vertical Navigation Page

Vertical Navigation or VNAV is a function that calculates when to start descending at a specified vertical speed so that you'll arrive at a target altitude (perhaps the traffic pattern altitude if you wish) at some specified distance from a waypoint, such as your destination airport. The system makes these calculations and graphically shows where the descent begins and ends. In the original G1000 software, this function was on a dedicated third page in the FPL group. In the Perspective and later G1000 versions, vertical navigation is incorporated into the MFD's main FPL flight plan page.

To create a descent profile with the original G1000 software, push the FPL key on the MFD and twist the small FMS knob to the Vertical Navigation page, the last page in the group.† Push the FMS knob, which highlights the first field in the TARGET POSITION FIELD window (figure 9-29). Use the FMS knobs to enter the desired distance from the destination waypoint and press the ENT key. Then use the small FMS knob to select whether you want to arrive "Before" or "After" the waypoint and press the ENT key. Next, use the large and small FMS knobs to enter the destination identifier and press the ENT key.

Now use the FMS knobs to enter your desired altitude (such as the traffic pattern altitude) in the TARGET ALTITUDE window and press the ENT key. Next, use the small FMS knob to select "Above WPT," if you want the target altitude calculated with reference to the waypoint elevation, or "MSL," if it's to be referenced to mean sea level. Finally, use the FMS knobs to enter your desired descent rate in the TARGET VERTICAL SPEED window and press the ENT key.

The VNAV function is now active. If you'd like to receive alert messages on the PFD, press the MENU key, scroll to select "VNAV messages ON?" and press the ENT key. One minute prior to starting your descent, you'll see "APPR VPROF – Approaching VNAV Profile," displayed as an alert message. At 500 feet above the target altitude, you'll see "APPR TRG ALT" displayed.

You can use the Vertical Navigation page to monitor your progress. For example, the map on this page graphically marks the beginning and end points of your descent with curved lines (figure 9-30). Also, you can compare the "Vertical Speed Required" field on this page with your actual descent rate to help you fly the descent profile you've created.

If you'd prefer to monitor other MFD pages, such as the Navigation Map page, you might want to have VSR (vertical speed required) displayed on the MFD in the Navigation Status Bar. If so, go to the System Setup page and set one of the fields in the MFD DATA BAR FIELDS window to VSR. Finally, if you wish to restore the Vertical Navigation page to its default values, press MENU, scroll to "Restore Page Defaults" and press the ENT key (figure 9-31).

† For vertical navigation in the Perspective and later G1000 versions, see pages 214-17

Some early G1000-equipped aircraft were placarded "Use of VNAV is prohibited." This was required for FAA certification since, at that time, the VNAV software held settings from prior flights and would continue to generate messages on subsequent flights. Later software versions reset the VNAV page to its default values each time the system is powered up. The placard is no longer required for planes with revised software.

Also, in early software revisions the curved lines marking the beginning and end of descent appeared only on the Vertical Navigation page. Some later revisions display these lines on other MAP group pages too.

Summary

Programming the GPS receiver is probably the most challenging issue for many pilots and instructors—particularly those who didn't grow up using computers. All time spent learning to program the GPS receiver will pay huge dividends. Nothing eliminates stress in the cockpit more than knowing that you can program the GPS to do what you want it to do. If possible, review this chapter and use the G1000 or Perspective PC Trainer software to solidify your understanding. If you're an instrument pilot, you'll also want to read Chapter 11.

It's important that you learn all you can about using the autopilot, which we discuss in the next chapter. The autopilot is a critical element in G1000-equipped aircraft and it will make your flying easier, safer and more pleasurable. It can be very useful in emergencies, though it may operate in fewer modes, as we'll discuss in Chapter 12.

Chapter 10:
Autopilot Operation

Historically, pilots have not received the level of training they need to fully understand and use the autopilot in their airplanes. That's probably because many flight instructors are not familiar with all of the operating modes and limitations of autopilots. Also, we may still have a bias in aviation that "real pilots" fly airplanes manually and that it's somehow "cheating" to use an autopilot and other cockpit automation. Nothing could be further from the truth.

To fly glass cockpit aircraft safely, you need to understand and use the autopilot often, while remaining proficient in flying the airplane manually. It's not that you need to use the autopilot because these aircraft are harder to fly. Rather, it's because using the autopilot frees you for more important tasks, like looking outside the cockpit for traffic. In training both new and experienced G1000 and Perspective pilots, I consistently find that use of and knowledge about the autopilot is one of the weaker skills of even proficient pilots. So I strongly encourage you to get to know your autopilot well.

Different manufacturers use different autopilots in their G1000-equipped aircraft. When the G1000 first started shipping in mid-2004, there was no integrated autopilot solution and so manufacturers used third-party autopilots such as the S-TEC 55X and King-Bendix KAP 140. Now, a fully integrated Flight Director and autopilot, the Garmin GFC 700 AFCS or Automatic Flight Control System, is available and some manufacturers have switched to this autopilot.

We'll talk first about the GFC 700 and then the KAP 140 autopilot. As always, refer to the approved Airplane Flight Manual Supplement for your autopilot and use it in preference to this book whenever a conflict exists.

Perspective

The Garmin GFC 700 autopilot in the Perspective operates in the same way as the GFC 700 used in the Garmin G1000. The most noticeable difference is the Perspective's new control panel (figure 15-16). Instead of separate UP/DOWN keys, a wheel is used to select climb and descent rates. The Perspective's IAS key performs the same function as the FLC key found in GFC 700-equipped G1000 aircraft. The Perspective also includes a new LVL key. It engages the autopilot, rolls the wings level, and maintains level flight. Note that the GFC 700 annunciators are in the PFD's AFCS Status bar, far from the autopilot keys. Pilots should look at the annuciators to verify every autopilot key press to avoid an automation surprise.

In the GA or Go Around mode, when the GA button is pushed, the autopilot remains on in the Perspective, but disconnects in the G1000. When selecting a pitch mode to climb or descend, if you forget to set an altitude reference with the ALT SEL knob and are climbing or descending away from the selected altitude, an ALTITUDE SELECT annunciator appears on the PFD.

GFC 700 Automatic Flight Control System (AFCS)

The Garmin integrated autopilot is one of the most capable found in general aviation aircraft, and it continues to evolve. One of the beauties of this autopilot is that you can preset all of its modes while on the

Figure 10-1 GFC 700 keys are on the MFD bezel and, in some aircraft, duplicated on the PFD. © *Max Trescott*

ground, and then, when you're in the air, you only need to press the AP key and the system will take over. It is innovative in that, instead of using a central computer, the intelligence is distributed among the separate servos that control pitch, roll, and trim (and the yaw damper where applicable).

Autopilots are notoriously difficult to maintain and this novel design is expected to improve reliability and performance. It's important to note, however, that the failure of other G1000 system components can cause the GFC 700 to have reduced functionality or become totally unusable. This is less of an issue in Perspective systems. For more information, read the section on Autopilot Failures later in this chapter.

At present, there are at least three different versions shipping in different aircraft. For example, the version in Beechcrafts has a yaw damper and the version in Cessnas has the capability to follow a vertical descent profile. The version used in early Columbias had neither. The autopilot and Flight Director keys are located on the bezel of the MFD (figure 10-1). In some aircraft, these keys are duplicated on the PFD. Describing all of the autopilot differences is beyond the scope of this book. You should read the Airplane Flight Manual Supplement for your aircraft so that you understand autopilot operation.

The Flight Director issues pitch and roll commands that are displayed on the PFD. It runs on software contained in the PFD and GIA#1, which is one of the GIA63 NAV/COM/GPS units. It generates magenta-colored command bars, or a "flying wedge" located just above the yellow inverted "V," displayed in the center of the PFD. The command bars move vertically to indicate a pitch command and bank left and right to indicate a roll. The command bars are removed from the display if attitude data becomes invalid or the Flight Director is turned off. To use the Flight Director manually, fly the airplane so that the lower inverted "V" remains tucked up tightly against the command bars. Or, press the AP key and the autopilot will control the plane to follow the guidance given by the Flight Director's command bars. Think of the Flight Director as the "brain" that gives cues to you or the autopilot, and the autopilot as the "muscle" that follows the brain.

Mode and status information for the GFC 700 is displayed in the AFCS Status bar, located at the top of the PFD under the Navigation Status bar (figure 10-2). Roll modes are displayed on the left of the display and pitch modes are on the right. Active modes are displayed toward the center of the status bar and appear in green. Armed modes which have been selected but have not yet engaged are displayed in white. Any time you see a mode listed, the Flight Director is on. If you see a green AP annunciator, then the autopilot is also on. An aural tone sounds when the autopilot is turned off; AP flashes in yellow if you disconnected it or AP flashes in red if the autopilot turned itself off.

One of the most common mistakes I see pilots make is confusing the Flight Director with the autopilot. Often, if the airplane is starting to bank and descend on its own, I hear pilots ask, "why is it doing

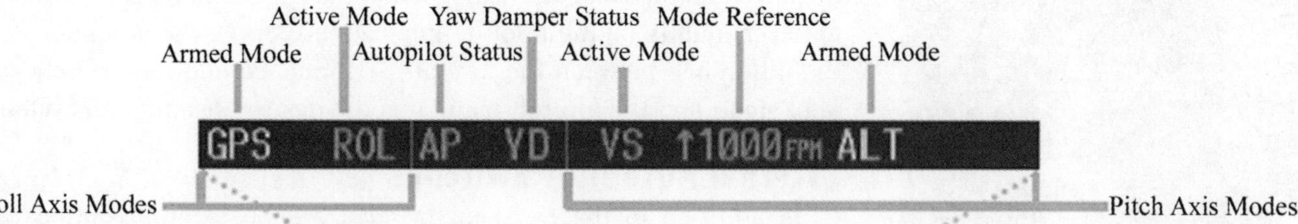

Figure 10-2 The AFCS Status bar is located at the top of the PFD. © *Garmin Ltd. or its affiliates*

that?" I'll ask them who's flying the plane, and they'll usually point at the command bars and say "the autopilot." Eventually, they realize that the Flight Director is on but the autopilot is off and that nobody is flying the airplane! You can avoid this situation by confirming that "AP" appears in the status bar anytime you think that you've engaged the autopilot.

You'll want to note the Autopilot System Status information, displayed above and to the left of the attitude indicator. You'll first notice this when the aircraft is turned on and the autopilot performs its preflight system test. At the completion of the test, a white PFT annunciator is displayed and an aural alert is heard (figure 10-3). If the preflight system tests fails, a red PFT annunciator is displayed. Other AFCS Warning and Caution annunciators are listed in Appendix H of this book and in the aircraft manuals.

Another annunciator, MAXSPD, flashes at the top of the airspeed indicator (figure 10-4) if Overspeed Protection is active. It's displayed when the Flight Director cannot maintain the reference speed without exceeding the autopilot's maximum airspeed limitation. This can occur if excessive power is used in a descent, or an excessive descent rate is selected. It's inactive in ALT, GS and GP modes.

TIP

I've talked with instructors around the country, and we all agree that each time you press a key on the autopilot, you must verify it by looking at the status bar. You need to confirm that the mode you think you selected is indeed shown on the status bar. Also, note whether it's already active, or whether it is armed to become active later. Checking the status bar after every push of an autopilot key will help you avoid an automation surprise. Another good practice is to read aloud the autopilot status indicators when you check them.

Roll and Pitch Modes

The integrated autopilot includes all of the same roll and pitch modes found in many autopilots, plus some advanced features. First, roll modes control lateral guidance, or the left/right motion of the airplane. To make things a little more confusing, one of the roll modes is named ROL or Roll Hold mode. In many autopilots, ROL mode keeps the wings level. In the GFC 700, ROL mode can also maintain a specific bank angle, as explained later in this chapter.

Pitch modes control the nose up or nose down motion of the airplane. You'll choose one of these modes whenever you want to change altitude or maintain your present altitude.

One way to visualize how the system works is to realize that the Flight Director always has two references or target values that it is trying to maintain. One is for lateral left/right guidance and the other is for pitch. For example, the lateral reference might be a heading it's trying to maintain, and the pitch reference might be a specific descent rate in feet per minute. The Flight Director measures the actual performance of the aircraft and compares it with the references. The difference between the actual performance and the references is then

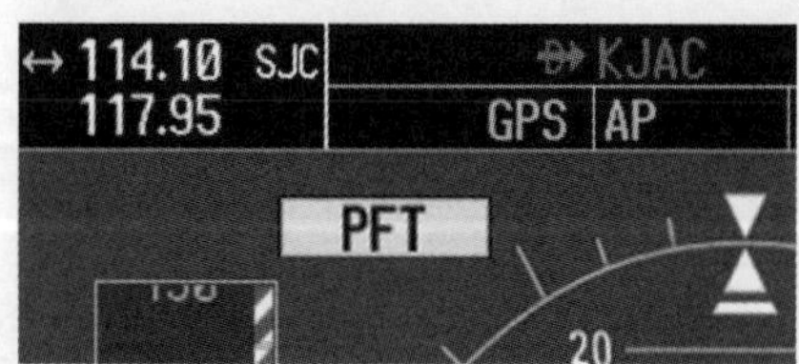

Figure 10-3 A white PFT and a loud alert indicate the completion of the autopilot's self-test. © *Garmin Ltd. or its affiliates*

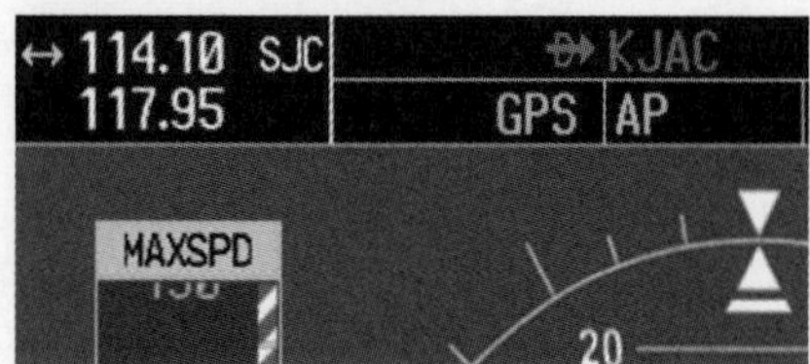

Figure 10-4 MAXSPD means you've exceeded the autopilot's maximum airspeed limitation. © *Garmin Ltd. or its affiliates*

Figure 10-5 On the Cessna 182 yoke, the CWS button is at the top, red AP DISC is in the center and dual trim switches are at the bottom. © *Max Trescott*

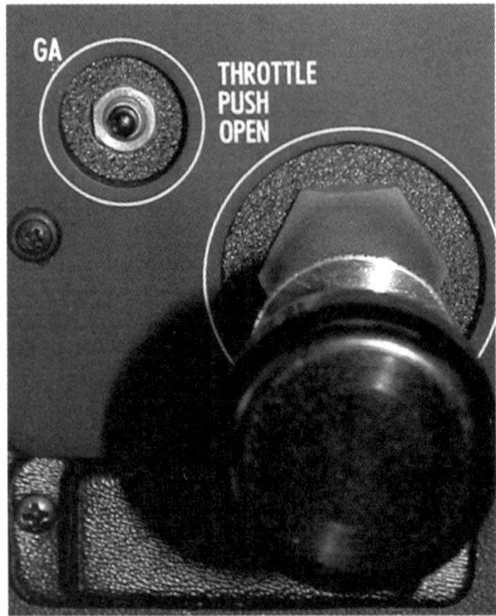

Figure 10-6 This GA button is conveniently located beneath your thumb when you advance the throttle for a go-around. © *Max Trescott*

displayed on the command bars. When the command bars are followed, either manually by the pilot or automatically when the autopilot is on, the difference between the aircraft performance and the references is kept small and the aircraft maintains the desired heading and pitch.

External Autopilot Switches

In addition to the keys on the MFD, some external buttons and switches are used for the autopilot. For example, in GFC 700-equipped aircraft, you'll find an AP DISC or Autopilot Disconnect button on the yoke or control stick (figure 10-5). This disengages the autopilot, Flight Director, yaw damper, and pitch trim operation. It's also used to mute the aural tone associated with the autopilot disconnecting.

A CWS or Control Wheel Steering button is found in all aircraft equipped with the Garmin integrated autopilot. When pressed and held, it temporarily disengages the autopilot and synchronizes the Flight Director command bars with the plane's current attitude. Upon release, in some modes, new reference points are transferred to the Flight Director, which will maintain the new altitude or attitude. For other modes, such as the Heading Select and Navigation modes, the Flight Director will revert to the reference in use prior to pushing and holding the CWS button. So for example, if you are in Navigation mode and push and hold the CWS button to steer around a cloud, upon release of the button the autopilot will re-intercept and fly the original course.

The GA or Go Around button disengages the autopilot and sets the Flight Director command bars for a climb pitch attitude with wings level (figure 10-6). It's useful for takeoffs, go arounds, and flying a missed approach. Its use is discussed later in the section on Other Pitch Modes.

Finally, MET or Manual Electric Trim switches are usually mounted on the yoke. These switches allow you to adjust the electric pitch trim. In some aircraft, the switches can also adjust aileron trim.

Engaging the Flight Director

Pressing the FD key, or any of the mode keys, engages the Flight Director. If the FD key is pressed, the Flight Director notes the aircraft's attitude at the moment the key is pushed and comes up in the Roll Hold and Pitch Hold modes. ROL and PIT are annunciated in the AFCS Status Bar and the command bars provide guidance to maintain the aircraft's current attitude. If, instead of pushing the FD key, a roll mode key is pushed, the system comes up in that roll mode and the Pitch Hold mode. If a pitch mode key is pushed, the Flight Director engages that pitch mode and the Roll Hold mode. Note that the term "Hold" in these modes can be misleading, as the Flight Director is just the brain, and cannot hold an attitude by itself—that's the work of the pilot or autopilot.

When ROL mode is engaged, the Flight Director maintains the

current bank angle, but only if it's greater than 6° and less than 22°. For bank angles less than 6°, the system assumes that the bank was unintentional and so it rolls the command bars level. For bank angles greater than 22°, it maintains a bank of 22°. Pitch can also be changed by pressing the UP and DN keys. Each press changes the pitch attitude by 0.5 degrees.

The reference for the Roll Hold and Pitch Hold mode can be modified by pressing the CWS button, rolling to new pitch and bank angles, and releasing the CWS button. The Roll Hold and Pitch Hold modes are handy for short periods of time when you want to maintain your current attitude. Generally they're not useful for more than a few minutes, since they don't know how to get you anywhere.

Other Roll Modes

Heading Select Mode

The Heading Select mode is one of the most common modes on any autopilot. It allows you to command the aircraft's heading by using the system's HDG knob to turn the HSI's heading reference bug to the desired heading. The Flight Director and autopilot, if it's engaged, will then turn to the selected heading. You'll find this mode useful while being vectored by ATC or for flying an intercept angle to join a course to be flown with the autopilot's Navigation mode.

Before engaging the Heading Select mode, you may want to first push the HDG knob on the PFD or MFD so that the heading reference bug is synchronized with your current heading. That way, the aircraft won't begin an immediate turn when you engage the mode. Next, press the HDG key to engage the Heading Select mode and a HDG annunciator will appear in green in the active roll mode field. Finally, turn the HDG knob to whatever heading you desire. Headings are commanded in the direction you've selected, even if the turn exceeds 180°. However, if the turn is more than 340°, the Flight Director will reverse to turn in the opposite direction.

Note that the CWS button will not change the heading selected with the HDG knob. If you push the CWS button and hand-fly the aircraft, upon releasing the CWS button, the aircraft will turn back to the heading set by the HDG knob.

Navigation Mode

The Navigation mode is one of the most useful modes. When engaged, the Flight Director will track any VOR, localizer or GPS signal selected on the HSI. This mode is used primarily while en route, whereas Approach mode, described below, is generally used to track navigation signals when flying an instrument approach. Nonetheless, Navigation mode can be used for non-precision GPS approaches and localizer approaches that don't require glide slope or glide path tracking.

To engage the Navigation mode, press the NAV key. A GPS, VOR, or LOC (localizer) annunciator is displayed in the AFCS Status bar if a

Figure 10-7 Navigation mode is active and tracking a VOR signal. *© Garmin Ltd. or its affiliates*

valid signal is selected on the HSI (figure 10-7). If there is more than one dot of deflection of the HSI's D-bar when the mode is engaged, the annunciators will be white indicating that the Navigation mode is armed. In this case, you must use HDG mode to steer the aircraft closer to the desired course until Navigation mode becomes active. As the course pointer's D-bar gets close to centering, Navigation mode becomes active, and the GPS, VOR, or LOC annunciator appears in green. Note that there's no NAV annunciation on the GFC 700; instead annunciators are shown for the selected navigation source.

Whenever a VOR course pointer is selected on the HSI, you should select a desired course using the CRS knob. If you want to fly from your present position directly to the VOR, press the CRS knob to center the CDI needle. For GFC 700 installations without a BC key, you'll need to use Navigation mode to track the backcourse of a localizer. This is the opposite direction from the front course for which the localizer was primarily designed. When tracking a backcourse, use the CRS knob to select the heading of the localizer's front course in order to display the proper orientation on the HSI. Note that BC (backcourse mode) is automatically displayed whenever you're on a ground track that is more than 105° from the localizer's front course.

Approach Mode

Approach mode is used to fly VOR, localizer, ILS, and GPS instrument approaches. It is more sensitive than Navigation mode when tracking VOR signals and it can also capture and track the glide slope associated with an ILS approach. For systems with WAAS-capable GPS receivers, it can also track the vertical glide path of an LPV, LNAV/VNAV, or LNAV+V approach.

To engage the Approach mode, press the APR key. A GPSa, VAPP, or LOC annunciator will appear in green in the AFCS Status bar when the mode becomes active, depending upon whether you're flying a GPS, VOR, or ILS approach. If a valid ILS frequency is tuned on the NAV receiver selected on the HSI, a GS, glide slope, annunciator will appear in the AFCS Status bar (figure 10-8). It will initially be white, but later in the approach, when the Flight Director has intercepted and captured the glide slope, the GS annunciator will turn green (figure 10-9). If a LPV, LNAV/VNAV, or LNAV+V approach is loaded in the active flight plan, a GP, glide path, annunciator will appear in the AFCS Status bar. It will initially be white, but when the Flight Director captures the glide path, the GP annunciator will turn green.

Figure 10-8 Navigation mode is tracking a localizer and the glide slope is armed prior to GS intercept. *© Garmin Ltd. or its affiliates*

Figure 10-9 The Flight Director has intercepted and captured the glide slope. *© Garmin Ltd. or its affiliates*

Note that while descending on a glide slope or glide path, you can use the CWS button to hand-fly the airplane to a new position. However, once you release the CWS button, the Flight Director will fly the aircraft back to the glide slope or glide path.

Other Pitch Modes

Altitude Hold Mode

The Altitude Hold mode is used extensively during cruise to maintain level flight. In its simplest use, pressing the ALT key causes the Flight Director to capture the aircraft's current altitude as a reference altitude, which is then displayed in the AFCS Status Box to the nearest ten feet. The ALT annunciator appears in green in the AFCS Status Box and, if the autopilot is engaged, the aircraft will maintain the reference altitude.

Note that the reference altitude is independent of the Selected Altitude, set by the G1000 or Perspective's ALT knobs and displayed above the altimeter (figure 10-10). Thus turning the ALT knobs and changing the Selected Altitude will not change your altitude when the Altitude Hold mode is active. However, the ALT knobs are used for the Selected Altitude Capture mode described below.

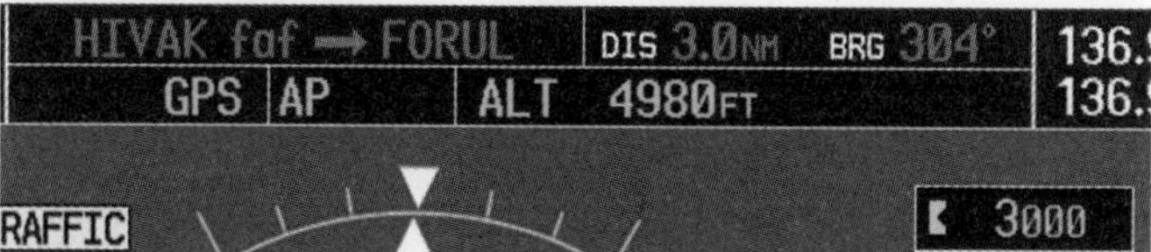

Figure 10-10 Aircraft is level at the 4980 feet reference altitude and the Selected Altitude is 3000 feet. *© Garmin Ltd. or its affiliates*

For small altitude changes while in Altitude Hold mode, press the CWS button, manually fly the aircraft to a new altitude and then release the CWS button. The Flight Director will maintain the new altitude. For large altitude changes, use any of the pitch modes with the Selected Altitude Capture mode.

Selected Altitude Capture Mode

Rather than push the ALT key to level off at a desired altitude, it's more convenient to preselect an altitude and let the autopilot level off for you when the aircraft reaches that altitude. To preselect an altitude, whether you're on the ground or in flight, use the G1000 or Perspective's ALT knobs to set the Selected Altitude displayed above the altimeter. The Selected Altitude Capture Hold mode is then armed automatically when the Flight Director is turned on, or if any of the following pitch modes are active: Pitch Hold, Vertical Speed, Flight Level Change, or Go Around. The current pitch mode remains active and displayed in green, and a white ALTS annunciator (ALT on early Columbia and Beechcraft models) appears in the AFCS Status Box. Depending upon the pitch mode in use, you may have to use the UP or DN key to initiate the climb or descent.

The ALTS annunciator is used to distinguish this mode from the Vertical Navigation mode, which uses an ALTV annunciator to indicate that the aircraft will level off at an altitude specified in the vertical flight plan. It's important for you to note which annunciator appears, since in the Vertical Navigation mode you can get either the ALTS annunciator or the ALTV annunciator, depending upon the altitude selected by the ALT knobs.

As the aircraft approaches the preselected altitude, the white ALTS annunciator extinguishes and is replaced with a blinking green ALTS annunciator and a white ALT annunciator. At 50 feet from the selected altitude, as the Flight Director is leveling off, both annunciators are extinguished and a green ALT annunciator will flash for up to ten seconds and then remain green, indicating that the Altitude Hold mode is now active.

In some early GFC 700 installations, while level in Altitude Hold mode, you had to first preselect an altitude before selecting a pitch mode. Otherwise the aircraft would remain in Altitude Hold mode. Now most GFC 700 installations allow a pilot to initiate a climb or descent by first pressing a pitch mode key and later preselecting an altitude at which to level off.

Vertical Speed Mode

The Vertical Speed mode is useful for maintaining a climb or a descent at a constant rate. My personal preference is to use this mode for descents and to use the FLC mode, described below, for climbs. To use it, preselect your desired cruise altitude with the ALT knobs and then push the VS key to engage Vertical Speed mode. A VS annunciator will appear in green in the active pitch mode field and the Flight Director will capture and maintain the aircraft's vertical speed. Then look at the Vertical Speed Reference Box at the top of the vertical speed indicator to verify the vertical speed captured (figure 10-11). You need to verify and change it if necessary because the Flight Director could capture an unrealistically high climb rate, which might cause the autopilot to pull the aircraft up into a stall. Note that during a climb, an aircraft's performance decreases with altitude and the vertical speed mode could put the aircraft into a stall later in the climb. This cannot happen with any FLC mode, which is why it's preferred for climbs.

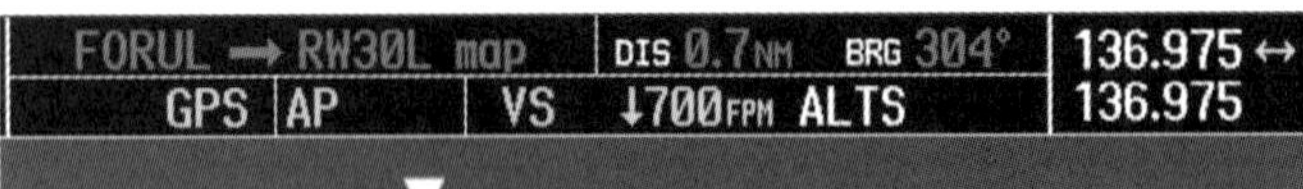

Figure 10-11 Always verify the vertical speed captured, in this case minus 700 feet per minute. *© Garmin Ltd. or its affiliates*

You can change the rate at any time by pressing the UP or DN keys, which will change the vertical speed in 100 feet per minute increments. You can also adjust the vertical speed by pressing the CWS button, manually flying the aircraft to a new vertical speed, and releasing the CWS button. Note that each installation has maximum vertical speed limits. For example, the maximum vertical speed limits for the Beechcraft G36 are +1500 and -3000 feet per minute.

Flight Level Change Mode

The Flight Level Change mode, also called Indicated Airspeed or IAS mode in the Perspective and some G1000 installations, is useful for changing altitude while maintaining the same airspeed. It's particularly useful in a climb, as it allows you to maintain a target climb airspeed, such as Vy, the best rate of climb, even as aircraft performance decreases. As with any altitude change, you should first preselect your new cruise altitude with the ALT knobs. Then press the FLC key. The system will acquire the aircraft's present speed as a reference and a FLC annunciator appears in green in the active pitch mode field.

To initiate the altitude change, however, you will also need to change the engine power or the FLC reference speed. For a climb, add power and the Flight Director will select a pitch that allows you to climb while maintaining the reference speed. Or, decrease the airspeed reference in 1-knot increments by pressing the UP key, and the aircraft will climb at its current power setting. For a descent, reduce power, or increase the FLC airspeed reference by pushing the DN key. Another way to adjust the FLC reference airspeed is to press the CWS button, manually fly the aircraft to a new airspeed and release the CWS button. The Flight Director will maintain the new reference speed.

Generally, the FLC or IAS reference can be adjusted again at any time until the aircraft reaches the selected altitude. However, that's not true in fast climbing aircraft such as Cessna Citations retrofitted with a G1000. The GFC 700 was certified differently for the Citation and its ALTS function begins to capture earlier than in other aircraft. For example, while climbing to 9,000 feet at 3800 fpm in a Citation, the IAS reference can no longer be changed as you pass through about 6,000 feet. Generally that's not an issue, however Citations departing IFR out of the Hayward, CA airport are instructed to initially climb to 2,000 feet. By the time a pilot engages the autopilot in IAS mode, the ALTS function is already starting to capture and the IAS reference cannot be changed in the climb. Thus for short initial climbs, pilots of these aircraft may want to use the Vertical Speed mode.

TIP

Always check the vertical speed reference soon after you engage the autopilot. If it captures an unrealistically high climb rate, the autopilot can pull the airplane into a stall.

Go Around Mode

The GA or Go Around mode is useful for takeoffs, go arounds, and flying a missed approach. When the GA button is pushed, it disengages the autopilot, except in the Perspective, and sets the Flight Director command bars for a climb pitch attitude. In Cessna and Beechcraft piston aircraft, it displays a 7° pitch up attitude. It also re-enables automatic sequencing of waypoints and selects GPS as the navigation source, thus eliminating the need to push the SUSP and CDI softkeys on a missed approach. When engaged, a green GA annunciator appears in the active fields of both the roll and pitch fields of the AFCS Status Bar, and the Altitude Hold mode is automatically armed. Any attempt to modify the aircraft's attitude while in this mode (e.g. with the UP or DN keys or the CWS button) results in reversion to the Pitch Hold and ROL modes.

Vertical Navigation Mode

Some GFC 700 autopilots include a VNV key, which enables it to follow a vertical descent profile specified in the active flight plan or to descend to a vertical altitude specified using the Direct-to key. It can be used for en route descents, and is a convenient way to meet ATC instructions to cross one or more fixes at specific altitudes. It cannot, however, be used for climbs or for flying the intermediate and final approach segments of an instrument approach procedure. It works only when GPS is selected as the navigation source on the HSI.

When engaged, the Vertical Navigation mode provides guidance to

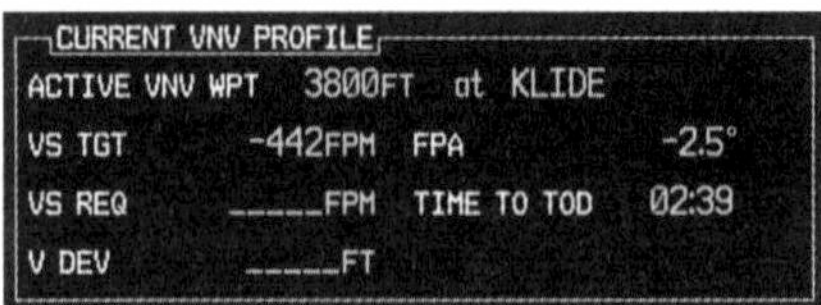

Figure 10-12 If you don't specify a VS TGT or FPA in the Current VNV Profile window, a minus 2.5° descent angle is used. *© Garmin Ltd. or its affiliates*

Figure 10-13 Vertical Path Tracking (VPTH) is armed and ALTV indicates this aircraft will descend to the altitude specified in the flight plan. *© Garmin Ltd. or its affiliates*

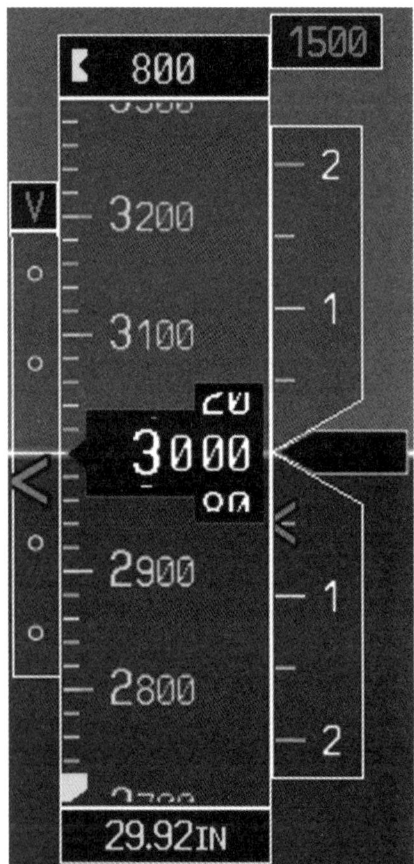

Figure 10-14 The vertical deviation indicator on the left shows the aircraft above the descent profile. The VS required indicator shows a -500 fpm descent is required to descend on the profile to the 1500 foot altitude specified in the flight plan. *© Garmin Ltd. or its affiliates*

descend to the higher of: 1) the Selected Altitude set by the ALT knobs (provided it's at least 75 feet below the current altitude) and indicated with an ALTS annunciator or, 2) the altitude specified for the active waypoint in the vertical flight plan and indicated with an ALTV annunciator. Thus if you intend to follow the vertical flight plan, you must remember to use the ALT knobs to select an altitude equal to or lower than the altitude in the vertical flight plan. Forgetting to set the ALT knobs can result in an automation surprise, when the autopilot levels off, or remains, at the Selected Altitude rather than the altitude specified in the flight plan.

To set up a vertical flight plan, use the FPL key on the MFD. Enter appropriate altitudes for each waypoint using the FMS knobs, or use altitudes filled in automatically from the system's database. Also, enter a target descent rate in feet per minute next to VS TGT, or specify a descent angle in degrees next to FPA (figure 10-12).

Then press the VNV key to arm the Vertical Path Tracking mode. A white VPTH annunciaton appears in the AFCS Status Bar, and a white GP annunciator also appears if the Approach mode is active. Note that a TOD label, for Top of Descent, appears on the Inset Map and Navigation Map page at the point where the vertical descent will begin. There are a variety of reasons why the Vertical Path Tracking mode might not become active at this point, and these are discussed at the end of this section.

When the aircraft is one minute away from TOD, "TOD within 1 minute" is annunciated in the Navigation Status bar (figure 10-13), and several new magenta-colored indicators appear on the PFD. The most important of these is a vertical deviation indicator, which appears to the left of the altimeter and is similar to the glide slope indicator except that it uses a magenta V on its side, rather than a green diamond, to indicate the target glide path. Like a glide slope indicator, the V moves down from the top of the indicator and when it's centered next to the altimeter, the aircraft is on the vertical descent path and can begin to descend. Full scale deflection of the vertical deviation indicator is plus and minus 1,000 feet. A vertical speed required indicator also appears and is indicated by a magenta V on its side in the vertical speed indicator. A VNAV Target Altitude, copied from the vertical flight plan, appears above and to the right of the Selected Altitude (figure 10-14).

About a minute later, as the aircraft reaches TOD and the Vertical Navigation mode becomes active, the white VPTH annunciator is extinguished and a green VPTH annunciator flashes for up to ten seconds and then remains green. At the same time, either a white ALTV or a white ALTS annunciator appears, depending upon whether the vertical flight plan altitude or the selected altitude is higher. When the aircraft is one minute away from BOD, or Bottom of Descent, "BOD within 1 minute" is annunciated in the Navigation Status bar.

As the aircraft approaches the VNAV Target Altitude, the white ALTV annunciator extinguishes and is replaced with a blinking green

ALTV annunciator and a white ALT annunciator. At 50 feet from the target altitude, as the Flight Director is leveling off, both annunciators are extinguished and a green ALT annunciator flashes for up to ten seconds and then remains green, indicating that the Altitude Hold mode is now active. The aircraft then flies level along the next leg. If additional descents are specified in the vertical flight plan, the Vertical Navigation mode is rearmed and the white ALTV annunciator reappears.

The Vertical Navigation mode, initiated with the VNV key, cannot be used to fly the intermediate or final approach segments of a LPV, LNAV/VNAV, or LNAV+V approach, unless the Approach mode is also selected. If both the VNV key and the APR key are pressed, and the VPTH and GP annunciators are both displayed, the autopilot initially descends using the vertical flight plan, and then uses the WAAS receiver's glide path to descend to the missed approach point. The VNV function can also be used when issued an ATC instruction to cross at a specific altitude over a waypoint not in your flight plan. To do this, use the Along Track Offsets function described in Chapter 14 to create a new waypoint and enter the crossing altitude. Then use the ALT knobs to select an altitude and press the VNV key.

Vertical Navigation Mode Limitations

As mentioned earlier, there is a variety of reasons that the Vertical Path Tracking mode might not become active. If the VNV key is pressed less than five minutes before TOD, the mode will activate as we've described in this section. However, if the VNV key is pushed more than five minutes before TOD, an additional acknowledgement is needed from the pilot once the aircraft is within five minutes of TOD. This can either be an additional press of the VNV key or any change in the Selected Altitude using the ALT knobs.

If the VNV key is pressed more than five minutes before TOD and no subsequent acknowledgement is made, at one minute prior to TOD, the white VPTH annunciator will flash every second for the next minute, signaling that an acknowledgement is required. If neither the VNV key is pressed nor the Selected Altitude is changed prior to TOD, the aircraft will not descend. If the VNV key is pushed after TOD, the aircraft will still not descend, since it is now above the vertical descent profile.

If you're beyond TOD and above the vertical descent profile, you may still be able to force capture of the descent profile, though it's not recommended if it would result in an excessive descent rate. If the white VPTH annunciator is on, press a pitch mode key, such as VS, and then press the DN key to select a descent rate equal to or greater than the rate indicated by the vertical speed required indicator, which is the magenta V to the right of the altimeter. As the magenta "V" in the vertical deviation indicator (to the left of the altimeter) centers, the Vertical Navigation mode becomes active, and the green VPTH annunciator appears.

TIP

If you push the VNV key more than 5 minutes prior to descent, you'll need to push it again later. But what if you're not sure if you need to push it again? At one minute prior to descent, look at the top of the PFD to see how many elements are flashing white. If only "TOD within 1 minute" is flashing, you don't need to push VNV again. If VPTH is also flashing at the same time, then you need to push the VNV key again. When using the VNV key, you need to constantly compare what the system will do next with your ATC instructions. If they disagree, you need to reprogram or disable the VNV function so that your flight path complies with ATC instructions.

The Vertical Path Tracking mode will not become active if any of the following occur:

- The CDI softkey is pressed deselecting GPS as the navigation source.
- The CNCL VNV softkey on the MFD's Active Flight Plan page is pressed.
- All vertical waypoints are deleted from the flight plan.
- The displays enter the Reversionary Mode.

When the Vertical Path Tracking mode is active, it may revert to Pitch Hold mode under certain conditions. If it does, Vertical Path Tracking mode is armed for a possible re-capture of the descent profile. Reversion to Pitch Hold mode occurs in the following circumstances if the vertical deviation from the descent profile:

- Exceeds 200 feet due to an overspeed condition.
- Exceeds more than 200 feet due to a flight plan change.
- Becomes invalid due to cross-track error from the intended course.
- Cannot be computed for leg types such as a hold or procedure turn.

Note that the altitudes in the vertical flight plan can be changed at any time before the Vertical Path Tracking mode becomes active. Also, once Vertical Path Tracking mode is active, the altitude for the flight plan's active waypoint can be increased to an altitude that's still below the aircraft's current altitude. However, selecting a new lower altitude for the active waypoint results in reversion to the Pitch Hold mode and Selected Altitude Capture mode.

Also, if the VS or FLC key is pressed while the Vertical Path Tracking mode is active, the Vertical Path Tracking mode and the appropriate altitude capture mode revert to armed. Vertical Path Tracking mode can become active again once:

- At least ten seconds have passed (to prevent immediate reactivation).
- Vertical deviation from the descent profile exceeded 250 feet but in now less than 200 feet.

Pressing the VNV key twice re-arms Vertical Path Tracking for immediate profile capture.

Backcourse Mode

The Backcourse mode is used whenever you're flying a localizer in the reverse direction. This occurs when you're flying a Localizer BC instrument approach, or when you're flying outbound on the front course of a localizer prior to the procedure turn inbound. In either case, use the CRS knob to set the HSI's course pointer to the localizer's front course.

If there's more than one dot of deflection of the CDI's D-bar, pressing the BC key arms the Backcourse mode and a white BC annunciator appears. When deflection is less than one dot, the Backcourse mode becomes active and a green BC annunciator appears. If you push the CWS button and hand-fly the aircraft, upon releasing the CWS button, the aircraft will re-intercept and track the backcourse.

Using the GFC 700

Prior to takeoff, you'll want to preset the Flight Director as part of your pre-takeoff checklist. Start by turning on the Flight Director by pressing any roll or pitch mode key or by pressing the FD key. If you press the FD key, the system comes up in the Pitch Hold and Roll Hold modes. Next set the heading bug for your initial heading and press the HDG key. Finally, set your initial altitude with the G1000 or Perspective's ALT knobs, and then press either the VS or FLC key and use the UP and DN keys to set your desired climb rate. Alternatively, if you'd prefer having a 7° pitch up guidance from the command bars during the initial climb, push the GA button to select Go Around mode.

After takeoff and above the minimum altitude for autopilot use, press the AP key and the autopilot will follow the guidance provided by the Flight Director. You'll find the minimum altitude for autopilot use in the aircraft's AFM Supplement. After leveling off, to initiate a subsequent altitude change, always start by using the ALT knobs to preselect an altitude. Then press a pitch key, such as the FLC or VS key. Finally, use the UP or DN key to set an appropriate climb or descent rate.

Common Errors

One common error in instrument flight is that pilots forget that their autopilot may revert from HDG, NAV, or APR mode to ROL mode when the HSI's navigation source is switched from GPS to one of the NAV receivers. If the reversion goes unnoticed, it results in the aircraft flying through the localizer. It's important that you know under which conditions this occurs in your aircraft. To the best of my knowledge, reversion to ROL mode always occurs when the navigation source is switched manually by pushing the CDI softkey. It also occurs when the CDI switches automatically with the G1000's ILS CDI Capture feature in the AUTO mode in KAP 140-equipped aircraft and in older GFC 700-equipped aircraft. Reversion to ROL mode does not occur in 2007 and later GFC 700-equipped Cessna 172, 182, and 206 aircraft when the CDI switches automatically, but it does occur when the CDI softkey is pushed. So depending upon your aircraft, you may want to wait until after you've selected the CDI to the proper source (e.g. to the appropriate NAV receiver when flying an ILS) before engaging the autopilot in approach mode. Or, you might choose to switch the CDI needle manually and then immediately re-engage the autopilot.

Another common error is the failure to properly preflight autopilots. Typically, this involves engaging the autopilot on the ground and then confirming that you can overpower the autopilot with the yoke. Then, press the autopilot disconnect switch and turn the yoke to verify that the control forces are less and that the autopilot disengaged. Finally,

TIP

Here's what I do to avoid an automation surprise when flying an ILS. In some aircraft, the KAP 140 autopilot reverts from NAV to ROL mode when the CDI switches automatically with the G1000's ILS CDI Capture feature. To avoid this, I usually switch the CDI needle myself. Generally, I'll do this immediately after a controller begins issuing headings to vector me for an approach. At that point, the GPS data on the CDI needle is of little value, so I push the CDI softkey to select the green CDI needle for the localizer. Since I'm in heading mode at this point, the autopilot doesn't revert to ROL mode when the CDI needle is changed. If I were in NAV mode when I switched the needle, immediately after pushing the CDI softkey, I would re-engage the autopilot's NAV mode.

Author Note

The discussion on testing MET switches applies specifically to Cessnas, which have dual trim switches. Some manufacturers have only a single trim switch. In all cases you should test the trim switches. Also note that pushing the pitch trim switch should disconnect the autopilot.

the Mechanical Electric Trim (MET) switches are tested. This involves confirming that the trim wheel does not move unless both switches are moved together in the same direction, that releasing one of the switches stops trim wheel movement, and that moving a single switch will not move the trim wheel. You'll also check to see that the AP disconnect button interrupts trim wheel motion. On the KAP 140, you need to hold the right MET switch in the up position for 5 seconds and verify that the PT (pitch trim) annunciator on the autopilot turns on. As always, read the Airplane Flight Manual Supplement for your autopilot for the exact preflight procedure.

Another common error is that pilots may try to move the yoke after the autopilot is engaged in flight. Typically, pushing or pulling on the yoke will cause the trim wheel to move in the opposite direction, creating heavy control forces if the autopilot disconnects. In the extreme, if you continue to push or pull the yoke, the trim wheel will move until it reaches one of the limits, potentially creating extremely heavy control forces and possible loss of control.

It's also not unusual for pilots to forget to apply proper rudder forces, particularly while climbing with the autopilot engaged. While you can fold your arms and just monitor the status of everything as the autopilot flies the plane, you still need to apply right rudder in a climb or, if the plane is so equipped, adjust the rudder trim. Pilots may also forget to adjust power when they initiate a climb or descent or when the autopilot levels off at the preselected altitude.

Autopilot Failures

Autopilots, like any other system, can fail. The consequences of a failure can be severe, so you should always monitor autopilot operation. For example, while on an instrument approach, some pilots keep their hand poised next to the yoke. That way, they can instantly grab the yoke and take control should the autopilot misbehave. When doing this, be careful not to apply any pressure to the yoke, so that the autopilot doesn't move the trim wheel against you as described in the previous section.

The autopilot uses rate of turn information to make all turns at the standard rate of 3° per second. So, for example, if you find the autopilot is banking excessively, say in excess of 30°, you might suspect that the autopilot is malfunctioning and you should disconnect it.

In the G1000, failure of some system components can also lead to the loss of some autopilot modes or, in some cases, render the autopilot totally unusable. In the Perspective system, the autopilot is affected by fewer of these component failures. For example, in early G1000 aircraft equipped with the GFC 700, loss of any of the following components leads to a complete loss of the GFC 700: PFD, ADC, AHRS, or GIA1. If GIA2 fails, the Flight Director will still function, though you will need to manually fly the airplane to follow the commands. If either GPS1 or GPS2, located within GIA1 and GIA2 respectively, were to fail, there would be no loss of functionality, as either GPS can take over for the other one.

If the MFD were to fail, you will lose GIA2, which is directly connected to most autopilots. For GFC 700-equipped aircraft, the autopilot will remain on in the active modes and will capture any armed modes. However, if your GFC 700 only has keys on the MFD bezel, you will be unable to change modes and once the autopilot is disconnected it cannot be re-engaged. The Flight Director will remain on, however, you will be unable to change modes or turn it off.

You can learn more about how component failures affect the autopilot in Chapter 12. You'll find a list of typical Warnings and Cautions for the Garmin AFCS Autopilot in Appendix H.

GFC 700 LIMITATIONS

Many pilots are unfamiliar with their autopilot limitations. Here's a list of some of the limitations for one GFC 700-equipped aircraft. Consult your Airplane Flight Manual Supplement for the limitations of your aircraft:

- Preflight test of autopilot, Flight Director, MET switches
- Pilot with seat belt fastened occupying the left pilot seat
- AP off during landings and takeoffs
- Max engagement 165 KIAS
- Minimum engagement 70 KIAS
- Electric Trim Max Operating Speed 175 KIAS
- Max fuel imbalance with autopilot engaged: 90 pounds
- AP disengaged below 200 feet for instrument approaches
- AP disengaged below 800 feet AGL for all other operations
- ILS Approaches limited to Category I
- Use of AP prohibited when audio panel is inoperative.
- Use of AP prohibited on missed approach until a rate of climb established to ensure altitude requirements will be met.

Maximum pitch and roll limits are also specified. For the Beechcraft G36, for example, the Flight Director cannot pitch more than 20° up or 15° down. Maximum bank angles are 22° and the maximum roll rate is 5 degrees per second.

Finally, it should be noted that some older G1000 installations cannot fly procedure turns and holding patterns automatically. In these aircraft, you'll need to manually steer the autopilot through these procedures using the Heading Select mode. Aircraft with updated system software, and all aircraft shipped with a WAAS-capable GPS receiver, can fly a hold using the autopilot's NAV mode with the GPS CDI pointer selected.

King/Bendix KAP 140 Autopilot

A large number of G1000-equipped aircraft, but no Perspective aircraft, were shipped with the KAP 140 autopilot, so we'll briefly discuss differences when using that autopilot. Note that some KAP 140 autopilot differences may exist among aircraft, so you should refer to your Airplane Flight Manual Supplement and use it in preference to this book if a conflict exists.

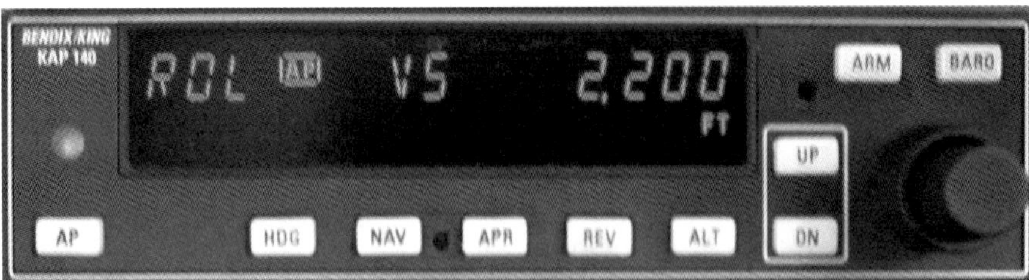

Figure 10-15 The KAP 140 initially engages in the ROL and VS modes. Here, the altitude preselect has been set to level off at 2,200 feet. © *Max Trescott*

One of the key differences is that the KAP 140 has less integration with the G1000. For example, there is no AFCS Status bar on the PFD and you must look at the autopilot to see in which modes it's operating. As you'd expect, most of the autopilot keys and the altitude preselect knobs are on the autopilot rather than on the MFD bezel. KAP 140 installations ship with an electric turn coordinator, not visible in the cockpit, which provides standard rate turn information and which must be working for autopilot operation. Finally, KAP 140-equipped G1000 aircraft do not ship with a Flight Director.

Soon after engine start, set the local barometric pressure on the KAP 140. Then, as part of the pre-takeoff checklist, you should preselect your cruise altitude using the knobs on the KAP 140. After takeoff, engage the KAP 140 autopilot by pushing the AP key for at least 0.25 seconds. The system will initially engage in the ROL and VS modes (figure 10-15). At this point, you'll probably want to synchronize the heading bug by pressing the HDG knob on the MFD and then select the HDG mode by pushing the HDG key on the KAP 140.

When the GFC 700 is in VS mode, it's easy to determine what vertical speed it has captured by looking at the top of the vertical speed indicator on the PFD. To see the KAP 140's vertical speed reference, you'll need to push either the UP or the DN key on the KAP 140 once. Pushing the UP or DN key additional times will change the vertical speed reference in 100 feet per minute increments. When you're in ALT mode, each push of the UP or DN key changes your altitude by 20 feet, though the original altitude continues to be displayed in the altitude preselect window.

Figure 10-16 The HDG and VS modes are active and the altitude hold mode is armed. © *Max Trescott*

Finally, you need to arm the KAP 140 so that it will level off at the preselected altitude. To do this, press the ARM key on the KAP 140 and verify that ALT mode is armed by looking for the label ALT in the lower half of the KAP 140 display (figure 10-16). Note that you'll get an aural altitude alert when you're 1000 feet from your preselected altitude. This is a good time to verify that you've preselected the correct altitude and that you've pressed the ARM key. For subsequent level-offs, you won't need to press the ARM key again as the KAP 140 automatically arms the ALT mode when you use the altitude preselect knobs to enter a new altitude.

Like the GFC 700, the KAP 140 has both an altitude hold mode and a vertical speed mode. However, the KAP 140 uses just a single key—the ALT key—to operate both of these modes. Pressing the ALT key toggles the KAP 140 between the two modes.

The KAP 140 also has both heading and navigation modes. Like the

GFC 700, the KAP 140 relies on a signal from the HDG knob on the PFD and MFD to provide the desired heading. To engage this mode, press the HDG key on the KAP 140 and steer with the HDG knob. Navigation mode, operated by pressing the NAV key on the KAP 140, can track a VOR, localizer, or GPS signal, depending upon which is selected on the CDI.

The KAP 140 has an approach mode engaged by pressing the APR key. For an ILS signal, it will also arm the glide slope mode and capture and track the signal at glide slope intercept. Like the GFC 700, the KAP 140 autopilot will revert to ROL mode if you push the CDI softkey and switch the HSI navigation signal source when the autopilot is engaged in HDG, NAV, or APR modes. To fly a backcourse approach, you'll need to push the REV key on the KAP 140 to account for the reverse sensing.

Some KAP 140-equipped aircraft, such as the original Diamond DA40 and Diamond DA42, provide a separate CWS switch on the control stick. This allows you to manually steer the aircraft to a new attitude or altitude, depending upon which autopilot mode is engaged.

The KAP140 is connected to the G1000 system via GIA2. So if GIA2 were to experience a complete failure, the KAP 140 would no longer receive navigational signals and won't operate in NAV or APR modes. If either GPS1 or GPS2 fails, the other one becomes the active GPS and there is no loss of autopilot functionality.

TIP

The vertical speed reference that is set when you first turn on the KAP 140 autopilot is displayed for three seconds. It's important that you verify and change it if necessary so that the autopilot doesn't pull the aircraft up into a stall. If don't look at the vertical speed reference in the first three seconds, you can display it again by pushing the UP or DN key once.

TIP

Pilots are often confused about when to use the ARM key on the KAP 140. Here's the story. Turning the altitude preselect knobs arms the Altitude Hold mode ONLY if the autopilot is already engaged. So if you preselect your first level off altitude on the ground before takeoff, Altitude Hold mode will not become engaged when you turn on the autopilot, since the autopilot was not engaged when you preselected the altitude. In that case, you need to press the ARM key. If the autopilot is engaged when you preselect subsequent altitudes, Altitude Hold mode arms automatically and you don't need to press the ARM key.

Limitations

Here are some, but not all, of the limitations for KAP 140 autopilot use in Cessna aircraft. It's important that you refer to your Airplane Flight Manual Supplement and understand all of the limitations of your autopilot.

- Preflight test procedures completed before flight
- Autopilot off during takeoff and landing
- Category I ILS approaches only
- Maximum airspeed: C172:140 kts; C182/C206:160 kts
- Minimum speeds: C172:70 kts; C182:80 kts; C206:90 kts
- Maximum flaps: 10°
- Maximum fuel imbalance: C172/C182:90 pounds; C206:100 lbs
- Must disconnect below 800 feet AGL (200 feet AGL if on approach)
- Autopilot disconnected before maneuvering manually with the yoke
- If red "PITCH TRIM" warning appears on G1000, you must follow the Recovery Procedure shown in the Emergency Procedures.
- Operation of the autopilot is prohibited when the audio panel is inoperative, since the warning tones are routed through it.

Note that if you fly the aircraft below the minimum airspeed, the pitch trim motor may lock out and the KAP 140 no longer operates. You'll receive a PITCH TRIM Warning annunciator on the G1000, PT illuminates on the KAP 140 display, and you'll receive a warning tone. To restore normal operation, cycle the autopilot circuit breaker. Note that if a pitch trim lockout occurs during an instrument approach, the safest course of action may be to discontinue the approach, climb, and fly the missed approach.

Summary

Like the Engine Indication System, autopilots are one of the few areas where there are large differences in operation across different G1000-equipped aircraft. Even different aircraft using the same autopilot have some differences in operation and limitations, so it's important that you become very knowledgeable about your particular autopilot.

Spend time learning how to use your autopilot and you will find that it's a helpful assistant that reduces your workload. In contrast, if you aren't familiar with all of the autopilot's modes and limitations, you may find yourself arm wrestling with the system, which won't be fun or safe, particularly, if you're in IMC.

If you're an instrument pilot, or want to learn about instrument procedures, you'll want to read Chapter 11 and the WAAS portion of Chapter 14. If not, you can skip ahead to Chapter 12 where we discuss dealing with component failures and emergencies.

Chapter 11:
Instrument Flying with the G1000

It's axiomatic that instrument pilots must know their aircraft avionics in great detail to successfully manage the many challenges of instrument flight. This is easier in non-TAA, since traditional VOR receivers operate similarly and pilots can often figure out how to use a receiver they haven't used before. In modern TAA, however, it may be impossible for even experienced instrument pilots to figure out the GPS. So when transitioning into a Perspective- or G1000-equipped aircraft, it's imperative that you study and understand the systems and gain experience in VFR conditions before flying in IMC.

To prepare for instrument flight, you must understand the flight planning functions covered in Chapter 9. Practice them on a PC using the Garmin PC Trainer software if possible. If you're flying with a WAAS-capable GPS, generally found in 2007 and later aircraft, then you'll need to read the 10-page WAAS section of Chapter 14. Read the TAA Instrument Scan section in this chapter and then fly multiple trips in VFR conditions to get familiar with using the flight planning functions. Next, become familiar with the instrument procedures in this chapter and fly IFR with a qualified flight instructor—preferably one who is factory trained and certified. Alternatively, practice instrument flight in VFR conditions with a qualified instructor or safety pilot.

Initially, fly instrument approaches with which you are familiar. Pay particular attention to flying missed approaches and how the button pushing varies with GPS versus other approach types. Next, learn to use arrival and departure procedures. Pay particular attention to Obstacle Departure Procedures (ODPs), which are not in the system database. You'll need to enter these manually and may need to use the OBS function.

Finally, get comfortable modifying flight plans quickly for the inevitable route changes from ATC. Also practice first entering one approach and then reprogramming the system to fly a different approach at the same airport.

Chapter 11 provides the fundamentals of using the G1000 and Perspective for instrument flying. Serious instrument pilots will want to get the new *Max Trescott's GPS and WAAS Instrument Flying Handbook*, which tells you what you need to know to safely operate modern GPS receiver systems so that you don't get stuck in the clouds wondering what button to push! To order, call 800-247-6553.

Using GPS

The system's GPS can be used to fly an entire instrument approach for any procedure in its database, provided "GPS" is in the title of the approach. For approaches that don't include "GPS" in the title, such as many VOR and all ILS approaches, GPS can be used up to the final approach course, which must be flown using a NAV receiver as the primary reference, and for the missed approach.

When loading an approach without GPS in the title, you'll be required to press the ENT key an additional time to acknowledge the message, "NOT APPROVED FOR GPS – GPS guidance is for monitoring only. Load approach?" (figure 11-1). The system will then use GPS for guidance to the approach, but the HSI will need to be switched to a NAV receiver before flying the final approach course. Note that in some aircraft, if the autopilot is engaged in NAV mode when the HSI is switched, the autopilot reverts to ROL mode.

To fly a GPS approach, the following criteria must be met prior to reaching a point 2 nm outside the final approach fix (FAF):

- System database is current
- GPS selected on HSI using CDI softkey
- Approach loaded and FAF is the active waypoint
- GPS in auto-sequencing mode (e.g. OBS softkey not pushed)
- APR annunciator appears at 2 nm outside of the FAF

TIP

Want to fly near perfect approaches? Updated versions of the G1000 and all G900X and Perspective systems include a Current Track Bug feature that makes it easy to determine the exact heading needed to correct for wind. It's a small magenta diamond near the top of the HSI that gives a visual representation of the TRK or ground track. To compensate for the wind, simply turn the plane to a heading where the bug aligns with the head of the HSI's course pointer. Tracking of GPS courses should be perfect.

There can be some scalloping of VOR radials and ILS courses along the ground, so using the Current Track Bug when flying with a VOR or ILS Course pointer displayed on the HSI may not be perfect. Nonetheless, the Current Track Bug should still give a very good indication of the heading that allows you to compensate for the wind when tracking a VOR or ILS course.

Three Ways to Fly IFR Approaches

Surprised? Most pilots know two ways to fly an approach: vectors and pilot navigation, also called own navigation. Flying via vectors is preferred, since it's less work for the pilot, though it's more work for the controller who issues a series of vectors or turns. The turns bring you onto a straight line, extending a number of miles from the airport, which is often, but not always, aligned with the runway's extended centerline. When the chips are down, e.g. you're tired, low on fuel or the weather's rotten, request vectors, as it will require less work and increase your chances for success.

Own navigation is used when aircraft are below radar coverage and ATC can neither see nor vector the aircraft. Aircraft can safely fly the approach on their own, provided they fly the instrument approach exactly as published. This can be more work than flying an approach via vectors, especially if it requires a procedure turn that takes you away from the airport before turning to fly inbound to the airport. Own navigation is used heavily in training, so pilots become familiar with it.

The third method, new in 2006, is that ATC can clear you direct to the intermediate fix and allow you to turn onto the intermediate segment without flying any course reversal charted at the IF. This is permitted if your IFR flight plan indicates an RNAV equipment suffix. When doing this, the controller is supposed to provide radar monitoring to the IF and advise you, at least 5 miles from the fix, to expect clearance direct to the IF. This allows you time to program your GPS to

TIP

When flying IFR, it's easy to forget that in some glass cockpit aircraft, the autopilot reverts from NAV to ROL mode when the HSI's course pointer is changed. Therefore I've created the acronym PICA—which is a typesetters' word referring to the height of a letter—to help you remember these steps.

Whenever you fly an approach, P is to push the PROC key, I is to inspect and verify every waypoint in the flight plan, C is to set the CDI softkey and A is to engage or re-engage the autopilot. For a non-instrument flight plan, use FICA—like the payroll tax in the United States—where F is for the FPL key and the remaining letters are the same.

fly to the intermediate fix. The controller must also assign an altitude to maintain until the IF and ensure that your aircraft is on a course that will intercept the intermediate segment at an angle not greater than 90° and is at an altitude that will permit a normal descent from the intermediate fix to the FAF. Information about this new option is in section 5-4-7 of the Aeronautical Information Manual.

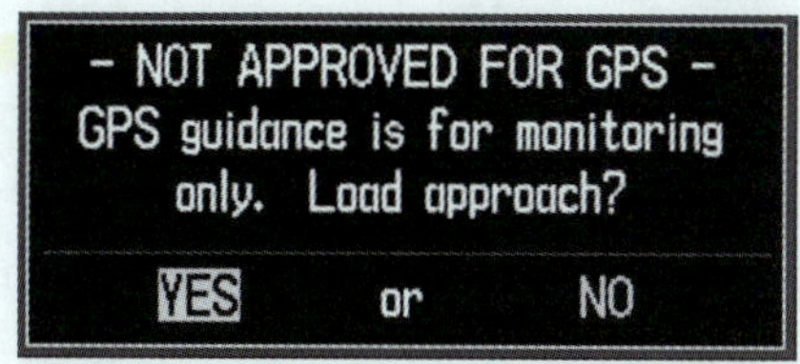

Figure 11-1 Any time you're not allowed to use GPS to navigate the final approach course, you'll see this message when you load the approach. *© Garmin Ltd. or its affiliates*

Specifying an IAF or VECTORS

It's important to let the controller know whether you plan to fly an approach with pilot navigation or vectors. If flying with pilot navigation, refer to your instrument approach plates to determine at which IAF you wish to begin the approach. When selecting an approach, the system requires you to choose either VECTORS or one of possibly several IAFs. Don't worry if the game plan changes after you've loaded the approach; you can always reload the approach with a different IAF or VECTORS provided you haven't passed the FAF.

In the past, experienced flight instructors recommended that you always specify an IAF when loading an approach, even if you were planning to fly the approach with vectors from the controller. The reason is that on early G1000 and Perspective systems, when you chose "VECTORS," the system deleted all waypoints except for the final approach fix and the missed approach point. That made flying an approach more difficult if you were unexpectedly cleared direct to one of the deleted waypoints. Also, when being vectored, it was harder to identify whether you were inside or outside of a deleted waypoint, making it more difficult to ascertain whether you were being vectored at a safe altitude. By specifying an IAF, even if you were not flying to that IAF, the system displayed more waypoints along the final approach course, improving position awareness. The disadvantage in loading an IAF instead of VECTORS when being vectored onto the final approach course was an additional step: activating a leg of the approach.

A recent software update to G1000 and Perspective systems eliminates these issues, now making it preferable to load an approach with VECTORS when being vectored to an approach. In the past when you loaded an approach with vectors or ACTIVATE VECTOR-TO-FINAL, the active leg was a course to fix leg, terminating at the FAF, which essentially extended the final approach segment as a longer straight line. That's still true, but now the system loads all approach waypoints that are within ± 3 degrees of the extended final approach segment.

In some cases a gap will be inserted on the map between the last en route waypoint and the course to fix leg. That way, the GPS will sequence from the en route waypoint to the course to fix leg rather than to the first waypoint of the approach.

Another change is that if there's another transition to the final approach fix that differs from the extended final approach course segment, that transition is displayed on the map, but the active leg will still be the course to fix leg terminating at the FAF.

Activating Approach Myth

In *Max Trescott's GPS and WAAS Instrument Flying Handbook*, I discuss in detail the huge misperception in general aviation that somehow a GPS receiver must be "activated" at some point before one can fly an approach. To briefly summarize that discussion, let me be clear on this point. You can fly any instrument approach, either via pilot navigation or vectors and never have to "activate the approach". Yet, I continually hear pilots say, "now I have to activate the approach," when in fact their GPS is already set up correctly for the approach. This probably stems from the two choices presented, LOAD or ACTIVATE, which may lead pilots to assume that if they initially choose LOAD instead of ACTIVATE that of course they will later need to activate something to fly the approach. There's at least one situation where trying to "activate the approach" can get a pilot into serious trouble. Imagine you're on the final approach course beyond the IAF or being vectored to final. Now, imagine you press the MENU key and select "ACTIVATE APPROACH." The autopilot will command a 180° turn to take you back to the initial approach fix, which is behind you! Should you find yourself in this, or some other situation involving an automation surprise, disconnect the autopilot and manually fly the airplane.

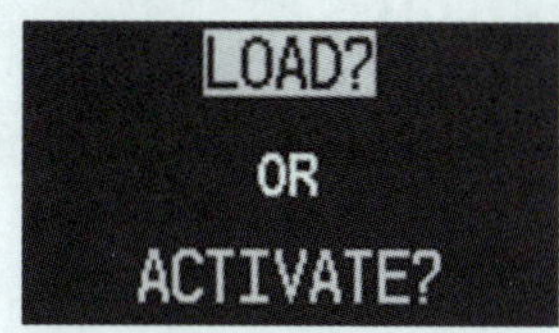

Figure 11-2 It's important that you understand the difference between loading and activating an approach. *© Garmin Ltd. or its affiliates*

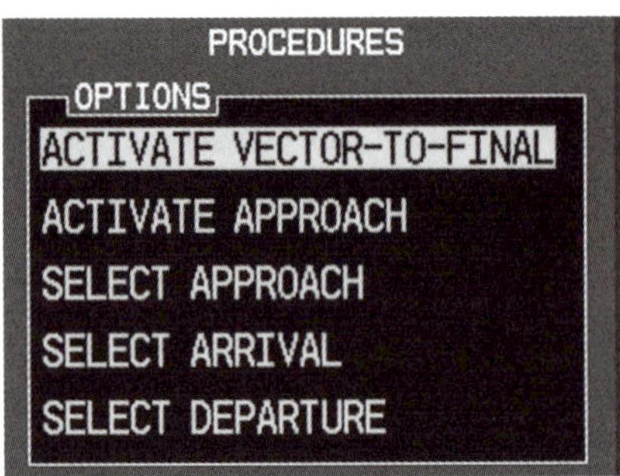

Figure 11-3 Select "ACTIVATE VECTOR-TO-FINAL" when ATC begins to vector you for the approach. *© Garmin Ltd. or its affiliates*

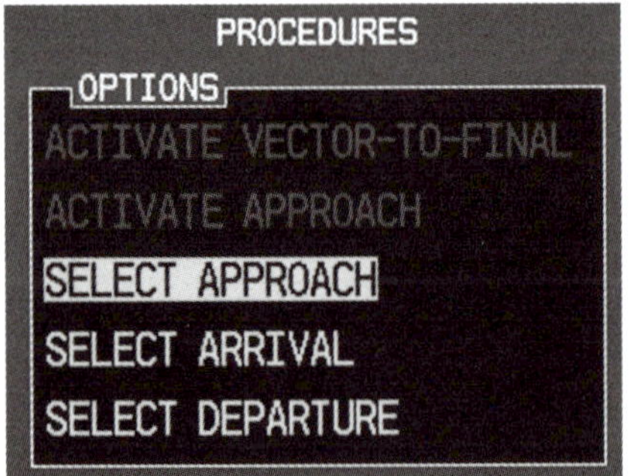

Figure 11-4 Press the PROC key to select an approach. *© Garmin Ltd. or its affiliates*

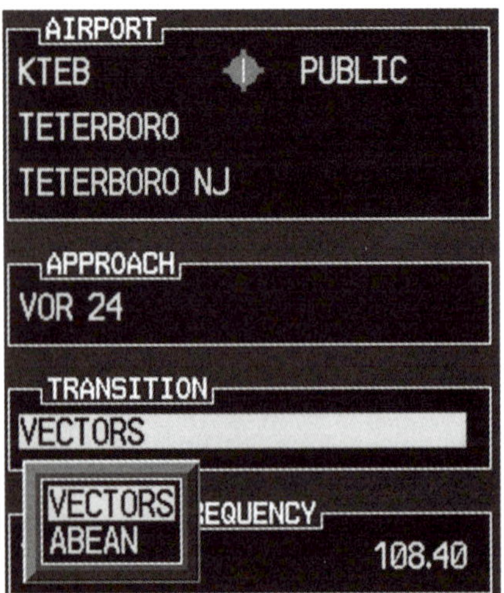

Figure 11-5 You'll need to choose whether to fly the approach via vectors or to start over an IAF. *© Garmin Ltd. or its affiliates*

LOAD versus ACTIVATE

When selecting an approach, you must choose to LOAD or ACTIVATE the approach (figure 11-2). Loading simply appends the approach to the end of your active flight plan, as you continue to navigate via all of the waypoints in your flight plan. Choose LOAD if you're selecting an approach while you're some distance away from the airport and you still need to navigate via intermediate waypoints before reaching the airport. Later, use the Direct-to key to go to the first waypoint on the approach, or press the PROC key and scroll to "ACTIVATE APPROACH," and press the ENT key to accomplish the same thing.

By contrast, ACTIVATE also adds the approach to the flight plan and the GPS begins course guidance to the first approach waypoint, skipping intermediate waypoints in your flight plan. This is fine once you've been instructed to fly directly to the IAF or the controller has begun issuing you vectors to the final approach course. If you follow the waypoints in sequence to the IAF, you don't need to do anything further.

Regardless of whether you LOAD or ACTIVATE an approach or specify an IAF or VECTORS, at any time you can press the PROC key, scroll to "ACTIVATE VECTOR-TO-FINAL" and press the ENT key (figure 11-3). The system will draw a magenta line extending out from the final approach course and ATC will turn you onto that course line.

After you load an approach, carefully review all of the waypoints in your flight plan to assure that they are correct. Never trust your life to flying IFR via a series of waypoints in a GPS until you have verified all of them. Generally, you'll find that your flight plan goes to the destination airport first and then to the instrument approach. You could delete the airport waypoint, but there's a better way. Instead use the Direct-to key to take you to the first waypoint in the approach. That way, if you have to change the approach, the system still knows your destination and you don't have to reenter it.

You must have an electronic or paper copy of the instrument procedure to fly an approach. The G1000 and Perspective do not include critical pieces of information such as altitudes to fly and the missed approach instructions, unless you have the optional Electronic Charts.

Selecting an Approach Using the PROC key

Garmin GNS 430 and GNS 530 users already know how to load approaches using my preferred method, the PROC key. Let's assume that you're currently navigating via Direct-to or a flight plan to your destination airport. If you're not, don't worry however. The process in selecting an approach is the same except for an extra step that prompts you to enter a destination airport.

Press the PROC key on either the PFD or MFD. Scroll using the large FMS knob to "SELECT APPROACH" and press the ENT key (figure 11-4). Then use either FMS knob to select an approach from the list available at the destination airport. Press the ENT key and scroll to select "VECTORS" or an IAF over which you'll start your approach and press the ENT key (figure 11-5). Press the ENT key again if you want to "Load" the approach, or scroll to "ACTIVATE?" if you're ready to activate and begin flying the approach. To activate an approach that has already been loaded, press the PROC key, scroll to select "ACTIVATE APPROACH" and press the ENT key.

LD DP | LD STAR | LD APR

Figure 11-6 From the Active Flight Plan page, you can use softkeys on the MFD to load an approach. © Garmin Ltd. or its affiliates

Using the MENU key

In early G1000 aircraft, you could also load an approach using the MENU key any time the Active Flight Plan window is open on either the PFD or MFD. First press the FPL key to open the Active Flight Plan window. Then press the MENU key and scroll to highlight "Load Approach." Press the ENT key and select the type of approach and your desired IAF or Vectors. Finally, scroll to either "LOAD?" or "ACTIVATE?" and press the ENT key.

INFO | DP | STAR | APR

Figure 11-7 To load an approach from the Airport Information page, press the PROC key or the APR softkey. © Garmin Ltd. or its affiliates

Using Softkeys on the MFD

In early G1000 aircraft, anytime the Active Flight Plan page is open, you can load an approach by pressing the LD APR softkey (figure 11-6). Use the large FMS knob to scroll to the AIRPORT, APPROACH and TRANSITION fields and the small FMS knob to enter an airport identifier and select the type of approach and desired IAF or Vectors. Scroll with the large FMS knob to "LOAD?" or "ACTIVATE?" and press the ENT key once or twice, depending upon the approach type.

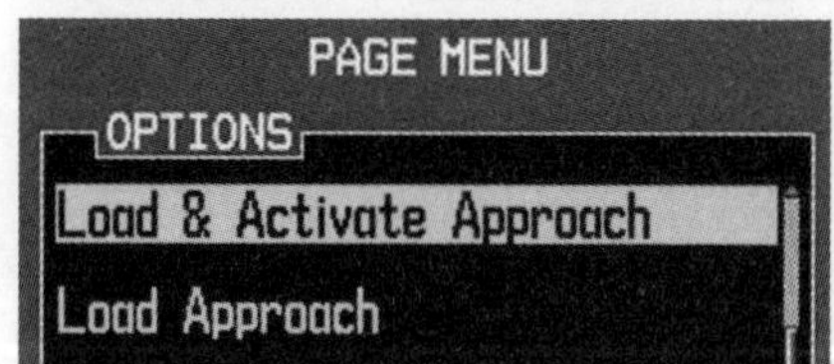

Figure 11-8 If you use the APR softkey to view an approach from the Airport Information page, you'll need to use the MENU key to load or activate it. © Garmin Ltd. or its affiliates

You can also select an approach from the Airport Information page, the first page in the WPT group. From this page, press the APR softkey (figure 11-7), and use the large FMS knob to scroll to the AIRPORT, APPROACH and TRANSITION fields (figure 11-5) and the small FMS knob to enter an airport identifier and select the type of approach and desired IAF or Vectors. Then—and here's where this differs from loading an approach from the Active Flight Plan page—press the MENU key and scroll to choose either "Load & Activate Approach" or "Load Approach" and press the ENT key once or twice, depending upon the approach type (figure 11-8).

APT | RNWY | FREQ | APR | | LD APR

Figure 11-9 You can load an approach from the Nearest Airports page with the PROC key or the APR softkey. © Garmin Ltd. or its affiliates

Finally, you can also select an approach from the Nearest Airports page, the first page in the NRST group. From this page, press the APR softkey, and use either FMS knob to select the desired approach. Then press the LD APR softkey (figure 11-9) and scroll with either FMS knob to select the desired IAF or Vectors from the TRANSITIONS field. Press the ENT key and scroll to either "LOAD?" or "ACTIVATE?" and press the ENT key once or twice, depending upon the approach type.

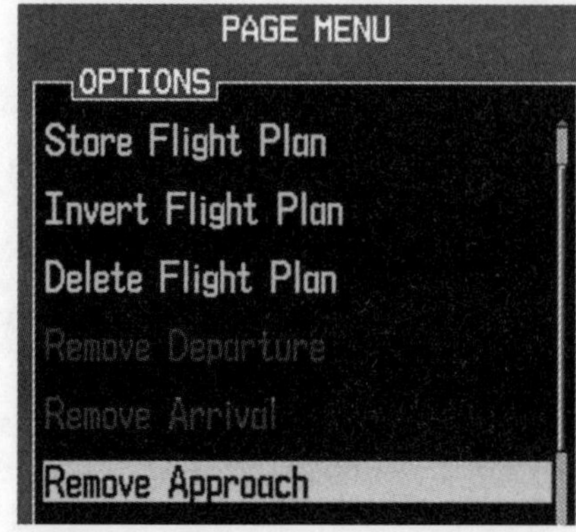

Figure 11-10 To remove an approach, use the MENU key. © Garmin Ltd. or its affiliates

Removing an Approach, Arrival or Departure Procedure

Plans often change while flying IFR and you may need to remove an instrument approach that you've already added to your flight plan. You

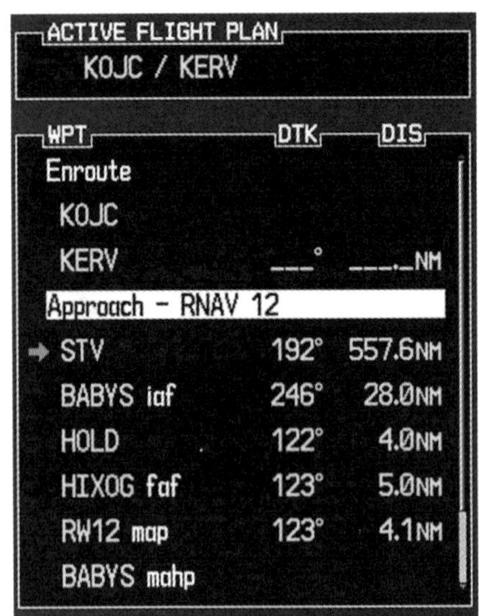

Figure 11-11 An easy way to delete a procedure is to highlight its name and press the CLR key. *© Garmin Ltd. or its affiliates*

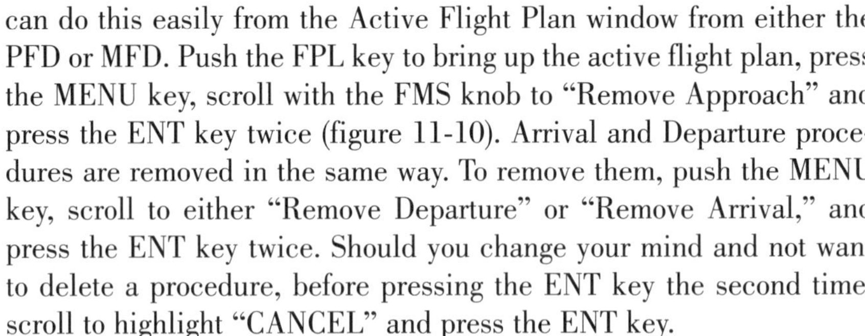

can do this easily from the Active Flight Plan window from either the PFD or MFD. Push the FPL key to bring up the active flight plan, press the MENU key, scroll with the FMS knob to "Remove Approach" and press the ENT key twice (figure 11-10). Arrival and Departure procedures are removed in the same way. To remove them, push the MENU key, scroll to either "Remove Departure" or "Remove Arrival," and press the ENT key twice. Should you change your mind and not want to delete a procedure, before pressing the ENT key the second time, scroll to highlight "CANCEL" and press the ENT key.

Approach, Arrival, and Departure Procedures are also easy to delete from within the Flight Plan window. Just look for the name of the procedure in the flight plan. For example, the name of an instrument approach procedure appears in white just above the initial approach fix (figure 11-11). To delete a procedure, scroll to highlight its name, push the CLR key and the ENT key.

Flying a VOR Approach with Vectors to Final

VOR approaches are more difficult to fly since, if GPS is not in the title of the approach, you have to switch the HSI's course pointer and in older G1000 systems set the CDI course. When radar service is available, instrument approaches are usually flown with vectors to the final approach course. There are two ways to select "vectors to final."

When the approach is first selected, you can choose "VECTORS" from the Transitions window and ACTIVATE the approach if you are on radar vectors and there are no other waypoints in your flight plan that you need to fly over before beginning the approach. Or, if you previously loaded an approach, with vectors or an IAF, and are now being vectored to final, press the PROC key, select "ACTIVATE VECTOR-TO-FINAL" and press the ENT key. Then follow the vectors provided by ATC to intercept the final approach course.

Using the system or Garmin's PC Trainer, enter a flight plan from KTOP to KOJC using any of the methods described in Chapter 9. With the Active Flight Plan window still open, press the LD APR softkey on the MFD or the PROC key on either display and select an approach. Choose the VOR RWY 36 with vectors to final and LOAD the approach by pressing the ENT key (figure 11-12). Notice you must press the ENT key twice.

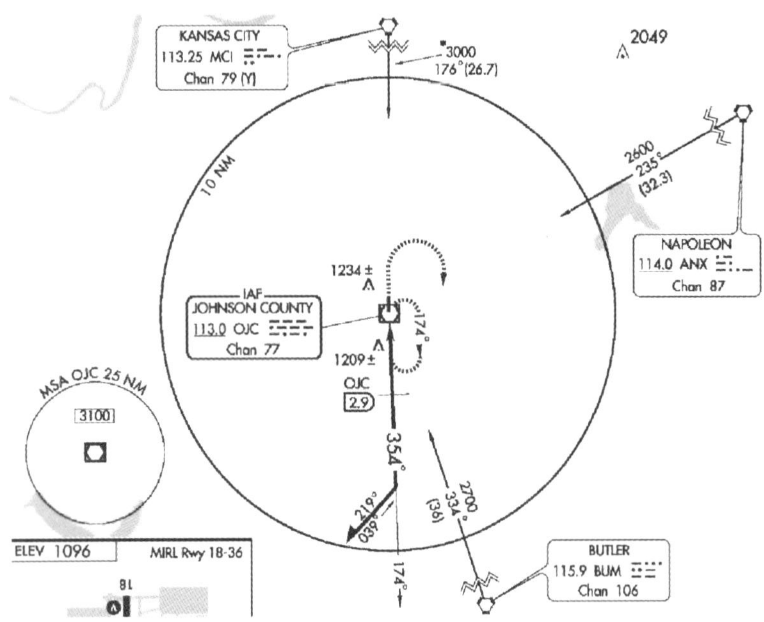

Figure 11-12 The VOR RWY 36 approach can be flown with vectors or by starting at OJC and flying a procedure turn.

After the first press, you'll see "NOT APPROVED FOR GPS – GPS guidance is for monitoring only" (figure 11-1). You'll get this warning for many VOR approaches and all localizer and ILS approaches whenever

"GPS" is not in the title of an approach. It's to remind you that you're not allowed to fly the final approach course of these approaches with GPS, so prior to intercepting the final approach course you must switch the HSI to display a VOR or LOCALIZER course pointer.

Next, review every waypoint in the flight plan to verify that it's correct (figure 11-13). In this example, we're flying with vectors, but if you were flying via own navigation, now would be the time to push the FMS knob, scroll to highlight the IAF and push the Direct-to key. Or, you could press the PROC key, select "ACTIVATE APPROACH" and press the ENT key.

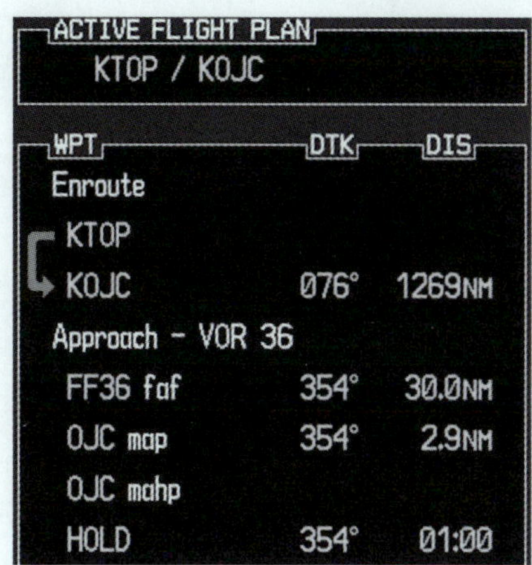

Figure 11-13 Here, the approach has been loaded but not activated, so you're still navigating directly to the airport. *© Garmin Ltd. or its affiliates*

Notice that the HSI displays "TERM," since you are within 30 miles of the departure or destination airport. Whenever you are in the terminal mode, the distance represented from the center of the CDI scale to a full left or full right deflection is 1 nm. Also, note that the system automatically loaded the VOR frequency into NAV1 and NAV2. If the GPS CDI was selected on the HSI, the frequency is loaded into the active field of both radios. If one of the VOR CDIs was selected, the VOR approach frequency is loaded into the standby field of the selected NAV radio. Verify that the Morse code identifier for the VOR appears next to the NAV radio frequency.

You'll need to get the weather. Load the appropriate frequency from the Airport Information page or, if you have data-link weather, review the textual METAR. Also note the minimums for the approach and brief yourself on the first few steps of the missed approach.

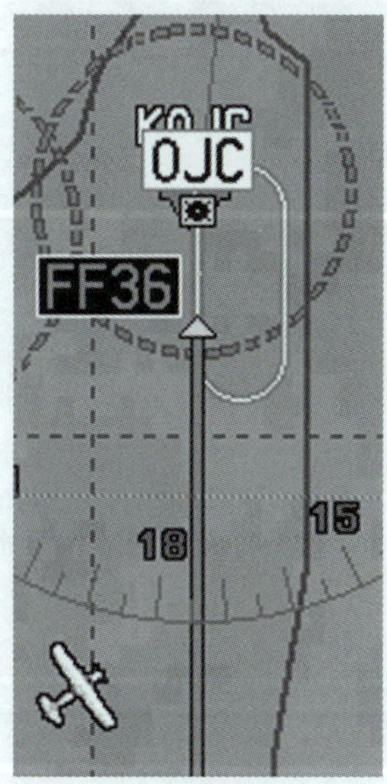

Figure 11-14 When flying vectors to final, you'll be intercepting a magenta line that's aligned with the final approach segment and terminates at the MAP. *© Garmin Ltd. or its affiliates*

Once ATC begins to vector you for the final approach, steer the plane using the autopilot's HDG mode and activate the approach. Press the PROC key, "ACTIVATE VECTOR-TO-FINAL" will be highlighted, and then press the ENT key. The system now draws a magenta line that extends approximately 30 nm from the final approach fix (figure 11-14). ATC then vectors you with a series of turns to intercept the final approach course outside the final approach fix.

As soon as ATC begins to issue vectors, push the CDI softkey to select NAV1 and verify the course is set to the 354° final approach course. While the system sets the CDI needle course for localizer, ILS and GPS approaches, in early G1000 aircraft, you had to set the course for VOR and localizer backcourse approaches! Immediately after pushing the CDI softkey, check the autopilot. If it reverted to ROL mode when the CDI changed, re-engage the autopilot in heading mode.

Figure 11-15 For approaches that don't allow GPS for navigating the final approach course, you'll receive an alert if you don't switch the CDI to a NAV radio. *© Garmin Ltd. or its affiliates*

After ATC issues the final vector and clears you for the approach, press the APR key on the autopilot to select the approach mode. At intercept, the autopilot will begin tracking the final approach course.

If you forget to switch the CDI and are still using the GPS, at 2 nm from the FAF the CDI scaling changes and the HSI displays ".3nm," the distance represented from the center of the scale to a full left or full right deflection. You will also see a softkey blinking "ADVISORY." Press the softkey and you'll be reminded to "Select NAV on CDI for approach" (figure 11-15). Just press the CDI softkey to display VOR 1 on the HSI, verify the course is set to the 354° final approach course, and press the APR key to re-engage the autopilot's approach mode.

NEXT DTK 354°

Figure 11-16 While on approach, you'll receive advance notice of each upcoming turn. *© Garmin Ltd. or its affiliates*

As you approach the FAF, "NEXT DTK 354°" is displayed in the PFD's Navigation Status bar (figure 11-16), reminding you of the desired ground track. At the FAF, begin your descent to the published altitude for this segment of the approach. For this approach, even lower minimums are available for DME-equipped aircraft that can identify a step down fix, an extra fix located between the FAF and missed approach point (MAP). GPS is a legal substitute for DME, so the G1000 and Perspective can fly to the lower minimums. To descend, preselect the next altitude on the autopilot, select the VS mode, set a descent rate and reduce power.

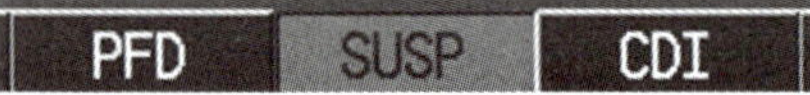

Figure 11-17 The SUSP softkey appears and auto-sequencing of waypoints is suspended at the MAP. *© Garmin Ltd. or its affiliates*

Approaching the MAP, "ARRIVING AT WAYPOINT" is displayed. As you cross the MAP, "SUSP" is displayed in the HSI and a SUSP softkey appears (figure 11-17). Also, note that the CDI TO/FROM triangle moves to the FROM position at the opposite end of the D-bar. (figure 11-18). Notice in the flight plan that automatic sequencing of waypoints stops. Now, you must disconnect the autopilot and either land or fly the missed approach instructions.

Figure 11-18 The TO/FROM arrow flips to FROM (triangle at bottom of figure) and SUSP is displayed in the HSI as you pass the MAP. *© Garmin Ltd. or its affiliates*

Flying the Missed Approach

Flying a missed approach is complex and rarely flown for real. Not only are you dealing with reconfiguring the aircraft, but you're also pushing multiple buttons on the G1000 or Perspective and on the autopilot. Let's list the activities.

For the aircraft, you'll need to add power, pitch to a climb attitude, trim the aircraft, verify that you have a positive rate of climb, and clean it up by raising flaps, opening cowl flaps and raising the landing gear. For the system, you'll need to press the SUSP softkey and, if you weren't flying a GPS approach, press the CDI softkey to select the GPS course pointer. For the autopilot, you'll disconnect it at the MAP, then select an altitude, the vertical speed or IAS mode, a climb rate or airspeed, heading or NAV mode to follow the first step in the missed approach instructions, and reengage the autopilot when you reach the minimum engagement altitude listed in Section 9 of your airplane's POH.

If your aircraft has a GA button, push it to reduce your workload. In most aircraft, it disconnects the autopilot, pushes the SUSP softkey, selects the GPS course pointer, and engages the Flight Director with a 7° pitch up attitude. In Perspective aircraft, the autopilot remains on when the GA button is pushed and you can climb out without disconnecting it.

Reduce workload further by performing some tasks before the MAP. Memorize the first two steps of the published missed approach, so you won't need to look down to read instructions when you're at minimums. Also, use the ALT knobs to preselect the missed approach holding alti-

TIP

When you're flying a holding pattern, you're expected to track the inbound course to the fix, as depicted by the magenta race track (figure 11-19). When flying outbound, you simply turn to the outbound heading (plus or minus wind correction) and accept whatever ground track you get. However, one DPE reports that with the advent of moving map displays, he sees some Instrument rating candidates try to track the outbound portion of the race track depicted on the screen. That is not the proper way to fly outbound when in a holding pattern.

tude. In the past, pilots would use the ALT knobs to set the approach minimums, however, that's now redundant with the PFD's BARO MINIMUMS feature.

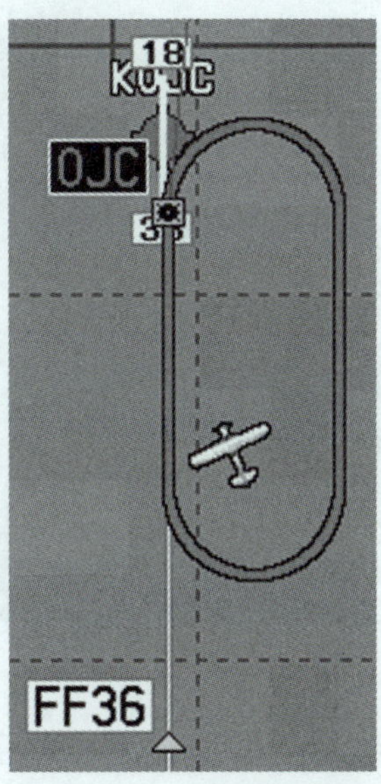

Figure 11-19 After flying outbound for a minute, turn and choose a heading that will intercept the inbound course to the holding fix. *© Garmin Ltd. or its affiliates*

There's a subtle difference in how the SUSP softkey works on older G1000 systems versus Perspective and later G1000 systems. In all aircraft, at the MAP the system displays "SUSP" in the HSI, the SUSP softkey appears and automatic sequencing of waypoints ceases. This reminds you to read the missed approach instructions and to perform any climb required prior to turning to the next waypoint. In older G1000 systems, it's advisable to delay pressing the SUSP softkey until reaching any altitude that may be required prior to a turn. That's because older systems don't consider the altitude you're at and immediately send you to the next waypoint, which may be through a mountain or other obstacle if you haven't first performed any required climb. Perspective and later G1000 systems avoid this problem by delaying presenting turn information until after you reach any required altitude. Thus in newer systems, you can push the SUSP key immediately after the MAP and safely follow all course guidance.

After initiating a missed approach, it's important to verify you're actually climbing. Whenever you are accelerating, somatogravic illusion can give you a false sense that you're climbing when you're actually flying straight and level or descending. Cross-checking the airspeed and vertical speed indicators is the only sure way to overcome this illusion.

As an example, let's continue the flight started in the previous section using the VOR Runway 36 approach into KOJC. As you crossed the MAP, "SUSP" appeared in the HSI, the SUSP softkey appeared and automatic sequencing of waypoints stopped. Push the GA button or disconnect the autopilot. In Perspective aircraft, the autopilot remains on when the GA button is pushed and you can climb out without disconnecting it. Apply climb power, pitch up, trim the aircraft and verify you have a positive rate of climb. Clean up the aircraft and following the missed approach instructions, climb to 1700 feet while tracking the 354° radial of the OJC VOR.

If you don't have a GA button, push the SUSP softkey and the CDI softkey to select the GPS course pointer. In early G1000 aircraft, you may want to delay this until you reach 1700 feet and are permitted to start a right turn. During the climb, preselect 2600 feet on the autopilot, set either the IAS or vertical speed mode, set a climb rate, select HDG or NAV mode and engage the autopilot after you're above its minimum altitude for use. A message like "Next DTK 192°" will appear with the course to the OJC VOR. Turn to the VOR, level off at 2600 feet and prepare to enter the hold at OJC.

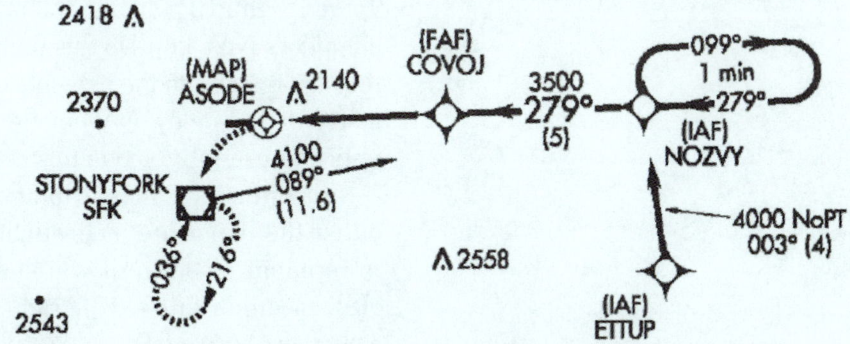

Figure 11-20 NoPT indicates that no procedure turn is required when starting this approach at the IAF at ETTUP.

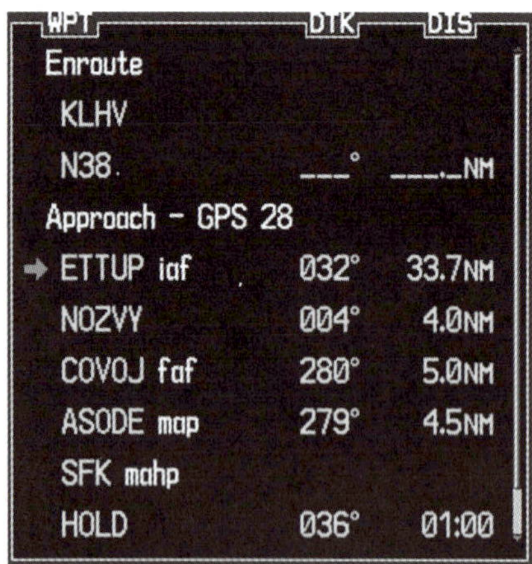

Figure 11-21 Since we activated this approach (instead of loading it), we're flying directly to ETTUP, the IAF.

© Garmin Ltd. or its affiliates

Approaching the hold, a message in the PFD's Navigation Status bar suggests a recommended holding entry procedure (e.g. HOLD PARALLEL, HOLD TEARDROP or HOLD DIRECT). In this case, a parallel entry is recommended. At the holding fix, the CDI triangle flips from "TO" to "FROM," automatic sequencing of waypoints ceases, "SUSP" is displayed in the HSI, and the SUSP softkey appears.

Early G1000s cannot fly a hold, so you'll need to use HDG mode or manually turn to a heading of 174° to parallel the holding course outbound. Perspective and updated G1000 systems do fly holds in NAV mode. All systems automatically time the outbound leg. Look for the time next to "HOLD" in your flight plan. After flying outbound for one minute, make a left turn (to remain within the hold's protected area) to a heading to intercept and track a 354° course back to the OJC VOR (figure 11-19). At the VOR, make a standard rate turn to the right to a heading of 174° and continue flying the holding pattern until you're ready to reattempt the approach, select another approach or choose another destination.

Flying a GPS Approach with Own Navigation

GPS approaches are among the easier approaches to fly, once you've set up your GPS receiver properly. Most can be flown from one or more initial approach fixes (IAF) without a procedure turn. Let's look at flying a GPS approach to N38, the Wellsboro-Johnston airport in Pennsylvania.

First create a flight plan from KLHV to N38. Then use the PROC key to load an approach. Choose the GPS Runway 28 approach and the ETTUP IAF (figure 11-20). Choose ACTIVATE if you're ready to proceed to ETTUP and press the ENT key. Then verify every waypoint in the flight plan. Press the FPL key and use the FMS knob to scroll through all of the waypoints (figure 11-21). Make sure you're flying directly to ETTUP and not to N38 first. Note on the chart that "NoPT" means no procedure turn is required or allowed, except with ATC permission, when flying from ETTUP to NOZVY.

Verify the GPS course pointer is selected on the HSI and press the autopilot's NAV key. Do this immediately after activating the approach, so that you're close to the magenta course line and navigation mode becomes active. If you delay, NAV mode remains armed and won't become active until you use HDG mode to steer the aircraft to intercept the course.

Since this is a short trip and you're never more than 30 miles from either the departure or destination airports, the GPS receiver remains in terminal mode until you start the approach. TERM appears in the HSI, meaning full left or right deflection equals 1 nm, or 2 nm total across the entire CDI.

As you approach each waypoint, PFD Navigation Status bar messages notify you of each turn. Approaching ETTUP, you'll see "NEXT DTK 004°" and then "TURN TO 004°." Approaching NOZVY, you'll see "NEXT DTK 280°" and then "TURN TO 280°."

TIP

When flying an approach, make sure that you monitor the HSI's CDI needle for primary course guidance. Many people watch the moving map and steer the plane to follow the map. While the map can be helpful, using the CDI needle allows you to track a course more accurately.

Prior to each waypoint where you can descend, preselect the next altitude on the autopilot. Then as you cross the waypoint, engage the vertical speed mode and set a descent rate.

You can leave the autopilot in NAV mode throughout the approach. The APR mode is only required for approaches with vertical guidance (e.g. ILS and some WAAS-based approaches). Reduce power for descent and increase the power as the autopilot levels off at each altitude.

Figure 11-22 At 2 nm from the final approach fix, "APR" appears in the HSI indicating the GPS has switched to approach mode. *© Garmin Ltd. or its affiliates*

At 2 nm from the FAF, COVOJ, "APR" appears (on non-WAAS GPS receivers) on the HSI, indicating the GPS receiver is in approach mode and that CDI scaling is now 0.3 nm from center to full left or full right deflection, or 0.6 nm across the full CDI scale (figure 11-22). At COVOJ, begin a descent to the published minimum altitude for the approach. As you approach ASODE, the MAP, "ARRIVING AT WAYPOINT" is displayed. As you cross the MAP, "SUSP" is displayed in the HSI, the SUSP softkey appears on the PFD, and the CDI TO/FROM triangle flips to FROM. Now, you must disconnect the autopilot and either land or fly the missed approach instructions.

Flying a GPS Approach from an IF

Let's now fly the same GPS approach at N38, but start instead at the IF NOZVY. All instrument approaches have an initial approach segment that begins at an initial approach fix or IAF, and ends where it joins the intermediate approach segment at the intermediate fix or IF. Starting an approach at the IF was always permissible if the fix was labeled IF/IAF. Generally, a racetrack holding pattern is depicted at a IF/IAF for a course reversal and altitude adjustment when starting a procedure at this fix.

To begin the approach, first navigate directly to NOZVY, cross the fix and turn to fly away from the airport. Then turn to reverse direction and cross NOZVY a second time. There are no requirements as to how you accomplish the 180° turn, except that all turns must be on the side of the course depicted by the racetrack symbol on the chart.

Prior to 2006, all instrument approaches starting at an IF/IAF with a racetrack were required to fly the course reversal. Now, pilots can navigate directly to any IF and skip any depicted course reversal if they approach the IF from a direction from which they can turn to final with less than a 90° turn. At N38, aircraft flying direct to NOZVY from 009° through 189° can skip the course reversal.

Again create a flight plan from KLHV to N38. Load the GPS Runway 28 approach and the NOZVY IAF. Choose ACTIVATE and press the ENT key. Note that the course to NOZVY is 029°, so a turn directly to COVOJ would exceed 90°. Thus a course reversal must be flown. Alternatively, we could ask ATC to vector us to a position from

TIP

When flying a non-precision approach to a non-towered airport, you may want to change one of the fields in the active flight plan to display CUM, which is the cumulative distance to the final waypoint. That way, you'll instantly know your distance to the airport and can report that distance when you call in on the CTAF to report your position and intentions. Whenever making these reports, give it in terms which a non-IFR pilot will understand. For example, don't just say that you're on the VOR 29 approach. Instead, state that you're 5 miles southeast of the airport on the VOR approach.

FLIGHT PLAN		
KLHV / N38		
	DTK	DIS
N38-GPS 28GPS LNAV+V		
NOZVY iaf	099°	10.3NM
HOLD	279°	01:00
COVOJ faf	279°	5.0NM
ASODE map	279°	4.5NM

Figure 11-23 The system automatically entered a HOLD at NOZVY, since we'll be entering from a direction that would require a turn of more than 90° to final. *© Garmin Ltd. or its affiliates*

where we can be cleared to fly direct to NOZVY and skip the procedure turn.

Push the FPL key, review the flight plan (figure 11-23) and you'll see a HOLD after NOZVY. Let's assume we're flying an older G1000 system that's unable to fly a hold in NAV mode. Approaching NOZVY, the PFD's Navigation Status bar displays "Hold Teardrop," the recommended holding entry for this direction of flight. Then "Turn right to 064° in 10 seconds" and Turn right to 064° now" are displayed. For older G1000 systems, push the autopilot's HDG key, turn to 064° and fly for one minute. Later G1000 versions and all Perspective aircraft can remain in NAV mode throughout the hold.

After a minute, turn right to 244° and then intercept the 279° course to NOZVY. Cross NOZVY and fly the remainder of the approach as described in the prior section.

Now let's fly the same GPS approach from a direction that allows us to skip the hold at NOZVY. Create a flight plan from KELM to N38. Load the GPS Runway 28 approach and the NOZVY IAF. The system then asks "Fly Course Reversal at NOZVY?" (figure 11-24). Choose NO, activate the approach, and push the autopilot's NAV key.

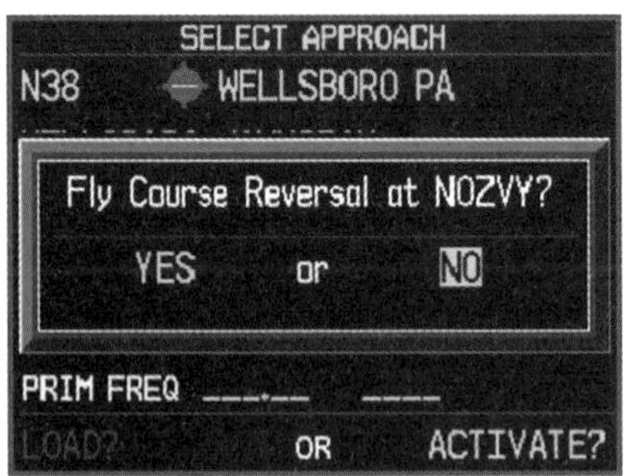

Figure 11-24 When loading an approach to start at an IF, the system often asks you whether you want to fly the course reversal. *© Garmin Ltd. or its affiliates*

ATC may specify in the approach clearance "*Cleared Straight-in* GPS Runway 28 approach" to ensure that the pilot understands that the hold is not to be flown. Approaching NOZVY, the PFD's Navigation Status bar displays "Turn right to 280° in 10 seconds" and Turn right to 280° now." Cross NOZVY and fly the remainder of the approach.

Sometimes you might not know whether you will need to fly a hold. If that were the case for this approach, you should load the HOLD at NOZVY. Later, if you don't need it, you can delete it by pushing the FPL key, scrolling to highlight HOLD, and pressing the CLR and ENT keys (figure 11-25). Deleting a hold is much easier than adding a hold, which requires reloading the entire approach.

Figure 11-25 Deleting a hold is easy. Just highlight HOLD in the flight plan with a cursor and press the CLR and ENT keys. *© Garmin Ltd. or its affiliates*

Flying an ILS Approach with Holding Pattern under Own Navigation

On an ILS approach, GPS can be used up to the final approach course, which must be flown using a NAV receiver as the primary reference, and for the missed approach. Prior to turning onto the final approach course, the CDI navigation source must be set to either NAV1 or NAV2 by pushing the CDI softkey on the PFD.

The system can make this switch for you automatically if the "ILS CDI CAPTURE" feature is enabled in "AUTO" mode. In some G1000 aircraft, the feature can be enabled and disabled using the System Setup page in the AUX page group (figure 7-48). In Perspective aircraft, the feature is always enabled.

When in "AUTO" mode, the system automatically switches the CDI from GPS to NAV1 as you intercept the final approach course, provided you are within about 1.2 nm left or right of course and less than 15 nm down the ILS course from the FAF. Note, however, that if you arrive at the ILS inside of the FAF, NAV1 or NAV2 must be set manually

NOTE: Be cautious when using the ILS CDI capture mode in early G1000 aircraft. If the autopilot is engaged in NAV or APR mode when the ILS auto capture occurs and the CDI switches to NAV1 or NAV2, the autopilot will revert to ROL mode. When this happens, you need to re-engage the autopilot's NAV or APR mode. This reversion to ROL mode doesn't occur in Perspective and 2007 and later GFC 700-equipped Cessnas.

A strategy for avoiding this is to switch the CDI source manually to NAV1 or NAV2 and then immediately re-engage the autopilot in NAV or APR mode. Some aircraft, such as early model Diamond DA40s, state in their limitations that the ILS CDI CAPTURE function must be set to Manual for autopilot coupled ILS approaches.

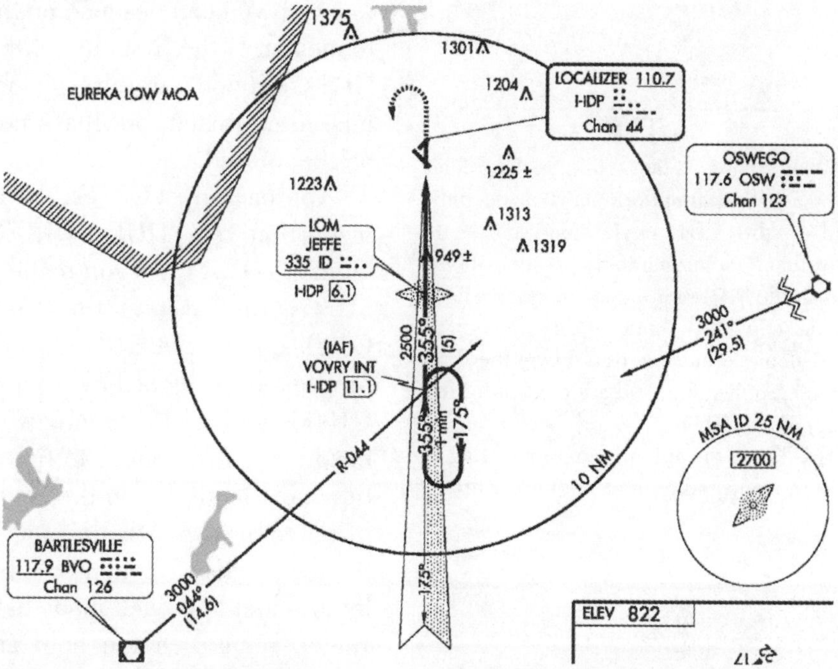

Figure 11-26 Since a holding pattern is depicted, the course reversal must occur at the hold when flying the approach under own navigation.

Let's fly an ILS approach to KIDP in Independence, Kan. First create a flight plan from KTUL to KIDP. Then use the PROC key to load an approach. Choose the ILS Runway 35 approach starting with the IAF at VOVRY (figure 11-26). Choose ACTIVATE and press the ENT key. Before proceeding, review every waypoint in the flight plan to verify that it's correct (figure 11-27). Then engage the autopilot in the NAV mode.

Check that the system loaded the ILS frequency into NAV1's active frequency (in Perspective and recent G1000 aircraft the frequency is loaded into both NAV1 and NAV2) and not the standby frequency. If the GPS course pointer was displayed on the HSI when the approach was loaded, it will be in the active frequency. Otherwise, it's loaded as the standby frequency and you'll need to push the Frequency Toggle key. Verify that the localizer's IIDP identifier appears next to the frequency in the NAV radio. Also, notice that the HSI displays "TERM" since you are within 30 miles of the departure or destination airport.

Prior to reaching the IAF, use a mnemonic like the "Four M's" to remember to push the MKR/MUTE key on the audio panel so that you can hear the Morse code audio as you pass over the markers. The four M's are: Mag compass, Markers, Minimums, and Missed approach.

With the G1000 and Perspective, you don't need the first M, since the HSI is automatically slaved to the magnetic compass and you never need to set it. Markers reminds you to turn on the marker audio with the MKR/MUTE key, minimums means to note the minimum altitude

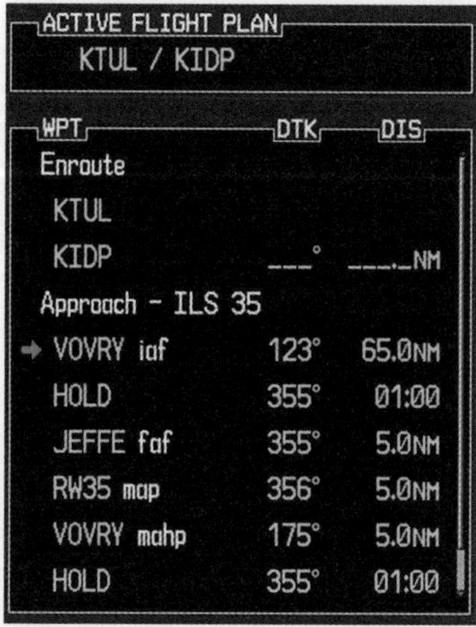

Figure 11-27 Early G1000 systems cannot fly a hold in NAV mode. You must use HDG mode or manually fly a 175° course outbound, not the 355° course shown next to HOLD. *© Garmin Ltd. or its affiliates*

to which you can descend on the approach and missed approach means to memorize the first step of the missed approach instructions. In non-GPS-equipped aircraft, you might have to set a NAV radio for the missed approach, but that's not necessary, since we'll always use GPS on the missed.

TIP

When flying vectors to an ILS, don't engage the autopilot's APR mode until after the CDI navigation source is switched either manually or automatically to the NAV radio. Instead, track a GPS course in NAV mode or fly vectors in HDG mode until you are given the final intercept heading and are cleared for the approach. Then select the APR mode. This keeps the autopilot from reverting to ROL mode and reduces button pushing.

Approaching VOVRY, the PFD's Navigation Status bar will recommend that you "HOLD DIRECT" to make the course reversal at the hold at VOVRY. As you reach VOVRY, auto-sequencing is suspended, SUSP is displayed on the HSI and the SUSP softkey appears. On early G1000s, push the HDG key on the autopilot and use the HDG knob to turn to a heading of 175° to make a direct entry into the hold. Updated G1000s and all Perspectives can fly a hold in NAV mode. Once on a heading of 175°, you can time outbound for 1 minute by watching the time next to HOLD in the Active Flight Plan window.

After timing outbound for a minute, make a right turn to intercept the localizer's 355° course inbound. Press the APR key on the autopilot to select approach mode to track the inbound course. If ATC directs you to remain in the hold at VOVRY, press the SUSP key before VOVRY, so the system won't auto-sequence to the next leg of the approach. When finished holding, press the softkey again.

Approaching VOVRY, "NEXT DTK 355° is displayed and the CDI will switch to NAV1 (figure 11-28), assuming the ILS CDI Capture function on the System Setup page is set for "AUTO." Alternatively, you can manually select NAV1 using the CDI key. Remember that in some aircraft, after the CDI is switched manually or automatically, the autopilot reverts to ROL mode and you will need to reengage approach mode. After engaging approach mode for an ILS approach, or any approach with vertical guidance, check to see that the autopilot's GS (glide slope) mode is armed.

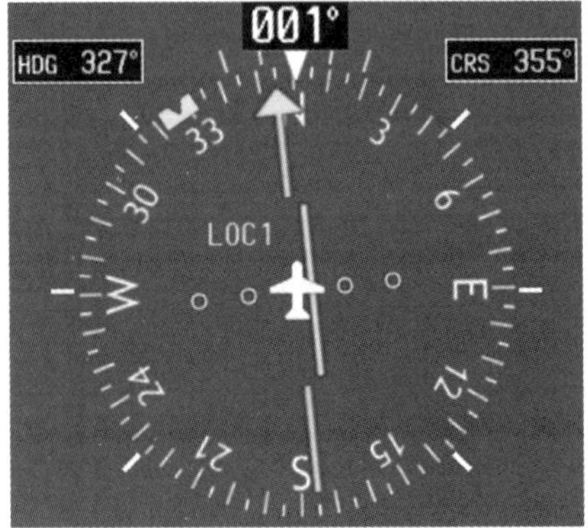

Figure 11-28 After the HSI switches to the NAV radio for an ILS approach, you may need to engage the autopilot in approach mode. *© Garmin Ltd. or its affiliates*

Inside VOVRY, you can descend to the next lower altitude published on the instrument approach chart. Note that auto-sequencing resumed, the HSI no longer displays SUSP and the SUSP softkey is gone. As you approach JEFFE, the green diamond representing the glide slope gradually moves down toward the center of the glide slope indicator. As it reaches the center, verify that the autopilot's GS mode is now active and reduce power for the descent. Nearing JEFFE, "NEXT DTK 356°" is displayed and you'll hear the Morse code for the outer marker. You can mute the Morse code audio by pressing the MKR/MUTE key one time.

As you near the MAP, "ARRIVING AT WAYPOINT" is displayed. At the MAP, auto-sequencing is suspended, SUSP is displayed on the HSI and the SUSP softkey appears. When you reach the minimum altitude for the approach, disconnect the autopilot and either land or initiate a climb to follow the missed approach instructions.

Loading an Arrival Procedure

An arrival procedure is used to transition an aircraft from the en route structure to an instrument approach. It also saves ATC time in issuing instructions, since it documents the route and altitudes for pilots to follow to reach an instrument approach. Pilots are required to have a copy of any arrival procedure that they are instructed to fly. If they don't have a copy on board the aircraft, they must not accept the arrival procedure and should ask for alternate routing instructions.

Generally, an arrival will start at one or more different points that form branches of the arrival. Like tributaries in a river, these branches will join at a single waypoint for which the arrival procedure is named. In selecting an arrival, you will be required to select the transition or branch of the arrival through which you'll be arriving and possibly the runway.

It's particularly important that you review all of the waypoints in your flight plan after loading an arrival and an approach. There are many overlapping waypoints between the en route structure, arrivals and approaches. For example, an arrival may end in a waypoint that is also the first waypoint that begins an approach. The system is designed to eliminate most of these redundant waypoints where overlaps occur, but it's still important that you review every waypoint in your flight plan for any possible errors.

Arrivals can be loaded in the same ways in which approaches can be loaded, except that they cannot be loaded from the Nearest Airports page.

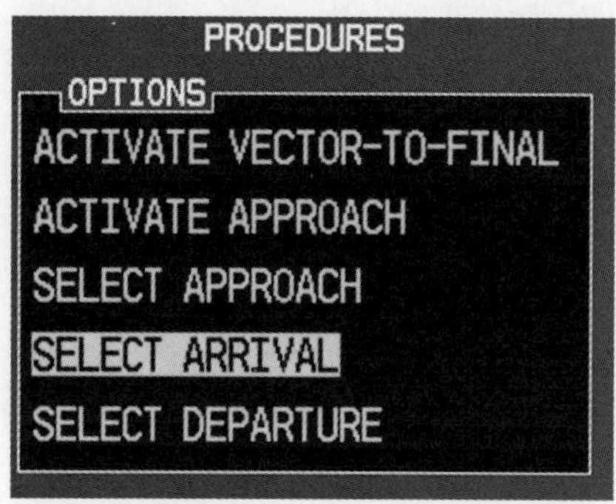

Figure 11-29 Press the PROC key to select an arrival procedure. *© Garmin Ltd. or its affiliates*

Using the PROC key

Press the PROC key on either the PFD or MFD. Scroll using the large FMS knob to "Select Arrival" and press the ENT key (figure 11-29). Then use either FMS knob to select an arrival from the list available at the destination airport. Press the ENT key and scroll to select the transition over which you'll begin the arrival and press the ENT key. In some cases, you'll also need to scroll to select and enter a runway number (figure 11-30). Finally, press the ENT key to "Load" the arrival.

Using Softkeys on the MFD

You can select an arrival from the Airport Information page, which is the first page in the WPT group. From this page, press the STAR softkey (figure 11-7), and use the large FMS knob to scroll to the ARRIVAL, TRANSITION and RUNWAY fields and use the small FMS knob to enter an arrival, transition and in some cases the runway. Finally, press the ENT key to "Load" the arrival.

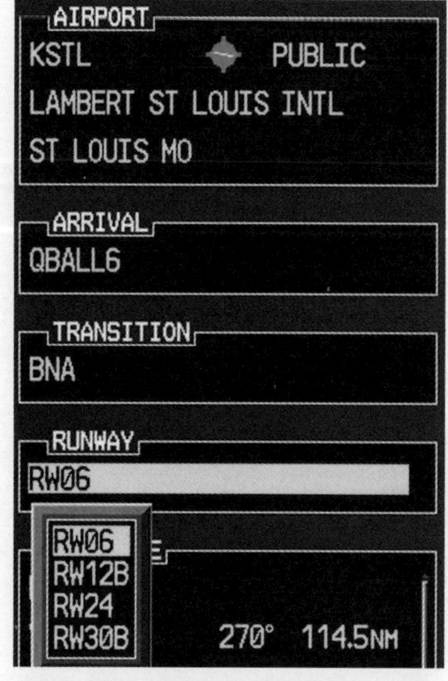

Figure 11-30 When you load an arrival procedure, you'll need to select a transition and sometimes a runway. *© Garmin Ltd. or its affiliates*

Loading a Departure Procedure

Departure procedures can be loaded in the same ways arrivals are loaded. Vector DPs, which are published as separate charts, are not in GPS databases, since these departure procedures are just a series of vectors. These should be flown with the autopilot's HDG mode until cleared direct to a waypoint.

ODPs, called textual DPs by Jeppesen, are also not included in GPS databases. ODPs can be found in the front of NACO chart books. Jeppesen textual DPs can be found on the page 11-1 airport taxi diagram, or for larger airports, on the back side of page 10-9A. OBS mode, discussed in the next section, is sometimes required to fly an ODP.

TIP

Load departure procedures before you load the rest of your flight plan. That way, the first leg of the departure procedure will be active. Otherwise, if you load the DP last, you'll need to active the first leg of the departure procedure.

Using the PROC key

Press the PROC key on either the PFD or MFD. Scroll using the large FMS knob to "Select Departure" (figure 11-31) and press the ENT key. Then use either FMS knob to select a departure procedure from the list available at the departure airport. Press the ENT key and then scroll to select the transition you'll take, press the ENT key, scroll to select and enter a runway number if necessary and press the ENT key. Finally, press the ENT key to "Load" the departure procedure.

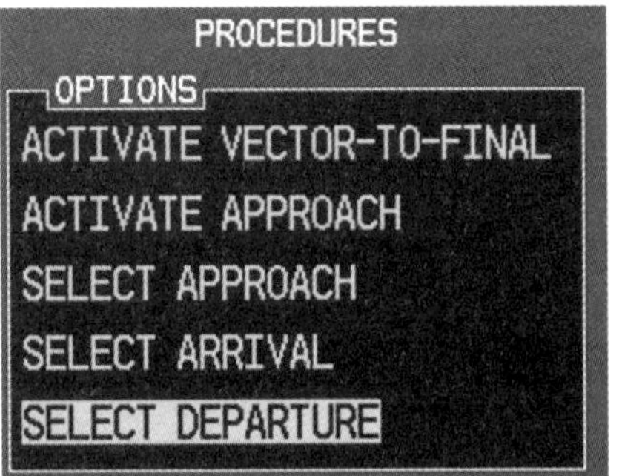

Figure 11-31 Press the PROC key to select a departure procedure. *© Garmin Ltd. or its affiliates*

Using Softkeys on the MFD

You can also select a departure procedure from the Airport Information page, which is the first page in the WPT group. From this page, press the DP softkey, and use the large FMS knob to scroll to the DEPARTURE, TRANSITION and RUNWAY fields and use the small FMS knob to enter a departure procedure, transition and in some cases the runway (figure 11-32). Finally, press the ENT key to "Load" the departure procedure.

AIRPORT
KSEA PUBLIC
SEATTLE TACOMA INTL
SEATTLE WA
DEPARTURE
BANGR3
RUNWAY
RW16L
TRANSITION
TOU

Figure 11-32 For departure procedures, you'll need to select a transition and sometimes a runway. *© Garmin Ltd. or its affiliates*

OBS Mode

GPS receivers, including the G1000 and Perspective, generally operate in leg mode, also called auto-sequencing mode, in which the GPS provides guidance between two successive waypoints in the flight plan. When a waypoint is reached, they automatically sequence to the next pair of waypoints.

A GPS can also operate in OBS mode, also called non-sequencing mode, where it deals with only a single waypoint, ignoring all other flight plan waypoints. Pilots can select and fly any random course line to and from the waypoint by turning the CRS knob. When in OBS mode, a GPS cannot sequence to the next waypoint in the flight plan, even after passing directly over the active waypoint. This mode is needed if you want to use the autopilot to fly some ODPs.

Note that you can set the active waypoint in your flight plan to use OBS mode and have the flight plan retain that information. To do this, press the FPL key on the PFD. The active waypoint will be the second waypoint in the active leg or whichever waypoint you set using the Direct-to key. Push the OBS softkey and turn the CRS knob to set the course for that waypoint. You can now push the OBS softkey to turn off OBS mode, since the OBS course is saved in the flight plan.

Using OBS mode on an Obstacle Departure Procedure

Often when you fly an ODP, you need to intercept and track a course to or from a VOR. You could do this using the NAV radios, however you'll then be switching back and forth between using the NAV radios and GPS. An alternative is to enter the VORs as waypoints in a GPS flight plan and use OBS mode to select the required course to or from the VORs. That way you can use a single GPS flight plan to fly the ODP and the route to your destination.

In this example, we'll simulate a flight from the Byron Airport, C83, in Byron, Calif. to the KMOD Airport in Modesto, Calif. First let's look at the ODP for Byron Airport (figure 11-33) and assume that we're departing from runway 30. The instructions are to make a "climbing right turn via heading 130° and ECA VORTAC R-250 to ECA before proceeding on course."

BYRON

TAKE-OFF MINIMUMS: **Rwy 23,** NA-obstacles.
Rwy 30, 200-1 or std. with a min. climb of 240' per NM to 300. Alternatively, with standard take-off minimums and a normal 200'/NM climb gradient, take-off must occur no later than 2000' prior to departure end of runway.

DEPARTURE PROCEDURE: **Rwy 5,** climbing right turn via heading 120° and ECA VORTAC before proceedingon course. **Rwy 12,** climbing left turn via heading 050° and ECA VORTAC R-250 to ECA VORTAC before proceeding on course. **Rwy 30,** climbing right turn via heading 130° and ECA VORTAC R-250 to ECA VORTAC before proceeding on course.

NOTE: **Rwy 5,** bush 17' from departure end of runway, 67' right of centerline, 6' AGL/52' MSL. **Rwy 12,** multiple trees and bush beginning 240' from departure end of runway, 286' right of centerline, up to 39' AGL/76' MSL. **Rwy 30,** multiple poles, building, and terrain beginning 66' from departure end of runway, 228' left of centerline, up to 65' AGL/225' MSL. Multiple poles beginning 949' from departure end of runway, 28' right of centerline, up to 42' AGL/103' MSL.

Figure 11-33 From runway 30, this ODP calls for a climbing right turn via heading 130° and the ECA VORTAC 250° radial to ECA before proceeding on course.

Since ODPs are not contained in the system database, we'll need to enter it manually. Enter a flight plan starting at C83, and then enter ECA and KMOD (figure 11-34). Note that the flight plan shows the active leg is from C83 to ECA. However, the ODP calls for us to track the 250° radial inbound to ECA, not the direct leg from C83 to ECA. To do that, push the OBS softkey. The flight plan now shows that ECA is the active waypoint.

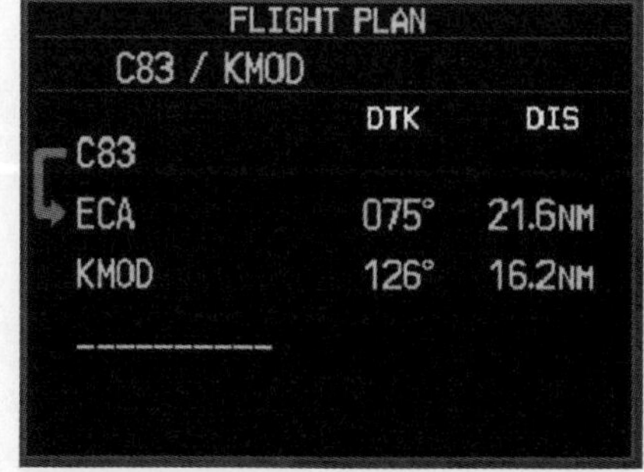

Figure 11-34 The active leg in this flight plan is from C83 to ECA. Now just push the OBS softkey and turn the CRS knob to set a course to fly to ECA. *© Garmin Ltd. or its affiliates*

Now turn the CRS knob to 070° and press the OBS softkey. Note that we've set the OBS to 070°, because we are flying inbound on the 250° radial. Had we been flying outbound on the 250° radial, our heading would have matched the radial number and we would have set the OBS to 250°.

After takeoff, use the autopilot's HDG mode to turn and fly a heading of 130°, an intercept angle to the 250° radial (figure 11-35). Then press the autopilot's NAV key. As the aircraft approaches the 250° radial, it will intercept it and fly toward the VORTAC. Upon reaching ECA, the flight plan sequences to the next leg from ECA to KMOD.

Using OBS mode to Fly an Unpublished Hold

OBS mode helps to visualize and fly unpublished holds. Suppose you receive the following holding instructions: "Hold southwest of the Crescent City VOR on the 245° radial with left turns. Expect further clearance at 0515 Zulu, current time is 0445 Zulu."

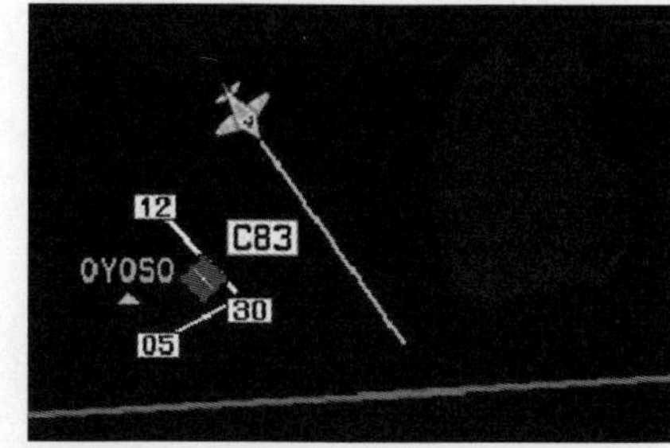

Figure 11-35 After takeoff, use the autopilot's HDG mode to turn and fly a heading of 130°, an intercept angle to the 250° radial. *© Garmin Ltd. or its affiliates*

To draw the hold on your chart, first locate the fix, Crescent City VOR. Then place the tip of a pen or pencil on the fix and draw a line along the 245° radial in the direction specified, in this case southwest. Then move your pen back to the fix where you started, drawing the inbound holding course. At the fix, begin drawing a left turn (figure 11-36) and continue drawing a racetrack.

To fly this hold, first enter CEC, the Crescent City VOR, as the active waypoint in a flight plan. Then press the OBS softkey to select non-sequencing or OBS mode. Next use the CRS knob to set 65°, the inbound course you'll fly when established in the hold. You'll now see

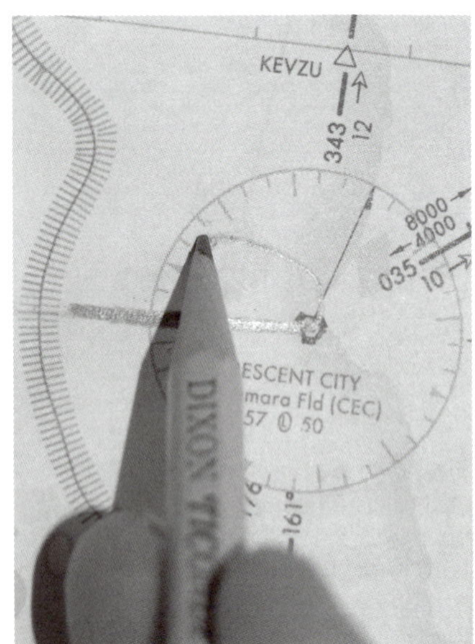

Figure 11-36 To draw a hold, first locate the fix. Place the tip of a pen or pencil on the fix and draw a line along a radial in the direction specified (in this case southwest on the 245° radial). Then move your pen back to the fix where you started and begin drawing the turn. *© Max Trescott*

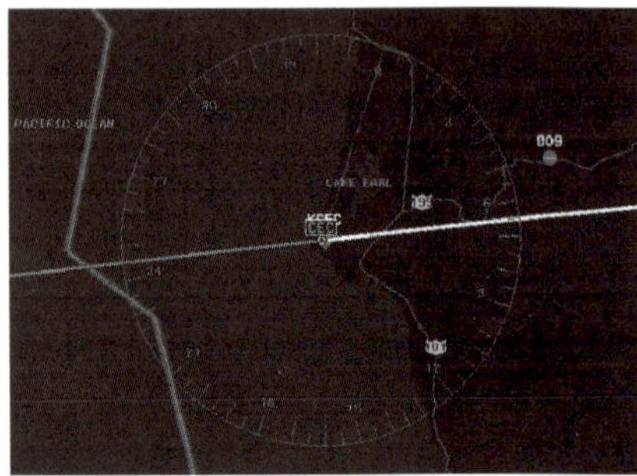

Figure 11-37 In OBS mode, you'll see a line, half white and half magenta, centered on the active waypoint. In this case, the CRS knob was turned to 65° to fly inbound on the CEC 245° radial. *© Garmin Ltd. or its affiliates*

a line crossing through the fix aligned with the CEC 245° radial. One half of the line is white and the other half is magenta (figure 11-37).

The G1000 and Perspective let you use only one GPS, so don't enter the OBS course (e.g. 65° in this example) prior to hold entry if you're still using the GPS for course guidance to the fix. Otherwise, if your autopilot is in NAV mode as you enter an OBS course, the autopilot will turn to fly a 45° intercept angle to the holding course. Or, if you'd like to set up the OBS course ahead of time, synchronize the heading bug with your current heading while the autopilot is tracking toward the fix and engage the autopilot's heading mode. Then push the OBS softkey and enter the 65° course with the CRS knob. Monitor the moving map to assure that heading mode takes you close to the holding fix.

For unpublished holds, you'll use the autopilot's heading mode to fly the hold entry and to fly outbound in the hold. Upon first reaching the holding fix, turn the heading knob to enter the hold and fly outbound. When you reverse course to fly inbound, press the autopilot's NAV key when you're within about 45° of the inbound course. The autopilot will intercept and track the holding course inbound toward the holding fix, provided that you're in OBS mode and have properly set the holding course. Upon reaching the fix, select heading mode and turn outbound. This combination of heading mode and NAV mode for flying a hold is the same whether you're using a WAAS-capable or non-WAAS GPS receiver.

Flying the DME Arc Approach

DME arc approaches require you to follow a curved path, defined by a specified DME distance from a VOR, for some portion of the approach. You can fly the approach via own navigation by navigating to one of the IAFs, or ATC can vector you to intercept the arc at an IAF or some intermediate point along the arc.

Let's look at flying a DME arc approach on a flight plan from KPAO to KWVI in Watsonville, Calif. (figure 11-38). First create a flight plan from KPAO to KWVI. Then load the VOR/DME-A approach starting with the IAF at JEJZE. Choose ACTIVATE and press the ENT key. Before proceeding, review every waypoint in the flight plan (figure 11-39) and verify that the VOR frequency 117.3 was loaded into NAV1. Then press the NAV key to engage the autopilot in navigation mode.

Note that GPS isn't in the title of the approach. Thus you can begin the approach using GPS, but must switch the CDI to a NAV radio to navigate the final approach course.

As you approach the IAF JEJZE, the GPS receiver will calculate when to start your turn onto the arc and your initial heading on the arc. If you're flying at about 120 knots, you'll see "NEXT DTK 004°" in the PFD's Navigation Status bar, notifying you of the turn and then "TURN TO 004°." At different groundspeeds, the initial heading will be slightly different. Then fly along the arc, keeping the GPS course pointer's D-bar centered.

If ATC vectors you to an intermediate point on the arc, you can activate the arc portion of your flight plan before reaching it. In the Active Flight Plan page, press the FMS knob and scroll to highlight "DME ARC." Then press the MENU key, highlight "Activate Leg" and press the ENT key. The arc portion of the approach will now be highlighted in magenta (figure 11-40). Intercept and fly along the arc.

Each time you reach a waypoint where you can descend, preselect the next altitude on the autopilot, engage the vertical speed mode and set a descent rate. Reduce the power as appropriate for descent and increase the power as the autopilot levels off at the new altitude.

As you approach KENIW, the PFD will display the messages "NEXT DTK 314°" and then "TURN to 314°." Start your turn and track the next segment to the FAF DYNER. Then push the CDI softkey to select NAV1. If you forget to do this, approaching DYNER the ALERTS softkey will blink. Push the ALERTS softkey to read the "Select NAV on CDI for approach" message.

Approaching the FAF, DYNER, "APR" or "LNAV" appears on the HSI, indicating that the GPS receiver is in approach mode. At DYNER, "NEXT DTK 314°" is displayed on the PFD and you can begin your descent to the published minimum altitude for the approach.

As you near the MAP, "ARRIVING AT WAYPOINT" is displayed. At the MAP, auto-sequencing is suspended, SUSP is displayed on the HSI, the CDI switches to a "FROM" indication and the SUSP softkey appears. You must then disconnect the autopilot and either land or initiate a climb to follow the missed approach instructions.

Flying a Course from Fix to Altitude

Some approaches include a leg where you need to climb to a particular altitude before proceeding to the next waypoint. For these legs, auto-sequencing is suspended and the SUSP softkey appears. When you reach the required altitude, simply press the SUSP softkey on the PFD and the flight plan will sequence to the next waypoint.

An example of this is the missed approach portion of the VOR/DME Runway 25 approach at KPMD (figure 11-41). You can load this approach in the G1000 software simulator and select vectors for the approach. At the MAP, auto-sequencing is suspended, SUSP is displayed on the HSI, the CDI switches to a "FROM" indication and the SUSP softkey appears.

If you press the SUSP softkey to re-enable auto-sequencing, the SUSP softkey will immediately reappear. This allows you to climb to 5000 feet, as listed in the flight plan, before flying to the next waypoint, which is the PMD VOR (figures 11-42 and 11-43). Once you reach 5,000 feet, press the SUSP softkey and you'll receive course guidance to PMD.

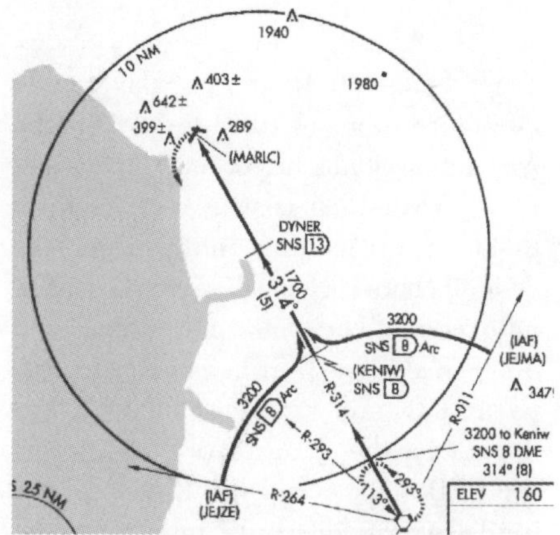

Figure 11-38 You can start this approach at IAFs on either end of the arc, or ATC can vector you to a mid-point of the arc.

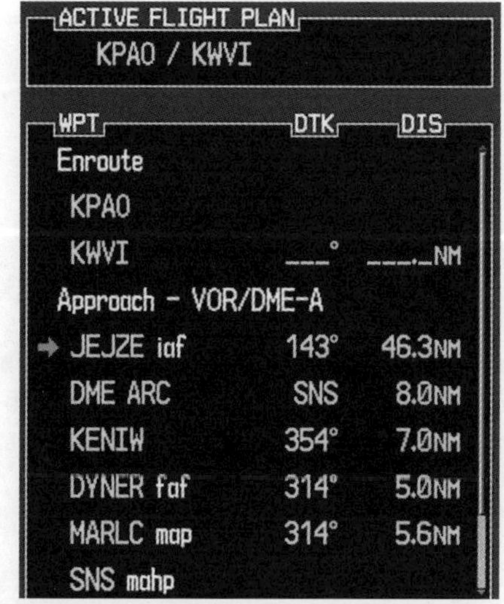

Figure 11-39 Review all steps in your flight plan. JEJZE, the IAF, is the active waypoint. *© Garmin Ltd. or its affiliates*

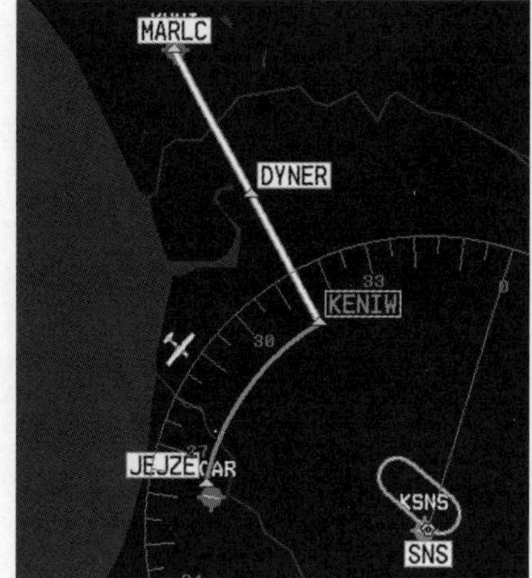

Figure 11-40 If vectored to the middle of an arc, activate the arc segment with the MENU key or the MFD's ACT LEG softkey. *© Garmin Ltd. or its affiliates*

TIP

When flying a DME arc, you may want to configure one of the fields in the Navigation Status bar of the MFD to display XTK, which is your crosstrack, or distance in nautical miles from the desired course. This will help you continually correct back toward the arc.

You can also use bearing pointers to help fly a DME arc. First, set the VOR frequency for the arc on NAV1. Then press the PFD softkey and the BRG1 softkey until NAV1 is displayed in a box to the lower left of the HSI. A green bearing pointer, which points to the VOR, also appears on the HSI. When flying the arc, choose a heading which keeps the bearing pointer approximately 90 degrees (plus or minus a few degrees for any wind correction) from your heading. While flying the proper heading on the arc, it will always point toward one of your wings, plus or minus the wind correction angle.

MISSED APPROACH: Climb to 5000 via PMD R-282 then climbing right turn to 7000 direct PMD VORTAC and hold. (TACAN aircraft climbing right turn to 5000 via R-298 to FISCH Int/14.3 DME and hold SE left turn 298° inbound.)

Figure 11-41 This missed approach procedure from Palmdale airport requires a climb before turning back to the VOR.

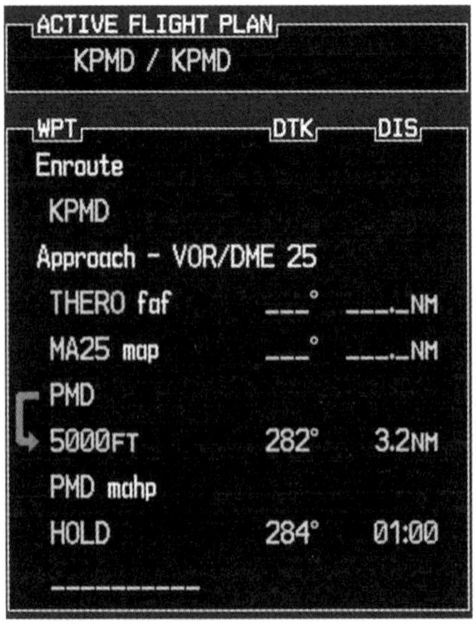

ACTIVE FLIGHT PLAN
KPMD / KPMD
WPT DTK DIS
Enroute
KPMD
Approach - VOR/DME 25
THERO faf ___° ___._NM
MA25 map ___° ___._NM
PMD
5000FT 282° 3.2NM
PMD mahp
HOLD 284° 01:00
____

Figure 11-42 When you reach the required altitude, press the PFD's SUSP softkey so that auto-sequencing will continue. *© Garmin Ltd. or its affiliates*

Flying a Course from Fix to Manual Sequence

This procedure is very similar to the Flying a Course from Fix to Altitude described above in that for a particular leg, auto-sequencing is suspended and the SUSP softkey appears. However, instead of waiting until you reach an altitude to press the SUSP softkey and fly to the next waypoint, you wait until you receive further instructions from ATC.

An example is the COASTAL TWO DEPARTURE from KBAF in Barnes, Mass. (figure 11-44). You can load this departure procedure in the G1000 software simulator by pressing the PROC key and selecting the "CSTL2" departure with a GEDIC transition departing from runway 02. Prior to departure, review each of the waypoints in your flight plan and check to see that MAN SEQ is the active leg. If it's not, scroll to highlight "MAN SEQ" in the Active Flight Plan window and activate the leg using the MENU key or the ACT LEG softkey on the MFD (figure 11-45).

As you depart, auto-sequencing is suspended and the SUSP softkey appears. Reading the departure procedure shows that after departure you are to fly vectors and altitudes assigned by ATC. Once you are cleared by ATC direct to the HFD VOR, press the SUSP softkey. This will re-enable auto-sequencing and provide you with course guidance to the next waypoint which is the HFD VOR.

TAA Instrument Scan

Learning good scanning techniques makes you a better instrument pilot. The techniques used in TAA differ from those used in traditional aircraft, though many instructors are unaware of the differences. One difference is that you'll want to scan more than just the PFD. After scanning the PFD indicators, check the MFD, then check the autopilot, and return to the PFD. For aircraft with the integrated GFC 700, the autopilot status bar is on the PFD, so modify your scan accordingly. Regardless of scan technique, most time is spent scanning the PFD and interpreting its indicators.

Round-gauge aircraft have "triangles of information" that can be cross-checked against each other. The airspeed, attitude indicator, altimeter and vertical speed indicator form a triangle that offers pitch information. The attitude indicator, turn coordinator and heading indicator form another triangle with bank information. After analyzing the PFD, I discovered it has "lines of information." Pitch information is conveyed along a horizontal line linking the airspeed, attitude indicator, altimeter, and vertical speed indicators. Bank information is in a vertical line formed by the attitude indicator, Heading Box, rate of turn indicator, and HSI.

Here's the scanning technique I teach my clients. First, scan from left to right along the horizon line, noting the four pieces of pitch related information. Start by looking at airspeed to get an idea of whether you need to make a pitch correction. Moving to the right, look at the attitude indicator's inverted "V" symbol and note the number of degrees it's located above or below the horizon. For each phase of flight, you should know the approximate number of degrees to which the V should be pitched. Begin making slight pitch corrections based upon what you saw on the airspeed and attitude indicators.

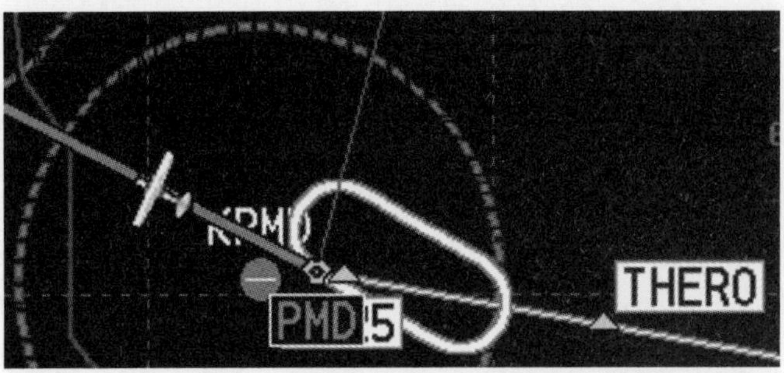

Figure 11-43 Continue to track the 282° radial and press the SUSP softkey at 5000 feet. *© Garmin Ltd. or its affiliates*

Moving to the right, note the altitude. Sometimes you'll want to read the 4 or 5-digit number representing altitude. However, it's more work to read and interpret digits than to look at an analog indication. Fortunately, the altitude reference bug provides an analog indication—provided you set your target altitude using the ALT knobs. Finally, note the vertical speed indication. Remember that while other instruments operate in real time, this instrument lags 4 to 6 seconds.

TAKE-OFF ALL RUNWAYS: Fly assigned heading and altitude for radar vectors to HFD VOR/DME. Thence. . . .
. . . . From over HFD VOR/DME proceed via the HFD R-143 to THUMB INT, then proceed via the HTO R-010 to YODER INT, then via the CCC R-057 to CCC VOR/DME. Then via (transition) or (assigned route). Expect clearance to requested flight level ten (10) minutes after departure.

Figure 11-44 This departure requires that you fly vectors before following the rest of the published procedure.

After completing a scan of the pitch indications along the horizon line, move your eye to the upper center of the PFD to begin scanning vertically from top to bottom for bank related indications. First, note the position of the attitude indicator's two triangles. If you're flying straight ahead, these triangles should be matched together. By consistently looking at and matching these triangles on every scan, you'll do a much better job of keeping the wings level and maintaining a heading. While scanning the triangles, glance just below them to note the position of the trapezoidal shaped slip/skid indicator. Use rudder inputs to position the indicator directly below the base of the triangle above it.

Move your eyes down to the Heading Box at the top of the HSI. Note whether the heading matches your desired heading and make small bank corrections if necessary. Next, inspect the turn rate indicator located along the top of the rotating compass card. In a turn, a magenta line or trend vector extends to the left or right to display the number of degrees the plane is projected to turn in the next 6 seconds. For a standard rate turn, bank the aircraft to an angle at which the trend vector matches one of the tick marks located 18° to the left and right of center. If you're over or under banking in a turn, make small corrections in bank angle to make the trend vector extend to one of the tick marks. If tracking a navigation signal, continue moving your eye down to the HSI's D-bar and begin correcting toward the desired course. Then repeat the entire scan.

ACTIVE FLIGHT PLAN
KBAF / GEDIC

WPT	DTK	DIS
Departure - CSTL2		
KBAF		
RW02		
MAN SEQ	026°	0.8NM
HFD		
THUMB	144°	11.0NM
YODER	192°	14.0NM
CCC	238°	29.9NM
GEDIC	216°	50.5NM

Figure 11-45 Fly vectors until cleared to HFD, then press the SUSP key. *© Garmin Ltd. or its affiliates*

Summary

It's imperative that you know how to use the flight planning and instrument procedures to fly safely in IMC. Practice in VFR conditions, in a simulator, or on the Garmin PC Trainer software so that when you fly in IMC you do so confidently.

In the next chapter, we talk about component failures and emergencies. TAA failures and the ways you need to respond are very different from traditional aircraft, so it's important to understand this material. Fortunately, in most failure scenarios, you'll have more redundancy and flying will be easier than partial panel flight in round-gauge aircraft.

Chapter 12:
Electrical Systems, Component Failures and Emergencies

Many experienced general aviation pilots, used to the vagaries of small plane electrical systems, have an instant visceral reaction to the idea of flying a glass cockpit that's dependent upon a plane's electrical system. That's not surprising, since many pilots have had one or more complete electrical failures. Given that, why would you trust your life to a glass cockpit? The answer is that just as the glass cockpit is not your father's Piper Cub, neither is the electrical system. Manufacturers have added more backup systems, but it's still key that you understand them so that you can effectively deal with failures in a G1000 or Perspective cockpit.

Most GA aircraft use a single alternator to generate power to recharge the aircraft's battery, which supplies electrical power for the aircraft. If the alternator fails, it's essential to identify this failure as soon as possible so that you can turn off unnecessary electrical equipment and conserve battery power. Unfortunately, warning systems are poor and many alternator failures go undetected until the battery is completely drained. While this is a non-emergency in daytime VFR conditions, it could be an emergency in IMC or at night if you're low on fuel and need power to activate pilot-controlled runway lighting.

General aviation aircraft certified for IFR operations have three gyroscopes: an attitude indicator, heading indicator and turn coordinator. A failure of all three of these while flying in IMC would be catastrophic, so the FAA requires a separate energy source for one of the gyroscopes. Typically, the attitude indicator and heading indicator are powered by an engine-driven vacuum pump and the turn coordinator is electric. This provides some redundancy if either the vacuum pump or the electrical system fails.

Electrical Systems

Glass cockpit aircraft instruments and displays are electric and the loss of electrical power renders them useless. Since this is unacceptable, the FAA requires an alternate power source and manufacturers have chosen to meet this requirement in different ways. First, most manufacturers have split the avionics bus into at least two buses. One, an "Essentials bus," powers only the most important equipment, such as the AHRS, ADC, PFD and one radio. The other bus supplies power to all avionics, including those on the Essentials bus. Upon loss of an alternator, you should follow your aircraft manufacturer's instructions for turning off unnecessary equipment while maintaining power to the Essentials bus. Also, since you'll receive a Warning annunciator almost immediately upon loss of the alternator, you'll be able to take action immediately and save more power than you usually can in a conventional GA aircraft.

Next, every manufacturer has a second or "standby" battery in their G1000 or Perspective aircraft to provide at least 30 minutes of power to some subset of equipment. In some cases, the standby battery powers the PFD and the Essentials bus; in other cases it powers a backup electric attitude indicator. The method of activation also varies by manufacturer. Some standby batteries take over automatically while others require that you turn on a switch to activate them. In the Tiger AG-5B, the standby battery is the same size as the main battery!

Finally, all manufacturers provide a set of traditional mechanical instruments for backup. Typically these are an airspeed indicator, attitude indicator and altimeter. In some cases, such as Cessna and Tiger, a vacuum pump is used to drive the standby attitude indicator and it will continue to operate after all electrical power is lost as long as the engine continues to run and the vacuum pump doesn't fail. In other cases, manufacturers use electric attitude indicators as a standby instrument. Note: vacuum pumps typically fail every 500 to 1000 hours. Therefore, you should check the vacuum pump on each flight and, if it has failed, replace it immediately so that it will continue to be available as a backup.

The best insurance against an electrical failure is a second alternator. That way, if one alternator fails, the second alternator will provide some current and continue to charge the battery. Depending upon the alternator's capacity and the electrical load on the battery, you may still have to turn off some unnecessary equipment. However, in this case, you can probably continue to your destination, whereas in a single alternator aircraft you may need to divert to a nearby airport, particularly if you're flying in IMC or at night.

Cessna 182 Electrical System

Figure 12-1 shows a simplified schematic of the electrical system for a Cessna 182. Note that this is a single alternator system and that power passes from the alternator through the alternator control unit (ACU) to the battery. In addition to regulating the voltage to an appropriate level for the battery, the ACU also has an overvoltage detection circuit that looks for any voltage spikes that might signal a problem with the charging system. Should it detect an overvoltage condition, it

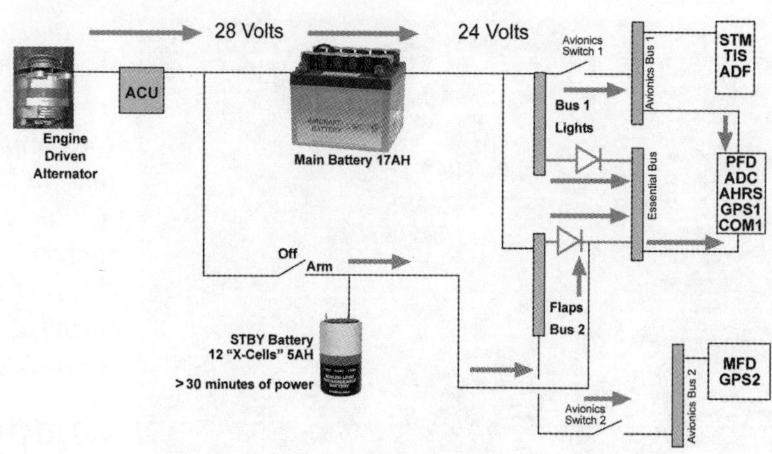

Figure 12-1 Understand your electrical system so you can effectively deal with emergencies.

will trip the alternator off line, the battery will begin to discharge and you'll receive a LOW VOLTS Warning annunciation on the PFD.

At this point, you should follow the instructions in your POH, which may instruct you to turn the left half of the Master switch off and then back on again. If the overvoltage condition was of a transient nature, the alternator will come back on line and you can resume normal operation. If, however, the alternator immediately trips off line again, you should suspect an electrical system problem and not reset the Master switch again.

The battery is connected to Bus1 and Bus2, which provide power to the lights, flaps and other equipment. Note that Bus1 also supplies power to Avionics Switch1, which supplies power to Avionics Bus#1. Likewise, Bus2 supplies power through Avionics Switch2 to Avionics Bus#2.

The Essentials bus powers the PFD, ADC, AHRS, GEA 71 Engine/Airframe Unit, one GIA 63 that provides GPS1 and COM1 and the standby instrument lights. It receives power from Bus1, Bus2 and Avionics Bus#1. This provides a high level of redundancy should one or more of the buses fail. Nonessential avionics, such as the Stormscope, MFD and second GIA 63 are powered through the Avionics 1 and 2 switches, which can both be turned off to conserve power in an emergency.

The ACU also supplies power to the standby battery and keeps it continuously charged as long as the STBY BATT switch is in the ARM position. Should the alternator fail and the main battery subsequently be totally drained, the standby battery will continue to power the Essentials bus for at least 30 minutes. This will allow you to continue to aviate, navigate and communicate using the PFD and the GPS, COM and NAV radio contained in one of the GIA 63 LRUs.

Note that diodes connect Bus1 and Bus2 to the Essentials bus. These are one-way devices and, if the main battery fails, they will block current from the standby battery and Essentials bus from powering any equipment on Bus1 or Bus2. Avionics Bus1 and Bus2 also would not receive power, which further helps conserve energy from the standby battery.

If the standby battery fails, all power to the G1000 system will be lost and both displays will be blank. At this point, you can continue to fly using the three standby instruments; however, you'll no longer have any navigation or communication capabilities. Hopefully by this point, you will have reached VMC and can land safely.

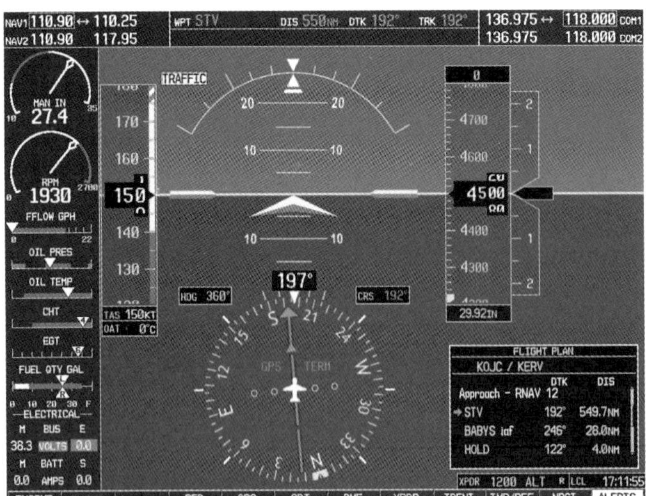

Figure 12-2 If a display fails, the primary flight instruments and engine indication system are combined and shown on the remaining screen.
© Garmin Ltd. or its affiliates

You may want to consider adding a handheld aviation radio to your flight bag. If you lose total power, it may be useful for contacting ATC to advise them of your situation and receive landing instructions. Note that while these radios can receive from a considerable distance, they will usually only transmit a few miles from the plane unless you have a way to connect an external antenna to the radio. Any avionics shop can install a connection so that your handheld radio can transmit more effectively.

Component Failures

A critical part of all pilot training is understanding and dealing with system malfunctions. It's so important that the Practical Test Standards (PTS) for the private certificate and instrument rating require DPEs to test candidates on system malfunctions. In traditional aircraft, this might be a no flaps landing to simulate an electrical system failure or a partial panel approach to simulate a vacuum pump failure.

In a G1000- or Perspective-equipped aircraft, an examiner might simulate the failure of the PFD, ADC or AHRS. All pilots flying TAA need to understand the impact of component failures in their aircraft and how to respond to them. In addition, flight instructors and DPEs must know how to teach and to simulate the failures. The impact of component failures on the autopilot is particularly complex and varies by autopilot and aircraft manufacturer. Table 12-1 summarizes the impact of component failures on autopilots.

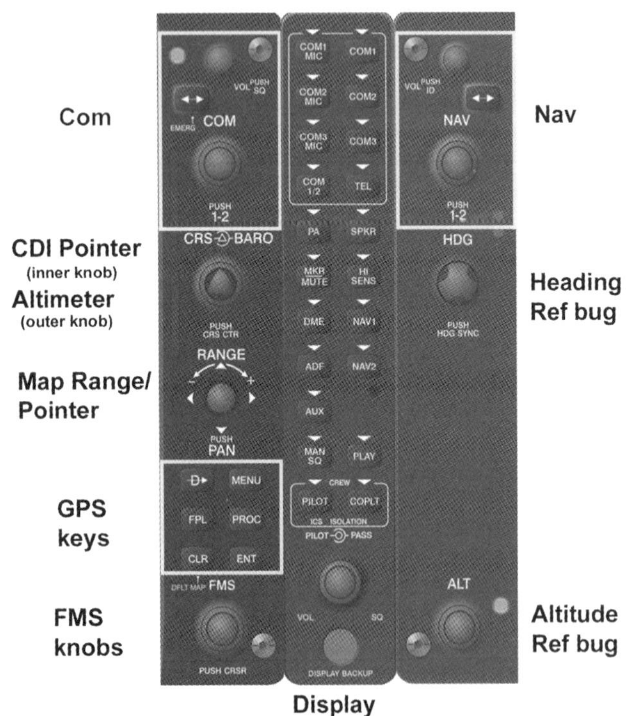

Figure 12-3 Push the Display Backup button whenever you detect a display failure.

Display Failures

The G1000 was the first glass cockpit to provide redundancy for PFD failures. Thus in the unlikely event that the PFD fails, you can still see the primary instruments, though they are displayed on the MFD. This "reversionary mode" occurs automatically if the system detects a failure through its fault monitoring system, or manually if you notice a failure not detected by the system and press the large, red Display Backup button located between the Perspective's displays (figure 15-1) and on the G1000 audio panel (figure 12-3).

In reversionary mode, the system combines the engine indication system from the MFD with the primary flight instruments from the PFD and sends the data to both displays (figure 12-2). That way, you'll still have access to the most important information, regardless of which display fails. You will however lose the MFD's maps. Early G1000 versions also lost the PFD's Inset Map; current G1000 and Perspective systems retain the Inset Map in reversionary mode. For installations with two audio panels, only the Display Backup button on the pilot's side audio panel is enabled.

It's important to remember that when one display fails, you'll also lose one of the GIA 63 units. This means that you'll lose one GPS receiver, one COM radio and one NAV receiver. Which one you lose depends on which display fails:

- PFD failure results in loss of GIA1 (COM1, NAV1 and GPS1)
- MFD failure results in loss of GIA2 (COM2, NAV2 and GPS2)

Loss of the PFD doesn't affect the KAP 140 autopilot. However loss of the PFD causes the GFC 700 in the Perspective to revert to ROL and ALT modes. In some other aircraft, a loss of the PFD leads to a complete loss of the GFC 700 autopilot.

In older G1000 aircraft, the autopilot was connected only to GIA2, which communicates with the system through the MFD. If the MFD failed, the system could not send NAV data to the autopilot. In Perspective and later model G1000 aircraft, the autopilot is connected to both GIA1 and GIA2. In these aircraft, the autopilot continues to operate in some capacity even if the MFD has failed. In some GFC 700-equipped aircraft, if the MFD fails, the autopilot will remain on in the active modes and will capture any armed modes. However, you will be unable to change modes and once the autopilot is disconnected it cannot be re-engaged. The Flight Director will remain on, however you will be unable to change modes or turn it off. In KAP 140-equipped aircraft, loss of the MFD results in loss of NAV and APR modes, and you'll need to use HDG or ROL mode.

Impact on Autopilot

Component Failure	**Perspective**	**GFC 700 Cessna 172**	**KAP 140**
PFD[1.]	Autopilot reverts to ROL + ALT modes	Lose autopilot	No impact on autopilot
AHRS[2.]	Lose autopilot	Lose autopilot	Lose HDG, NAV, APR
ADC	Lose autopilot	Lose autopilot	Lose ALT capture
GIA1	Reverts to ROL and PIT modes. Can be re-engaged.	No impact on autopilot	No impact on autopilot
GIA2	No impact on autopilot	Lose autopilot	Lose NAV, APR
MFD[3.]	No impact on autopilot	Autopilot remains on but modes cannot be changed	Lose NAV, APR

1. GIA1 also lost when PFD fails
2. Magnetometer data lost when AHRS fails
3. GIA2 also lost when MFD fails

Table 12-1

Radio, Transponder and Audio Panel Failures

The G1000 includes two GIA 63 units, each of which contains a COM, NAV and GPS receiver. Failure of an entire unit is unlikely, since each of the components within the LRU is independent. Should GPS1 fail, the GPS2 receiver in the second GIA 63, GIA2, will take over navigation of an active flight plan without any pilot intervention.

In older G1000, GFC 700 equipped aircraft like the Columbia 400, the Flight Director software ran only on GIA1. In these aircraft, loss of

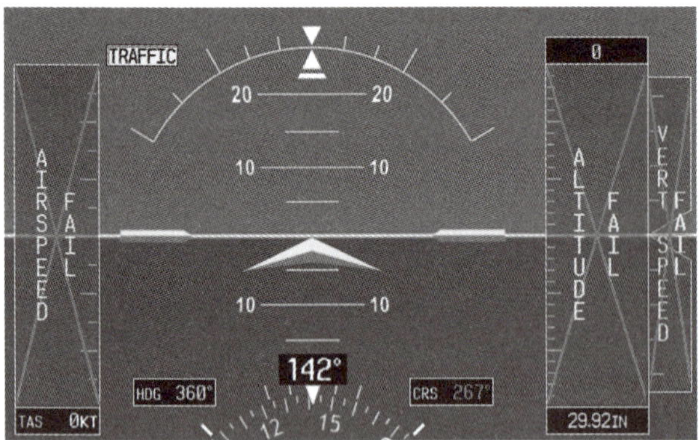

Figure 12-4 Loss of the ADC causes Xs to be placed over airspeed, true airspeed, altitude, vertical speed and OAT indicators. *© Garmin Ltd. or its affiliates*

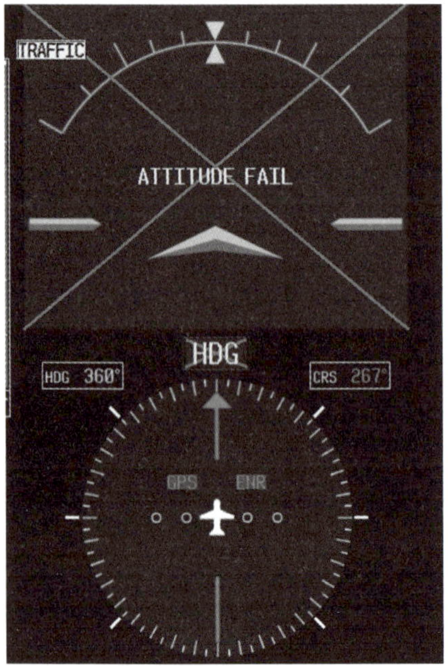

Figure 12-5 Loss of the AHRS leads to Xs being placed over the attitude indicator and HDG box and the background turns black. *© Garmin Ltd. or its affiliates*

GIA1 results in loss of the autopilot and Flight Director. If GIA2 fails, the autopilot is lost but the Flight Director continues to work. For Perspective and newer GFC 700 aircraft, see Table 12-1 for the effects of a loss of GIA1 or GIA2. In KAP 140 equipped aircraft, a loss of GIA2 renders the autopilot unable to track a signal using the NAV or APR modes, but all other modes will work.

If the failure of a COM or NAV radio is detected, the system will place a red "X" over the COM or NAV frequency display to indicate the failure. If a failure in a COM radio's tuning mechanism is detected, the GIA 63 will automatically tune that radio's active field to 121.5, the emergency frequency. In the event of an audio panel failure, the pilot's headset will be automatically connected to COM1. If the transponder fails, a red "X" appears over the transponder window in the lower right corner of the PFD.

ADC and AHRS Failures

The ADC receives and processes the pitot and static system inputs to generate airspeed, altimeter and vertical speed information for the PFD and to provide Mode C altitude information to the transponder. It also measures total air temperature and uses this data to calculate density altitude, true airspeed and outside air temperature (OAT).

If the ADC fails, the PFD will display a red "X" over the airspeed, altimeter, vertical speed and outside air temperature indicators (figure 12-4), your transponder will no longer send altitude data and TIS traffic will no longer be displayed. If this occurs, you should refer to the standby altimeter and airspeed indicator installed in your aircraft.† If air temperature data is lost, a red "X" will appear on the outside air temperature and true airspeed windows. In Perspective and other GFC 700 equipped aircraft, loss of the ADC results in loss of the autopilot. However, the Flight Director will continue to work, though the Vertical Speed, Altitude Hold and Flight Level Change modes will be inoperative. In the case of the KAP 140 autopilot, loss of the ADC doesn't affect the roll modes, but does result in the loss of the altitude preselect. You can still use the VS and ALT modes, but you'll need to manually press the ALT key to level off at a desired altitude.

The AHRS receives magnetic heading information from the magnetometer and provides attitude and rate of turn information to the PFD. If the system detects that the AHRS has failed, a large red "X" is displayed over the attitude indicator and HDG box on the PFD and the background turns black (figure 12-5). If just the magnetometer fails, then only compass data is lost and a red X is displayed over the Heading box.

If the AHRS fails, you should fly with reference to your aircraft's

† For details on managing failures in aircraft with dual AHRS and/or dual ADCs, see Chapter 15.

standby attitude indicator. You may also want to configure the Track Vector and the Nav Range Ring on the MFD, since these will help you easily identify your ground track. Also, consider setting one of the MFD Navigation Status Bar fields to XTK so that you can easily identify your deviation from course. In Perspective and GFC 700-equipped aircraft, loss of the AHRS results in loss of the autopilot and the Flight Director. In KAP 140-equipped aircraft, loss of the AHRS results in the loss of all roll modes except for ROL mode; pitch modes are unaffected.

Instructors and examiners are encouraged to simulate the loss of either the AHRS or ADC by dimming the PFD by pressing the MENU key on the PFD as described in Chapter 4. Or, you can create overlays, using the transparency film used for giving presentations on an overhead projector, that block out the appropriate portions of the PFD to simulate different failures. The pilot should respond by flying the aircraft with reference to the MFD and standby instruments and by engaging the autopilot in ROL mode.

The ROL mode simply keeps the wings level and will not maintain a heading over time. In an emergency, changes in course can be made by overpowering the autopilot by gently turning the yoke. CAUTION: Read the limitations on your autopilot, as some do not permit overpowering it using the yoke. However, in an emergency, use your best judgment as to what to do.

CAUTION: If you choose to overpower the yoke to make a turn, be careful not to push or pull on the yoke, as this will cause the elevator trim wheel to trim against the pressure until it reaches its limits. If the autopilot then disconnects, you will have the extremely high control pressures associated with the trim wheel being at its limits, *which could lead to loss of control of the airplane.* One technique to turn the yoke, to the left for example, without pushing or pulling is to gently push down on the top left of the yoke while pushing up with the other hand on the bottom right of the yoke.

Alternate Ways to Simulate Failures

It's possible to simulate failures by pulling circuit breakers, though some manufacturers and FAA Advisory Circulars discourage this since it can shorten the life of the circuit breakers. Some manufacturers put the AHRS and ADC on the same circuit breaker, and in these aircraft you won't be able to fail them separately. If you were to do this, simulate loss of the AHRS by pulling the AHRS circuit breaker. The pilot should control the plane by using the remaining PFD instruments and standby attitude indicator and engage the autopilot in ROL mode.

Loss of the ADC could be simulated by pulling the ADC circuit breaker. The pilot should control the plane by using the PFD's attitude indicator and the standby altimeter and airspeed indicator and engage the autopilot. Note: pulling the ADC circuit breaker causes the loss of altitude information for the transponder. Therefore you should avoid doing this while in Class B or C airspace or within the 30 nm Mode C veil that surrounds Class B airports. This will also result in the loss of Mode S TIS data, since traffic information is not sent to aircraft which are not transmitting altitude information.

Loss of the PFD could be simulated by pulling the PFD circuit breaker. The pilot should press the Display Backup button on the audio panel and control the plane using the MFD. Note: Pulling the PFD breaker prevents the tuning of NAV1 and COM1 frequencies. Therefore, you should be using COM2 if you pull the PFD circuit breaker. In some installations, pulling the PFD breaker also shuts off the front avionics fan.

Engine Indication System Failures

All engine and airframe information, including RPM, manifold pressure, oil temperature and pressure, electrical system, EGT, CHT, fuel and vacuum data is processed by the GEA 71 Engine/Airframe Interface. It also provides all Warning, Caution and Alert annunciations to the PFD.

While it's possible that the entire GEA 71 could fail, it's more likely that a single element, such as an EGT probe to a particular cylinder, will fail. When a failure occurs, a red "X" will appear over the data in the MFD's engine display that is no longer valid.

Emergencies

Covering all possible emergencies that you might encounter is beyond the scope of this book. You're encouraged to read Section 3 Emergency Procedures of your POH so that you are familiar with all emergency procedures for your particular aircraft. Here are several features common to most Perspective- and G1000-equipped aircraft that are useful in emergencies.

NRST Softkey and NRST pages

GPS receivers have revolutionized finding the nearest airport during an emergency. In addition to calling ATC and asking for vectors to a suitable airport, you can find the information yourself on the system. This has the advantage that you can continually monitor your progress toward an airport.

The fastest and easiest way to get information on the nearest airport is to push the NRST softkey on the PFD. This provides basic information on the nearest airports, including runway lengths and communication frequencies. You can also quickly load a frequency by scrolling to it and pressing the ENT key. A full description appears in Chapter 4.

The MFD's NRST pages can provide even more detailed information about each airport, including runway designations, length and width. The NRST Airport page is easy to reach by turning the MFD's large FMS knob several clicks clockwise. It should be the first page displayed in the group. Full details on this and other NRST pages appear in Chapter 7.

Radio Communications

The system makes it easy to get to the emergency frequency of 121.5 MHz. Pushing and holding the Frequency Toggle key for two seconds loads the emergency frequency into the active frequency for which toggling is enabled. Also, should a COM radio fail, that radio defaults to 121.5 MHz. If both displays were to fail, the pilot's headset is automatically connected to 121.5 MHz.

Checklists

In an emergency, your adrenaline will be pumping and it will be easy to overlook something. So train yourself to use a checklist during an emergency. That way, you can methodically work through the problem even if you're not thinking straight.

Perspective aircraft have electronic checklists, though not all G1000-equipped aircraft do. To access checklists in the Perspective and later G1000 versions, turn the large FMS knob to select the √LST group on the MFD. In older aircraft, you'll need to press the CHKLIST softkey followed by the EMERGCY softkey.

Backup Equipment

You may want to carry a portable GPS receiver and handheld radio with you for backup. Handheld radios are most effective when connected to an external antenna, and any avionics shop can set this up for you.

Summary

Understanding electrical systems is important whether you're analyzing which aircraft to buy or learning to deal with emergencies in the aircraft you fly. All TAA offer the potential for increased safety in an emergency, but to take advantage of it, you must understand their systems, the impact of a component failure and how to react to it. Studying and understanding the systems ahead of time will make you more secure in the knowledge that you know what to do when a failure occurs. You'll also enjoy flying more!

So far, we've talked about the individual elements of the system and how to operate them. Now, let's put it all together and take a flight. To help develop a routine to use each time you fly, read the following chapters: Chapter 13 for the G1000 and Chapter 15 for the Perspective.

Chapter 13: Flying a Trip Behind the G1000

Let's take a trip and fly behind a G1000-equipped Cessna 172. We've picked that aircraft since, over the last 50 years, more of them have been built than any other GA aircraft. Therefore, more readers are likely to be familiar with it and can spot the differences in the way a G1000-equipped version is flown. Also, these aircraft are becoming more available as rental aircraft, so if you're a renter pilot, you may find one to fly. If you fly a different G1000-equipped aircraft, you'll find that many of the steps outlined here will still apply to your aircraft.

Some pilots still fly 172s using mental checklists. However, the FAA continues to put a strong emphasis on the use of actual checklists, and given the added complexity of the glass cockpit aircraft, it's imperative that you use one. You can use the manufacturer supplied checklist—either on paper or an electronic version in the G1000—buy a third-party checklist or create your own.

Note that the procedures provided here are generic and where they differ from your POH or checklist, you should use those in preference to this book. Also, many routine steps are left out, as our purpose in this section is to highlight differences in flying a G1000-equipped aircraft, not to list every step required to fly a 172.

Required Equipment & Limitations

As a pilot, you're hopefully aware that the FAA specifies in FAR 91.205 the equipment required to be operational in your aircraft for day VFR, night and IFR flight. If any of this equipment is not operational, you're not allowed to fly the aircraft unless you get a ferry permit from the FAA to allow you to bring the aircraft back to a place where it can be repaired.

Manufacturers can specify additional required equipment. You may find this in the back of Section 6 Weight & Balance of your POH and also in Section 2 Operating Limitations. For the Cessna 172, you'll find the Kinds of Operation Equipment List (KOEL) in Section 2 which tells you which equipment is required for different types of operation.

Perspective

Pilots flying Perspective-equipped aircraft can skip this chapter and instead read the Flying a Trip Behind the SR22 Perspective section of Chapter 15.

For example, the forward and aft avionics fans are required for any flight, while the PFD bezel lighting (of the keys on the PFD) is only required for Night IFR operations. Also, the strobe lights are required, while the beacon on the tail is not. Interestingly, the standby battery is not required for any type of flight, though according to the notes it is "recommended." You'll want to study this table so that you understand what equipment is required for different types of flight. You'll also want to understand all other limitations listed in Section 2.

Preflight

Many of the preflight items, particularly those that relate to the airframe, will be familiar to any 172 pilot. Some of them, however, are unique to G1000-equipped C172s. For example, you must verify that the G1000 Cockpit Reference Guide is in the aircraft and accessible to the pilot, since it's listed in the KOEL as required equipment for any flight.

Part of the checklist includes verifying that the avionics switches are off and then turning on the Master switches and verifying that the PFD display comes on. Note that the PFD operates with the avionics switches off, since it receives power through the Essentials bus. Also—and this will be a surprise to many pilots—the PFD is on when you start the engine.

About 15 to 20 seconds after the PFD comes on, check to see that all "Xs" over the engine indicators are gone. The data is considered valid whenever the pointers on these gauges are visible. The ADC will come up next and "Xs" over the pitot-static instruments will be removed. The display remains dark (with no brown and blue background representing the ground and sky) until attitude data becomes available. After a total of about 60 seconds, the AHRS will come up and all "Xs" should be removed from the display.

Next, you'll check the fuel gauges and verify that various annunciators are on or off as specified by the checklist. For example, the LOW FUEL L and LOW FUEL R annunciators should be off while LOW VACUUM should be on. If you've added fuel, you'll need to set the fuel totalizer so that the proper amount of fuel is reflected when using the Trip Planning page and the Fuel Range Ring. To do this, press the ENGINE and then the SYSTEM softkeys on the PFD. If you filled the fuel tanks, press the RST USED softkey, which is the only one available on some early versions of the G1000 software. Later versions have additional softkeys that allow you to increment or decrement the totalizer by the number of gallons added or removed from the tanks.

Next, you need to verify operation of the forward and aft avionics fans, since these are required equipment. You'll turn on the Avionics Bus#1 switch and listen for the forward fan. Note that you can also put your hand on top of the glare shield and feel air from the fan. Then turn off the Avionics Bus#1 switch, turn on the Avionics Bus#2 switch and listen for the aft avionics fan.

As part of your preflight inspection, verify that the air inlet for the rear avionics fan is not blocked by any object, such as a plastic bag for example. Inlets are located on the rear bulkhead. The C172's inlet is in the lower right corner (figure 13-1), the C182's is in the middle and the C206's is in the upper left corner. Blockage reduces airflow to the G1000 electronics mounted in the tailcone and could lead to overheating. Not all manufacturers' G1000-equipped aircraft have avionics fans, so these steps won't apply to all aircraft.

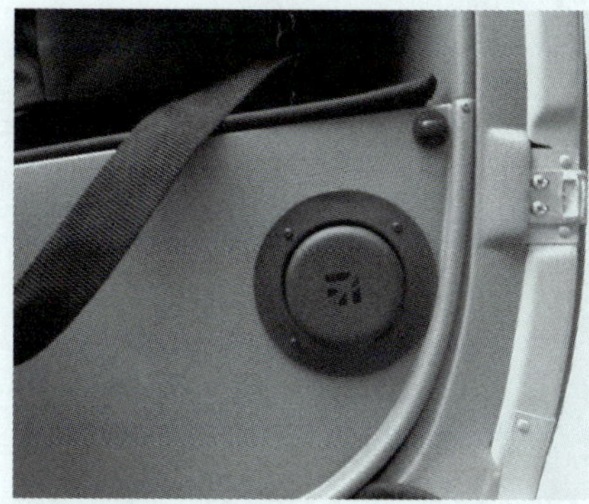

Figure 13-1 Be careful not to block airflow to the avionics vent in the aft bulkhead.

Starting the Engine

Prior to engine start, verify that Avionics Switch1 and Switch2 are both off. You'll also move the STBY BATT switch to the TEST position and hold it there for 20 seconds to verify that the green LED does not go out. This puts a test load on the battery to check its capacity.

Then, move the STBY BATT switch to the ARM position and verify that the PFD comes on. In the ARM position, the battery is connected to the Essentials bus. Should the main battery become fully discharged, the standby battery will automatically provide power to the Essentials bus if it's in the ARM position (figure 13-2).

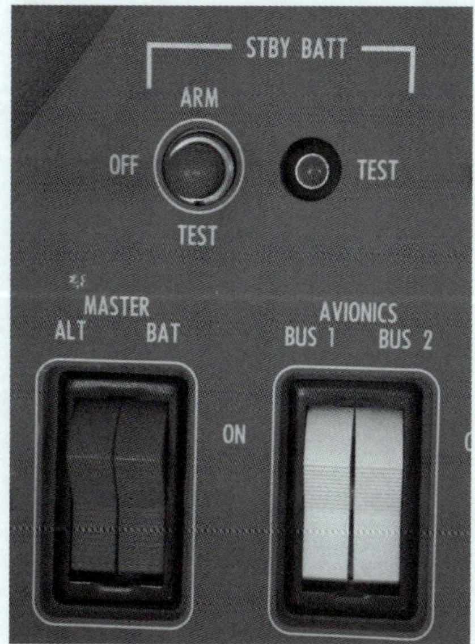

Figure 13-2 The STBY BATT switch stays in the ARM position during flight.

Next, look at the Engine Indication System on the PFD and verify that there are no red "Xs" on any of the indicators. Then, check the Essentials bus voltage for at least 24 volts, the main bus for 0 volts and the standby battery for a discharge. Also, verify that the STBY BATT annunciator appears on the PFD. Turn on the strobe lights (since these are the anticollision lights required per the KOEL), turn on both Master switches (ALT and BAT) and, after priming, start the engine. If you don't hear noise from the fuel pump while priming, you might have only the STBY BATT switch on. If so, turn on the Master switches.

After engine start, check the oil pressure and then verify that both the main and standby batteries show a positive charge, which indicates that the alternator is now charging the batteries. Verify that the LOW VOLTS annunciator is now off and turn on the Avionics Bus #1 and Bus #2 switches.

Prior to Taxi

As the MFD completes its self-test, read the aircraft model number at the top of the screen to verify that it matches your type of aircraft. It's possible for an avionics technician to load the wrong software into your G1000 during maintenance, which is why you need to check this. Check the database expiration date at the bottom of the MFD screen to verify that the databases are current. If you pressed the ENT key before looking for the database date and the MFD's opening screen is gone, you can go to the System Status page to find the database dates.

Next, select the System Status page in the AUX group of pages. Scroll with the FMS knobs so that you can see all system components listed on the page. Verify that there is a checkmark under the Status column for every component listed to confirm that the entire G1000 system is operating properly. Go to the GPS Status page and press the GPS1 and GPS2 softkeys to verify that both GPS receivers are receiving multiple satellites. Finally, check the HSI. If a yellow "INTEG" annunciator appears, there aren't enough satellites to perform a RAIM test and you shouldn't use the GPS for primary navigation guidance.

Next, load the appropriate frequencies into your radio by using the Airport Information page. For example, you'll first want to load the ATIS or AWOS frequency and then load frequencies for clearance delivery or ground control and request taxi instructions. Finally, load the tower frequency. Remember to use this page to save time entering frequencies both at your departure and destination airports.

Before Takeoff

To check the flight instruments, verify that there are no red "Xs" over any of the indicators. Next, enter the altimeter setting into three places: the PFD using the BARO knob, the standby altimeter and the autopilot using the knobs on the KAP 140.

Enter your first level-off altitude in two places: the G1000 using the ALT knobs and the autopilot using the KAP 140 knobs. The former sets the cyan altitude reference bug and the altitude reference window above the altimeter. The latter preselects the altitude at which the autopilot will level off and maintain altitude with the ALT mode.

Next, check the standby instruments to see that they are operating properly. Then perform the autopilot preflight and Manual Electric Trim tests. These tests require a number of steps, but are essential for determining that the autopilot and electric trim system are performing correctly before takeoff.

During the engine runup, do the usual test of the magnetos and carburetor heat. When asked to check the vacuum indicator, you'll need to look in the EIS section of the MFD. Note: some G1000-equipped aircraft don't have a vacuum pump and others, like the Tiger AG-5B, use a separate vacuum indicator on the instrument panel. Finally, you'll check that all annunciators on the PFD are off, check to see that the engine doesn't quit when the throttle is retarded to idle and then return it to 1000 rpm.

Set Avionics

Prior to takeoff, set all COM and NAV radio frequencies that you can. For example, load the departure control frequency from the Airport Information page and any VOR frequencies you may need. Also, set the CDI softkey to either VOR or GPS navigation, depending upon which you are using.

If you're not using VOR navigation, enter your flight plan into the GPS. It's much faster, easier and safer to do this while you're still on the ground. After entering all of the waypoints, scroll through the entire flight plan to verify that each one was entered correctly.

Next, set the heading reference bug to the departure runway heading. That way, you are all set to engage the autopilot during your climb out. Verify that the autopilot is off and prepare for takeoff.

Takeoff and Climb

After takeoff, engage the KAP 140 autopilot after you are more than 800 feet above the ground. This is fairly simple to do if you remember that you will be working your way across the autopilot from left to right and that you'll need to push at least four keys in the process.

First, push the AP key on the KAP 140 autopilot and verify that ROL mode is now displayed on the top line of the display, which shows active modes. Verify that VS is shown on the top line, indicating that this mode is active and that the autopilot captured the aircraft's vertical speed at the time you pressed the AP key.

Next, press the HDG or NAV key, depending upon whether you will steer the aircraft with the G1000's HDG knob or have the autopilot track the navigation source you selected on the HSI with the CDI softkey. If you press the HDG key, HDG will be displayed on the top half of the display indicating that it's the active mode and the plane will immediately start turning to whatever heading you've selected with the G1000's HDG knob.

If you press the NAV key, NAV will appear on the KAP 140 display. If it appears on the top line, it's because you're relatively close to the desired course and the autopilot is now tracking the navigation signal. If NAV appears on the lower half of the display, the NAV mode is armed and will remain armed until you steer the airplane, presumably with the HDG mode, close enough to the desired course for the autopilot to capture the course.

Next, press either the UP or DN key to display the vertical speed that the autopilot captured. It's important that you do this, as sometimes autopilots capture a higher than desired vertical speed, leading to a nose-high attitude and the possibility of a stall. If you want to change the vertical speed reference, push the UP or DN key again to change the reference in 100 feet per minute increments.

Finally, press the ARM key and verify that ALT appears on the lower half of the KAP 140 display indicating that the altitude hold mode is armed to level off and maintain the altitude you preselected. As you continue to climb, go through your aircraft's climb checklist.

At 1000 feet from your preselected altitude, the autopilot will emit a chime sound through the audio panel. This is a reminder to check that the altitude hold mode is armed. Whenever you hear the chime, look for the ALT label on the bottom half of the KAP 140 display and call out "1000 feet to go, altitude armed."

As you reach your preselected altitude, verify that the autopilot actually levels off and that ALT is now displayed on the top half of the KAP 140 display. Altitude hold mode is now active. Then, set cruise power, lean the engine and go through your cruise checklist.

GFC 700 Autopilot

If the G1000-equipped Cessna 172 you fly has a GFC 700 autopilot, the steps you'll follow will differ slightly from the flight described in this chapter.

Before takeoff, you can push the GA or Go Around button, which turns on the GFC 700's Flight Director and sets the command bars for a 7° pitch up attitude. You'll only have to enter your first level-off altitude once; use the G1000's ALT knobs.

During the climb, instead of turning on the autopilot with the AP key as you would with the KAP 140, preset your desired autopilot modes on the Flight Director first. For example, press the IAS or FLC key and the airspeed at which you'd like to climb. Use the ALT knobs to set your desired level-off altitude if it differs from the one you set on the ground. ALTS will be displayed in white at the top of the PFD, indicating that the altitude hold mode is armed to level off and maintain the altitude you preselected. Then press the NAV key or set the heading bug and press the HDG key. Only after all the modes are set correctly, press the AP key. If GPS is displayed in white at the top of the PFD, the NAV mode is armed and won't become active until you steer the airplane closer to the desired course with the HDG mode.

Cruise

Throughout the entire flight, you need to search for traffic visually. The mode S transponder and optional TAS devices help you do this. Generally, you'll leave the MFD set on the Navigation Map page, with TRAFFIC selected along with other features you desire. Note that if you have the Navigation Map zoomed out, the traffic, which only displays out to 7 miles, is tightly clustered in the center of the screen. Thus, whenever you receive a traffic alert, you may want to turn the small FMS knob one click so you can see the dedicated Traffic Map page. If you leave that page set for the 12-mile range, you'll see all data available from the mode S transponder.

During the flight, you may want to check the weather at your destination or along your route. Turn to the Weather Data Link page, or Airport Information page, and see whether the weather or the forecast has changed since you took off. You might also want to monitor the ATIS of airports en route, since this might give you an early warning of changing weather. If you're in IMC, doing this will keep you apprised of possible options if an electrical system failure or other problem occurs.

You'll also want to enable the Fuel Range Ring or use the Trip Planning page to monitor whether adverse winds might require an unplanned fuel stop. Remember that this fuel information will be accurate only if you correctly set the fuel totalizer before you took off.

Night Flight

Any night flight brings additional risks and requires additional planning. For example, a high percentage of night accidents occur during approach and descent to the destination, since it's harder to spot terrain. The accident rates are highest in dark night conditions with no moonlight. Also cockpit lighting can be an issue. G1000-equipped aircraft can make contributions in both areas.

At night, turn down the brightness of the displays so that your eyes can better adapt to darkness and you can see more outside the cockpit. The first thing you'll notice when you use the instrument panel lighting knobs to dim the displays is that they both dim together. However, you'll probably want to dim the MFD even more than the PFD. To dim it separately, press the MENU key on the PFD and follow the instructions in Chapter 4.

When on the Navigation Map page, you may want to press the MAP and TOPO softkeys to turn off the topographical information, since it adds to the overall brightness. Don't do this, however, if you need the topographical information to enhance the overall safety of your flight.

One of the greatest contributions that the G1000 brings to night flight is terrain awareness. This can be activated by pushing the MAP and TERRAIN softkeys from the Navigation Map page. Alternatively, you can use the Terrain Proximity page in the MAP page group. During the flight, make sure that you avoid any areas painted in yellow or red. *I strongly urge you to use terrain awareness capability at night,* or whenever you're uncertain about surrounding terrain. Many fatal accidents would be avoided if every pilot had this capability and used it.

Approach for landing

As you approach your destination, you'll want to prepare early for landing. This includes starting your descent, getting the ATIS information and determining your entry into the airport traffic pattern. If you want the G1000 to calculate the start of your descent, push the FPL key and turn to the third page in this group, the Vertical Navigation page.† Set the parameters for your descent, such as your desired descent rate, final target altitude and distance from the airport at which you'll reach the target altitude. Then press the MENU key, select "VNAV Messages On?" and the G1000 will notify you when to start your descent.

The Airport Information page provides information that you'll want to know about your destination airport. First, use it to load the ATIS or AWOS frequency into a COM radio and pick up the current weather as soon as you can. If possible, figure out from the winds which runway you're likely to use. Also, note whether the surface winds are vastly different from your winds aloft, which may suggest the presence of wind shear and turbulence. While you're loading frequencies from this page, remember to load tower and ground frequencies too.

Next, use the map on this page, which is always North Up, to orient yourself for your arrival. To do that, look at the bottom of the HSI and determine the direction from which you're arriving. Plan your entry by looking at the map and runways and visualizing from which quadrant of the map you're arriving. After you've planned your entry, return to the Navigation Map page.

Landing

Prior to landing, you'll need to disconnect the autopilot before descending below 800 feet AGL. If you're on an instrument approach, however, you can leave the autopilot engaged until 200 feet AGL. It's been observed in some manufacturers' aircraft that the autopilot may trip off as you add the first notch of flaps, particularly at higher speeds. This occurs when pitch acceleration forces exceed +1.4Gs or -0.6Gs and results in a TRIM FAIL annunciator appearing on the PFD. To avoid this, put the first notch of flaps in slowly, or slow down before adding the first notch of flaps.

Once you've safely entered the traffic pattern, you may want to turn off the TERRAIN softkey, particularly at night. Otherwise, you may get distracted as the MFD turns completely red during landing. You may also want to go to the Traffic Map page and press the STANDBY softkey if you anticipate a busy traffic pattern that will continually generate traffic alerts as you land.

† For vertical navigation in later G1000 versions, see pages 214-17.

After landing, taxi off the runway, stop and go through your After Landing checklist using either the G1000 electronic checklist or any other checklist. Prior to shutdown, note the tach time in the EIS section of the MFD. Then follow the Securing checklist to shut down your airplane.

Note that the PFD remains on after the airplane is shut down! You must remember to turn the STBY BATT switch off before you leave the airplane. Otherwise, the PFD and other equipment on the Essentials bus will completely discharge the standby battery.

Flying Other G1000-equipped Aircraft

The overall process of flying other G1000-equipped aircraft is similar to our description of flying the Cessna 172. There are differences, however, and we'll discuss some of these, particularly as they relate to the G1000. Also, refer to the Appendix, where you'll find a table of differences among G1000-equipped aircraft.

First, electronic checklists were not shipped with many early versions of the G1000. Their availability varies by manufacturer. Also, you might not need to listen for avionics fans during the preflight as not all manufacturers include these.

In some aircraft, such as the Diamond DA40, the PFD and MFD both come on when you turn on the Master switch, so you'll see both during engine start. Also, the Diamond DA40 and DA42 don't have a standby battery for the PFD, so you won't be testing a battery before flight. Instead, they have a separate battery for the standby attitude indicator.

One of the greatest differences among G1000-equipped aircraft is the autopilot. Differences exist even with aircraft using the same autopilot. For example, early model Cessna and Diamond aircraft were both equipped with the KAP 140, but only the Diamond aircraft included Control Wheel Steering capability. And while Cessna's KAP 140 implementation had GPS roll steering capability, KAP 140-equipped Diamond's did not. Integrated autopilots, such as the GFC 700, let you preselect the altitude from the G1000. Describing all of the autopilot differences is beyond the scope of this book. You should read the Airplane Flight Manual Supplement for your aircraft so that you understand autopilot operation.

The Mooney M20M and M20R include a separate annunciator panel to display Warning and Caution alerts. Therefore, they do not use the Annunciator window in the G1000. While the G1000 in these aircraft will still display the lower level "Advisory" alerts via the ALERTS softkey, it will not display any of the higher level Warning and Cautions.

However, the G1000 does include additional indicators in the Mooney aircraft. For example, it includes Rudder Trim, Elevator Trim and Flap Indicators. All of these are located on the MFD below the engine information.

The Warning and Caution alerts vary considerably across aircraft. The Appendix lists the Warnings and Cautions that appear in the G1000's Annunciator window for the different aircraft. For example, the Beechcraft G36 includes a GEAR UP Warning, while the Diamond DA42 includes left and right GBOX TEMP warnings when temperatures in the gearboxes exceed 120°C.

Summary

Flying G1000-equipped aircraft is truly enjoyable. To get the most out of the experience, you'll want to make sure that you take advantage of the many features that reduce your workload and enhance overall safety. Also, it's imperative that you read the POH and the G1000 Cockpit Reference Guide for your aircraft

If you're on the fence and aren't sure that flying a G1000-equipped aircraft will make a difference, consider this. I spent over 25 years working in the high-tech industry and was initially skeptical, since I'd seen many cases of technological solutions that didn't make any additional contribution toward solving a real world problem. Hence, I was prepared to believe that this was yet another misapplication of technology.

After the first flight, however, I was convinced that being able to aviate, navigate and communicate from a single display makes a major contribution to the overall ease and safety of flying an aircraft. This feature alone would have eliminated some IFR accidents where pilots were distracted by adjusting radios or the transponder and failed to maintain the aircraft in the proper attitude. Also, the enhanced positional awareness reduces a pilot's mental workload and increases safety. Finally, having an excellent autopilot frees a pilot for other tasks and makes flight in IMC more pleasant.

If you're used to flying older Cessna 172s, you'll find that not only is the G1000 a major change, but even the aircraft handling characteristics are better than those of older aircraft. If you're looking for something fun and sporty to fly, try a Diamond DA40, with its outstanding visibility and docile stall characteristics. If fast is the name of your game, you can't beat the new G1000-equipped Mooneys, Beechcraft and Columbia 350i and 400i. And of course, for just pure fun and economy, there's the Tiger AG-5B. Regardless of which airplane you choose, you'll find that the G1000 makes a substantial positive difference in your flying experience.

Chapter 14:
Advanced G1000 and Perspective Features

Many advanced features have been released since the Garmin G1000 was introduced. Since many readers are already familiar with the basic G1000 features, we've chosen to discuss these features in a new chapter, rather than integrate them into prior chapters. Readers flying older G1000 aircraft can skip this chapter, while pilots flying Perspective and upgraded G1000 and G900X aircraft will want to read it in detail.

Let's review the topics we'll cover, which are ordered similarly to the chapter order of this book. There are new features and minor enhancements to the PFD. New features include a new Current Track Bug that makes it easy to figure out how much wind correction you need to track a course. Enhancements include a revised Navigation Status bar and new options for displaying wind data.

Flight plans are enhanced with timesaving features such as the ability to enter waypoints into a flight plan from lists of Recent, Nearest, or Flight Plan waypoints. Vertical navigation, in conjunction with the autopilot's VNV key discussed in Chapter 10, is now possible using direct-to navigation or a series of descent altitudes in a flight plan. Other new features include along track offsets, parallel track and—drum roll please—the long awaited airways!

The MFD has new features and enhancements, including SafeTaxi Diagrams that help you find your way around some of the larger airports. Optional electronic charts are now available for some aircraft; you can choose to subscribe to either Jeppesen charts or the government NACO charts.

We'll also cover the basics of WAAS, the Wide Area Augmentation System. These advanced GPS receivers make it possible to fly instrument approaches with ILS-like precision to hundreds of airports in North America. Finally, there's a new Dead Reckoning mode that keeps track of your position if the GPS fails.

There are also new options available for purchase through your avionics shop. The GDL 90 ADS-B transceiver and GSR 56 Iridium

Perspective

When the Perspective was first introduced, it included most, but not all features listed in Chapter 14. Experienced Perspective pilots will want to read the end of this chapter to learn about newer features, such as the Profile View for the Navigation Map page, importing/exporting flight plans, dual navigation database, selected altitude intercept arc, and AOPA Directory. New Perspective pilots will want to read this entire chapter.

Figure 14-1 The Current Track Bug, below the number "7," shows the ground track. Turning left 7° would align the bug with the CDI needle and compensate for the wind drift. *© Garmin Ltd. or its affiliates*

transceiver are described in Chapter 3. Cessna offers a Search and Rescue (SAR) option that lets search crews incorporate search patterns into a flight plan. Search types include parallel track, sector, and expanding square search patterns.

New PFD Features and Enhancements

Current Track Bug

The Current Track Bug is an extremely useful new feature. It's very small and barely mentioned in the manuals, so it's possible that you haven't noticed it. It's a small magenta diamond near the top of the HSI (figure 14-1) that gives a visual representation of the TRK or ground track formerly displayed in the PFD's Navigation Status Bar. Using the bug helps you quickly identify a heading that exactly compensates for the wind so you can parallel the desired course. The CDI's D-bar is still used to tell you whether you are to the left or right of the desired course.

GPS users learn over time to fly whatever heading causes the DTK, or desired ground track, and TRK numbers to be identical. For example, if the desired track to your destination is 270°, and your TRK, the plane's current track over the ground, is 265°, then you need to turn the plane 5° to the right to parallel the desired course.

It's even easier to do this visually with the Current Track Bug. Simply turn the plane so that the bug aligns with the head of the GPS CDI needle. Note, however, that you don't "chase" the Current Track Bug as you do the CDI's D-bar. If the Current Track Bug is to the left of the CDI needle, you need to turn to the right. The Current Track Bug will move to the right as the aircraft turns right.

You can also use the Current Track Bug when flying with a VOR or ILS needle displayed on the CDI. GPS courses aren't always aligned exactly with VOR and ILS courses, so the HSI's D-bar may not be exactly correct. However, the Current Track Bug should still give a very good indication of the heading that allows you to compensate for the wind when tracking a VOR or ILS course.

Navigation Status Bar

The Navigation Status bar has changed significantly. The original format (figure 4-3), contained the active waypoint, distance to that waypoint, desired track (DTK) to the waypoint and ground track (TRK). The new format shows the Direct-to symbol and waypoint when flying with Direct-to navigation. When flying an active flight plan leg, it displays the beginning and ending waypoints separated by an arrow (figure 14-2).

Figure 14-2 The bearing updates in real time, continuously showing the ground track required to the active waypoint. *© Garmin Ltd. or its affiliates*

The distance to the active waypoint is still displayed, however DTK and TRK are replaced with BRG, or bearing to the active waypoint. DTK and TRK are useful, since by flying to keep TRK close to DTK, you could maintain a flight path parallel to the desired course. However if you were left or right of course, these numbers couldn't guide you back to the course—you'd need to reference the D-bar to do that. Note that DTK and TRK are available elsewhere on the PFD. DTK is listed in the flight plan, and the new Current Track Bug is a visual representation of TRK. Also, you can set up the MFD's Navigation Status bar to display DTK and TRK. Note: the latest Perspective software displays ETE, not BRG.

The advantage of bearing information is that it provides a continuous update of the ground track required to reach the active waypoint. In a zero wind condition, flying a heading equal to BRG will take you directly to the active waypoint. Automatic Direction Finder (ADF) receivers also display bearing information, and pilots familiar with these know that if there is any wind, continually matching the aircraft's heading to BRG results in flying a curved path to the waypoint. The easiest way to resolve the wind issue with the G900X and G1000 is to fly a heading that causes the Current Track Bug to remain on a course that matches the BRG displayed. For example, if the BRG says 326°, fly whatever heading is required to make the Current Track Bug remain at 326°.

Wind Data Window

The new Wind Data window is an obvious change to the PFD. Older G1000s have a Wind Vector that can be displayed on the PFD's Inset Map and in the upper right corner of the MFD. Those Wind Vectors are still displayed, but now pilots have additional options.

The Wind Data window is displayed above and to the left of the HSI, just below the heading box. There are three ways to configure it. To choose one, press the PFD softkey and then the WIND softkey. This brings up four new softkeys (figure 14-3).†

OPTN 1 | OPTN 2 | OPTN 3 | OFF

Figure 14-3 Press the PFD and WIND softkeys to show the four wind display softkeys. *© Garmin Ltd. or its affiliates*

Pressing the OPTN 1 softkey brings up a box with two arrows and two numbers that resolve the wind vector into its two components (figure 14-4). The number below the vertical arrow shows the amount of headwind or tailwind in knots, and the number next to the horizontal arrow shows the amount of left or right crosswind. This option is particularly useful for identifying the crosswind component while on final approach to land.

Pressing the OPTN 2 softkey displays a single arrow that shows the wind direction and the total wind velocity in knots. This is similar to the format used to display wind on the MFD. It's particularly useful for identifying changes in wind direction and strength and you may want to use it while flying en route.

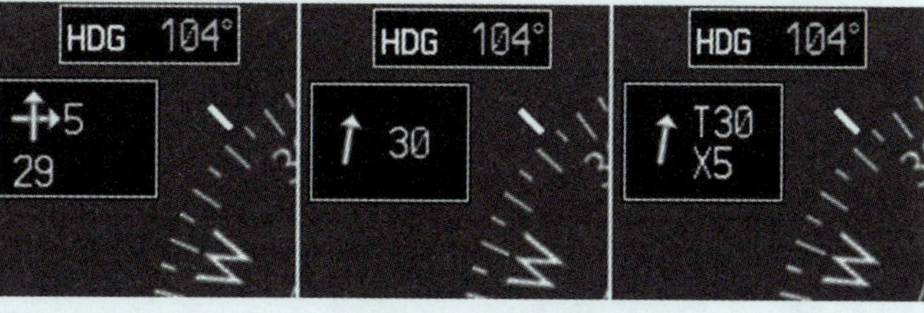

Figure 14-4 From left to right, Options 1, 2 and 3 displaying the same wind. *© Garmin Ltd. or its affiliates*

The OPTN 3 softkey combines the options. It shows a single vector for wind direction and two numbers for the strength of the headwind or tailwind and crosswind in knots. We recommend that you always display the Wind Data window. If you choose to turn it off, press the PFD, WIND and then the OFF softkeys.

† The Perspective has two wind options. See Figure 15-4.

Altitude Alerting

Altitude alerting is associated with the selected altitude displayed at the top of the altimeter (figure 14-43). Typically, the altitude you select with the G1000's ALT knobs is displayed with cyan or light blue digits on a black background. As you approach the selected altitude, you'll now get a series of warnings that alert you to verify that level off at the selected altitude actually occurs.

When your altitude comes within 1,000 feet of the selected altitude, the box flashes for three seconds and then the altitude displays in reverse video with black text on a light blue background and an aural alert sounds. As you come within 200 feet of the selected altitude, the text flashes for three seconds and reverts to the original blue text on a black background. Subsequently, if you deviate from that altitude by more than 200 feet, the digits will appear yellow on black to draw your attention to the deviation.

Radio Changes

In the past, "TX" or "RX" was displayed between the standby and active COM frequencies when the radio was transmitting or receiving a signal. Now "SO" is also displayed when the radio squelch is open.

Transponder

The FMS knobs can now be used to enter a transponder code, though our preference is still to use softkeys. To use the knobs, push the XPDR and CODE softkeys and turn the small FMS knob to enter the first two digits of the squawk code. Then turn the large FMS knob one click to the right, use the small FMS knob to enter the last two digits, and press the ENT key.

A new GND softkey sets the mode-S transponder in Ground mode and displays a green GND annunciator next to the transponder code. In Ground mode, mode A and C data is not transmitted, but acquisition squitter continues. Squitter allows the aircraft to be known to ground-based stations and to reply to discrete Mode S interrogations.

PFD Display Changes

A number of minor changes were made to the PFD. The most important of these is that the Inset Map is now displayed when the system is in reversionary mode. The map appears in the lower right corner in the same space used when the FPL, MENU, NRST, TMR/REF or ALERTS keys are pushed. Note that you can still push any of these keys, however, the Inset Map will disappear and be replaced by one of five windows. Pushing the same key a second time restores the Inset Map.

There are changes to the Inset Map. A new TRFC-2 softkey removes all map information except TIS or TAS traffic (figure 14-5A). When NEXRAD is selected for display, the letters NR, for NEXRAD, appear in the lower right corner of the map and age information appears in the upper right corner. For example, if NEXRAD data was received 3 minutes ago, "NR: 3m" is displayed. Remember, however, that NEXRAD data is already at least eight minutes old when you receive it. Thus in this example, the data is actually at least 11 minutes old!

When a traffic advisory or TA occurs, the Inset Map is automatically enabled and displays the traffic. Now, distance and direction to the traffic appear in yellow at the bottom of the map. If the traffic is beyond the Inset Map's scale and cannot be displayed, "TA OFF SCALE" appears at the bottom of the map.

There are two changes associated with the HSI. The first is that whenever the D-bar shows a full scale deflection, XTK and the distance from the course line in nautical miles appear in the HSI (figure 14-5). For example, in the Terminal mode, which has a full scale deflection of 1 nm, as full scale deflection is reached, "XTK 1.01 NM" is displayed in magenta. Also, changing the HSI format now requires pushing an additional softkey. After pushing the PFD softkey, one must now push the new HSI FRMT softkey to reach the 360 HSI and ARC HSI softkeys.

The softkeys for selecting barometric pressure units also changed. Formerly, you would push the PFD softkey and then the METRIC softkey. Now you push the PFD softkey and the ALT UNITS softkey to bring up a new level of softkeys. Pushing the IN or HPA softkeys select barometric pressure display in inches or hectopascals respectively. Pushing the METERS softkey changes the altitude display from feet to meters.

Figure 14-5 The desired course is 1.27 nm to the left, and the aircraft is correcting toward the course. *© Garmin Ltd. or its affiliates*

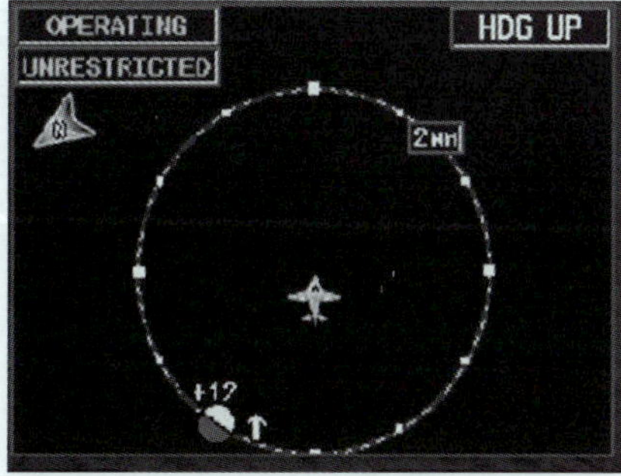

Figure 14-5A A new feature lets you dedicate the PFD's Inset Map to traffic. Press the INSET softkey and select the new TRFC-2 softkey.

Flight Planning

Enhancements

Two new enhancements save you time entering identifiers into a flight plan. Other new features let you create a vertical descent profile, an along track offset, or add airways to a flight plan.

The first enhancement lets you choose a waypoint from up to five lists of waypoints: FPL (flight plan), NRST, Recent, USER and AIRWAY. If the waypoint you want is on one of these lists, you can enter it faster with this feature than by twisting the FMS knobs. To use this method, press the FPL key to open the flight plan, turn the small FMS knob one click to the right to open the Waypoint Information window, and then one click to the left to open a new window with the pull-down lists (figure 14-6). The first list shown is FPL. To access the NRST and Recent lists, turn the small FMS knob. When you see the list you want, turn the large FMS knob to move the cursor down to the list of identifiers. Then turn either FMS knob to highlight an identifier on the list. Press the ENT key twice to add the identifier to the flight plan.

Another change is that when you press the FPL key, a flashing cursor is already present. Previously after pushing the FPL key, you needed to push the FMS knob to get a cursor, so this change saves a step. Note that in the past the cursor came on at the end of the flight plan. It now comes on highlighting the active waypoint.

Figure 14-6 When entering waypoints, twist the small FMS knob one click to the right and one click to the left to bring up this shortcut screen.
© Garmin Ltd. or its affiliates

Direct-to Vertical Navigation

Vertical flight planning to manage descents is now available. The Direct-to key on either the PFD or MFD can be used to create an altitude constraint if you're referencing just a single waypoint for your descent. This can be used, for example, to command an aircraft to cross a waypoint at a certain altitude or to arrive at pattern altitude a mile or two from a destination airport using the autopilot's VNV key, described in Chapter 10. Vertical Navigation using multiple altitude constraints is also available using the MFD's FPL key, and we describe that later in this section.

To create an altitude constraint for a single waypoint, press the Direct-to key on either the PFD or MFD. Enter the waypoint using the FMS knobs and scroll with the large FMS knob to the ALT field (figure 14-7). Use the large and small FMS knobs to enter an altitude and press the ENT key. Then use the small FMS knob to select MSL or AGL, and press the ENT key. For example, if you've entered 1000 feet and select AGL, guidance will be provided to 1000 feet above the airport's field elevation.

Figure 14-7 This Direct-to window is set to provide vertical navigation to the 900 foot MSL pattern altitude 2 miles before arriving at the destination.
© Garmin Ltd. or its affiliates

Finally, use the small FMS knob to enter a negative number in the OFFSET field and press the ENT key. This creates a target location, some number of miles before the direct-to waypoint, to which you'll descend. If you want to descend to a location beyond a waypoint, use the Along Track Offsets.

The Direct-to key can also be used to create an altitude constraint in conjunction with a waypoint already loaded in a flight plan. This creates a descent path from an aircraft's current altitude to the waypoint altitude. It also removes any altitude constraints in the flight plan for waypoints prior to the direct-to waypoint. Altitude constraints after the direct-to waypoint are retained. To use it, highlight a waypoint in the active flight plan, push the Direct-to key, scroll to enter the altitude constraint, AGL or MSL, any offset distance, and press the ENT key.

The vertical constraint portion of Direct-to navigation can be cancelled separately, while still retaining Direct-to course guidance. To clear a vertical constraint, press the Direct-to key and the MENU key (figure 14-8). Scroll to highlight "Clear Vertical Constraints" and press the ENT key.

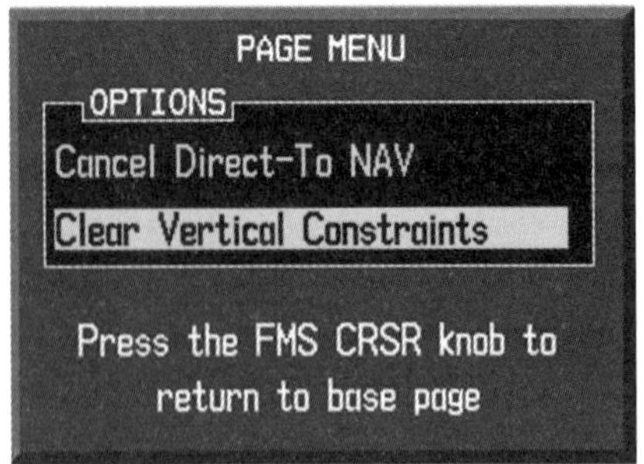

Figure 14-8 Pressing the Direct-to key and the MENU key gives you the option of clearing vertical constraints.
© Garmin Ltd. or its affiliates

Vertical Flight Plans

The MFD's Flight Plan group now has two pages instead of three. The third page, originally used for Vertical Navigation, is combined with the Active Flight Plan on page one. The second page, the Flight Plan Catalog page, remains unchanged. All vertical navigation is done from the MFD's Active Flight Plan page, or with the Direct-to key.

Entering a vertical flight plan is relatively easy. In addition to adding waypoints to the Active Flight Plan page, use the FMS knobs to enter altitudes on the same line with each corresponding waypoint. The GFC 700 autopilot's vertical navigation function, enabled with the VNV key, can then follow a flight plan's descent profile; it cannot command a climb. There are several nuances to properly using the VNV key, so you'll want to read Chapter 10 carefully.

VIEW | VNV PROF | CNCL VNV | VNV D→ | ATK OFST | ACT LEG | SHW CHRT | CHKLIST

Figure 14-9 The VNV Direct-to softkey lets you initiate vertical descent guidance immediately. *© Garmin Ltd. or its affiliates*

Once you've entered all of the altitude constraints in a flight plan, you can easily reference any of these altitudes for a descent without affecting lateral guidance to any intermediate waypoints in the flight plan. From the MFD's Active Flight Plan page, press the VNV Direct-to softkey (figure 14-9) to initiate vertical descent guidance. This opens a new window asking if you'd like to activate descent guidance (figure 14-10). If you didn't highlight a waypoint, the window chooses the next valid altitude shown in light blue text in the flight plan. Alternatively, if you highlighted a subsequent waypoint or altitude prior to pushing the VNV Direct-to softkey, that altitude is referenced. Pressing the ENT key confirms activation and immediately activates descent guidance.

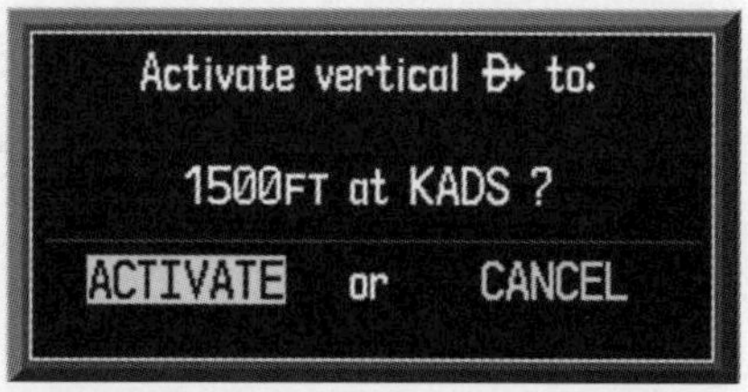

Activate vertical D→ to:
1500FT at KADS ?
ACTIVATE or CANCEL

Figure 14-10 In this case, KADS was either the next waypoint with a valid altitude, or the waypoint highlighted before pressing the VNV Direct-to softkey. *© Garmin Ltd. or its affiliates*

When an arrival or approach procedure is added to a flight plan, the system includes any altitudes that can be retrieved from its database. It only contains "Cross at" altitudes; "Expect to cross at" altitudes are not in the database, but can be entered manually. Some of these altitudes have restrictions, such as cross "At" or "At or below" the altitude. These restrictions are indicated by bars added above and/or below the altitudes (figure 14-11).

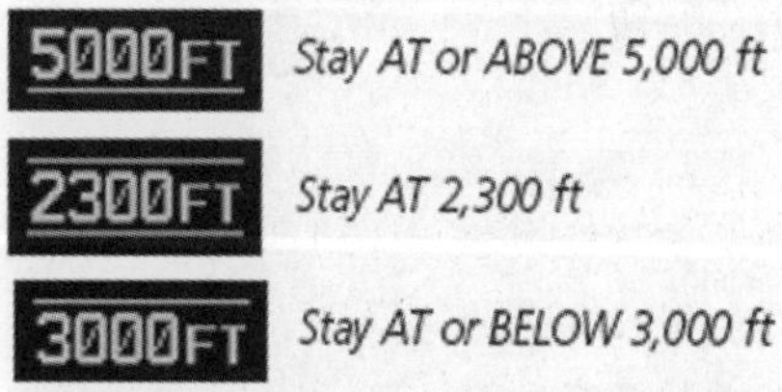

5000FT *Stay AT or ABOVE 5,000 ft*
2300FT *Stay AT 2,300 ft*
3000FT *Stay AT or BELOW 3,000 ft*

Figure 14-11 Restrictions are shown with bars above and/or below an altitude. *© Garmin Ltd. or its affiliates*

Different types of text are used in the altitude column of the Active Flight Plan to indicate how each altitude is treated (figure 14-12). Large blue altitudes entered by the pilot and small blue altitudes, retrieved from the system's database, are used to determine vertical speed or provide deviation guidance. Large white altitudes are the system's estimate of the aircraft's altitude as it crosses a waypoint and are not used for vertical guidance. Small white altitudes from the system's database are displayed as a reference, but are not used for vertical guidance. Light blue subdued text (not shown) cannot be used for vertical guidance. Altitudes can be designated for vertical guidance by pressing the ENT key, or un-designated by pressing the CLR key.

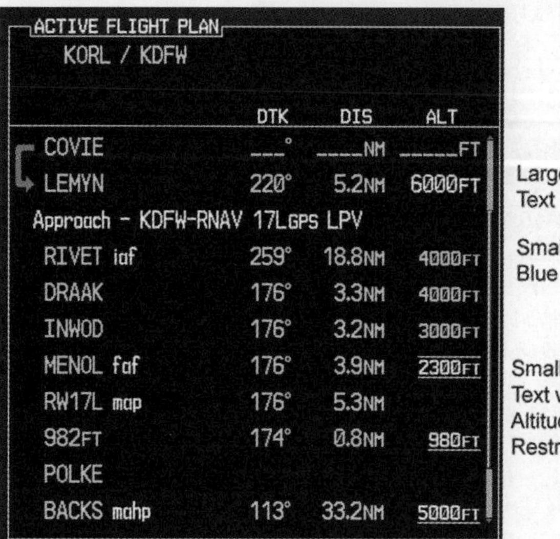

Figure 14-12 White altitudes are system estimates of the aircraft's altitude; blue altitudes are used for vertical guidance. *© Garmin Ltd. or its affiliates*

After entering altitudes in the flight plan, you must enable a descent profile, which is the rate at which the descents will occur. To do this from the Active Flight Plan page, push the ENBL VNV softkey (figure 14-13), or press the MENU key, scroll to highlight "Enable VNV," and press the ENT key. This populates the Current VNV Profile window of the flight plan (figure 14-14) with a Flight Plan Angle (FPA) that varies by aircraft and a Vertical Speed Target (VS TGT) that displays the number of feet per minute required to achieve the FPA at your present ground speed. For example, for an aircraft with a default FPA of -2.5° flying at a ground speed of 100 knots, a VS TGT of -442 fpm is displayed.

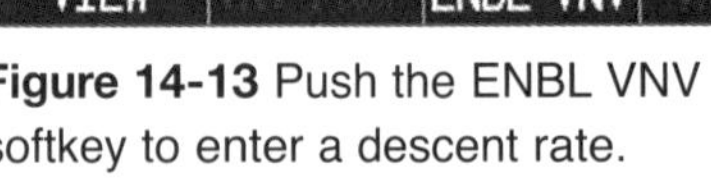

Figure 14-13 Push the ENBL VNV softkey to enter a descent rate. *© Garmin Ltd. or its affiliates*

You can fly a different descent profile by scrolling with the large FMS knob to highlight and enter data in the VS TGT or FPA field. You can also move the cursor to the VS TGT field by pressing the VNV PROF softkey (figure 14-9), or by pressing the MENU key, scrolling to highlight "Select VNV Profile Window," and pressing the ENT key. Use the small FMS knob to set a VS TGT, such as -500 feet per minute, and press the ENT key. If you'd prefer to descend at a specific angle, scroll to the FPA field and use the small FMS knob to select an angle, for example -3°, and press the ENT key.

CURRENT VNV PROFILE			
ACTIVE VNV WPT	4000FT at RIVET iaf		
VS TGT	-442FPM	FPA	-2.5°
VS REQ	_____FPM	TIME TO TOD	09:48
V DEV	_____FT		

Figure 14-14 The Flight Plan Angle (FPA) defaults to -2.5°, or you can specify a different FPA or Vertical Speed Target (VS TGT). *© Garmin Ltd. or its affiliates*

You can disable the vertical flight plan from the Active Flight Plan page by pushing the CNCL VNV softkey (figure 14-9) or by pressing the MENU key, scrolling to highlight "Cancel VNV," and pressing the ENT key (figure 14-15). This clears the Current VNV Profile window and places dashes in all data fields. It also removes the vertical deviation and VS required indicators from the PFD (figure 10-14).

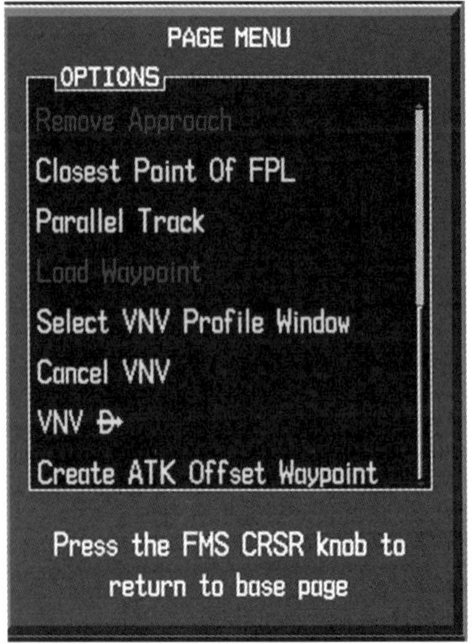

Figure 14-15 You can disable the vertical flight plan from the Active Flight Plan page by pressing the MENU key and scrolling to "Cancel VNV." *© Garmin Ltd. or its affiliates*

Along Track Offsets

Along Track Offsets is a new feature that lets you take an existing waypoint in a flight plan and create a new waypoint adjacent to it, but offset by the number of miles you specify. The new waypoint can be offset before the original waypoint if a negative number is specified, or after it if a positive number is entered. You might use this function in combination with a vertical flight plan if, for example, you wish to descend to the traffic pattern altitude two miles before an airport. Offset waypoints are neither permitted after the final approach fix of an approach nor beyond the last waypoint in a flight plan.

To create an along track offset from the PFD or MFD, press the FPL key, highlight an existing waypoint, press the MENU key, scroll to "Create ATK Offset Waypoint" and press the ENT key. Then turn the small FMS knob to enter a positive or negative number of miles and press the ENT key. Or, from the MFD's active flight plan, highlight an identifier and press the ATK OFST softkey. Use the small FMS knob to enter a positive or negative number of miles and press the ENT key. A new waypoint name is created using the same identifier name with the number of nautical miles it's offset.

There are a few caveats for any vertical navigation and along track offsets. First, you are still responsible for terrain and obstacle clearance at all times. For example, if there's a hill near your destination, setting an along track offset to arrive at pattern altitude prior to the airport may descend you into terrain. Ideally, these features should be programmed while on the ground or at a safe altitude. In some cases, it will make more sense to manually fly the aircraft, rather than go "heads down" to program a feature in a busy environment or close to your destination.

Parallel Track

The Parallel Track function creates a course parallel to the flight plan but offset from that course by as little as 1 nm or as much 99 nm. Its only practical use of which we are aware is to allow pilots to fly to the left or right of center of an airway, presumably to avoid other traffic on the airway. However, this is counter to FAA recommendations to always fly on the center of airways. That's because the obstacle clearance (the number of feet of protection a pilot has from the rocks) for airways is predicated upon pilots flying on their center. Failure to do so could result in a CFIT (controlled flight into terrain) accident. Hence, we discourage using this function for the purpose of flying offset from the center of an airway.

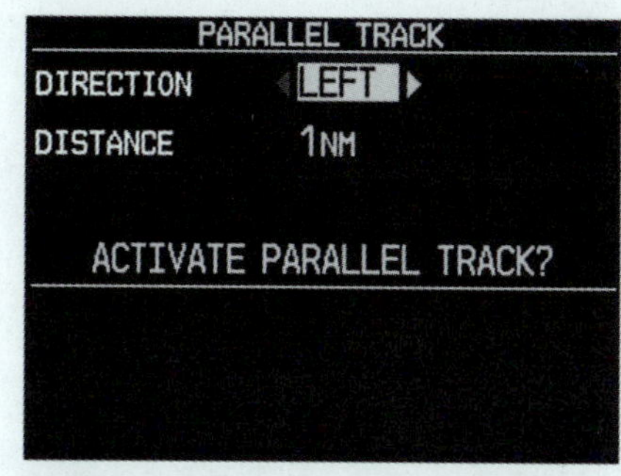

Figure 14-16 Don't use the parallel track function to fly offset from the center of an airway. *© Garmin Ltd. or its affiliates*

Creating a parallel track is easy. From the flight plan page, press the MENU key, scroll to "Parallel Track" and press the ENT key. In the Parallel Track window (figure 14-16), turn the small FMS knob to select "Right" or "Left" of track and press the ENT key. In the DISTANCE field, turn the small FMS knob to select the number of miles to offset the parallel track from the flight plan and press the ENT key. "ACTIVATE PARALLEL TRACK?" is now highlighted. Press the ENT key to confirm.

On the PFD and MFD maps, new course lines parallel to the flight plan courses are displayed. The course line parallel to the active leg in the flight plan is magenta and course guidance along this leg is provided to the autopilot. In the flight plan, "-p" is added to the end of each waypoint identifier to signify that a parallel track is active. To cancel the parallel track, press the MENU key, scroll to "Parallel Track" and press the ENT key. "CANCEL PARALLEL TRACK?" is now highlighted. Press the ENT key to confirm.

There are a number of limitations to the use of a parallel track. First, you must have an active flight plan or be using the Direct-to function to fly to a waypoint. Once enabled, the parallel track is cancelled if you subsequently use the Direct-to key, load an approach or holding pattern. Also, course changes of greater than 120° and edits to the active leg of the flight plan will cancel the parallel course. Finally, a parallel track is not saved when a flight plan is stored in the flight plan catalog.

Airways

Airways are virtual highways in the sky used extensively by aircraft on IFR flight plans. In the past, pilots referred to charts to identify the VORs and fixes, also called intersections, that defined the twists and turns of these higheays. Now the Perspective, G900X and updated G1000s not only display airways on the MFD, but also let pilots add them to flight plans. This simplifies the work of loading and flying an IFR flight plan.

The most common airways are low altitude Victor airways and high altitude Jet Routes. Both are defined with VORs and fixes. Five letter identifiers are used to name fixes, often located at the intersection of

TOPO | TERRAIN | AIRWAYS | STRMSCP | NEXRAD | XM LTNG

Figure 14-17 Press the MAP and AIRWAYS softkeys to choose which airways to display. *© Garmin Ltd. or its affiliates*

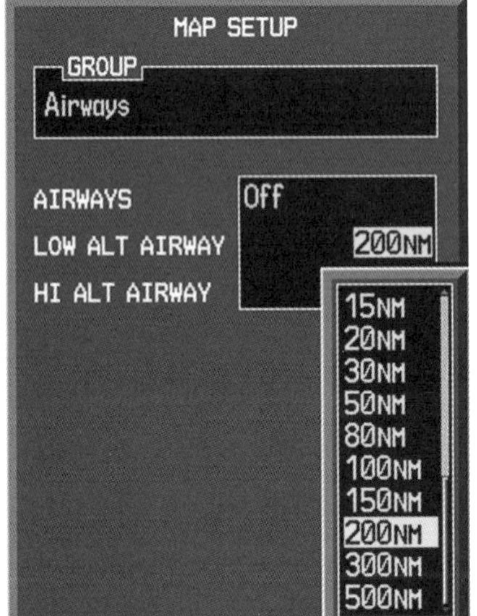

Figure 14-18 Press the MENU key, select "Map Setup," and choose the "Airways" group to configure the maximum map range at which airways are displayed. *© Garmin Ltd. or its affiliates*

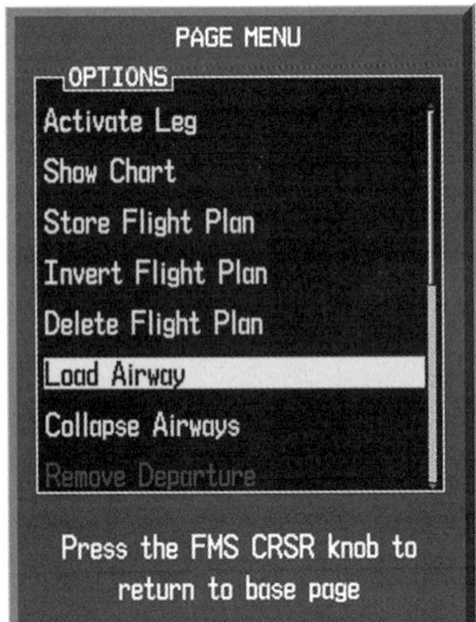

Figure 14-19 From the PFD or MFD, press the MENU key and select "Load Airway" to begin adding an airway to a flight plan. *© Garmin Ltd. or its affiliates*

radials from two or more VORs. Victor airways, with names like V334, exist from 1200 feet AGL up to 18,000 feet MSL, and Jet Routes, with names like J110, are above 18,000 feet MSL.

Q-routes and T-routes, relatively new types of airways defined by GPS waypoints, are also available in the G900X and G1000. They were created to handle the increasing density of air traffic and to take advantage of the widespread availability of GPS. T-routes are low altitude airways and Q-routes are high altitude airways.

Displaying Airways on the MFD

Airways are only displayed on the MFD, since the PFD Inset Map is small. The easiest way to display them is to push the MFD's MAP softkey, which brings up a second level of softkeys (figure 14-17) that now includes an AIRWAYS softkey. Pushing this softkey cycles the display through four states, and the softkey label changes to indicate the current state. The softkey labels and their states are:

- AIRWAYS – Airways not displayed.
- AIRWY ON – All airways displayed.
- AIRWY LO – Victor airways and T-routes displayed.
- AIRWY HI – Jet Routes and Q-routes displayed.

You can also select the maximum map range at which airways are displayed using a new screen under the MFD's Map Setup. Push the MENU key, Map Setup should be highlighted, and press the ENT key. In the GROUP field, scroll with the small FMS knob to select AIRWAYS and press the ENT key. Scroll with the large FMS knob to select the LO ALT AIRWAY or HI ALT AIRWAY field and then turn the small FMS knob to select the maximum map range at which the airways will still be displayed (figure 14-18). Note that you can also use this screen to select which airways are displayed, though it's probably easier to use the AIRWAYS softkey described above. However, if you choose to use this screen, scroll to the AIRWAYS field and use the small FMS knob to select one of the four choices.

Loading Airways into a Flight Plan

Airways can be loaded from either the PFD or MFD, though you may prefer to do it from the MFD, since the system graphically displays the airways and fixes as you scroll through choices. Also, note that the airway display and flight plan functions are separate, so you can load airways regardless of whether they are displayed on the MFD. Finally, we recommend that you first load any Departure Procedure and Arrival Procedure before you load an airway, as this helps the system recommend the correct airways and exit points.

To load an airway, you need to press the FPL key to display the active flight plan. Then choose the airway insertion point as you would for any waypoint insertion, by scrolling with the large FMS knob to highlight the waypoint that will come after the airway. From either the

PFD or MFD, press the MENU key, scroll to highlight "Load Airway" and press the ENT key (figure 14-19). There is a shortcut which is faster, but it works only on the MFD. Once you've selected the airway insertion point, instead of pressing the MENU key, turn the small FMS knob one click to the right and push the LD AIRWY softkey that appears.

Next, from the Airway Loading page (figure 14-20), use either FMS knob to select an airway from the pull-down list and press the ENT key. Then use either FMS knob to select the waypoint from which you will exit the airway and press the ENT key (figure 14-21). Note that as you scroll through the lists of airways and exit points, the MFD map is updated to show the current selection. Also, a preview list, to the right of the airway and exit pull-down lists, shows the bearings and distances for the airway segments. Finally, "LOAD?" should be highlighted. Press the ENT key to confirm and load the airway into the flight plan.

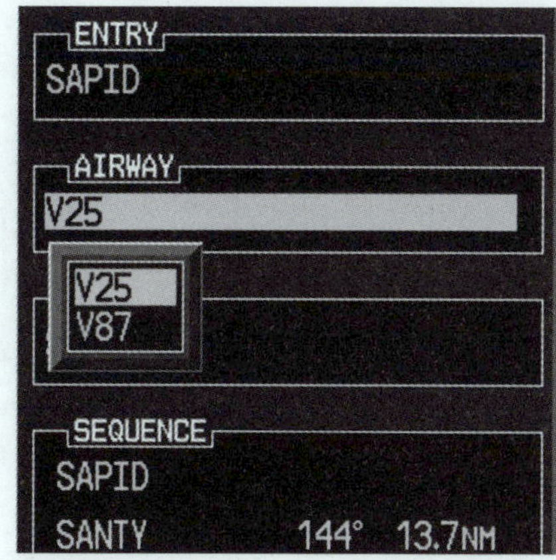

Figure 14-20 Use either FMS knob to select an airway. *© Garmin Ltd. or its affiliates*

Figure 14-21 You must select the waypoint from which you will exit an airway. *© Garmin Ltd. or its affiliates*

Note that the Load Airway menu selection will not appear if a valid airway insertion point wasn't highlighted. This occurs if:

- No waypoint was highlighted with the cursor.
- The first waypoint in the flight plan was selected.
- There are no airways in the database for the waypoint selected.
- The waypoint selected is on an arrival or an approach procedure.

It is acceptable to insert an airway when highlighting a waypoint on a departure procedure or another airway.

Display of Airways in a Flight Plan

Looking at the MFD flight plan, you'll now see a white header that says "Airway" followed by the name of the airway and the identifier for the exit waypoint (figure 14-22). The header on the PFD flight plan is similar but doesn't include the word "Airway." Indented beneath the header is a list of waypoints that define the airway. Should you wish to delete an entire airway, scroll with the FMS knobs to highlight the white header, press the CLR key and the ENT key. You can also delete the airway and replace it with another airway by highlighting the header, pressing the MENU key, selecting "Load Airway" and selecting a new airway and exit waypoint.

ACTIVE FLIGHT PLAN
KHAF / KLAX

	DTK	DIS	ALT
KHAF			_____FT
SAPID	___°	____NM	_____FT
Airway - V25.VTU			
SANTY	___°	____NM	_____FT
SNS	116°	29.0NM	_____FT
PRB	127°	76.0NM	_____FT
RZS	135°	81.4NM	_____FT
VTU	110°	42.9NM	_____FT
KLAX	094°	33.6NM	_____FT

Figure 14-22 To delete an airway, highlight the white airway identifier and press the CLR and ENT keys. *© Garmin Ltd. or its affiliates*

Note that the flight plan doesn't display all waypoints along an airway. It shows beginning and end points and waypoints that define turns along the airway. Other intermediate waypoints along straight legs of an airway are not shown. You can however manually insert any of these missing waypoints. You might choose to do this to make it easier to determine your distance to a fix, or to provide additional references if you're later given vectors.

To insert an additional waypoint within an airway, scroll to highlight the waypoint after the missing waypoint and turn the small FMS one

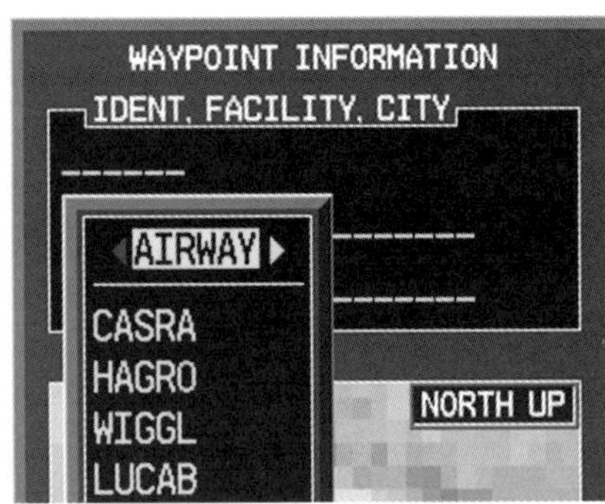

Figure 14-23 To insert a waypoint in an airway, scroll to highlight the waypoint after the new waypoint, turn the small FMS knob to the left, and scroll to select a waypoint. *© Garmin Ltd. or its affiliates*

click to the left. This brings up a new window with the word "Airway" (figure 14-23). Scroll with the large FMS knob to select the desired waypoint and press the ENT key twice. The new waypoint is now displayed in the flight plan. You can also insert a waypoint that's not along an airway. If you do that, the system breaks the airway into two segments.

If there is a long list of waypoints displayed in your flight plan, you may want to collapse airways, so that you see only two lines for each airway: a revised white airway header that includes "(collapsed)" and the exit waypoint. To do this while viewing the active flight plan page on either the PFD or MFD, press the MENU key, scroll to select "Collapse Airways" and press the ENT key. Note that the Flight Plan always displays three waypoints: the From, To and Next waypoints. Hence, the airway on which you're located is automatically expanded to show these points. You can also manually expand all airways to show all waypoints by pressing the MENU key, scrolling to select "Expand Airways" and pressing the ENT key.

Here are a few other considerations when using airways. Some airways are one-way, however the system does not have the capability to indicate this. Also, flight plans with airways can be saved. However, when the GPS database is later updated, the airway may be deleted from the flight plan. This can occur if the new database no longer contains the airway entry or exit waypoints or the airway identifier. Finally, in the unlikely event that there is not enough room in a flight plan to insert an airway, "Flight Plan is full. Remove unnecessary waypoints" is displayed.

MFD Changes

The MFD is now upgraded to include SafeTaxi and a number of minor enhancements. Electronic charts, available at an additional cost, are discussed in the next section.

SafeTaxi

GPS technology makes it easy to navigate the skies. So easy that sometimes the biggest challenge on a flight is trying to taxi at an unfamiliar airport. If you've flown into a large metropolitan airport with its labyrinth of runways and taxiways, particularly at night, you understand. Garmin's new SafeTaxi takes a quantum leap forward in solving this problem.

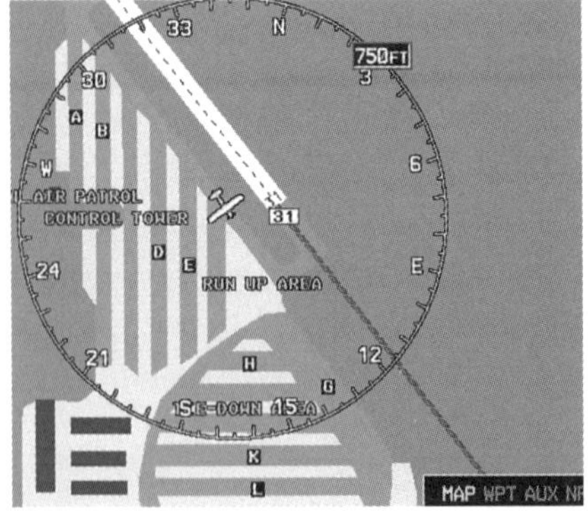

Figure 14-24 Here, the Navigation Map is set to the 3000 foot range to get a good view of the SafeTaxi diagram. *© Garmin Ltd. or its affiliates*

SafeTaxi is a set of more than 700 diagrams for U.S. airports. The talented staff at Garmin uses data from the FAA's Safe Flight 21 program and the government NACO instrument charts to create these diagrams. Best of all, the system places a moving airplane symbol on the map, so you can instantly identify your position on the airport (figure 14-24).

The diagrams show lots of detail. As you might expect, they include runways and taxiways and show the numbers and letters used to identify them. They also display many landmarks including ramps, buildings, FBOs, and control towers. To see this level of detail, you may have to zoom in using the Range knob.

Finding the SafeTaxi diagrams is easy. They are available on virtually every map that includes an airport, including the PFD's Inset Map and the MFD's Navigation Map, Weather Data Link, and Trip Planning pages and pages in the Waypoint and Nearest page groups. To see the SafeTaxi diagram on one of these pages, simply zoom in using the Range knob.

SafeTaxi diagrams are configured in the same way as other map features by setting the maximum map range at which the diagrams still appear. To do this, press the MFD's MENU key. "Map Setup" should be highlighted, so just press the ENT key. Then turn the small FMS knob to select the "Aviation" group and press the ENT key. Scroll with the large FMS knob to highlight "SAFETAXI" and turn the small FMS knob to select the map range above which SafeTaxi diagrams will no longer be displayed (figure 14-25). When I set map features, I usually select the highest map range available, which in this case is the 20-nautical mile range. Finish by pressing the ENT key and the FMS knob.

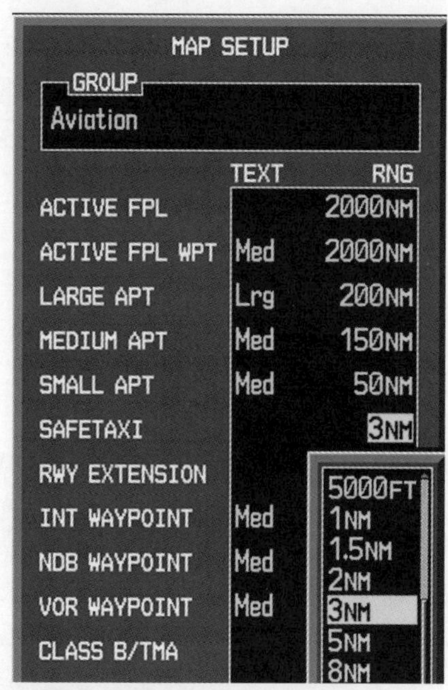

Figure 14-25 Press the MENU key, select "Map Setup," and choose the "Airways" group to set the map range beyond which SafeTaxi diagrams are no longer displayed. *© Garmin Ltd. or its affiliates*

Note that the DCLTR softkey affects the amount of SafeTaxi information displayed on the PFD's Inset Map and the MFD's Navigation Map page. SafeTaxi diagram labels are removed when the DCLTR-1 softkey is displayed and SafeTaxi diagrams are removed entirely when the DCLTR-3 softkey is displayed.

SafeTaxi diagrams are stored on the new, larger 2 Gigabyte SD memory cards that also store the terrain, obstacles and FliteCharts databases. These are the cards located in the lower of the two memory card slots in the PFD and MFD. They must remain in these slots, since the data from them is not downloaded into the system. Pull the cards, and you'll lose SafeTaxi, terrain data and other information.

The SafeTaxi database is updated for a subscription fee on a 56-day cycle. You can tell whether the database is current by looking at the MFD's startup page (figure 14-26). After the MFD is cycled beyond this page, you can still access the expiration information by going to the System Status page in the Auxiliary page group.

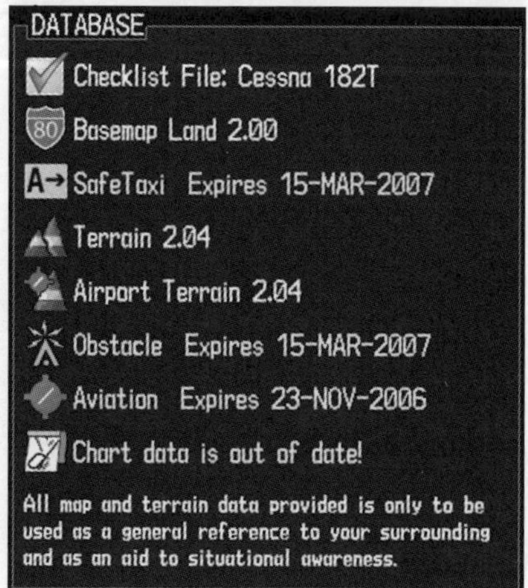

Figure 14-26 Upon power up, the new MFD "splash screen" shows expiration dates immediately without scrolling. *© Garmin Ltd. or its affiliates*

Active Flight Plan Changes

The MFD's active flight plan is enlarged to use half of the display. In addition, a new VIEW softkey brings up an additional layer of softkeys that allow you to modify the flight plan (figure 14-27). Pressing the WIDE softkey expands the active flight plan to the full width of the display and compresses the map to the lower left corner. Pressing the NARROW softkey restores the flight plan to the previous view.

The "Change Fields" Menu option is no longer available. This command previously let pilots select the fields displayed in flight plans. The only choice available now is the CUM softkey, which changes the distances in the flight plan to cumulative distances. We recommend you use this setting when flying instrument approaches, particularly into non-towered or non-radar airports, to make it easier to announce your total distance from the airport. Pressing the LEG-LEG softkey returns the flight plan to displaying distances for each leg.

MFD Map Setup

There are also changes to the MFD's Map Setup. First, under the Group field, you'll find an additional choice called "Airways," described earlier. In the Map group, there are several changes. In the AUTO ZOOM field, there are now four choices that are self-explanatory: Off, MFD Only, PFD Only, and All On (figure 14-28).

Figure 14-27 Press the CUM softkey to see cumulative distances to your destination. *© Garmin Ltd. or its affiliates*

Indented below this are three new fields: MAX LOOK FWD, MIN LOOK FWD, and TIME OUT. These let you adjust parameters that control auto-zoom. Previously, the auto-zoom feature kept the active waypoint displayed while progressively zooming the map to lower and lower ranges as you approached a waypoint, stopping at the 1.5 nm range. These range changes occurred frequently as you approached a waypoint and were so annoying that some pilots left auto-zoom off. The new parameters make auto-zoom more useful and, since they're based on time rather than distance, the feature works equally well for slower aircraft and VLJs.

The first two fields adjust the maximum and minimum ranges used, based upon the distance between the center of the map (or from the airplane symbol when in the North Up orientation) to the top of the display and the groundspeed of the aircraft. The maximum field can be set from 0 to 999 minutes. For example, if you set a MAX LOOK FWD time of 5 minutes and are in an aircraft traveling at 120 kts, or 2 nm/minute, then the aircraft will travel 10 nm in 5 minutes. To show the distance you'll travel in 5 minutes in the top half of the map, auto-zoom uses a maximum map range of 20 nm. If the field is set to zero, auto-zoom uses a maximum range of 2000 nm.

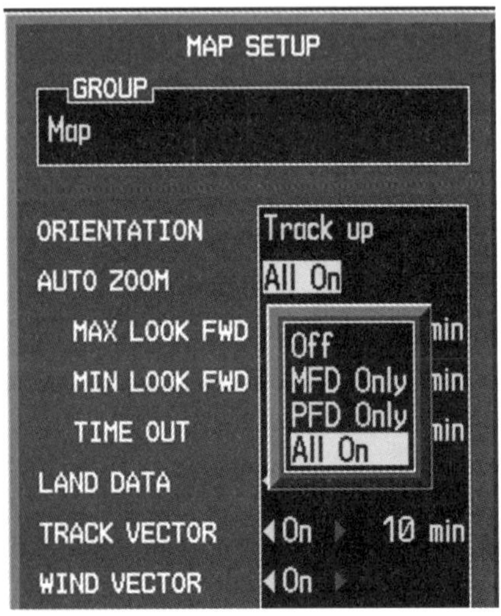

Figure 14-28 Press the MENU key, select "Map Setup," and choose the "Map" group to configure Auto-Zoom options. *© Garmin Ltd. or its affiliates*

The MIN LOOK FWD field can be set from 0 to 99 minutes. Using our example, when this field is set to 1 minute, for an aircraft traveling at 120 kts, or 2 nm/minute, auto-zoom uses a minimum map range of 4 nm. If the field is set to zero, auto-zoom uses a minimum range of 1.5 nm. You can always override auto-zoom by manually selecting a map range using the Range knob. If you do, auto-zoom will not resume making changes for at least the number of minutes set in the TIME OUT field. That field can be set from 0 to 99 minutes.

Another change to the Map group is that the Track Vector is a solid blue line (figure 15-13) and its length can be changed. Formerly, its length was fixed at one minute. Now, using Map Setup, you can choose a Track Vector as short as 20 seconds or as long as 20 minutes.

In the Weather Group, the field formerly labeled CELL MOVEMENT is now labeled NEXRD CELL MOV. In the Aviation Group, the field formerly labeled OTHER AIRSPACE is now labeled OTHER/ADIZ and there's a new field labeled TFR. In the Land Group there's a new field labeled RAILROAD.

MAP Group Changes

- GPS course lines and the destination airport were originally shown only on the Navigation Map page. Now these can also be viewed on the Traffic Map, Stormscope, Weather Data Link, Terrain Proximity, and TAWS pages.
- The Traffic Map page has a new TNA MUTE softkey that mutes "TIS not available" aural alerts. For aircraft equipped with a Honeywell TAS, a TEST softkey generates a test display with examples of each type of traffic symbol and generates a "TAS System Test OK" aural alert.
- On the Weather Data Link page, panning the map pointer displays cloud top altitude information.
- The TAWS Map page has a new INHIBIT softkey for inhibiting TAWS-B aural alerts. There is also a new MENU key option for "Show Aviation Data" which alternates with "Hide Aviation Data."

WPT Group Changes

- Some Airport Information page MENU key options are renamed. Selections for arrival, approach, and weather pages previously used the format "View Arrival." These selections now use the format "Show Arrival Page."
- On the User Waypoint Information page, the MENU key selection "View Recent User WPT List" no longer exists.

AUX Group Changes

- The System Status page has new ANN TEST and ARFRM softkeys. When the former is pressed, it causes the annunciators to light on the audio panel. The latter softkey selects the AIRFRAME window for scrolling.
- On the GPS Status page, the Satellite Status page has changed. EPE, DOP, and HUL are no longer shown and are replaced with EPU, HDOP, HFOM, and VFOM. There are two new softkeys RAIM and SBAS that alternate with each other. The letter "D" appears at the bottom of the vertical bars for each satellite for which WAAS correction data is available.

  The SBAS (Satellite-Based Augmentation System) softkey lets you deselect WAAS reception, which may improve GPS performance when flying outside of the WAAS coverage area (most of North America), such as when flying over the ocean. To deselect WAAS, push the SBAS softkey, push the FMS knob to highlight WAAS, and press the ENT key.
- On the System Setup page, TAS is an additional choice for display on the MFD Navigation Status bar. There is a new DFLTS

softkey. You can no longer change the map datum. The ILS CDI CAPTURE choice is gone (CDI selection is automatic). For WAAS-capable systems, in the GPS CDI SELECTED field, the 5.0 nm choice is replaced with 2.0 nm, the WAAS CDI sensitivity in the enroute mode.

Under DISPLAY UNITS, the NAV ANGLE choices include MAGNETIC(°), but no longer include AUTO. The PRESS field is deleted and a new WEIGHT field has been added.

- A LOCK softkey on the XM Information page saves GDL 69A activation data when the XM service is configured. It's not used for normal operation, but there are no adverse effects if it's pushed. There are new fields for AUDIO SIGNAL STRENGTH and DATA SIGNAL STRENGTH
- On the System Status page, under DATABASE, there are new fields for version, region and expiration information for SAFETAXI and CHARTS.

NRST Group Changes

- On the Nearest Airports page, in the APPROACHES window, the name of approaches are now prefixed with the identifier for the associated airport.

Electronic Charts

Instrument pilots need charts to fly IFR and now, for an additional fee, they can display IFR charts on the system. Furthermore they have two choices: Jeppesen charts, called ChartView, or government NACO charts, purchased through Garmin, called FliteCharts. At this writing, the Jeppesen subscriptions are more expensive but are updated more frequently, contain some additional chart types outlined below, display local airport NOTAMs, and superimpose an aircraft symbol on charts to show your position. NACO charts don't show aircraft position, but of course you can find that on any system map page.

Savvy pilots will want to carry a backup in the form of paper or a portable electronic device for at least two reasons. Foremost is redundancy. In the event of an electrical system failure and a subsequent draining of the main battery, electronic charts become inaccessible, since the standby battery powers only the PFD, not the MFD where charts are located. Also, some pilots may prefer to have a paper copy in front of them even when using electronic charts. That's because if you want a single piece of information, it's sometime faster to glance at a paper chart, than to push softkeys or pan with the joystick.

Most of the features and softkeys used to access charts are the same for both chart options. Therefore we'll describe their use simultaneously, noting any differences. As always, refer to your Aircraft Flight Manual as the final authority on operating the G1000 and Perspective's electronic charts.

There are several ways to access charts. The easiest is to let the system choose a default chart. Another way is to use the softkeys and FMS knobs to choose a chart yourself, though it requires more steps. Finally, if you start with the default chart, but it's not the one you need, you can still manually select any chart. We'll talk first about the chart defaults.

Electronic Chart Defaults

Charts are always selected from one of the following MFD pages: the Navigation Map page, Active Flight Plan page, or Nearest Airports page. From any of these pages, press the SHW CHRT softkey, to display a chart, whether you're using the default chart or manually selecting a chart. Alternatively, press the MENU key, scroll to "Show Chart" and press the ENT key. Generally, you'll fly with an active flight plan or a direct-to destination, and these will determine which default chart is presented. If, however, you don't have an active flight plan, the system defaults to the Airport Diagram (figure 14-29) if you're on the ground, or to the Airport Diagram of the nearest airport if you're in the air.

If you have an active flight plan, the default chart presented when the SHW CHRT softkey is pushed changes depending on whether you're on the ground or which waypoint is active in the flight plan. If you're on the ground, the system always defaults to the Airport Diagram, even if you have an active waypoint. Once the aircraft takes off however, the default becomes the chart appropriate for the active waypoint in your flight plan. For example, if you have a departure procedure loaded and the active waypoint is part of that procedure, the default is the chart for that departure procedure. Likewise, if you have an arrival procedure loaded and the active waypoint is part of that procedure, the default is the chart for that arrival procedure. Finally, if the active waypoint is part of an instrument procedure you've loaded, the default is the chart for that instrument procedure. Note that when an en route waypoint, such as a VOR, is the active waypoint, the system doesn't have a default chart and if you push the SHW CHRT softkey, you'll receive a "No chart associated with selected waypoint" message.

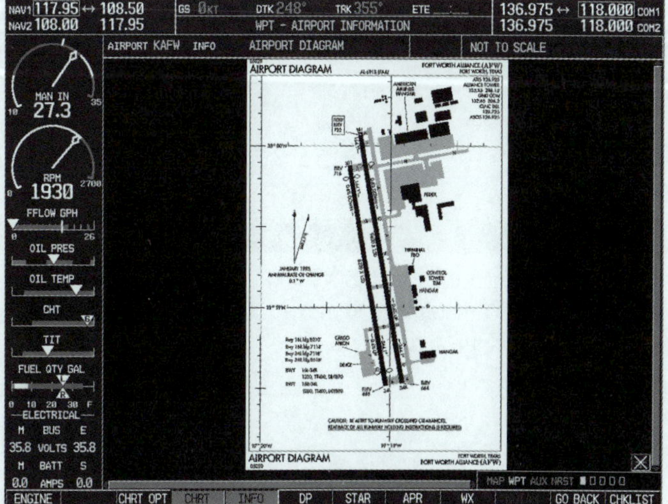

Figure 14-29 Without an active flight plan, electronic charts default to the Airport Diagram. © Garmin Ltd. or its affiliates

Pressing the SHW CHRT softkey brings up the default charts we have discussed, but it also brings up additional softkeys that access other charts (figure 14-30). This second layer of softkeys brings up charts for a single default airport, usually your departure airport when you're on the ground, or the airport associated with any active waypoint in the flight plan. Thus if you're sitting on the ground at San Jose, Calif., with a flight plan to Los Angeles, Calif., pushing the DP, STAR and APR softkeys all bring up charts for San Jose—unless you've gone into the flight plan and made one of the waypoints in the arrival or approach procedures the active waypoint. In that case, the DP, STAR and APR softkeys bring up charts for Los Angeles.

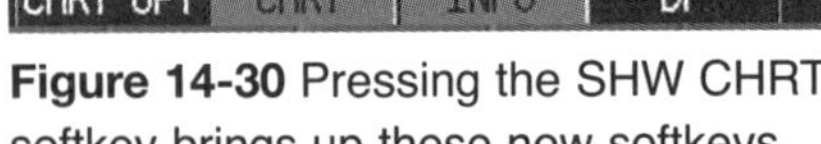

Figure 14-30 Pressing the SHW CHRT softkey brings up these new softkeys. *© Garmin Ltd. or its affiliates*

Note that there's a quick shortcut for changing the airport to which the DP, STAR and APR softkeys default without having to change the active waypoint in a flight plan. Using this same example, if you've entered a flight plan, are on the ground at San Jose and want to review charts for Los Angeles, after pressing the SHW CHRT softkey, push the MENU key, scroll to highlight "View Destination Airport" and press the ENT key (figure 14-31). Now the DP, STAR and APR softkeys will bring up charts for your destination airport.

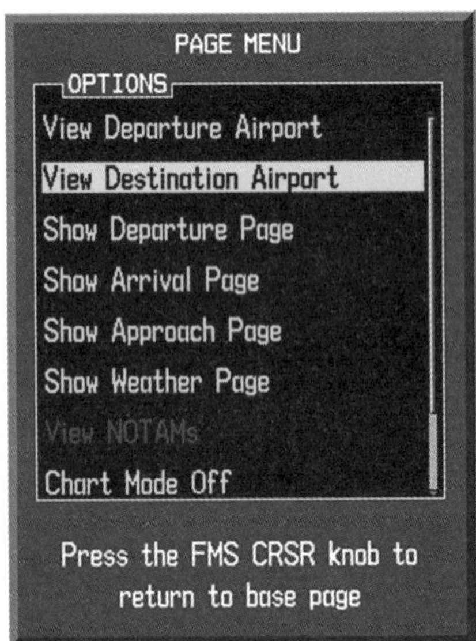

Figure 14-31 Select "View Destination Airport" to force electronic charts to default to the destination airport. *© Garmin Ltd. or its affiliates*

Jeppesen charts have an additional NOTAM softkey displayed for selected airports. Pressing the softkey displays recent local NOTAM information applicable to the current chart revision cycle.

Chart Options

Once a chart is selected, the Range/Joystick knob can be turned to zoom a chart in or out. This changes the chart mileage scale, shown above and to the right of Jeppesen Charts (NACO charts are not scaled). Pushing the Joystick up and down lets you scroll through an entire chart. In addition, the Joystick can be moved left and right on NACO charts, allowing you to pan the entire chart. For both chart types, pressing the Joystick centers the chart on the display.

Additional viewing options are available by pressing the SHW CHRT softkey and the CHRT OPT softkey, which bring up a new layer of softkeys (figure 14-32).

The ALL softkey is initially grayed out indicating that the entire chart is shown. The FIT WDTH softkey expands or contracts charts so that the full width of the chart matches the width available in the current display. The FULL SCN softkey toggles the display between a view in which a chart shares space with the Airport Information or weather along the right side of the display, and one in which the full screen is available for displaying a chart. These softkeys also change the position of the pull-down windows used for manually selecting charts. When the FULL SCN softkey is selected and grayed out, the selection windows are along the top of the display (figure 14-33); when the FULL SCN softkey is unselected, the selection windows appear along the right side of the display (figure 14-34).

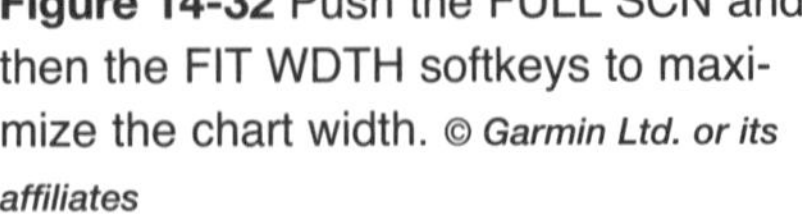

Figure 14-32 Push the FULL SCN and then the FIT WDTH softkeys to maximize the chart width. *© Garmin Ltd. or its affiliates*

Jeppesen charts have four additional softkeys used to view one quarter of a chart. The HEADER softkey displays the top of the chart including the briefing strip. The PLAN softkey shows the graphical plan view of the approach. The PROFILE softkey shows the descent profile. Finally, the MINIMUMS softkey shows visibility and descent minimums.

Selecting Electronic Charts Manually

Chart defaults save time, since you avoid manually entering airport identifiers and selecting charts from a list. However, charts can also be selected manually, and a few chart types are only selected this way.

Charts are always selected from one of the following MFD pages: the Navigation Map page, Active Flight Plan page, or Nearest Airports page. From any of these pages, press the SHW CHRT softkey. Then use a softkey to choose a chart type. Note that the INFO softkey is already grayed out and an Airport Diagram chart displayed. For different chart types, push the DP, STAR, or APR softkey to find a departure procedure, arrival, or instrument procedure chart.

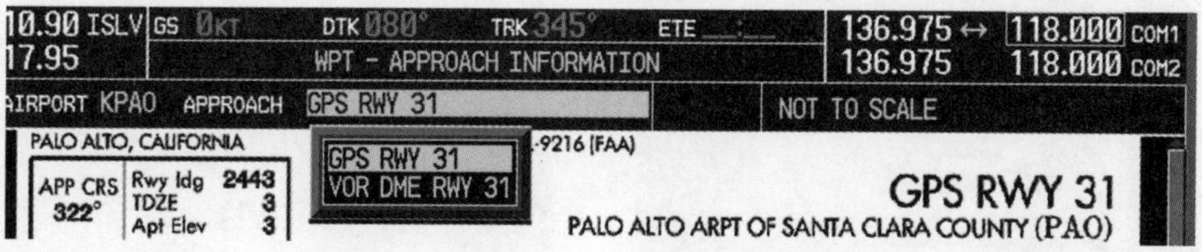

Figure 14-33 When the FULL SCN softkey is selected and grayed out, manual chart selection windows are along the top of the display. *© Garmin Ltd. or its affiliates*

Next, press the FMS knob to get a cursor. The identifier for the default airport will be highlighted. To choose a different airport, start by turning the small FMS knob, then alternate between the large and small FMS knobs to enter the identifier and press the ENT key. Then scroll with the large knob to the INFO, DEPARTURE, ARRIVAL, or APPROACH window, depending upon whether the INFO, DP, ARRIVAL, or APR softkey was pushed. Scroll with the small FMS knob to select a chart from the list and press the ENT key. The selected chart is then displayed. Remember that these chart selection pull-down windows are along the top of the display when the FULL SCN softkey is selected and grayed out and along the right side of the display when the FULL SCN softkey is unselected.

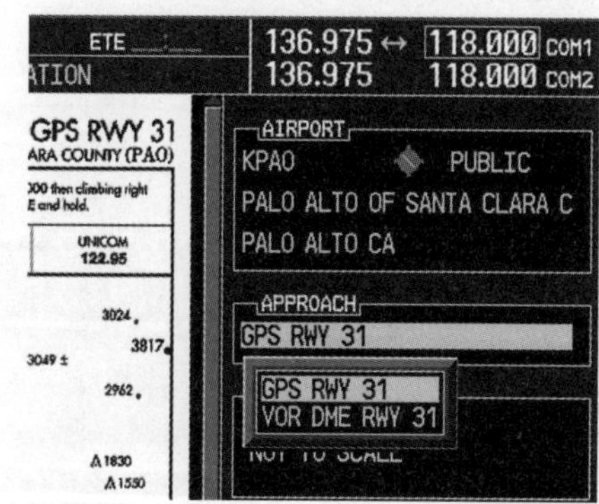

Figure 14-34 When the FULL SCN softkey is unselected, manual chart selection windows appear along the right side of the display. *© Garmin Ltd. or its affiliates*

The following charts can only be selected manually. These include charts for:

- Takeoff Minimums
- Alternate Minimums (NACO only)
- Class B Airspace (Jeppesen only)
- Airline Parking Gate Coordinates (Jeppesen only)
- Airline Parking Gate Location (Jeppesen only)

To select one of these charts, press the SHW CHRT softkey, then either the INFO or WX softkey. Push the FMS knob to enter the airport identifier as described above and scroll to the INFO window (figure 14-35) to select one of these charts and press the ENT key.

Chart Setup

There are two chart display options: Day View with a white background and Night View with a black background. An Auto mode is available to switch automatically between the modes, based upon the intensity of the ambient light. To select a mode, press the SHW CHRT softkey and then the MENU key. Scroll to select "Chart Setup" and press the ENT key. Then scroll with the large FMS knob to highlight the FULL SCREEN, COLOR SCHEME, or percentage field (figure 14-36). FULL SCREEN allows you to use the small FMS knob to select the full screen chart view "On" or "Off". You'll probably never use it, however, as it's easier to push the FULL SCN softkey to achieve the same thing.

COLOR SCHEME lets you use the small FMS knob to select "Day,"

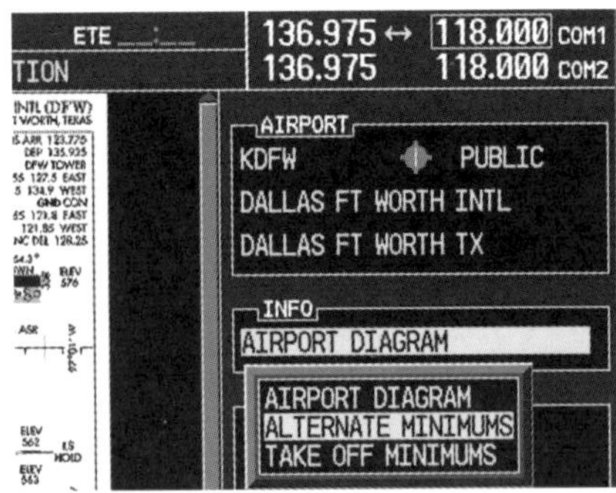

Figure 14-35 Some charts, like Takeoff Minimums, can only be selected manually after first pushing the INFO or WX softkey and then entering an airport identifier. *© Garmin Ltd. or its affiliates*

"Auto," or "Night." In Auto mode, the system uses the percentage field to determine at what ambient light intensity the system switches between day and night views.

MENU Key Options

There are many MENU options available including (figure 14-31):

- View Departure Airport (Sets departure airport as default).
- Show Departure Page (Shows departure charts for default airport).
- Show Arrival Page (Shows arrival charts for default airport).
- Show Approach Page (Shows approach charts for default airport).
- Show Weather Page (Shows weather and Airport Diagram for default airport).
- Chart Mode Off (Turns off chart and displays Airport Information page).
- Chart Set Up (Changes chart background color for day or night).
- Go Back to Previous Page (Returns to previous page).

After pushing the DP, STAR or APR softkeys, the following options also become available by pressing the MENU key (figure 14-37):

- View FPL Departure Chart (shows chart if a DP is loaded in the flight plan).
- View FPL Approach Chart (shows chart if an approach is loaded in the flight plan).
- Show Info Page (Shows Airport Diagram and Airport INFO for default airport).
- Load Departure (Lets you load a departure procedure).
- Load Arrival (Lets you load an arrival procedure).
- Load Approach (Lets you load an approach procedure).

Figure 14-36 Press the SHW CHRT softkey, the MENU key and scroll to highlight the COLOR SCHEME field to manually set charts for Day View or Night View. *© Garmin Ltd. or its affiliates*

WAAS – Wide Area Augmentation System

Some G1000's, including all 2007 and later Cessna models and all Perspective and G900X installations, include WAAS-capable GPS receivers. Some older G1000 aircraft can now be upgraded with WAAS receivers. One way to tell if a G1000 aircraft has a WAAS-capable receiver is to look at the approach names when you select them with the PROC key. If you see "LPV" listed after an approach, then it has a WAAS-capable receiver. If you see "Unavail" (figure 14-38) listed after an approach, then the airplane doesn't have a WAAS-capable receiver. Another way is to go to the AUX group's GPS Status page and look at the bottom of the vertical bars. A "D" at the bottom of the bars indicates differential GPS or WAAS. We'll briefly discuss WAAS here, but the best way to learn about it is with *Max Trescott's GPS and WAAS Instrument Flying Handbook* (see inside back cover for details). In additional to four hours of tutorial information, it includes several interactive simulators that let you practice loading WAAS instrument approaches.

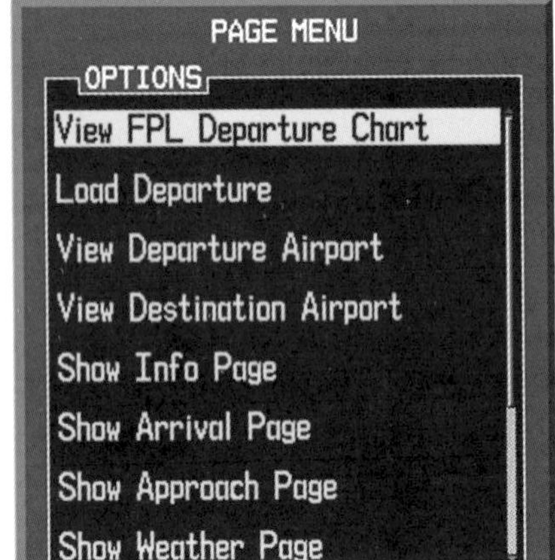

Figure 14-37 Press SHW CHRT and either the DP, STAR or APR softkey and then the MENU key to display these options. *© Garmin Ltd. or its affiliates*

WAAS is an acronym for Wide Area Augmentation System. To augment something is to make it larger in size, number, or strength. In this case, the FAA has augmented the basic GPS system to compensate for errors and to improve the accuracy available to pilots. It's a wide area system because the correction signals pilots use are broadcast over a very wide area—North America.

The new WAAS infrastructure includes WAAS Reference Stations, which are GPS receivers at 38 precisely surveyed locations around North America. Each station compares its actual location with the location calculated using GPS satellites, and correction signals are calculated. Uplink stations transmit the correction data to several new satellites in geosynchronous orbit. The satellites retransmit the data to WAAS receivers on the same frequency used by the GPS satellites.

A WAAS-capable GPS receiver, in addition to decoding information from the GPS satellites, is set up to decode information from the WAAS geosynchronous satellites. The result is that WAAS-capable GPS receivers are able to eliminate much of the error in the GPS system and identify an aircraft's position with sufficient accuracy to allow instrument approaches to be flown to within 200 feet above the ground. Also, WAAS receivers have the capability to ignore data from malfunctioning satellites and to continue computing their position with the remaining satellite signals. Also, in the en route mode, full scale deflection of the CDI is 2 miles for a WAAS capable receiver, versus the 5-mile sensitivity used by non-WAAS capable receivers.

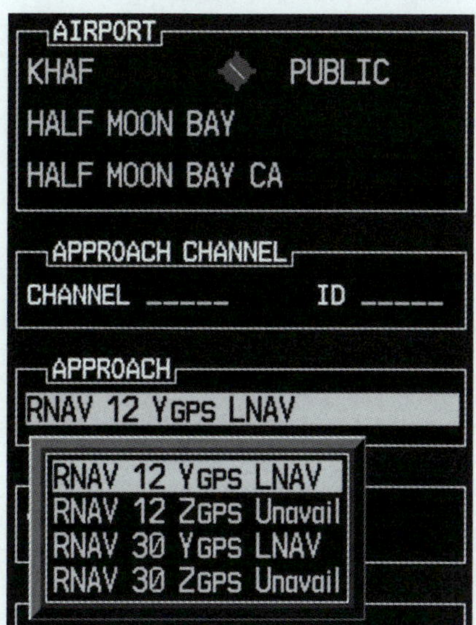

Figure 14-38 If an approach says "Unavail", your system is not WAAS-capable. *© Garmin Ltd. or its affiliates*

WAAS Minimums

Now let's talk about the different type of WAAS minimums. You'll probably be surprised to learn that with a WAAS-capable receiver, you can now fly four different types of GPS minimums (figure 14-39). We'll briefly mention the four types, and then cover them in more detail.

LPV is a new minimums category that provides vertical guidance. It allows you to use your GPS receiver to fly an approach in much the same way that you currently fly an ILS. It usually provides the lowest minimums available with a GPS receiver.

LNAV/VNAV minimums are flown by airliners with special equipment and you can now fly these approaches with a WAAS receiver. These minimums are usually higher than LPV minimums, since the approaches were designed to be flown with older, less accurate equipment, and hence have larger protected areas.

LNAV minimums are the ones flown with older GPS approach receivers. Pilots have flown these approaches for a number of years and they are also available with WAAS receivers. They are non-precision approaches and no vertical guidance is provided.

Many WAAS approaches include circling minimums, similar to circling minimums for any other approach chart.

There's a fifth option, LNAV+V, though technically it's not a minimums category and it's not listed in chart minimums. When available, your WAAS receiver provides an advisory glide slope for guidance down to non-precision LNAV minimums. The minimums are the same as for a LNAV approach, but LNAV+V lets you easily set up a stabilized approach at a constant descent rate to reach those minimums. Now let's examine each of the minimums in detail.

CATEGORY	A	B	C	D
LPV DA	1236-1½ 418 (500-1½)			
LNAV/ VNAV DA	1368-2 550 (600-2)			
LNAV MDA	2100-1¼ 1282 (1300-1¼)	2100-1½ 1282 (1300-1½)	2100-3 1282 (1300-3)	
CIRCLING	2100-2 1282 (1300-2)		2100-3 1282 (1300-3)	

RIVERSIDE, CALIFORNIA

Figure 14-39 For LNAV+V minimums, use the LNAV line.

LPV Approaches

When LPV minimums were first offered, these approaches could go as low as 250 feet above the ground. Now, we will start to see LPV approaches with minimums as low as 200 feet, identical to that of a category I ILS. Basically, LPV is a near-precision GPS approach that provides Localizer Performance with Vertical guidance. In fact, that's how it is defined in the new FAA Instrument Procedures Handbook.

LPV, when available, is the top line in the minimums section for most RNAV GPS approaches, and it will usually have the lowest minimums for an approach. It is always followed by the letters DA, decision altitude. Decision altitudes are only specified on precision approaches with vertical guidance, and the point at which you reach the decision altitude is often not marked on instrument approach charts. Here's a critical point: When flying to LPV minimums, you cannot wait for your GPS to count down to zero miles to identify when to fly the missed approach, since it's displaying the distance to the runway threshold and not to the decision altitude. Instead, you need to watch your altimeter.

In many cases, the minimums for a LPV approach are much lower than for a non-precision GPS approach. In order to allow you to descend that much lower, the FAA needed to design smaller protected areas, to squeeze the approaches in among the many obstacles that exist along an approach. Then, in order to assure that you stay within the protected area, new criteria were developed for the accuracy of a WAAS-capable GPS receiver.

On a traditional non-precision approach, a GPS receiver needs a lateral accuracy of 0.3 nautical miles to assure that an aircraft stays in an even larger protected area. Prior to permitting you to fly with LPV minimums, a WAAS receiver is required to calculate its current accuracy or Horizontal Position Level (HPL). This is the maximum distance in meters from your present position to the position where the GPS thinks you are, with a probability of 99.99999% (figure 14-40). To allow an approach, the HPL value must be less than the Horizontal Alarm Limit (HAL), which is 40 meters or about 164 feet, considerably less than the 0.3 nautical miles or approximately 1800 feet required on non-precision GPS approaches. It must also calculate the Vertical Position Level (VPL), which must be less than the Vertical Alarm Limit (VAL), which is 50 meters to allow an LPV approach with 250-foot minimums, and 35 meters to allow an LPV approach with 200-foot minimums.

Now let's look at the CDI sensitivity on an LPV approach. To review, when a basic, non-precision GPS approach is flown, plus and minus 1-

nautical mile linear scaling is provided until 2 nautical miles prior to the FAF, where the sensitivity increases to plus and minus point 0.3 nm for the final approach segment. The CDI sensitivity for an LPV approach is also plus and minus 1 nautical mile for the intermediate segment, however at 2 miles prior to the FAF, it starts to change smoothly so that at the FAF it is either 0.3 nautical miles or 2°, whichever is less.

The 2° angle is typically used, though it does vary depending upon the length of the final approach segment. For final approach segments less than 8.2 nautical miles long, the CDI scales to 2° at the FAF, which is less than the plus and minus 0.3 nautical mile sensitivity of a non-precision GPS approach, but comparable to the sensitivity of an ILS approach (figure 14-41). For final approach segments longer than 8.2 nautical miles, the CDI scaling remains fixed at 0.3 nautical miles beyond the FAF and switches to a 2° angle when it equals 0.3 nm sensitivity. This is to achieve performance equivalent to a non-precision GPS approach, and better than the sensitivity of an ILS at the same distance from a runway.

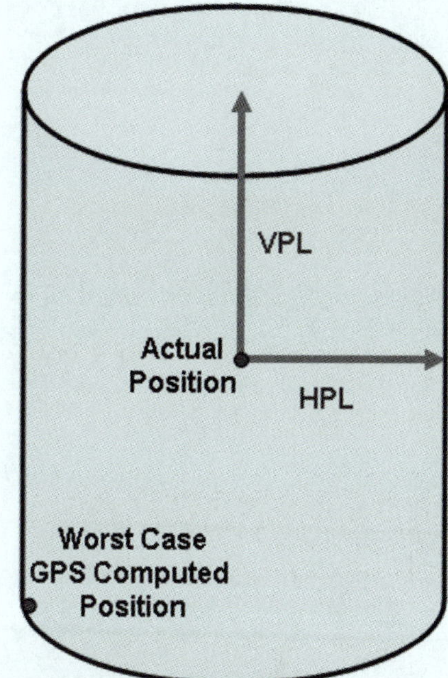

Figure 14-40 A VPL signal quality of better than 50 meters is required to turn on the LPV annunciator that authorizes you to fly an LPV approach.

Finally, as you get very close to the runway, the CDI scaling of an LPV approach will change from angular to linear, so that it doesn't become ultrasensitive, as it does when flying an ILS signal close to the runway. The CDI sensitivity on an LPV approach is set so that the total width is usually 700 feet at the runway threshold or plus and minus 350 feet for full scale left or right deflection of the CDI needle. With a traditional mechanical HSI or OBS with five dots to the left and right of center, each dot represents 70 feet. On the G1000, which has two small circles left and right of center, each circle represents 175 feet.

LNAV/VNAV Approaches

Now let's examine LNAV/VNAV minimums. From a practical standpoint, you'll probably use these minimums only when no LPV minimums are designated, since LNAV/VNAV minimums are almost always higher than LPV minimums. Oddly, your GPS may annunciate LNAV+V for some LNAV/VNAV approaches because advisory glide slopes are new and database suppliers used to use LNAV+V to indicate a LNAV/VNAV approach. So if your chart says an approach has LNAV/VNAV minimums, but your GPS annunciator shows LNAV+V, then you can fly the approach to LNAV/VNAV minimums. Like LPV minimums, LNAV/VNAV minimums are specified with a DA or decision altitude.

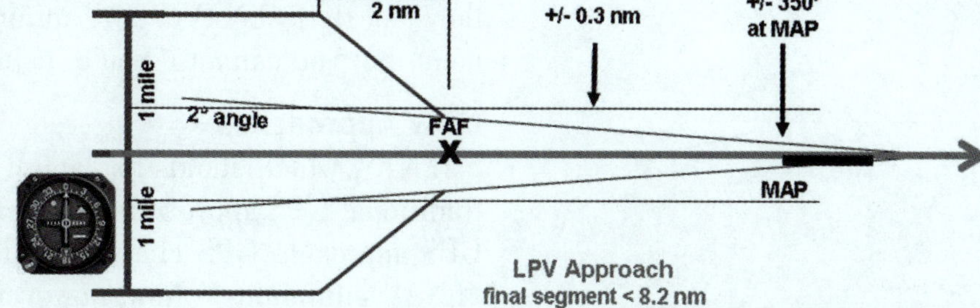

Figure 14-41 CDI sensitivity decreases to a 2° angle on the final segment of an LPV approach. *© Garmin Ltd. or its affiliates*

A variety of equipment can be used to fly LNAV/VNAV minimums. Most GA pilots will use a WAAS receiver, but airliners certified to fly these approaches can use barometric-VNAV systems, sometimes known as baro-VNAV systems, which combine an IFR GPS receiver with an additional barometric pressure input. There are a number of limitations that apply to the airliners, and these are found in the notes on RNAV GPS instrument charts. Ironically, these notes don't apply to you when flying with a less expensive, state-of-the-art WAAS receiver.

First, as you may remember, altimeters are affected by non-standard pressure and temperature. The differences due to pressure are generally much larger than those due to temperature, so most of the time pilots can successfully fly by correcting only for non-standard pressure. That's what you are doing when you twist a knob to set your altimeter. Airline pilots also set their baro-VNAV systems to the local pressure setting when flying an LNAV/VNAV approach.

However, there's no second knob that lets you adjust your altimeter for non-standard temperature. Our inability to correct for this error can be a serious problem as we get close to the ground in extremely cold weather, as it is for airliners flying LNAV/VNAV approaches that rely on outside air pressure to determine their altitude. Thus some LNAV/VNAV approaches have notes for lower temperature limits that apply to the airlines, but not to WAAS receivers. In a few cases, you will also see notes for high temperature limits for LNAV/VNAV approaches. That's because in hot weather, temperature errors will generate a vertical descent that exceeds the maximum 3.5° slope permitted for an LNAV/VNAV approach. Again, these notes only apply to the airlines, and not to a WAAS receiver.

Remote altimeter settings are not permitted for use by airliners with baro-VNAV systems, since the farther you are from the altimeter setting source, the greater the possible error when you use that altimeter setting. Again, these notes only apply to the airlines, and you can use a remote altimeter setting specified on an LNAV/VNAV approach with a WAAS receiver.

It's not unusual to see a note that reads: "WAAS VNAV NA" on instrument charts for airports outside of the WAAS coverage area in Hawaii, Alaska, and Puerto Rico. In these cases, the airlines win, since they can fly to LNAV/VNAV minimums with their baro-VNAV equipment, but you cannot if you're using a WAAS receiver.

LNAV Approaches

LNAV, which stands for lateral navigation, is a fancy name for the traditional GPS approaches pilots fly. In the past, with just one type of GPS approach, GPS charts just listed "GPS minimums," rather than "LNAV minimums." Now, however, with multiple types of minimums, traditional GPS approach minimums needed a name.

There is no vertical guidance provided for LNAV approaches. Hence these are non-precision approaches, and the minimums are published as an MDA, or minimum descent altitude. These MDAs are treated the same as MDAs for any other non-precision approach, and you are not allowed to descend below them until you're in a position to land. LNAV approaches can be flown with a traditional approach-certified GPS receiver, a WAAS-capable receiver, or an RNP 0.3 certified system. Any other RNAV systems require special approval to fly these approaches.

LNAV+V Approaches

Some LNAV approaches have an advisory glide slope. These approaches use the same non-precision minimums as LNAV approaches, but the advisory glide slope is flown similarly to an ILS. The purpose of the glide slope is to provide a stable descent rate down to the MDA. Historically, many instructors have taught students to "dive and drive" at each step down of a non-precision approach, but the FAA has determined that the high descent rates used for this contribute to an increase in accidents. Hence, the FAA now recommends that stable descent rates be used on all non-precision approaches, and advisory glide slopes help pilots determine appropriate descent rates.

Flying an LPV Approach from an IAF

Now let's fly the RNAV (GPS) RWY 30Z approach, which has LPV minimums, into Half Moon Bay, Calif. (figure 14-42). When selecting an approach, you'll be asked to choose VECTORS, or one of possibly several IAFs. It's important to know before you load the approach which IAF you plan to use if using pilot navigation, or whether you want the controller to vector you to the approach. You can later switch between vectors or different IAFs if the game plan changes—and you have permission from ATC—provided you haven't passed the FAF. Any change made after the FAF cancels the GPS's approach mode. Let's plan on flying to the IAF at SAPID this time. Later we'll show you some interesting new gotchas in the WAAS-capable receivers that you'll want to remember when flying an approach with vectors.

Selecting a WAAS approach is the same as selecting any other approach. First press the PROC key. "SELECT APPROACH" should already be highlighted. If it's not, scroll with the large FMS knob to highlight it. Then press the ENT key.

Use either FMS knob to select an approach from the list available at the destination airport. In this case, choose the RNAV 30 Z GPS approach. Then press the ENT key and scroll to select the IAF at SAPID and press the ENT key. Since we're ready to fly directly to SAPID now, scroll with the large knob to "ACTIVATE?" and press the ENT key.

We've created a new acronym, PICA, for whenever you load an instrument procedure. Anyone familiar with typesetting and layout will know that a pica is a unit of measure that indicates the size of a letter on a page. In teaching people to fly glass cockpits, we've

TIP

Always specify an IAF when loading an approach, even if planning to fly an approach with vectors from the controller. If you choose "VECTORS," on some approaches, GPS receivers will delete some of the waypoints along the final approach course. This makes flying the approach more difficult if you're later told to fly directly to one of those waypoints, or if you need to descend at one of these points. You may want to "activate" the leg (see page 139) that you're intercepting.

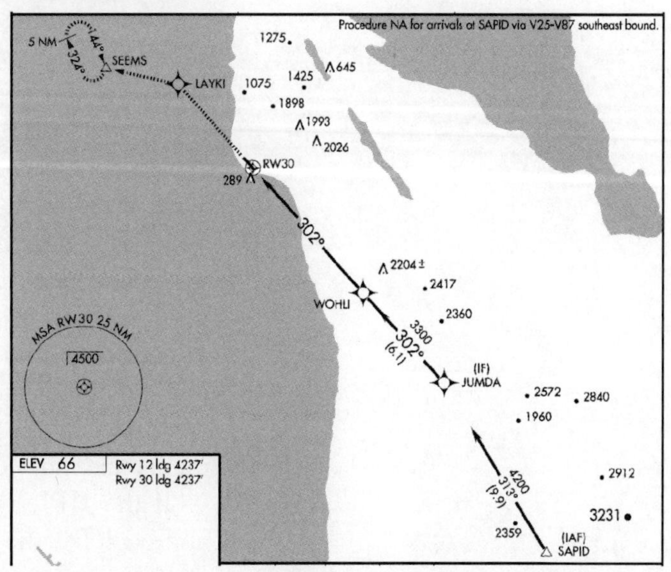

Figure 14-42 A narrow LPV approach allows low minimums in spite of the adjacent mountain ridge.

observed that people consistently miss one or more important steps when setting up an instrument approach. PICA is designed to help you remember to check all of these steps every time you select an approach.

The "P" is for pressing the PROC key, which we've already done. The "I" in PICA is to Inspect every waypoint in the flight plan to verify that it is correct. Make sure, for example, that you're flying directly to SAPID and not to KHAF first, which would be the case if you had pressed LOAD instead of ACTIVATE. Use the "C" in PICA to confirm that the GPS CDI needle is selected and set for the correct course by pressing the CDI softkey on the PFD. Finally, the "A" in PICA is a reminder to check the Autopilot and confirm that it is still engaged in the NAV or navigation mode.

Approaching the IAF at SAPID, you'll see a 10-second countdown on the GPS telling you to expect a turn to a heading of 314°. The countdown feature is a nice improvement over non-WAAS G1000 GPS receivers, which gave a shorter warning of upcoming turns that was easier to miss. At the end of the countdown, if you need to make a right turn, the GPS will display "Turn right to 314° now." If you're using the autopilot, the plane will intercept the approach course near the IAF and begin flying inbound. After you're established on the final approach course inbound, push the autopilot's APR key to engage the approach mode.

After this turn, the GPS auto-sequences and JUMDA becomes the active waypoint. This is a good time, if you haven't already, to get the AWOS weather for Half Moon Bay and to complete the pre-landing checklist. Approaching JUMDA, the GPS will start a countdown again followed by "Left turn to 302° now."

After passing JUMDA, the GPS auto-sequences again. WOHLI, which is the final approach fix, becomes the active waypoint and we can begin our descent to 3,300 feet.

As soon as the final approach fix becomes the active waypoint, the WAAS receiver evaluates the satellites and WAAS correction signals. Then it calculates the HPL and VPL and compares them to the HAL and VAL limits for the approach. If the receiver's analysis shows that we have a satellite signal of sufficient quality to fly to LPV minimums, we'll see the green TERM annunciator replaced with a green LPV annunciator, and we can continue flying the approach. A yellow LPV annunciator means that the current HPL and VPL values are not yet adequate for the approach. That's an early indication that LPV minimums may not be approved unless the satellite signal improves.

If the HPL and VPL exceed the HAL or VAL limits at the final approach fix, the approach minimums will be automatically downgraded. If this approach also had LNAV minimums—which it doesn't in this case—we might see the LNAV annunciator instead and a message that the approach was downgraded. We could then continue flying the approach to the LNAV minimums. In the unlikely event that the receiver was unable to meet the signal integrity requirements for any minimums, the receiver would display a message telling you to abort the approach.

At 2 miles from WOHLI, the WAAS receiver will switch from terminal mode to approach mode. The CDI scaling is smoothly reduced from plus and minus 1.0 nm full scale left or right deflection to either 0.3 nautical miles, or 2° full scale deflection, whichever is less at the FAF. Ultimately, scaling decreases to 2° on the final approach segment. On the missed approach, the scaling returns to 0.3 nautical miles, after we press the SUSP softkey.

If we're at 3,300 feet at WOHLI, our vertical deviation indicator, which is a magenta diamond (figure 14-43), will be centered, so it's time to start descending along the glide path. When flying an LPV approach, full scale up or down deflection is 15 meters, about 50 feet. When flying LNAV/VNAV and LNAV+V approaches, full scale deflection is 45 meters, a little less than 150 feet.

Assuming you get a local altimeter setting, you'll continue this approach down to the decision altitude of 363 feet. Note that when we reach the decision altitude, we are not yet at the runway threshold, to which the GPS is currently counting down the mileage. For this particular approach, we are still 0.7 nautical miles away.

If you have the runway in sight when you reach the decision altitude, you can land. Otherwise you must immediately initiate a go around, as you are NOT permitted to continue flying level looking for the airport. This is in sharp contrast to a non-precision LNAV approach, where you could continue flying level to the missed approach point at the runway threshold. But that is not permitted on an LPV or LNAV/VNAV approach, since they use decision altitudes.

With a decision altitude, if you don't see the airport at that point, you must immediately start a climb and follow the missed approach instructions. You can then re-engage the autopilot during the climb out, after you reach the minimum altitude specified in the limitations for your particular autopilot.

About 20 seconds later (depending upon groundspeed), as you're climbing out on our missed approach, "ARRIVING AT WAYPOINT" is displayed. About 10 seconds later, as you cross the RW30 waypoint, "SUSP" is displayed, indicating that automatic sequencing of waypoints has stopped, and the CDI TO/FROM arrow flips to FROM.

Flying an LPV Approach with Vectors

We'll talk in a few minutes about flying the missed approach. But before we do that, let's talk about a major "gotcha" when flying this same approach with vectors. Experienced GPS users are likely to get trapped by this until they understand why a WAAS-capable GPS receiver operates differently when flying with vectors.

First, imagine we've drawn a line at the FAF perpendicular to the final approach course. The line cuts the approach in half and we'll label the area closest to the airport "inside the FAF" and the other area

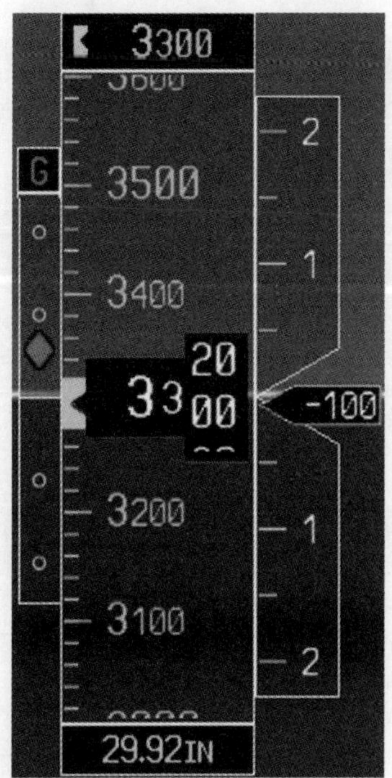

Figure 14-43 This aircraft is almost at WOHLI, and it's slightly below the glide path. *© Garmin Ltd. or its affiliates*

"outside the FAF." Flying an LPV approach with vectors is the same as flying any other approach with vectors if you are outside the FAF when you select "Vectors" when loading an approach or when you choose "Activate Vector-to-Final?"

Imagine, however, that you are flying from a direction that requires you to fly by an airport before you turn around to intercept an approach to fly back to the airport. Now you may be inside the FAF when you select "Vectors" or "Activate Vector-to-Final?" (figure 14-44). When you do, the SUSP annunciator is displayed. If you're a GPS pro, you know that when you see SUSP, it means that auto-sequencing of waypoints in the flight plan is suspended. As an experienced GPS pro, you might press the SUSP softkey to restart auto-sequencing, which would be incorrect. Pushing it a second time only makes things worse.

The FAA's TSO-C146a specification requires WAAS receivers to annunciate legs that are not auto-sequenced. Therefore, whenever you're inside the FAF and you select Vectors or Activate Vectors-to-Final, the SUSP annunciation will come on. That is normal for a WAAS-capable receiver. Do not push the SUSP softkey to try to make the SUSP annunciation go away. In fact, don't do anything. The SUSP annunciation will go away automatically when you're outside the FAF, and on a ground track that's within 45° of the published inbound course.

If you forget and do press the SUSP softkey, the first press will cause the GPS to activate the leg in the flight plan closest to you. If you press the SUSP softkey a second time, it puts the GPS in OBS mode and your approach is no longer active. By the way, if you wait until you are outside of the FAF, and then push the SUSP softkey, the SUSP annunciation goes away and you can proceed normally. Of course, it would have gone away by itself if you waited another minute or two until you were on a 45° intercept angle to the final approach course.

The best way to recover from these accidental pushes of the SUSP softkey is to reactivate vectors to final. Just press the PROC key, scroll with the large FMS knob to highlight "Activate Vector-to-Final?" and press the ENT key. The SUSP annunciator will come on again and you can continue with the approach. Then fly the headings given to you by the controller, intercept the final approach course, and fly the approach.

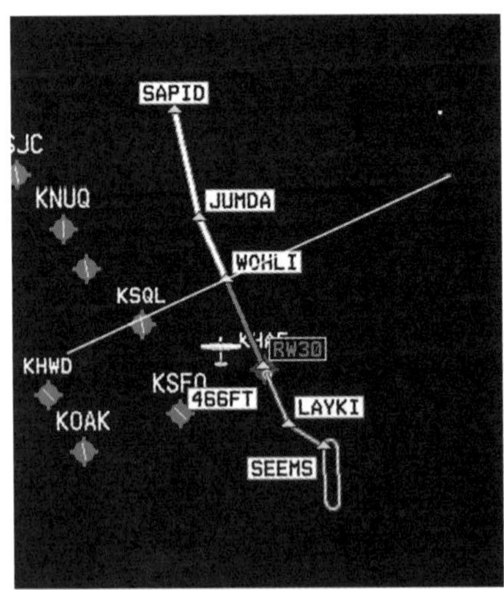

Figure 14-44 This aircraft is in the area inside the FAF at WOHLI, so the SUSP annunciator comes on when the approach is loaded with vectors or a leg is activated. *© Garmin Ltd. or its affiliates*

Flying the Missed Approach

Now let's talk about flying the missed approach using the RNAV (GPS) 30 Z example. Note that there are differences compared with non-WAAS-capable GPS receivers.

You'll recall we started our climb at the DA before reaching the missed approach waypoint, which is usually at the runway threshold for LPV approaches. Later in the climb, as we cross the missed approach waypoint, the GPS receiver will annunciate "ARRIVING WPT." Then

"SUSP" is displayed, indicating that automatic sequencing of waypoints was stopped, the CDI TO/FROM arrow flips to FROM, and the vertical deviation indicator is flagged off to show the loss of glide path (figure 14-45). Also, the CDI scaling switches from a full scale left and right deflection of 350 feet to 0.3 nautical miles, considerably tighter than the 1 nautical mile used by non-WAAS-capable GPS receivers when flying the missed approach segment.

Fortunately, the first segment of a missed approach for an LPV approach is required to be aligned with the final approach course, so you won't have to make any turns immediately. Read the missed approach directions carefully to determine when you can push the SUSP softkey to re-enable auto-sequencing, which will provide course guidance to the missed approach holding waypoint. If you're tracking straight ahead to a missed approach point directly in front of you, as you are on a LPV approach, you should be able to push the SUSP softkey to extinguish the SUSP annunciator almost immediately after it comes on during your climb out.

However, if the missed approach instructions were to read something like "climb to 3000 feet and then turn left to" a waypoint, you'd need to wait until reaching 3,000 feet, or the altitude specified, prior to pushing the SUSP softkey and initiating a turn. With older G1000 software, if you push SUSP too soon, the GPS gives turn guidance to your autopilot before you've reached the altitude at which you're permitted to start a turn, which could send you into an obstacle! New G1000 and Perspective systems delay any turn until any required altitude is reached.

Figure 14-45 You must begin flying the missed approach at the decision altitude, which occurs before reaching the missed approach waypoint, indicated here by the SUSP annunciator. *© Garmin Ltd. or its affiliates*

In our present example, we can push the SUSP softkey immediately after the SUSP annunciator comes on, since our missed approach instructions are to climb to 6,000 feet direct to LAYKI. Once we press the SUSP softkey, the SUSP annunciator is extinguished and the LPV annunciator is replaced with a MAPR annunciator. That indicates that the GPS receiver is providing missed approach signal integrity, meaning that the CDI full scale left or right deflection is now 0.3 nautical miles.

The system displays, "Next DTK 302° now" which confirms that we should continue climbing straight ahead. At LAYKI, our missed approach instructions tell us to fly a 267° track to SEEMS. As we approach LAYKI, the GPS gives us the 10 second countdown by displaying "Turn left to 267° in 10 seconds." It then displays "Turn left to 267° now," and the GPS gives the autopilot course guidance to SEEMS.

This is when the magic begins. If we check the flight plan, it tells us that after SEEMS, our next waypoint is "HOLD" with a DTK of 144°. In non-WAAS GPS receivers, that was a subtle warning that the GPS would be telling the autopilot to turn to 144°, which is not the correct heading for entering this hold. Experienced GPS pilots are used to the fact that GPS receivers will not fly hold entries, and that they must switch the autopilot to heading mode and manually fly the airplane to enter the hold.

The new WAAS-capable GPS receivers are much smarter. Not only can they fly the proper entry into a hold, they can also continue to fly the hold for you. Getting back to our example, 20 seconds out from SEEMS, we get a 10-second warning to "Hold Teardrop." Next, we'll get a 10-second countdown that says "Next DTK 310° in 10 seconds." On the moving map, you'll also see a dashed white line depicting the course required, in this case, for a teardrop entry (figure 14-46).

As we cross SEEMS, the SUSP annunciation appears, the dashed line becomes magenta showing us that it's the active leg we'll follow to fly a teardrop entry, and the GPS gives the autopilot instructions to turn to a heading of 310° to track the teardrop entry.

Looking at the approach chart, we can see that the missed approach holding course is on the 144° track to SEEMS, and that it uses 5-nautical mile legs. Looking at our flight plan, next to the "HOLD" waypoint, we can see the distance counting up (figure 14-47). As this value approaches 5 nautical miles, we get a 10-second countdown message that says "Turn right to 144° in 10 seconds," followed by a "Turn right to 144° now" annunciation. The GPS then gives course guidance to the autopilot to turn and follow a 144° track to SEEMS.

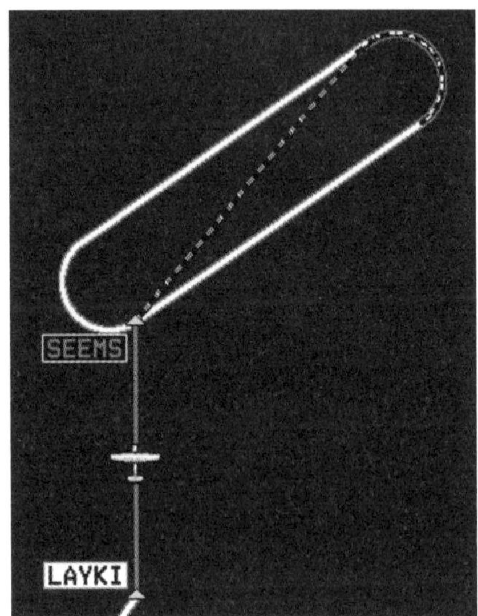

Figure 14-46 The dashed line shows the path the autopilot will fly to make a teardrop entry. *© Garmin Ltd. or its affiliates*

As the aircraft rolls out onto the 144° course, note that the SUSP annunciator stays on. This lets us know that the GPS will continue to fly the holding pattern until we provide it with new instructions in the flight plan. This feature takes most of the work out of flying a holding pattern, and frees pilots to devote time to more important tasks, such as deciding their next course of action.

By the way, pushing the SUSP softkey won't make the SUSP extinguish unless you have another waypoint in your flight plan after "hold." That makes sense. Turning off SUSP would turn on auto-sequencing, but there wouldn't be a waypoint to sequence to. If you do enter a waypoint after "HOLD" and press the SUSP softkey, SUSP will extinguish, but the GPS will continue to fly the hold until the next time it reaches the missed approach holding waypoint, which in this case is SEEMS. At SEEMS, it will activate the leg from "HOLD" to your next waypoint, and provide course guidance along that leg.

FLIGHT PLAN

KHAF / KHAF

	DTK	DIS
466FT	___°	____NM
LAYKI		
SEEMS mahp	___°	____NM
→ HOLD	144°	3.1NM

Figure 14-47 The distance for the HOLD waypoint counts up as you fly outbound. *© Garmin Ltd. or its affiliates*

Flying LNAV/VNAV and LNAV+V Approaches

LNAV/VNAV approaches are loaded and flown in the same way that LPV approaches are flown. The difference is that when the final approach waypoint becomes the active waypoint, either LNAV/V or LNAV+V is annunciated on the HSI, depending upon which was coded into the GPS database. Remember, that if there are LNAV/VNAV minimums for an approach and the system annunciates LNAV+V, you can fly the approach to LNAV/VNAV minimums.

LNAV+V approaches are non-precision approaches, but there are no chart minimums designated LNAV+V. Instead, you'll use the LNAV minimums to fly these approaches. Originally, there was no easy way to know ahead of time whether a particular LNAV approach had an advisory glide slope, except to fly an approach in a WAAS-equipped aircraft or with Garmin's PC Trainer software and see whether LNAV or LNAV+V is annunciated when the FAF is the active waypoint. Now, when you load an approach, you should see LNAV+V listed next to the approach name when you select the approach, and in your flight plan.

When flying a LNAV or LNAV+V approach, you'll descend just to the MDA specified on the LNAV line of the minimums section of the chart. However if LNAV+V is annunciated, a vertical deviation indicator appears, and you can use it to fly the advisory glide slope either manually or with the autopilot. For LNAV and LNAV+V approaches, if you arrive at the MDA prior to the missed approach point, you are permitted to fly level all the way to the missed approach point as you look for the airport.

Dead Reckoning Mode

The new Dead Reckoning mode is not something you can select, however, if there is a loss of GPS signal integrity while flying en route, you'll be happy that you have it. Essentially it provides an estimated position, based upon your last known GPS position, combined with continuous updates of airspeed and heading data. However, the system will only go into this mode when operating in the ENR or en route mode (more than 30 miles from the departure or destination airport), or when operating in the OCN or oceanic mode. In other phases of flight, such as in the TERM, APR or MAPR (missed approach) modes, a loss of GPS signal integrity causes the message "NO GPS POSITION" to appear on both the PFD and MFD maps, and dead reckoning information is not provided.

When the dead reckoning mode is active, "DR" is displayed in yellow above and to the right of the airplane symbol on the HSI (figure 14-48). All other GPS derived information also appears in yellow to alert you to the degraded position accuracy. This includes the Navigation Status bar's distance and bearing information, and the HSI's GPS bearing pointers and Bearing Information window distances. The Current Track Bug and the Wind Data window also appear in yellow. A "GPS NAV LOST" alert message is also generated, which causes the ALERTS softkey to flash white. On the MFD, a yellow DR appears on the map just below the airplane symbol, and all GPS related data in the Navigation Status bar is displayed in yellow.

When operating in the DR mode, the position information should be considered increasingly unreliable. If you should subsequently lose heading and/or airspeed data, the position may become very unreliable and should not be used for navigation. While in DR mode, the autopilot cannot be coupled to the GPS, so you'll need to operate it in the Heading Select mode or some other roll mode. TAWS and Terrain Proximity are also disabled, and any distances in the Nearest information pages may be inaccurate.

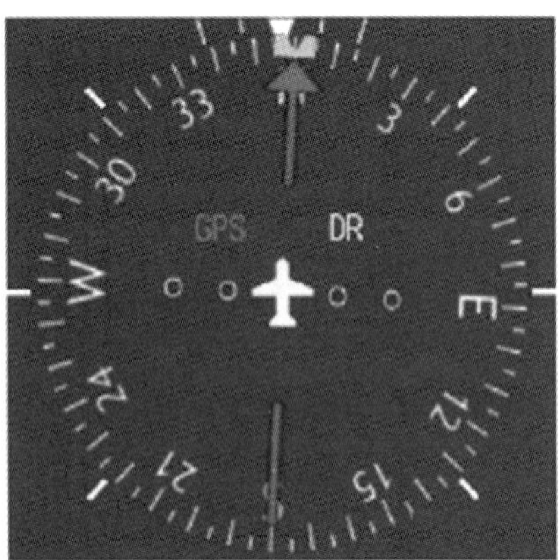

Figure 14-48 If you lose GPS signal integrity, the dead reckoning mode provides guidance, but it loses accuracy over time. *© Garmin Ltd. or its affiliates*

Synthetic Vision Technology

Synthetic Vision Technology (SVT), introduced by Garmin in April 2008, became available first on the Diamond DA40 and was later certified in aircraft from other manufacturers. It's a software option, priced under $10,000, which can be added to G1000-equipped aircraft of manufacturers who've done the additional certification work required. SVT is standard with the Perspective glass cockpit.

SVT adds a forward-looking view that renders a 3D image of terrain, traffic, obstacles and runways ahead. It is based upon the aircraft's current GPS position, heading, attitude and a terrain database. SVT is not intended for primary navigation, but merely as a backup to enhance situation awareness. The user manuals clearly state that due to accuracy and reliability limitations, SVT must not be used as the sole basis for decisions on maneuvering to avoid terrain, traffic or obstacles.

The terrain image is displayed on the entire PFD, and shows through the instrument indicators (figure 15-18). Due to the resolution of the database, nine arc-second squares are used, some smoothing of peaks and valleys may occur. The field of view is 30 degrees to the left of center and 35 degrees to the right, since the terrain display is centered on the attitude indicator and HSI, which are located to the left of center on the G1000 and Perspective PFD. Terrain above your altitude appears above the horizon line and is colored in red to indicate the potential danger ahead. Impact markers, displayed as Xs in the Inset Map, show where impact is projected to occur if the aircraft continues on its present course.

Other major elements of the system projected on the PFD are:

- Flight Path Marker – Shows where the aircraft is going.
- Zero Pitch Line – Shows aircraft's current altitude versus terrain.
- Traffic – Symbols that change position and size.
- Obstacles – Symbols that enlarge as you approach obstacles.
- Runways – Depicts runway identifier and centerline.
- Airport Signs – Indicate nearby airports.
- Gridlines – Add texture to terrain.

Operation

Operation of SVT is simple; four clearly labeled softkeys are used to enable the system. First press the PFD softkey, which accesses a variety of functions including SVT. Then press the SYN VIS softkey. This brings up the four SVT softkeys (figure 14-49). To use any of these keys, you must first press the SYN TERR softkey, which brings up the 3D terrain display and enables the three other softkeys.

Pressing the other SVT softkeys layers additional information onto the 3D display.

- PATHWAY – rectangular boxes for course guidance.
- HRZN HDG – horizon heading marks and digits.
- APTSIGNS – signposts for nearby airports.

Flight Path Marker

The flight path marker (FPM) is my favorite feature. It appears at ground speeds greater than 30 knots and projects the aircraft's path based upon the current winds, aircraft speed and heading. This differs from the attitude indicator's airplane symbol, which depicts the aircraft's current heading.

The FPM can help identify potential conflicts before a TAWS alert occurs. When the flight path marker is below terrain or obstacles, your current path is taking you below those objects. It can also be used to precisely maintain altitude in a turn, For example, I once checked out a pilot in a SR22 who lost over 200 feet in his first steep turn. On the very next turn, he had less than 20 feet of altitude deviation after I told him to hold the FPM on the zero pitch line. SVT's zero pitch line, drawn completely across the display, depicts the aircraft's current altitude versus the horizon.

Figure 14-49 Push the PFD and SYN VIS softkeys to bring up these four softkeys that control Synthetic Vision. *© Garmin Ltd. or its affiliates*

A pilot can also use the FPM to determine the descent angle needed to a runway by simply maneuvering the aircraft to position the FPM at the beginning of the SVT runway depiction. Of course the pilot would still need to manage power and airspeed and be aware that in some cases this method might result in an unsafe descent angle. The FPM also makes it easy to fly through the boxes depicted when Pathways are enabled.

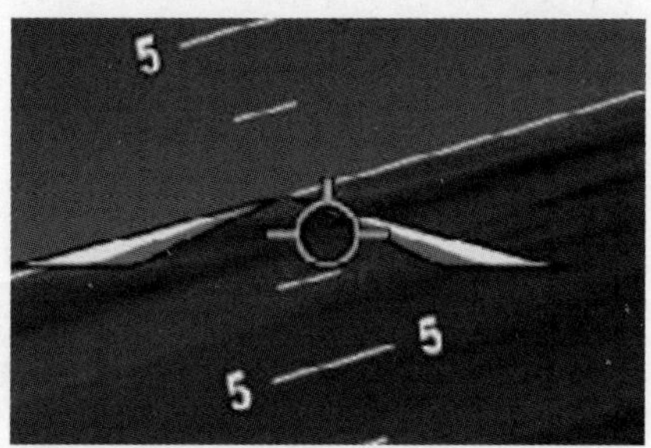

Figure 14-50 Although the inverted-V airplane symbol shows the aircraft pitched to 0°, the round Flight Path Marker shows the aircraft is descending *© Garmin Ltd. or its affiliates*

Pathways

When the PATHWAY softkey is selected, highway in the sky (HITS) guidance is provided by displaying a series of rectangles that a pilot flies through to maintain the desired course. NASA originally developed this concept and their testing showed that it let pilots fly a more precise path though at the cost of a pilot higher workload. Positioning the FPM in the center of each rectangle should reduce the workload, though Garmin's own testing showed that some pilots still find it easier to fly a course using the conventional flight director.

Most of the time, the rectangles are 700 feet wide and 200 feet tall. However, when flying an approach, the width is 700 feet or half of the full-scale CDI deflection, whichever is less. Also on approach, the height is 200 feet or half of the full-scale deflection of the vertical deviation indicator, whichever is less. The rectangles are magenta when flying the active leg of a GPS flight plan, white when flying a GPS leg that is not active, and green when flying an ILS or localizer. Pathways are not displayed when leg sequencing is suspended, such as after the MAP before the SUSP softkey is pressed, or on any flight plan leg that would lead to intercepting a leg in the wrong direction.

Pathways are displayed at the higher of the selected altitude (set with the ALT knobs) or the flight plan altitude. Descent profiles are displayed when a descent is programmed in the profiles window of the MFD's flight plan. No profile is shown for climbs; instead, the rectangles are depicted level at the selected altitude. This is due to the various climb performance variables that could, under some circumstances, result in a climb pathway that could lead to a stall.

Traffic

Traffic is displayed as either a white diamond, or for nearby traffic, as a yellow "sun" on the PFD. The symbols move across the PFD depending on intruder traffic location. The symbols also grow in size as the traffic gets closer. As traffic approaches within 1,000 feet laterally of the aircraft, traffic symbols are removed, as they may mislead pilots as to actual intruder aircraft location, due to the inaccuracies in traffic systems.

Terrain Alerting

SVT includes a terrain awareness system, but it is less capable than the TAWS option available. While the terrain and obstacle color displays are the same, TAWS uses more sophisticated algorithms to determine an aircraft's distance from terrain and obstacles. Where both systems are installed, TAWS takes precedence over SVT terrain warnings. SVT requires a valid 3-D GPS position and valid terrain/obstacle database in order to generate warnings.

SVT's terrain system uses yellow to indicate terrain and obstacles that are between 100 feet and 1,000 below the aircraft. Red is used to indicate terrain and obstacles that are above the aircraft or as little as 100 feet below the aircraft. The colors change automatically as the aircraft altitude varies. X symbols, generated by FLTA alerts described in the TAWS-B section of Chapter 7, are displayed in the Inset map to display potential impact points.

Other SVT Features

Standard tower symbols, like those used on sectional charts and on the PFD and MFD, are used to display obstacles. The symbols are drawn in perspective view, based upon their distance and height relative to the aircraft. Obstacles more than 1,000 feet below the aircraft are not displayed. Obstacles do not change color to warn of a potential conflict until a FLTA alert occurs.

When on the surface, runway texture, identifiers and centerline stripes are displayed. Generally the stripes appear within a couple of feet of where they are actually located. Thus on takeoff, pilots will see the runway stripes on the PFD positioned relatively closely to those they view outside the window.

When in the air, runways ahead of the aircraft are displayed as a white rectangle in perspective view. The rectangle grows in size as you approach and eventually the runway identifier is also displayed. When an instrument approach is loaded, a second larger rectangle is displayed making it easier to spot the runway.

Pressing the APTSIGNS softkey activates airport signs. Signs for an airport first appear without the identifier when an aircraft is about 15 nm away. At approximately 8 nm, the airport identifier appears and at about 4.5 nm, the sign is removed.

Pressing the HRZN HDG softkey activates the display of tick marks and compass headings along the zero pitch line. Compass headings, synchronized with the HSI, are displayed in 30° increments, meaning that there are never more than three visible on the PFD.

The field of view displayed (figure 14-51) on the PFD can be represented on the PFD by a pair of V-shaped, dashed lines extending in front of the airplane symbol. This field of view symbol can be turned on and off using the MFD's Map Setup option. To do this, press the MENU key, choose Map Setup and press the ENT key. Turn the large FMS knob to highlight the GROUP field and press the ENT key. Scroll with either FMS knob to select Aviation and press the ENT key. Then scroll with the large FMS knob to highlight the FIELD OF VIEW field and turn the small FMS knob to select On or Off. Press the FMS knob to return to the Map page.

Latest Features

This section covers features new to the G1000. Many of these features were first introduced in the Perspective and more recently added to the G1000.

Importing/Exporting Flight Plans

Perspective and some G1000 aircraft have the capability to import and export flight plans. This lets you create a flight plan at home on commercial flight planning software, export the flight plan to a SD data card, place the SD card in the MFD's top card slot, and import it to the Flight Plan Catalog page. Jeppesen FlightStar, Seattle Avionics Voyager and FltPlan.com havc this capability.

Flight Data Logging

A new Flight Data Logging feature automatically stores critical flight and engine data on an SD data card inserted into the top card slot of the MFD. Approximately 1,000 flight hours can be recorded for each 1GB of available space on the card.

When the MFD is powered on, data is written to the SD card once a second. Logged data is stored using a file name that includes the date in the format: dataYYYY_MM_DD.csv. The file is created any time an SD card is in the MFD's upper slot and can be viewed with Microsoft Excel and other applications that recognize the .csv file format. Generally, the factory will have supplied a card for this. One place to view engine data collected on the card is www.cirrusreports.com.

You can view the status of the Flight Data Logging feature on the AUX-UTILITY page. If no SD card is inserted, "NO CARD" is displayed. While data is being written to the SD card, "LOGGING DATA" is displayed.

Auxiliary Video

The G1000 system provides a control and display interface to an optional auxiliary video system. The system can display video for up to two inputs. The G1000 implementation is similar to the Enhanced Vision System for the Perspective, described in Chapter 15.

Dual Navigation Database

This feature lets each display store an upcoming navigation database on the bottom SD card so that the system can automatically load it to replace the active database when the new database becomes effective. The next cycle becomes available seven days prior to its effective date. Upon power-up, the system checks the active and standby databases. If the standby database is current and the active database is out of date, the standby database is copied to the active database location, which takes about 45-55 seconds.

Selected Altitude Intercept Arc

During a climb or descent, a light blue Selected Altitude Intercept Arc (figure 14-52) appears on the Navigation Map page at the estimated position the aircraft will intercept the Selected Altitude. To enable this feature, press the MENU key, select "Map Setup" and press the ENT key, scroll to select the "Map" group and press the ENT key. Then scroll down using the large FMS knob opposite SEL ALT ARC and use the small FMS knob to select "ON." Push the FMS knob to remove the Map Setup window.

Profile View

The Profile View (figure 14-53) shows pilots how terrain, obstacles and winds aloft may impact their projected flight path. First introduced in Perspective, it's now available on the G1000. When selected, it creates a new window at the bottom of the MFD's Navigation Map Page with a side view of the aircraft and upcoming terrain and obstacles. Headwind and tailwind components for winds aloft data are displayed up to 3,500 feet above and below your aircraft's present altitude. It does not give aural alerts or cautions or display potential impact points.

To enable the Profile View, from the Navigation Map page press the MAP softkey. Then press the PROFILE softkey, which turns the softkey gray and displays the Profile View window at the bottom of the page. Another way to turn the Profile View on and off is to press the MENU key, scroll to select "Show Profile View" or "Hide Profile View" and press the ENT key.

The Profile Path, a white rectangle on the main Navigation Map, outlines the area analyzed for the Profile View. The rectangle length in nautical miles, which is always half of the Navigation Map range, is displayed in the lower right of the Profile View window. White range markers along the length of the rectangle match range markers on the distance scale inside the Profile View window whenever the profile range is at least 4 nm.

The width of the Profile Path is identical to the full-scale left and right deflection of a WAAS-capable GPS CDI needle. Thus the rectangle width is 4 nm in enroute mode, 2 nm in terminal mode and 0.6 nm in approach mode.

The Profile View window depicts a side view outline of terrain. Color is added to the outline when Terrain mode is enabled. To enable Terrain, from the MFD's Navigation Map page, press the MAP softkey and then the TERRAIN softkey. Yellow indicates terrain and obstacles that are between 100 feet and 1,000 below the aircraft. Red indicates terrain and obstacles that are above the aircraft or as little as 100 feet below the aircraft. The colors change automatically as aircraft altitude varies.

Note that terrain and obstacle data will not be displayed when the Navigation Map range is larger than the Map Setup range setting for Terrain Data and Obstacle Data. See Chapter 7 and Figure 7-15 for details on setting these parameters. When the Navigation Map range is set for less than 2 nm, data is removed from the Profile View window and PROFILE NOT AVAILABLE is displayed.

You can turn the Profile Path rectangle on and off, or set a maximum map range above which it is not displayed. You can also turn the display of winds on or off. To access these functions, press the MENU key, select "Map Setup" and press the ENT key, scroll to select the "Profile" group and press the ENT key. Then scroll down using the large FMS knob to select a particular field (figure 15-54). Use the small FMS knob to turn functions on or off and to select the maximum map range at which the Profile Path rectangle will be displayed.

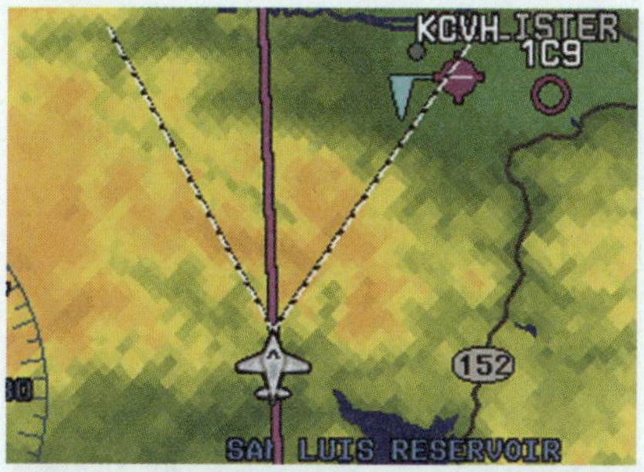

Figure 14-51 The field of view symbol, two dashed white lines, shows the area represented by SVT terrain. *© Garmin Ltd. or its affiliates*

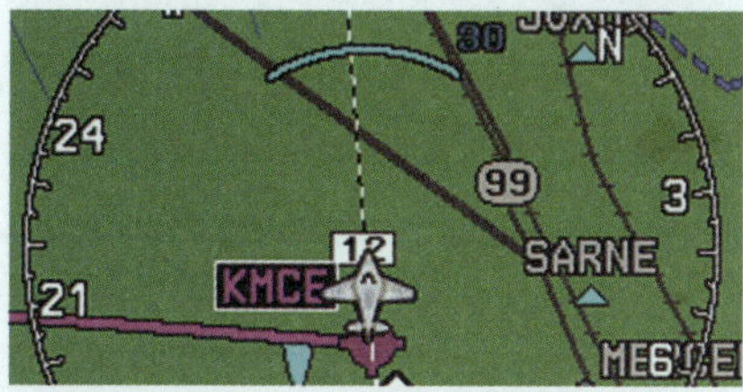

Figure 14-52 The Selected Altitude Intercept Arc, a blue curved line, shows where the aircraft will reach the selected altitude. The white dashed line is a Runway Extension. *© Garmin Ltd. or its affiliates*

AOPA Directory

In the past, you could not use the G1000 to find an airport's traffic pattern altitude or whether right or left traffic is used. Now you can often find that information in the Aircraft Owners and Pilots Association (AOPA) Airport Directory database (figure 14-55). To view directory information from the Airport Information page, press the INFO Softkey until INFO-2 is displayed.

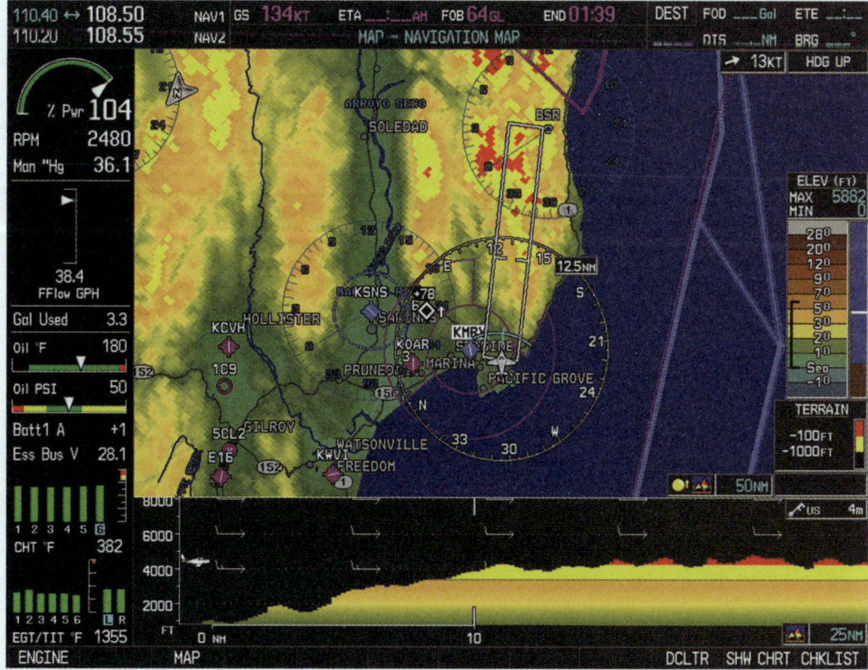

Figure 14-53 A white rectangle shows the area analyzed for the profile view. The profile view displays high terrain in yellow and red when TERRAIN is turned on. *© Garmin Ltd. or its affiliates*

Summary

Garmin continues to add more advanced features to their glass cockpit systems and pilots continue to benefit from them. In 2008, Garmin released the Perspective glass cockpit, which you could think of as the G1000+, since it adds new features not found in the

G1000. These differences are discussed in the next chapter. Savvy G1000 pilots will want to monitor the Perspective's evolution to learn about features that may get added to future G1000 software revisions.

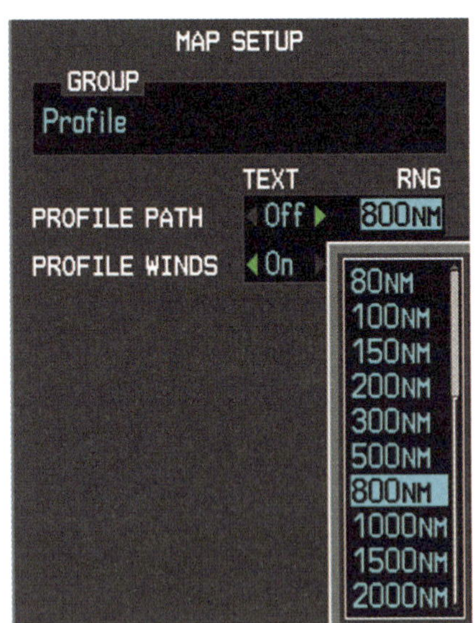

Figure 14-54 To modify the Profile View, press the MENU key, select "Map Setup" and press the ENT key, scroll to select the "Profile" group and press the ENT key. *© Garmin Ltd. or its affiliates*

Figure 14-55 To view the AOPA Directory, go to the Airport Information Page and press the INFO softkey until the new INFO-2 softkey is displayed.
© Garmin Ltd. or its affiliates

Chapter 15:

Flying the Perspective Glass Cockpit

In May 2008, Cirrus Design announced the Perspective glass cockpit for the SR22, now also available for the SR20. The Perspective's software is nearly identical to the G1000 and exceptions are pointed out in this chapter. Therefore, Perspective pilots may want to skim this chapter first to understand the differences and then read the entire book from Chapter 1. Pilots familiar with the G1000 and the Garmin GFC 700 autopilot will quickly adapt to flying the Perspective glass cockpit, once they note the new locations for knobs and autopilot keys.

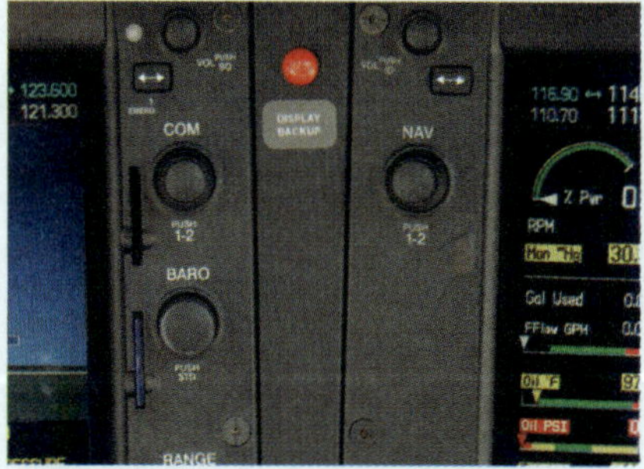

Figure 15-1 Push the red Display Backup button, located between the PFD and MFD, if either display fails.

Perspective Hardware

The most obvious difference between the Perspective and the G1000 is the hardware. Perspective aircraft use either 10- or 12-inch displays for the PFD and MFD and they have fewer knobs; the G1000's redundant knobs along the left side of the PFD and the right side of the MFD are eliminated. The Display Backup button, found at the bottom of the audio panel in G1000-equipped aircraft, is at the top of the display between the radio controls (figure 15-1). In the center console, there's a new keypad for data entry and an autopilot control panel. Many Perspective aircraft have a second AHRS and some have a second ADC.

PFD

Physically, the Perspective PFD differs from G1000 displays in that it has no knobs or keys along the left side of the display (figure 15-2). The CRS, HDG and ALT knobs, located on the PFD and MFD in G1000 systems, are found on the Perspective's center console. As a result, the BARO knob, located in the center of the PFD's right bezel, is a separate standalone knob, not part of a pair of concentric knobs. This makes it easier to identify the knob and adjust the altimeter setting. The other knobs along the PFD's right bezel are the same as the G1000.

A major change is that % Power is displayed in the upper left of the PFD, instead of the NAV frequencies found on the G1000. In reversionary mode, the NAV frequencies are displayed. The PFD's background

Perspective

The Perspective continues to evolve rapidly. Early Perspective users will want to read about new features now also available in the G1000 and listed in Chapter 14. These include Importing/Exporting Flight Plans, Flight Data Logging, Dual Navigation Database, Selected Altitude Intercept Arc, Map Profile, and the AOPA Directory. The Perspective also includes two features originally only in jet aircraft: the Baro Transition Alert and selection of the type of airplane symbol and command bars used on the attitude indicator, both described in Chapter 16.

Recent minor changes in the Perspective are that ETE replaces the BRG field at the top of the PFD and Pilot Profiles can now be imported and exported with an SD memory card. When IFR, a low altitude annunciator appears if you're at least 164 feet below the FAF altitude.

Figure 15-2 The Perspective features a 12-inch Primary Flight Display. © *Max Trescott*

colors are also different. On the G1000, the top half of the background is solid blue and the bottom half is brown. By contrast, the Perspective PFD uses color gradients. At the top of the display, dark blue fades to give way to light blue at the horizon line. Below the horizon line, either a light orange/tan color gradually becomes a dark brown at the bottom of the display or Synthetic Vision is displayed.

The Current Track Bug is easier to identify, since it has a series of dashed lines connecting it to the center of the HSI (figure 15-3). Look for full details on this extremely useful feature on the second page in Chapter 14. The bug is easy to miss in G1000 implementations, since it is often hidden behind the white pointer at the top of the HSI or behind the light blue heading bug. In the Perspective you can't miss it. And that's good, because this bug helps you quickly identify a heading that exactly compensates for the wind so you can parallel the desired course. By turning the plane so that the bug aligns with the top of the HSI's course pointer when the D-bar is centered, you can nail every instrument approach!

Figure 15-3 The Perspective's Current Track Bug is easier to spot because of its dashed lines. © *Garmin Ltd. or its affiliates*

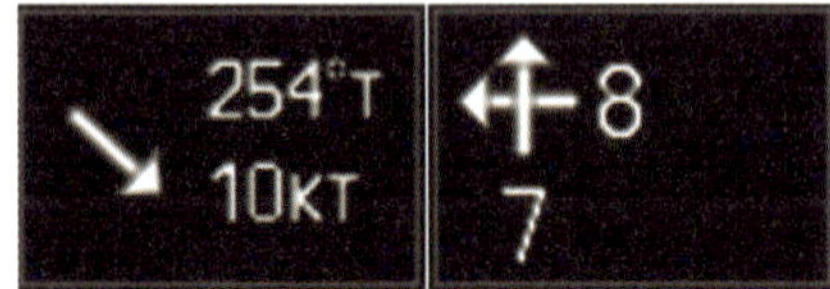

Figure 15-4 Pressing the PFD softkey and then the WIND softkey brings up two options for displaying a wind vector. © *Garmin Ltd. or its affiliates*

PFD Softkeys

In the lower left, a new SENSOR softkey brings up additional keys that let you select which AHRS and ADC is used to display instrument indications on the PFD; these keys do not allow you to select which unit is connected to the autopilot. Comparators evaluate the outputs of each ADC and AHRS and indicate if there's a discrepancy. If a unit fails, the good unit is automatically connected to the autopilot. ADC and AHRS failures are discussed in greater detail later in this chapter.

Pressing the PFD softkey and then the WIND softkey brings up two options for displaying a wind vector (the G1000 has three options). Pressing the OPTN 1 softkey displays a single arrow showing the wind direction (figure 15-4). Numbers indicate the wind direction in degrees and the total wind velocity in knots. I prefer this option in the cruise phase of flight.

Pressing the OPTN 2 softkey displays two arrows and two numbers that resolve the wind vector into its components. The number below the vertical arrow shows the amount of headwind or tailwind in knots; the number next to the horizontal arrow shows the amount of left or right crosswind. This option is particularly useful for identifying the crosswind component while on final approach to land. To see both formats simultaneously on the PFD, turn on the Inset Map. Then use the console's MENU key and the MAP SETUP option to enable WIND VECTOR on the MFD and Inset Map. Then press the PFD, WIND and OPTN 1 softkeys.

Pressing the PFD and then the ALT UNITS softkey brings up additional softkeys. Pushing the METERS softkey adds a meters display to the altimeter and Reference Altitude. The IN (inches) and HPA (hectopascals) softkeys change the format in which the barometric setting is displayed.

Pressing the PFD and then the STD BARO (Standard Baro) softkey sets the barometric setting to standard pressure of 29.92 inches or 1013 hectopascals.

Figure 15-5 Push the COM knob to switch the radio controls, on COM1 in this image, to COM2. © *Max Trescott*

COM and NAV Radios

Unlike the redundant COM and NAV radio displays found on the G1000, the Perspective displays these frequencies in only one location. The COM frequencies are displayed in the upper right of the PFD (figure 15-5) and the NAV frequencies are displayed in the upper left of the MFD (figure 15-6). The redundant COM and NAV radio controls found on G1000 displays are eliminated, leaving the Perspective with one set of COM and one set of NAV controls, located adjacent to their respective frequency displays. The radios can also be tuned with the knobs on the Control Unit in the central console.

Figure 15-6 Both active NAV frequencies remain white until you select NAV1 or NAV2 with the CDI softkey. © *Max Trescott*

The Perspective's COM and NAV radios are operated the same as the G1000 radios. Like most modern radios, both an active and a standby frequency are shown for each NAV and COM radio. The active frequency is the one ready for use, and the standby frequency is where new frequencies are loaded. Unlike most radios, however, the frequencies aren't labeled! Active frequencies—the ones closer to the center of the display—are displayed using numbers slightly larger than the standby frequencies. On the G1000, the numbers are the same size.

Like the G1000, the selected frequency—the one actually in use—is displayed in green. For NAV radios, a frequency is selected if its corresponding green course pointer, selected with the CDI softkey, is displayed on the HSI. When the GPS course pointer is selected on the HSI, both active NAV radio frequencies are white. The selected COM frequency, displayed in green, is the active frequency selected on the audio panel for transmitting.

Color also indicates which radios the NAV and COM knobs are currently tuning. Understanding this is important since the frequency selection and volume control knobs are shared and can only control one radio at a time. Garmin 430/530 users are already accustomed to sharing a single set of concentric frequency selection knobs that control one radio at a time and are switched between radios by pushing the center of either the NAV or COM knobs. That's also true on the Perspective and G1000, but what's unique is that the volume controls are also shared! So, it's important to know which radio the knobs are controlling.

Cyan (light blue) is the color for objects that are user adjustable and it's used to indicate the radio being operated by the bezel controls. On the G1000, a cyan colored rectangle surrounds the standby frequency and a cyan double arrow is located between the active and standby fields. The Perspective is similar, though it doesn't have a colored rectangle. Instead, the radio being tuned by the tuning knobs is indicated with a cyan double arrow and its standby frequency is displayed in cyan. Pushing the button in the center of the NAV or COM knobs selects the other radio for adjustment and moves the cyan colors up or down between radios 1 and 2.

There are three ways to manually tune the radios, one of which is identical to the G1000. To tune a radio the G1000 way, look for the cyan arrow. If it's on the correct radio, turn the concentric NAV or COM knobs on the displays to set the new frequency. The large knob sets the MegaHertz numbers to the left of the decimal point and the small knob sets the kiloHertz numbers. To tune the other radio, first push the button in the center of the NAV or COM knobs to move the cyan colors up or down to the other radio.

To use a frequency you've entered, you'll need to swap the frequencies in the active and standby fields. To do this, push the Frequency Toggle key, marked with a double-headed arrow. This transfers the frequency you've entered in the standby field to the active field toward the center of the screen, where it can now be used. The final step is to use the audio panel to select the active COM frequency or the PFD's CDI softkey to select the active NAV radio frequency.

Figure 15-7 Using the number pad may be the fastest way to enter a radio frequency. *© Max Trescott*

Frequencies can also be entered from the Control Unit in the central console in two ways. To enter a COM or NAV frequency, first press the COM or NAV key respectively. Then use the center console's FMS knobs to enter a COM or NAV frequency.

Perhaps the fastest way to enter a single frequency is to use the number pad on the Control unit. Auto-tuning, described at the end of this section, may be the fastest way to enter multiple frequencies associated with a single airport. To enter a frequency with the number pad, first press the Control Unit's COM or NAV key to place the tuning selection box on the COM or NAV frequencies. If it's on the correct radio, type the numbers of the radio frequency using the number pad (figure 15-7). To tune the other radio, push the center of the COM/NAV knob before entering a radio frequency with the number pad or the COM/NAV knobs. When finished, you may want to push the FMS key, to return the Control Unit's FMS knobs to a known state.

Frequencies can be auto-tuned from virtually any MFD page listing a frequency or from the nearest airports by pushing the PFD's NRST/REF softkey. To auto-tune a frequency, press the FMS knobs to get a cursor, scroll with the large FMS knob to highlight a frequency and press the ENT key. There are a number of other radio features that are common to both the Perspective and G1000. Consult Chapter 5 for full details.

Figure 15-8 Early Perspective aircraft use the GMA 347 audio panel. © *Max Trescott*

Audio Panel

Perspective aircraft use the GMA 347 (figure 15-8) and, beginning in 2012, the GMA 350 (figure 15-9). Pressing the COM1/MIC or COM2/MIC key selects a radio for transmitting. Push the COM1 or COM2 key when you want to listen to two radios simultaneously, such as when you're listening to the ATIS on approach to an airport. The NAV keys let you listen to a navigation radio. The COM 1/2 key on the GMA 347 lets the pilot and copilot talk simultaneously on separate radios; pressing both MIC keys simultaneously enables this mode on the GMA 350.

Figure 15-9 Beginning in 2012, the GMA 350 audio panel was installed in Perspective aircraft © *Garmin Ltd. or its affiliates*

Both audio panels have a built-in marker beacon receiver used to identify marker locations on an ILS approach. To hear marker beacon Morse code audio, push the MKR/MUTE key to illuminate its annunciator. When the marker beacon is audible, pushing the MKR/MUTE key again mutes the audio. The SENS key on the GMA 347 increases the sensitivity of the marker beacon receiver. The GMA 350 uses an external switch to set marker sensitivity.

On the GMA 347, intercom volume is set with a pair of concentric knobs on the left for the pilot and another pair on the right for the copilot and passengers. The inner knobs control the intercom volume. Pulling the inner right volume knob lets you control the passenger's intercom volume. On the GMA 350, turning the outer knob positions a cursor. When the cursor is on PILOT, COPLT, or PASS, the inner knob adjusts the intercom volume for that listener.

Automatic squelch is enabled on each microphone input, but a manual squelch is available if initial syllables are clipped (squelch too tight) or you hear continuous background noise (squelch open). On the GMA 347, to enable manual squelch press the left center knob. Then turn the left outer knob to set the pilot's squelch. Turn the right outer knob to set the copilot and passenger's squelch. Do NOT press the left inner knob again, or the squelch will revert to automatic mode. On the GMA 350, turn the large knob to put the cursor on MAN SQ. Then turn the smaller knob to where the background noise first goes away.

The intercom has multiple isolation modes that provide a variety of ways to isolate the pilot, copilot, crew (both the pilot and copilot), and passengers from each other. For everyone to be connected on the GMA

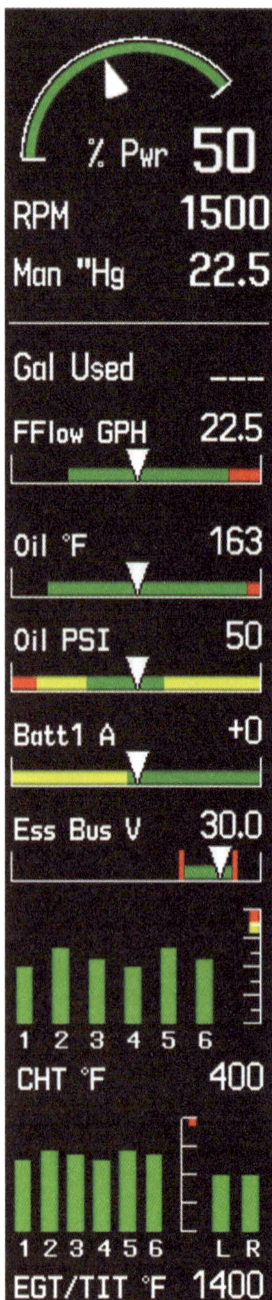

Figure 15-10 Typical Engine page from Cirrus Design SR22T. *© Garmin Ltd. or its affiliates*

347, the PILOT and COPLT LEDs are out, but on the GMA 350 the PILOT, COPLT, and PASS keys must all be lit.

A digital recorder can play back COM audio. Pressing the PLAY key once plays back the most recent transmission. Pressing the key twice plays the next oldest transmission and additional key presses bring up earlier transmissions in sequence.

The SPKR key is used to direct audio from any of the radios over the speaker. A Passenger Address mode lets you make in-cabin announcements over the aircraft's speaker. To enable it on either audio panel, hold the SPKR key for two seconds and then make your announcement.

Engine Indication System

The engine indication system (EIS) is the portion of Perspective and G1000 systems that varies the most from manufacturer to manufacturer and even across airplane models within a manufacturer's line of aircraft. Therefore, it's important that you become familiar with the documentation for the engine indication system in the aircraft you fly and follow that documentation wherever it may conflict with this book.

Like all G1000 aircraft, the Perspective EIS displays critical data along the left side of the MFD during flight (figure 15-10). When the Display Backup button is pressed to put the system into Reversionary mode, the EIS data is combined with PFD data and displayed on both the PFD and MFD. Data displayed includes % power, rpm, manifold pressure, electrical and fuel data and optional ice protection information.

Color is significant. Green bands indicate normal ranges of operation; yellow and red bands indicate caution and warning, respectively. White or uncolored bands are for areas outside of normal operation. If instrument data is invalid or unavailable, a red "X" is displayed across the instrument.

Pressing the MFD's ENGINE softkey displays the EIS – Engine page (see Appendix D). This is a full screen MFD page that displays all engine, fuel, fuel calculations, electrical, and air density data. It also includes oxygen and ice protection information for aircraft in which these options are installed. Many pilots like displaying this page for takeoff, so that they can easily verify that the engine is developing full power on the takeoff roll. It's also the page that you'll want to use for leaning, accessing the anti-icing system controls and for accessing the fuel totalizer if you didn't set it properly after engine start. Note: displaying this page removes traffic displays from the MFD. When using this page, configure the PFD's Inset Map to display traffic information and monitor it there.

You can lean the engine manually by watching the temperatures as you adjust the mixture, or you can press the ASSIST softkey, described in Chapter 6, to aid in the process. Some aircraft, such as the SR22T are leaned by setting a target fuel flow while monitoring the fuel flow indicator. Generally, you lean after you've reached your cruise altitude and have set the power as recommended by the aircraft manufacturer.

though some aircraft can be leaned during climb. It's important to note that you should follow the leaning instructions in your POH rather than the general instructions provided here.

For aircraft with an optional ice protection system or Flight into Known Icing (FIKI) system, a gauge on the EIS – Engine page indicates the amount of TKS fluid in each tank. Operation of these systems is beyond the scope of this book. Refer to your aircraft's POH and a factory trained flight instructor for operating details.

Fuel Totalizer

One of the EIS's most important functions is the fuel totalizer, which displays the fuel flow rate, the number of gallons used and the number of gallons remaining in the fuel tanks. However, in order to work correctly, *it is critical that you reset the fuel totalizer whenever you add fuel to the tanks.* Also, the fuel range ring and trip planning functions, described in Chapter 7, will not indicate properly if the fuel quantity is not reset.

In G1000 systems, it's easy to overlook resetting the fuel totalizer. But the Perspective glass cockpit differs in that it forces you to view the Initial Usable Fuel screen after engine startup, as it's one of the MFD pages that you need to cycle through before reaching the main MFD pages. You can also access this page at any time by pressing the MFD's ENGINE and FUEL softkeys.

When the Initial Usable Fuel page is displayed (figure 15-11), press either the FULL or TAB softkeys, depending upon the level to which the fuel tanks have been filled. Or, if you added a specific number of gallons and the fuel is not full or at the tabs, enter the number of gallons added to the plane. Use the large FMS knob to change the fuel totalizer in 10 gallon increments and the small FMS knob for 1 gallon increments. When you're finished, press the SAVE softkey.

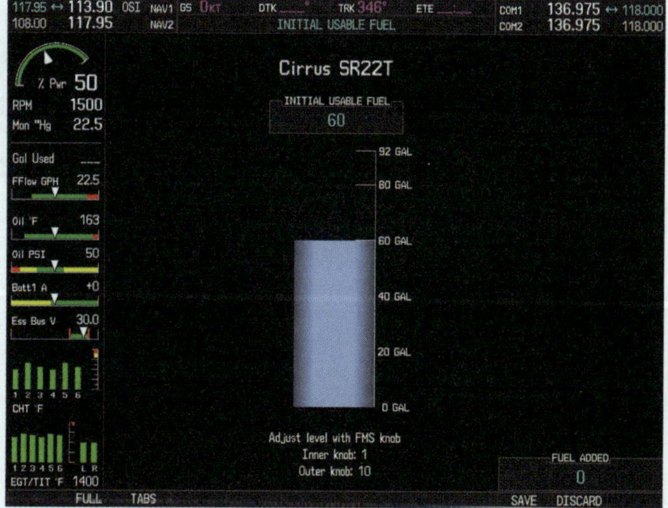

Figure 15-11 The Initial Fuel page lets you set the full totalizer to account for any fuel that you've added to the plane.
© Garmin Ltd. or its affiliates

Fuel issues represent 12% of all General Aviation accidents, yet they are among the easiest of accidents to avoid. Always be conservative in your fuel calculations. Whenever I set the fuel totalizer, I generally subtract 5 gallon as an additional fuel buffer. I'll joke with pilots that I'm subtracting one gallon for my wife, one for each of my kids and so on. It helps make the point that you never want to run short of fuel and should set the fuel totalizer so that you are guaranteed to have more fuel than is displayed.

MFD

Like the Perspective's PFD, the MFD differs from G1000 displays in that it has no knobs or keys, in this case, along the right side of the display (figure 15-12). The CRS, HDG and ALT SEL knobs are found only on the Perspective Control Unit (figure 15-7). The only knobs on

Figure 15-12 The Perspective features a 12-inch Multifunction Display. *© Max Trescott*

the MFD's left bezel are for controlling the NAV radios.

In the upper right of the MFD, a new Destination Airport Information window appears instead of the COM frequencies displayed in the upper right of the G1000's MFD. The window includes the destination airport identifier, fuel remaining at airport (FOD), distance, estimated time en route and bearing to airport. The destination airport is automatically selected.

The destination airport is defined as:

1) The last airport in the active flight plan if:
- No arrival or approach is loaded, or
- An arrival waypoint is part of the active leg and no approach is loaded, or
- The active leg is past the MAP

2) The airport prior to the procedure(s) if:
- An arrival or approach are loaded but not active

3) The airport associated with the approach if:
- An arrival waypoint is part of the active leg and an approach is loaded, or
- The approach is active

4) The direct-to waypoint if:
- The direct-to waypoint is not in the active flight plan and is an airport.

Otherwise, the destination airport is undefined and all of the fields in the Destination Airport Information window are filled with dashes.

To display traffic on the Navigation Map page, the page must in the Heading Up orientation. This often confuses G1000 pilots, who are used to being able to see traffic on this page regardless of orientation. Apparently when Perspective was certified, the FAA felt that other map orientations could confuse pilots about where to look out the window for traffic.

Figure 15-13 The length of the track vector can be specified in minutes or seconds using the keypad's MENU key. *© Garmin Ltd. or its affiliates*

The Perspective also has a different track vector from the G1000 track vector shown in figure 7-11. The Perspective's track vector is a solid blue line segment that extends to a selectable distance as short as 30 seconds or as long as 20 minutes using the MENU key and the Map Setup command (figure 15-13). Another difference is that the vector can show up to 90° of a turn in the 30 and 60 second modes.

Later model Perspective aircraft, and earlier ones updated with software version 4 or later, can import and export flight plans, letting you create a flight plan at home and later upload it into the aircraft. This feature, available in a few G1000-equipped aircraft including the TBM 850, is described at the end of Chapter 14.

MFD Page Navigation

Page navigation on the Perspective's MFD varies depending upon the version of software installed in the aircraft. In early Perspective aircraft, page navigation is identical to that used in the G1000 (figure 7-3). The pages are organized into four chapters or page groups, selected by turning the large FMS knob. The groups are MAP, WPT (waypoint), AUX (auxiliary) and NRST (nearest). As you turn the large knob, the label for the group selected is highlighted in cyan. Note: there's also a fifth page group that's activated by pushing the FPL key, discussed in Chapter 9.

Next to the group labels are a series of open squares that represent the number of pages in the currently selected group. One of the squares will always be filled in, indicating the page within the group that's currently displayed. You can select other pages in the group by turning the small FMS knob. Each page has a name and you'll find it at the top of the MFD display, below the Navigation Status bar.

Organizationally, the most commonly used groups and pages are located at each end, so that you can reach them quickly. For example, twisting both knobs to the far left selects the Navigation Map page, which is probably the one used most in flight. Twisting the large knob to the far right brings up the Nearest Airports page, which may be important in an emergency.

If you ever get lost while navigating the pages and want to get back to a known state, push the CLR key and hold it for two seconds. This will take you to the Navigation Map page, the first page in the MAP group. You can then get to any other page easily from this known position.

Later model Perspective aircraft, and earlier ones updated with software version 4 or later, still use the large and small FMS knobs to navigate the pages, however a different page guide is used for navigation. On these later systems, the page guide disappears from the lower right a few seconds after you stop turning the FMS knobs, slightly increasing the MFD's display area. The number of seconds for this timeout is user-settable.

The page groups selected with the large FMS knob are MAP, WPT (waypoint), AUX (auxiliary), FPL, √LST (checklist), NRST (nearest) and EIS (Engine Indication System). In addition, rather than using empty squares to represent the pages in each group, the page guide displays the page names for every page in the currently selected group (figure 15-14). Turning the small FMS knob selects a page in the current group. Both the current group and the current page name are highlighted in cyan.

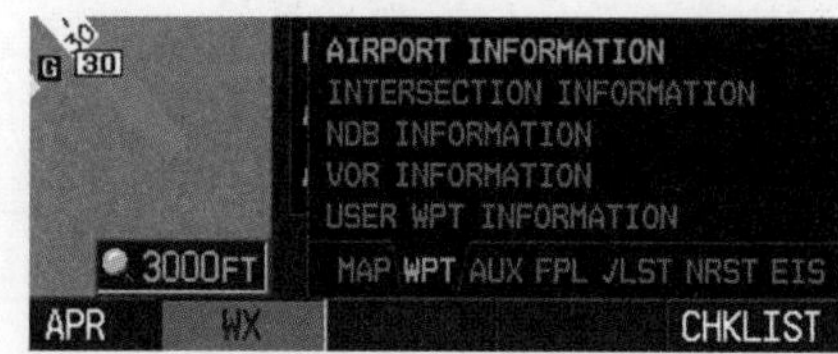

Figure 15-14 The Perspective MFD page guide displays page names for the selected group. Here, the Airport Information page in the WPT group is selected. *© Garmin Ltd. or its affiliates*

Users can configure the number of clicks of the FMS knobs it takes to display the page guide and to change the currently selected page. When CHANGE ON 1st CLICK is configured off, the first click of the

Figure 15-15 Use the AUX – System Setup page to configure how long the MFD's page guide remains on the screen before timing out. *© Garmin Ltd. or its affiliates*

FMS knob displays the page guide, but does not navigate away from the currently selected page. A second click of the FMS knobs is required to change to a different page. When CHANGE ON 1st CLICK is configured on, the first click of a FMS knob displays the page guide and changes the page displayed on the MFD. For example, if you're on the main Map page, a single click of the small FMS knob will select the Traffic page. Experienced pilots who know the page layout will probably prefer this latter configuration.

To configure this feature, go to the AUX – System Setup page, the fourth page in the AUX group. Press the FMS knob to get a cursor and scroll with the large FMS knob to highlight the CHANGE ON 1st CLICK field (figure 15-15). Then turn the small FMS knob to select ON or OFF. To change the number of seconds required before the page guide times out and is removed from the display, turn the large FMS knob to highlight the TIMEOUT SECONDS field. Then turn the small FMS knob to select the number of seconds. Press the FMS knob to remove the cursor.

Perspective Autopilot

The Garmin GFC 700 autopilot used in the Perspective glass cockpit operates in the same way as the GFC 700 used in the Garmin G1000 and described in detail in Chapter 10. The most noticeable difference is that the Perspective uses a new control panel (figure 15-16), located in the center console. Instead of separate UP/DOWN keys, a wheel is used to select climb and descent rates. The Perspective's IAS (Indicated Airspeed) key performs the same function as the FLC (Flight Level Change) key found in GFC 700-equipped G1000 aircraft.

An optional yaw damper is available. Without the yaw damper, pilots need to push and hold the rudder pedals appropriate to the climb, descent or turn they're performing.

The Perspective also includes a new LVL key. When pressed, it engages the autopilot, rolls the wings level, and maintains an aircraft attitude that provides level flight. It does not track a course or heading or maintain an altitude. Pressing the LVL key cancels any armed or active modes. After the LVL key is pushed, other modes can be selected by pressing other autopilot mode keys.

Pilots familiar with Avidyne Entegra glass cockpits and transitioning into the Perspective will want to note key differences between the Perspective's autopilot and S–TEC autopilots used in many Entegra systems. First, the annunciators for the Perspective autopilot are in the AFCS Status bar near the top of the PFD, far away from the autopilot keys in the center console. But S–TEC autopilot users are accustomed to seeing annunciations just above the autopilot keys.

A common error I see transitioning pilots make is that they don't look at the AFCS Status bar after they've pushed an autopilot key. Thus they don't know whether they actually set the mode they think they selected. Pilots should verify every autopilot key press to avoid an automation surprise. It's also important to note whether a mode is already active or armed to become active later.

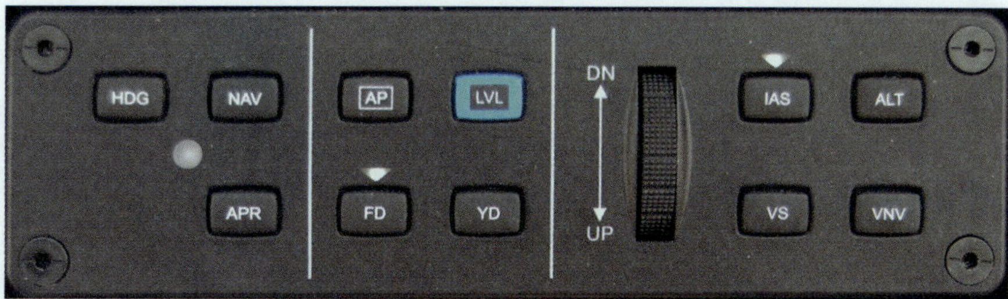

Figure 15-16 A separate control panel, the GMC 705, controls the autopilot in the Cirrus Perspective. It substitutes a wheel for the UP/DOWN buttons and adds a new LVL key. *© Max Trescott*

Pilots new to using the GFC 700 may also fail to realize that pushing autopilot mode keys (with the exception of the LVL key) only engages the Flight Director. Since they see the Flight Director's command bars and the roll and pitch mode annunciations in the PFD's AFCS Status bar, they often believe that the autopilot is engaged. However, pilots must always push the AP key to engage the autopilot (unless they've pushed the LVL key). If they don't see a green AP annunciator in the PFD's AFCS Status bar, the autopilot is not engaged.

Enhanced Vision System

An Enhanced Vision System (EVS) that uses an external infrared camera is a Perspective option. It's designed to enhance situation awareness at night or in haze, however it cannot see through clouds. It generates a black and white image, viewed on the AUX group Video page, in which hotter objects (such as runways and lights) appear whiter on the display. The EVS recalibrates itself every 5 minutes, or when manually initiated by the pilot, to optimize the image. When this occurs, the image is interrupted for 1 second. If the video signal is completely interrupted, No Video or NO DATA AVAILABLE may appear on the display.

When the AUX – Video page is displayed on the MFD, softkeys become available to control the EVS. Pressing the VID ZM+ and VID ZM- softkeys switches the display magnification between 1X and 2X. Normally, the Video page is split with EVS on top and a map displayed on the bottom half of the page. Pushing the HIDE MAP softkey removes the map and expands the EVS view to fill the entire page (figure 15-17). Pushing the HIDE MAP softkey again restores the map and the split view.

Pressing the SETUP softkey brings up a new level of softkeys. The CNTRST- and CNTRST+ softkeys change the display contrast, the BRIGHT- and BRIGHT+ softkeys change the display brightness and the SAT- and SAT+ softkeys change the display saturation. Changes are made in 5% increments from 0 to 100%. These adjustments can also be made by pressing the MENU key and choosing a menu option

TIP

Some of the GFC 700 keys toggle between two different modes. For example, pressing the HDG key toggles between HDG and ROL modes. As a result, pilots often push the correct key but don't get the desired mode, since they don't check the AFCS Status bar before or after they pressing a key. One Cirrus CSIP flight instructor recommends the following procedure when pushing autopilot keys:

1) Look at the current modes annunciated.
2) Push an autopilot key to make a change.
3) Confirm the change on the AFCS Status bar.

System Failures

Most Perspective aircraft have dual AHRS for redundancy, so that the loss of one AHRS in some cases allows the autopilot to continue to be used, though it may disconnect and need to be re-engaged.

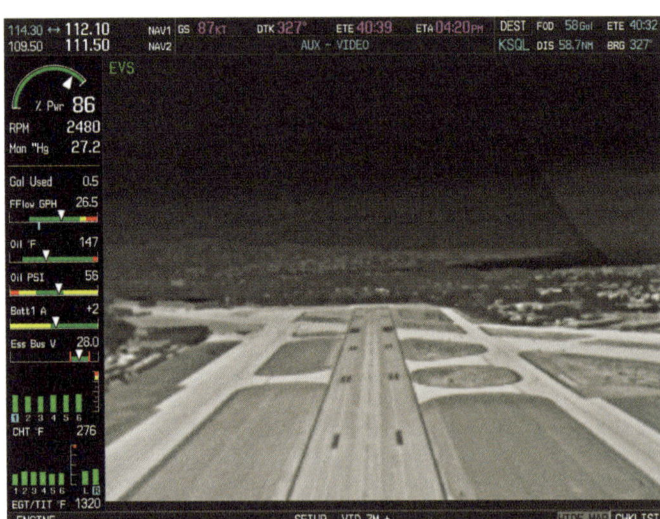

Figure 15-17 Hotter objects appear whiter, making it easier to spot the runway and obstacles at night or in haze.
© Garmin Ltd. or its affiliates

While dual ADCs are also available, relatively few aircraft are shipped with a second ADC. Comparators are used to compare the critical values generated by dual sensors to detect: 1) a significant discrepancy between their outputs or 2) the failure of a unit. In the former case, a discrepancy results in a MISCOMP (miscompare) annunciator appearing in the Comparator Window, which appears in the upper right of the PFD. In the latter case, when there is no data from one or both units of a particular type, a NO COMP (no compare) annunciator appears.

Generally, a MISCOMP annunciation is worse than a NO COMP, since the system cannot determine which sensor is accurate and must ignore both. As long as a MISCOMP is displayed, the autopilot cannot be engaged. Generally the system quickly recognizes which sensor has failed and the MISCOMP annunciation becomes a NO COMP, allowing the pilot to re-engage the autopilot.

System Failures with Redundant AHRS

In Perspective systems with dual AHRS, a MISCOMP annunciation appears for the following differences in outputs:

- HDG MISCOMP — heading difference > 6 degrees
- PIT MISCOMP — pitch difference > 5 degrees
- ROL MISCOMP — roll difference > 6 degrees

When one of these MISCOMPs appears in the Comparator Window, the autopilot disconnects and the autopilot disengage chime is heard. If just the magnetometer fails, then only compass data is lost and a red X is displayed over the Heading box.

Usually the Perspective system quickly recognizes which AHRS has failed. When it does, a MISCOMP annunciation is replaced by a NO COMP annunciation, meaning there is no data from one or both AHRS. If only AHRS1 has failed, the Reversionary Sensor Window appears on the right side of the PFD, and a USING AHRS2 annunciation appears. The pilot should then reengage the autopilot.

In some cases, a MISCOMP remains. You can try to identify the erratic unit and pull its circuit breaker so the MISCOMP becomes a NO COMP and you can re-engage the autopilot. To identify the best AHRS, press the PFD's SENSOR softkey and select the AHRS units one at a time. Compare each unit with the standby attitude indicator, any visual references you may have, or even the GPS TRK (ground track) to determine if the aircraft is changing its heading in a turn. If you can identify the erratic AHRS, pull its circuit breaker. After the MISCOMP annunciator disappears, attempt to re-engage the autopilot.

If all AHRS data is lost, you should fly with reference to your aircraft's standby attitude indicator. You may also want to configure the Track Vector and the Nav Range Ring on the MFD, since these will help you easily identify your ground track. Also, consider setting one of the MFD Navigation Status Bar fields to XTK (crosstrack) so that you can easily identify your course deviation. Note that if the magnetometer or both AHRS fail, any MFD maps that use a heading up orientation, such as the Traffic and Stormscope pages, will automatically switch to a Track Up orientation.

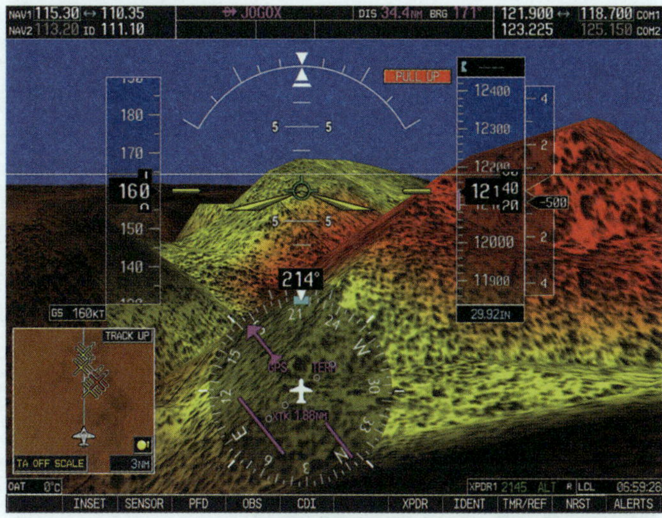

Figure 15-18 The Flight Path Marker, shows the projected path of the aircraft, in this case into the side of the mountain. *© Garmin Ltd. or its affiliates*

System Failures with Redundant ADCs

In those few aircraft with dual ADCs, no pilot action is required in the case of an ADC failure. If the comparator detects a significant difference between the ADCs, a MISCOMP annunciator appears in the Comparator Window. The system then automatically connects the operating ADC to the autopilot and switches the PFD to display its output.

If a NO COMP message appears, then there is no data from one or both ADCs. If only ADC1 has failed, the system automatically switches the autopilot to the operating ADC and the autopilot does not disengage. The Reversionary Sensor Window appears on the right side of the PFD and a USING ADC2 annunciation appears. Again, no pilot action is required.

Insertion Point and Quick Select Box

Garmin 430/530 and G1000 users have to remember that new waypoints are added before, not after the flight plan cursor. Later software updates to the Perspective continuously display a small triangle indicating that new waypoints are inserted above the MFD's flight plan cursor (figure 15-19). Also, Perspective users no longer have to first push the FMS knob to get a cursor; they can just start typing in a new identifier or altitude. That's because a new Quick Select Box of dashed white lines shows the cursor position even when the cursor is off. The box's position can be moved with the joystick.

Weather from MFD Flight Plan

A Selected Waypoint Weather window has been added to the bottom of the MFD's Flight Plan to display textual METAR data. A small flag appears in the flight plan next to airports and waypoints with nearby weather information. To view METAR data, scroll the cursor or the Quick Select Box over the desired waypoint. For non-airport waypoints, the distance and direction from the waypoint to the nearby airport with weather information is listed.

ESP: Electronic Stability and Protection

The optional ESP works to maintain the aircraft within normal pitch, roll, and airspeed parameters by automatically engaging one or more servos when the aircraft is near a defined pitch, roll, and/or airspeed operating limit. Pilots will perceive a resistance to their control movements as the system tries to return the aircraft to more normal operating parameters. If the aircraft deviates further from the desired attitude or airspeed, the system applies increasing force. A pilot can override ESP by pressing and holding the AP DISC autopilot disconnect switch.

ESP is enabled from the System Setup page in the AUX group. From that page, press the SETUP2 softkey. Scroll the cursor to the STABILITY & PROTECTION field and turn the small FMS knob to enable or disable ESP. When ESP in enabled, double tick marks appear on the roll scale of the attitude indicator to indicate the limits where the system will engage and then disengage. Initially, they indicate 45°. If the aircraft exceeds 45°, the system engages and the double tick marks move to 30°, where ESP will disengage.

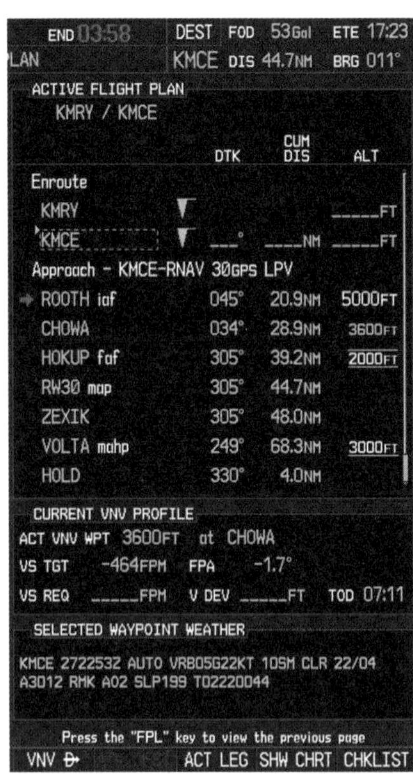

Figure 15-19 A small triangle indicates that new waypoints are inserted above the dashed white line cursor position. Note the blue flags indicating METARs available for KMRY and KMCE. KMCE weather is displayed at the bottom.
© Garmin Ltd. or its affiliates

Hypoxia Recognition

This optional feature detects pilot incapacitation by monitoring elapsed time since the most recent Perspective system key push, excluding the audio panel and push-to-talk switches. If a period of inactivity exceeds a system limit, which is shorter at higher altitudes, an "ARE YOU ALERT?" message is generated that causes the ALERTS softkey to flash white. Pressing the ALERTS or any other softkey or turning any knob resets the system. If the alert is not acknowledged within 60 seconds, a "HYPOXIA ALERT" message is generated and a yellow CAUTION softkey flashes. If that alert is not acknowledged within 60 seconds, an "AUTO DESCENT" Warning is displayed and "Automatic descent to 14,000FT in 60 seconds" is displayed in the Alerts window. If no interaction occurs, the GFC 700 autopilot descends to 14,000 feet in IAS mode at the maximum allowable airspeed for the aircraft. If no pilot interaction occurs after four minutes at 14,000 feet, the system descends to 12,500 feet.

Underspeed Protection

This feature monitors the airspeed when the autopilot is on and can initiate a descent to maintain a safe airspeed. At a speed between 80-90 knots, depending upon flap settings and whether TKS FIKI is on or off, an aural "AIRSPEED" alert is sounded. If the aircraft slows an additional 4 to 10 knots, depending upon configuration, a yellow MINSPD annunciator appears above the airspeed indicator. If the aircraft continues to slow and the stall warning sounds for at least one second, ROL and PIT modes become active and a pitch reference is selected to maintain a speed that's at least two knots above stall speed. Or, if the Vertical Speed or VNV mode was active, a pitch reference is selected to fly at the minimum commandable autopilot speed. An aural "AIRSPEED" alert will sound every five seconds and an UNDERSPEED PROTECT ACTIVE warning appears. After power is added and airspeed increases, the autopilot will revert to the vertical mode that was active before the underspeed condition.

Flying a Trip Behind the SR22 Perspective

We've discussed the Perspective system in general. Now let's take a trip and fly behind a Perspective-equipped Cirrus SR22T on a typical flight. We've chosen this aircraft because it was the first to include the Perspective glass cockpit and because it's one of the most popular aircraft in its class. If you fly a different Perspective-equipped aircraft, you'll find that many of the steps outlined here will still apply to your aircraft.

Note that the procedures provided here are generic and where they differ from your POH or checklist, you should use those in preference to this book. Also, many routine steps are left out, as our purpose in this section is to highlight differences in flying a Perspective-equipped aircraft, not to list every step required to fly a SR22.

Required Equipment and Limitations

First, before flying, you'll want to review the Garmin Reference Manual and your aircraft's POH to determine what limitations apply. Here are some typical system Limitations, however, you will need to read your manuals to get a complete list of all limitations that apply to your aircraft.

Operation is prohibited beyond 70° North and South latitude and in a few other areas close to these extreme northern and southern regions. Navigation cannot be predicated upon use of terrain or obstacle data displayed on the system, so you'll need to find another way to be absolutely certain that you avoid all obstacles and terrain. Use of the Traffic Map to maneuver to avoid traffic is prohibited. You can use the map to help you spot the traffic, but you're not supposed to maneuver to avoid the traffic until you actually see it, since the system is not a certified TCAS that gives instructions for avoiding other traffic.

Use of the Weather Map for hazardous weather penetration, such as thunderstorms is prohibited. Instead, you want to use the system's weather capabilities to fly well around weather. Don't use it to try and pick your way through holes that you think you see on the display.

As a pilot, you're hopefully aware that the FAA specifies in FAR 91.205 the equipment required to be operational in your aircraft for day VFR, night and IFR flight. If any of this equipment is not operational, you're not allowed to fly the aircraft unless you get a ferry permit from the FAA to allow you to bring the aircraft back to a place where it can be repaired. Manufacturers can also specify additional required equipment.

Some of the equipment always required by the FAA includes certain flight instruments, namely the airspeed indicator, altimeter and compass. Engine related instruments such as a tachometer, oil pressure and temperature and fuel gauges are also required.

Figure 15-20 Turning on Battery 2 powers the essentials bus, which feeds the PFD, AHRS, ADC and GIA1. It's a good way to check if the avionics cooling fan is working. *© Max Trescott*

Figure 15-21 If a flap light comes on when Battery 2 is on but Battery 1 is off, it means a diode has failed and Battery 2 is also powering the main electrical buses. Battery 2 would then drain rapidly if you have an alternator failure. *© Max Trescott*

You'll want to go to the Kinds of Operation Equipment List, or KOEL, in Section 2 of your POH to learn what equipment your aircraft manufacturer requires for different types of operation.

For example, in the Cirrus SR22, the Garmin Perspective Cockpit Reference Guide is required to be easily accessible by the pilot while in flight. The anti-collision light in the Cirrus SR22 is the strobes, so your strobes must be operational. Cirrus requires that the fuel flow indicator and ammeter be operational.

For night flight, the FAA requires navigation lights and a source of electrical power. Cirrus requires that the backlighting work for the PFD and MFD, so you'll need to check this before you go. In early model aircraft, the standby instruments were not backlit, so you were required to bring a flashlight.

It's equally important to read the Kinds of Operation Equipment List in section 2 of the POH to see what's never required. Interestingly, Battery 2 is not required for VFR flight, but is required for IFR flight. We recommend it even in VFR conditions, particularly if there's any chance that you may encounter IMC conditions during your flight. Some other things that are never required are the cylinder head temperature and exhaust temperature gauges and the wheel fairings.

Preflight

Part of the preflight includes turning on Battery (figure 15-20), verifying that the PFD display comes on and listening for the avionics cooling fan. You'll also verify that the flap position light is out, which confirms that Battery 2 is powering only the essentials bus. If the flap light is on (figure 15-21), it means that a diode has failed and that Battery 2 is also powering the main buses which, in an emergency, would waste power on unnecessary items. Note that the PFD operates with the avionics switches off, since it receives power through the Essentials bus. Also—and this will be a surprise to many pilots—the PFD and MFD are on when you start the engine.

About 15 to 20 seconds after the PFD comes on, check to see that all red "Xs" over the engine indicators are gone. The data is considered valid whenever the pointers on these gauges are visible. The ADC will come up next and "Xs" over the pitot-static instruments will be removed. The display remains dark (with no brown and blue background representing the ground and sky) until attitude data becomes available. After a total of about 60 seconds, the AHRS will come up and all "Xs" should be removed from the display.

Starting the Engine

After engine start, check the oil pressure and then verify that the alternator shows a positive charge and is now charging the batteries. Turn on the Avionics Bus and check the database expiration date at the bottom of the MFD screen to verify that the databases are current.

If you've added fuel, you'll need to set the fuel totalizer so that the proper amount of fuel is reflected when using the Trip Planning page and the Fuel Range Ring. This screen comes up after you push the MFD's ENT key several times to get though the initial screens. Then press either the FULL or TABS softkey, depending upon how much fuel is on board. Or, if you added a specific number of gallons, turn the small and large FMS knobs to add fuel in 1 and 10 gallon increments and press the SAVE softkey.

Next, go to the GPS Status page and press the GPS1 and GPS2 softkeys to verify that both GPS receivers are receiving multiple satellites. Finally, check the HSI. If a yellow "INTEG" annunciator appears, there aren't enough satellites to determine your position and verify integrity and you shouldn't use the GPS for primary navigation guidance.

Next, load the appropriate frequencies into your radio by using the Airport Information page. For example, you'll first want to load the ATIS or AWOS frequency and then load frequencies for clearance delivery or ground control and request taxi instructions. Finally, load the tower frequency. Remember to use this page to save time entering frequencies both at your departure and destination airports.

Before Takeoff

Before takeoff, check the flight instruments and verify that there are no red "Xs" over any of the indicators. Next, enter the altimeter setting into the system using the BARO knob and set the standby altimeter. Enter your first level-off altitude using the ALT SEL knob. Then perform the autopilot preflight and the usual engine run-up.

Prior to takeoff, set all COM and NAV radio frequencies. Also, set the CDI softkey to either VOR or GPS navigation, depending upon which you are using. If you're not using VOR navigation, enter your flight plan into the GPS. It's much faster, easier and safer to do this while you're stopped on the ground. After entering all of the waypoints, scroll through the entire flight plan to verify that each one was entered correctly. You may also want to look at the map to verify that the route looks correct.

Next, set up the Flight Director so that you are ready to engage the autopilot during your climb out. Press the GA switch to set the Flight Director for Take off mode. Then set the heading reference bug to the initial assigned heading. If the runway heading is your on-course heading, then you can also set press the HDG key to set the Flight Director's heading mode. If you'll initially be flying the runway heading before an assigned heading, leave the Flight Director in GA mode for takeoff and press the HDG key when you're able to turn on course. Verify the green GA and/or HDG annunicators in the AFCS Status bar displayed at the top of the PFD. Also, verify the green AP annuciator is off, indicating the autopilot is off, and prepare for takeoff.

Takeoff and Climb

After the aircraft is stable in climb and you've completed post-takeoff tasks such as raising the flaps, choose a pitch mode like IAS by pressing the IAS key and verify that the green IAS annunciator appears. If you weren't at the desired airspeed when you pushed the IAS key, roll the UP/DN wheel a few clicks as necessary to set the desired airspeed in the AFCS Status bar. Finally, verify that the white ALTS annunciator appears, indicating that the altitude hold mode is armed to level off at the preselected altitude. When you are more than 400 feet above the ground, push the AP key to engage the autopilot and verify that the green AP annunciator appears.

To track a course, select the desired navigation source, GPS, NAV1 or NAV2, with the CDI softkey. Then push the autopilot's NAV key and verify that a GPS or VOR annunciator appears. If it's green, it's because you're relatively close to the desired course and the autopilot is now tracking the navigation signal. If it's white, the NAV mode is armed and will remain armed until you steer the airplane with the HDG knob to an angle that will intercept the desired course or if your clearance permits (e.g. a VFR departure), you can push the Direct, ENT, ENT keys to redraw the desired course from your present position to the active waypoint.

As you continue to climb, go through your aircraft's climb checklist. At 1000 feet from your preselected altitude, the selected altitude flashes. This is a reminder to check that the autopilot levels off at the selected altitude. Look for the white ALTS annunciator and call out "1000 feet to go, altitude armed." At 200 feet below the selected altitude you'll hear the autopilot chime. As you reach your preselected altitude, verify that the autopilot actually levels off and that ALT is now displayed in green. Altitude hold mode is now active.

Then set cruise power and go through your cruise checklist. Next, lean the engine per the Airplane Flight Manual. In the case of the turbo SR22, you'll probably set the mixture to a specific fuel flow in gallons per hour, depending upon the percent power you desire. For other aircraft, you might go to the MFD and press the ENGINE and ASSIST softkeys for assistance in leaning.

Cruise

Throughout the entire flight, you need to search for traffic visually. Generally, you'll leave the MFD set on the Navigation Map page, with TRAFFIC and PROFILE selected along with other features you desire. Note that if you have the Navigation Map zoomed out, the traffic will be tightly clustered in the center of the screen. Thus, whenever you receive a traffic alert, you may want to turn the small FMS knob one click so you can see the dedicated Traffic Map page, or look for the yellow dot on the PFD.

During the flight, you may want to check the weather. Use the MFD's flight plan (figure 15-19) or Airport Information page for METARs. For other weather data, turn to the Weather Data Link page. You might also want to monitor the ATIS of airports en route, since this might give you an early warning of changing weather. You'll also want to enable the Fuel Range Ring or use the Trip Planning page to monitor whether adverse winds might require an unplanned fuel stop. Remember that this fuel information will be accurate only if you correctly set the fuel totalizer before you took off.

Night

Any night flight brings additional risks and requires additional planning. For example, a high percentage of night accidents occur during approach and descent to the destination, since it's harder to spot terrain. The accident rates are highest in dark night conditions with no moonlight. Also cockpit lighting can be an issue.

At night, turn down the brightness of the displays so that your eyes can better adapt to darkness and you can see more outside the cockpit. You'll probably want to dim the MFD even more than the PFD using the MENU key on the PFD. To dim it separately, press the MENU key on the PFD and follow the instructions in Chapter 4.

While on the Navigation Map page, you may want to press the MAP and TOPO softkeys to turn off the topographical information, since it adds to the overall brightness. One of the greatest contributions that the system brings to night flight is terrain awareness. This can be activated by pushing the MAP and TERRAIN softkeys from the Navigation Map page. Alternatively, you can use the Terrain Proximity page in the MAP page group. During the flight, make sure that you avoid any areas *painted in yellow or red. I strongly urge you to use terrain awareness capability or SVT at night*, or whenever you're uncertain about surrounding terrain. Many fatal accidents would be avoided if every pilot had this capability and used it. If you have the optional EVS, consider displaying it during the descent, approach and landing phases.

Approach for Landing

As you approach your destination airport, you'll want to prepare early for landing. This includes starting your descent, getting the ATIS information and determining your entry into the airport traffic pattern. If you want the Perspective to calculate the start of your descent, push the FPL key and enter target altitudes into the MFD's vertical flight plan. Then press the ENBL VNV softkey and set your desired descent rate in the VNV Profile window below your flight plan. Press the MENU key, select "VNAV Messages On?" and the Perspective will notify you when to start a descent.

The Airport Information page provides information that you'll want to know about your destination airport. First, use it to load the ATIS or AWOS frequency into a COM radio and pick up the current weather as soon as you can. If possible, figure out from the winds which runway you're most likely to use. Also, note whether the surface winds are vastly different from your winds aloft, which may suggest the presence of wind shear or turbulence. While you're loading frequencies from this page, remember to load tower and ground frequencies too.

Next, use the map on this page, which is always North Up, to orient yourself for your arrival. To do that, look at the bottom of the HSI and determine the direction from which you're arriving. Plan your entry by looking at the map and runways and visualizing from which quadrant of the map you'll be arriving. After you've planned your entry, return to the Navigation Map page.

Landing

Prior to landing, you'll need to disconnect the autopilot before descending below 1000 feet AGL, unless you're on an instrument approach. Once you've safely entered the traffic pattern, you may want to turn off the TERRAIN softkey, particularly at night. Otherwise, you may get distracted as the MFD turns completely red during landing. Audio alerts from the traffic system are inhibited whenever the flaps are not fully retracted, though you can still visually monitor traffic.

After landing, taxi off the runway, stop and go through your After Landing checklist. Then follow the Shutdown checklist to shut down your airplane.

Summary

The Perspective software is expected to evolve rapidly and some features found only in the Perspective will undoubtedly be added to future G1000 software revisions. In the next chapter, we'll talk about some G1000 features currently found only in VLJs.

Chapter 16:
Very Light Jets and Turboprops

Historically, aircraft avionic systems evolved slowly. Products stayed on the market for many years with few changes until they were replaced by entirely new models. The G1000 and Perspective break that paradigm. First, with two large software-driven displays, new features can continually be added in far less time than it took to design, manufacture, and release traditional avionics. In some cases, the features may be included in a major software revision and will appear in all G1000 and Perspective aircraft as the manufacturers upgrade the software in their aircraft. In other cases, new features may be specific to a particular manufacturer or airframe.

A multiple bus architecture that includes Ethernet, RS-232 and ARINC 429 makes it easy for new devices to be designed and connected to the system. These could be new LRUs that plug into the system card cage or external devices that connect to the system. To get an idea of how rapidly change occurs, examine the new features, many of which we predicted in earlier editions of this book, introduced since the G1000 started shipping in 2004.

New Jet & Turboprop Features:

- Radar Altimeter
- TCAS II
- AC-U-KWIK directory
- Class A TAWS

New Perspective features:

- Hypoxia Recognition
- ESP: Electronic Stability and Protection
- Overspeed and Underspeed Protection

New software features, depending upon the manufacturer, include:

- Electronic Checklists
- Obstruction database
- Bearing Pointers
- Flight Director
- Electronic approach charts

- Airways on maps and in flight plans
- Synthetic Vision Technology (SVT)
- Terrain Profile View
- AOPA Directory
- Flight Data Logging
- Auxiliary Video
- Import/Export Flight Plans

New devices supported include:

- GDL 69A Data Link Weather & Radio module
- DME and ADF receivers
- GFC 700 integrated autopilot
- GWX 68 Weather Radar
- TAS Systems from Garmin, L-3, Honeywell and Avidyne
- TAWS-B Terrain Warning System
- WAAS-enabled version of the GPS receivers that allows you to fly precision approaches with ILS-like performance
- GDL 90 ADS-B Transceiver
- Alphanumeric keypad
- Carbon Monoxide monitor
- GSR 56 Iridium Transceiver for voice and text data and worldwide weather

Given the number of enhancements that have occurred in the first eight years, imagine the new features and modules that may become available over the next 10 years. The biggest change of all, of course, was the introduction of the G1000 into the next generation of aircraft—the Very Light Jets.

Very Light Jets

Not only are these exciting times for avionics, but we're witnessing the development of an entirely new class of aircraft—the Very Light Jets. These aircraft, enabled by the development of smaller, low cost jet engines, are attracting considerable attention.

Figure 16-1 Cessna Mustang cockpit mockup. © *Max Trescott*

When first announced, some of the early orders were placed for less than $1 million. As with almost all aircraft development, the costs have risen over time and most VLJs will probably ship out at over $2 million.

G1000 equipped VLJs

We'll talk about the Cessna Mustang, as it's representative of how other VLJs and turboprops are equipped. It uses a three-display version of the G1000, with the two outer displays configured as identical PFDs, a 15-inch MFD located in the center of the instrument panel and dual audio panels (figure 16-1). Diamond is using 12-inch PFDs and a 15-inch MFD in the D-Jet.

One of the best features is the full alphanumeric keypad located near the center of the console where either pilot can access it easily. This should save knob twisting when entering identifiers into a flight plan. An alphanumeric keypad is shipped in most jet and turboprop implementations and in some piston systems, including the Cirrus SR20 and SR22 and the Cessna/Columbia 350 and 400. GA pilots can only hope that keypads will eventually become available in all G1000-equipped aircraft.

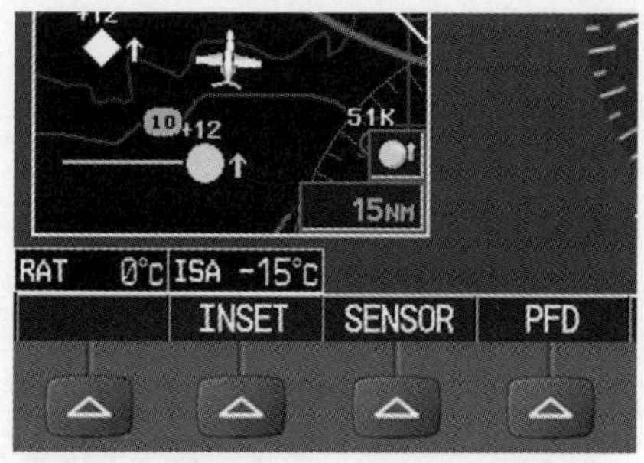

Figure 16-2 The Mustang's SENSOR softkey brings up new softkeys for the ADC and AHRS. © Garmin Ltd. or its affiliates

All G1000-equipped VLJs and turboprops use the new GFC 700 autopilot. However, unlike most piston-engine installations, where the autopilot keys are on the MFD bezel, the Mustang has a separate GMC 710 Control unit and it includes some new functions. A SPD key on the GMC 710 toggles the airspeed reference, displayed at the top of the airspeed indicator and used by the autopilot's FLC mode, between Indicated Airspeed (IAS) and Mach units. A Bank key selects and deselects Low Bank Mode, which limits the maximum commanded roll angle to 18°. Low Bank Mode is automatically activated above 29,850 feet and deactivated when descending through 29,650 feet.

Figure 16-3 These softkeys let you manually select an ADC or AHRS. © Garmin Ltd. or its affiliates

The Mustang is also equipped with an Emergency Descent Mode (EDM) that is activated automatically when cabin pressurization is lost above 30,000 feet MSL. EDM automatically selects FLC mode with the Selected Altitude set to 15,000 feet and Heading Select mode with a Selected Heading set to 90° left of the current heading. When the red EDM annunciator appears on the PFD, pilots should reduce the throttles to idle and extend the speed brakes to achieve the maximum descent rate.

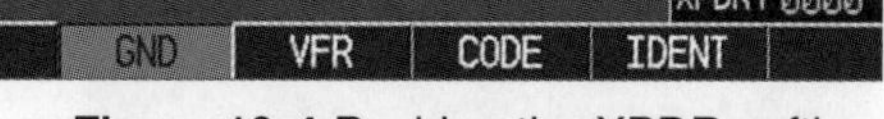

Figure 16-4 Pushing the XPDR softkey let's you select between two transponders. © Garmin Ltd. or its affiliates

Reliability is critical, and jet manufacturers try to remove single points of failure. For example, the Cessna Mustang uses two ADCs and two AHRSs, since these devices are so critical to generating the flight instrument displays. Pressing the Mustang's SENSOR softkey on the PFD (figure 16-2) brings up a new level of softkeys (figure 16-3) that let you select which ADC and AHRS are used to present information on the PFD. If differences in the data generated from each sensor exceed a specified amount, a Comparator Window appears in the upper right corner of the PFD which displays the discrepancy. If sensor values are unavailable, NO COMP is displayed in the Comparator Window.

Figure 16-5 Press the PFD key to bring up these softkeys that let you select between two aircraft presentations on the HSI. © Garmin Ltd. or its affiliates

Two transponders provide additional redundancy. Pressing the XPDR softkey brings up a new level of softkeys (figure 16-4) that include a XPDR1 and XPDR2 softkey. The transponder in use is also shown in the Transponder window, next to the squawk code. Flight crews can also enter a Flight ID of up to seven characters. To enter a Flight ID, push the TMR/REF softkey, scroll to FLT ID, use the FMS knobs to enter an ID, and press the ENT key.

A Baro Transition Alert can be set to notify pilots as they climb or

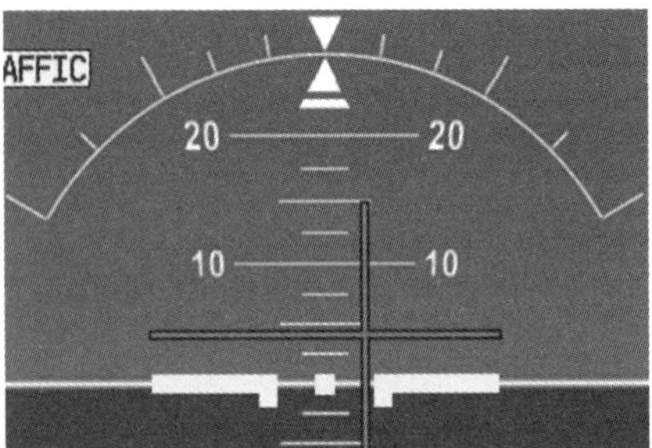

Figure 16-6 The X POINTR softkey selects this airplane symbol on the HSI. *© Garmin Ltd. or its affiliates*

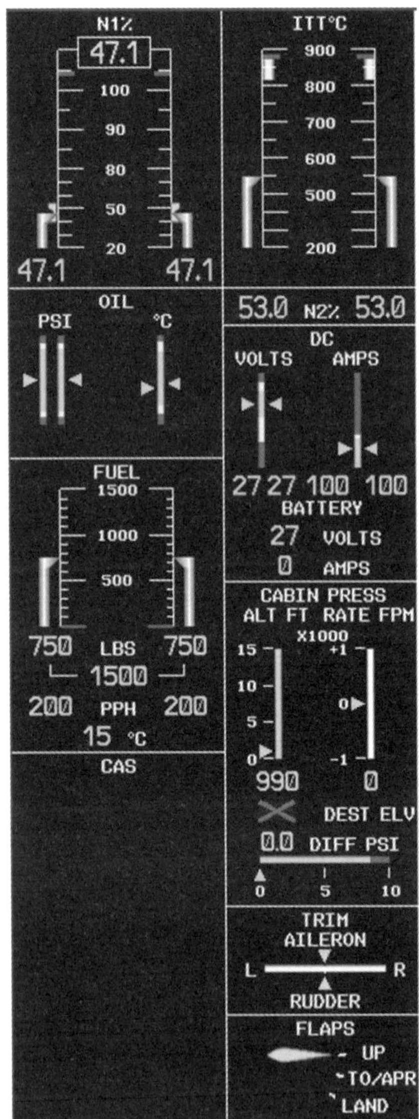

Figure 16-7 All Mustang engine instruments are shown simultaneously, resulting in a slightly smaller map area on the MFD *© Garmin Ltd. or its affiliates*

descend through the transition altitude, which is 18,000 feet in the U.S., but differs by country. The alert flashes the barometric pressure setting in light blue until the pressure setting is changed. The feature can be enabled or disabled and a transition altitude set from the AUX – System Setup page (figure 7-45).

You can also select the type of airplane symbol and command bars used on the attitude indicator. Press the PFD and FD FRMT softkeys to bring up a new level of softkeys (figure 16-5). The SNGL CUE softkey selects the inverted V symbol and command bars (figure 4-6) used in most G1000 aircraft, while the X POINTR softkey selects a miniature airplane symbol and command bars that use a vertical and a horizontal line (figure 16-6).

Below the Inset map are new temperature displays for Ram Air Temperature (RAT) and deviation from International Standard Atmosphere (ISA) (figure 16-5). Another difference is that the current Mach number is displayed below the Airspeed indicator for airspeeds at or above Mach 0.4 or at altitudes above 27,120 feet.

While most G1000 aircraft have one set of V speeds displayed next to the airspeed indicator, the Mustang has two: a set for takeoff and another for landing. Takeoff speeds include V1, Vr, V2, and Venr. Landing speeds include Vref and Vapr. To choose which speeds are displayed, press the TMR/REF softkey, then the MENU key, scroll to select the desired speeds to display and press the ENT key. You can select any combination of the takeoff and landing speeds on or off.

If the altimeter settings on the two PFDs differ by more than 0.02 in Hg, the readouts turn yellow. To synchronize the settings so that the same altimeter setting is shown on both PFDs, press the PFD's MENU key, scroll to highlight the "BARO SYNC" field, turn the small FMS knob to select ON and press the MENU key. The setting will remain synchronized for the entire flight. The same screen is also used to synchronize the CDIs so that the same navigation source is displayed on both PFDs. Once set, synchronization is not turned off until the power is cycled.

As you might expect, the Engine Indication System (EIS) varies considerably from piston-powered engine displays. A single display shows all parameters simultaneously, so no engine softkeys are required. The top left portion of the Mustang EIS displays N1 fan rotation speed for the left and right engines (figure 16-7). Percentage values are displayed graphically with sliders and numerically below the sliders. If the N1 values drop below 20%, the sliders are removed while the digital readout remains. The target N1 value is shown at the top in light blue.

Oil pressure and temperature are shown below the N1 display. When these are in the normal green operating range, no numeric values are displayed. Below this is the fuel display. Fuel quantities for each tank in pounds is displayed graphically with sliders and numerically below the sliders. Below this, fuel flow for each engine in pounds per hour is displayed along with the fuel temperature.

The top right portion of the Mustang EIS displays Interstage Turbine Temperatures (ITT) with a slider scale in °C. Digital readouts, not provided during normal operation, appear below the sliders during engine start, for temperatures below 200°C, and when values are in the caution or warning range. When the engine igniters are on, IGN annunciators appear in green at the top of the sliders.

GS 300KT DTK 269° TRK 271° ETE 04:13 | AUX - WEIGHT PLANNING

PAYLOAD (LB)		FUEL (LB)	
BASIC EMPTY WEIGHT	5350	ZERO FUEL WEIGHT	6040
PILOT & STORES	+ 200	FUEL ON BOARD	+ 2600
BASIC OPERATING WEIGHT	5550	AIRCRAFT WEIGHT	8640
PASSENGERS # 2 AT 200 (EACH) =	400	EST. LANDING WEIGHT	8640
CARGO	+ 90	EST. LANDING FUEL	2600
ZERO FUEL WEIGHT	6040	FUEL RESERVES	- 0
		EXCESS FUEL	2600

Figure 16-8 All of the information for the Weight Planning page is displayed in the upper right corner of the page. © *Garmin Ltd. or its affiliates*

Below this are the N2 values. These digital readouts appear in white during engine start and change to green for normal operating conditions. Below this is the electrical display, which shows the generator voltage and current on vertical scales and as a digital readout.

Cabin pressurization information is shown below the electrical display. The vertical scales show pressure altitude on the left and pressure change rate in 1000 foot increments on the right. Digital readouts appear beneath both scales. Below this, the destination elevation is shown and a horizontal scale indicates the pressure differential in pounds per square inch. At the very bottom, position indicators are displayed for aileron trim, rudder trim, and flaps.

Weight and balance calculations are a snap, as the Cessna Mustang has a new Weight Planning page, the first page in the AUX group, that lets you enter payload and fuel information (figure 16-8). That way, you'll never have an excuse not to do a full weight and balance calculation before every takeoff.

To start, press the EMPTY WT softkey to select the BASIC EMPTY WEIGHT field. Then use the small FMS knob to enter the aircraft's empty weight and press the ENT key. Next, highlight the PILOT & STORES field and use the small FMS knob to enter the weight. Continue in this fashion to enter the number of passengers, their average weight, and the cargo weight. These numbers are summed and displayed in the ZERO FUEL WEIGHT fields.

Next, highlight the FUEL ON BOARD field and use the small FMS knob to enter the number of pounds of fuel on board. Alternatively, you can load the fuel value measured by on board sensors. To load that value, press the FOB SYNC softkey, or press the MENU key, highlight "Synchronize Fuel on Board," and press the ENT key. Finally, scroll to FUEL RESERVES and use the small FMS knob to enter the weight of your reserve fuel.

When the aircraft is in the air and a destination entered in the flight plan, additional fuel calculations are displayed. These include the estimated landing weight, estimated landing fuel weight and excess fuel weight. Some of these weights display in amber if certain conditions are not met. These include:

- the zero fuel weight if greater than the maximum allowed

Figure 16-9 Flying prototype of Cessna Mustang on display.
© Max Trescott

Figure 16-10 Diamond D-Jet.
© Diamond Aircraft Industries, Inc.

Figure 16-11 Flying prototype of the HondaJet. *© Honda*

- the aircraft weight if greater than the maximum allowed takeoff weight
- the estimated landing weight if greater than the maximum allowed landing weight
- the estimated fuel at landing weight and excess fuel weight if the estimated landing fuel weight is less than the fuel reserve weight, or in red if it's zero or negative.

A high percentage of software features in Perspective- and G1000-equipped piston-powered aircraft have found their way directly into G1000-equipped VLJs. Therefore, one of the best ways to learn to fly a G1000-equipped VLJ is to train with a factory certified instructor in any G1000 aircraft available. Here's a brief description of G1000-equipped VLJ and turbine aircraft that have been announced.

Cessna CitationJet

In 2010, Cessna began offering a G1000 integrated Flight deck retrofit to operators of the popular CitationJet (Model 525, serial numbers 0001-0359). The upgrade features a large 12-inch MFD in the center of the panel, flanked by 10.4-inch PFDs at the pilot and copilot positions. The retrofit includes Garmin's GWX™ 68 digital color weather radar. The upgrade is available through Cessna's Citation Service Centers.

Cessna Mustang

Cessna is the world's largest supplier of business jets and single-engine aircraft. They are one of the few companies that spans the full price performance range of GA aircraft. Hence, they should have a strong market advantage in reaching VLJ customers who fall solidly between these two marketplaces. The Mustang (figure 16-9) received type certification in September, 2006, and is built in Independence, Kan.

Diamond D-Jet

Diamond is a relative newcomer to the GA market, but has established itself as an innovative designer and manufacturer. Unlike most other manufacturers that are planning to build 6-passenger, twin engine jets, Diamond's design is for a pilot plus 4-passenger, single engine jet (figure 16-10). At under $2 million, it may be among the least expensive VLJs. Customer deliveries are planned for 2014. Diamond has production facilities in Austria and Canada.

HondaJet

After 20 years of research, Honda announced plans to produce their $4.5 million HondaJet, which should begin shipping in 2013 (figure 16-11). The HondaJet is a composite-fuselage, six-place twin jet with an innovative over-the-wing engine mount. It's being built in Greensboro, North Carolina.

Figure 16-12 Flight deck of the Embraer Phenom. *© Embraer*

Embraer

Embraer selected the G1000 for both their Very Light Jet and Light Jet aircraft, known respectively as the Phenom 100 and Phenom 300 (figure 16-12). The Phenom 100 accommodates four passengers at speeds up to Mach 0.7 and a maximum altitude of 41,000 feet. Over 240 of these jets have shipped since December 2008. The current price is about $3.6 million. The Phenom 300 seats nine and travels at up to Mach 0.78 at a maximum altitude of 45,000 feet. The Phenom 100 is built in Brazil and Melbourne, FL and the Phenom 300 is built in Brazil.

Figure 16-13 Cirrus Aircraft Vision SF50 jet. *© Cirrus Aircraft*

Cirrus Vision SF50

The Cirrus SF50 jet will use the Perspective glass cockpit. The aircraft is powered by a single Williams FJ33-4A-19 engine, producing 1,900 pounds-force of thrust and is projected to cruise at about 300 knots (figure 16-13). It will seat seven people and be equipped with a Ballistic Recovery Systems parachute. The current price is $1.72 million. The first production-conforming jet in slated to fly in 2014 and customer deliveries are planned for 2015.

Turboprops

Quest Aircraft Company KODIAK

Quest Aircraft's KODIAK is a 10-place, single-engine turboprop utility airplane (figure 16-14). This float capable aircraft is designed for part 135 charter and scheduled flight operations. It's also expected to be used for humanitarian and mission needs around the world, because of its rugged aluminum construction, superior STOL performance, and high useful load.

Figure 16-14 The KODIAK has STOL performance and a high useful load. *© Quest Aircraft*

Figure 16-15 The Cessna Caravan, one of the longest serving single-engine turboprops, will sport the G1000 in 2008. *© Cessna Aircraft Company*

Figure 16-16 The experimental Epic LT can now be built with a Garmin G900X panel. *© Max Trescott*

Figure 16-17 The King Air C90, 200, B200, 300, and 350 can be retrofitted with a Garmin G1000. *© Max Trescott*

The KODIAK offers turbine reliability and has the ability to land on unimproved surfaces. Its flight deck features a three-panel G1000 system with two PFDs flanking a centrally located MFD. The first customer delivery was in December 2007 and the base price in 2005 was $1,111,000.

Cessna Caravan

The Cessna Caravan is a 10-place, single-engine turboprop utility aircraft and short-haul regional airliner (figure 16-15). It was originally certified in 1984 with round gauges, and started shipping with a G1000 panel beginning in mid-2008. The Caravan is available in several configurations, including a cargo version used extensively by FedEx. It uses the 675 hp Pratt & Whitney PT6A-114 engine and has a maximum speed of 186 knots and range of 932 nm.

Epic

Epic Aircraft is in the midst of a transition from selling experimental aircraft to introducing certified aircraft. The Epic LT is the experimental aircraft (figure 16-16) and builders now have the option of installing the G900X. The certified version, the Epic Dynasty, will be available with the G1000. With its 1200 shp Pratt & Whitney PT6-67A, the Epic LT delivers speeds of up to 330 knots at its 28,000 foot service ceiling. The kit price of the Epic LT was $1.1 million in 2004. Following a Chapter 7 liquidation in 2010, a Russian company, Engineering LLC, purchased Epic in 2012 and announced plans to type certify the Epic LT.

King Air G1000 Retrofit

In 2006, Garmin announced that the King Air C90 (figure 16-17) would be the first aircraft in the G1000 retrofit program, and installations began in 2007. Later, the King Air 200, B200, 300 and 350 were added to the program. A three-display configuration is used that includes a 15-inch MFD and the GFC 700 autopilot. Standard features include WAAS, dual AHRS and dual RVSM-capable air data computers. SVT, Class A TAWS, and Electronic Stability and Protection (ESP) are available as options.

EADS Socata TBM 850

In 2007, EADS Socata announced the G1000

would be incorporated in future TBM 850 (figure 16-18) aircraft. In 2011, the company announced they will begin offering a G1000 retrofit for TBM 700A and 700B models. The three-display configuration includes a 15-inch MFD and the GFC 700 autopilot. EADS Socata claims that the TBM 850 is the world's fastest turboprop, with a maximum cruising speed of 320 knots at 26,000 feet.

Figure 16-18 The EADS Socata TBM 850 was upgraded in early 2008 to include the G1000. *© EADS Socata*

Piper Meridian

In 2009, Piper began shipping the G1000 as an option on the Piper Meridian, the company's flagship, six-seat, cabin–class turboprop (figure 16-19). The standard configuration includes two PFDs, a 15-inch MFD, GFC 700 autopilot and Synthetic Vision. For redundancy, it includes dual AHRS, ADCs, transponders, and audio panels. The Meridian sells for approximately $2.1 million and flies at 260 knots using a 500 shp, Pratt & Whitney PT6A-42A.

Figure 16-19 The G1000 became an option on the Piper Meridian in 2009. *© Piper Aircraft*

Summary

Whether you're a student pilot, G1000-equipped aircraft owner or potential owner, I hope this book has enriched your knowledge and appreciation for the revolution that is occurring with glass cockpits in general aviation. If you're a prospective owner, of either a piston-powered aircraft or VLJ, start flying current G1000-equipped aircraft so that you'll be fully prepared when your new aircraft arrives. If you're a skeptic as I was and are not convinced that the G1000 glass cockpit simplifies operation and enhances safety, I encourage you to get instruction in one of these aircraft and find out for yourself.

This is a rapidly changing environment and you'll want to stay tuned to developments as they emerge. New features and devices are likely to be announced every few months and additional manufacturers will undoubtedly select the G1000 to equip their aircraft. It's an exciting time to be involved in general aviation and glass cockpit technology. If you're not already involved, now is the time to jump in! Enjoy the ride.

Appendix A:
Guide to G1000-Equipped Aircraft

Cessna 172

Cessna 172 G1000 Cockpit

Cessna 182

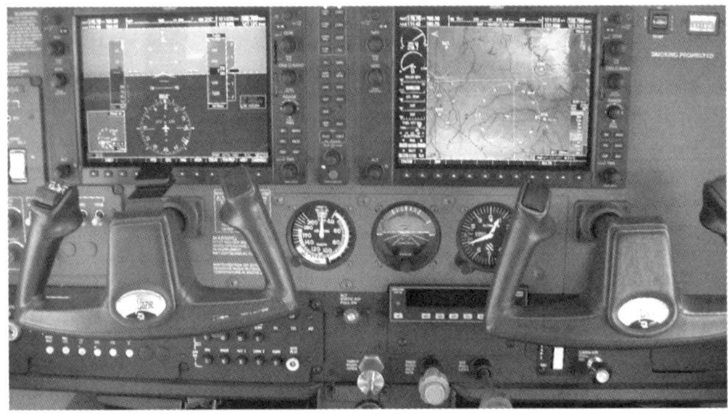
Cessna 182 G1000 Cockpit

Cessna T206

Cessna T206 G1000 Cockpit

Beechcraft G36 Bonanza

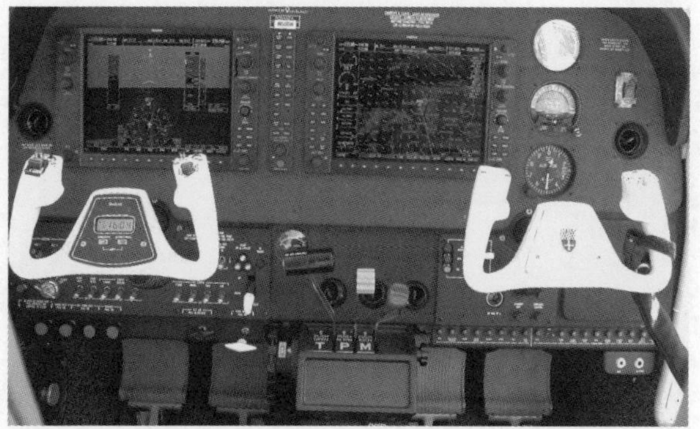

Beechcraft G36 G1000 Cockpit

Columbia © Columbia Aircraft

Columbia G1000 Cockpit © Columbia Aircraft

Diamond DA40

Diamond DA40 G1000 Cockpit

Diamond DA42

Diamond DA42 G1000 Cockpit

Mooney Ovation 20R

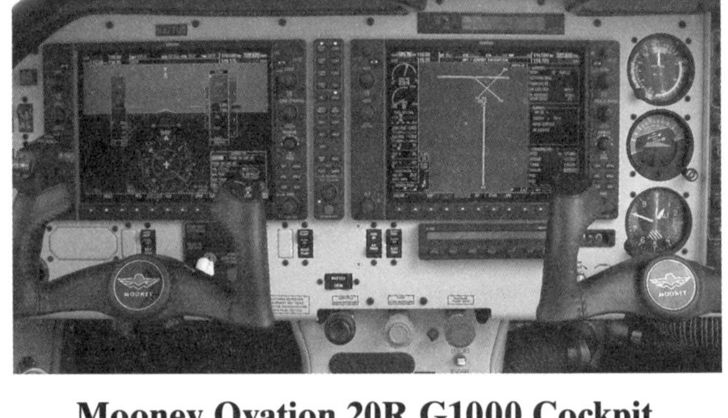

Mooney Ovation 20R G1000 Cockpit

Tiger AG-5B

Tiger AG-5B G1000 Cockpit

Cirrus SR22T Perspective

Cirrus SR22T Perspective Cockpit

Piper Saratoga TC © Piper Aircraft

Piper Saratoga II TC G1000 Cockpit © Piper Aircraft

Appendix B:
G1000 Feature Differences by Aircraft Manufacturer

Feature	Beechcraft G36 & G58	Cessna 172, 182, 206	Cessna 350 & 400	Diamond DA40 & DA42	Mooney M20M, M20R & M20TN	Cirrus SR22
Checklists	Future	Yes	No	Future	Yes	Yes
Pilot Profiles	Yes	Future	Yes	Yes	Yes	Yes
Engine/Flight time (on Engine (SYSTEM page)	No	Engine hours (tach)	Total Time in Service (>60 kts)	Total Time in Service (airborne)	Engine hours (tach)	No
Vacuum gauge	No	Yes	No	No	Yes**	No
Standby battery for PFD	Yes	Yes	Yes	No***	Yes	Yes
Alphanumeric keypad	No	No	Yes	No	No	Yes
Annunciator window	Yes	Yes	Yes	Yes	Not used (uses Alerts softkey)	Yes
Alert Levels	<u>3 levels</u> Warning Caution Advisory	<u>3 levels</u> Warning Caution Advisory	<u>3 levels</u> Warning Caution Advisory	<u>3 levels</u> Warning Caution Advisory	<u>1 level</u> Advisory	<u>3 levels</u> Warning Caution Advisory
Fuel flow sensor	Yes	Yes	Yes	Yes	Yes	Yes
Fuel Used (for trip planning & fuel range ring)	Reset Full & add/subtract	Reset Full† & add/subtract	Reset Full & add/subtract	Reset Full & add/subtract	Reset Full & add/subtract	Reset Full & add/subtract
Maximum Fuel Indication per tank	G36: 37 of 37 gallons G58: 89 of 89 gallons	182/206 35 of 44.5 gallons	49 of 49 gallons	DA40:17 of 20 gallons DA42:25 of 25 gallons	44.5 of 55 gallons	Mechanical Fuel Guages
VSpeed bugs	Yes	Yes	Yes	Yes	Yes	Yes
Rudder Trim Indication	No	No	No	No	Yes	No
Flap Indication	No	No	No	No	Yes	No
Elevator Trim Indication	No	No	Yes	No	Yes	No
Oxygen Indicator	No	No	Yes	No	No	Yes
Alternators	Two	One	Two	DA40 One DA42 Two	Two	Two
Aileron Trim Indictor	No	No	Yes	No	No	No

Feature	Beechcraft G36 & G58	Cessna 172, 182, 206	Cessna 350 & 400	Diamond DA40 & DA42	Mooney M20M, M20R & M20TN	Cirrus SR22
Weather Radar Garmin GWX 68	G36: No G58: Yes	No	No	No	No	No
TAWS	Yes	Option	Yes	Yes: DA40 XL only	No	Yes
CO Detector	No	Yes	Yes	Yes: DA40 XL only	No	Yes
Volume % displayed	Yes	Yes	Yes	Yes*	Yes	Yes
RX displayed on COM	Yes	Yes	Yes	Yes*	Yes	Yes
COM 1/2 key enabled	Yes	No	No	Yes on both	No	Yes
Obstacle database	Yes	Yes*	Yes	Yes*	Yes	Yes

* Early software versions lacked this capability which is now shipped in new planes
** Vacuum pump drives panel annunciator, but not displayed in G1000
*** Standby battery only operates backup attitude indicator
† Early software versions shipped with only the Reset Full capability

Autopilot Differences by Aircraft Manufacturer

Feature	Beechcraft G36 & G58	Cessna 172, 182, 206	Cessna 350 & 400	Diamond DA40 & DA42	Mooney M20M, M20R & M20TN	Cirrus SR22
Autopilot	GFC 700	KAP 140 GFC 700*	GFC 700	KAP 140 GFC 700 **	S-Tec 55X GFC 700 ***	GFC 700
GPS roll steering Integration with autopilot	Yes	Yes	Yes	No†	Yes, GPSS standard	Yes
G1000 ALT reference knob integrated with Autopilot	Yes	No†	Yes	No†	Yes	Yes
CWS with A/P	Yes	No†	Yes	Yes	Yes	No
Vertical Speed & glide slope	Yes	Yes	Yes	Yes	Yes	Yes
Altitude preselect	Yes	Yes	Yes	Yes	Yes	Yes

* 2007 and later 182 and 206; 2008 and later 172
** 2007 and later DA40XL and DA40XLS
*** May, 2006 and later
† Yes in GFC 700-equipped versions

Appendix C: G1000 Warnings and Cautions by Aircraft Manufacturer

Beechcraft G36 Aircraft Warnings and Cautions

Warning Alerts – Red Text Label	Alerts Window Message	Audio Alert
GEAR UP	Gear up	Continuous Aural Tone
ALT 1 INOP	Alternator 1 offline	Repeating Tone
ALT 2 INOP	Alternator 2 offline	Repeating Tone
ALT 1-2 INOP	Alternator 1 and 2 offline	Repeating Tone

Caution Alerts – Yellow Text Label	Alerts Window Message	Audio Alert
AC DOOR EXTD	Air conditioner on and door extended	Single Chime
STARTER ENGD	Starter relay has power applied	Single Chime
BUS1 VOLT HI	Bus 1 voltage greater than 30 VDC	Single Chime
BUS2 VOLT HI	Bus 2 voltage greater than 30 VDC	Single Chime
AFT DOOR	Aft door not latched	Single Chime

Beechcraft G58 Baron Aircraft Warnings and Cautions

Warning Alerts – Red Text Label	Alerts Window Message	Audio Alert
GEAR UP	Gear up	Continuous Aural Tone
L ALT INOP	Left alternator offline	Repeating Tone
R ALT INOP	Right alternator offline	Repeating Tone
L-R ALT INOP	Right and Left alternators offline	Repeating Tone

Caution Alerts – Yellow Text Label	Alerts Window Message	Audio Alert
L START ENGD	Left starter relay has power applied	Single Chime
R START ENGD	Right starter relay has power applied	Single Chime
LBUS VOLT HI	Left bus voltage greater than 30 VDC	Single Chime
RBUS VOLT HI	Right bus voltage greater than 30 VDC	Single Chime
LBUS VOLT LO	Left bus voltage less than 24V. Suppressed below 500 RPM	Single Chime
RBUS VOLT LO	Right bus voltage less than 24V. Suppressed below 500 RPM	Single Chime
AFT DOOR	Aft door not latched	Single Chime
L AIR PUMP	Press Low – Ops in icing conditions not approved	Single Chime
R AIR PUMP	Press Low – Ops in icing conditions not approved	Single Chime

Cessna Aircraft Warnings and Cautions (See Cessna 350/400 below)

Warning Alerts – Red Text Label	Audio Alert
OIL PRESSURE	Continuous Aural Tone
LOW VOLTS	Continuous Aural Tone*
HIGH VOLTS	Continuous Aural Tone
CO LVL HIGH	Continuous Aural Tone
PITCH TRIM	No Tone

* Tone inhibited when aircraft is on the ground.

Caution Alerts – Yellow Text Label	Audio Alert
LOW VACUUM	Single Aural Tone
LOW FUEL L	Single Aural Tone
LOW FUEL R	Single Aural Tone
STBY BATT	Single Aural Tone
PROP HEAT*	Single Aural Tone

* for T182, T206, and 206 with Prop De-Ice

Cessna 350/400 Aircraft Warnings and Cautions

Warning Alerts – Red Text Label	Alerts Window Message	Audio Alert/Voice Message
DOOR OPEN	Door not secured	Chime/"Door Open"
FUEL VALVE	Fuel tank is not correctly selected or in OFF posistion	Chime/"Fuel Valve"
L BUS OFF	No power on the left bus	Chime/None
R BUS OFF	No power on the right bus	Chime/None
CO LVL HIGH	Carbon Monoxide level is too high	Chime/"Carbon Monoxide"
OIL PRES LOW	Low oil pressure	Chime/"Oil Pressure Low"

Caution Alerts – Yellow Text Label	Alerts Window Message	Audio Alert/Voice Message
L ALT OFF	Left alternator offline	Single Chime/"Left Alternator Out"
R ALT OFF	Right alternator offline	Single Chime/"Right Alternator Out"
FUEL PUMP	Fuel pump is operating	Single Chime/"Fuel Pump On"
L LOW FUEL	Low fuel in the left fuel tank	Single Chime/None
R LOW FUEL	Low fuel in the right fuel tank	Single Chime/None
RUDR LMTR*	Rudder limiter is engaged	Single Chime/None
STARTER ENGD	Starter relay has power applied	Single Chime/None
OXYGEN	Oxygen system neeeds attention or is off	Single Chime/None
OXYGEN PRES	Pressure above 12000 ft and oxygen system off	Single Chime/None
OXYGEN QTY	Oxygen quantity below 250 psi	Single Chime/None

* Cessna 350 only

Mooney Alerts

Mooney aircraft use an external annunciator located above the G1000 displays to display warning and caution annunciations. These aircraft do not use the Alerts Annunciation window on the G1000 PFD.

Mooney Annunciator Panel

Diamond DA40 and DA40F Aircraft Warnings and Cautions

Warning Alerts – Red Text Label	Alerts Window Message	Audio Alert
OIL PRES LO	Oil pressure is below 25 psi	Continuous Aural Tone
FUEL PRES LO	Fuel pressure is below 14 psi	Continuous Aural Tone
FUEL PRES HI	Fuel pressure is greater than 35 psi	Continuous Aural Tone
ALTERNATOR	Alternator Failed. Battery is only electric source	Continuous Aural Tone
STARTER ENGD	Starter is engaged	Continuous Aural Tone
DOOR OPEN	Canopy and/or rear door is not closed and locked	Continuous Aural Tone
TRIM FAIL	Autopilot automatic trim is inoperative	Continuous Aural Tone

Caution Alerts – Yellow Text Label	Alerts Window Message	Audio Alert
L FUEL LOW	Left fuel quantity is less than 3 gallons (+/- one gallon)	Single Aural Tone
R FUEL LOW	Right fuel quantity is less than 3 gallons (+/- one gallon)	Single Aural Tone
LOW VOLTS	On-board voltage is below 24V	Single Aural Tone
PITOT FAIL	Pitot heat is inoperative	Single Aural Tone
PITOT OFF	Pitot heat is off	Single Aural Tone

Diamond DA42 Aircraft Warnings and Cautions

Warning Alerts – Red Text Label	Alerts Window Message	Audio Alert
L/R ENG TEMP	Left/right engine coolant temp is >105 deg C	Continuous Aural Tone
L/R OIL TEMP	Left/right engine oil temp is greater than 140 deg C	Continuous Aural Tone
L/R OIL PRES	Left/right engine oil pressure is less than 1.2 bar	Continuous Aural Tone
L/R ENG FIRE	Left/right engine fire detected	Continuous Aural Tone
L/R GBOX TEMP	Left/right engine gearbox temp is >120 deg C	Continuous Aural Tone
L/R ALTN AMPS	Left/right engine alternator output is >60 amps	Continuous Aural Tone
L/R STARTER	Left/right engine starter is engaged	Continuous Aural Tone
L/R FUEL TEMP	Left/right fuel temp is greater than 75 deg C	Continuous Aural Tone
DOOR OPEN	Front, rear or baggage door is not closed	Continuous Aural Tone
AP TRIM FAIL	Autopilot automatic trim is inoperative	No Tone

Caution Alerts – Yellow Text Label	Alerts Window Message	Audio Alert
L/R ECU A FAIL	Left/right engine ECU A has failed	Single Aural Tone
L/R ECU B FAIL	Left/right engine ECU B has failed	Single Aural Tone
L/R FUEL LOW	Left/right engine main fuel tank is low	Single Aural Tone
L/R ALTN FAIL	Left/right engine alternator has failed	Single Aural Tone
L/R VOLTS LOW	Left/right bus voltage is less than 25 volts	Single Aural Tone
L/R COOL LVL	Left/right engine coolant level is low	Single Aural Tone
L/R AUX FUEL E	Left/right auxiliary fuel tank is empty	Single Aural Tone
PITOT FAIL	Pitot heat has failed	Single Aural Tone
PITOT HT OFF	Pitot heat is off	Single Aural Tone
STAL HT FAIL	Stall warning heat has failed	Single Aural Tone
STAL HT OFF	Stall warning heat is off	Single Aural Tone
L/R AUX FUEL E	Left/Right auxiliary fuel tank is empty	Single Aural Tone
DEICE LVL LO	De-icing fluid level is low	Single Aural Tone
DEICE PRES HI	De-icing pressure is high	Single Aural Tone
DEICE PRES LO	De-icing pressure is low	Single Aural Tone
STICK LIMIT	Stick limiting system has failed	Single Aural Tone

Cirrus SR22 Warnings and Cautions

Warning Alerts – Red Text Label	Alerts Window Message	Audio Alert
ANTI ICE CTL	Tank valves cannot close	Repeating Double Chime
ANTI ICE QTY	Fluid quantity is low	Repeating Double Chime
AOA OVERHEAT	AOA probe is overheated	Repeating Double Chime
AUTO DESCENT	Aircraft descending	Repeating Double Chime
BRAKE TEMP	Brake temperature high	Repeating Double Chime
CHT	Cylinder temperature high	Repeating Double Chime
CO LVL HIGH	Carbon monoxide level high	Repeating Double Chime
DUCT OVERHEAT	Cabin heat duct temperature high	Repeating Double Chime
ESS BUSS	Check essential power bus voltage	Repeating Double Chime*
FUEL FLOW	Check fuel flow	None
FUEL QTY	Check fuel tank levels	Repeating Double Chime
M BUS 1	Check main power bus 1 voltage	Repeating Double Chime
M BUS 2	Check main power bus 2 voltage	Repeating Double Chime
MAN PRESSURE	Check manifold pressure	Repeating Double Chime (after 30 seconds)
OIL PRESSURE	Oil pressure is out of range	Repeating Double Chime*
OIL TEMP	Oil temperature is high	Repeating Double Chime
OXYGEN FAULT	Oxygen system fault	Repeating Double Chime
OXYGEN QTY	Oxygen quantity is low	Repeating Double Chime
RPM	Check engine RPM	Repeating Double Chime
STALL	Stall warning	Tone
START ENGAGED	Starter is engaged	Repeating Double Chime
TIT	TIT temperature is high	Repeating Double Chime
UNDERSPEED PROTECT ACTIVE	None	"Airspeed"

Caution Alerts – Yellow Text Label	Alerts Window Message	Audio Alert
ALT 1	Check alternator 1 current	Double Chime*
ALT 2	Check alternator 2 current	Double Chime*
ALT AIR OPEN	Alternate air door is open	Double Chime
ANTI ICE HEAT	Stall warning/AoA heater failed	Double Chime*
ANTI ICE LEVEL	TKS fluid quantity unreliable	Double Chime
ANTI ICE PRESSURE	TKS pressure abnormal	Double Chime
ANTI ICE QTY	TKS imbalance or low quantity	Double Chime
ANTI ICE SPEED	Airspeed too low/high for ice protection	Double Chime*
AP MISCOMPARE	Autopilot is not available	Double Chime
AP/PFD DIF ADC	Autopilot and PFD using different ADCs	Double Chime
AP/PFD DIF AHRS	Autopilot and PFD using different AHRS	Double Chime
AVIONICS OFF	Avionics master switch is off	Double Chime
BATT 1	Check battery 1 current	Double Chime*
BRAKE TEMP	Brake temperature is high	Double Chime
CHT	Cylinder temperature high	Double Chime
FLAP OVERSPEED	Flaps extended beyond airspeed limits	Double Chime
FUEL FILTER	Fuel filter in bypass	Double Chime
FUEL QTY	Check fuel tank levels	Double Chime
HYPOXIA ALERT	Hypoxia caution alert	Double Chime
M BUS 1	Check main power bus 1	Double Chime*
M BUS 2	Check main power bus 2	Double Chime*
MAN PRESSURE	Check manifold pressure	None
NO ADC MODES	Autopilot air data modes not available	Double Chime
NO VERT MODES	Autopilot vertical modes not available	Double Chime
OIL PRESSURE	Oil pressure is out of range	Double Chime*
OIL TEMP	Oil temperature is high	Double Chime
OXYGEN QTY	Oxygen quantity is low	Double Chime
OXYGEN RQD	Oxygen is required	Double Chime
PARK BRAKE	Parking brake is set	None
PITOT HEAT FAIL	Pitot heat failure	Double Chime
PITOT HEAT REQD	Pitot heat is required	Double Chime*
START ENGAGED	Starter is engaged	Double Chime

* Tone inhibited when aircraft is on the ground.

Appendix D:
G1000 Engine Instrumentation Systems by Manufacturer

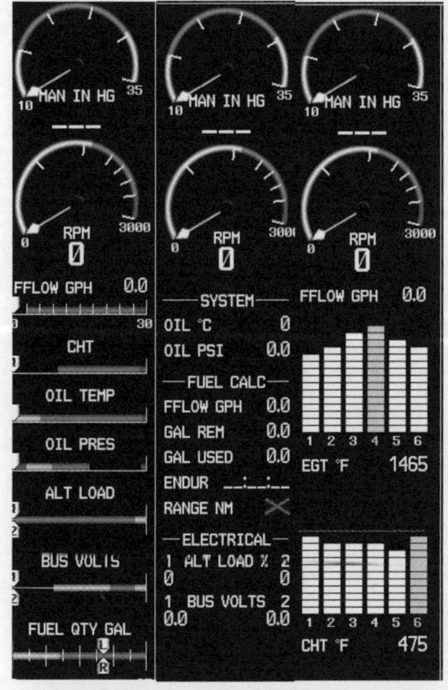

Beechcraft G36

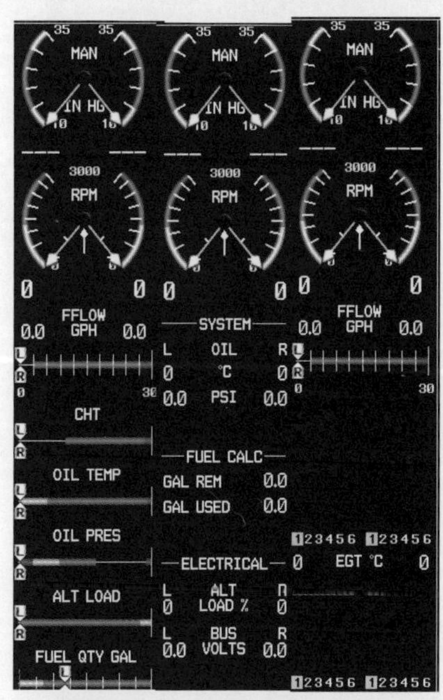

Beechcraft G58 Baron

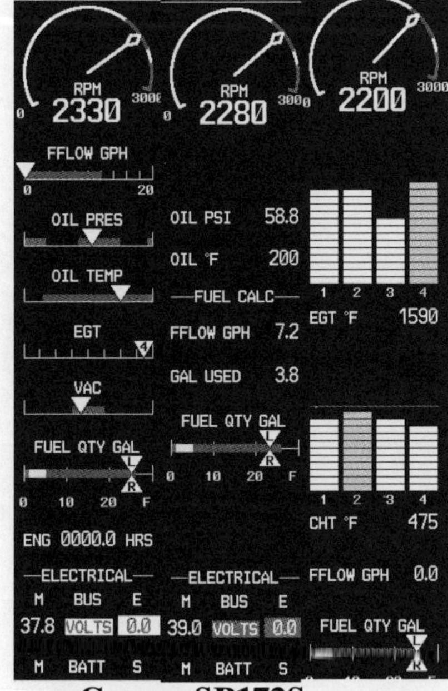

Cessna SP172S

Cessna 182T

Cessna T206H

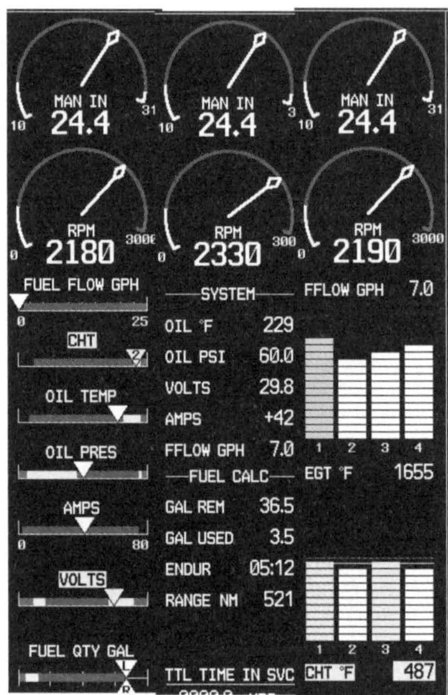

Diamond DA40

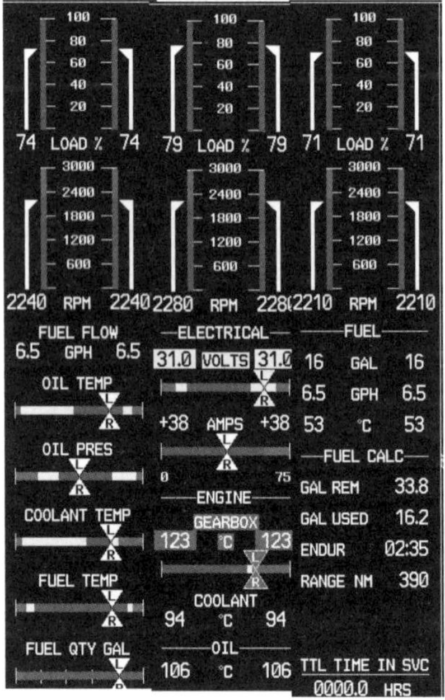

Diamond DA42

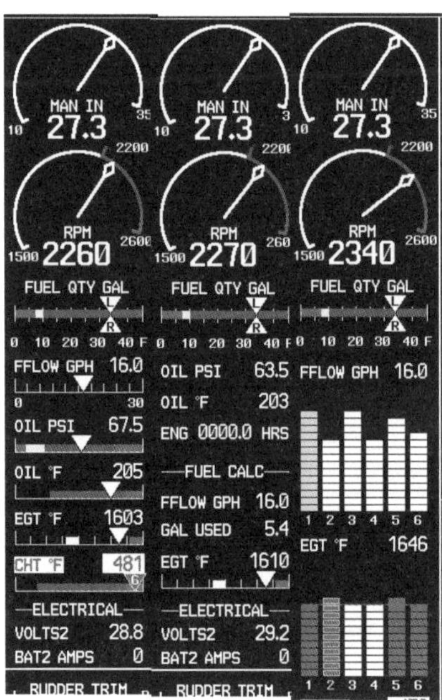

Mooney M20

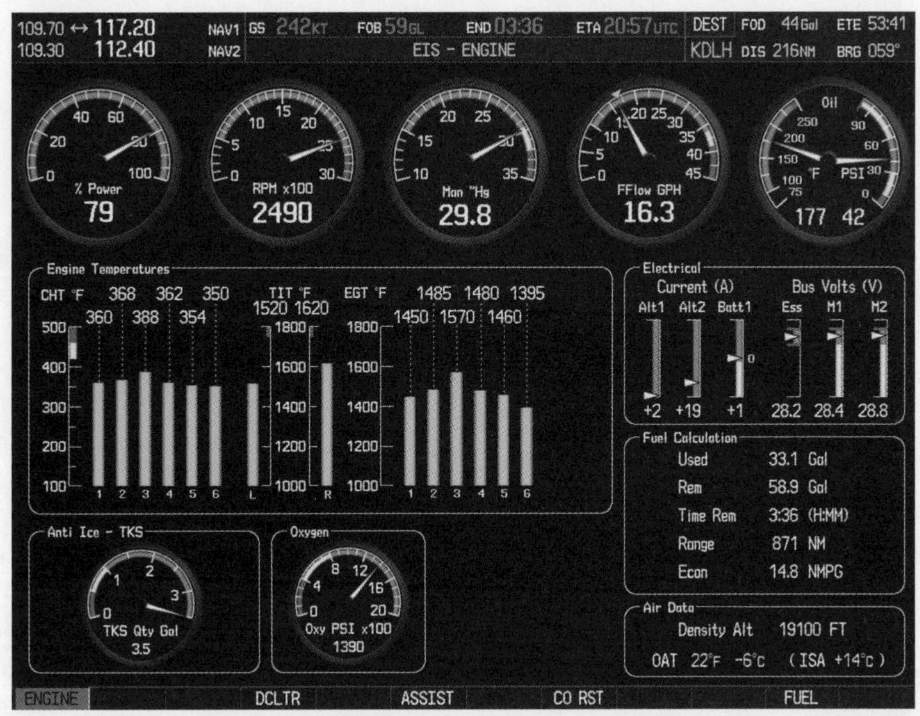

Engine Page of Cirrus SR22

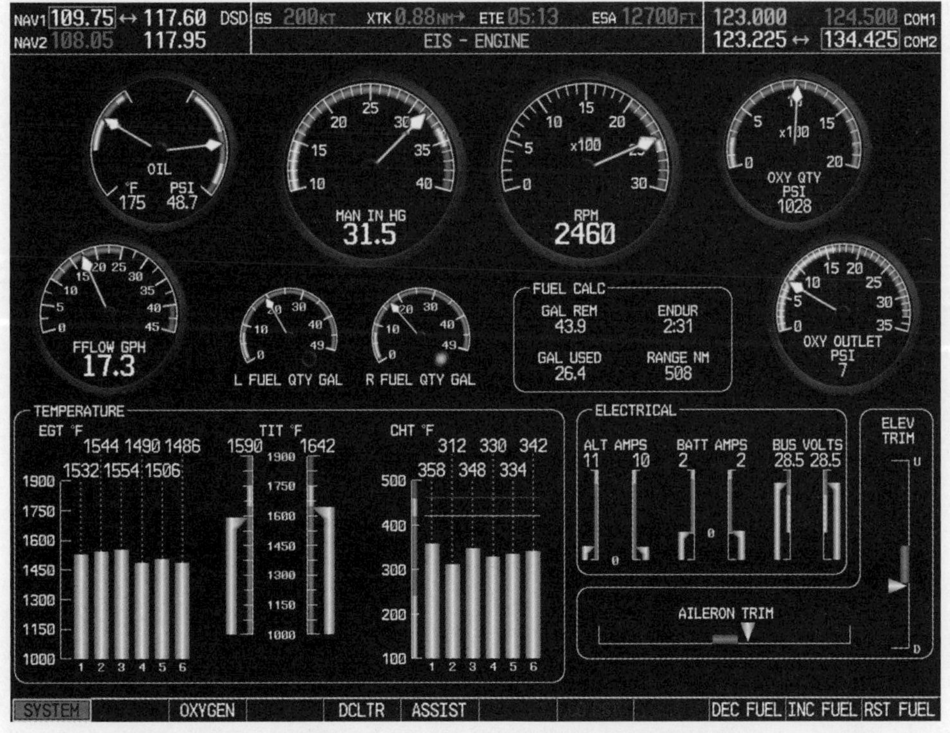

Actual inflight screen capture of Columbia 400i System page. Engine is operating lean of peak.

Appendix E: Declutter levels for Navigation Map page

Columns list information removed at each level by pressing DCLTR softkey on MFD

Always Displayed	**No Declutter**	**Declutter(-1)**	**Declutter(-2)**	**Declutter(-3)**
Flight Plan course lines	All Features visible	River/Lakes Names	User Waypoints	Airports
Flight Plan waypoints		Land/Country Text	Latitude/ Longitude Grid	Lightning Strike Data
Rivers/Lakes		Towns & Cities	VORs	NEXRAD data
Topographical data		Freeways	NDBs	Traffic Symbols
Terrain Proximity		Roads & Highways	Intersections	Traffic Labels
Map Borders		Railroads	Special Use airspace (except MOA, Restricted, TFR and Prohibited)	MOA,Restricted, TFR and Prohibited
Bearing Lines		Political Boundaries		

Appendix F: Comparison of Garmin G1000 with GNS 430 and GNS 530

Feature	G1000	GNS 430/GNS 530
Stored Flight Plans	99	20
User Interface Organization	4 Groups + FPL group	4 Groups + FPL group
Winds Aloft	Displayed on MFD	AUX page
True Airspeed	Displayed on PFD	AUX page
Nearest	NRST chapter & PFD Softkey	NRST chapter
Frequency load from Waypoint database into COM & NAV	Yes	Yes
Select DP, STAR, Approach	PROC & MENU keys & MFD softkeys	PROC key
HOLD outbound timing	Yes	Yes
Announce start of Procedure Turn	Yes	Yes
FPL creation	Identifiers or "Point & Shoot" with joystick on MFD map	Enter identifiers
Hold entry type recommendation	Yes	Yes
Auto-switch CDI pointer from GPS to Localizer upon capture	Yes	Yes
Vertical Navigation	Yes with graphical start and end points	Yes
Real-time weather display	Optional. Many weather products. See Chapter 8.	Optional. Only NEXRAD & METARS displayed.
RMI bearing pointers	Yes	No, but 530 displays radial
Automatically SUSP waypoint sequencing at missed approach point	Yes	Yes
Automatically re-start sequencing when inbound from procedure turn	Yes	Yes
Automatic Trip Planning Page	Yes – AUX page	Yes – AUX page
Fuel Range Ring	Yes—graphical display	No
Airport Information	All on one page	Spread over 6 pages
Runway Maps	Yes	Yes

Appendix G:

TAWS Alert Summaries

For aircraft with TAWS, such as the Columbia 350i and 400i and Beechcraft G58 Baron.

Alert Type	PFD/MFD TAWS Page Annunciation	MFD Map Page Pop-Up Alert	Aural Message
Excessive Descent Rate Warning (EDR)	PULL UP	PULL-UP	"Pull Up"
Reduced Required Terrain Clearance Warning (RTC)	PULL UP	TERRAIN - PULL UP or TERRAIN AHEAD - PULL UP	"Terrain, Terrain; Pull Up, Pull Up" or "Terrain Ahead, Pull Up; Terrain Ahead, Pull Up"
Imminent Terrain Impact Warning (ITI)	PULL UP	TERRAIN AHEAD - PULL UP or TERRAIN - PULL UP	Terrain Ahead, Pull Up; Terrain Ahead, Pull Up" or "Terrain, Terrain; Pull Up, Pull Up"
Reduced Required Obstacle Clearance Warning (ROC)	PULL UP	OBSTACLE - PULL UP or OBSTACLE AHEAD - PULL UP	"Obstacle, Obstacle; Pull Up, Pull Up" or "Obstacle Ahead, Pull Up; Obstacle Ahead, Pull Up"
Imminent Obstacle Impact Warning (IOI)	PULL UP	OBSTACLE AHEAD - PULL UP or OBSTACLE - PULL-UP	"Obstacle Ahead, Pull Up; Obstacle Ahead, Pull Up" or "Obstacle, Obstacle; Pull Up, Pull Up"
Reduced Required Terrain Clearance Caution (RTC)	TERRAIN	CAUTION - TERRAIN or TERRAIN AHEAD	"Caution, Terrain; Caution, Terrain" or "Terrain Ahead; Terrain Ahead"
Imminent Terrain Impact Caution (ITI)	TERRAIN	TERRAIN AHEAD or CAUTION - TERRAIN	"Terrain Ahead; Terrain Ahead" or "Caution, Terrain; Caution, Terrain"
Reduced Required Obstacle Clearance Caution (ROC)	TERRAIN	CAUTION - OBSTACLE or OBSTACLE AHEAD	"Caution, Obstacle; Caution, Obstacle" or "Obstacle Ahead; Obstacle Ahead"
Imminent Obstacle Impact Caution (IOI)	TERRAIN	OBSTACLE AHEAD or CAUTION - OBSTACLE	"Obstacle Ahead; Obstacle Ahead" or "Caution, Obstacle; Caution, Obstacle"
Premature Descent Alert Caution (PDA)	TERRAIN	TOO LOW - TERRAIN	"Too Low, Terrain"
Altitude Callout "500"	None	None	"Five-Hundred"
Excessive Descent Rate Caution (EDR)	TERRAIN	SINK RATE	"Sink Rate"
Negative Climb Rate Caution (NCR)	TERRAIN	DON'T SINK or TOO LOW - TERRAIN	"Don't Sink" or "Too Low, Terrain"

Alert Type	PFD/MFD TAWS Page Annunciation	MFD Pop-Up Alert	Aural Message
TAWS System Test Fail	TAWS FAIL	None	"TAWS System Failure"
TAWS Alerting is disabled	TAWS INHB	None	None
No GPS position or excessively degraded GPS signal	TAWS N/A	None	"TAWS Not Available"
System Test in progress	TAWS TEST	None	None
System Test pass	None	None	"TAWS System Test OK"

Appendix H: AFCS Autopilot Alert Summaries

Warnings and Cautions annunciations for the Garmin AFCS Autopilot in the Beechcraft G58 Baron. Annunciations may vary slightly in other aircraft.

Alert Condition	Annunciation	Description
Rudder Mistrim Right	RUD→	Yaw servo providing sustained force Ensure Slip/Skid Indicator centered; observe maximum fuel imbalance limits
Rudder Mistrim Left	←RUD	
Aileron Mistrim Right	AIL→	Roll servo providing sustained force in indicated direction Ensure Slip/Skid Indicator centered; observe maximum fuel imbalance limits
Aileron Mistrim Left	←AIL	
Elevator Mistrim Down	↓ELE	Pitch servo providing sustained force Apply nose-down/up control wheel force upon AP disconnect
Elevator Mistrim Up	↑ELE	
Pitch Trim Failure (or Stuck **MEPT** Switch)	PTRM	If AP engaged, take control of the aircraft and disengage AP If AP disengaged, move **MEPT** switches separately to unstick
Yaw Damper Failure	YAW	Yaw Damper control failure; AP inoperative
Roll Failure	ROLL	Roll axis control failure; AP inoperative
Pitch Failure	PTCH	Pitch axis control failure; AP inoperative
System Failure	AFCS	AP and MEPT are unavailable; FD may still be available
Preflight Test	PFT	Performing Preflight System Test; Aural alert sounds at completion
	PFT	Preflight system test failed

Glossary

Active Leg — The segment of a route currently being traveled. A segment is defined by two sequential waypoints in the active flight plan.

ACU — Alternator Control Unit. Regulates the voltage generated by the alternator to a lower level to charge the battery.

ADC — Air Data Computer. Provides data from the pitot-static system (airspeed, altitude, etc).

ADF — Automatic Direction Finder. An aircraft receiver that receives low frequency signals such as those from NDBs and AM broadcast stations and includes an indicator needle that points in the direction of the station.

AFCS — Automatic Flight Control System. Garmin's name for the Flight Director and GFC 700 integrated autopilot in the G1000 system.

AHRS or AHARS — Attitude Heading and Reference System. Provides heading, attitude and rate of turn information.

AIRMET — An advisory of weather that is significant, but of lower intensity than a SIGMET. This weather should be considered hazardous to single engine and other light aircraft.

Almanac Data — Information transmitted by each GPS satellite on the orbit and health of every satellite in the GPS constellation. Almanac data allows a GPS receiver to rapidly acquire satellites when it's first turned on.

ALT — Altitude. On the G1000, the ALT knobs are used to set the altitude reference, which is the target altitude you want to fly. For G1000 aircraft with integrated autopilots, the ALT knob also preselects the altitude at which the autopilot will level off and maintain altitude.

Altimeter — Instrument for determining elevation based upon changes in pressure.

ARTCC — Air Route Traffic Control Center. Better know as "Center." Provides radar separation service for aircraft flying outside of metropolitan areas and at higher altitudes across the United States.

ASOS — Automated Weather Observing System. Unattended, computer driven weather observation station for airports. Observations are generally updated every minute and are broadcast over aviation frequencies and are available via telephone.

ATC — Air Traffic Control. Generic name for the many different services that provide separation service for aircraft in flight.

ATIS — Automatic Terminal Information Service. Short taped message about current weather conditions for an airport that is updated hourly, generally by an air traffic controller trained as a weather observer.

AWOS — Automated Weather Observing System. Similar to ASOS.

Bearing — The compass direction from a position to a destination, measured to the nearest degree. In GPS receivers, bearing usually refers to the direction to a waypoint.

CAT — Clear Air Turbulence. Turbulence that occurs when the sky is clear of clouds. It's frequently found at high altitudes and is associated with the jet stream or mountains.

CDI — Course Deviation Indicator. A needle or display that shows the amount of error from the desired course. For a VOR, the error is shown in degrees. For a GPS course, the error is based upon the crosstrack error (XTK) in nautical miles from the desired course.

CFIT — Controlled Flight Into Terrain. An accident or incident in which an airplane, under the full control of the pilot, is flown into terrain, obstacles, or water.

CHT — Cylinder Head Temperature. Engine temperature measured in the block of metal that forms the top of an engine cylinder.

Course — The direction from a route waypoint to the next waypoint in a route segment.

Crosstrack Error (XTK) — The distance in nautical miles from the desired course.

CWS — Control Wheel Steering. A function available for some autopilots that allows a pilot to momentarily interrupt autopilot control, manually fly to a new altitude or attitude, and then allow the autopilot to continue to control the airplane with the new reference.

Desired Track (DTK) — The compass course in degrees between two adjacent waypoints in a GPS flight plan.

Dilution of Precision (DOP) — A measure of the satellite geometry relative to your position. A low DOP value indicates better relative geometry and higher corresponding accuracy.

DIS — Distance in nautical miles. This is one of the fields that is available for display on the G1000's Navigation Status bar and in the flight plans.

DME — Distance Measuring Equipment. Aircraft equipment for measuring the slant range in nautical miles from the aircraft to an appropriately equipped VOR station on the ground. Most DME receivers can also generate groundspeed and time to the station information.

DOP — See Dilution of Precision.

DP — Departure Procedure. An instrument procedure written for a particular airport which, if followed correctly, guarantees terrain clearance for departing aircraft.

DPE — Designated Pilot Examiner. FAA designee who administers oral and flight tests for pilots licenses.

DTK — See Desired Track.

EFAS — En route Flight Advisory Service. Generally called "Flight Watch," it's a network of government stations across the United States that provide in-flight weather information to pilots on 122.0 MHz from 6AM to 10PM local time.

EGT — Exhaust Gas Temperature. The temperature measured in the exhaust gases as they leave the engine.

EIS — Engine Indication System. Garmin's name for the multiple screens on the MFD that display engine data. These displays vary considerably across different manufacturers' implementations of the G1000.

Ephemeris Data — Current satellite position and timing information transmitted as part of a satellite's data message. A set of ephemeris data is valid for several hours.

EPE — See Estimated Position Error.

EPU — Estimated Position Uncertainty. A statistical estimate of the 95% accuracy boundary around a position. It's defined as the radius of a circle, centered on an estimated horizontal position, such that there is a 5% probability of the actual position being outside the circle.

ESA — En route Safe Altitude. The recommended minimum altitude within ten miles left or right of the desired course on an active flight plan or Direct-to course.

ETA — Estimated Time of Arrival. The estimated time at which you'll arrive at a GPS waypoint.

Estimated Position Error — A measurement of horizontal position error in feet or meters based upon several factors including DOP and satellite signal quality.

ETE — Estimated Time En route. The estimated time in hours and minutes that it will take you to go from your present position to a waypoint based upon your current course and groundspeed.

FADEC — Full Authority Digital Engine Control. Electronic system that manages the fuel-air mixture and ignition timing for an engine. It reduces pilot workload, increases efficiency, and lowers fuel burn.

FAF — Final Approach Fix. The point at which the final segment of an instrument approach begins. For non-precision approaches, this is designated by a Maltese cross. For precision approaches, it's at the glide slope intercept point.

FITS — FAA Industry Training Standards. Joint FAA and industry program for improving TAA training. It makes heavy use of scenario-based training.

Flight Director — Software which provides pitch and roll commands that are displayed on the PFD. You can either manually fly the airplane to follow the commands, or engage the autopilot and have it follow the commands for you.

FPL — Flight Plan. Key on the G1000 that opens the Active Flight Plan window.

FMS — Flight Management System. Computerized avionics found on most commercial aircraft that uses positional data from a GPS or other system to locate the aircraft. It's generally linked to an autopilot and a MFD.

Frequency — The number of repetitions per unit time of a complete waveform, particularly of a radio wave.

FSS — Flight Service Station. A network of government stations that open and close aircraft flight plans and initiate a search process for overdue aircraft. They also provide weather information when EFAS is closed.

G.A.— General Aviation. Aircraft and flight hours flown by other than major and regional airlines or the military.

GPS — Global Positioning System. A global navigation system based on 24 satellites and spare satellites orbiting the earth, which provides precise position information for navigation.

HDOP — Horizontal Dilution of Precision. The number of GPS satellites received and their relative positions or geometry to each other, affects the quality of longitude and latitude coordinates generated by a GPS receiver. HDOP is a measure of that quality, using a scale from 0.0 to 9.9, with lower numbers representing better accuracy.

Heading — The direction in which an airplane is pointed. Heading differs from course to the extent necessary to counteract the force of the wind.

HFOM — Horizontal Figure of Merit. A measure of horizontal position uncertainty, in feet or meters, reported by a GPS receiver, that defines a 95% containment value on the accuracy of a position fix.

HI — Heading Indicator. Instrument that shows the current magnetic heading of an aircraft. In older aircraft, this is a gyro-based instrument which needs to be manually synchronized with the compass. In modern TAA, the heading indicator is part of the PFD and it is continuously synchronized with the magnetometer.

HIWAS — Hazardous In-flight Weather Advisory Service. Taped broadcast of weather over a wide region which is broadcast over a subset of VOR stations across the United States.

HSI — Horizontal Situation Indicator. Cockpit instrument that combines a Heading Indicator with a heading bug and a VOR/ILS CDI needle.

HUL — Horizontal Uncertainty Level. An estimate of horizontal position uncertainty, based on measurement inconsistency, which bounds the true error with high probability.

IAF — initial approach fix. The point at which an instrument approach procedure begins if it is flown under own navigation. Instrument approaches flown with vectors from ATC do not need to pass over an IAF.

IFR — Instrument Flight Rules. The set of rules used when flying an airplane on an instrument flight plan.

ILS — Instrument Landing System. A precision instrument approach that provides horizontal and vertical guidance and consists of a localizer, glide slope and usually one or more marker beacons.

IMC — Instrument Meteorological Conditions. Weather conditions that are less than VFR minimums (generally 3 miles visibility and 1000 feet cloud ceilings) that require a pilot to fly primarily by reference to instruments.

KOEL — Kinds of Operation Equipment List. A matrix found in the POH of TAA which details which equipment is required for different types of flights, such as VFR, IFR, day and night.

Latitude — A position's distance north or south of the equator, measure by degrees from zero to 90. One degree of latitude equals 60 nautical miles.

LCD — Liquid Crystal Display. A flat, glass screen found in laptop computers and avionics used to show moving maps and other information. Characters are generated on it by applying an electric current that arranges liquid crystal molecules sandwiched between two layers of glass to act as light filters.

Leg (Route) — A portion of a route defined by two sequential waypoints in a flight plan.

Longitude — The distance east or west of the prime meridian measured in degrees. The prime meridian runs from the north pole to the south pole through Greenwich, England.

LRU — line replaceable unit. A modular piece of electronic equipment that can easily be removed and swapped with another identical unit to make servicing faster and easier.

MAP — missed approach point. The end point of the final approach segment, generally located close to the approach end of a runway. It's the point at which a pilot must decide whether to land or to go around and fly the missed approach procedure.

Mean Sea Level — The average level of the ocean's surface as measured by the level halfway between mean high and low tide. Used as a baseline for determining land elevation.

MET — Manual Electric Trim. Switch or switches, generally located on the pilot's yoke, which allows you to adjust the airplane's elevator trim control.

METAR — an hourly weather observation taken between 45 minutes after the hour until the hour at an airport with a weather observer.

MFD — Multifunction Display. Provides navigation, maps, and other functions. It's generally located in front of the copilot or, in 3-display cockpits, between the pilot and copilot.

MOA — Military Operations Area. Special use airspace designed to separate certain nonhazardous military activities from IFR traffic and to identify for VFR traffic where these activities are conducted. Pilots don't require permission to enter these areas but may want to contact a FSS or ATC to determine if the area is active or "hot."

MSA — Minimum Safe Altitude. Altitudes depicted on approach charts which provide at least 1,000 feet of obstacle clearance within a 25-mile radius of the navigation facility upon which the procedure is predicated.

MSL — Mean Sea Level. It defines zero elevation for a local area.

MVFR — Marginal Visual Flight Rules. Refers to flight conditions with 3-5 miles of visibility or ceilings between 1000 and 3,000 feet.

Nautical Mile — A unit of length used in navigation. It's equal to about 6,076 feet or about 1.15 statute miles.

NDB — Non-Directional Beacons. Low frequency transmitters, generally associated with an instrument procedure, which generate a signal that can be received by an aircraft with an ADF receiver.

NEXRAD — Next Generation Radar. A network of 159 independent WSR-88D Weather Surveillance Radar Doppler systems first deployed in 1988 and operated by the National Weather Service (NWS). It covers most of the contiguous U.S., Alaska and Hawaii.

NLDN — National Lightning Data Network. Private network of equipment that locates the position of cloud-to-ground lightning strikes in the United States. The data is available through a weather subscription service.

NOTAM — Notice to Airmen. A communication from the FAA containing information concerning the establishment, condition or change in any aeronautical facility, service, procedure or hazard, the timely knowledge of which is essential to personnel concerned with flight operations.

NWS — National Weather Service. U.S. government agency responsible for observing and forecasting weather.

OAT — Outside Air Temperature. The G1000 calculates this by measuring the total air temperature and then subtracting the heating effects of the airplane moving through the air.

PFD — Primary Flight Display. Displays the traditional six instruments and other data.

POH — Pilot Operating Handbook. The manual that's supplied with a new aircraft.

RAIM — Receiver Autonomous Integrity Monitoring. A GPS receiver system that can detect whether it is receiving correct information from the satellites that is sufficiently accurate for use in flying an instrument approach.

RMI — Radio Magnetic Indicator. Instrument traditionally found in airliners. It combines a heading indicator with a bearing pointer and gives pilots a direct reading of the radial on which they're located. TAA aircraft use their computing power to generate the same type of information with bearing pointers.

Route — A series of waypoints entered into a flight plan which defines a desired navigation path.

RPM — Rotations Per Minute.

PROC — Procedure. Key on the G1000 used to select instrument procedures.

RVR — Runway Visual Range. The distance measured by transmissometers at some larger airports to directly measure the visibility along a runway with an instrument approach. Aircraft are not permitted to land if the measured RVR is below the visibility requirements specified in a particular instrument approach.

Selective Availability — Random error which the government can intentionally add to GPS satellite signals to degrade GPS position accuracy for civilian use. It was turned off in the 1990's and is not currently in use.

SIGMET — A forecast of weather that extends over a widespread area and is potentially hazardous to all types of aircraft.

Squitter — Random transmissions of a transponder's 24-bit identification address, sent periodically, regardless of the presence of interrogations. The purpose of squitter is to alert Mode S ground stations and Traffic Avoidance System (TAS) equipped aircraft to the presence of a Mode S-equipped aircraft.

STAR — Standard Arrival Procedure. An instrument procedure written for a particular airport which, if followed correctly, safely transitions an aircraft from the en route structure to an instrument procedure for an airport.

Stormscope — A passive device that detects electrical discharges—usually associated with thunderstorms—within a 200 nm radius of the aircraft. In the G1000, the system measures the bearing and distances to the discharges, and displays them on the Stormscope Map page.

TA — Traffic Advisories. An alert that's issued when another aircraft is within ½ mile horizontally and 500 feet vertically of your position.

TAA — Technically Advanced Aircraft. Includes aircraft with at least a GPS and moving map display. Also includes all airplanes with glass cockpits.

TAF — Terminal Aerodrome Forecast. A concise forecast of conditions expected during a 24-hour period within a five mile range of an airport's runways.

TAS — Traffic Advisory System. An active traffic surveillance system which broadcasts a signal that interrogates the Mode C transponders of nearby aircraft, displays their location, and provides an aural alert informing the pilot of a TA.

TAWS — Terrain Awareness & Warning System. Most G1000-equipped aircraft contain Terrain Awareness, which requires that you look at the display to note higher terrain. TAWS, available in G1000-equipped Beechcraft and Columbia aircraft, gives an aural terrain warning.

TBO — Time Between Overhaul. A specification used to estimate the useful life of an engine in hours.

TCA — Terminal Control Area. An area surrounding busy airports in which all traffic operating is separated and controlled by ATC. The term is no longer used in the United States, but is still used in some countries.

TCAS — Traffic Collision Avoidance System. An airborne system developed by the FAA that operates independently from the ground-based Air Traffic Control (ATC) system. TCAS was designed to increase cockpit awareness of proximate aircraft and to serve as a "last line of defense" for the prevention of mid-air collisions. It's generally found on commercial and business aircraft.

TCAD — Traffic Collision Avoidance Device. A passive traffic surveillance system which gathers information from transponders interrogated from multiple sources, regardless of geography or proximity to ATC radar sites. It cannot detect aircraft whose Mode C transponders are not being interrogated by ground radar or TCAS or TAS equipment.

TFR — Temporary Flight Restriction. A regulatory action issued via the U.S. Notice to Airmen (NOTAM) system to restrict certain aircraft from operating within a defined area, on a temporary basis, to protect persons or property in the air or on the ground.

TFT — Thin Film Transistor. A Liquid Crystal Display (LCD) technology.

TIS — Traffic Information Service. An in-cockpit display of nearby traffic provided by an uplink from appropriately equipped FAA approach radar sites.

TIT — Turbine Inlet Temperature. The temperature of the exhaust gases entering a turbocharger. The TIT is often used for accurate leaning of turbocharged engines.

TKE — Track Angle Error. The angle difference between the desired track and your current track.

TMA — Terminal Maneuvering Area. A term used in some countries to describe an area surrounding busy airports in which all traffic operating is separated and controlled by ATC.

Track — Your current direction of travel relative to the ground.

TRK — See Track

TRSA — Terminal Radar Service Area. Similar to Class C airspace except that pilot participation is voluntary. However, if you request radar service in a TRSA, you're required to follow all ATC instructions you receive.

UTC — Universal Coordinated Time. Also called GMT or Zulu time, it's based upon the time at Greenwich, England.

VFOM — Vertical Figure of Merit. A measure of vertical position uncertainty, in feet or meters, reported by a GPS receiver, that defines a 95% containment value on the accuracy of a position fix.

VFR — Visual Flight Rules. The set of rules used when not flying on an instrument flight plan and in VMC conditions.

VHF — Very High Frequency. The frequency range from 30 to 300 MHz. The propagation of signals in this band is generally limited to line-of-sight conditions.

VLJ — Very Light Jets. A new class of small jet aircraft enabled by the development of small jet engines.

VMC — Visual Meteorological Conditions. Weather conditions that are greater than VFR minimums (generally 3 miles visibility and 1000 feet cloud ceilings).

VNAV — Vertical Navigation. Creates a 3-D profile to guide an airplane to a target altitude and location.

VOR — VHF Omni-directional Radio-range. VORs are a system of navigation aids that operate within the 108.0 to 117.95 MHz frequency band. They are subject to line-of-sight restrictions, and the range varies proportionally to the altitude of the receiving equipment.

VSR — Vertical Speed Required. The descent rate in feet per minute required at the present groundspeed to reach a target altitude at a waypoint.

WAAS — Wide Area Augmentation System. An extremely accurate navigation system developed for civil aviation that has the ability to provide horizontal and vertical navigation for precision approach operations. It uses a network of precisely-located ground reference stations that monitor GPS satellite signals and generate a correction message that is sent to user receivers via navigation transponders on geostationary satellites.

Waypoint — A location stored in a GPS. This can either be a pre-defined location, such as an airport or VOR, or a user-defined location, such as your house.

XPDR — Transponder. Airborne equipment which, when interrogated by ground-based radar equipment, sends a signal that enhances the aircraft's display on radar and may transmit altitude and other information.

XTK — See Crosstrack Error.

Index

140° arc view, 25
360 HSI softkey, 25, 213
360 softkey, 83
360° softkey, 80
ACT LEG softkey, 140
Activating
  a previously stored flight plan, 142
  an instrument approach, 170
  leg in a flight plan, 140
  VECTOR-TO-FINAL, 170, 236
Active Flight Plan page, 136, 214
  activating a leg, 140
  changing fields, 137
  creating a new flight plan, 137
  deleting a flight plan, 141
  deleting a waypoint, 139
  direct to a flight plan waypoint, 139
  inserting waypoints, 138
  inverting a flight plan, 140
  storing a flight plan, 141
  using recent waypoints, 138
active frequency, 40
active leg information, 137
AC-U-KWIK directory, 267
ADC, 14, 162
  failure, 194
  failure dual systems, 259
ADF, 35
ADF key, 47
ADS-B, 16, 115, 130, 209, 268
advisory glide slope, 230, 231, 238
ADVISORY softkey, 28
AFCS, 149
  Status bar, 152
AFCS Status bar, 147
AGE label, 78
AHRS, 3, 14, 17, 162
  failure, 194
  failure dual systems, 257
  reinitialization, 14
Air Data Computer. *See* ADC
Air Reports, 129
AIREPS, 124, 129
AIRMETs, 125
Airport Directory, 245
Airport Information page, 87
  enter airport or city name, 88
  flying direct to, 135
  INFO softkey, 89
  loading frequencies, 43, 90
  orientation, 88
  Runway window, 89
  selecting a departure procedure, 182
  selecting an approach, 171
  selecting an arrival procedure, 181
  weather, 90
Airport Signs on Synthetic Vision, 240
Airspace Alerts box, 103
Airspace Alerts window, 112
airspeed
  calibrated, 97
  indicator, 22
  reference bugs, 23, 32, 270
  trend vector, 23
AIRSPEED alert, 260
Airways, 217
  AIRWAYS softkey, 218
  collapsing, 218, 220
  displaying, 218
  expanding, 220
  inserting waypoint within, 219
Alerts, 28
  arrival, 104
  VNAV arrival, 146
ALERTS softkey, 28
ALL softkey, 226
Along Track Offsets, 159, 214, 216
ALT key (autopilot), 155, 164
ALT knobs, 24
ALT softkey, 31
ALT UNITS softkey, 213, 249
alternator, 189
  failure, 28, 55
altimeter, 24, 270
Altitude alerting, 212
altitude constraints, 214
Altitude Hold mode, 155
altitude reference box, 24
altitude reference bug, 24
ALTITUDE SELECT annunciator, 147
ALTS annunciator, 158
ALTV annunciator, 158
ANN TEST softkey, 223
annunciators, 28
AOPA Directory, 245
AP DISC button, 152, 162
AP disconnect button, 152, 162
AP key, 164
Approach frequencies, 89
Approach mode, 159
  autopilot, 154, 161
  GPS, 27
APR, 27
APR key (autopilot), 165
APR softkey, 110, 171, 225
APTSIGNS softkey, 240, 242
ARC HSI softkey, 25, 213
ARC softkey, 80, 83
ARFRM softkey, 223
arrival alerts, 104
Arrival frequencies, 89
Arrival Procedure, 181
ASSIST softkey, 56
ATIS, 43
ATK Offset Waypoint, 216
ATK OFST softkey, 216
Attitude Heading Reference System. *See* AHRS
attitude indicator, 23
audio panel, 14, 45, 163
  failure, 194
  passenger address, 46
  Perspective, 251
AUTO DESCENT Warning, 260
AUTO softkey, 95
Automatic Direction Finder, 35
automation surprise, 161
autopilot, 16
  altitude preselect, 164
  common errors, 161
  failures, 162
  Garmin. *See* GFC 700
  KAP 140, 16, 163–65
  keys, 150
  limitations, 163
  LVL key, 256
  operation, 203
  Perspective, 256
  preflight, 161, 163
auto-zoom, 63, 71, 222
AUX key, 47
Aviation Data
  Show or Hide, 83
Aviation Weather Watches, 124
Avidyne, 1, 78
  Entegra, 256
AWOS, 43
BACK softkey, 29, 30
Backcourse mode, 160, 165
backlighting, 37
backup instruments, 17, 190
bank indications, 23
Bank key, 269
BARO knob, 25, 247
BARO MIN, 33
barometric setting box, 25
base reflectivity, 119
battery
  main, 191
  standby, 55, 190
BC annunciator, 160
BC key, 160
beam tilt angle, 119
bearing, 104, 210
bearing pointer
  Perspective, 19
bearing pointers, 35
Beechcraft
  autopilot, 24, 150, 155, 206

autopilot limitations, 156
Flight Director, 157, 163
G36, 207
GEAR UP Warning, 207
King Air, 274
radar in Baron, 16, 117
TAWS, 68
BKSP softkey, 31
BOD, 158
BRG, 210
BRG1 and BRG2 softkeys, 36
Cancel
Direct-to navigation, 133
Cautions, 28
CDI, 25
setting scale, 105
CDI auto-capture, 105
CDI box, 105
CDI softkey, 26, 160, 161, 173
CELL mode, 80
CELL MOV softkey, 126
Celsius, selecting, 103
Center frequencies, 111
Cessna, 1, 16, 17, 190
autopilot, 16, 24, 157, 161, 206
C172, 199–206
C182, 190
C206, 53, 54, 59
C400. *See* Corvalis
Caravan, 274
Citation autopilot, 157
electrical system, 189–91
Engine page, 53
Flight Director, 157
KAP 140, 163, 206
KAP 140 limitations, 165
maximum fuel indications, 54
Mustang jet, 11, 12, 15, 24, 268–72
Changing
display units, 102
fields, 221
Navigation Status bar fields, 104
ChartView, 224
checklists, 64, 197
chevrons, 23
CHKLIST softkey, 65, 197
CHRT OPT softkey, 226
CHT, 51
Cirrus Design, 1, 247
SR22, 260–66
SR22 Feature Comparison, 280
Vision SF50 jet, 273
Warnings and Cautions, 284
City Forecasts, 123
Class B/C/D, 74
alerts, 103
CLD TOP softkey, 128
cleaning display, 7
clear air mode, 119
clearance recorder, 49
Closest Point of FPL, 145
CLR key, 63, 64
CNCL VNV softkey, 160, 216
CODE softkey, 31
color, use of, 20
Columbia. *See* Corvalis
COM 1/2 key, 46
COM knobs, 40
COM radio, 13
auto-tuning, 250
failure, 194
operation, 41
Perspective, 249
setting channel spacing, 105
COM1 key, 45
COM1 MIC key, 45
command bar, 23
common errors, 161
Comparator Window, 258, 269
composite reflectivity, 119
configuring map, 66
Control Unit, Perspective, 250
Control Wheel Steering. *See* CWS
Convective Outlook, 129
Convective SIGMET, 125
coolant temperature gauge, 59
COPLT key, 49
Copy a Stored Flight Plan, 144
Corvalis (Columbia)
autopilot, 24, 150
carbon monoxide monitor, 4
GDU 1042, 12
keypad, 15
lean of peak, 57
System page, 55, 56, 57, 284
TAWS, 68
COUNTY softkey, 123
County warnings, 123
Course
from Fix to Altitude, 185
from Fix to Manual Sequence, 186
course deviation indicator, 25
auto-capture, 105
re-scaling, 28
setting scale, 105
use of, 26
course pointer, 26
course reversal, 180
Course to Waypoint function, 135
Creating
Descent profiles, 145–46
new flight plan, 137–38, 142–43
pilot profiles, 106
waypoints, 92
crossing restrictions, 157, 214
crosstrack error, 104, 187, 259
CRS knob, 26, 182
CUM softkey, 221
Cumulative Distance, 137
Current Icing Product, 129
Current Track Bug, 210, 248
cursor, 64, 213
CWS, 152, 161
switch, 165
CYL SLCT softkey, 56
cylinder head temperature, 51
Data link lightning, 127
database, updating, 244
D-bar, 27
dBZ, 119
DCLTR softkey, 29, 66, 221
Dead Reckoning mode, 239
DEC FUEL softkey, 58
de-cluttering screen, 66
Deleting
a stored flight plan, 144
active flight plan, 141
all stored flight plans, 144
vertical constraint, 214
waypoints, 93
waypoints in a flight plan, 139
density altitude, 97
Departure Procedures, 90, 181
departure time, 98
descent profile, 146, 214
descent profiles, SVT, 241
Desired Track, 22, 71, 104, 137
Destination Airport Information window, 254
DFLTS softkey, 37
Diamond, 1, 16, 53
autopilot, 17, 206
DA40, 53, 54, 57, 58, 105, 165, 206
DA42, 53, 55, 56, 58, 59, 206, 207
D-Jet, 208, 272
KAP 140, 165, 206
maximum fuel indication, 54
roll steering, 206
standby instruments, 17, 59
Synthetic Vision Technology, 240
digital clearance recorder, 49, 252
dilution of precision, 100
Direct-to key, 131–33, 214
Direct-to Navigation, 133
by facility or city name, 135
canceling, 133
Nearest Airport, 133
to a flight plan waypoint, 134, 139
using MFD joystick, 136
versus flight plan, 131
vertical, 214
via a specified course, 135
Direct-to page, 133
display
backlighting, 37
backup, 50, 192, 247
cleaning, 7
failure, 192
Perspective, 247
Display Backup button, 14, 50, 192, 196, 247
distance, 104
Distance Measuring Equipment, 34
DME, 34
softkey, 35
Tuning box, 35
DME arc approach, 184
DME key (audio panel), 47
DME/ADF softkey, 35
DN key, 164
DP softkey, 182, 225
DTK, 104
DTK Up map orientation, 71
dual navigation database, 244
EADS Socata TBM 850, 274
ECHO TOP softkey, 126
Echo tops, 126
Edit
Flight Plan, 138–41
Stored Flight Plan, 143
EGT, 52
electrical system, 55, 189–91
electronic charts, 224, 225
electronic checklists, 64, 197
Electronic Stability and Protection, 260
Email messages, 17
EMERGCY softkey, 65, 197
emergencies, 196
Display Backup button, 14, 50
NRST softkey, 33
setting 121.5, 41
Emergency Descent Mode, 269
EMPTY WT softkey, 271
en route safe altitude, 95, 104
ENBL VNV softkey, 215, 265
endurance, 97
engine indication system, 51
Cessna Mustang, 270
failure, 196
Perspective, 252
engine load indicator, 53
Engine page, 52
ENGINE softkey, 56, 252
Engine/Airframe Unit, 15
Enhanced Vision System, 257
ENR, 27
enroute mode, 27
Enroute Safe Altitude, 137
ENT key, 64
entering
airport identifiers, 89, 213
data, 64
Epic Aircraft, 274

ESA, 104
ESP, 260
Essentials bus, 55, 190
estimated position error, 100
estimated time en route, 95, 104, 137
estimated time of arrival, 95, 104, 137
ETA, 104
ETE, 104
EVS, 257
exhaust gas temperature, 52
exporting flight plans, 243
FAA, 16
FAA Industry Training Standards, 6
FAF, 28
FD FRMT softkey, 270
FD key, 152
feet, selecting, 103
field of view, 243
fields
    changing in a flight plan, 137
    changing in Navigation Status bar, 104
FIKI, 253
final approach fix, 28
FIS-B weather, 16, 115, 130
FIT WDTH softkey, 226
FITS, 6
FLC key, 147
Flight Data Logging, 61, 243
Flight Director, 149–53, 161, 162, 163, 193, 194, 263
Flight ID, 269
Flight into Known Icing, 253
Flight Level Change mode, 156
Flight Path Marker, 241
Flight Plan
    activating a leg, 140
    activating a previously stored, 142
    airways, 218
    altitudes and text colors, 215
    changing fields, 137
    copy a stored, 144
    creating a new, 137–38, 143, 142–43
    deleting, 141
    deleting a stored, 144
    deleting a waypoint, 139
    deleting all stored, 144
    direct-to a flight plan waypoint, 134, 139
    edit a stored, 144
    importing, 243
    inserting waypoints, 138, 213
    inverting an active, 140
    inverting and activating a stored, 143
    sorting stored, 145
    storing a, 141
    using recent waypoints, 138
    vertical, 158, 214
Flight Plan Catalog
    activating a previously stored flight plan, 142
    copy a stored flight plan, 144
    creating a new flight plan, 138, 143
    deleting a stored flight plan, 144
    deleting all stored flight plans, 145
    edit a stored flight plan, 144
    importing a flight plan, 243
    inverting and activating a stored flight plan, 143
    sorting flight plans, 145
Flight Plan Navigation, 136
flight timer, 98
Flight Watch, 81, 115, 124
FlightStar, 243
FliteCharts, 224
FltPlan.com, 243
flux valve, 15
FMS knobs, 61
    entering data, 64
    selecting pages, 63
FOB SYNC softkey, 271
FPA, 158
FPL key, 63, 136, 213
free/slave switch, 25
Freezing Level, 128
FREQ softkey, 110, 111, 113
frequencies
    Approach, 89
    Arrival, 89
    ATIS or AWOS, 89
    Center, 111
    Flight Service Station, 111
    nearest, 111
Frequencies window, 89
frequency
    active, 40
    auto-tuning, 43
    display, 39
    selected, 40
    standby, 40
Frequency Toggle key, 40
FRZ LVL softkey, 129
FSS frequencies, 111
fuel
    gauges, 54
    imbalance, 165
    leaning, 52
    low fuel indicator, 4
    mismanagement, 4, 54
    planning, 96
    range ring, 8, 69
    remaining, 97
    required, 97
    statistics, 94
    totalizer, 58, 253
fuel flow indicator, 53
fuel flow rate, 96
fuel on board sensors, 97
Fuel page, 59
Fuel Range Ring, 8, 69
FUEL softkey, 253
FULL SCN softkey, 226
GA button, 152, 157, 263
GAL REM softkey, 58
gallons, selecting, 103
Garmin
    Data Link, 15
    Flight Data Services, 17, 115, 130
    GNS 430/GNS 530, 5, 7, 20, 40, 63, 131, 142
    GTS 800 TAS, 78
    integrated autopilot, 149
    weather service, 17
GDC 74A, 14
GDL 69/GDL 69A, 15, 115
GDL 90 ADS-B Transceiver, 16, 130
GDU 1040/1042/1043/1044B, 12
GEA 71, 15
gearbox temperature indicator, 59
geodetic sea level, 83
GFC 700, 17, 149, 161, 203, 214, 256, 269
GIA 63, 13
GIA1, 162, 193
GIA2, 162, 165, 193
glass cockpit
    benefits, 2, 5
    electrical systems, 2
glide slope indicator, 24
GMA 1347, 14, 45
GMA 347, 14, 45, 47, 251
GMA 350, 14, 45, 47, 251
GMC 705, 17
GMC 710, 17, 269
GMU 44, 15
GND softkey, 212
Go Around button, 152, 263
Go Around mode, 147, 157, 161
GP annunciator, 159
GPS
    active, 13, 99
    approach mode, 27
    enroute mode, 27
    failure, 193
    flying approach, 176
    hot spare, 13
    loss of signal integrity, 239
    receiver, 13
    roll steering, 17
    terminal mode, 27
    updating database, 13
GPS approach, 168
GPS Status page, 99
GPS1 softkey, 100
gridlines on Synthetic Vision, 240
ground track bug, 210
groundspeed, 104
    average, 98
GRS 77, 14
GSL, 83
GSR 56, 17
gyro, mechanical, 17
Hazardous Inflight Weather Advisory Service, 42
HDG key (autopilot), 153, 164
HDG knob, 25, 153, 164
HDG MISCOMP, 258
HDG mode, 164
HEADER softkey, 226
Heading Box, 25
heading reference bug, 26
Heading Select mode, 153
Heading Up map orientation, 71
Hectopascals, selecting, 103
HI SENS key, 47
highway in the sky, 241
HITS, 241
HIWAS, 42
holding entry procedure, 176
Holding Pattern, 163, 183
HondaJet, 273
horizontal situation indicator, 25
horizontal uncertainty level, 100
HPA softkey, 249
HRZN HDG softkey, 240, 243
HSI, 25, 213
HSI FRMT softkey, 213
Hurricane Tracks, 130
HYPOXIA ALERT message, 260
Hypoxia Recognition, 260
IAS key, 147, 256, 264
IAS mode, 156
icing, 129
Icing Supercooled Large Droplets, 130
IDENT softkey, 31
identifying a station, 26
IFR
    accidents, 5
    freezing level, 128
    GPS approach, 168
    information (Airport Info page), 90
    low, 122
    own navigation, 168
    procedure turn, 168
    vectors, 168
IFR (see also Instrument Approach), 122
IFR Rating round gauges, 9
ILS, 24, 42, 43, 92
    flying an approach, 178
    using SVT Pathways, 241
ILS CDI auto-capture, 105, 161, 178, 224
importing flight plans, 243
IN softkey, 249
INC FUEL softkey, 58
Indicated Airspeed Mode, 156

INFO-2 Softkey, 245
infrared camera, 257
INHIBIT softkey, 223
Initial Usable Fuel screen, 253
inner marker, 47
Inserting
  waypoints into a flight plan, 138
insertion point, 259
Inset Map, 29, 212, 249
INSET softkey, 29
Instrument Approach
  ACTIVATE VECTOR-TO-FINAL, 236
  auto-tuning frequencies, 44
  DME arc approach, 184
  flying hold, 238
  flying ILS, 178
  GPS approach, 176
  load using softkeys, 171
  LOAD versus ACTIVATE, 170
  Missed Approach, 174, 236
  procedure turn, 168
  procedures, 90
  removing an approach, 171
  round gauge vs. glass cockpit, 9
  selecting an approach, 170
  vectors, 168, 233, 235
  VECTOR-TO-FINAL, 170
  VOR approach, 172
instrument scan technique, 186
INTEG label, 26, 202
Intercept Arc, 244
intercom, 48
  isolation modes, 49
  Perspective, 251
  setting squelch, 48
  setting volume, 48
Intersection Information page, 90
Inverting
  a flight plan, 140
  and activating a stored flight plan, 143
Iridium Transceiver, 17, 115
Jeppesen
  charts, 224
  FlightStar, 243
Jet Routes, 217
joystick, 30, 136
KAP 140, 161, 163–65
  limitations, 165
  operation, 203
  PITCH TRIM warning, 165
keypad, 15, 247
kilograms, selecting, 103
Kinds of Operation Equipment List, 199
King Air, 274
King/Bendix, 163
KODIAK, 273
L3 Skywatch, 78
land data, 72
laser-ring gyro, 14
LD AIRWY softkey, 219
LD APR softkey, 110
LD DP softkey, 182
Lean page, 56
LEAN softkey, 56
leaning, 52, 56
  SR22T, 252
LEGEND softkey, 126, 128
LEG-LEG softkey, 222
lighting, 13
  setting display, 37
lightning
  Data link, 127
  Stormscope Map page, 79
Limitations
  G1000, 18
  GFC 700, 163
  KAP 140, 165
  Perspective, 18
line replaceable units, 11
liters, selecting, 103
LNAV approach, 229, 232
LNAV/VNAV approach, 229, 231, 238
LNAV+V approach, 229, 233, 238
Loading
  Arrival Procedures, 181
  Departure Procedures, 181
  instrument approach, 170
localizer, 27
LOCK softkey, 224
low altitude annunciator, 247
Low Bank mode, 269
low fuel indicator, 4
LPV approach, 159, 229
LRU, 11
LTNG softkey, 127
LVL key, 147
Mach number, 270
magnetic north, 102
magnetic variation, 103
magnetometer, 15
MAN SQ key, 48
manifold pressure gauge, 53
MANUAL softkey, 96
map datums, 103
map orientation, 71
map pointer
  display elevations, 67
Map Setup, 66, 222
MAP softkey, 66
MAPR annunciator, 239
marker beacon, 24, 46, 251
MAXSPD annunciator, 151
MDA/DA bug, 32, 33
memory cards, 13
MENU key, 64
Messages
  Airspace Alert, 103
  arrival alert, 104
  NOT APPROVED FOR GPS, 172
  RAIM, 101
  reminder, 98
  TAWS, 86
  TIS status, 78
  Traffic, 29
  VNAV alert, 146
MET, 152
METAR, 121, 259
METAR softkey, 30, 122
METERS softkey, 213, 249
meters, selecting, 103
METRIC softkey, 25, 37, 213
Metric, selecting, 103
MFD
  changing Navigation Status bar, 104
  entering data, 64
  failure, 163, 193
  frequency auto tuning, 43
  navigating the pages, 63, 255
  organization, 63
  Perspective, 253
microfiber cloth, 7
middle marker, 46
minimum safe altitude, 104
minimums alerting, 32
MINIMUMS softkey, 226
MINSPD annunciator, 260
MISCOMP, 258
Missed Approach, 174
MKR/MUTE key, 47, 251
MOAs displayed, 74
Mode S transponder, 30
Mooney
  annunciator panel, 206, 282
  autopilot, 16, 24
  tachometer, 58
  trim and flap indicators, 206
MORE WX softkey, 123
Morse code identifier, 26, 42
MSA, 104
Multifunction Display. *See* MFD
MUSIC 1, 47
MUSIC 2, 48
music muting, 48
MVFR, 122
NACO charts, 224
NARROW softkey, 221
NASA, 241
National Lightning Detection Network, 127
NAV key, 153
NAV knobs, 40
NAV radio, 13
  auto-tuning ILS frequencies, 44
  operation, 42
  Perspective, 249
Nav Range Ring, 70, 195, 259
NAV1 key, 47
Navigation Map page, 65, 244, 245
  auto-zoom, 71, 222
  aviation data labels, 74
  configuring options, 66
  fuel range ring, 69
  joystick for direct to navigation, 136
  land data features displayed, 75
  map orientation, 71
  Map Setup, 66, 222
  nav range ring, 70
  obstacle data, 72
  terrain information, 67
  topographical and terrain ranges, 73
  topographical information, 66
  track vector, 70, 222
  traffic information, 68
  traffic on Perspective, 254
  traffic ranges, 73
  weather ranges, 73
  Weather softkeys, 68
  wind vector, 70
Navigation mode, 153
Navigation Status bar (MFD), 62
  changing fields, 104
Navigation Status bar (PFD), 22, 210
NDB, 47
NDB Information page, 91
NDBs displayed, 74
Nearest Airports
  flying direct to, 34, 133
  loading frequency, 34, 43
  NRST softkey, 43
  setting criteria, 106
  softkey, 33
  window, 33
Nearest Airports page, 109
  loading frequencies, 44
  selecting an approach, 171
Nearest Airports window (PFD), 133
Nearest Airspaces page, 112
Nearest Frequencies page, 111
  loading frequencies, 44
Nearest Intersections page, 110
  flying direct to, 136
Nearest NDB page, 110
  flying direct to, 136
Nearest User Wpts page, 111
Nearest VOR page, 111
  flying direct to, 136
  loading frequencies, 44
NEW softkey, 138
NEXRAD Radar, 117, 212
NEXRAD softkey, 30, 69, 116
night flight, 204, 265
NO COMP, 258

NO GPS POSITION, 239
non-sequencing mode, 182
North Up map orientation, 71
NOT APPROVED FOR GPS message, 172
NOTAM softkey, 226
NR annunciator, 212
NRST softkey, 33, 133, 196
NTSB Glass Cockpit Study, 2
OBS mode, 182–84
OBS softkey, 182
OBS/SUSP softkey, 36
obstacle database, 72
obstacles on Synthetic Vision, 240
odometer, 98
offset waypoints, 216
oil pressure gauge, 54
oil temperature gauge, 54
ON softkey, 31
OPERATE softkey, 76
outer marker, 46
outside air temperature, 14, 22, 36
Overspeed Protection, 267
own navigation, 168
OXYGEN softkey, 59
PA key, 46
page guide, 63
panning pointer, 30
Parallel Track function, 217
Passenger Address, 46
PATHWAY softkey, 240
Pathways, 241
Perspective, 209, 247–66
  AHRS failure, 257
  alphanumeric keypad, 15
  audio panels, 14, 251
  autopilot, 256
  bearing pointers, 19, 36
  COM and NAV radios, 249
  Control Unit, 253
  current track bug, 19
  Destination Airport Information, 254
  Destination Airport Window, 61
  Display Backup Button, 50
  displaying traffic on Nav map, 254
  displays, 12
  Electronic Stability & Protection, 260
  Engine Indication System, 51, 252
  Enhanced Vision System, 257
  Flight Director, 257
  Flying trip in a SR22, 260–66
  fuel totalizer, 51, 253
  heading box, 26
  Hypoxia Recognition, 260
  intercom, 251
  LVL key, 256
  manual squelch, 48
  MFD, 253
  MFD page navigation, 255
  page navigation, 61
  passenger address, 46
  PFD, 19, 247
  Quick Select Box, 259
  radios, 20, 39
  squelch, 251
  Synthetic Vision Technology, 240
  Track Vector, 254
  Underspeed Protection, 260
  Usable Fuel Screen, 253
  Waypoint Weather window, 259
  yaw damper, 256
PFD, 6, 19
  controls knobs, 21
  failure, 192, 193
  Perspective, 19, 247
  softkey, 25, 35, 37, 211, 213
PFT annunciator, 151
Phenom 100 and 300, 272–73
PILOT key, 49
Pilot Profiles, 106, 247
Pilot Reports, 129
Piper Meridian, 275
PIREPS, 124, 129
PIT MISCOMP, 258
pitch indications, 23
PITCH TRIM warning, 165
pitot-static system, 14
PLAN softkey, 226
PLAY key, 49
pounds, selecting, 103
precipitation mode, 119
Precipitation Type at Surface, 120
preflight, 200
Primary Flight Display. *See* PFD
primary flight instruments, 20
PROC key, 63, 170
procedure turn, 163, 168
PROFILE NOT AVAILABLE, 245
Profile Path, 244
PROFILE softkey, 226, 244
Profile View, 61, 244
PT annunciator, 162
Q-routes, 218
Quest Aircraft, 273
Quick Select Box, 139, 259
racetrack, 183
radar
  age of NEXRAD data, 120
  airborne, 16
  NEXRAD, 117
  NEXRAD versus airborne, 116
Radar Altimeter, 267
radio controls, 20
Radio Magnetic Indicator, 35
RAIM, 100, 202
RAIM softkey, 223
rain, 119
Ram Air Temperature, 270
range knob, 63
rate of turn indicator, 25
Receiver Autonomous Integrity Monitoring. *See* RAIM
reference bug, 23
  altitude, 24
  heading, 26
  setting airspeed, 32
reflectivity, 119
remaining distance, 137
reminder messages, 98
Removing an approach, 171
RENAME softkey, 93
Restricted airspace, 74, 112, 132
  alerts, 103
reversionary mode, 50, 192, 212, 247, 252
RMI, 35
RNWY softkey, 110
ROL MISCOMP, 258
ROL mode, 161, 164
Roll Hold mode, 152
roll steering, 17
round gauges, IFR training, 9
RST FUEL softkey, 58
RST USED softkey, 58
runway diagrams, 220
Runway Extensions, 74, 75
runway information, 89
Runway window, 110
runways on Synthetic Vision, 240
SafeTaxi diagrams, 220
safety, 4
  systems, 2
Satellite imagery, 128
satellite radio system, 107
Satellite Status window, 100
SBAS softkey, 223
scanning, 3, 186
Scheduler, 98
SD-type memory card, 13
Search and Rescue option, 210
Seattle Avionics Voyager, 243
Selected Altitude Intercept Arc, 244
selected frequency, 40
Selecting
  Arrival Procedures, 181
  Departure Procedures, 181
  HSI navigation source, 26
  instrument approach, 170
  radio frequencies, 21
SENSOR softkey, 248, 258, 269
SETUP2 softkey, 260
Severe Weather Storm Tracks, 126
SFC OFF softkey, 127
SHW CHRT softkey, 225
SIG/AIR softkey, 125
SIGMETs, 125
SiriusXM, 15, 107, 115
situational awareness, 3
SKYWATCH, 78–79
slip/skid indicator, 24
SNGL CUE softkey, 270
SO annunciator, 212
softkeys, 20, 29
software version, 109
somatogravic illusion, 86
Sorting flight plans, 145
SPECI, 121
speed bugs, 23, 32
  enabling, 32
SPKR key, 46, 252
squelch
  COM radios, 41
  intercom, 48
  Perspective, 251
SR22. *See* Cirrus Design
Standard Arrival Procedures, 90
standard rate turn, 25
standby battery, 55
standby frequency, 40
standby instruments, 17, 190
  electric standby attitude indicator, 17
STANDBY softkey, 76
STAR, 90
STAR softkey, 181, 225
STBY BATT switch, 201
STBY softkey, 31
STD BARO softkey, 37, 249
S-TEC
  55X, 149
  autopilots, 256
Storing a Flight Plan, 141
Storm Prediction Center, 124
Stormscope Map page, 79, 259
Stormscope vs. XM lightning, 127
STRIKE mode, 80
Strike Rate, 80
STRMSCP softkey, 30, 68
stuck microphone, 41
sunrise and sunset times, 96
Surface Analysis Weather maps, 126
SUSP annunciator, 236, 237
SUSP softkey, 174, 237
SVT, 240
SYN TERR softkey, 240
SYN VIS softkey, 240
Synthetic Vision Technology, 25, 240–43
System page (engine), 57
System Setup page, 101
SYSTEM softkey, 57, 200
System Status page, 108
system time box, 22, 36
TA OFF Range message, 78
TAA, 4
TACAN, 92
tach time, 58
tachometer, 53
TAF, 122
TAS, 78
TAWS, 68, 83–86, 223, 242, 268

Excessive Descent Rate Alert, 86
Five Hundred Foot Alert, 86
Forward Looking Terrain Avoidance, 84
Negative Climb Rate Alert, 86
page, 83
Premature Descent Alert, 85
TBM 850, 274
Technically Advanced Aircraft, 4
TEL key, 46
Temporary Flight Restrictions, 120
TERM, 27
terminal mode, 27
Terrain Alerting on SVT, 242
terrain data
setting ranges, 73
side view, 245
Terrain Proximity Map, 82
TERRAIN softkey, 30, 67
terrain warning system, 68
text messages, 17
TFRs, 120
thermocouple, 51
thunderstorms, 120, 123, 127
Tiger, 53
autopilot, 16, 24
engine pages, 53, 55
fuel flow rate, 57–58
standby battery, 190
Total Time in Service, 58
vacuum indicator, 202
vacuum pump, 17, 59, 190
time, 22
setting local, 36, 101
Timer/References window, 31
timers, 98
general purpose, 31
up or down, 98
TIS, 76
TIT, 52
TKE, 104
TKS fluid, 253
TMR/REF softkey, 31
TNA MUTE softkey, 223
TOD, 158
TOD annunciator, 159
TOPO softkey, 29, 67
topographical data
displaying legend, 67
setting ranges, 73
total air temperature, 14
Total Time in Service, 58
totalizer, 58, 253
tower symbols, 242
Track Up map orientation, 71
Track Vector, 70, 222, 259
Perspective, 254
Traffic Advisories, 28, 74, 77, 213
displaying on Perspective, 254
Traffic Advisory Systems (TAS), 75, 78–79
Traffic Information Service (TIS), 76
Traffic Map page, 75, 259
Traffic on Synthetic Vision, 242
TRAFFIC softkey, 29
transponder, 30, 212
altitude mode, 31
failure, 194
ground mode, 212
status bar, 22, 30–31, 269
trend vector, 23
airspeed, 23
altitude, 24
standard rate turn, 25
TRFC COAST message, 78
TRFC RMVD message, 78
TRFC-1, -2 softkey, 29
TRFC-2 softkey, 212
trim, 152, 162
TRIM FAIL annunciator, 205
Trip Planning page, 94
trip statistics, 95
TRK, 104
T-routes, 218
true airspeed, 23, 97
true north, 102
tuning frequencies, 39
turbine inlet temperature, 52
turbocharging, 52, 53, 56, 57
turbulence, 120, 126
turbulence forecast, 129
turn coordinator, 24
turn rate indicator, 25
Underspeed Protection, 260
units, changing, 102
Universal Coordinated Time, 101
unpublished holds, 183
unusual attitude, 23
UP key, 164
updating database, 244
User Waypoint Information page, 92
USING ADC2 annunciation, 259
USING AHRS2 annunciation, 258
Utility page, 98
vacuum gauge, 59
vacuum pump, 3, 17, 59
vectors, 168, 170, 233, 235
vertical deviation indicator, 158
Vertical Navigation, 214
altitude constraints, 214
direct-to, 214
flight plan (new), 158, 214
page (old), 146
VNAV arrival alerts, 146
Vertical Navigation (autopilot), 157
limitations, 159
Vertical Path Tracking mode, 158–60
vertical speed indicator, 24
Vertical Speed mode, 156
vertical speed required, 104, 146
indicator, 158
Very Light Jets, 268
VFR, 122
VFR softkey, 31
Victor airways, 217
video, auxiliary, 243
VIEW softkey, 80, 83, 221
Visibility product, 130
VNAV, 146
VNAV Target Altitude, 158
VNV Direct-to softkey, 215
VNV key, 157, 159, 160, 214
VNV PROF softkey, 216
VNV Profile window, 215
VOL/PUSH ID knob, 42
VOL/PUSH SQ knob, 41
volume
intercom, 48
NAV and COM, 41
VOR Information page, 91
loading frequencies, 44
VORs displayed, 74
VORTAC, 92
VPTH annunciator, 158, 159
VS mode, 164
VSR, 104
WAAS, 228, 229–39, 268
WAAS receiver, 159
Warnings, 20, 28, 207
Waypoint Information box, 138
waypoints
changing, 93
creating, 92
deleting, 93
offset, 216
Weather
Airport Information page, 90
Data Link page, 115
METAR in flight plan, 259
setting data ranges, 73
subscription, 115
Weight Planning page, 271
WIDE softkey, 221
Wind Data window, 211
WIND OFF softkey, 128
WIND softkey, 211, 248
Wind Vector, 70, 211, 248
Winds Aloft, 128
WPTS softkey, 95
WX LGND softkey, 30
WX softkey, 122
WX-500 Weather Mapping Sensor, 79
WxWorx, 115
X POINTR softkey, 270
XM Information page, 107
XM LTNG softkey, 30, 69, 127
XM Satellite. *See* SiriusXM
XPDR softkey, 31, 269
XTK, 104, 213, 259
yaw damper, 12, 150, 256
Zero Pitch Line, 240
zoom
Inset map, 30
Navigation Map, 63
Zulu time, 36

Get the New IFR Book that Gives ALL the Details for operating:

- G1000 and Perspective
- Garmin 430 and 430W
- Garmin 530 and 530W
- G900X and GNS 480
- Bendix King KLN 94

"Max Trescott has done it again... This book is an absolute must-have for your flying library if you're an instrument rated pilot or are working on your instrument rating. It's a comprehensive no-nonsense guide to understanding and flying GPS approaches."

— Rod Machado

Don't get stuck in the clouds wondering which button to push!

Get the one book that tells pilots what they need to know to safely fly using a modern GPS receiver and autopilot. Most books treat GPS as a subtopic and don't tell everything you need to know about using GPS. *Max Trescott's GPS and WAAS Instrument Flying Handbook* recognizes that GPS is at the center of modern cockpits and not just add-on equipment. Designed for both VFR and IFR pilots, the book uses NTSB reports and NASA ASRS pilot reports to illustrate pitfalls in using—and misusing—GPS equipment. Dozens of practical GPS and IFR tips are included. Learn about the common "gotchas" in GPSs and autopilots that trip up even experienced pilots.

Learn What All Pilots Should Know

- The big differences between the Direct-to key and using a flight plan.
- Getting started entering flight plans.

Learn the Right Way to Load Approaches including:

- The myth of needing to "activate the approach".
- Why you'll never want to load an approach with an IAF—even when receiving vectors to final.
- When to Load versus to Activate an instrument approach.
- Why pushing the SUSP key gets you in trouble when loading an instrument approach.

Learn About Flying Instrument Approaches

- How to fly ALL instrument approach types.
- Why checking RAIM alone isn't sufficient with a WAAS-capable GPS receiver.
- How to use your autopilot along every step of the approach.
- Why your autopilot may fail to couple to an ILS glide slope.
- Why some missed approaches begin before a GPS counts down to zero.

Learn About WAAS and other New Capabilities

- Details on new minimums: LPV, LNAV/VNAV, LNAV, LNAV+V, and LP.
- How to tell if a GPS is certified to use new WAAS-based approaches.
- Different regulations that apply to WAAS-based GPS receivers.
- Loading airways and flying GPS-based T- and Q-route airways.

$39.95

To Order: Call 800-247-6553 or go to: www.G1000Book.com